THE HUMAN MOSAIC

TENTH EDITION

THE HUMAN MOSAIC

A Thematic Introduction to Cultural Geography

TERRY G. JORDAN-BYCHKOV
University of Texas at Austin

MONA DOMOSH
Dartmouth College

RODERICK P. NEUMANN
Florida International University

PATRICIA L. PRICE
Florida International University

W.H. FREEMAN AND COMPANY
New York

PUBLISHER: **Sara Tenney**

ACQUISITIONS EDITOR: **Jason Noe**

DEVELOPMENTAL EDITOR: **Nick Tymoczko**

MARKETING MANAGER: **Scott Guile**

PROJECT EDITOR: **Jane O'Neill**

TEXT DESIGNER: **Jerry Wilke**

COVER DESIGNER: **Victoria Tomaselli**

ILLUSTRATION COORDINATORS: **Shawn Churchman** and **Bill Page**

ILLUSTRATIONS: **maps.com**

PHOTO EDITORS: **Patricia Marx** and **Elyse Rieder**

PHOTO RESEARCHER: **Laura Nash**

PRODUCTION COORDINATOR: **Susan Wein**

MEDIA AND SUPPLEMENTS EDITOR: **Lisa Samols**

COMPOSITION AND LAYOUT: **Sheridan Sellers,**
    W. H. Freeman and Company Electronic Publishing Center

MANUFACTURING: **Quebecor World**

Note: Photographs not otherwise credited are the property of Scott, Foresman and Company.

FRONTLINE/World is a trademark of WGBH Educational Foundation.
Frontline is a registered trademark of WGBH Educational Foundation.

Library of Congress Control Number: 2005927280

ISBN 0-7167-6384-2
EAN 9780716763840

Printed in the United States of America

First printing

W. H. Freeman and Company
41 Madison Avenue
New York, NY 10010
Houndmills, Basingstoke RG21 6XS, England

www.whfreeman.com

CONTENTS IN BRIEF

SPECIAL FEATURES

PRACTICING GEOGRAPHY

DOING GEOGRAPHY

SEEING GEOGRAPHY

Culture in a Globalizing World

Focus On

Dear Colleague,

The Human Mosaic is the cultural geography textbook I was privileged to write with the man who first envisioned it, Terry Jordan-Bychkov. As you may know, since the publication of the last edition, Terry died of cancer. He will be sorely missed in the geography community. But it was Terry's wish that *The Human Mosaic* continue, and I'm honored to lead the effort to carry his unique vision for the book into the future.

The tenth edition of *The Human Mosaic* is once again published by W. H. Freeman and Company, our home for the past two editions. As always, it follows Terry's original concept of exploring central geographic topics (demography; agriculture; the city; religion; language; ethnicity; politics; industry; and folk, indigenous, and popular culture) through a framework of five enduring themes—culture region, cultural diffusion, cultural ecology, cultural interaction, and cultural landscape. Terry adopted these themes as a means of allowing students to make sense of the numerous and diverse elements of cultural geography and the world around them. Most important, the tenth edition remains true to Terry's insistence that each new edition accurately and vividly reflect global realities and the current state of geographic studies.

Terry was as well positioned as anyone to appreciate the need for such an approach and equally qualified to effectively accomplish it. His research covered regions ranging from the American West and the Upland South to Australia and the farthest corners of Russia, and his travels took him around the world—from England to Greece, from India home to Texas. The tenth edition reflects the diversity of this world and the generous and ecumenical spirit with which Terry Jordan, as both a scholar and a person, approached it. In the process, the tenth edition extends the legacy of the book he wrote to help guide students toward an equally generous worldview.

Sincerely,
Mona Domosh
AUGUST 2005

Geography is a diverse academic discipline. It concerns place and region and employs diverse methodologies from the social sciences, humanities, and earth sciences. Geographers deal with a wide range of subjects, from spatial patterns of human occupancy to the interaction between people and their environments. The geographer strives for a holistic view of the Earth as the home of humankind.

Because the world is in constant flux, geography is an ever-changing discipline. Geographers necessarily consider a wide range of topics and view them from several different perspectives. They continually seek new ways of looking at the inhabited Earth. For example, the rise of feminist perspectives has enabled geographers to see the world anew by pointing out that the spaces we use every day are shaped and used differently because our societies are profoundly structured by gender roles. Another example is the importance of globalization to our world today. This has led geographers to new and incisive engagements with concepts such as transnationalism and postcolonialism. Every revision of an introductory text such as *The Human Mosaic* requires careful attention to such changes and innovations that are ongoing in the dynamic field that is cultural geography.

The Five Themes

The Human Mosaic has always been built around **five themes:** culture region, cultural diffusion, cultural ecology, cultural interaction, and cultural landscape. These five themes are introduced and explained in the first chapter and serve as the framework for the 11 topical chapters that follow. Each theme is applied to a variety of geographical topics: religion, language, ethnicity, politics, demography, agriculture, industry, the city, and types of culture. This thematic organization allows students to relate to the most important aspects of cultural geography at every point in the text. As instructors, we have found that beginning students learn best when provided with a precise and useful framework, and the five-themes approach provides such a framework for understanding cultural geography. A small icon accompanies each theme as a visual reminder to students when these themes recur throughout the book. They will see:

 Culture Region

 Cultural Diffusion

 Cultural Ecology

 Cultural Interaction

 Cultural Landscape

In our classroom experience, we have found the thematic framework to be highly successful. Our *culture region* theme appeals to students' natural curiosity about the differences between places. *Cultural diffusion* conveys the dynamic aspect of culture particularly relevant to this age of incessant and rapid change. Students acquire an appreciation for how cultural traits spread (or do not spread) from place to place. The topics employed to illustrate the concepts of diffusion include many examples to which college students can relate, such as reggae and rap music, computer technology and the Internet, and the impact of globalization on consumer goods around the world. *Cultural ecology* addresses the complicated relationship between culture and the physical environment. With today's complex and often controversial relationship between the natural environment and our globalizing world, the tensions and the alliances that arise from this relationship are now at the forefront of this theme. *Cultural interaction* permits students to view culture as an interrelated whole, in which one facet acts on and is acted on by other facets—a key to understanding our complicated world. Last, the theme of *cultural landscape* heightens students' awareness of the visible character of places and regions.

Coverage and Organization

The Human Mosaic continues to provide balanced coverage between traditional geographical topics (culture, land use, political patterns, human adaptation to environment, environmental modification) and major new issues (globalization, political economy, feminism, global warming, transnationalism, and the digital age). We think that this balance exposes students to the breadth of cultural geography today. Adhering to a thematic organization, the book covers the following topic areas:

CHAPTER 1   Cultural Geography: Science and Art introduces the student to the field and explains the five themes of culture region, cultural diffusion, cultural ecology, cultural interaction, and cultural landscape, which are used throughout the text.

CHAPTER 2   Many Worlds: Geographies of Cultural Difference raises students' awareness of cultural diversity and examines the large array of cultural perspectives that shape how people understand and organize space and place.

CHAPTER 3   The Geography of Religion: Spaces and Places of Sacredness covers the interwoven cultures of religions, how they vary from place to place, and how sacredness profoundly shapes the world around us.

CHAPTER 4   Speaking About Places: The Geography of Language introduces the student to the geographical branch of geolinguistics and the spatial groupings of languages, with particular emphasis on the flexibility of languages to adapt to the changing needs of their users.

CHAPTER 5   Ethnic Geography: Homelands and Islands examines the spatial and ecological aspects of ethnicity as well as the tensions between globalization of some cultural trends and the trend toward ethnic awareness around the world.

CHAPTER 6   Political Geography: A Divided World addresses the geographical aspects of human political behavior, illustrated by the breakup of empires, the drawing of international boundaries, and voting patterns.

CHAPTER 7   Geodemography: Peopling the Earth looks at the distribution of people across the Earth and the spatial variations of birthrates, health, population growth, and other demographic traits that exist in different regions.

CHAPTER 8   Agricultural Geography: Food from the Good Earth examines types of agriculture, the ecology of farming and herding, the diffusion of elements of agriculture, the interaction between agriculture and other aspects of culture, and the visible variations revealed in agricultural landscapes.

CHAPTER 9   Industries: A Faustian Bargain explores industry and the industrial revolution through the eyes of the cultural geographer, with particular attention to recent global shifts in manufacturing and its uneven spatial distribution.

CHAPTER 10   Urbanization: The City in Time and Space looks at overall patterns of urbanization, how urbanization

began and developed, and the differing forms of global and globalizing cities.

CHAPTER 11   Inside the City: A Cultural Mosaic complements Chapter 10 by focusing on patterns within cities such as spatial differences, regional differences, and city structures.

CHAPTER 12   One World or Many? The Cultural Geography of the Future addresses the interactive relationship between globalization and the diversity of cultural geographies.

New to the Tenth Edition

Welcoming Two New Coauthors *The Human Mosaic* has undergone constant transformations throughout its nine editions, but it has stayed true to its original ecumenical vision of the world and of the discipline. That vision remains with this tenth edition, now coauthored with two highly accomplished geographers and teachers: Rod Neumann and Patricia Price, both of Florida International University. With Rod's expertise on the political ecology of Africa and Patricia's on the cultural and urban geography of Latin America and the U.S-Mexican border region, we believe we have created a new edition that speaks to students' needs to understand an increasingly interconnected and global world.

In this edition, you will find new perspectives and features:

Increased Emphasis on Globalization, Interconnectedness, and Transnational Activities To give students a better understanding of the entire world and of the processes and effects of globalization, the new edition has several new features:

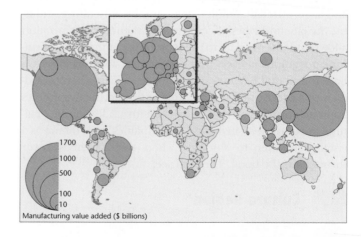

Figure 9.10 **Map of world manufacturing production.**
(Adapted from Dicken, 2003.)

■ Dozens of new and expanded international examples complement *The Human Mosaic*'s strengths while broadening the text's investigation into culture.

■ New **Culture in a Globalizing World** boxes move beyond typical economics-centered discussions to focus on the dynamic interaction of globalization and culture. They explore specific ways in which globalization is reshaping cultural practices around the globe—and, in turn, how the practices are shaping globalization.

■ A thoroughly revised Chapter 12—One World or Many? The Cultural Geography of the Future—offers a more balanced view of globalization while also emphasizing its relevance.

More Exposure to Modern Geographic Methods and Ways of Thinking In the new edition, **three critical thinking features** work together to introduce students to geographic methods and to help them develop an active-learning mind-set:

■ Updated **Seeing Geography** photo essays ask students to analyze photographic landscapes from a geographic perspective.

■ New **Practicing Geography** interviews feature today's leading cultural geographers discussing how they ask and answer questions, giving students a sense of geography's contribution to our understanding of important contemporary issues. We would like to thank our colleagues who graciously agreed to be interviewed for these boxes:

Chapter 1 Denis Cosgrove, *Univerisity of California, Los Angeles*

PRACTICING GEOGRAPHY

Denis Cosgrove

(Courtesy of Denis E. Cosgrove.)

When cultural geographer Denis Cosgrove rides the bus through West Los Angeles on his way to work at UCLA, or when he takes his Sunday walks through the green spaces of London, as he does often in the summer months on his visits to his former hometown, he is "practicing" geography. As he says, "the world/landscape around me is a primary source of questions . . . life is a field course."

Cosgrove, the Humboldt Chair of Geography at UCLA, and one of the most prominent cultural geographers in the English-speaking world, has explored through a series of

Chapter 2 Gregory Knapp, *University of Texas*
Chapter 3 Kenneth Foote, *University of Colorado*
Chapter 4 Allan Pred, *University of California, Berkeley*
Chapter 5 Daniel Arreola, *Arizona State University*
Chapter 6 Katharyne Mitchell, *University of Washington*
Chapter 7 Rachel Silvey, *University of Colorado*
Chapter 8 Karl Zimmerer, *University of Wisconsin, Madison*
Chapter 9 Amy Glasmeier, *Penn State*
Chapter 10 Kris Olds, *University of Wisconsin, Madison*
Chapter 11 Susan Hanson, *Clark University*
Chapter 12 Susan Mains, *University of the West Indies*

■ New **Doing Geography** exercises at the end of each chapter ask students to put geographic skills into practice, in ways that are enlightening, fun, and manageable for instructors.

A Stronger Initial Introduction to Geographic Perspectives Chapter 1 now presents a better balance between contemporary theory and classic geographic concepts, made evident through these elements:

■ A rewritten discussion of the book's five themes (culture region, cultural diffusion, cultural ecology, cultural interaction, and cultural landscape) to reflect current geographic scholarship

■ An expansion of the core theme of cultural ecology to include political-economic influences, reflecting the discipline's current conviction that cultural ecology should include political and economic forces operating on regional, national, and global scales

■ New and increased coverage of globalization and interconnectedness, giving students a firmer foundation in this crucial aspect of geographic exploration by relating it to their own lives

Revised Map Program To accommodate the changes of a world in flux, the authoritative map program retains its characteristic elegance and clarity while conveying the latest geographic information.

Thoroughly Updated All statistics have been updated, when available, to 2005, reflecting censuses worldwide.

Retained from the Highly Acclaimed Earlier Editions

We have retained the basic, classroom-tested devices that underlie *The Human Mosaic*'s earlier success:

Reflecting on Geography questions scattered through each chapter are intended to help students apply what they have just learned to real-world situations.

Focus On boxes, which appear from one to five times in each chapter, present illustrative examples or highlight relevant studies that students will find interesting.

Relevant web sites are listed at the end of each chapter to lead students to related materials bearing on the chapter's topic.

Figure captions in most cases contain questions relevant to what is being shown. Our maps and photos are not decoration but vital parts of the learning process.

Media and Supplements

The tenth edition is accompanied by a superior media and supplements package that facilitates student learning and enhances the teaching experience. For students, we have seamlessly integrated topics from the text with the companion web site; thus, the latest technology is being used to reinforce concepts from the text. For instructors, we have created a full-service ancillary package that will help in the preparation of lectures and exams, particularly in regard to electronic classroom presentations.

Aids for Student Learning

Atlas

Rand McNally's Atlas of World Geography,
paperback, 176 pages

This is available packaged with the text (ISBN 0-7167-7616-2), or with the text and *Student Study Guide* (ISBN 0-7167-7619-7), or with the text and *Exploring Human Geography with Maps* (ISBN 0-7167-7618-9).

Mapping Exercise Workbook

Exploring Human Geography with Maps,
Margaret Pearce, Ohio University, ISBN 0-7167-4917-3

This full-color workbook uses cartographic visualization to make maps into tools for the exploration and representation of geographic ideas. It directly addresses the concepts of *The Human Mosaic*, chapter by chapter, and it includes activities accessible through *The Human Mosaic Online* at http://www.whfreeman.com/jordan. Three types of activities occur in each chapter: Exploring Geographic Information Visually, Interpreting the Language of Maps, and Other Ways of Mapping.

Study Guide

Student Study Guide, by Michael Kukral, Rose-Hulman Institute of Technology, ISBN 0-7167-7256-6

The new and updated *Student Study Guide* provides a tremendous learning advantage for students using *The Human Mosaic*. This best-selling supplement contains updated practice tests, chapter learning objectives, key terms, and sections on map reading and interpretation. A highly integrated manual, the *Student Study Guide* supports and enhances the material covered in *The Human Mosaic* and guides the student to a clearer understanding of cultural geography.

Self-Study on the Web

The Human Mosaic Online:
http://www.whfreeman.com/jordan

The companion web site serves as an online study guide. The core of the site is a range of features that encourage critical thinking and assist in study and review. Features include:

Web Activities from *Exploring Human Geography with Maps*, by Margaret Pearce, Ohio University

Review Quizzes for each chapter, by A. Steele Becker, University of Nebraska, Kearney, and Jacqueline V. Becker

Aids for the Instructor

Presentation

Instructor's Resource CD-ROM and Web Site,
ISBN 0-7167-7402-X

Both resources contain *all* the text images available in JPEG format and as Microsoft PowerPoint™ slides for use in classroom presentations. The labels on the images have been enlarged for better projection quality. The *Instructor's Resource CD-ROM* also contains chapter outlines on Microsoft PowerPoint™, as well as the *Test Bank* as chapter-by-chapter Microsoft Word™ files that can be easily modified by the instructor.

Slide Set with Lecture Notes,
ISBN 0-7167-1486-8

This is a set of 100 images with accompanying explanatory lecture notes for presentations.

Overhead Transparencies,
ISBN 0-7167-1318-7

This is a handy set of 100 key maps and figures from the text for classroom presentation.

NEW FRONTLINE/World™ Video Anthology

Available in VHS (ISBN 0-7167-2837-0) and DVD
(ISBN 0-7167-2838-9)

Drawn from the acclaimed PBS series FRONTLINE/World, these ten video segments, each between 10 and 20 minutes long, concern matters both current and relevant. Taken together, the book and the videos are an especially engaging educational resource.

NEW FRONTLINE/World™ Instructor Video Guide

by Jason Dittmer, Georgia Southern University,
ISBN 0-7167-2835-4

This guide provides background information and offers ideas and resources for connecting the videos with classroom discussions and homework assignments.

FRONTLINE/World™ videos available on VHS or DVD include the following:

India "Hole in the Wall: Opening the door to cyberspace"
Mexico "A Death in the Desert: The fatal journey of a migrant worker"
Guatemala/Mexico "Coffee Country: Can fair trade save the farm?"
Spain "The Lawless Sea: Investigating a notorious shipwreck"
Moscow "Rich in Russia: A brave new world of young capitalists and tycoons"
Iraq "The Road to Kirkuk: After Saddam's terror, can Kurds and Arabs live together?"
Nigeria "The Road North: What the Miss World riots reveal about a divided country"
Bhutan "The Last Place: Television arrives in a Buddhist kingdom"
Hong Kong "Chasing the Virus: Trying to stop the deadly SARS epidemic"
Cambodia "Pol Pot's Shadow: Searching for a mysterious executioner"

Course Management

All instructor and student resources are also available via WebCT and Blackboard to enhance your course. W. H. Freeman and Company offers a course cartridge that populates your course web site with content tied directly to the book.

Assessment

Test Bank, by Douglas Munski,
University of North Dakota

The *Test Bank* is available on the *Instructor's Resource* CD-ROM and can also be accessed via the book's companion web site under the password-protected "For Instructors" section. The *Test Bank* is carefully designed to match the pedagogical intent of the text. It contains more than 1000 test questions (multiple-choice and true/false). The files are provided as chapter-by-chapter Microsoft Word files that are easy to download, edit, and print.

Acknowledgments

No textbook is ever written single-handedly or even "double-handedly." An introductory text covering a wide range of topics must draw heavily on the research and help of others. In various chapters, we have not hesitated to mention a great many geographers on whose work we have relied. We apologize for any misinterpretations or oversimplifications of their findings that may have resulted because of our own error or the limited space available.

Many geographers contributed advice, comments, ideas, and assistance as this book moved from outline through draft to publication from the first edition through the tenth. We would like to thank those colleagues who contributed their helpful opinions during the **revision of the tenth edition:**

W. Frank Ainsley, University of North Carolina, Wilmington; Timothy Bawden, University of Wisconsin, Eau Claire; Brad Bays, Oklahoma State University; Gigi Berardi, Western Washington University; Daniel Borough, California State University, Los Angeles; Patricia Boudinot, George Mason University; Wayne Brew, Montgomery County Community College; Michael J. Broadway, Northern Michigan University; Scott S. Brown, Francis Marion University; Merel J. Cox, Pennsylvania State University, Altoona; Christina Dando, University of Nebraska, Omaha; Robin E. Datel, California State University, Sacramento; James A. Davis, Brigham Young University; Richard Deal, Western Kentucky University; Lorraine Dowler, Pennsylvania State University; D. J. P. Forth, West Hills College; Jeffrey J. Gordon, Bowling Green State University; Qian Guo, San Francisco State University; Andy Herod, University of Georgia; Elliot P. Hertzenberg, Wilmington College; Ronald Isaac, Ohio University; Brad Jokisch, Ohio University; James R. Keese, Cal Poly State University; Artimus Keiffer, Wittenberg University; Edward L. Kinman, Longwood University; Marti L. Klein, Saddleback College; Olaf Kuhlke, University of Minnesota, Duluth; Paul R. Larson, Southern Utah University; Peter Li, Tennessee Technological University; Jose Javier Lopez, Minnesota State University, Mankato; John Milbauer, Northeastern State University; Cynthia A. Miller, Minnesota State University, Mankato; Karen M. Morin, Bucknell

University; Garth A. Myers, University of Kansas; Michael G. Noll, Valdosta State University; Ann M. Oberhauser, West Virginia University; Bimal Paul, Kansas State University; Erik Prout, Texas A&M University; Virginia M. Ragan, Maple Woods Community College; Henry O. Robertson, Louisiana State University, Alexandria; Robert Rundstrom, University of Oklahoma, Norman; Norman H. Runge, University of Delaware; Lydia Savage, University of Southern Maine; Steven M. Schnell, Kutztown University of Pennsylvania; Cynthia S. Simmons, Michigan State University; Emily Skop, University of Texas, Austin; Christa Smith, Clemson University; Anne K. Soper, Indiana University; Jonathan Taylor, California State University, Fullerton; Thomas Terich, Western Washington University; Ralph Triplette, Western Carolina University; Ingolf Vogeler, University of Wisconsin, Eau Claire; Barney Warf, Florida State University; W. Michael Wheeler, Southwestern Oklahoma State University; Donald Zeigler, Old Dominion University.

We would also like to thank those colleagues who offered helpful comments during the **preparation of earlier editions:**

Jennifer Adams, Pennsylvania State University; Christopher Airriess, Ball State University; Nigel Allan, University of California, Davis; Thomas D. Anderson, Bowling Green State University; Timothy G. Anderson, Ohio Wesleyan University; Patrick Ashwood, Hawkeye Community College; Nancy Bain, Ohio University; A. Steele Becker, University of Nebraska, Kearney; Sarah Bednarz, Texas A&M University; Craig S. Campbell, Youngstown State University; Marcelo Cruz, University of Wisconsin, Green Bay; Matthew Ebiner, El Camino College; Carolyn Gallaher, American University; Charles F. Gritzner, South Dakota State University; Sally Gros, University of Oklahoma, Norman; Jennifer Helzer, California State University, Stanislaus; Cecelia Hudleson, Foothill College; Gregory Jean, Samford University; Vandara Kohli, California State University, Bakersfield; Debra Kreitzer, Western Kentucky University; Michael Kukral, Ohio Wesleyan University; Hsiang-te Kung, Memphis University; William Laatsch, University of Wisconsin, Green Bay; Ann Legreid, Central Missouri State University; Ronald Lockmann, California State University, Dominiquez Hills; Jesse O. McKee, University of Southern Mississippi; Wayne McKim, Towson State University; Douglas Meyer, Eastern Illinois University; Klaus Meyer-Arendt, Mississippi State University; John Milbauer, Northeastern State University; Cynthia A. Miller, Syracuse University; Glenn R. Miller, Bridgewater State College; Don Mitchell, Syracuse University; James Mulvihill, California State University, San Bernardino; Douglas Munski, University of North Dakota; Thomas Orf, Prestonburg Community College; Brian Osborne, Queen's University; Kenji Oshiro, Wright State University; Bimal K. Paul, Kansas State University; Jeffrey P. Richetto, University of Alabama; Robert Rundstrom, University of Oklahoma; Stephen Sandlin, California State University, Pomona; Lydia Savage, University of Southern Maine; Andrew Schoolmaster III, University of North Texas; Roger W. Stump, State University of New York at Albany; Thomas M. Tharp, Purdue University; Ralph Triplette, Western Carolina University; Daniel E. Turbeville III, Eastern Washington University; Ingolf Vogeler, University of Wisconsin; Philip Wagner, Simon Fraser State University; Barbara Weightman, California State University, Fullerton; David Wilkins, University of Utah; Douglas Wilms, East Carolina State University; Donald Zeigler, Old Dominion University.

Our thanks also go to various staff members of W. H. Freeman and Company whose encouragement, skills, and suggestions have created a special working environment and to whom we express our deepest gratitude. In particular, we thank Jason Noe, acquisitions editor for geography; Sara Tenney, publisher, and a strong supporter of our book from the first; Nick Tymoczko, developmental editor par excellence; Scott Guile, marketing manager; Jane O'Neill, project editor; Vicki Tomaselli, designer; Sheridan Sellers, compositor and page makeup artist; Bill Page, illustration coordinator; Laura Nash and Elyse Reider, photo researchers, and Patricia Marx, photo editor; Susan Wein, production coordinator; Philip McCaffrey, managing editor; Ellen Cash, vice president of production; Lisa Samols, media and supplements editor; Karen Osborne, copy editor; and Eleanor Wedge, proofreader. At Dartmouth College, Chongwon J. Char served as an excellent and tireless research assistant. The beneficial influence of all these people can be detected throughout the book.

Finally, we dedicate this book to Terry Jordan-Bychkov. He loved exploring the world—its diverse peoples and places as far away as Siberia and as close as Texas—and sharing the excitement of that exploration with his students, friends, and family. It was Terry's vision, energy, intellect, and passion that made this book happen in the first place and that sustained it through nine editions. His spirit is reflected on every page.

Terry G. Jordan-Bychkov was the Walter Prescott Webb Professor in the Department of Geography at the University of Texas at Austin. He earned his PhD at the University of Wisconsin at Madison. A specialist in the cultural and historical geography of the United States, Jordan-Bychkov was particularly interested in the diffusion of Old World culture to North America that helped produce the vivid geographical mosaic evident today. He served as president of the Association of American Geographers in 1987 and 1988 and earlier received an Honors Award from that organization. He wrote on a wide range of American cultural topics, including forest colonization, cattle ranching, folk architecture, and ethnicity. His scholarly books include *The European Culture Area: A Systematic Geography*, 4th edition (with Bella Bychkova Jordan, 2002), *Anglo-Celtic Australia: Colonial Immigration and Cultural Regionalism* (with Alyson L. Greiner, 2002), *Siberian Village: Land and Life in the Sakha Republic* (with Bella Bychkova Jordan, 2001), *The Mountain West: Interpreting the Folk Landscape* (with Jon Kilpinen and Charles Gritzner, 1997), *North American Cattle Ranching Frontiers* (1993), *The American Backwoods Frontier* (with Matti Kaups, 1989), *American Log Building* (1985), *Texas Graveyards* (1982), *Trails to Texas: Southern Roots of Western Cattle Ranching* (1981), and *German Seed in Texas Soil* (1966). Having been fascinated with maps and landscapes since childhood, Jordan-Bychkov became a geography major during his college freshman year. For him, the most rewarding aspect of geography was field research. His only hobby was travel.

Mona Domosh is a professor of geography at Dartmouth College. She earned her PhD at Clark University. Her research has examined the links between gender ideologies and the cultural formation of large American cities in the nineteenth century, particularly in regard to such critical but vexing distinctions as consumption/production, public/private, masculine/feminine. She is currently engaged in research that takes the ideological association of women, femininity, and space in a more postcolonial direction by asking what roles nineteenth-century ideas of femininity, masculinity, consumption, and "whiteness" played in the crucial shift from American nation-building to empire-building. Domosh is the author of *Invented Cities: The Creation of Landscape in 19th-Century New York and Boston* (1996); the coauthor, with Joni Seager, of *Putting Women in Place: Feminist Geographers Make Sense of the World* (2001); and the coeditor of *Handbook of Cultural Geography* (2002).

Rod Neumann is an associate professor of geography in the Department of International Relations at Florida International University. He earned his PhD at the University of California at Berkeley. He has studied the complex relationships between human culture and the natural environment through a specific focus on national parks, wildlife conservation, and forest use and management. He combines the analytical tools of cultural and political ecology and landscape studies in his research. He has conducted fieldwork primarily in sub-Saharan Africa but also has research interests in Central America and the U.S. West. He is the author of *Imposing Wilderness: Struggles of Livelihoods and Nature Preservation in Africa* (1998) and *Making Political Ecology* (2005), and the coauthor, with Eric Hirsch, of *The Commercialization of Non-Timber Forest Products* (2000).

Patricia L. Price is an associate professor of geography at Florida International University. She earned her PhD at the University of Washington. Trained as a development and urban geographer, she has inexorably gravitated to the field of cultural geography and incorporated all three approaches into her scholarship. She is fascinated by landscapes and how they provide an understanding of ways in which humans form attachments to place. The scale of the very local—minds, bodies, and neighborhoods—has been a key focus of her work. Connecting the long-standing theme of humanistic scholarship in cultural geography to more recent critical approaches best describes her ongoing project. From her initial field research in urban Mexico, she has extended her focus to the U.S.-Mexican border and, most recently, to south Florida as a borderland of sorts. Price is the author of *Dry Place: Landscapes of Belonging and Exclusion* (2004), which centralizes the role of narrative in historical claims to the U.S. Southwest and northern Mexico as well as in contemporary imaginations of identity, faith, and nation in the borderlands. One of her most recent projects is a study of social banditry and popular religiosity in northern Mexico, which she would like to extend to a book-length project. As the tenth edition of *The Human Mosaic* went to press in 2005, she was engaged in a two-year field research project in the East Little Havana neighborhood of Miami. This project, sponsored by the National Science Foundation, brought together a total of six researchers and many more graduate and undergraduate research assistants in Miami, Phoenix, and Chicago. Together, they are exploring how established Latina/o residents of inner-ring ethnic enclave neighborhoods deal with changes arising from gentrification and ongoing immigration.

THE HUMAN MOSAIC

Why is it difficult for most of us to interpret this image as a map?

Aboriginal Painting of Arnhem Land, Northern Territory, Australia. *(Penny Tweedie/CORBIS.)*
Turn to Seeing Geography on page 28 for an in-depth analysis of the above question.

CULTURAL GEOGRAPHY

Science and Art

MOST OF US ARE BORN GEOGRAPHERS. We are curious about the distinctive character of places and peoples. We think in terms of territory and space. Take a look outside your window right now. The houses and commercial buildings, streets and highways, gardens and lawns, all tell us something interesting and profound about who we are as a culture. If you travel down the road, or on a jet to another region or country, that view outside your window will change, sometimes subtly, sometimes drastically. Our geographical imaginations will push us to look and think and begin to make sense of what it is going in these different places, environments, and landscapes. It is this curiosity about the world—about how and why it is structured the way it is, what it means, and how we can go about changing it—that is at the heart of cultural geography. You are already cultural geographers; we hope that our book will make you better ones.

If every place on Earth were identical, we would not need geography, but each is unique. Every place, however, does share characteristics with other places. Geographers define the concept of **region** to mean a grouping of similar places. The existence of different regions endows the Earth's surface with a magical quality. Places possess an emotional significance that contributes profoundly to our identity as individual human beings: we all must belong somewhere to be complete persons. Geography as an academic discipline is an outgrowth of both our curiosity about lands and peoples other than our own and our need to come to grips with the place-centered element within our souls. Because geographers deal with these fundamentally important issues, they have, over the centuries, generated a number of concepts that have literally changed the world (see Focus On: Seven Cultural Geographical Ideas That Changed the World).

Seven Cultural Geographical Ideas That Changed the World

1. Maps
2. Human adaptation to habitat
3. Human transformation of the Earth
4. Sense of place

5. Spatial organization and interdependence
6. Central place theory (see Chapter 10)
7. Megalopolis (see Chapter 10)

Abridged from Hanson, 1996

Our natural geographical curiosity and intrinsic need for identity were long ago reinforced by pragmatism, the practical motives of traders and empire builders who wanted information about the world for the purposes of commerce and conquest. This concern for the practical aspects of geography first arose thousands of years ago among the ancient Greeks, Romans, Mesopotamians, and Phoenicians, the greatest traders and empire builders of their times. They cataloged factual information about locations, places, and products. Indeed, **geography** is a Greek word meaning literally "to describe the Earth." Not content merely to chart and describe the world, these ancient geographers soon began to ask questions about why cultures and environments differ from place to place, initiating the study of what today we call geography.

When professional, academic geographers consider the differences and similarities among places, they want to understand what they see. They first find out exactly what variations exist among regions and places by describing them as precisely as possible. Then they try to decide what forces made these areas different or alike. Geographers ask *what? where? why?* and *how?*

What Is Cultural Geography?

Cultural geography forms one part of the discipline of geography, complementing physical geography (the part that deals with the natural environment). To understand the scope of cultural geography, we must first discuss the various meanings of **culture.**

There are many definitions of culture, some broad and some narrow. For the purposes of this book, we define culture as learned collective human behavior, as opposed to innate, or inborn, behavior. These learned traits form a way of life held in common by a group of people. Learned similarities in speech, behavior, ideology, livelihood, technology, value system, and society bind people together. Culture,

defined in this way, involves a communication system of acquired beliefs, memories, perceptions, traditions, and attitudes that serves to shape behavior. We can think of this communication system as a set of "stories" that groups of people tell about themselves. These "stories" can take the form of narratives, such as creations myths, Hollywood films, and novels, or can be more broadly conceived, as in the clothes we wear, the foods we eat, the ways we worship, the governments we accept as legitimate, the way we form families, and so on. As geographers, we tend to be interested in these stories as they take shape in particular places, environments, and landscapes.

A particular culture is not a static, fixed phenomenon, nor does it always govern its members. Rather, as geographers Kay Anderson and Fay Gale put it, "culture is a *process* in which people are actively engaged." It is a dynamic mix of symbols, beliefs, language, and practices. Individual members can and do change a culture, which means that ways of life constantly change and that tensions between opposing views are usually present. Contestation and change are part of the human condition and are reflected in culture. Cultures are never internally homogeneous because individual humans never think or behave in exactly the same manner. Within each culture are persons of different gender, creativity, age, sexual orientation, and so on.

Cultural geography, then, is the study of the relationships among space, place, environment, and culture. It examines in what ways culture is expressed and symbolized in the landscapes we see around us, including homes, commercial buildings, roads, agricultural patterns, gardens, and parks. It is concerned both with how we understand, give meanings to, and derive meanings from landscapes, places, and environments, and with the roles that those landscapes, places, and environments play in shaping and changing culture. It analyzes the ways in which language, religion, the economy, government, and other cultural phenomena vary or remain constant from one place to another and provides a perspective for understanding how

Figure 1.1 **Two traditional houses of worship.** Geographers seek to learn how and why cultures differ, or are similar, from one place to another. Often the differences and similarities have a visual expression. In what ways are these two structures—one a Catholic church in Honduras and the other a Buddhist temple in Laos—alike and different? *(Left: Rob Crandall/Stock Connection/Alamy; Right: Peter Adams/Alamy.)*

people function spatially and identify with place and region (Figure 1.1).

In seeking explanations for cultural diversity and place identity, geographers consider a wide array of causal factors. Some of these involve the **physical environment:** terrain, climate, natural vegetation, wildlife, variations in soil, and the pattern of land and water. Because we cannot understand a culture removed from its physical setting, cultural geography offers not only a spatial perspective but also an ecological one. One of the distinctive attributes of geography is the way it bridges the social and earth sciences to study people in their habitats. For this reason, geographers tend to resist the increasing fragmentation of learning into highly specialized, segregated academic disciplines. We seek an integrative view of humankind in its physical environment.

Geography does not offer easy explanations for cultural phenomena because many complex forces are at work and all of them are interconnected in very complicated ways. The complexity of the forces that affect culture can be illustrated by an example drawn from agricultural geography: the distribution of wheat cultivation in the world. If you look at Figure 1.2, you can see important areas of wheat cultivation in Australia but not Africa, in the United States but not Chile, in China but not Southeast Asia. Why does this spatial pattern exist? Partly it results from environmental factors such as climate, terrain, and soils. Some regions have always been too dry for wheat cultivation. The land in others is too steep or infertile. Indeed, there is a strong correlation between wheat cultivation and midlatitude climates, level terrain, and good soil.

Still, we should not place exclusive importance on such physical factors. People can modify the effects of climate through irrigation; the use of hothouses; or the development of new, specialized strains of wheat. They can conquer slopes through terracing, and they can make poor soils productive through fertilization. For example, farmers in mountainous parts of Greece traditionally wrested an annual harvest of wheat from tiny terraced plots where soil had been trapped behind hand-built stone retaining walls. Even in the United States, environmental factors alone cannot explain the curious fact that major wheat cultivation is concentrated in the semiarid Great Plains, some distance from states such as Ohio and Illinois, where the climate for growing wheat is better. The cultural geographer knows that wheat has to survive in a cultural environment as well as a physical one.

Ultimately, agricultural patterns cannot be explained by the characteristics of the land and climate alone. Many factors complicate the distribution of wheat, including people's tastes and traditions. Food preferences and taboos, often backed by religious beliefs, strongly influence the choice of crops to plant. Some cultural groups prefer dark bread made from rye flour. Other groups, particularly Native Americans, would rather eat breads made from maize, a crop given a religious role in their traditional way of life (see Focus On: "When Jesus Came, the Corn Mothers Went Away," in Chapter 3). Obviously, wheat will not

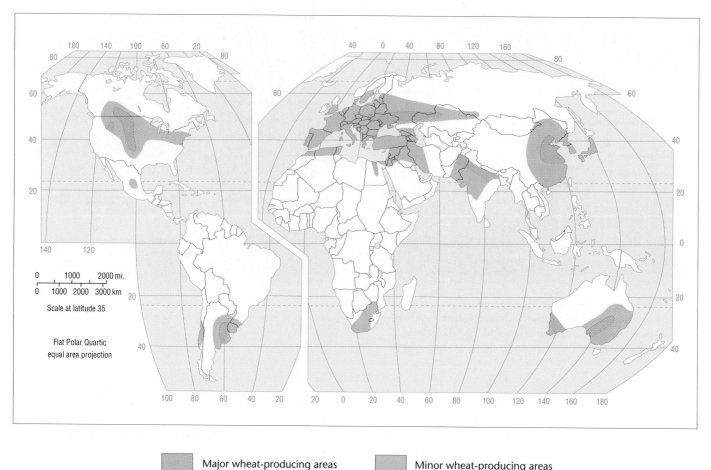

Major wheat-producing areas   Minor wheat-producing areas

Figure 1.2 **Areas of wheat production in the world today.** These culture regions are based on a single trait: the importance of wheat in the agricultural system. This map tells us what and where. It raises the question of why. What causal forces might be at work to produce this geographical distribution of wheat farming?

"thrive" in such cultural environments. Where wheat bread is preferred, people are willing to put great efforts into overcoming hostile physical surroundings. They have even created new strains of wheat, thereby decreasing the environment's influence on the distribution of wheat cultivation. Other factors, such as public policies, can also encourage or discourage wheat cultivation. For example, tariffs protect the wheat farmers of France and other European countries from competition with more efficient American and Canadian producers.

This is by no means a complete list of the forces that affect the geographical distribution of wheat cultivation. It should be clear, though, that the contemporary map of wheat production reflects the push and pull of many factors. The distribution of all cultural elements is a result of the constant interplay of diverse factors. Cultural geography is the discipline that seeks such explanations.

Themes in Cultural Geography

Our study of cultures is organized around five geographical concepts or themes: culture region, cultural diffusion, cultural ecology, cultural interaction, and cultural landscape. These themes are stressed throughout the book and give structure to each chapter.

 Culture Region

Phrased as a question, the theme of culture region could be "How are cultures and cultural traits grouped or arranged geographically?" Places and regions provide the essence of geography. How and why are places alike or different? How do they mesh together into functioning spatial networks? How do their inhabitants perceive them and identify with them? These are central geographical questions. A **culture region,** then, is a geographical unit based on characteristics and functions of culture. Three types of culture regions are recognized by geographers: formal, functional, and vernacular.

Formal Culture Regions A **formal culture region** is an area inhabited by people who have one or more cultural traits in common, such as language, religion or system of livelihood. It is an area, therefore, that is relatively homogeneous with regard to one or more cultural traits. Geographers use this concept to map spatial differences throughout the world. For example, an Arabic-language formal culture region can be drawn on a map of languages and would include the areas where Arabic is spoken, rather than, say, English or Hindi or Mandarin. Similarly, a wheat-farming formal culture region would include the parts of the world where wheat is a major crop (look again at Figure 1.2).

The examples of Arabic speech and of wheat cultivation represent the concept of formal culture region at its simplest level. Each is based on a single cultural trait. More commonly, formal culture regions depend on multiple related traits (Figure 1.3). Thus, an Inuit (Eskimo) culture region might be based on language, religion, economy, social organization, and type of dwellings. The culture region would reflect the spatial distribution of these five Inuit cultural traits. Districts in which all five of these traits are present would be part of the culture region. Similarly, Europe can be subdivided into several multitrait regions (Figure 1.4).

Formal culture regions are the geographer's somewhat arbitrary creations. No two cultural traits have the same distribution, and the territorial extent of a culture region depends on what and how many defining traits are used (Figure 1.5). Why *five* Inuit traits, not four or six? Why not *foods* instead of (or in addition to) dwelling types? Consider, for example, Greeks and Turks, who differ in language and religion. Formal culture regions defined on the basis of speech and religious faith would separate these two groups. However, Greeks and Turks hold many other cultural traits in common. Both groups are monotheistic, worshipping a single god. In both groups, male supremacy and patriarchal families are the rule. Certain folk foods, such as shish kebab, are enjoyed by both. Whether Greeks and Turks are placed in the same formal culture region or in different ones depends entirely on how the geographer chooses to define the culture region. That choice in turn depends on the specific purpose of research or teaching that the culture region is designed to serve. Thus, an infinite number of formal culture regions can be created. It is unlikely that any two geographers would use exactly the same distinguishing criteria or place cultural boundaries in precisely the same location.

The geographer who identifies a formal culture region must locate *cultural borders.* Because cultures overlap and mix, such boundaries are rarely sharp, even if only a single cultural trait is mapped. For this reason, we find cultural *border zones* rather than lines. These zones broaden with each additional cultural trait that is considered, because no two traits have the same spatial distribution. As a result, instead

Figure 1.3 **A traditional market on the island of New Guinea.** Various facets of a multitrait formal culture region can be seen here, including the wares for sale and the people's clothing. *(Muchtar Zakaria/APPhoto.)*

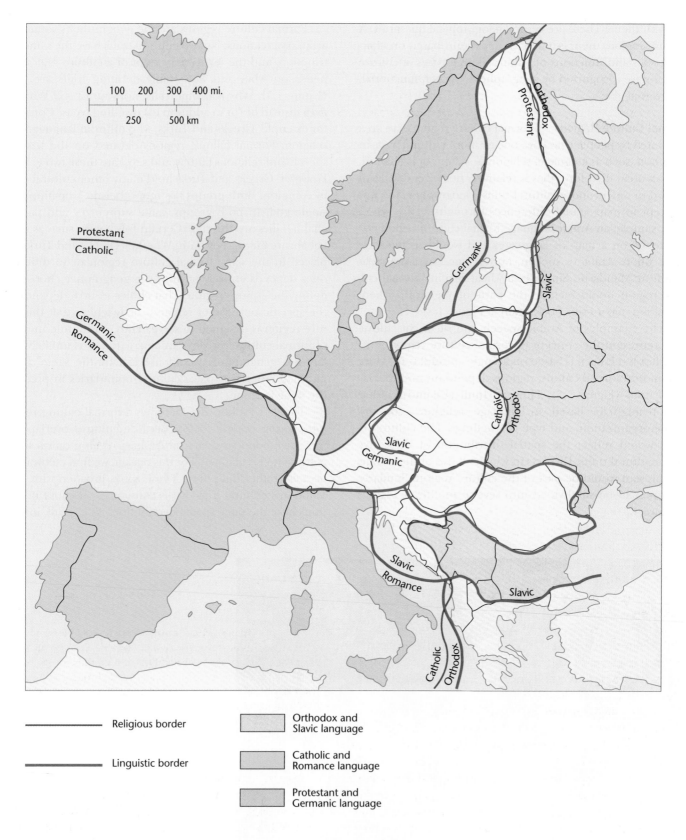

Figure 1.4 Formal culture regions of Europe based on only two traits: language and religion.
Notice how transitional areas appear between such culture regions even when only two traits are used to define them. What does this teach us about boundaries between cultures?

of having clear borders, formal culture regions reveal a center or core where the defining traits are all present. Away from the central core, the characteristics weaken and disappear, as is suggested in Figures 1.4 and 1.5. Thus, many formal culture regions display a **core-periphery** pattern.

In a real sense, then, the human world is chaotic. No matter how closely related two elements of culture seem to be, careful investigation always shows that they do not cover exactly the same area. This is true regardless of what degree of detail is involved. What does this chaos mean to the cultural geographer? First, it tells us that every cultural trait is spatially unique and that the explanation for each spatial variation differs in some degree from all others. Second, it means that culture changes continually throughout an area and that every inhabited place on Earth has a unique combination of cultural features. No place is exactly like another.

Does this cultural uniqueness of each place prevent geographers from seeking explanatory theories? Does it doom them to explaining each locale separately? The answer must be no. The fact that no two hills or rocks, no two planets or stars, no two trees or flowers are identical has not prevented geologists, astronomers, and botanists from formulating theories and explanations based on generalizations.

Functional Culture Regions The hallmark of a formal culture region is cultural homogeneity. Moreover, it is abstract rather than concrete. By contrast, a **functional culture region** need not be culturally homogeneous; instead, it is an area that has been organized to function politically, socially, or economically as one unit. A city, an independent state, a precinct, a church diocese or parish, a trade area, a farm, and a Federal Reserve Bank district are all examples of functional regions. Functional culture regions have **nodes,** or central points where the functions are coordinated and directed. Examples of such nodes are city halls, national capitals, precinct voting places, parish churches, factories, and banks. In this sense, functional regions also possess a core-periphery configuration, in common with formal culture regions.

Many functional regions have clearly defined borders. A metropolitan area is a functional region that includes all the land under the jurisdiction of a particular urban government (Figure 1.6). The borders of this functional region may not be so apparent from a car window, but they will be clearly delineated on a regional map by a line distinguishing between one jurisdiction and another. Similarly, each state in the United States and each Canadian province is a functional region, coordinated and directed from a capital, with government control extended over a fixed area with clearly defined borders.

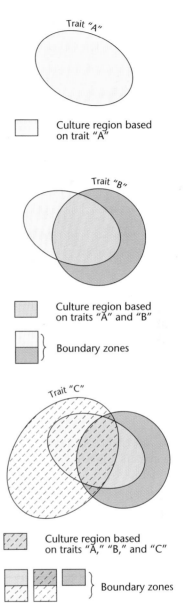

Figure 1.5 Hypothetical formal culture regions based on one, two, and three traits. Notice that no two traits have the same spatial distribution. With each additional trait, the core of the region grows smaller and the boundary zone broader. Imagine how complicated the pattern would become were 5, 10, or 100 traits included. Do you understand now why each place on Earth is unique?

Not all functional culture regions have fixed, precise borders, however. A good example is a daily newspaper's circulation area. The node for the paper would be the plant where it is produced. Every morning, trucks move out of the plant to distribute the paper throughout the city. The newspaper may have a sales area extending into the city's suburbs, local bedroom communities, nearby towns, and rural

Figure 1.6 **Aerial view of Denver.** This image clearly illustrates the node of a functional region—here, the dense cluster of commercial buildings—that coordinates activities throughout the area that surrounds it. Can you identify the border of this functional region? Why or why not? (*Jim Wark/Airphoto.*)

areas. There its sales area overlaps the sales territories of competing newspapers published in other cities. It would be futile to try to define exclusive borders for such an area. How would you draw a sales area boundary for the *New York Times*? Its Sunday edition is sold in some quantity even in California, thousands of miles from its node, and it is published simultaneously in different cities.

Functional culture regions generally do not coincide spatially with formal culture regions, and this disjuncture often creates problems for the functional region. Germany provides an example (Figure 1.7). As an independent state, Germany forms a functional culture region. Language provides a substantial basis for political unity. However, the formal culture region of the German language extends beyond the political borders of Germany and includes part or all of eight other independent states. More important, numerous formal culture regions have bo rders cutting through German territory. Some of these have endured for millennia, causing differences among northern, southern, eastern, and western Germans. These contrasts make the functioning of the German state more difficult and help explain why Germany has been politically fragmented more often than unified.

Vernacular Culture Regions A **vernacular culture region** is one that is *perceived* to exist by its inhabitants, as evidenced by the widespread acceptance and use of a special regional

name. Figure 1.8 reveals one such popular region in the United States, "Dixie." Some vernacular regions are based on physical environmental features; others find their basis in economic, political, or historical characteristics. Vernacular regions, like most culture regions, generally lack sharp borders, and the inhabitants of any given area may claim residence in more than one such region. They vary in scale from city neighborhoods to sizable parts of continents.

At a basic level, the vernacular region grows out of people's sense of belonging and identification with a particular region. By contrast, many formal or functional culture regions lack this attribute and, as a result, are far less potent geographical entities. Self-conscious regional identity has major political and social ramifications.

REFLECTING ON GEOGRAPHY

What examples can you think of that show how identification with a vernacular region is a powerful political force?

Vernacular culture regions often lack the organization necessary for functional regions, although they may be centered around a single urban node, and they frequently do not display the cultural homogeneity that characterizes formal regions. They are a type unto themselves—a type rooted in culture itself.

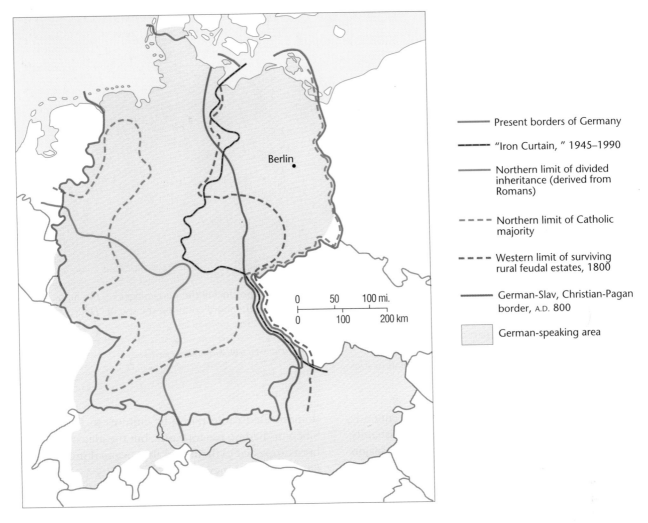

Berlin

Present borders of Germany

"Iron Curtain, " 1945–1990

Northern limit of divided inheritance (derived from Romans)

Northern limit of Catholic majority

Western limit of surviving rural feudal estates, 1800

German-Slav, Christian-Pagan border, A.D. 800

German-speaking area

0   50   100 mi.
0   100   200 km

Figure 1.7 **East versus west and north versus south in Germany.** As a political unit and functional culture region, Germany must overcome the disruptions caused by numerous formal culture regions that tend to make the sections of Germany culturally different. Formal and functional culture regions rarely coincide spatially. How might these sectional contrasts cause problems for modern Germany?

 ## Cultural Diffusion

How did the various elements of cultures spread to the culture regions where they occur today? How do ideas, practices, behaviors, and technologies spread geographically, or why do they not spread? These questions define our second theme, **cultural diffusion.**

Regardless of type, the culture regions of the world evolved through communication and contact among people (see Focus On: Cultural Diffusion: A 100 Percent American). As Figure 1.9 shows, each element of culture originates in one or more places and then spreads. Some innovations occur only once, and geographers can sometimes trace a cultural element back to a single place of origin. In other cases, **independent invention** occurs: the same or very similar innovation is separately developed at different places by different peoples. The study of cultural diffusion—the geographical origin and spread of ideas and innovations—is a very important theme. Through the study of diffusion, the cultural geographer can begin to understand how spatial patterns in culture emerged and evolved. After all, any culture is the product of almost countless innovations that spread from their points of origin to cover a wider area.

Types of Diffusion Geographers, drawing heavily on the research of Torsten Hägerstrand, recognize several different kinds of diffusion (see Figure 1.9). **Relocation diffusion** occurs when individuals or groups with a particular idea or practice migrate from one location to another, thereby

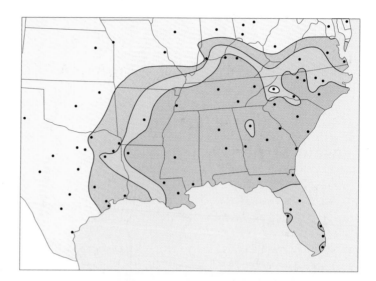

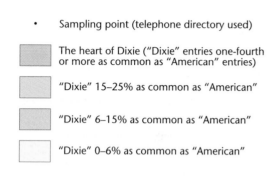

- Sampling point (telephone directory used)

The heart of Dixie ("Dixie" entries one-fourth or more as common as "American" entries)

"Dixie" 15–25% as common as "American"

"Dixie" 6–15% as common as "American"

"Dixie" 0–6% as common as "American"

Figure 1.8 **Dixie: a vernacular region.** "Dixie" is loaded with historical and cultural connotations. The territorial extent of Dixie was determined by counting the number of times it appeared in telephone directories as part of the name of business establishments. The total for each city was then divided by the entries for "American," to adjust for the different population sizes of the cities, producing the percentages on the map. The higher the number, the more common the use of "Dixie." Make a count of regional terms in your telephone directory. Does the place where you live lie within a vernacular region such as Dixie? *(After Reed, 1976: 932, with modifications for Texas.)*

bringing it to their new homeland. Religions frequently spread this way. An example is the migration of Christianity with European settlers who came to America. In **expansion diffusion,** ideas or practices spread throughout a population, from area to area, in a snowballing process, so that the total number of knowers or users and the areas of occurrence increase.

Expansion diffusion can be further divided into three subtypes. In **hierarchical diffusion,** ideas leapfrog from one important person to another or from one urban center to another, temporarily bypassing other persons or rural territory. We can see hierarchical diffusion at work in everyday life by observing the acceptance of new modes of dress or foods. For example, sushi restaurants originally diffused from Japan in the 1970s very slowly, as many people were reluctant to try raw fish. In the United States the first restaurants appeared in the major cities of Los Angeles and New York. Only gradually throughout the 1980s and 1990s did sushi eating become more common in the less urbanized parts of the country. By contrast, **contagious diffusion** involves the wavelike spread of ideas in the manner of a contagious disease, moving throughout space without regard to hierarchies. Hierarchical and contagious diffusion often work together. The worldwide spread of HIV/AIDS provides a sobering example of how these two types of diffusion can reinforce each other (Figure 1.10). Sometimes a specific trait is rejected but the underlying idea is accepted, resulting in **stimulus diffusion.** For example, early Siberian peoples domesticated reindeer only after exposure to the

domesticated cattle raised by cultures to their south. The Siberians had no use for cattle, but the idea of domesticated herds appealed to them, and they began domesticating reindeer, an animal they had long hunted.

If you throw a rock into a pond and watch the spreading ripples, you can see them become gradually weaker as they move away from the point of impact. In the same way, diffusion becomes weaker as a cultural innovation moves away from its point of origin. That is, diffusion decreases with distance. An innovation will usually be accepted most thoroughly in the areas closest to where it originates. Because innovations take increasing time to spread outward, time is also a factor. Acceptance generally decreases with distance and time, producing what geographers call **time-distance decay.** Modern mass media, however, have greatly accelerated diffusion, diminishing the impact of time-distance decay.

In addition to the gradual weakening or decay of an innovation through time and distance, barriers can retard its spread. **Absorbing barriers** completely halt diffusion, allowing no further progress. For example, in 1998 the fundamentalist Islamic Taliban government of Afghanistan decided to abolish television, videocassette recorders, and videotapes, viewing them as "causes of corruption in society." As a result, the cultural diffusion of television sets was reversed, and the important role of television as a communication device to facilitate the spread of ideas was eliminated.

Extreme examples aside, few absorbing barriers exist in the world. More commonly, barriers are permeable,

FOCUS ON

Cultural Diffusion: A 100 Percent American

Our solid American citizen awakens in a bed built on a pattern that originated in the Near East but that was modified in northern Europe before it was transmitted to America. He throws back covers made from cotton, domesticated in India; or linen, domesticated in the Near East; or silk, the use of which was discovered in China. All of these materials have been spun and woven by processes invented in the Near East. He slips into his moccasins, invented by the Indians of the Eastern woodlands, and goes to the bathroom, whose fixtures are a mixture of European and American inventions, both of recent date. He takes off his pajamas, a garment invented in India, and washes with soap, invented by the ancient Gauls. He then shaves—a masochistic rite that seems to have been derived from either Sumer or ancient Egypt. . . . On his way to breakfast, he stops to buy a paper, paying for it with coins, an ancient Lydian invention.

At the restaurant, a whole new series of borrowed elements confronts him. His plate is made of a form of pottery invented in China. His knife is of steel, an alloy first made in southern India; his fork, a medieval Italian invention; and his spoon, a derivative of a Roman original. . . . When our friend has finished eating, . . . he reads the news of the day, imprinted in characters invented by the ancient Semites upon a material invented in China by a process invented in Germany. As he absorbs the accounts of foreign trouble, he will, if he is a good, conservative citizen, thank a Hebrew deity in an Indo-European language that he is 100 percent American.

From Linton, Ralph. 1936. *The Study of Man: An Introduction.* Englewood Cliffs, N.J.: Prentice-Hall. © 1936, renewed 1964: 326–327. Adapted by permission of Prentice-Hall, Inc., Englewood Cliffs, N.J.

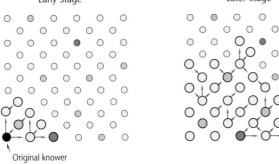

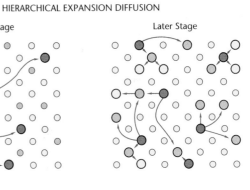

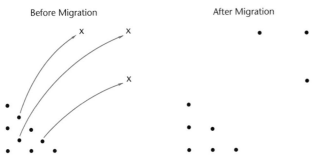

Figure 1.9 Types of cultural diffusion. These diagrams are merely suggestive; in reality, spatial diffusion is far more complex. In hierarchical diffusion, different scales can be used, so that, for example, the category "very important person" could be replaced by "large city."

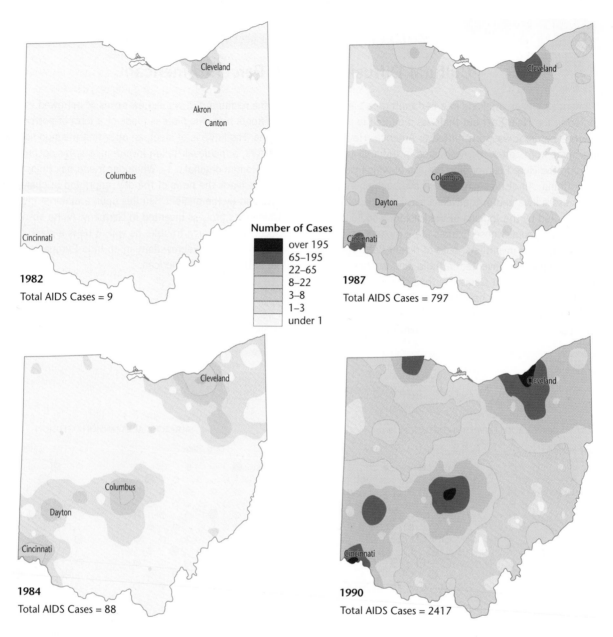

Number of Cases
- over 195
- 65–195
- 22–65
- 8–22
- 3–8
- 1–3
- under 1

1982
Total AIDS Cases = 9

1987
Total AIDS Cases = 797

1984
Total AIDS Cases = 88

1990
Total AIDS Cases = 2417

Figure 1.10 **Diffusion of HIV/AIDS in Ohio.** As you can see from this map, HIV/AIDS spread through both hierarchical and contagious diffusion processes. Do you think a similar pattern is evident at the national scale? At the global scale? *(Source: Gould, 1993.)*

allowing part of the innovation wave to diffuse through but acting to weaken or retard the continued spread. When a school board objects to students with tattoos or body piercings, the principal of a high school may set limits by mandating that these markings are covered by clothing. However, over time, those mandates may change as people get used to the idea of body markings. More likely than not, though, some mandates will remain in place. In this way, the principal and school board act as a **permeable barrier** to cultural innovations.

REFLECTING ON GEOGRAPHY

The Internet has certainly made the diffusion of many forms of cultural change much more rapid. Some scholars have argued that in fact the Internet has eliminated barriers to diffusion. Can you think of examples where this is true? Untrue?

Acceptance of innovations at any given point in space passes through three distinct stages. In the first stage, acceptance takes place at a steady, slow rate, perhaps because the innovation has not yet caught on, the benefits have not been adequately demonstrated, or a product is not readily available. During the second stage, acceptance grows rapidly and the trait spreads widely, as with a fashion style or dance fad. Often diffusion on a microscale exhibits what is called the **neighborhood effect,** which means that acceptance is usually most rapid in small clusters around an initial adopter. Direct exposure to an innovation is the best advertisement. In the third stage, acceptance grows at a slower rate than in the second, perhaps because the fad is passing or because an area is already saturated with the innovation.

Although all places and communities hypothetically have equal potential to adopt a new idea or practice, diffusion typically produces a core-periphery spatial arrangement, the same pattern observed earlier in our discussion of culture regions (see Figures 1.4 and 1.5). Hägerstrand of-

fered an explanation of how diffusion produces such a regional configuration. The distribution of innovations can be random, but the overlap of new ideas and traits as they diffuse through space and time is greatest toward the center of the region and least at the peripheries (Figure 1.11). As a result of this overlap, more innovations are adopted in the center, or core, of the region.

Some other cultural geographers, most notably James Blaut and Richard Ormrod, regard the Hägerstrandian concept of diffusion as too narrow and mechanical because it does not give enough emphasis to cultural and environmental variables and because it assumes that information automatically produces diffusion. As a result, nondiffusion—the failure of innovations to spread—is more prevalent than diffusion, a condition Hägerstrand's system cannot accommodate. Similarly, the Hägerstrandian system relies solely on communication and, implicitly, on the assumption that all

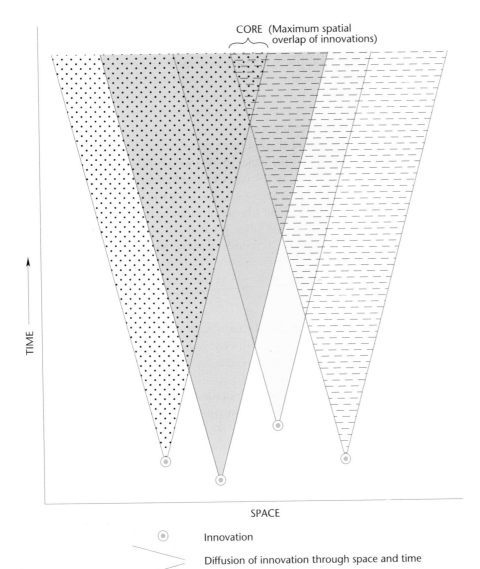

CORE (Maximum spatial overlap of innovations)

TIME

SPACE

⊙ Innovation

◇ Diffusion of innovation through space and time

Figure 1.11 Evolution of regional core and periphery from a random distribution of innovations and an equal rate of cultural diffusion in space and time. This scheme was proposed by Torsten Hägerstrand at a symposium on diffusion held at Texas A&M University in 1984. Can you see how time and space work together to produce core and periphery?

innovations are beneficial throughout geographical space. In reality, *susceptibility* to an innovation is far more crucial, especially in a world where communication is so rapid and pervasive that it renders the friction of distance almost meaningless. The inhabitants of two regions will not respond identically to an innovation, and the geographer must seek to understand this spatial variation in receptiveness to explain diffusion or the failure to diffuse. Within the context of their culture, people must perceive some advantage before they will adopt an innovation.

Globalization The modern technological age, in which improved worldwide transport and communications allow the instantaneous diffusion of ideas and innovations, has given rise to the phenomenon called **globalization.** This term refers to a world increasingly linked under the rule of capitalist economics and politics, in which international borders are diminished in importance and a worldwide marketplace is created. Some scholars have suggested that globalizing processes and an accompanying ease of diffusion will work to homogenize peoples, breaking down culture regions and eventually producing a single global culture. Throughout *The Human Mosaic,* we will return to this concept, testing its validity and measuring its consequences.

 Cultural Ecology

How do groups of people interact with Earth's biophysical environment, and in what ways do the culture and politics of those groups affect their ecological situation and resource use? These questions define our third theme, **cultural ecology.** Cultural geographers view the relationship between people and nature as a two-way interaction. People's cultural values, beliefs, perceptions, and practices have ecological impacts, and ecological conditions in turn influence cultural perceptions and practices. The cultural geographer must study the interaction between culture and environment to understand spatial variations in culture.

The term *ecology* was coined in the nineteenth century to refer to a new biological science concerned with studying the complex relationships among living organisms and their physical environment. Later, another concept, the **ecosystem,** was introduced to describe a territorially bounded system consisting of interacting organic and inorganic components. Plant and animal species were said to be adapted to specific conditions in the ecosystem and functioned to help keep the system stable over time.

Geographers borrowed these ideas to help them understand the interactions between environment and culture. They studied "human ecosystems" and sought to give culture a central role in human adaptation to the environment.

The focus of early cultural ecology, then, was to analyze the ecological interactions of isolated groups to determine how well their cultures adapted them to specific environments.

It soon became clear, however, that human cultural interactions with the environment were far too complex to be analyzed with concepts borrowed from biology. Furthermore, the idea that culture groups interacted with their ecosystems in isolation from larger-scale political, economic, and social forces was difficult to defend. We can readily observe, for example, that trade goods come into communities, agricultural commodities flow out, money circulates, taxes are collected, and people migrate in and out for work. So geographers use the term *ecology* in a much broader way than do physical scientists, reflecting the fact that studies of local human-environment relations need to include political, economic, and social forces operating on national, and even global, scales.

The theme of cultural ecology, the meeting ground of cultural and physical geographers, has traditionally provided a focal point for the academic discipline of geography. In fact, some geographers have proposed that geography *is* cultural ecology, that the study of the intricate relationships between people and their physical environments unites cultural and physical geography to form the entire academic discipline. Although few accept this narrow definition of geography, most will agree that an appreciation of the complex people-environment relationship is necessary for concerned citizens of the twenty-first century.

Through the years, cultural geographers have developed various perspectives on the interaction between humans and the land. Four schools of thought have developed: environmental determinism, possibilism, environmental perception, and humans as modifiers of the Earth. Two of these, you will recall, are listed among the cultural geographical ideas that have changed the world (refer again to Focus On: Seven Cultural Geographical Ideas That Changed the World.)

Environmental Determinism During the late nineteenth and early twentieth centuries, many geographers accepted **environmental determinism:** the belief that the physical environment is the dominant force in shaping cultures and that humankind is essentially a passive product of its physical surroundings. Humans are clay to be molded by nature. Similar physical environments produce similar cultures.

For example, environmental determinists believed that peoples of the mountains were predestined by the rugged terrain to be simple, backward, conservative, unimaginative, and freedom loving. Dwellers in the desert were likely to believe in one god but to live under the rule of tyrants. Temperate climates produced inventiveness, industriousness, and democracy. Coastlands pitted with fjords produced great navigators and fishermen. Environmental determinism had serious consequences, particularly during the time of European colonization in the late nineteenth century. For example, many Europeans saw Latin American native inhabitants as lazy, childlike, and prone to vices such as alcoholism because of the tropical climates that cover much of this region. Living in a tropical climate supposedly ensured that people didn't have to work very hard for their food. Europeans were able to rationalize their colonization of large portions of the world in part along climatic lines. Because the natives were "naturally" lazy and slow, the European reasoning went, they would benefit from the presence of the "naturally" stronger, smarter, and more industrious Europeans who came from more temperate lands.

Determinists overemphasize the role of environment in human affairs. This does not mean that environmental influences are inconsequential or that cultural geographers should not study such influences. Rather, the physical environment is only one of many forces affecting human culture and is never the sole determinant of behavior and beliefs.

Possibilism   Since the 1920s, **possibilism** has been the favored view among geographers. Possibilism is the belief that people, rather than their environments, are the primary architects of culture (Figure 1.12). Possibilists claim that any physical environment offers a number of possible ways for a culture to develop. In this way, the local environment helps shape its resident culture. However, a culture's way of life ultimately depends on the choices people make among the possibilities that are offered by the environment. These choices are guided by cultural heritage and are shaped by a particular political and economic system. Possibilists see the physical environment as offering opportunities and limitations; people make choices among these to satisfy their needs. In short, local traits of culture and economy are the products of culturally based decisions made within the limits of possibilities offered by the environment.

Most possibilists think that the higher the technological level of a culture, the greater the number of possibilities and the weaker the influences of the physical environment. Technologically advanced cultures, in this view, have achieved some mastery over their physical surroundings. Geographers Jim Norwine and Thomas Anderson, however, warn that even in these advanced societies "the quantity and quality of human life are still strongly influenced by the natural environment," especially climate. They argue that humankind's control of nature is anything but supreme and perhaps even illusory. One only has to think of the devastation caused by the December 2004 tsunami in the Indian Ocean to underscore the often illusory character of the control humans think they have over their physical surroundings (see Focus On: "The Facts Are Incontestable").

FOCUS ON

"The Facts Are Incontestable": Two Views of Creative Genius

An Environmental Determinist's View

The absence of artistic and poetic development in Switzerland and the Alpine lands [may be ascribed] to the overwhelming aspect of nature there, its majestic sublimity which paralyzes the mind. . . . This position [is reinforced] by the fact that . . . the lower mountains and hill country of Swabia, Franconia and Thuringia, where nature is gentler, stimulating, appealing, and not overpowering, have produced many poets and artists. The facts are incontestable. They reappear in France in the geographical distribution of the awards made by the Paris Salon of 1896. Judged by these awards, the [people of the] rough highlands . . . are singularly lacking in artistic instinct, while art flourishes in all the river lowlands of France. . . . French men of letters, by the distribution of their birthplaces, are essentially products of fluvial valleys and plains, rarely of upland and mountain.

From Semple, 1911. Copyright © 1939 by Carolyn W. Keene

A Possibilist's View

All [European] patent offices report the Swiss as the foremost inventors. . . . A partial list of books published in different countries showed Switzerland to be far ahead of any other country in this sphere. . . .

The Swiss themselves attribute much importance in the growth of their industries to the religious persecutions in neighboring countries in the sixteenth and seventeenth centuries—persecutions which drove thousands of intelligent men . . . into Switzerland. The revocation of the Edict of Nantes . . . in 1685 is credited with driving sixty thousand Huguenots from France into Switzerland. They founded the silk industry of Zurich and Bern. It was a Huguenot who founded the watch business at Geneva. . . . Spanish persecution in the Low Countries and Swiss neutrality during the Thirty Years' War added to the human resources of Switzerland.

From Jefferson, 1929: 660–661

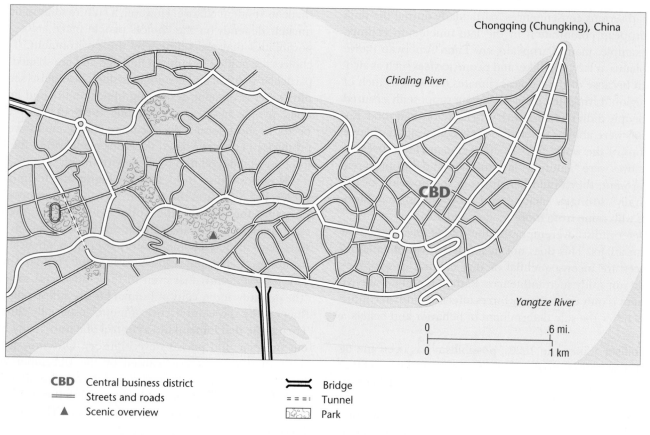

Chongqing (Chungking), China

Chialing River

CBD

Yangtze River

| 0 | | .6 mi. |
| 0 | | 1 km |

CBD Central business district
Streets and roads
▲ Scenic overview

Bridge
Tunnel
Park

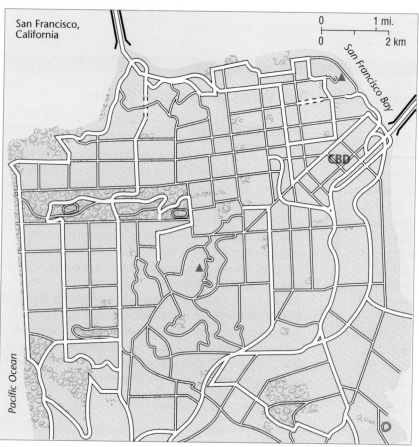

San Francisco, California

| 0 | | 1 mi. |
| 0 | | 2 km |

San Francisco Bay

CBD

Pacific Ocean

Figure 1.12 Chongqing (Chungking) and San Francisco. Both of these cities are among the largest in their respective countries. Both developed on elongated, hilly sites flanked on all but one side by water, and both were connected in the twentieth century by bridges leading to adjacent land across the water. In certain other respects, too—such as the use of tunnels for arterial roads—the cities are similar. Note, however, the contrast in street patterns. In Chongqing the streets were laid out to accommodate the rugged terrain, but in San Francisco relatively little deviation from a gridiron pattern was permitted. Note, too, that although San Francisco has a much smaller population than Chongqing, it covers a far larger area. What do these contrasts suggest about the relative merits of environmental determinism and possibilism? About the role of culture?

Environmental Perception Another approach to the theme of cultural ecology focuses on how humans perceive nature. Each person and cultural group has mental images of the physical environment, shaped by knowledge, ignorance, experience, values, and emotions. To describe such mental images, cultural geographers use the term **environmental perception.** Whereas the possibilist sees humankind as having a choice of different possibilities in a given physical setting, the environmental perceptionist declares that the choices people make will depend more on what they perceive the environment to be than on the actual character of the land. Perception, in turn, is colored by the teachings of culture.

Some of the most productive research done by geographers in environmental perception has been on the topic of **natural hazards,** such as flooding, hurricanes, volcanic eruptions, earthquakes, insect infestations, and droughts. All cultures react to such hazards and catastrophes, but the reaction varies greatly from one cultural group to another. Some peoples reason that natural disasters and risks are unavoidable acts of the gods, perhaps even divine retribution. Often they seek to cope with the hazards by placating their gods. Others hold government responsible for taking care of them when hazards yield disasters. In Western culture, many groups regard natural hazards as problems that can be solved by technological means. In the United States, one of the most common manifestations of this belief has been the widespread construction of dams to prevent flooding. Similarly, many Westerners and others think that the effects of drought can be mitigated by the development of better irrigation systems.

In virtually all cultures, people knowingly inhabit hazard zones, especially floodplains, exposed coastal sites, drought-prone regions, and the environs of active volcanoes (Figure 1.13). More Americans than ever now live in areas likely to be devastated by hurricanes along the coast of the Gulf of Mexico and atop earthquake faults in California. How accurately do they perceive the hazard involved? Why have they chosen to live there? How might we minimize the eventual disasters? The cultural geographer seeks the answers to such questions and aspires, with other geographers, to mitigate the inevitable disasters through such devices as land-use planning.

Perhaps the most fundamental expression of environmental perception lies in the way different cultures see nature itself. We must understand at the outset that nature is a culturally derived concept that has different meanings to different peoples. In the **organic view,** held by many traditional groups, people are part of nature. The habitat possesses a soul, is filled with nature spirits, and must not be offended. By contrast, most Western peoples believe in the **mechanistic view of nature.** Humans are separate from and hold dominion over nature. They see the habitat as an integrated system of mechanisms governed by external forces that can be rendered into natural laws and understood by the human mind.

Humans as Modifiers of the Earth Many cultural geographers, observing the environmental changes people have wrought, emphasize humans as modifiers of the habitat. This presents yet another facet of cultural ecology. In a sense, the human-as-modifier school of thought is the

Figure 1.13 **People often settle in natural hazard areas,** exposing themselves to the hazard of an earthquake and resultant landslide, as here, in the Central American country of El Salvador, where more than 1200 people died on January 13, 2001. Why would people choose to live in such a place? (*La Prensa Grafica/ AP Photo.*)

opposite of environmental determinism. Whereas the determinists proclaim that nature molds humankind, those cultural geographers who study the human impact on the land assert that humans mold nature.

We now know that even seemingly innocuous behavior, repeated for millennia, for centuries, or in some cases for mere decades, can have catastrophic effects on the environment. Plowing fields and grazing livestock can eventually denude regions (Figure 1.14). The use of certain types of air conditioners or spray cans apparently has the potential to destroy the planet's very ability to support life. Clearly, access to energy and technology is the key variable that controls the magnitude and speed of environmental alteration. Geographers seek to understand and explain the processes of environmental alteration as they vary from one culture to another and, through *applied geography,* to propose alternative, less destructive modes of behavior.

Cultural geographers began to concentrate on the human role in changing the face of the Earth long before the present level of ecological consciousness developed. They learned early on that different cultural groups have widely different outlooks on humankind's role in changing the Earth. Some, such as those rooted in the mechanistic tradition, tend to regard environmental modification as divinely approved, viewing humans as God's helpers in completing the task of creation. Some other groups, organic in their view of nature, are much more cautious, taking care not to offend the forces of nature. They see humans as part of nature, meant to be in harmony with their environment (for more on this topic, see Chapter 3).

Figure 1.14 **Human modification of the Earth includes severe soil erosion.** This erosion could have been caused by road building or poor farming methods. The scene is in the Amazon Basin of Brazil. How can we adopt less destructive ways of modifying the land? *(Michael Nichols/National Geographic.)*

Gender differences can also play a role in the human modification of the Earth. **Ecofeminism,** a term derived from a book by Karen Warren, maintains that because of socialization, women have been better ecologists and environmentalists than men. (We should not forget that the modern environmental preservation movement grew in no small part out of Rachel Carson's book *Silent Spring.*) Traditionally, women—as childbearers, gardeners, and nurturers of the family and home—dealt with the daily chores of gaining food from the earth, whereas men—as hunters, fishers, warriors, and forest clearers—were involved with activities that were more associated with destruction. Whether or not we agree with this rather deterministic and essentializing viewpoint (understanding gender differences as biologically determined rather than culturally constructed), we can see that in many situations through time, and around the globe, women and men have had different relationships to the natural world.

 Cultural Interaction

How do the many different traits within a culture influence one another? That is the central concern in our fourth theme, **cultural interaction.** An explanation of the relationships among culture, space, place, environment, and landscape requires us to consider a whole range of cultural, economic, and social factors. The geographer recognizes that all facets of culture are systemically and spatially intertwined. In short, cultures are complex wholes rather than conglomerations of unrelated traits. The theme of cultural interaction finds a place on the list of cultural geographical ideas that changed the world as "spatial organization and interdependence" (refer again to Focus On: Seven Cultural Geographical Ideas That Changed the World). Cultural interaction reflects the geographer's awareness that the immediate causes of some cultural phenomena are other cultural phenomena. A change in one element of culture requires accommodating changes in others.

For example, religious belief has the potential to influence a group's voting behavior, diet, shopping patterns, type of employment, and social standing. Traditional Hinduism, the majority religion of India, segregates people into social classes called castes and specifies what forms of livelihood are appropriate for each. The Mormon faith, among others, forbids the consumption of alcoholic beverages, tobacco, and certain other products, thereby influencing both the diet and the shopping patterns of its adherents. In countless other ways, one facet of a culture influences other facets. The geographer must examine how these intracultural forces help determine variations in all aspects of the culture.

The theme of cultural interaction, if improperly used, can lead the geographer to **cultural determinism.** Advocates of this extreme viewpoint, developed in reaction to the earlier environmental determinism, maintain that the physical environment is inconsequential as an influence on culture. Any facet of a culture, they would argue, is shaped entirely by other facets. Cultural interaction, for them, offers all the explanations for spatial variations. People and culture are the active forces; nature is irrelevant. You should be wary of such claims. Julian Steward, a noted cultural ecologist, warned us long ago of "the fruitless assumption" that all culture comes from culture. Nonetheless, understanding the complex relationships among different aspects of culture is one of the important tasks for cultural geographers. Below we outline the various approaches that geographers have used to explain and understand these relationships.

REFLECTING ON GEOGRAPHY

Think of examples that might support the statement that "the immediate causes of some cultural phenomena are other cultural phenomena."

Spatial Models Geographers have employed several different approaches in studying cultural interactions, approaches that range from the scientific to the artistic. Those who view cultural geography as a **social science** believe that we should apply the scientific method to the study of people. Emulating physicists and chemists, they devise theories and seek regularities or universal spatial principles that apply across cultural lines, explaining all of humankind. These principles ideally become the basis for laws of human spatial behavior. **Space** is the word that perhaps best connotes this approach to cultural geography (see Doing Geography at the end of the chapter).

Social scientists face a difficult problem. They have no laboratories in which to test their theories; the world is their laboratory. The controlled experiments of the physical sciences are thus far more complicated, if not impossible, for cultural geographers. One solution to this problem is the technique known as **model** building. Aware that many causal forces are involved in the real world, they set up artificial model situations to focus on one or more potential factors. Hägerstrand's diagrams of different types of diffusion and of the evolution of core-periphery patterns are examples of spatial models (see Figure 1.9). Some model-building geographers are more sensitive to cultural variables. They devise *culture-specific* models to describe and explain certain facets of spatial behavior within specific cultures. They still seek regularities and spatial principles, but more modestly, within the bounds of individual cultures. For example, several geographers proposed a model for Latin American cities in an effort to stress similarities among them and to understand certain underlying causal forces (Figure 1.15). Obviously, no actual city in Latin America conforms precisely to their uncomplicated geometric plan. Instead, they deliberately generalized and simplified so that an urban type could be recognized and studied. The model will look strange to a person living in a city in the United States or Canada, for it describes a very different kind of urban environment, based in another culture.

Sense of Place Other geographers seek to understand the uniqueness of each region and place. Just as *space* identifies the perspective of the model-building geographer, **place** is the key word connoting this more humanistic view of geography. The geographer Yi-Fu Tuan coined the word *topophilia,* literally "love of place," to describe people who exhibit a strong sense of place and the geographers who are attracted to the study of such places and peoples. Geographer Edward Relph tells us that "to be human is to have and know your place" in the geographical sense. Sense of place is among the geographical ideas that changed the world, as you will recall from earlier in this chapter. This perspective on cultural geography values subjective experience over objective scientific observation. It focuses on understanding the complexity of different cultures and how those cultures give meaning to and derive meaning from particular places.

Power and Ideology Cultures, though, are rarely if ever homogeneous. Often certain groups of people have more power in society, and their beliefs and ways of life dominate and are considered the norm, while other groups of people with less power may participate in alternative cultures. These divisions are often based on gender, economic class, racial categories, ethnicity, or sexual orientation. The social hierarchies that result are maintained, reinforced, and challenged through many means, including brute force, but culture, too, plays a major role. Some geographers study ideology—a set of dominant ideas and beliefs—in relationship to place, environment, and landscape in order to understand how power works culturally. For example, most nations maintain a set of powerful beliefs about their relationships to the land, some holding to the idea that there is a deep and natural connection between a particular territory and the people who have inhabited it. These ideas often form part of a national identity and are expressed so routinely in poems, music, laws, and rituals that people accept these ideas as truths. Yet immigrants to that culture and country, and people who have been marginalized by this culture, may hold very different ideas of identity with the land. Cultural and political conflict may result. Uncovering and analyzing the connections between ideology and power,

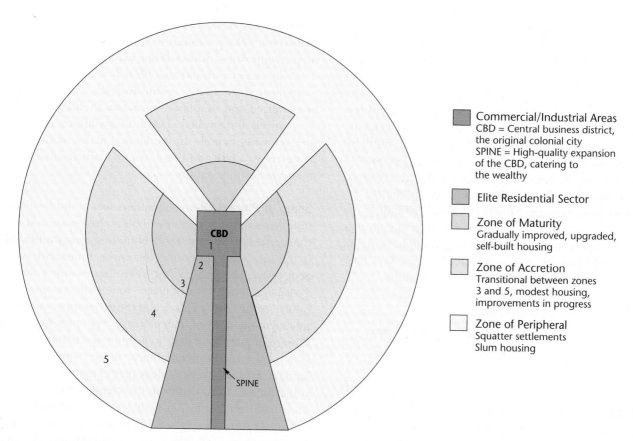

 (legend)

Commercial/Industrial Areas
CBD = Central business district,
the original colonial city
SPINE = High-quality expansion
of the CBD, catering to
the wealthy

Elite Residential Sector

Zone of Maturity
Gradually improved, upgraded,
self-built housing

Zone of Accretion
Transitional between zones
3 and 5, modest housing,
improvements in progress

Zone of Peripheral
Squatter settlements
Slum housing

Figure 1.15 **A generalized model of the Latin American city.**
Urban structure differs from one culture to another, and in many
ways the cities of Latin America are distinctive, sharing much in
common with one another. Geographers Ernst Griffin and Larry
Ford developed the model diagrammed here to help describe and
explain the processes at work shaping the cities of Latin America.
In what ways would this model not be applicable to cities in the
United States and Canada? *(After Griffin and Ford, 1980: 406.)*

then, are often integral to the geographer's task of understanding the diversity within a culture.

These different approaches to thinking about cultural
geography are both necessary and healthy. These groups ask
different questions about place and space; not surprisingly,
they often obtain different answers. The model-builders
tend to minimize diversity through their search for universal causal forces; the humanists examine diversity *among* cultures and strive to understand the unique; those who look to
power and ideology focus on diversity and contestation
within cultures. All lines of inquiry yield valuable findings.
We present all of these perspectives within the theme of
cultural interaction and more generally throughout *The
Human Mosaic.*

 Cultural Landscape

What are the visible expressions of culture? What do culture
regions look like? These questions provide the basis of our

fifth and final theme, the **cultural landscape.** The cultural
landscape is comprised of all the built forms that cultural
groups create in inhabiting the Earth—roads, agricultural
fields, cities, houses, parks, gardens, commercial buildings,
and so on. Cultures shape their own landscapes out of the
natural habitat. Every inhabited area has a cultural landscape, fashioned from the natural landscape, and each
uniquely reflects the culture or cultures that created it (Figure 1.16). Landscape mirrors culture, and the cultural geographer can learn much about a group of people by carefully
observing and studying the landscape. Indeed, so important
is this visual record of cultures that some geographers regard landscape study as geography's central interest.

Why is such importance attached to the cultural landscape? Perhaps part of the answer is that it visually reflects
the most basic strivings of humankind: for shelter, food, and
clothing. In addition, the cultural landscape reveals peoples' different attitudes toward the modification of the
Earth. It also contains valuable evidence about the origin,
spread, and development of cultures, for it usually preserves

Figure 1.16 **Terraced cultural landscape of an irrigated rice district in Yunnan Province, China.** In such areas, the artificial landscape made by people overwhelms nature and forms a human mosaic on the land. Why is rice cultivated in such hilly areas in Asia, whereas in the United States rice farming is confined to flat plains? *(Stone.)*

various types of archaic forms. Dominant and alternative cultures use, alter, and manipulate landscapes to express their diverse identities. Every cultural landscape, then, is an accumulation of human artifacts, each of which tells us something important about the people who have created it.

This potential for interpretive analysis attracts many geographers to studying the cultural landscape, for such visible evidence can reveal much about a past long forgotten by the present inhabitants and about the choices made and changes wrought by a people. The idea that cultural landscapes possess interpretive potential was introduced into geography by the German scholar August Meitzen. Long ago, in observing the rural cultural landscape of central Europe, Meitzen wrote that "we walk in every village, in a sense, among the ruins of antiquity." At every step we encounter built landscape features that, once we learn to decipher them, can reveal ancient cultural diffusions, past adaptations to the environment, and cultural changes through time. Echoing Meitzen, American geographer Peirce Lewis concluded that "one can read the landscape as we do a book." Taking this idea one step further, the geographer might go so far as to say that if you show us the landscape in which you live, we will tell you who you are, and vice versa—if we know something about who you are, we can surmise some of the important elements of your landscape.

Aside from containing archaic forms, landscapes also convey revealing messages about the present-day inhabitants and cultures. All humanized landscapes bear cultural meaning. Lewis further proposed that "the cultural landscape is our collective and revealing autobiography, reflect-

ing our tastes, values, aspirations, and fears in tangible forms." Cultural landscapes offer "texts" that geographers read to discover dominant ideas and prevailing practices within a culture, as well as less dominant and alternative forms within that culture. This "reading," however, is often a very difficult task, given the complexity of cultures, cultural change, and recent globalizing trends that can obscure local histories (see Culture in a Globalizing World).

REFLECTING ON GEOGRAPHY

As we will learn throughout this book, landscapes are often created from more than one set of cultural values and beliefs, oftentimes in conflict with each other. How then can we "read" conflict into the landscape, when it appears so natural and unified? What sort of information would we need?

Geographers have pushed the idea of "reading" the landscape further in order to focus on the symbolic and ideological qualities of landscape. In other words, landscape elements such as houses and road patterns can be understood not only as reflections of the functional needs of a culture for housing and transport but also as expressions of the values, beliefs, and meaning systems—the symbols and ideologies—of particular cultures. In fact, as geographer Denis Cosgrove has suggested (see Practicing Geography on page 26), the very idea of landscape itself was ideological, in that its development in the Renaissance served the interests of the new elite class for whom agricultural land was valued not for its productivity but for its use as a visual subject. Land, in

CULTURE IN A GLOBALIZING WORLD

"Reading" Globalization in a Medieval Square

Visitors to Warsaw in 2002 would no doubt have toured Market Square in the center of the city's Old Town. Here, apparently surrounded by seventeenth- and eighteenth-century buildings, they could shop in market stalls and sit down for coffee at outdoor, umbrella-covered tables, basking in the feel of medieval history. "Reading" the landscape around them, however, would have been a difficult task. Some of the buildings were obscured, draped in large swaths of fabric displaying advertisements for mobile phones and fast food. Even if they could have seen the buildings, however, their readings would have been incomplete at best. Weren't they sitting in an authentic late-medieval market square? Well, sort of. Almost all the buildings on the square had been destroyed by bombing in World War II. When the square was reconstructed in the 1950s, the government decided it should be rebuilt not as it was in 1939, but instead to resemble a "pure" mercantile square of the seventeenth and eighteenth centuries, with no "modern" buildings included. So, in 2002, they were sitting in a square built in the 1950s to resemble what the government thought it looked like in late-medieval times—a newly remodeled version of a 1950s, socialist vision of the mercantile past. On top of this, its recent restoration had been funded by Western companies, which were now advertising their wares on the buildings. Here's how design historian David Crowley describes it:

> Warsaw today has the atmosphere of a city where commercial interests have the upper hand, even in those parts so strongly weighted with national meaning. International corporations wish to be seen as the patrons of Warsaw's revival, drawing prestige by association with it traditional core. Citibank no doubt gained some prestige in the eyes of potential clients in the city when they

Market Square in Warsaw. Most tourists dining in the outdoor cafés don't realize that the historical buildings surrounding them were actually built in the 1950s, not the 1650s. Can you think of other examples of tourists being "fooled" by the apparent authenticity of buildings? *(Carmen Redondo/CORBIS.)*

sponsored the apparent reconstruction of the façade of the former Town Hall. In similar spirit, restoration work on the Old Town and Royal Castle—sacred spaces in the city's mythology—was funded in summer 2002 by Western European and North American corporations. In return for their gifts, they were given permission to drape colossal billboards across these buildings. The picturesque facades that make up the western and northern sides of the Old Town Square—the central attraction of the city to its small tourist trade—were almost obscured by spectacular inducements to buy shampoo and mobile phones. At the same time the southern elevation of the Royal Castle became a frame for a long advertisement for instant coffee.*

*Crowley, David. 2003. *Warsaw*. London: Reaktion Books.

---

other words, was important to look at as a scene, and the actual workings that were necessary for agriculture were thus hidden from these views. If you go to an art museum, for example, it will be difficult, if not impossible, to find in the Italian Renaissance room any landscape paintings that depict agricultural laborers (Figure 1.17).

Closer to home, we need only to look outside our windows to see other symbolic and ideological landscapes. One of the most familiar and obvious **symbolic landscapes** is the

urban skyline. Composed of tall buildings that normally house financial service industries, it represents to others the power and dominance of finance and economics within that culture (Figure 1.18). On the other hand, other cities are dominated by tall structures that have little to do with economics but more with religion. In medieval Europe, for example, cathedrals and churches rose high above other buildings, symbolizing the centrality and dominance of Catholicism in this culture.

Even the most mundane landscape element can be interpreted as symbolic and ideological. The typical middle-class, suburban, American or Canadian home, for example, can be interpreted as an expression of a dominant set of ideas about culture and family structure (Figure 1.19). These homes are often comprised of living room, dining room, kitchen, and bedrooms, all separated by walls. The cultural assumptions built into this division of space include the assumed value of individual privacy (everyone has their own bedroom), the idea that certain functions should be spatially separate from others (cooking, eating, socializing, sleeping), and the notion that a family is comprised of a mother, father, and children (indicated by the "master" bedroom and smaller "children's" bedrooms). Thus, even the most common of landscapes can be seen as symbolic of a particular culture and built from ideological assumptions.

As we have seen, the physical content of the cultural landscape is both varied and complex. To better study and understand these complexities, geographical studies focus on three principal aspects of landscape: settlement forms, land-division patterns, and architectural styles. In the study of *settlement forms*, cultural geographers describe and explain the spatial arrangement of buildings, roads, and other features that people construct while inhabiting an area. One of the most basic ways in which geographers categorize settlement forms is to examine their degree of **nucleation,** a term that refers to the relative density of landscape elements. Urban centers are of course very nucleated, while rural, farming areas tend to be much less nucleated, what geographers call **dispersed.** Another

Figure 1.17 **Landscape triptych panel by Fra Angelico, fifteenth century.** Notice the depiction of the beautiful and orderly agricultural landscape outside the city walls but the absence of people actually doing the work to maintain that order. Why aren't the laborers depicted? (*Archivo Iconografico, S.A./CORBIS.*)

Figure 1.18 **Yokohama at dusk.** This skyline is a powerful symbol of the economic importance of the world's largest city, Tokyo-Yokohama. What landscape form best symbolizes your town/city? (*Jose Fuste Raga/CORBIS.*)

Figure 1.19 **American ranch house.** The horizontally expansive ranch is a common house form in the United States and Canada. Can you think of other countries where ranch houses are also common? *(Robert Holmes/ CORBIS.)*

common way to think about settlement forms is the degree to which they appear standardized and planned, such as the grid form of much of the American West (Figure 1.20), versus the degree to which the forms appear to be organic, that is, to have been built without any apparent geometric plan, such as the central areas of most European cities. Thinking about settlement forms in terms of these two basic categories helps geographers begin their analysis of the relationships between cultures and the landscapes they produce.

Land-division patterns indicate the uses of particular parcels of land and as such reveal the way people have divided the land for economic, social, and political uses. Within a particular nucleated settlement form—a city, for example—you can see different patterns of land use. Some areas are devoted to economic uses, others to residential, political (city hall, for example), social, and cultural uses. Each of these areas can be further divided. Economic uses can include offices for financial services, retail stores, warehouses, and factories. Residential areas are often divided into middle-class, upper-class, and working-class districts and/or are grouped by ethnicity and race (see Chapter 11). Such patterns of course vary a great deal from place to place and culture to culture, as we will see throughout this book. One of the best ways to glimpse settlement and land-division patterns is through an airplane window. Looking down, you can see the multicolored abstract patterns of planted fields, as vivid as any modern painting, and the regular checkerboard or chaotic tangle of urban streets.

Figure 1.20 **The town of Westmoreland in the Imperial Valley of California.** It's difficult to find a more regularized, geometric land pattern than this. Why do you think much of the American West was divided into these rectangles? *(Jim Wark/Airphoto.)*

Figure 1.21 **Folk and popular architecture both reflect culture.** This log house, near Ottawa in Canada, is a folk dwelling and stands in sharp contrast to the professional architecture of the Toronto skyline. What conclusion might a perceptive person from another culture reach (considering the "virtues" of height, durability, and centrality) about the ideology of the culture that produced the Toronto landscape? *(Left: Courtesy of Terry G. Jordan-Bychkov; Right: Photodisc.)*

Perhaps no other aspect of the human landscape is as readily visible from ground level as the *architectural style* of a culture. Geographers look at the exterior materials and decoration, as well as the layout and design of the interiors. Styles tend to vary both through time, as cultures change, and across space, in the sense that different cultures adopt and invent their own stylistic detailing according to their own particular needs, aesthetics, and desires. Thus, examining architectural style is often useful when trying to date a particular landscape element or when trying to understand the particular values and beliefs that cultures may hold. In North American culture, different building styles catch the eye: modest white New England churches and giant urban cathedrals; hand-hewn barns and geodesic domes; wooden one-room schoolhouses and the new windowless school buildings of urban areas; shopping malls and glass office buildings. Each tells us something about the people who designed, built, or inhabit these spaces. Thus, architecture provides a vivid record of the resident culture (Figure 1.21). For this reason, cultural geographers have traditionally devoted considerable attention to examining architecture and style in the cultural landscape.

Conclusion

As we have seen and will continue to see, the interests of cultural geographers are diverse. It might seem to you, con-fronted by the various themes, subject matter, viewpoints, and methodologies described in this chapter, that cultural geographers run off in all directions, lacking unity of purpose. What does a geographer who studies architecture have in common with a colleague who studies the political and cultural causes of environmental degradation? What interests do an environmental perceptionist and a student of cultural diffusion share? Why do scholars with such apparently different interests belong in the same academic discipline? Why are they all geographers?

The answer is that regardless of the particular topic the cultural geographer studies, she or he necessarily touches on several or all of the five themes we have discussed. The themes are closely related segments of a whole. Spatial patterns in culture, as revealed by maps of culture regions, are reflected in and expressed through the cultural landscape, require an ecological interpretation, are the result of cultural diffusion, and suggest the workings of cultural interaction.

As an example of how the various themes of cultural geography overlap and intertwine, let us look at one element of architecture that most North Americans will be familiar with: the ranch-style, single-family house (see Figure 1.19). This house type is defined by its one-story height and its linearity from side to side. These houses are found throughout much of the United States and to a lesser extent in Canada, though they are rare in other countries. They are obviously part of the cultural landscape, and their spatial distribution constitutes a formal culture region that can be mapped.

PRACTICING GEOGRAPHY

Denis Cosgrove

(Courtesy of Denis E. Cosgrove.)

When cultural geographer Denis Cosgrove rides the bus through West Los Angeles on his way to work at UCLA, or when he takes his Sunday walks through the green spaces of London, as he does often in the summer months on his visits to his former hometown, he is "practicing" geography. As he says, "the world/landscape around me is a primary source of questions . . . life is a field course."

Cosgrove, the Humboldt Chair of Geography at UCLA, and one of the most prominent cultural geographers in the English-speaking world, has explored through a series of scholarly articles and books (for some of these, see Ten Recommended Books on Cultural Geography, at the end of this chapter) the relationships between landscape and culture in Renaissance Italy, nineteenth-century England, and twentieth-century America. His fascination with these places and times, and his enthusiasm for the study of geography in general, began early, when he was a child in Liverpool, England. His walks were important then, too. "Being raised in a great port city where our Sunday walks were often along the docks, seeing great cargo ships with words like Montevideo and Cape Town and Lagos on their sterns . . .

and being given a globe at the age of eight and seeing dotted lines crossing the oceans to these same places with 'Distance to Liverpool' printed on these steamship routes . . . made me realize that I lived in a place that mattered on the globe."

Today Cosgrove finds himself working as much inside as out, often in archives, looking at historical documents and closely reading maps and other images that express relationships between particular cultures and their landscapes. For example, in one of his recent projects Cosgrove explored how the development of aerial views in the twentieth century—both air photos and drawings—"was a uniquely appropriate way of making sense of the new landscapes emerging then in the American West." To make this rather abstract idea more concrete, he focused his study on a particular person who was a newspaper artist in Los Angeles in the mid-twentieth century. Focusing on one person, he says, allowed him "to make contact with a life in the world with all its complexity and use it to make more general points about how geographies come about." His approach is based more in the humanities than in the social sciences, interpretative instead of explanatory. And, above all, it involves "a great respect for the role of imagination (my own and others') in the ways that we shape the world."

Geographers who study such houses also need to employ the other themes of cultural geography to gain a complete understanding. They can use the concept of cultural diffusion to learn when and by what routes this building style emerged and diffused and what barriers hindered its diffusion. In this particular case, geographers would be led back to the early years of the twentieth century, when the first suburban housing was being built outside of urban centers. In this case, land was relatively inexpensive, allowing for a house type that occupied a wide expanse of space. What's more, they would learn that the design influences of Frank Lloyd Wright and his vision for an organic architecture that would mirror nature were dominant, which laid the path for successful and widespread diffusion. Further, the cultural geographer would need an ecological interpretation of the ranch house. What materials were required to build such a house? Did the style vary in the different climatic and ecological regions in which such houses were built? Finally, the cultural geographer would want to know how the use of ranch houses was integrated

with other facets of the culture. Did changes in the economy and standard of living lead people to accept ranch houses? Did changes in technology lead to more elaborate houses? Why did it become the quintessential house type in post–World War II America, featured in many of its popular TV shows? Do these humble structures possess a symbolism related to traditional American values and virtues? Thus, the geographer interested in housing is firmly bound by the total fabric of cultural geography, unable to segregate a particular topic such as ranch houses from the geographical whole. Culture region, cultural landscape, cultural interaction, cultural ecology, and cultural diffusion are interwoven.

In this manner, the cultural geographer passes from one theme to another, demonstrating the holistic nature of the discipline. In no small measure, it is this holism—this broad, multithematic approach—that distinguishes the cultural geographer from other students of culture. We believe that, by the end of the course, you will have gained a new perspective on the Earth as the home of humankind.

DOING GEOGRAPHY

Space, Place, and Knowing Your Way Around

We started this chapter by saying that most of us are born geographers, with a sense of and curiosity about the places and spaces around us. Think, for example, of the place you call home. You are probably familiar enough with its streets and buildings and greenspaces, and with the people who inhabit these spaces, to make connections among them—you know how to "read" the place. There are many other places, however, where this is not the case. Most of you have had the experience of going somewhere new, where it is difficult to find your way around, literally and metaphorically. Many of you, for example, are attending a college or university far from home, while others have experienced the disorienting feeling of moving from one home to another, whether across town or across continents. How did you find your way? How did the "strange" space become a familiar place?

This activity requires you to draw on your own experiences to understand two fundamental concepts in cultural geography, space and place. Geographers tend to use the term *space* in a much more abstract way than *place*—as a term that describes a two-dimensional location on a map. *Place,* on the other hand, is a less dry term, one that is used to describe a location that has meaning. Your college campus, for example, may have been just an abstract space located on a map when you applied to the school, yet now it is a place because you have filled it with your own meanings.

Drawing on your own experiences, pick one particular space that for you has become a place. First, identify what you knew about this space beforehand and how you knew this (for example, perhaps you looked the place up in an atlas or saw it in a movie). Second, in narrative form, describe the process whereby that space became a place for you. Third, identify in what ways you learned how to "read" this place. In other words, how did you learn to see this particular location as a three-dimensional, meaningful place that is different from what you knew of it as a "space." Fourth, use your experiences to discuss the following questions: Do you have to live in a place to really "know" it? Must one experience a space for it to become a place?

Geography on the Internet

You can learn more about the discipline of geography and the subdiscipline of cultural geography on the Internet at the following web sites:

American Geographical Society
http://www.amergeog.org

America's oldest geographical organization, with a long and distinguished record; publisher of the *Geographical Review.*

Association of American Geographers
http://www.aag.org/

The leading organization of professional geographers in the United States. This site contains information about the discipline, the association, and its activities, including annual and regional meetings.

National Geographic Society
http://www.nationalgeographic.com/

An organization that has, for over a century, served to popularize geography with active programs of publishing and television presentations prepared for the public.

Royal Geographic Society/Institute of British Geographers
http://www.rgs.org/

Explore the activities of these allied British organizations, whose collective history goes back to the Age of Exploration and Discovery in the 1800s . . . and don't forget to visit The Human Mosaic Online at http://www.whfreeman.com/jordan/index.htm

Sources

Anderson, Kay, and Gale, Fay. 1999. *Cultural Geographies.* Melbourne: Pearson Education.

Blaut, James M. 1977. "Two Views of Diffusion." *Annals of the Association of American Geographers* 67: 343–349.

Carson, Rachel. 1962. *Silent Spring.* Boston: Houghton Mifflin.

Gould, Peter. 1993. *The Slow Plague: A Geography of the AIDS Pandemic.* Cambridge: Blackwell.

Griffin, Ernst, and Larry Ford. 1980. "A Model of Latin American City Structure." *Geographical Review* 70: 397–422.

Hägerstrand, Torsten. 1967. *Innovation Diffusion as a Spatial Process.* Allan Pred (trans.). Chicago: University of Chicago Press.

Hanson, Susan E. (ed.). 1996. *Ten Geographic Ideas That Have Changed the World.* New Brunswick, N.J.: Rutgers University Press.

Jefferson, Mark. 1929. "The Geographic Distribution of Inventiveness." *Geographical Review* 19: 649–661.

Lewis, Peirce. 1983. "Learning from Looking: Geographic and Other Writing About the American Cultural Landscape." *American Quarterly* 35: 242–261.

Linton, Ralph. 1936. *The Study of Man: An Introduction.* Englewood Cliffs, N.J.: Prentice-Hall.

Meitzen, August. 1895. *Siedelung und Agrarwesen.* 3 vols. and atlas. Berlin: Wilhelm Hertz.

Norwine, Jim, and Thomas D. Anderson. 1980. *Geography as Human Ecology?* Lanham, Md.: University Press of America.

Ormrod, Richard K. 1990. "Local Context and Innovation Diffusion in a Well-Connected World." *Economic Geography* 66: 109–122.

Reed, John S. 1976. "The Heart of Dixie: An Essay in Folk Geography." *Social Forces* 54: 925–939.

Relph, Edward. 1981. *Rational Landscapes and Humanistic Geography.* New York: Barnes & Noble.

Semple, Ellen Churchill. 1911. *Influences of Geographic Environment.* New York: Henry Holt.

SEEING GEOGRAPHY

Why is it difficult for most of us to interpret this image as a map?

Aboriginal Painting of Arnhem Land, Northern Territory, Australia.

Aboriginal Topographical Painting of Arnhem Land

As the title indicates, this is an Aboriginal painting that depicts a portion of Arnhem Land, which is located in the northeast corner of the Northern Territory, Australia. Like all maps, it is a two-dimensional rendering of three-dimensional space. In other words, it is an attempt to represent land and location on a flat surface. All cultures devise certain symbols that allow for these representations to be understood. On USGS (United States Geological Survey) maps, for example, a standardized set of symbols represent such things as roads, rivers, and cities. Similarly, this map is filled with symbols that represent such features as watering holes (the circular figures) and community sites (the curved figures).

As we've learned throughout this chapter, different cultures create and experience landscapes differently. Here we can see that different cultures also represent their landscapes differently. This image is part of a long tradition of Australian Aboriginal topographic representations that reflect their particular culture and their views of the lands they occupy. In general, these representations are religious in nature, depicting myths about the sites and travels of ancestors. Most of these myths concern a spiritual identification between people and their lands. Hence, these maplike representations are not meant as objective measurements of land, as in degrees of longitude and latitude, or miles and kilometers. Instead they communicate meanings about the sacred relationships between people and their physical environment.

To most Western and American eyes, then, these images do not look like maps, since we neither recognize the symbols that Aboriginal peoples use to translate three-dimensional spaces into two dimensions, nor do we think of maps as meaningful in and of themselves. Most likely Western maps would look very odd to Aboriginal eyes. One of the goals of studying cultural geography, as we will see throughout this book, is to appreciate this diversity—this mosaic—of relationships between peoples and the places they inhabit, shape, and represent. ■

Steward, Julian H. 1976. *Theory of Cultural Change.* Urbana: University of Illinois Press.

Warren, Karen J. (ed.). 1997. *Ecofeminism: Women, Culture, Nature.* Bloomington: Indiana University Press.

Ten Recommended Books
on Cultural Geography

(For additional suggested readings, see *The Human Mosaic* web site: www.whfreeman.com/jordan)

Anderson, Kay, Mona Domosh, Steve Pile, and Nigel Thrift (eds.). 2003. *Handbook of Cultural Geography.* London: Sage Publications. An edited collection of essays that push the boundaries of cultural geography into such subdisciplines as economic, social, and political geography.

Blunt, Alison, Pyrs Gruffudd, Jon May, Miles Ogborn, and David Pinder (eds.). 2003. *Cultural Geography in Practice.* London: Arnold Publishing. An edited collection of essays that take a very practical view of what it mean to actually conduct research in the field of cultural geography.

Cosgrove, Denis. 1998. *Social Formation and Symbolic Landscape.* Madison: University of Wisconsin Press. The landmark study that outlines the relationships between the idea of landscape and social and class formation in such places as Italy, England, and the United States.

Cosgrove, Denis, and Stephen Daniels (eds.). 1990. *The Iconography of Landscape: Essays on the Symbolic Representation, Design and Use of Past Environments.* Cambridge: Cambridge University

Press. An important collection of essays that foreground an ideological reading of landscape.

Foote, Kenneth E., Peter J. Hugill, Kent Mathewson, and Jonathan M. Smith (eds.). 1994. *Re-Reading Cultural Geography.* Austin: University of Texas Press. A beautifully compiled representative collection of some of the best works in American cultural geography at the end of the twentieth century, and a useful companion to the book edited by Wagner and Mikesell.

Goudie, Andrew. 2000. *The Earth Transformed: An Introduction to Human Impacts on the Environment,* 5th ed. Cambridge, Mass.: MIT Press. A fine introduction to the theme of cultural ecology—in particular, habitat modification—as viewed by a British geographer.

Jackson, Peter. 1992. *Maps of Meaning.* New York: Routledge. A concise introduction to the many perspectives of cultural geography, filled with interesting examples.

Mitchell, Don. 1999. *Cultural Geography: A Critical Introduction.* New York: Blackwell. An introductory text on cultural geography written to emphasize the material and political elements of the discipline.

Tuan, Yi-Fu. 1974. *Topophilia: A Study of Environmental Perception, Attitudes, and Values.* Englewood Cliffs, N.J.: Prentice-Hall. A Chinese-born geographer's innovative and imaginative look at

people's attachment to place, a central concern of cultural geography.

Wagner, Philip L., and Marvin W. Mikesell. 1962. *Readings in Cultural Geography.* Chicago: University of Chicago Press. A classic collection, edited by two distinguished Berkeley-trained cultural geographers, presenting the subdiscipline as it was at mid-twentieth century and developing the device of five themes.

Journals in Cultural Geography

Annals of the Association of American Geographers. Volume 1 was published in 1911. The leading scholarly journal of American geographers.

Cultural Geographies (formerly known as *Ecumene*). Volume I was published in 1994.

Journal of Cultural Geography. Published semiannually by the Department of Geography, Oklahoma State University, Stillwater, Okla. Volume 1 was published in 1980.

Progress in Human Geography. A quarterly journal providing critical appraisal of developments and trends in the discipline. Volume 1 was published in 1977.

Social and Cultural Geography. Volume 1 was published in 2000 by Routledge, Taylor, & Francis Ltd. in Great Britain.

What makes one father-daughter pair so very different from the other?

Two American father-daughter couples. *(Left: Richard T. Nowitz/Corbis; Right:Rob Gage/FPG International.)*

Turn to Seeing Geography on page 63 for an in-depth analysis of the above question.

MANY 2 WORLDS
Geographies of Cultural Difference

NO MATTER WHERE WE LIVE, IF YOU LOOK carefully you will constantly be reminded of how important the expression of cultural identity is to people's daily lives. In many cities, the geography of cultural difference is inscribed in the names of urban neighborhoods. By geography of cultural difference, we mean not only the geographic distribution of different cultures but also the way that difference is created or reinforced by geography. For example, in the United States the history of legally enforced spatial segregation of "whites" and "blacks" has been important in establishing and maintaining cultural differences between these groups. Many of the areas to which African-Americans were confined were formerly given pejorative and racist names like "Darktown." "Chinatown," "Little Italy," "Little Havana," and "Germantown" are other examples of urban neighborhoods, where spatial segregation of groups was sometimes legally enforced and sometimes established voluntarily. Often these neighborhoods have distinctive landscapes that provide visible clues about the predominant culture of the residents.

One may encounter startling and abrupt cultural differences over relatively short distances. Take one region, south Florida, for example. Beyond Miami's urban limits, physically defined by the dike that holds back the Everglades wetlands, the cultural landscape abruptly shifts. Travel due west and one soon enters a Native American community delineated by the boundaries of the Miccosukee Indian Reservation, with its distinctive palmetto-thatched "chikee" shelters and roadside tourist attractions. Travel northwest and one quickly arrives in a rural agricultural landscape. Here the cultural mix is comprised of descendents of Anglo farmers from Georgia who cultivate family landholdings, African-American workers and small business owners, and Caribbean Basin migrant laborers employed by corporate agribusinesses. Here one is just as likely to hear Haitian Creole or Mayan as English. Indeed, the area is said to have the highest concentration of native Mayan speakers outside of Guatemala.

In our globalizing world, similar cases of many different cultures existing within the confines of relatively small spaces are common. This phenomenon suggests that while we share the same space, we simultaneously inhabit many different worlds viewed through the lens of culture and identity. These worlds reflect and shape our identities along lines of ethnicity, class, nationality, race, gender, and sexuality. A single *place* may be attractive to one group but repellent to another. The same landscape may hold different meanings for different culture groups. In short, we live in not one world, but many, and we experience not one geography, but many geographies.

What does it mean to speak of "geographies" in the plural? Isn't there just one "geography"? The plural form emphasizes that there is no single way of seeing the land and the landscape. Cultural geography studies have shown, for example, that women and men often experience the same places in different ways. A certain street corner or tavern might be a comfortable and familiar hangout for men but a threatening or uncomfortable zone that women avoid. Similarly, a person confined to a wheelchair is likely to have a very different view of movement through space than a person who can walk. Where an ambulatory person may be barely conscious of curbs and steps, a person in a wheelchair sees barriers to be bypassed through careful route planning. To speak of geographies, then, is to go beyond the physical qualities of our world and raise new questions about the different meanings that people give to places and landscapes, how these relate to their sense of self and belonging, and how, in multicultural societies, we deal with these different meanings politically and socially.

Many Cultures

Because of the influences of globalization, an increasing number of societies, including our own, are multicultural. Let's explore how this fact relates to multiple geographies by first thinking a bit more about cultures and how we identify, categorize, and delineate them spatially. According to literary critic and cultural theorist Raymond Williams, *culture* is one of the two or three most complicated words in the English language. When the term was initially used in fifteenth-century English, it meant to cultivate or husband nature, as in agriculture or horticulture. But in the late eighteenth and early nineteenth centuries, an important

shift in meaning occurred. People began to speak of "cultures" in the plural form. Specifically, they began thinking about "European culture" in relation to other cultures around the world. As Europe modernized and urbanized in the nineteenth century, a new term was invented, **folk culture,** to distinguish traditional, rural life ways of life from new urban, industrial ones. Today we take it for granted that we think in terms of multiple, distinct cultures that we can locate geographically.

As noted in Chapter 1, even when we develop solid criteria in order to delineate a culture geographically, we find that it is not internally homogeneous. We mentioned gender and sexuality as two among many possible ways in which cultures can be quite diverse and heterogeneous. Sometimes groups within a dominant culture become distinctive enough that we label them **subcultures.** These can be the result of resistance to the dominant culture or they can be the result of a distinct religious, ethnic, or national group forming an enclave community within a larger culture.

Thinking of cultures in the plural is a complicated affair and an important component of cultural geography. The list of possible cultures and subcultures that one might identify would seem to be endless. We cannot attempt that here, but we will look at a few major categories of culture groups to illustrate the idea of geographies of difference.

Cultures are classified using many different criteria. The concept of culture includes both material and nonmaterial elements. **Material culture** includes all objects or "things" made and used by members of a cultural group: buildings, furniture, clothing, artwork, musical instruments, and other physical objects. The elements of material culture are visible. **Nonmaterial culture** includes the wide range of beliefs, values, myths, and symbolic meanings that are transmitted across generations of a given culture. Cultures may be categorized and geographically located using criteria based on either or both of these features.

One distinction between categories of culture, which we have already suggested, is *folk culture* versus *popular culture.* The word **folk** describes a rural people who live in an old-fashioned way—a people holding to a lifestyle less influenced by modern technology. Folk cultures are rural, cohesive, conservative, largely self-sufficient groups that are homogeneous in custom and ethnicity, with a strong family or clan structure and highly developed rituals. Order is maintained through sanctions based in religion or the family, and interpersonal relationships are strong. Most goods are handmade, and a subsistence economy prevails. Individualism is generally weakly developed in folk cultures, as are social classes. In the poorer countries of the underdeveloped world, some aspects of folk culture still exist, though few if any peoples have been left untouched by the forces of globalization. In industrialized countries such as the United

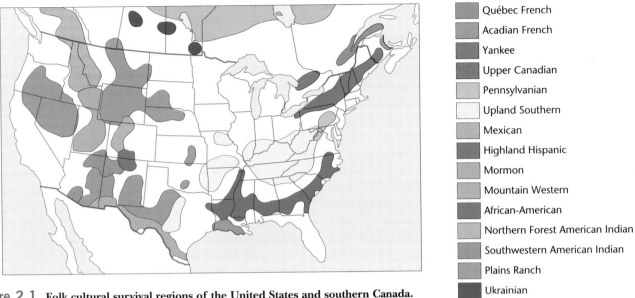

▪	Québec French
▪	Acadian French
▪	Yankee
▪	Upper Canadian
▪	Pennsylvanian
▫	Upland Southern
▪	Mexican
▪	Highland Hispanic
▪	Mormon
▪	Mountain Western
▪	African-American
▪	Northern Forest American Indian
▪	Southwestern American Indian
▪	Plains Ranch
▪	Ukrainian

Figure 2.1 **Folk cultural survival regions of the United States and southern Canada.** All are now in decay and retreat, and no true folk cultures survive in North America.

States and Canada, unaltered folk cultures no longer exist, though many remnants can be found (Figure 2.1). **Folk geography,** a term coined by Eugene Wilhelm, may be defined as the study of the spatial patterns and ecology of these traditional groups.

Popular culture, by contrast, is generated from and concentrated mainly in urban areas, broadly defined (Figure 2.2). Popular material goods are mass-produced by machines in factories, and a cash economy, rather than barter or subsistence, dominates. Relationships among individuals are more numerous but less personal than in folk cultures, and the family structure is weaker. Mass media such as film, print, television, radio, and, increasingly, the Internet are more influential in shaping popular culture. People are more mobile, less attached to place and environment. Secular institutions of authority—such as the police, army, and

Figure 2.2 **Popular culture is reflected in every aspect of life,** from the clothes we wear to the recreational activities that occupy our leisure time. *(Left: Alex Majoli/Magnum; Right: Stuart Franklin/Magnum.)*

courts—take the place of family and church in maintaining order. Individualism is strongly developed.

Another major category is **indigenous culture.** A simple definition of *indigenous* is "native" or "of native origin." In the modern world of sovereign nation-states, the word has acquired a much greater cultural and political meaning. In fact, the International Labor Organization's (ILO) Indigenous and Tribal Peoples Convention 169 (Article 1.1) presents a legal definition that recognizes indigenous peoples as comprising a distinct culture. According to the ILO, indigenous peoples are self-identified tribal peoples whose social, cultural, and economic conditions distinguish them from the national society of their host state. Indigenous peoples are regarded as descending from peoples present in the state territory at the time of conquest or colonization. Indigenous cultures are, in effect, those peoples that were colonized—mostly, but not exclusively—by European cultures and are now minorities in their homelands. This definition is applied globally, suggesting that indigenous cultures worldwide share common traits and face similar perils and opportunities. The United Nations helped focus global attention on indigenous cultures when it declared 1995–2004 to be the International Decade of the World's Indigenous People.

In reality, all of culture presents a continuum rather than easily distinguished categories. Many gradations are possible among cultures, and much heterogeneity exists within cultures. We can use our five themes of cultural geography—*region, diffusion, ecology, interaction,* and *landscape*—to study geographies of cultural difference.

 ## Regions of Difference

How do cultures vary geographically? Some cultures exhibit major variations from place to place with minor variations over time. Others display less difference from region to region but change rapidly over time. For this reason, the theme of culture region is particularly well suited to the study of cultural difference. *Formal* culture regions can be delineated on the basis of both material and nonmaterial elements.

Material Folk Culture Regions

In many parts of the world, remnants of material folk culture persist. Although folk culture has largely vanished from the United States and Canada, vestiges remain in various areas of both countries. Figure 2.1 shows culture regions in which the material artifacts of 15 different North American folk cultures survive in some abundance, but even these artifacts are disappearing. Each region possesses many distinctive relics of material culture.

For example, the strongly Germanic *Pennsylvanian* folk culture region features an unusual Swiss-German type of barn, distinguished by an overhanging upper-level "forebay" on one eave side (Figure 2.3). In contrast, barns are usually attached to the rear of houses in the *Yankee* folk region, which is also distinguished by an elaborate traditional gravestone art, featuring "winged death heads." The *Upland South* is noted in part for the abundance of a variety of distinctive house types built using notched-log construction. The *African-American* folk region displays such features as the "scraped-earth" cemetery, from which all grass is laboriously removed to expose the bare ground (Figure 2.4); the banjo, an African instrument by origin; and head kerchiefs worn by women. Grist windmills with sturdy stone towers and *pétanque,* a bowling game played with small metal balls, among other traits characterize the *Québec French* folk region. The *Mormon* folk culture is iden-

Figure 2.3 A multilevel barn with projecting "forebay," central Pennsylvania. Every folk culture region possesses distinctive forms of traditional architecture. Of Swiss origin, the forebay barn is one of the main identifying material traits of the Pennsylvanian folk culture region. This barn type crossed the Atlantic with German-speaking Swiss colonists in the 1700s. *(Courtesy of Terry G. Jordan-Bychkov.)*

tifiable by distinctive hay derricks and clustered farm villages conforming to a checkerboard street pattern. The western *Plains Ranch* folk culture produced such material items as the "beef wheel," a windlass used during butchering (Figure 2.5). These examples of material artifacts are only a few of the many that survive from various folk regions.

Is Popular Culture Placeless?

Superficially at least, popular culture varies less from place to place than does folk culture. In fact, Canadian geographer Edward Relph goes so far as to propose that popular culture produces a profound **placelessness,** a spatial standardization that diminishes regional variety and demeans the human spirit. Others observe that one place seems pretty much like another, each robbed of its unique character by the pervasive influence of a continental or even worldwide popular culture (Figure 2.6). When compared with regions and places produced by folk culture, rich in their uniqueness (Figure 2.7), the geographical face of popular culture often seems expressionless. The greater mobility of people in popular culture weakens attachment to place and compounds the problem of placelessness. Moreover, the spread of McDonald's, Levi's, CNN, shopping malls, and much else further adds to the sense of placelessness.

But is popular culture truly regionless and placeless? Many cultural geographers are more cautious about mak-

Figure 2.5 **"Beef wheel" in the ranching country of the Harney Basin in central Oregon.** This windlass device hoists the carcass of a slaughtered animal to facilitate butchering. Derived, as was much of the local ranching culture, from Hispanic Californians, the beef wheel represents the folk material culture of ranching. *(Courtesy of Terry G. Jordan-Bychkov.)*

Figure 2.4 **A "scraped-earth" folk graveyard in East Texas.** The laborious removal of all grass from such cemeteries is an African-derived custom. Long ago, this practice diffused from the African-American folk culture region to Caucasians in the southern coastal plain of the United States to become simply a "southern" custom. How might such cultural diffusion across racial lines occur? *(Courtesy of Terry G. Jordan-Bychkov.)*

ing such a sweeping generalization. In *The Clustering of America,* Michael Weiss argues that "American society has become increasingly fragmented" and identifies 40 "lifestyle clusters" based on postal zip codes. "Those five digits can indicate the kinds of magazines you read, the meals you serve at dinner," and what political party you support. "Tell me someone's zip code and I can predict what they eat, drink, drive—even think." The lifestyle clusters, each of which is a formal culture region, bear Weiss's colorful names—such as "Gray Power" (upper-middle-class retirement areas), "Old Yankee Rows" (older ethnic neighborhoods of the Northeast), and "Norma Rae–Ville" (lower- and middle-class southern mill towns, named for the Sally Field movie about the tribulations of a union organizer in a textile manufacturing town) (Figure 2.8). Old Yankee Rowers, for example, typically have a high school education, enjoy bowling and ice hockey, and are three times as likely as the average American to live in row houses or duplexes. Residents of Norma Rae–Ville are mostly nonunion factory workers, have trouble earning a living, and consume twice as much canned stew as the

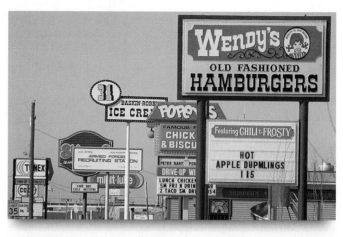

Figure 2.6 **Placelessness exemplified: scenes almost anywhere, developed world.** Guess where these pictures were taken. The answers are provided at the end of the chapter.

Compare these views to Figure 2.8. *(See also Curtis, 1982. Photo at left: Donald Dietz/Stock Boston, Inc.; Top Right: David Frazier/Photo Researchers; Bottom Left: Courtesy of Terry G. Jordan-Bychkov.)*

national average. In short, a whole panoply of popular sub-cultures exists in America and the world at large, each possessing its own belief system, spokespeople, dress code, and lifestyle.

REFLECTING ON GEOGRAPHY

Do you live in a "placeless" place, in "nowhere U.S.A."? If not, how is a distinctive regional form of popular culture reflected in your region?

Indigenous Culture Regions

Worldwide, large concentrations of indigenous populations exist outside of the strong influence of national cultures and the effective control of governments located in faraway capital cities. National control by a central government is often weakened by minimal infrastructure, rough topography, or

harsh environmental conditions. That is, concentrations of indigenous peoples are generally in areas with few roads or modern communications systems, such as mountainous areas, vast arid and semiarid regions, or large expanses of forest or wetlands. These concentrations constitute indigenous culture regions.

The so-called Hill Tribes of South Asia are a good example. Mountain ranges, including the Chittagong Hills, the Assam Hills, and the Himalayas, surround the fertile valleys and deltas around which the ancient South Asian Hindu and Islamic civilizations were centered. Various indigenous peoples occupy these highland regions, which are remote from the lowland centers of authority and culturally distinct from them (Figure 2.9). A series of indigenous culture regions ringing the valleys of South Asia thus exists, occupied by what the British colonial authorities referred to as Hill Tribes. Most of these peoples practice some version of **swidden agriculture** (see Chapter 8), hold Christian or animist

Figure 2.7 Retaining a sense of place: a hill town in Cappadocia Province, Turkey. This town, produced by a folk culture, exhibits striking individuality. How can you tell that this is not a popular culture landscape? *(Courtesy of Terry G. Jordan-Bychkov.)*

beliefs, and speak languages distinct from those spoken in the lowlands. A similar pattern of highland indigenous culture regions can also be identified in the countries of Southeast Asia, such as Myanmar and Thailand, where culture groups such as the Shan and Karen have populations in the millions.

Indigenous culture regions also persist in Central and South America. There is a distinct Mayan culture region that encompasses parts of Mexico, Belize, Guatemala, and Honduras (Figure 2.10). Concentrations of Mayan speakers are especially common in rugged highlands and tropical forests. In South America, another concentration of indigenous peoples exists in sections of the Andes Mountains. This area constituted the geographic core of the Inca

Figure 2.8 Three examples of the 40 lifestyle clusters in U.S. popular culture. Any of the 200 television market areas that contained individual zip code areas with above-average occurrence of the lifestyle indicated are shaded in their entirety, even though only a portion of the market area was so characterized. For a description of each lifestyle, see the text. Are these regions accurately described? What would you change? *(Adapted from Weiss, 1988: 307, 335, 362.)*

Figure 2.9 A Murong tribesman with his children in the indigenous culture region of Bangladesh's Chittagong Hill Tracts. *(Shehzad Noorani/Peter Arnold.)*

civilization, which thrived between A.D. 1300 and 1533 and incorporated several major linguistic groups under its rule. Today, up to 55 percent of the national populations of Andean countries such as Bolivia, Peru, and Ecuador are indigenous. On the slopes and in the high valleys of the Andes, Quechua and Aymara speakers constitute an overwhelming majority, signifying another indigenous culture region (Figure 2.11).

Food and Drink

A persistent formal regionalization of popular culture is vividly revealed by what foods and beverages are consumed, which varies markedly from one part of a country to another and throughout different parts of the world. The highest per capita levels of U.S. beer consumption occur in the

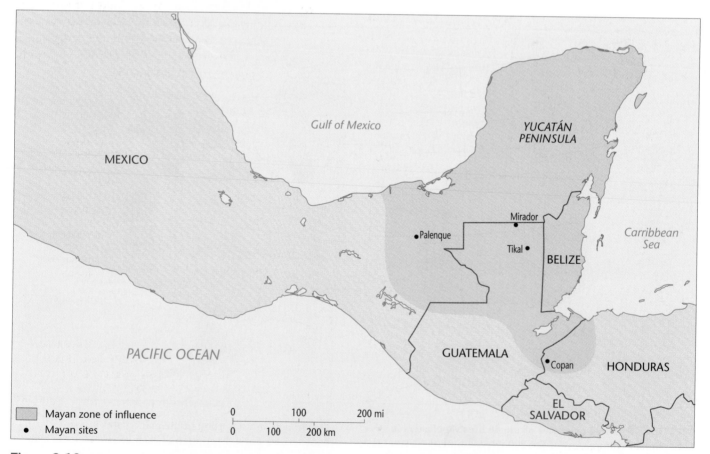

Figure 2.10 **The Mayan culture region in Middle America.** The ancient Mayan Empire collapsed centuries ago, but its Mayan-speaking descendents continue to occupy the region today. In many cases Mayan communities, after centuries of political and economic marginalization, are today actively struggling to have their land rights recognized by their respective governments.

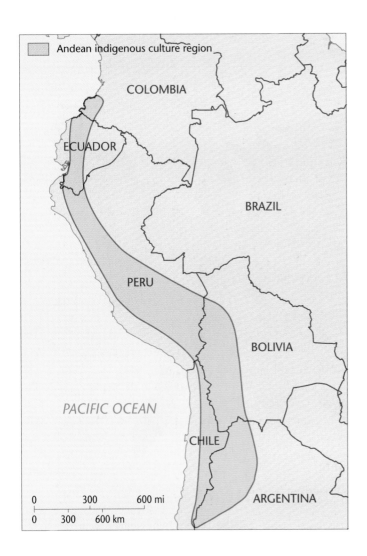

Figure 2.11 **The indigenous culture region of the Andes, including Quechua- and Aymara-speaking peoples.** This is the core of the ancient Inca Empire, where today many of the indigenous people speak their mother language rather than Spanish. *(Adapted from de Blij and Muller, 2004.)*

West, with the notable exception of Mormon Utah. Whiskey made from corn, manufactured both legally and illegally, has been a traditional southern alcoholic beverage, whereas wine is more common in California.

Foods consumed by members of the North American popular culture also vary from place to place. In the South, grits, barbecued pork and beef, fried chicken, and hamburgers are far more popular than elsewhere in the United States, whereas more pizza and submarine sandwiches are consumed in the North, the destination for many Italian immigrants. Indeed, pizza diffused to the southern states only in the mid-1950s.

Fast food might seem to epitomize popular culture, yet its importance varies greatly within the United States (Figure 2.12). The stronghold of the fast-food industry is the American South; the Northeast has the fewest fast-food restaurants. Such differences undermine the geographical uniformity or placelessness supposedly created by popular culture. Music provides another example.

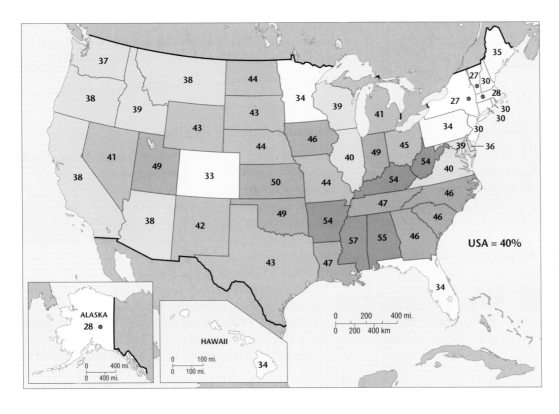

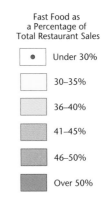

Figure 2.12 **Fast-food sales as a share of total restaurant sales, by state, 1997.** What does this illustration suggest about the convergence hypothesis, which holds that regional cultures in America are collapsing into a national culture? *(From* Restaurant Business. *See also Roark, 1985.)*

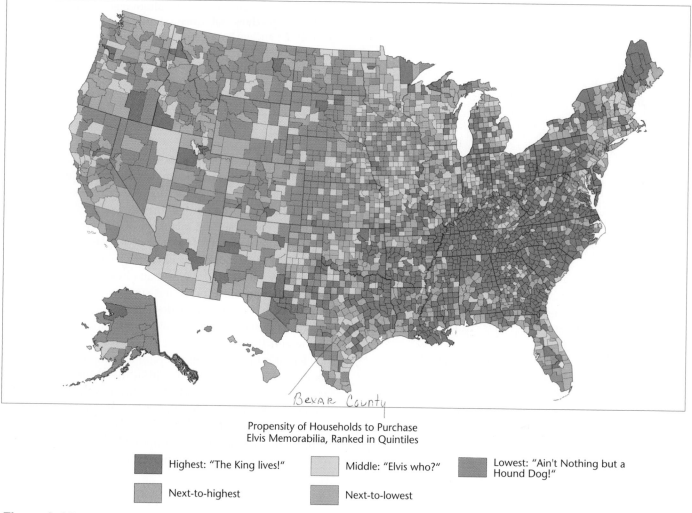

Propensity of Households to Purchase
Elvis Memorabilia, Ranked in Quintiles

⬛	Highest: "The King lives!"	⬜	Middle: "Elvis who?"	⬛	Lowest: "Ain't Nothing but a Hound Dog!"
⬛	Next-to-highest	⬛	Next-to-lowest		

Figure 2.13 **Purchases of Elvis Presley memorabilia, 1990s.** The hotbeds of Elvis adoration lie mainly in the eastern United States, while most westerners can take him or leave him. What cultural factors might underlie this "fault line" in the geography of popular culture? *(Redrawn, based on data collected by Bob Lunn of DICI, Bellaire, Texas, and published by Edmonson and Jacobson, 1993.)*

Popular Music

Popular culture has spawned many different styles of music, all of which reveal geographical patterns in levels of acceptance. Elvis Presley epitomized both popular music and the associated cult of personality. Even today, a generation after his death, he retains an important place in American popular culture.

Elvis also illustrates the vivid geography of that culture. In the sale of Presley memorabilia, the nation reveals a split personality. The main hotbeds of Elvis worship lie in the eastern states, while the King of Rock and Roll is largely forgotten out West. Although it raises more questions than it answers, Figure 2.13 leaves no doubt that popular culture varies regionally.

Vernacular Culture Regions

Rather than being the intellectual creation of professional geographers, a **vernacular culture region** is the product of the spatial perception of the population at large—a composite of the mental maps of the people. Such regions vary greatly in size, from small districts covering only part of a city or town to huge, multistate areas. Like most other geographical regions, they often overlap and usually have poorly defined borders.

Almost every part of the industrialized Western world offers examples of vernacular regions based in the popular culture. Figure 2.14 shows some sizable vernacular regions in North America. Geographer Wilbur Zelinsky compiled these regions by determining the most common name for

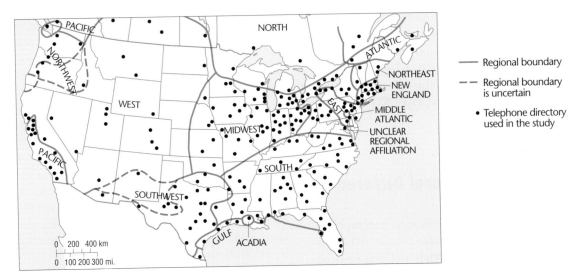

Figure 2.14 Some vernacular regions in North America.
Cultural geographer Wilbur Zelinsky mapped these regions on the basis of business names in the white pages of metropolitan telephone directories. Why are names containing "West" more widespread than those containing "East"? What might account for the areas where no region name is perceived? *(Adapted from Zelinsky, 1980a:14.)*

businesses appearing in the white pages of urban telephone directories. One curious feature of the map is the sizable, populous district—in New York, Ontario, eastern Ohio, and western Pennsylvania—where no regional affiliation is perceived. Using a different source of information, geographer Joseph Brownell sought to delimit the popular "Midwest" in 1960 (Figure 2.15). He sent out questionnaires to postal employees in the midsection of the United States, from the Appalachians to the Rockies, asking each whether, in his or her opinion, the community lay in the "Midwest." The

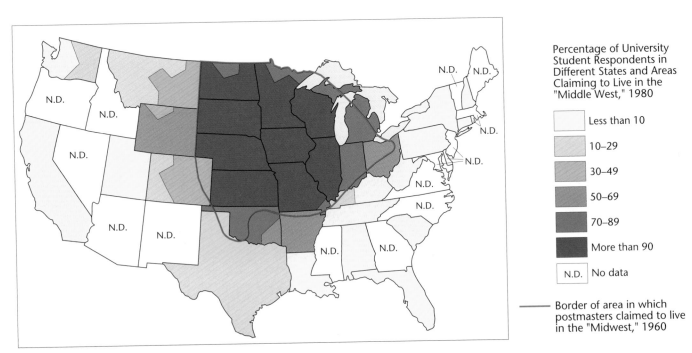

Percentage of University Student Respondents in Different States and Areas Claiming to Live in the "Middle West," 1980

- Less than 10
- 10–29
- 30–49
- 50–69
- 70–89
- More than 90
- N.D. No data

— Border of area in which postmasters claimed to live in the "Midwest," 1960

Figure 2.15 The vernacular Middle West or Midwest Two surveys, taken a generation apart and using two different groups of respondents, yielded similar results. *(Sources: Brownell, 1960:83; Shortridge, 1989.)*

results identified a vernacular region in which the residents considered themselves midwesterners. A similar survey done 20 years later, using student respondents, revealed a core-periphery pattern for the Midwest (see Figure 2.15). As befits an element of popular culture, the vernacular region is often perpetuated by the mass media, especially radio and television.

Diffusion and Cultural Difference

Do elements of folk culture spread through geographical space differently from those of popular culture? Whereas folk culture spreads by the same models and processes of diffusion as popular culture, diffusion operates more slowly within a folk setting. The relative conservatism of such cultures produces a resistance to change. The Amish, for example, as one of the few surviving folk cultures, are distinctive today simply because they reject innovations that they believe to be inappropriate for their way of life and values.

Agricultural Fairs

An example of the progress of diffusion in a folk setting can be seen in the spread of the American agricultural fair, usually held at the county level. The county fair originated in the Yankee folk region in Pittsfield, Massachusetts, in 1810 and spread first to western New England and the adjacent Hudson Valley by expansion diffusion. From that source region it diffused westward into the American heartland, the Midwest, where it gained its widest acceptance (Figure 2.16).

Usually promoted by agricultural societies, the fairs originally served an educational purpose, as places where farmers could learn about improved methods and breeds. Soon an element of entertainment was added, represented by a racetrack and midway; competition for prizes for superior agricultural products became common. By the early twentieth century, the agricultural fair had diffused through most of the United States, although farmers in culture regions such as the Upland South did not accept it as readily or fully as did midwesterners.

Blowguns: Diffusion or Independent Invention?

Often the path of past diffusion of an item of material culture is not clearly known or understood, presenting geographers with a problem of interpretation. The blowgun is a good example. A hunting tool, it is a long, hollow tube through which a projectile is blown by the force of one's breath. Geographer Stephen Jett mapped the distribution of blowguns, which he discovered were used in societies in both the Eastern and Western Hemispheres, all the way

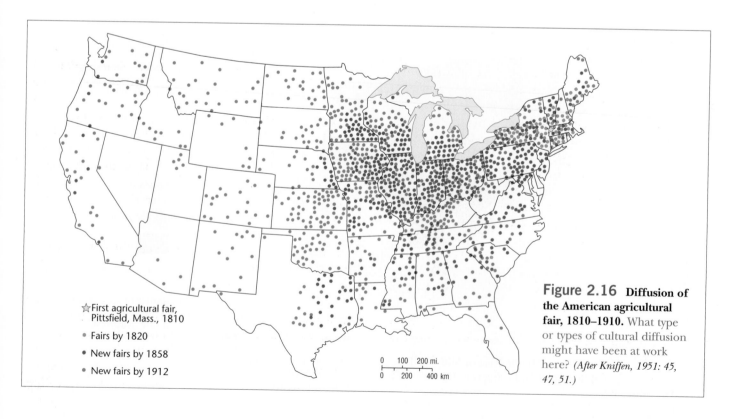

☆ First agricultural fair, Pittsfield, Mass., 1810

• Fairs by 1820

• New fairs by 1858

• New fairs by 1912

Figure 2.16 Diffusion of the American agricultural fair, 1810–1910. What type or types of cultural diffusion might have been at work here? *(After Kniffen, 1951: 45, 47, 51.)*

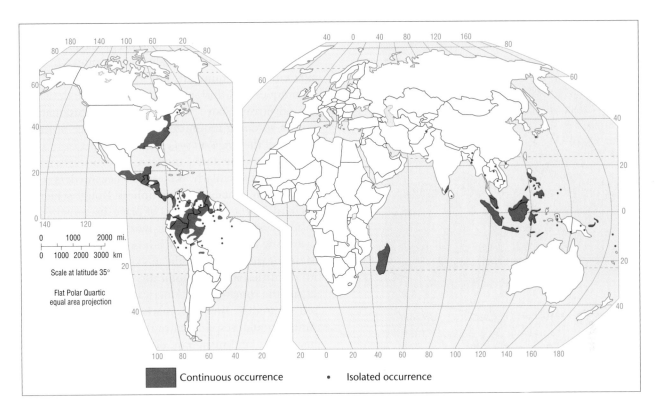

Continuous occurrence • Isolated occurrence

Figure 2.17 **Former distribution of the blowgun among Native Americans, South Asians, Africans, and Pacific Islanders.** The blowgun occurred among folk cultures in two widely separated areas of the world. Was this the result of independent invention or cultural diffusion? What kinds of data might one seek to answer this question? Compare and contrast the occurrence in the Indian and Pacific ocean lands to the distribution of the Austronesian languages (see Chapter 4). *(Source: Jett, 1991: 92–93.)*

from the island of Madagascar, off the east coast of Africa, to the Amazon rain forests of South America (Figure 2.17).

Indonesian peoples, probably on the island of Borneo, appear to have first invented the blowgun. It became their principal hunting weapon and diffused through much of the equatorial island belt of the Eastern Hemisphere. How, then, do we account for its presence among Native American groups in the Western Hemisphere? Was it *independently invented* by Native Americans? Was it brought to the Americas by *relocation diffusion* in pre-Columbian times? Or did it spread to the New World only after the European discovery of America? We do not know the answers to these questions, but the problem presented is one common to cultural geography, especially when studying the traditions of nonliterate cultures, which precludes the use of written records that might reveal such diffusion. Certain rules of thumb can be employed in any given situation to help resolve the issue. For example, if one or more nonfunctional features of blowguns, such as a decorative motif or specific terminology, occurred in both South America and Indonesia, then the logical conclusion would be that cultural diffusion explained the distribution of blowguns.

Diffusion in Popular Culture

Hierarchical diffusion often plays a greater role in popular culture because popular society, unlike folk culture, is highly stratified by socioeconomic class. For example, the spread of McDonald's restaurants—beginning in 1955 in the United States and, later, internationally—occurred hierarchically for the most part, revealing a bias in favor of larger urban markets (Figure 2.18). Further facilitating the diffusion of popular culture is the fact that *time-distance decay* is weaker in such regions, largely because of the reach of mass media.

Sometimes, however, diffusion in popular culture works differently, as a study of Wal-Mart revealed. Geographers Thomas Graff and Dub Ashton concluded that Wal-Mart initially diffused from its Arkansas base in a largely *contagious* pattern, reaching first into other parts of Arkansas and neighboring states. Simultaneously, as often happens in the spatial spread of culture, another pattern of diffusion was at work, one Graff and Ashton called *reverse* hierarchical diffusion. Wal-Mart initially located its stores in smaller towns and markets, only later spreading into cities—the precise reverse of the way hierarchical diffusion normally works. This

Figure 2.18 **Another McDonald's opens in Moscow.**
McDonald's, which first spread to Moscow about 1987, has always
preferred hierarchical diffusion. Of all McDonald's outlets
worldwide today, about 45 percent are located in foreign countries,
almost always in large cities. *(Courtesy of Terry G. Jordan-Bychkov.)*

combination of contagious and reverse hierarchical diffusion led Wal-Mart to become the nation's largest retailer in
only 30 years. A different kind of diffusion, *relocation diffusion,* in 1995 brought Wal-Mart into Canada, when it purchased 122 stores from rival Woolco and soon became that
country's largest discount retailer in total sales.

Before the advent of modern transportation and mass
communications, innovations usually required thousands of
years to complete their areal spread, and even as recently as
the early nineteenth century the time span was still measured
in decades. In regard to popular culture, modern transportation and communications networks now permit cultural diffusion to occur within weeks or even days. The propensity for
change makes diffusion extremely important in popular culture. The availability of devices permitting rapid diffusion enhances the chance for change in popular culture.

Advertising

The most effective device for diffusion in popular culture, as
Zelinsky suggests, confronts us almost every day of our lives.
Commercial advertising of retail products and services bom-
bards our eyes and ears, with great effect. Using the techniques of social science, especially psychology, advertisers

have learned how to sell us products we do not need. The
skill with which advertising firms prepare commercials often
determines the success or failure of a product. In short, popular culture is equipped with the most potent devices and
techniques of diffusion ever devised. These devices of market advertising have accelerated the diffusionary process
and in so doing minimized the importance of *time-distance
decay* and the *neighborhood effect.*

At the same time, modern advertising is very place-
conscious, particularly as messages became less textual and
increasingly visual. As geographers Douglas Fleming and
Richard Roth noted, images of place are a vital component
in many ads and are used to market products and services
by linking them to popular, admired places. The "Marlboro
Man" cigarette ads provide an excellent example, and even
in countries as geographically and culturally distant as
Egypt, the romanticized American West is used effectively to
sell cigarettes. Isn't it remarkable that Egyptian Muslim
Arabs should respond favorably to a symbol-laden place
image of a land most have never seen or ever hope to see?
Such is the power of diffusion in popular culture.

Communications Barriers

Although the communications media create the potential
for almost instant diffusion over very large areas, this can be
greatly retarded if access to the media is denied or limited
(see Focus On: The Geography of Rock and Roll). *Billboard,*
a magazine devoted largely to popular music, described one
such barrier. A record company executive complained that
radio stations and disk jockeys refused to play "punk rock"
records, thereby denying the style an equal opportunity for
exposure. He claimed that punk devotees were concentrated in New York City, Los Angeles, Boston, and London,
where many young people had found the style reflective of
their feelings and frustrations. Without access to radio stations, punk rock could diffuse from these centers only
through live concerts and the record sales they generated.
The publishers of *Billboard* noted that "punk rock is but one
of a number of musical forms which initially had problems
breaking through nationally out of regional footholds," for
Pachanga, ska, pop/gospel, "women's music," reggae, and
"gangsta rap" experienced similar difficulties. Similarly,
Time Warner, a major distributor of gangsta rap music, endured scathing criticism from the U.S. Congress in 1995 because of potentially offensive or deleterious aspects of this
genre. This eventually led the company to sell the subsidiary
label that recorded this form of rap. To control the programming of radio and television, or distribution generally,
is to control much of the diffusionary apparatus in popular
culture. The diffusion of innovations ultimately depends on
the flow of information.

The Geography of Rock and Roll

Diffusion occurs rapidly in popular culture. The rock-and-roll musical style arose in the early 1950s, achieved its maximum diffusion within a decade, then gave way to other, often derivative, forms of music. Its chief personality, Elvis Presley, was only 42 years old at the time of his death in 1977, yet the heyday of early rock and roll had ended a decade and a half before he died.

The hearth (creative center) of rock and roll, about 1952 or 1953, was the Upper Delta country along the Mississippi River, centered on Memphis, Tennessee. Elvis, Little Richard, Fats Domino, Chuck Berry, and Jerry Lee Lewis, the chief practitioners of rock and roll, all worked in the Upper Delta. The style developed as a blending of African-American rhythm and blues and Hill Southern white rockabilly, a fast-tempo country-and-western style. Diffusion was achieved through the radio and from sales of inexpensive 45-rpm records, coupled with live concerts. The spread occurred most rapidly between 1955 and 1958;

after 1963, rock and roll was in decline, although it influenced many subsequent musical styles, including the Beatles.

Barriers were encountered in the diffusion. Parental opposition to the music and lyrics as "degraded" led to the banning of rock and roll on radio stations in some cities. The barriers proved to be permeable—explicit sexual references, so common in rhythm and blues and vintage rock and roll, were softened. "Roll with me, Henry" became the less suggestive "Dance with me, Henry." Hierarchical diffusion was clearly evident. Early adopters were inquisitive, gregarious young people, trendsetters in their generation. From them acceptance spread down through lower hierarchies until only a hard core of nonaccepters remained. Similar trendsetters abandoned rock and roll for other rock styles after about 1963, and the major musical phenomenon of the 1950s went into decline.

Adapted from Francaviglia, 1973

Government censorship, as opposed to mere criticism, also creates barriers to diffusion, though of varying degrees of effectiveness. In 1995 the Islamic fundamentalist regime in Iran, opposed to what it perceived as the corrupting influences of Western popular culture, outlawed television satellite dishes in an attempt to prevent citizens from watching programs broadcast in foreign countries. The Taliban government of Afghanistan went even further, banning all television sets. Control of the media can greatly control people's tastes in, preferences in, and ideas about popular culture. Even so, repressive regimes must cope with a proliferation of communication methods, including fax machines and the Internet. So pervasive has cultural diffusion become that the insular, isolated status of nations is probably no longer attainable for very long, even under totalitarian conditions.

Although newspapers are potent agents of diffusion in popular culture, they also act as selective barriers, often reinforcing the effect of political boundaries. For example, between 20 and 50 percent of all news published in Canadian newspapers is of foreign origin, whereas only about 12 percent of all news appearing in U.S. papers comes from foreign areas.

REFLECTING ON GEOGRAPHY

Because Canadian newspapers devote so much more coverage to international stories than U.S. newspapers, are Americans more provincial than Canadians as a result?

Diffusion of the Rodeo

Barriers of one kind or another usually weaken the diffusion of elements of popular culture before they become ubiquitous. The rodeo provides an example. Rooted in the ranching culture of the American West, it has never completely escaped that setting (Figure 2.19). That is, the *neighborhood effect* is evident, even in popular culture.

Like so many elements of popular culture, the modern rodeo had its origins in folk tradition. Taking their name from the Spanish *rodear,* "to round up," rodeos began simply as roundups of cattle in the Spanish livestock ranching system in northern Mexico and the American Southwest. Anglo-Americans adopted Mexican cowboy skills in the nineteenth century, and cowboys from adjacent ranches began to hold contests at roundup time. Eventually, some cowboy contests on the Great Plains became formalized, with prizes awarded.

The transition to commercial rodeo, with admission tickets and grandstands, came quickly as an outgrowth of the formal cowboy contests. One such affair, at North Platte, Nebraska, in 1882, led to the inclusion of some rodeo events in a Wild West show at Omaha in 1883. These shows, which moved by railroad from town to town in the manner of circuses, were probably the most potent agent of early rodeo diffusion. Within a decade of the Omaha event, commercial rodeos were being held independently of Wild West shows in several towns, such as Prescott, Arizona, by 1888. Spreading

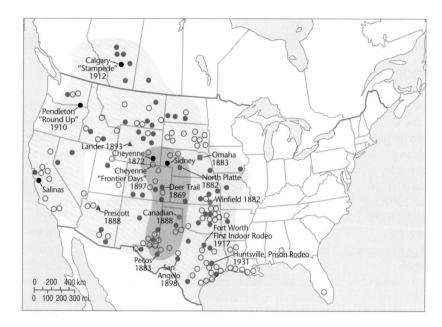

Figure 2.19 Origin and diffusion of the American commercial rodeo. Derived originally from folk culture, rodeos evolved through formal cowboy contests and Wild West shows to emerge, in the late 1880s and 1890s, in their present popular culture form. The border between the United States and Canada proved no barrier to the diffusion, although Canadian rodeo, like Canadian football, differs in some respects from the U.S. type. What barriers might the diffusion have encountered? *(Sources: Frederickson, 1984; Pillsbury, 1990b.)*

rapidly, commercial rodeos appeared throughout much of the West and parts of Canada by the early 1900s. At Cheyenne, Wyoming, the famous Frontier Days rodeo was first held in 1897. By World War I, the rodeo had also become an institution in the provinces of western Canada, where the Calgary Stampede began in 1912.

Today, rodeos are held in 36 states and three Canadian provinces. The state of Oklahoma's annual calendar of events lists no fewer than 98 scheduled rodeos, including many that explicitly bridge racial and gender gaps. Rodeos have received the greatest acceptance in the popular culture found west of the Mississippi and Missouri rivers (see Figure 2.19). *Absorbing* and *permeable barriers* to the diffusion of commercial rodeo were encountered at the border of Mexico, south of which bullfighting occupies a dominant position, and in the Mormon culture region centered in Utah.

 Ecologies of Difference

What is the nature of the relationship between ecology and cultural difference? Do different cultures and subcultures differ in their interactions with the physical environment?

Indigenous Ecology

Many observers believe that indigenous peoples possess a very close relationship with and great deal of knowledge about the physical environment. In many cases, indigenous cultures have developed sustainable land-use practices over generations of experimentation in a particular environmental setting. As a consequence, academics, journalists, and even corporate advertisers often portray indigenous peoples as defenders of endangered environments, such as tropical rain forests. It was not always this way. Especially during the height of European **colonialism,** indigenous populations (then considered colonial subjects) were often accused of destroying the environment. The then-common belief that indigenous land-use practices were destructive helped Europeans to justify colonialism by claiming they were saving colonial subjects from themselves. In hindsight it is easy to see that this belief was related to now-discredited European ideas of the racial inferiority of colonized peoples.

Debate continues today, with some observing that while indigenous cultures may once have lived sustainably, globalization is making their knowledge and practices less useful. Others note that it is impossible to generalize about sustainability in indigenous cultures because they vary greatly in their use of the environment from place to place and are internally heterogeneous. A key discussion centers on the role of indigenous peoples in conserving global biodiversity. In part this reflects the reality that indigenous peoples often occupy territories that Western scientists view as critical to global biodiversity conservation (Figure 2.20). For example, 85 percent of national parks and other pro-

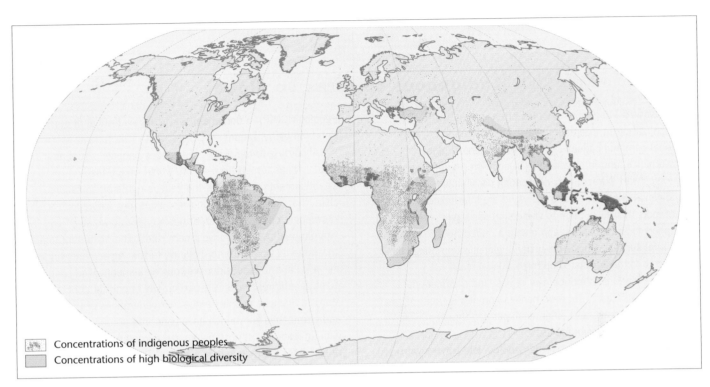

Concentrations of indigenous peoples
Concentrations of high biological diversity

Figure 2.20 **The global congruence of cultural and biological diversity.** Conservationists are aware that many of the world's most biologically diverse regions are occupied by indigenous cultures. Many suggest, therefore, that cultural preservation and biological preservation should go hand in hand. *(Adapted from IDRC, 2004.)*

tected areas in Central America and 80 percent in South America have resident indigenous populations. There is also close geographic correspondence between indigenous territories and tropical rain forests not only in Latin America but also in Africa and Southeast Asia. Tropical rain forests, while covering only 6 percent of the Earth's surface, are estimated to contain 60 percent of the world's biodiversity. With the rise of genetic engineering, tropical forests are viewed by conservationists and corporations alike as in situ gene banks. As multinational biotechnology companies look to the tropics for genetic resources for use in developing new medicines or crop seeds, indigenous peoples are increasingly vocal about their proprietary rights over the biodiversity of their homelands (see Culture in a Globalizing World).

Faced with these issues, cultural geographers generally emphasize the continued importance of indigenous knowledge for environmental management and of indigenous land-use practices for sustainable development. Initially geographers focused on the *adaptive strategies* of indigenous cultures in relation to ecological conditions. Later they came to realize that externally generated political and economic forces were just as important in shaping cultural-ecological relationships. A look at the work of a few key cultural geographers will illustrate the implications of this idea.

Local Knowledge

Much of the interest in indigenous perceptions and practices falls under the rubric of **indigenous technical knowledge (ITK).** This is a concept that anthropologists and geographers developed to describe the detailed local knowledge about the environment and land use that is part of many indigenous cultures. Geographer Paul Richards, for example, suggested that ITK is in many cases superior to Western scientific knowledge and therefore should be considered in environmental management and agricultural planning. In his study of West African cultures, *Indigenous Agricultural Revolution,* Richards documented the subtle and extensive knowledge about local soils, climate, and plant life. This local-scale knowledge provides the foundation for people to experiment with new crops and agricultural techniques, while also allowing them to successfully adjust to changing social and environmental conditions.

Sometimes, however, the global economy applies such pressure to local **subsistence economies** that they become ecologically unsustainable. Subsistence economies are those that are oriented primarily toward production for local consumption, rather than the production of commodities for sale on the market. When an indigenous society organized for subsistence production begins producing

CULTURE IN A GLOBALIZING WORLD

Indigenous Cultures Go Global

The world's indigenous peoples often interact with globalization in interesting ways. On the one hand, new global communications systems, institutions of global governance, and international NGOs are providing indigenous peoples with extraordinary networking possibilities. Local indigenous peoples around the world are now linked in global networks that allow them to share strategies, rally international support for local causes, and create a united front to defend cultural survival. On the other hand, globalization brings the world to formerly isolated cultures. Global mass communications introduce new values, and multinational corporations' search for new markets and new sources of gas, oil, genetic, forest, and other resources can threaten local economies and environments.

Both aspects of indigenous peoples' interactions with globalization were evident at the World Trade Organization's (WTO) Ministerial Conference in Cancún, Mexico, in 2003. Hosted by the Mayan community in nearby Quintana Roo, indigenous peoples' organizations from around the world gathered for the conference. Though not officially part of the conference, they came together there to strategize ways to forward their collective cause of cultural survival and self-determination, gain worldwide publicity, and protest the WTO's vision of globalization. One outcome of this meeting was the International Cancún Declaration of Indigenous Peoples (ICDIP), a document that is highly critical of current trends in globalization.

According to the ICDIP, indigenous peoples' situation globally "has turned from bad to worse" since the establishment of the WTO. Indigenous rights organizations claim that "our territories and resources, our indigenous knowledge, cultures and identities are grossly violated" by international trade and investment rules. The document urges governments worldwide to make no further agreements under the WTO and to reconsider previous agreements. The control of plant genetic resources is a particularly important concern. Many indigenous peoples argue that generations of their labor and cumulative knowledge have gone into producing the genetic resources that transnational corporations are trying to privatize for their own profit. The ICDIP asks that future international agreements ensure "that we, Indigenous Peoples, retain our rights to have control over our seeds, medicinal plants and indigenous knowledge."

Globalization is clearly a critical issue for indigenous cultures. Some argue that globalization, because it facilitates the creation of global networks that provide strength in numbers, may ultimately improve indigenous peoples' efforts to control their own destinies. The future of indigenous cultural survival will ultimately depend on how globalization is structured and for whose benefit.

for an external market, social, ecological, and economic difficulties often ensue.

Global Economy

Geographer Barney Nietschmann's classic study of the indigenous Miskito communities living along the Caribbean coast of Nicaragua showed how external markets can undermine local subsistence economies. Miskito communities had developed a subsistence economy founded on land-based gardening and the harvesting of marine resources, including green turtles. The value of green turtles increased dramatically when companies moved in to process and export turtle products (meat, shells, leather). They paid cash and extended credit so that the Miskito could harvest turtles year-round instead of seasonally. Subsistence production in other areas suffered as labor was directed to harvesting turtles. Turtles became scarcer, so more labor time was required to hunt them in a desperate effort to pay debts and buy food. Ulti-

mately, the turtle population was decimated and the subsistence production system collapsed.

This study might sound like yet another tragic story of "disappearing peoples" or a "vanished way of life," but it didn't end there. Nietschmann continued his research with Miskito communities into the 1990s (he died in 2000), discovering, among other things, that the Miskito people did not disappear but continued to defend their cultural autonomy in the face of great external pressures from globalization. They responded to the collapse of their resource base by creating in 1991, in cooperation with the Nicaraguan government, a protected area as part of a local environmental management plan. They were supported in this endeavor by academics, international conservation nongovernmental organizations (NGOs), and the Nicaraguan government. Known as the Cayos Miskitos and Franja Costera Marine Biological Reserve, it encompasses 13,000 square kilometers of coastal area and offshore keys with 38 Miskito communities. This is an ongoing experiment. Miskito communities continue to struggle with outsiders for control over their land and resources in the reserve. There are hopeful signs, however, that the government is cooperating in this struggle and that both the natural resource base and the Miskito people will benefit from this project.

The Miskito case demonstrates the resiliency of indigenous cultures, the limits of ITK, and the potency of global economic forces. It thus reflects some of the most recent studies of the cultural and political ecology of indigenous peoples, such as those conducted by geographer Anthony Bebbington. Bebbington has done research among the indigenous Quichua populations in the Ecuadorian Andes to assess how they interact with modernizing institutions and practices. He found that while the Quichua people often possess extensive knowledge about local farming and resource management, ITK alone is not sufficient to allow them to prosper in a global economy. As a consequence, they have sought the support and knowledge of government agencies, the Catholic Church, and NGOs. He further found that indigenous Quichua communities use outside ideas and technologies to promote their own cultural survival, attempting, in essence, to negotiate their interactions with globalization on their own terms. (For more information on other research in the Quichua region, see Practicing Geography.)

REFLECTING ON GEOGRAPHY

Contrary to their current popular image, indigenous cultures do cause environmental damage. Can you think of an example?

Folk Ecology

As with indigenous cultures, ideas persist about folk cultures' particular ability to sustainably manage the environment. For example, their close ties to the land and local environment enhance the *environmental perception* of folk groups. This becomes particularly evident when they migrate. Typically, they seek new lands similar to the one left behind. A good example can be seen in the migrations of Upland Southerners from the mountains of Appalachia between 1830 and 1930. As the Appalachians became increasingly populous, many highlanders began looking elsewhere for similar areas to settle. In their migrations, they usually moved in clan or extended-family groups. Initially, they found an environmental twin of the Appalachians in the Ozark-Ouachita Mountains of Missouri and Arkansas. Somewhat later, others sought out the hollows, coves, and gaps of the central Texas Hill Country. The final migration of Appalachian hill people brought some 15,000 members of this folk culture to the Cascade and Coast mountain ranges of Washington State between 1880 and 1930 (Figure 2.21).

Gendered Ecology

We stressed in Chapter 1 and earlier in this chapter that cultures are heterogeneous and that gender is one of the principal areas of difference within cultures. Geographers and other social scientists have documented significant

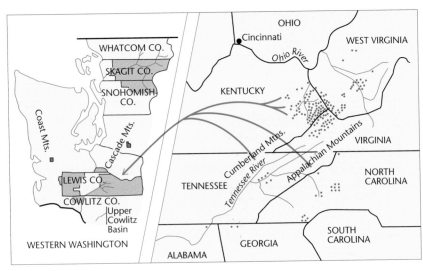

Figure 2.21 The relocation diffusion of Upland Southern hill folk from Appalachia to western Washington. Each dot represents the former home of an individual or family that migrated to the Upper Cowlitz River basin in the Cascade Mountains of Washington State between 1884 and 1937. Some 3000 descendants of these migrants lived in the Cowlitz area by 1940. What does the high degree of clustering of the sources of the migrants and subsequent clustering in Washington suggest about the processes of folk migrations? How should we interpret their choices of familiar terrain and vegetation for a new home? Why might members of a folk society who migrate choose a new land similar to the old one? (*After Clevinger, 1938: 120; Clevinger, 1942:4.*)

Gregory Knapp

(Courtesy of Gregory Knapp.)

"As a Berkeley student in the 1960s, I was surrounded by folks who thought they had straightforward answers to the world's problems. I was one of them, too, for a while." So recalls Professor Gregory Knapp, whose early undergraduate studies were shaped by his participation in Berkeley street protests. Moving on from the Berkeley scene, he dropped out and began his search for greater understanding of the world's complexities.

His journey led him eventually to discover two things that have shaped his life ever since: the discipline of geography and a love of fieldwork. "My defining experience was a three-month field course through Mexico, Belize, and Guatemala in 1976," he explains. "By the end of the trip I had fallen in love with the region's natural and cultural diversity. I've retained a love of fieldwork, as well as an appreciation for originality and creativity, ever since." He returned to Berkeley, finished his degree, and went on to study geography at the University of Wisconsin, where he earned his doctorate after conducting research in the Andes.

He continues today to conduct research in the indigenous Quichua region of the Ecuadorian Andes, further fueling his enthusiasm for fieldwork. For Professor Knapp, the "ability to explore new landscapes, follow up on surprising juxtapositions, and talk late into the night about what local people find important is incredibly stimulating! These days, I find a lot of concern for 'sustainability,' for the children retaining their heritage along with an ability to pursue a livelihood. I think geographers have a lot to contribute in this area."

In the field, he tries to balance a variety of research methods. A long-term perspective is important, which means repeated visits to sites over the years and close attention to archival materials. Diversity matters, too, and it is important to gather views across ethnic, gender, and class lines. Overall, "probably the most important method in a region like the Andes is open-ended conversation."

His recent accidental discovery of unpublished information has led to a new line of research on religion in the Quichua region. This discovery raises an important question: Although Christian missionaries are everywhere, why do some people convert and others not? "The patterns of conversion are an important part of the human mosaic, and the patterns are turning out to be surprising in this region." He also continues to update his work on cultural and political ecology in the Andes. In particular, he is studying the "role of irrigation in providing a flexible adaptive strategy for regional folk cultures that are no longer 'indigenous' in self-definition but that are not in any simple way homogenized or national either."

Reflecting his undiminished enthusiasm for exploration and sense of wonder regarding natural and cultural diversity, he offers a bit of advice for students of cultural geography everywhere: "It is always a good idea to follow up on the surprising and unexpected. We live in an amazing and ultimately unpredictable world."

differences between men's and women's relationships with the environment. This observation holds for popular, folk, and indigenous cultures. *Ecofeminism* is one way of thinking about how gender influences our interactions with nature. This concept, however, might seem to suggest that there is something inherent or essential about men and women that makes them think and behave in particular and different ways toward the environment. While many cultural geographers would argue against such essentialism, few would disagree that gender is an important variable in cultural and political ecology.

Diane Rocheleau's work on women's roles in the management of **agroforestry** systems is illustrative. Agroforestry systems are farming systems that combine the growing of trees with the cultivation of agricultural crops. Agroforestry is practiced by folk and indigenous cultures across the trop-ical world and has been shown to be a highly productive and ecologically sustainable practice. It is common in these production systems for men and women to have very distinct roles.

After conducting studies for many years first in East Africa and later in the Dominican Republic, Rocheleau was able to derive general themes regarding the way human-environment relations are gendered, not only in agro-forestry systems but also in many rural and urban environments. Together with two colleagues, she identified three themes: gendered knowledge, gendered environmental rights, and gendered environmental politics. First, because women and men often have different tasks and move in different spaces, they possess different and even distinct sets of knowledge about the environment. Second, men and women have different rights, especially with regard to the

Figure 2.22 Traffic jam in Yellowstone National Park at the height of the summer tourist season. *(Klein/Hubert/Peter Arnold.)*

ownership and control of land and resources. Third, for reasons having to do with their responsibilities in their families and communities, women are often the main leaders and activists in political movements concerned with environmental issues. Taken together these themes suggest that environmental planning or resource management schemes that do not address issues of gendered ecology are likely to have unintended consequences, some of them negative for both women and environmental quality.

Ecology of Popular Culture

Because popular culture is largely the product of industrialization and the rise of technology, it is less directly tied to the physical environment than folk and indigenous cultures, which is not to say that it does not have an enormous impact on the environment. Gone is the intimate association between people and land known by our folk ancestors. Gone, too, is our direct vulnerability to many environmental forces, although the security is more apparent than real. People functioning within popular cultures have enormous potential for producing ecological disasters. Also, because popular culture encourages little intimate contact with and knowledge of the physical world, our *environmental perceptions* can become quite distorted.

Popular culture makes heavy demands on *ecosystems.* This is true even in the seemingly benign realm of recreation. Recreational activities have increased greatly in the world's economically affluent regions. Many of these activities require machines, such as snowmobiles, off-road vehicles, and jet skis, that are powered by internal combustion engines and have numerous adverse ecological impacts ranging from air pollution to soil erosion. In national parks and protected areas worldwide, affluent tourists in search of nature have overtaxed protected environments and wildlife and produced levels of congestion approaching those of urban areas (Figure 2.22).

Such a massive presence of people in our recreational areas inevitably results in damage to the physical environment. A study by geographer Jeanne Kay and her students in Utah revealed substantial environmental damage done by off-road recreational vehicles, including "soil loss and long-term soil deterioration." One of the paradoxes of the modern age and popular culture seems to be that the more we cluster in cities and suburbs, the greater our impact on open areas; we carry our popular culture with us when we vacation in such regions.

 Interaction and Difference

In the inner workings of folk and popular cultures, how do the various elements of culture interact with one another? In folk cultures, for example, an *organic* view of nature tends to reduce practices that destroy habitats. Strong group identity tends to weaken individualism, and conservatism hinders change. Thus a set of core beliefs common in folk cultures interact to limit the degree of environmental disturbance.

Cultural interaction, however, is most directly and visibly at work in popular culture. Increased leisure time, instant communications, greater affluence for many people, heightened mobility, and weakened attachment to family and place—all attributes of popular culture—have the potential, through interaction, to cause massive spatial restructuring. Most social scientists long assumed that the result of such globalizing forces and trends, especially mobility and the electronic media, would be the homogenization of culture, wherein the differences among places are reduced or eliminated. This assumption is called the **convergence hypothesis;** that is, cultures are converging, or becoming more alike. In the geographical sense, this would yield *placelessness,* a concept discussed earlier in the chapter.

Impressive geographical evidence can be marshaled to support the convergence hypothesis. Wilbur Zelinsky, for example, compared the given names of people in various parts of the United States for the years 1790 and 1968 and found that a more pronounced regionalization existed in the eighteenth century than in the mid-twentieth century. The personal names that the present generation of parents bestow on children vary less from place to place than did those of our ancestors two centuries ago.

Mapping Personal Preference

Countering the convergence hypothesis is the greater individualism and resistance to conformity characteristic of popular culture. What is the geographical result of heightened individualism and personal preference? Geographer Ronald Abler concluded that individualism—coupled with increasingly rapid communications media, abundant leisure, and widespread wealth—has the ability to create a new regionalism in popular culture, allowing for cultural divergence rather than convergence. Free exercise of individual preferences could create a new spatial order. If people decide to pursue their chosen lifestyles in geographical proximity to others who share their preferences and orientations, then a spatial restructuring will certainly occur. Hints of this trend are seen in certain segregated communities where only the elderly live, as in Sun City, Arizona, and in the residential concentration of gay people in certain districts within cities such as San Francisco (Figure 2.23).

The media cater to and help promote such restructuring. Special-interest media, or "narrowcasting," to use Abler's term, can help produce and nurture a spatially diverse popular culture. For example, 141 radio stations in the United States and Canada are oriented to African-Americans. Cable television stations now aim most programming at specific audiences, in a process known as target marketing. In Zelinsky's words, "The increasingly free exercise of individual preferences as to values, pleasures, self-improvement, social and physical habitat, and general lifestyle in an individualistic, affluent national community may have begun to alter the spatial attributes of society and culture."

Place Images

The same media that serve and reflect the rise of personal preference—movies, television, photography, music, advertising, art, and others—often produce *place images,* a subject studied by geographers Brian Godfrey and Leo Zonn, among others. Place, portrayer, and medium interact to produce the image, which, in turn, colors our perception of and beliefs about places and regions we have never visited.

The images may be inaccurate or misleading, but they nevertheless create a world in our minds that has an array of unique places and place meanings. Our decisions about tourism and migration can be influenced by these images. For example, through the media, Hawaii has become in the American mind a sort of earthly paradise peopled by scantily clad, eternally happy, invariably good-looking natives who live in a setting of unparalleled natural beauty and idyllic climate. People have always formed images of faraway places. Through the interworkings of popular culture, these images proliferate and become more vivid, if not more accurate.

 ## Landscapes of Difference

Do folk and popular cultures look different? Does each have a distinctive cultural landscape? The theme of cultural landscape reveals the important differences between *and among* folk and popular cultures.

Folk Architecture

Every folk culture produces a highly distinctive landscape. One of the most visible aspects of these landscapes is **folk architecture.** These traditional buildings illustrate the theme of cultural landscape in folk geography.

Folk architecture springs not from the drafting tables of professional architects but from the collective memory of groups of traditional people (Figure 2.24). These buildings—whether dwellings, barns, churches, mills, or inns—are based not on blueprints but on mental images that change little from one generation to the next. In this sense, it is an architecture without architects. Folk buildings are extensions of a culture and its region. They help shape the unique character of each folk culture region and offer a highly visible aspect of the human mosaic. Folk architecture is marked not by refined artistic genius or spectacular, revolutionary design but rather by traditional, conservative, and functional structures. Expect from it a simple beauty, a harmony with the physical environment, a visible expression of folk culture. Material composition, floor plan, and layout are important ingredients of folk architecture, but numerous other characteristics help classify farmsteads and dwellings. The form or shape of the roof, the placement of

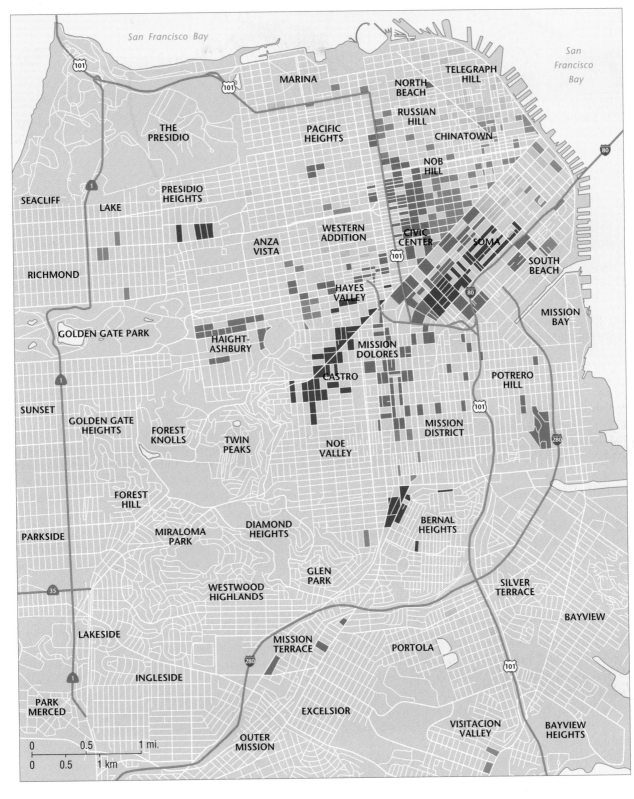

Average Opening Date of Gay, Lesbian, Bisexual, and Transsexual Gathering Places

1953–1959	1959–1966	1966–1972	1972–1978	1978–1985

Figure 2.23 Changing gay/lesbian/bisexual/transsexual residential and social space in San Francisco. Such lifestyle segregation and its rapid diffusion typify popular culture. *(Source: Scott, in progress.)*

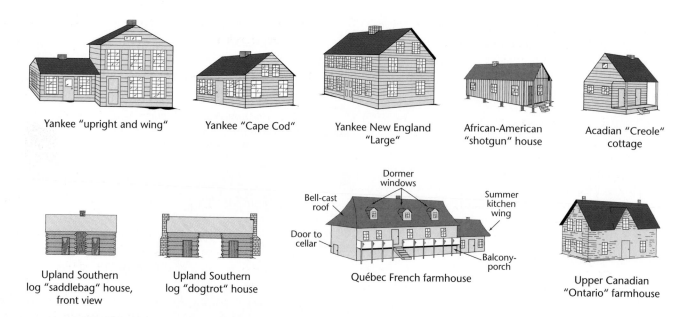

Figure 2.24 **Selected folk houses.** Six of the 15 folk culture regions of North America are represented (see Figure 2.1). *(After Glassie, 1968; Kniffen, 1965.)*

the chimney, and even such details as the number and location of doors and windows can be important classifying criteria. E. Estyn Evans, a noted expert on Irish folk geography, considered roof form and chimney placement, among other traits, in devising an informal classification of Irish houses.

The house, or dwelling, is the most basic structure that people erect, regardless of culture. For most people in nearly all folk cultures, a house is the single most important thing they ever build. Folk cultures as a rule are rural and agricultural. For these reasons, it seems appropriate to focus on the folk house.

Folk Housing in Sub-Saharan Africa

Throughout East Africa and southern Africa, rural family homesteads take a common form. Most consist of a compound of buildings called a *kraal,* a term related to the English word *corral* and used across the region. The compound typically includes a main house (or houses in polygamous cultures), a detached building in the rear for cooking, and smaller buildings or enclosures for livestock.

All construction is done with local materials. Small, flexible sticks are woven in between poles that have been driven into the ground to serve as the frame. Then a mixture of clay and animal dung is plastered against the woven sticks, layer by layer, until it is entirely covered. Dried tall grasses are tied together in bundles to form the roof. In a recent innovation, rural people who can afford the expense have replaced grass with corrugated iron sheets. In some societies

the dwellings are round, in others square or rectangular. You can often tell when you have entered a different culture region by the change in house types.

One of the most distinctive house types is found in the Ndebele culture region of southern Africa, which stretches from South Africa north into southern Zimbabwe. In the rural parts of Ndebele region, people are farmers and livestock keepers and live in traditional kraals. What makes these houses distinctive is the Ndebele custom of painting brightly colored designs on the exterior house walls and sometimes on the walls and gates surrounding the kraal. The precise origins of this custom are unclear, but it seems to date to the mid-nineteenth century. Some suggest that it was an assertion of cultural identity in response to their displacement and domination at the hands of white settlers. Others point to a religious or sacred role.

What is clear is that the custom has always been the purview of women, a skill and practice passed down from mother to daughter. Many of the symbols and patterns are associated with particular families or clans. Initially, women used natural pigments from clay, charcoal, and local plants, which restricted their palette to earth tones of brown, red, and black. Today many women use commercial paints—expensive, but longer lasting—to apply a range of bright colors, limited only by the imagination. Another new development is in the types of designs and symbols used. People are incorporating modern machines such as automobiles, televisions, and airplanes into their designs. In many cases, traditional paints and symbols are blended with the modern to produce a synthetic design of old and new. Ndebele house painting is developing and evolving in new directions, all the while continuing to signal a persistent cultural identity to all who pass through the region.

Folk Housing in North America

In the United States and Canada, folk architecture today is a relict form preserved in the cultural landscape. For the most part, popular culture, with its mass-produced, commercially built houses, has so overwhelmed the folk traditions that few folk houses are built today, yet many survive in the refuge regions of American and Canadian folk culture (see Figures 2.1, 2.24).

Yankee folk houses are of wooden frame construction, and shingle siding often covers the exterior walls. They are built with a variety of floor plans, including the *New England "large"* house, a huge two-and-a-half-story house built around a central chimney and two rooms deep. As the Yankee folk migrated westward, they developed the *upright-and-wing* dwelling. These particular Yankee houses are often massive, in part because the cold winters of the region forced most work to be done indoors. By contrast, Upland Southern folk houses are smaller and built of notched logs. Many houses in this folk tradition consist of two log rooms, with either a double fireplace between, forming the *saddlebag* house, or an open, roofed breezeway separating the two rooms, a plan known as the *dogtrot* house (Figure 2.25). An example of an African-American folk dwelling is the *shotgun* house, a narrow structure only one room in width but two, three, or even four rooms in depth. Acadiana, a French-derived folk region in Louisiana, is characterized by the half-timbered *Creole cottage,* which has a central chimney and built-in porch. Scores of other folk house types survive in the American landscape, although most such dwellings now stand abandoned and derelict.

Canada also offers a variety of traditional folk houses (see Figure 2.24). In French-speaking Québec, one of the common types consists of a main story atop a cellar, with attic rooms beneath a curved, bell-shaped (or *bell-cast*) roof. A balcony-porch with railing extends across the front, sheltered by the overhanging eaves. Attached to one side of this type of French-Canadian folk house is a summer kitchen that is sealed off during the long, cold winter. Often the folk houses of Québec are built of stone. To the west, in the Upper Canadian folk region, one type of folk house occurs so frequently that it is known as the *Ontario farmhouse.* One-and-a-half stories in height, the Ontario farmhouse is usually built of brick and has a distinctive gabled front dormer window.

Now, using the sketches shown in Figure 2.24 and descriptions of eastern North American folk houses, identify the four houses illustrated in Figure 2.26 (answers are located at the end of the chapter).

The interpretation of folk architecture is by no means a simple process. Folk geographers often work for years trying to "read" such structures, seeking clues to diffusion and traditional adaptive strategies. The old problem of *independent invention* versus diffusion is raised repeatedly in the folk

Figure 2.25 A dogtrot house, typical of the Upland Southern folk region. The distinguishing feature is the open-air passageway, or dogtrot, between the two main rooms. This house is located in central Texas. *(Courtesy of Terry G. Jordan-Bychkov.)*

Figure 2.26 **Four folk houses in North America.** Using the sketches in Figure 2.24 and the related section of the text, determine the regional affiliation and type of each. The answers are provided at the end of the chapter. *(Courtesy of Terry G. Jordan-Bychkov.)*

landscape, as Figure 2.27 illustrates. Precisely because interpretation is often difficult, however, geographers find these old structures challenging and well worth studying. Folk cultures rarely leave behind much in the way of written records, making their landscape artifacts all the more important in seeking explanations.

Landscapes of Popular Culture

Popular culture permeates the landscape of countries such as the United States, Canada, and Australia, including everything from mass-produced suburban houses to golf courses and neon-lit strips. So overwhelming is the presence of popular culture in most American settlement landscapes that an observer must often search diligently to find visual fragments of the older folk cultures. The popular landscape is in continual flux, for change is a hallmark of popular culture.

Few aspects of the popular landscape are more visually striking than the ubiquitous commercial malls and strips on urban arterial streets, which geographer Robert Sack calls *landscapes of consumption* (see Figure 2.6). In an Illinois college town, two other cultural geographers, John Jakle and Richard Mattson, made a study of the evolution of one such strip. During a 60-year span, the street under study changed from a single-family residential area to a commercial district (Figure 2.28). The researchers suggested a five-stage *model* of strip evolution, beginning with the single-family residential period, moving through stages of increasing commercialization, which drives owner-residents out, and culminating in stage 5, where the residential function of the street disappears and a totally commercial landscape prevails. Business properties expand so that off-street parking can be provided. Public outcries over the ugliness of such strips are common. Even landscapes such as these are subject to interpretation, however, for the people who create them perceive them differently. For example, geographer Yi-Fu Tuan suggests that a commercial strip of stores, fast-food restaurants, filling stations, and used-car lots may

a

b

Figure 2.27 **Two polygonal folk houses.** (a) A Buriat Mongol yurt in southern Siberia, near Lake Baikal. (b) A Navajo hogan in New Mexico. The two dwellings, almost identical and each built of notched logs, lie on opposite sides of the world, among unrelated folk groups who never had contact with each other. Such houses do not occur anywhere in between. Is cultural diffusion or independent invention responsible? How might a folk geographer go about finding the answer? *(Part a, Courtesy of Terry G. Jordan-Bychkov; Part b, Courtesy of Stephen C. Jett.)*

appear as visual blight to an outsider, but the owners or operators of the businesses are very proud of them and of their role in the community. Hard work and high hopes color their perceptions of the popular landscape.

Perhaps no landscape of consumption is more reflective of popular culture than the indoor shopping mall, numerous examples of which now dot both urban and suburban landscapes. Of these, the largest is West Edmonton Mall in the Canadian province of Alberta. Enclosing some 5.2 million square feet (483,000 square meters) and completed in 1986, West Edmonton Mall employs 18,000 people in more than 600 stores and services, accounts for nearly one-fourth of the total retail space in greater Edmonton, earned 42 percent of the dollars spent in local shopping centers, and experienced 2800 crimes in its first nine months of operation. Beyond its mere magnitude, West Edmonton Mall boasts a water park, a sea aquarium, an ice-skating rink, a mini–golf course, a roller coaster, 19 movie theaters, and a 360-room hotel. Its "streets" feature motifs from such exotic places as New Orleans, represented by a Bourbon Street complete with fiberglass ladies of the evening. Jeffrey Hopkins, a geographer who studied this mall, refers to this as a "landscape of myth and elsewhereness," a "simulated landscape" that reveals the "growing intrusion of spectacle, fantasy, and escapism into the urban landscape."

Leisure Landscapes

Another common feature of popular culture is what geographer Karl Raitz labeled *leisure landscapes*. Leisure landscapes are designed to entertain people on weekends and vacations;

often they are included as part of a larger tourist experience. Golf courses and theme parks such as Disney World are good examples of such landscapes. *Amenity landscapes* are a related landscape form. These are regions with attractive natural features such as forests, scenic mountains, or lakes and rivers that have become desirable locations for retirement or vacation homes. One such landscape is in the Minnesota North Woods lake country, where, in a sampling of home ownership, geographer Richard Hecock found that fully 40 percent of all dwellings were not permanent residences but instead weekend cottages or vacation homes. These are often purposefully made rustic or even humble in appearance.

The past, reflected in relict buildings, has also been incorporated into the leisure landscape. Most often, collections of old structures are relocated to form "historylands," often enclosed by imposing chain-link fences and open only during certain seasons or hours. If the desired bit of visual history has perished, Americans and Canadians do not hesitate to rebuild it from scratch, undisturbed by the lack of authenticity—as, for example, at Jamestown, Virginia, or Louisbourg on Cape Breton Island, Nova Scotia. Normally the history parks are put in out-of-the-way places and sanitized to the extent that people no longer live in them. Role-playing actors sometimes prowl these parks, pretending to live in some past era, adding "elsewhenness" to "elsewhereness."

Elitist Landscapes

A distinctive aspect of popular culture is the development of social classes. A small elite group—consisting of persons of wealth, education, and refined taste—occupies the top

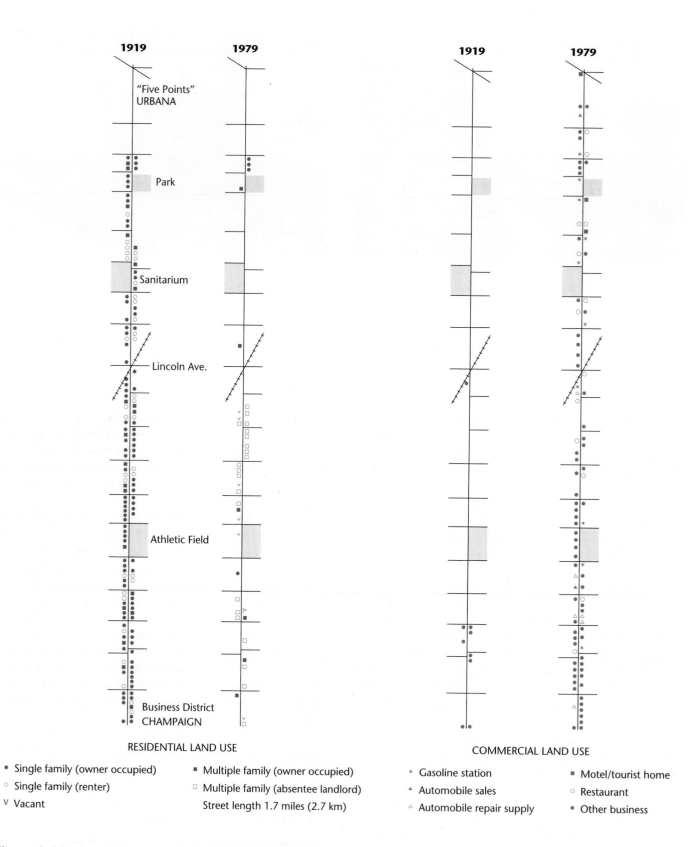

RESIDENTIAL LAND USE

COMMERCIAL LAND USE

- Single family (owner occupied)
- Single family (renter)
- Vacant
- Multiple family (owner occupied)
- Multiple family (absentee landlord)

Street length 1.7 miles (2.7 km)

- Gasoline station
- Automobile sales
- Automobile repair supply
- Motel/tourist home
- Restaurant
- Other business

Figure 2.28 **The evolution of a commercial strip in Champaign-Urbana, Illinois, 1919–1979.** Popular culture reshaped a landscape. Is the older or newer landscape "better"? Why? *(Adapted from Jakle and Mattson, 1981: 14, 20.)*

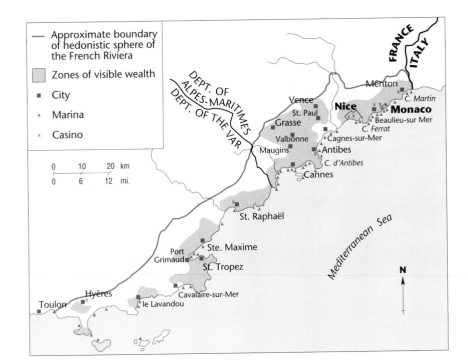

Figure 2.29 **The distribution of elitist or hedonistic cultural landscape on the French Riviera.** What forces in the popular culture generate such landscapes? *(Adapted from Gade, 1982: 22.)*

position in popular cultures. The important geographical fact about such people is that because of their wealth, desire to be around similar people, distinctive tastes, and hedonistic lifestyles, they can and do create distinctive cultural landscapes, often over fairly large areas.

Daniel Gade, a cultural geographer, coined the term *elitist space* to describe such landscapes, using the French Riviera as an example (Figure 2.29). In that district of southern France, famous for its stunning natural beauty and idyllic climate, the French elite applied "refined taste to create an aesthetically pleasing cultural landscape" characterized by preservation of old buildings and town cores, a sense of proportion, and respect for scale. Building codes and height restrictions, for instance, are rigorously enforced. Land values, in response, have risen, making the Riviera ever more elitist, far removed from the folk culture and poverty that prevailed there before 1850. Farmers and fishermen have almost disappeared from the region, though one need drive but a short distance, to Toulon, to find a working seaport. It seems, then, that the different social classes generated within popular culture become geographically segregated, each producing a distinctive cultural landscape (Figure 2.30).

America, too, offers elitist landscapes. An excellent example is the *gentleman farm,* an agricultural unit operated for pleasure rather than profit (Figure 2.31). Typically, gentleman farms are owned by affluent city people as an avocation, and such farms help to create or maintain a high social standing for those who own them. Some rural landscapes in America now contain many such gentleman farms; perhaps

most notable among these places are the inner Bluegrass Basin of north-central Kentucky, the Virginia Piedmont west of Washington, D.C., eastern Long Island in New York, and parts of southeastern Pennsylvania. Gentleman farmers engage in such activities as breeding fine cattle, racing horses, or hunting foxes.

Geographer Karl Raitz performed a study of gentleman farms in the Kentucky Bluegrass Basin, where their concentration is so great that they constitute the dominant feature of the cultural landscape. The result is an idyllic scene, a rural landscape created more for appearance than for function. Raitz provided a list of visual indicators of Kentucky gentleman farms: wooden fences, either painted white or creosoted black; an elaborate entrance gate; a fine handpainted sign giving the name of the farm and owner; a network of surfaced, well-maintained driveways and pasture roads; and a large, elegant house, visible in the distance from the public highway through a lawnlike parkland dotted with clumps of trees and perhaps a pond or two. So attractive are these estates to the eye that tourists travel the rural lands to view them, convinced they are seeing the "real" rural America, or at least rural America as it ought to be.

REFLECTING ON GEOGRAPHY

Can you think of other types of landscapes of popular culture to go with consumption, leisure, and elitist landscapes?

Figure 2.30 The cultural landscape of the affluent in Port of Fontvieille, Monaco. *(Sergio Pitamitz/Age Fotostock.)*

The American Scene

In an article entitled "The American Scene," geographer David Lowenthal attempted to analyze the cummulative visible impact of popular culture on the American countryside. Lowenthal identified the main characteristics of popular landscape in the United States, including: the "cult of bigness"; the tolerance of present ugliness to achieve a supposedly glorious future; emphasis on individual features at the expense of aggregates, producing a "casual chaos"; and the preeminence of function over form.

The American fondness for massive structures is reflected in edifices such as the Empire State Building, the Pentagon, the San Francisco–Oakland Bay Bridge, and Salt Lake City's Mormon Temple. Americans have dotted their cultural landscape with the world's largest of this or that, perhaps in an effort to match the grand scale of the physical environment, which includes such landmarks as the Grand Canyon, the towering redwoods of California, and the Rocky Mountains.

Americans, argues Lowenthal, tend to regard their cultural landscape as unfinished. As a result, they are "predisposed to accept present structures that are makeshift, flimsy, and transient," resembling "throwaway stage sets." Similarly, the hardships of pioneer life perhaps preconditioned Americans to value function more highly than beauty and form. The state capitol grounds in Oklahoma City are adorned with little more than oil derricks, standing above busy

Figure 2.31 **Gentleman farm in the Kentucky Bluegrass region near Lexington.** Here is "real" rural America as it should be (but never was). *(Courtesy of Terry G. Jordan-Bychkov.)*

Figure 2.32 Oil derrick on the Oklahoma state capitol grounds.
The landscape of American popular culture is characterized by
such functionality. The public and private sectors of the economy
are increasingly linked in the popular culture. Is criticism of such
a landscape elitist and snobbish? *(See also Robertson, 1996. Photo
courtesy of Terry G. Jordan-Bychkov.)*

pumps drawing oil and the wealth that comes with it from
the Sooner soil—an extreme but revealing view of the American landscape (Figure 2.32).

Furthermore, individual landscape features take prece-
dence over the groupings in which they appear. Five buildings or houses in a row may display five different
architectural styles, and rarely is an attempt made to erect as-
semblages of structures that "belong" together. "Places are
only collections of heterogeneous buildings." To be worthy,
each structure must be unique and eye-catching, and architects in the popular culture vie with one another in producing attention-grabbing edifices. Each fast-food chain seems
to require its own outlandish style of structure to facilitate instant visual recognition by potential customers.

Conclusion

In this chapter we have just scratched the surface of the
complex nature of the geography of multiculturalism. Using
the cases of folk, popular, and indigenous cultures, we
learned that there are many ways of perceiving and being in
the landscape. We have also seen how each of these cultural
categories is in turn internally heterogeneous, with significant differences occurring among gender, class, and ethnic
groups. Religion, often a defining element of cultural difference, is also vitally important. Chapter 3 is devoted to this
major cultural trait.

DOING GEOGRAPHY

Self-Representation of Indigenous Culture

The world has been witnessing the reassertion of indigenous
culture after 500 years of marginalization. For centuries, the
roar of dominant national cultures drowned out indigenous
peoples' voices. As a result, members of dominant national
cultures—academics, missionaries, government officials, and
journalists—have been largely responsible for writing about
the histories and cultures of indigenous peoples. This has
begun to change as some indigenous groups have prospered
economically and as the indigenous rights movement gains
increasing support worldwide. Today, more and more
indigenous peoples have taken charge of representing
themselves and their cultures to the outside world, by
building museums, producing films, hosting conferences, and
creating web sites.

This exercise requires you to study carefully one of these
platforms for cultural expression: self-produced indigenous
peoples' web sites. First, you will need to do a little
background research on the names and locations of major
indigenous cultures. You can use the web sites listed at the
end of this chapter to help you get started. Second, it is
important to verify that the web sites you are studying are
self-produced. Confirm that the site is produced by a tribal or
indigenous organization, not through an external NGO,
national government, corporation, or university. Third, think
about how you are going to analyze the content of the web
site in order to draw conclusions about the self-representation
of indigenous cultures.

Here are a few suggestions and possibilities. Try to focus
on questions of geography: How do indigenous groups speak
about their relationship to the land and the environment?
What do they say about territorial claims and homelands?
What roles do maps play on the web sites? What are their
ideas on biodiversity conservation and bioprospecting (the
search for genetic resources and other biological resources)?
Think about possibilities for comparison. For example, how
does what you learn from self-produced web sites compare to
what you knew from other sources or from your own beliefs
and assumptions? Are there regional differences in terms of
the quantity and content of web sites? Do you find common
themes across or within regions? Are there indigenous cultures
that produce contrasting or competing representations? (For
example, do some indigenous cultures have more than one
self-generated web site and do they present different ideas?)
What major issues and challenges does the site highlight and
how do these relate to globalization?

Cultures on the Internet

You can learn more about the main categories of culture discussed in the chapter on the Internet at the following web sites:

American Memory, Library of Congress

http://rs6.loc.gov

A project of the Library of Congress that presents a history of American popular culture, complete with documentation and maps.

Cultural Survival

http://www.cs.org/

The interactive web site of Cultural Survival, an organization that promotes the human rights and goals of indigenous peoples. Many timely indigenous cultural issues and important links can be found here.

First Peoples Worldwide

http://www.firstpeoples.org/

This group promotes an indigenous-controlled international organization that advocates for indigenous self-governance and culturally appropriate economic development.

International Folk Culture Center, San Antonio, Texas

www.ifccsa.org

This site has information on diverse aspects of folk culture, including traditional dress and the Virtual Museum of World Instruments.

Manchester Institute for Popular Culture, Manchester, U.K.

http://www.mmu.ac.uk/h-ss/mipc/

This site is dedicated to the academic study of popular culture, based at the Manchester Metropolitan University.

Native Lands

http://www.nativelands.org/

Native Lands deals with biological and cultural diversity in Latin America. It is very involved in mapping projects to help secure indigenous territorial claims and protect tropical forests.

Pioneer America Society

http://www.uncwil.edu/people/ainsleyf/pas/pas.htm

The leading professional organization of geographers interested in both folk and popular cultural landscapes. The site describes its activities and publications, including its journal, *Material Culture*.

Popular Culture Association

http://www2.h-net.msu.edu/~pcaaca/

A multidisciplinary organization dedicated to the academic discussion of popular culture, where activities of the association are discussed.

Sources

Abler, Ronald F. 1973. "Monoculture or Miniculture? The Impact of Communication Media on Culture in Space," in David A. Lanegran and Risa Palm (eds.), *An Invitation to Geography*. New York: McGraw-Hill, 186–195.

Alcorn, J. 1994: Noble Savage or Noble State? Northern Myths and Southern Realities in Biodiversity Conservation. *Ethnoecologica* 2(3): 7–19.

Bebbington, A. 1996. "Movements, Modernizations, and Markets: Indigenous Organizations and Agrarian Strategies in Ecuador," in R. Peet, and M. Watts (eds.), *Liberation Ecologies: Environment, Development, Social Movements*. London: Routledge, 86–109.

Bebbington, A. 2000. "Reencountering Development: Livelihood Transitions and Place Transformations in the Andes. *Annals of the Association of American Geographers* 90(3): 495–520.

Brownell, Joseph W. 1960. "The Cultural Midwest." *Journal of Geography* 59: 81–85.

Clevinger, Woodrow R. 1938. "The Appalachian Mountaineers in the Upper Cowlitz Basin." *Pacific Northwest Quarterly* 29: 115–134.

Clevinger, Woodrow R. 1942. "Southern Appalachian Highlanders in Western Washington." *Pacific Northwest Quarterly* 33: 3–25.

Curtis, James R. 1982. "McDonald's Abroad: Outposts of American Culture." *Journal of Geography* 81: 14–20.

de Blij, Harm, and Peter Muller. 2004. *Geography: Realms, Regions and Concepts*, 11th ed. New York: Wiley.

Edmonson, Brad, and Linda Jacobsen. 1993. "Elvis Presley Memorabilia." *American Demographics* 15(8): 64.

Evans, E. Estyn. 1957. *Irish Folk Ways*. London: Routledge & Kegan Paul.

Fleming, Douglas K., and Richard Roth. 1991. "Place in Advertising." *Geographical Review* 81: 281–291.

Francaviglia, Richard V. 1973. "Diffusion and Popular Culture: Comments on the Spatial Aspects of Rock Music," in David A. Lanegran and Risa Palm (eds.), *An Invitation to Geography*. New York: McGraw–Hill, 87–96.

Frederickson, Kristine. 1984. *American Rodeo from Buffalo Bill to Big Business*. College Station: Texas A&M University Press.

Gade, Daniel W. 1982. "The French Riviera as Elitist Space." *Journal of Cultural Geography* 3: 19–28.

Godfrey, Brian J. 1993. "Regional Depiction in Contemporary Film." *Geographical Review* 83: 428–440.

Goss, Jon. 1999. "Once-upon-a-Time in the Commodity World: An Unofficial Guide to the Mall of America." *Annals of the Association of American Geographers* 89: 45–75.

Graff, Thomas O., and Dub Ashton. 1994. "Spatial Diffusion of Wal-Mart: Contagious and Reverse Hierarchical Elements." *Professional Geographer* 46: 19–29.

Hecock, Richard D. 1987. "Changes in the Amenity Landscape: The Case of Some Northern Minnesota Townships." *North American Culture* 3(1): 53–66.

Holder, Arnold. 1993. "Dublin's Expanding Golfscape." *Irish Geography* 26: 151–157.

Hopkins, Jeffrey. 1990. "West Edmonton Mall: Landscape of Myths and Elsewhereness." *Canadian Geographer* 34: 2–17.

IDRC. 2004. Web site of the International Development Research Centre at http://web.idrc.ca/en/ev-1248-201-1-DO_TOPIC.html.

International Cancún Declaration of Indigenous Peoples. 2003. Prepared during the Fifth WTO Ministerial Conference, Cancún, Mexico. From http://www.ifg.org/programs/indig/CancunDec.html.

International Labor Organization. 1989. Indigenous and Tribal Peoples Convention. From http://members.tripod.com/PPLP/ILOC169.html.

SEEING GEOGRAPHY

What makes one father-daughter pair so very different from the other?

Two American father-daughter couples.

American Fathers and Daughters

Here we see two father-daughter couples, walking hand in hand down the street. They both live in the United States. But they also live in different worlds: folk and popular.

How can we tell? Well, the clothes they wear provide perhaps the main clue. The father and daughter on the left belong to the *Amish* religion, which has rejected most modern inventions and fads, retaining instead the folk lifestyle of the preindustrial age. Their clothing differs little from that of their ancestors in Pennsylvania two centuries ago. They are farmers rather than city dwellers. You can be sure that they will not get in a car and drive home, because they still prefer horse-drawn buggies.

The couple on the right is dressed very differently and clearly belongs to the popular culture. They may be going to buy a pizza or board a subway to go home. The father appears to be a businessman, and he certainly is not a farmer accustomed to working in fields with a horse-drawn plow.

And how do we know all this about their parallel, separate worlds? Mainly through the theme of cultural landscape. The clothing people wear can best be regarded as part of the visible culture—in other words, the landscape. ■

Jakle, John A., and Richard L. Mattson. 1981. "The Evolution of a Commercial Strip." *Journal of Cultural Geography* 1(2): 12–25.

Jett, Stephen C. 1991. "Further Information on the Geography of the Blowgun and Its Implications for Early Transoceanic Contacts." *Annals of the Association of American Geographers* 81: 89–102.

Kay, Jeanne, et al. 1981. "Evaluating Environmental Impacts of Off-Road Vehicles." *Journal of Geography* 80: 10–18.

Kimber, Clarissa T. 1973. "Plants in the Folk Medicine of the Texas-Mexico Borderlands." *Proceedings, Association of American Geographers* 5: 130–133.

Kimmel, James P. 1997. "Santa Fe: Thoughts on Contrivance, Commoditization, and Authenticity." *Southwestern Geographer* 1: 44–61.

Kniffen, Fred B. 1951. "The American Agricultural Fair." *Annals of the Association of American Geographers* 41: 43–54.

Kniffen, Fred B. 1965. "Folk-Housing: Key to Diffusion." *Annals of the Association of American Geographers* 55: 549–577.

Kunstler, James H. 1993. *The Geography of Nowhere: The Rise and Decline of America's Man-Made Landscape.* New York: Simon & Schuster.

Lowenthal, David. 1968. "The American Scene." *Geographical Review* 58: 61–88.

McDowell, L. 1994. "The Transformation of Cultural Geography, in D. Gregory, R. Martin, and G. Smith (eds.), *Human Geography: Society, Space, and Social Science.* Minneapolis: University of Minnesota Press, 146–173.

Miller, E. Joan Wilson. 1968. "The Ozark Culture Region as Revealed by Traditional Materials." *Annals of the Association of American Geographers* 58: 51–77.

Mings, Robert C., and Kevin E. McHugh. 1989. "The RV Resort Landscape." *Journal of Cultural Geography* 10: 35–49.

Nietschmann, B. 1973. *Between Land and Water: The Subsistence Ecology of the Miskito Indians, Eastern Nicaragua.* New York: Seminar Press.

Nietschmann, B. 1979. "Ecological Change, Inflation, and Migration in the Far West Caribbean." *Geographical Review* 69: 1–24.

Pillsbury, Richard. 1990a. "Striking to Success." *Sport Place* 4(1): 16, 35.

Pillsbury, Richard. 1990b. "Ride 'm Cowboy." *Sport Place* 4: 26–32.

Pillsbury, Richard. 1998. *No Foreign Food: The American Diet in Time and Place.* Boulder, Colo.: Westview Press.

Price, Edward T. 1960. "Root Digging in the Appalachians: The Geography of Botanical Drugs." *Geographical Review* 50: 1–20.

Raitz, Karl B. 1975. "Gentleman Farms in Kentucky's Inner Bluegrass." *Southeastern Geographer* 15: 33–46.

Raitz, Karl B. 1987. "Place, Space and Environment in America's Leisure Landscapes." *Journal of Cultural Geography* 8(1): 49–62.

Relph, Edward. 1976. *Place and Placelessness*. London: Pion.

Richards, P. 1975. "'Alternative' Strategies for the African Environment. 'Folk Ecology' as a basis for Community Oriented Agricultural Development," in P. Richards (ed.), *African Environment, Problems and Perspectives*. London: International African Institute, 102–117.

Richards, P. 1985. *Indigenous Agricultural Revolution*. London: Hutchinson.

Roark, Michael. 1985. "Fast Foods: American Food Regions." *North American Culture* 2(1): 24–36.

Robertson, David S. 1996. "Oil Derricks and Corinthian Columns: The Industrial Transformation of the Oklahoma State Capitol Grounds." *Journal of Cultural Geography* 16: 17–44.

Rocheleau, D., B. Thomas-Slayter, and E. Wangari (eds.). 1996. *Feminist Political Ecology: Global Issues and Local Experiences*. New York: Routledge.

Rooney, John F., Jr. 1969. "Up from the Mines and Out from the Prairies: Some Geographical Implications of Football in the United States." *Geographical Review* 59: 471–492.

Rooney, John F., Jr. 1988. "Where They Come From." *Sport Place* 2(3): 17.

Rooney, John F., Jr., and Paul L. Butt. 1978. "Beer, Bourbon, and Boone's Farm: A Geographical Examination of Alcoholic Drink in the United States." *Journal of Popular Culture* 11: 832–856.

Rooney, John F., Jr., and Richard Pillsbury. 1992. *Atlas of American Sport*. New York: Macmillan.

Sack, Robert D. 1992. *Place, Modernity, and the Consumer's World: A Rational Framework for Geographical Analysis*. Baltimore: Johns Hopkins University Press.

Scott, Damon. In progress. "The Gay Geography of San Francisco." PhD dissertation. University of Texas at Austin.

Shortridge, Barbara G. 1987. *Atlas of American Women*. New York: Macmillan.

Shortridge, James R. 1989. *The Middle West: Its Meaning in American Culture*. Lawrence: University Press of Kansas.

Shuhua, Chang. 1977. "The Gentle Yamis of Orchid Island." *National Geographic* 151(1): 98–109.

Tuan, Yi-Fu. *Topophilia*. Englewood Cliffs, N.J.: Prentice-Hall, 1974.

Weiss, Michael J. 1988. *The Clustering of America*. New York: Harper & Row.

Wilhelm, Eugene J., Jr. 1968. "Field Work in Folklife: Meeting Ground of Geography and Folklore." *Keystone Folklore Quarterly* 13: 241–247.

Williams, R. 1976. *Keywords: A Vocabulary of Culture and Society*. New York: Oxford University Press.

Zelinsky, Wilbur. 1974. "Cultural Variation in Personal Name Patterns in the Eastern United States." *Annals of the Association of American Geographers* 60: 743–769.

Zelinsky, Wilbur. 1980a. "North America's Vernacular Regions." *Annals of the Association of American Geographers* 70: 1–16.

Zelinsky, Wilbur. 1980b. "Selfward Bound? Personal Preference Patterns and the Changing Map of American Society." *Economic Geography* 50: 144–179.

Zonn, Leo (ed.). 1990. *Place Images in Media: Portrayal, Experience, and Meaning*. Savage, Md.: Rowman & Littlefield.

Ten Recommended Books
on Geographies of Difference

For additional suggested readings, see *The Human Mosaic* web site: www.whfreeman.com/jordan

Burgess, Jacquelin A., and John R. Gold (eds.). 1985. *Geography, the Media, and Popular Culture*. New York: St. Martin's Press. The geography of popular culture is linked in diverse ways to the communications media, and this collection of essays explores facets of that relationship.

Carney, George O. (ed.). 1998. *Baseball, Barns and Bluegrass: A Geography of American Folklife*. Boulder, Colo.: Rowman & Littlefield. A wonderful collection of readings that, contrary to the title, span the gap between folk and popular culture.

Ensminger, Robert F. 1992. *The Pennsylvania Barn: Its Origin, Evolution, and Distribution in North America*. Baltimore: Johns Hopkins University Press. A common American folk barn, part of the rural cultural landscape, provides geographer Ensminger with visual clues to its origin and diffusion; a fascinating detective story showing how geographers "read" cultural landscapes and what they learn in the process.

Glassie, Henry. 1968. *Pattern in the Material Folk Culture of the Eastern United States*. Philadelphia: University of Pennsylvania Press. Glassie, a student of folk geographer Fred Kniffen, considers the geographical distribution of a wide array of folk culture items in this classic overview.

Jackson, Peter, and Jan Penrose (eds.). 1993. *Constructions of Race, Place, and Nation*. Minneapolis: University of Minnesota Press. An edited collection that examines the way in which the ideas of racial and national identity vary from place to place; rich in empirical research.

Jordan, Terry G., Jon T. Kilpinen, and Charles F. Gritzner. 1997. *The Mountain West: Interpreting the Folk Landscape*. Baltimore: Johns Hopkins University Press. Reading the folk landscapes of the American West, three geographers reach conclusions about the regional culture and how it evolved.

Price, Patricia. 2004. *Dry Place: Landscapes of Belonging and Exclusion*. Minneapolis: University of Minnesota Press. Price explores the narratives that have sought to establish claims to the dry lands along the U.S.-Mexico border, demonstrating how stories can become vehicles for reshaping places and cultural identities.

Skelton, Tracey, and Gill Valentine (eds.). 1998. *Cool Places: Geographies of Youth Cultures*. London: Routledge. The engaging essays in *Cool Places* explore the dichotomy of youthful lives by addressing the issues of representation and resistance in youth culture today. Using first-person vignettes to illustrate the wide-ranging experiences of youth, the authors consider how the media have imagined young people as a particular community with shared interests and how young people resist these stereotypes, instead creating their own independent representations of their lives.

Weiss, Michael J. 1994. *Latitudes and Attitudes: An Atlas of American Tastes, Trends, Politics, and Passions*. New York: Little, Brown.

Using marketing data organized by postal zip codes, Weiss reveals the geographical diversity of American popular culture.

Zelinsky, Wilbur. 1992. *The Cultural Geography of the United States,* 2nd ed. Englewood Cliffs, N.J.: Prentice-Hall. This revised edition of a sprightly, classic book, originally published in 1973, reveals the cultural sectionalism in modern America in the era of popular culture, with attention also to folk roots.

Journals
in Folk and Popular Cultural Geography

Journal of Popular Culture. Published by the Popular Culture Association from 1967 until its demise in 2002. Volume 1 appeared in 1967. See in particular Vol. 11, No. 4, 1978, a special issue on cultural geography and popular culture.

Material Culture: Journal of the Pioneer America Society. Published three times annually, this leading periodical specializes in the subject of traditional American material culture. Volume 1 was published in 1969, and prior to 1984 the journal was called *Pioneer America.*

Answers

Figure 2.6 The scenes were taken in the following unplaces: McDonald's in Tokyo, Wendy's in Idaho, and Pampas Grill in Finland.

Figure 2.26 (a) French-Canadian farmhouse, Port Joli, Québec; (b) New England "large" house, New Hampshire; (c) Yankee upright-and-wing house, Massachusetts; (d) shotgun house, Alleyton, Texas.

*How can an ordinary landscape, such as a
parking lot, become a sacred space?*

**Parking lot shrine to the Virgin of Guadalupe, Self-Help Graphics and Art,
East Los Angeles.** *(Courtesy of Patricia L. Price.)*

Turn to Seeing Geography on page 106 for an in-depth analysis of the above question.

THE GEOGRAPHY OF RELIGION

Spaces and Places of Sacredness

RELIGION IS A CORE COMPONENT of culture, lending vivid hues to the human mosaic. It provides a good place to begin our topical study of cultural geography. **Religion** can be defined as a relatively structured set of beliefs and practices through which people seek mental and physical harmony with the powers of the universe. It is often through the rituals provided by religion that the milestones along the course of our lives—birth, coming of age, marriage, and death—are observed and celebrated. Religions often attempt not just to accommodate but also to influence the awesome forces of nature, life, and death. Religions help people make sense of their place in the world. In literal terms, the word *religion*—derived from the Latin *religare*—means "to fasten loose parts into a coherent whole."

Religion very often lies at the root of conflict between cultural groups, for people seem less willing to tolerate, let alone to accommodate, differences in religious matters than differences in any other aspect of culture. Having attained some sort of harmony with the cosmos, we do not want to be told that our path is only one of many and possesses no exclusive claim to the truth. Catholics versus Protestants in Northern Ireland, Hindus versus Muslims in India, Catholics versus Orthodox versus Muslims in the Balkans, and Jews versus Muslims in the Middle East are all conflicts based at least in part in religion (refer later to Culture in a Globalizing World).

That said, religion is also often at the heart of how people with very different worldviews can come to understand one another. So, on the one hand, the conquest of the Americas by the Iberians (people of modern-day Spain and Portugal) was often a violent affair. The religious conversion of indigenous peoples to Christianity was at the heart of the political takeover. Temples were destroyed and violent coercion was often used to convert the

Figure 3.1 **The Virgin of Guadalupe.** This is the image that appeared to Juan Diego. As he opened his cape in the presence of Bishop Zumárraga of Mexico City, roses of Castille (a powerful symbol to Spaniards) fell onto the floor and this image was left behind. Her downcast gaze and dark features spoke to Mexican Indians, as did the red belt about her waist, which indicates that she is pregnant. *(Mark Lennihan/AP Photo.)*

heathen natives to Christianity. On the other hand, the Virgin of Guadalupe, who appeared to the Mexican Indian convert Juan Diego in 1531—just 10 years after Cortes's conquest of Mexico—is one of the most powerfully healing figures in the Americas to this day. Her portrait is a mixture of European and indigenous American symbols (Figure 3.1). In her kind manner of speaking to Juan Diego in Nahuatl (an indigenous language spoken by central Mexicans) and her resemblance to the earth goddess Tonantzín, she made sense to native Mexicans. For the Spaniards, dark-skinned Virgins had long been part of their religious symbolism. In the midst of the violence of conquest, then, the Virgin of Guadalupe provided a mother figure that was readily acceptable to native Mexicans, was familiar to Spaniards, and acted as a bridge by which people from these two very different cultures could understand one another.

In short, religion is at once a definitive trait of many cultural groups and a highly territorial phenomenon, with strong, often ancient, linkages to the spirit of place, ethnicity, and nationality. For these reasons, religion is a key element of cultural geography, one we need to consider early in our study.

Different types of religion exist in the world. One way to classify them is to distinguish between proselytic and ethnic faiths. **Proselytic religions,** such as Christianity, actively seek new members and aim to convert all humankind. They instruct their faithful to spread the Word to all the Earth, using persuasion and sometimes violence to convert the "heathen." The colonization of peoples and their lands is sometimes a result of the desire to convert them to the conqueror's religion. By contrast, each **ethnic religion** is identified with a particular ethnic or tribal group and does not seek converts. Judaism provides an example. Though a person can convert to Judaism, it is a complex process that has traditionally been discouraged. Basically, a Jew is anyone born of a Jewish mother. Proselytic religions sometimes grow out of ethnic religions—the evolution of Christianity from its parent Judaism is a good example.

Another distinction among religions is the number of gods worshipped. **Monotheistic religions,** such as Islam and

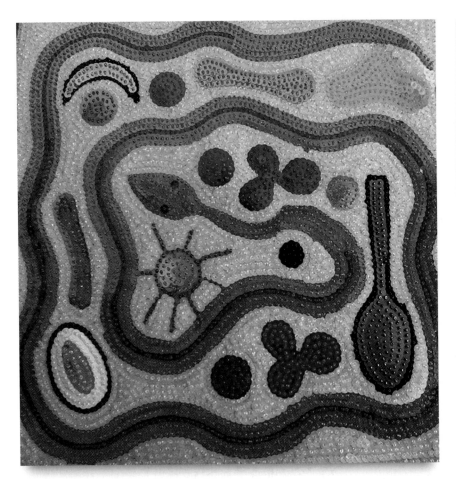

Figure 3.2 **Danbala and Saint Patrick.** Danbala in Haitian Voudou is parallel to the Catholic Saint Patrick, as both are associated with snakes. *(Left: Pierre Fugère Cherismé, Fonde-des-Negres, Haiti/Courtesy of Aid to Artisans, Inc.; Right: Mary Evans Picture Library.)*

Christianity, believe in only one god and may expressly forbid the worship of other gods or spirits. **Polytheistic religions** believe there are many gods. For example, Vodun (also spelled Voudou in Haiti or Voodoo in the southern United States) is a West African religious tradition with adaptations in the Americas wherever the enslavement of Africans was once practiced. Though, as with most major religions, there is one supreme god, it is the hundreds of spirits, or *Iwa*, that Vodun adherents turn to in times of need. Some of the better-known spirits in the Haitian Voudou tradition are Danbala Wedo, the peaceful snake-god who brings rain and fertility; Legba, the keeper of crossroads and doorways who is invoked at the beginning of all rituals; and Ezili Danto, the protective mother figure portrayed as a dark-skinned country woman.

Finally, the distinction between syncretism and orthodoxy is important. **Syncretic religions** combine elements of two or more different belief systems. Umbanda, a religion practiced in parts of Brazil, blends elements of Catholicism with a reverence for the souls of Indians, wise men, and historical Brazilian figures, along with a dash of nineteenth-century European spiritism. Caribbean and Latin American religious practices often combine elements of European, African, and indigenous American religions. Sometimes, in order to continue practicing their religions, people in this region would hide statues of Afrocentric deities within images of Catholic saints. Or they would determine which Catholic figures were most like their own deities. Note in Figure 3.2 the equation of Danbala, the snake-god of Haitian Voudou, with Saint Patrick, who is also associated with snakes. **Orthodox religions,** by contrast, emphasize purity of faith and are not open to blending with elements of other belief systems. The word *orthodoxy* comes from Greek and literally means "right" (*ortho*) "teaching" (*doxy*). Many religions, including Christianity, Judaism, Hinduism, and Islam, have orthodox strains. So, for instance, while some orthodox Jews closely follow a strict interpretation of the Oral Torah (a specific version of the Jewish holy book), moderate but observant Jews may observe only some or perhaps none of the dietary, marriage, and worship proscriptions observed by orthodox

CULTURE IN A GLOBALIZING WORLD

Religious Fundamentalism: A Global Response?

Throughout history, religions have been one of the main ways in which people have attempted to make sense of the changing world around them. Although we may associate globalization with the fast pace and seemingly shrinking world of the last 30 years or so, people from diverse cultures have been in contact across the globe for thousands of years. So how have religions helped people to cope with the changes brought by new ideas, new ways of doing things, and new belief systems?

One response is acceptance. The Muslim conquest of Iberia in the eighth century brought a centuries-long flourishing of culture to modern-day Spain and Portugal. Islamic rule here was noted for its humane and enlightened nature, while the rest of Western Europe languished in the Dark Ages. The Muslims who ruled Iberia were renowned for their religious tolerance, and they included Jews and Christians as valued members of their governmental, scientific, and artistic communities.

Another response is intolerance. When Buddhism branched off from Hinduism, its parent religion, not all Hindus were pleased at the way Buddhism replaced Hinduism in some areas. Angkor Wat (see Figure 12.11), a temple complex in Cambodia, is replete with bas-relief carvings of Buddha figures with their faces entirely chipped off or recarved to resemble Hindu deities. Hindus intolerant of the Khmer king Jayavarman VII's Buddhist beliefs were responsible for defacing these sacred images upon the king's death in A.D. 1220.

Today, many religions are experiencing intense fundamentalist movements, including Christianity, Judaism, Hinduism, and Islam. Fundamentalism means a return to the founding principles of a religion, which may include a literal interpretation of sacred texts and an attempt to follow the ways of a religious founder as closely as possible. Fundamentalists draw a sharp distinction between themselves and other practitioners of their religion whom

they do not believe to be following the proper religious principles, and between themselves and adherents of other faiths. Fundamentalism can be seen as an attempt to purify religious belief and practice in the face of modern influences that are thought to debase the religion. These tendencies have led to fundamentalists being viewed as antimodern and intolerant, although their possession of these traits is strongly disputed by fundamentalists themselves.

Fundamentalism is an emotionally charged term, because it is often used to portray its followers derogatorily as radical extremists. The tendency of the U.S. media to use the term *Islamic fundamentalists* as a synonym for *terrorists* is an unfortunate example of this. Yet there are connections between politics and religious fundamentalism. The political agenda of the U.S. government on matters of abortion, adoption, marriage, foreign policy, domestic security, and the curriculum in public schools has become notably influenced by conservative religious groups. Although not all these groups are entirely fundamentalist in nature, many do embrace fundamentalist Christian beliefs that espouse creationism and the sinfulness of homosexuality, as well as questioning the separation of church and state. *Islamism,* a political ideology based in conservative Muslim fundamentalism, holds that Islam provides the political basis for running the state. Similar to the influence of Christian fundamentalism, Islamist influences in several Muslim-majority countries have set a conservative social agenda and have strongly questioned the separation of church and state.

Is violence a necessary corollary to religious fundamentalism? No, but unfortunately the two have had a close historical association. From the Hindu backlash against Buddhism in thirteenth-century Cambodia to the ongoing conflict between Israelis and Palestinians, the bombings of dozens of abortion clinics in the United States in the 1980s and 1990s, and the Al-Qaeda–led assault on the World Trade Center in 2001, fundamentalism, intolerance, and violence have too often been the response to the threats perceived in increasing globalization.

Jews. Intolerance of other religions, or of those felt not to follow the proper ways, is associated with **fundamentalism** rather than orthodoxy. Many who consider themselves orthodox are also quite tolerant of other beliefs (see Culture in a Globalizing World).

The importance of religion to the contemporary study of cultural geography will be explored through our five

themes. First, religious beliefs differ from one place to another, producing spatial variations that can be mapped as **culture regions.** Second, these religions spread and evolved through **cultural diffusion** involving many sorts of interactions among peoples and places. Violent conquests, diasporas, and the geographic expansion of religions through conversion have all played a role in shaping the contemporary world map of religious belief. Third, the natural environment frequently plays an important part in faith-based belief structures, either because the forces of nature are viewed as potentially negotiable or because features of the natural landscape, such as rivers and mountains, are thought to exert a powerful influence over human destinies. Thus the ecology of religion is a key aspect of its cultural geography. Fourth, as the previous three points suggest, a complex and dynamic cultural interaction connects religion and other aspects of culture. Fifth, and finally, religious beliefs are often visible on the **cultural landscape.** For example, religious architecture, such as mosques, temples, and shrines, literally marks the landscape with the imprint of particular religious beliefs. How the spiritual shaping of some spaces as sacred comes about is an important statement about what, and who, matters, culturally speaking.

 ## Religious Culture Regions

What is the spatial patterning of religious faiths? How do religions function spatially? Because religion, like all of culture, has a strong territorial tie, functional, formal, and vernacular religious culture regions all abound. The most basic kind of formal religious culture region depicts the spatial distribution of religious faiths and denominations (Figure 3.3). Some parts of the world exhibit an exceedingly complicated pattern of religious adherence, and the boundaries of formal religious culture regions, like most cultural borders, are rarely sharp (Figure 3.4 on page 74). Persons of different faiths often live in the same province or town.

Judaism

Judaism is a 4000-year-old religion and the first great monotheistic faith to arise in southwestern Asia. It is the parent religion of Christianity and is also closely related to Islam. Jews believe in one God who created humankind for the purpose of bestowing kindness upon them. As with Islam and Christianity, people are rewarded for their faith, are punished for violating God's commandments, and can atone for their sins. The Jewish holy book, or *Torah,* is comprised of the first five chapters of the Hebrew Bible. In contrast to the other monotheistic faiths, Judaism does not actively seek new converts and has remained an ethnic religion through most of its existence.

Judaism has split into a variety of subgroups, partly as a result of the forced dispersal of the Jews from Palestine in Roman times and the subsequent loss of contact among the various colonies. Jews, scattered to many parts of the Roman Empire, became a minority group wherever they were found. In later times, they spread throughout much of Europe,

North Africa, and Arabia. Those Jews who lived in Germany and France before migrating to central and eastern Europe are known as the *Ashkenazim;* those who never left the Middle East and North Africa are called *Mizrachim;* and those from Spain and Portugal are known as *Sephardim.* Spain expelled its Sephardic Jews in 1492, the same year that Christopher Columbus set sail for the New World. It was not until the quincentennial of both events, in 1992, that the Spanish government issued an official apology for the expulsion.

The late nineteenth and early twentieth centuries witnessed large-scale Ashkenazic migration from Europe to America. The Holocaust that befell European Judaism during the Nazi years involved the systematic murder of perhaps a third of the world's Jewish population, mainly Ashkenazim. Europe ceased to be the primary homeland of Judaism, and many of the survivors fled overseas, mainly to the Americas and the newly created state of Israel. Today, Judaism has about 13 million adherents throughout the world. At present, roughly 6 million, or a little less than half, live in North America. Just over 5 million live in Israel.

Christianity

Christianity, a proselytic faith, is the world's largest religion, both in area and in number of adherents, claiming about a third of the global population (Table 3.1). Christians are monotheistic, believing that God is a trinity consisting of three aspects: the Father, the Son, and the Holy Spirit. Jesus Christ is believed to be the son of God who was given to mankind for the sake of human redemption some 2000 years ago. Through Jesus's death and resurrection, all of humankind is potentially redeemed from sin and provided eternal life in heaven.

TABLE 3.1	**Major Religions of the World**	
Religion	Adherents (millions)	As a Percentage of World Population
Christianity	2000	33
Islam	1155	19
Atheist or nonreligious	913	16
Hinduism	800	15
Chinese composite faiths	381	6
Buddhism	364	6
Animist/Shamanist	240	4
Other religions	110	2

2000 Britannica Book of the Year (Chicago: Encyclopedia Britannica);
World Almanac and Book of Facts 2001 (New York: World Almanac Books).

Major Religions

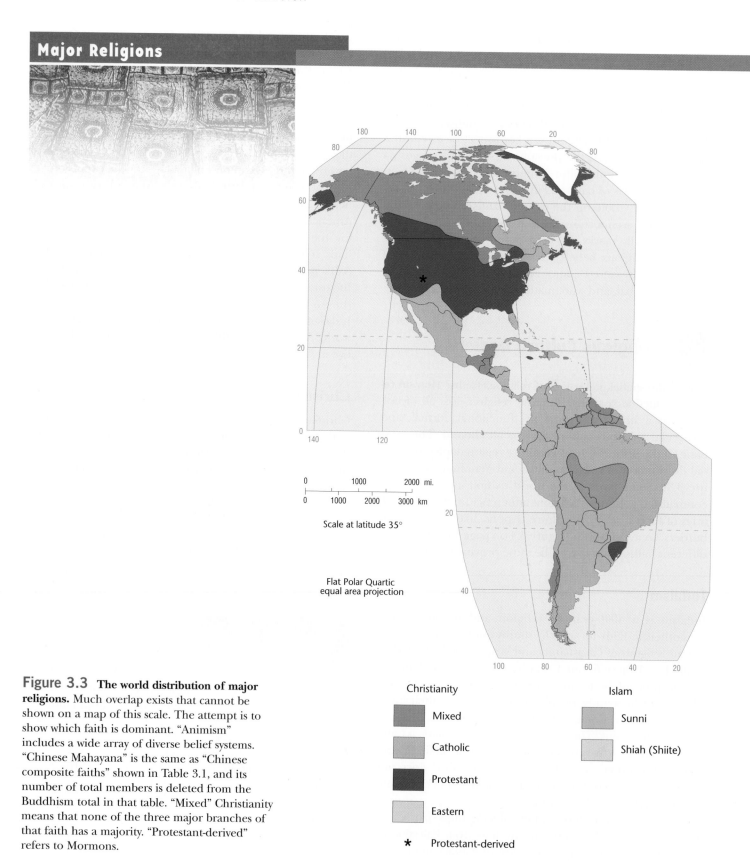

180 140 100 60 20 80 80

60

40

20

0

140 120

0   1000   2000 mi.
0   1000   2000   3000 km

Scale at latitude 35°

Flat Polar Quartic
equal area projection

20

40

100   80   60   40   20

Figure 3.3 **The world distribution of major religions.** Much overlap exists that cannot be shown on a map of this scale. The attempt is to show which faith is dominant. "Animism" includes a wide array of diverse belief systems. "Chinese Mahayana" is the same as "Chinese composite faiths" shown in Table 3.1, and its number of total members is deleted from the Buddhism total in that table. "Mixed" Christianity means that none of the three major branches of that faith has a majority. "Protestant-derived" refers to Mormons.

Christianity

- Mixed
- Catholic
- Protestant
- Eastern
- ★ Protestant-derived

Islam

- Sunni
- Shiah (Shiite)

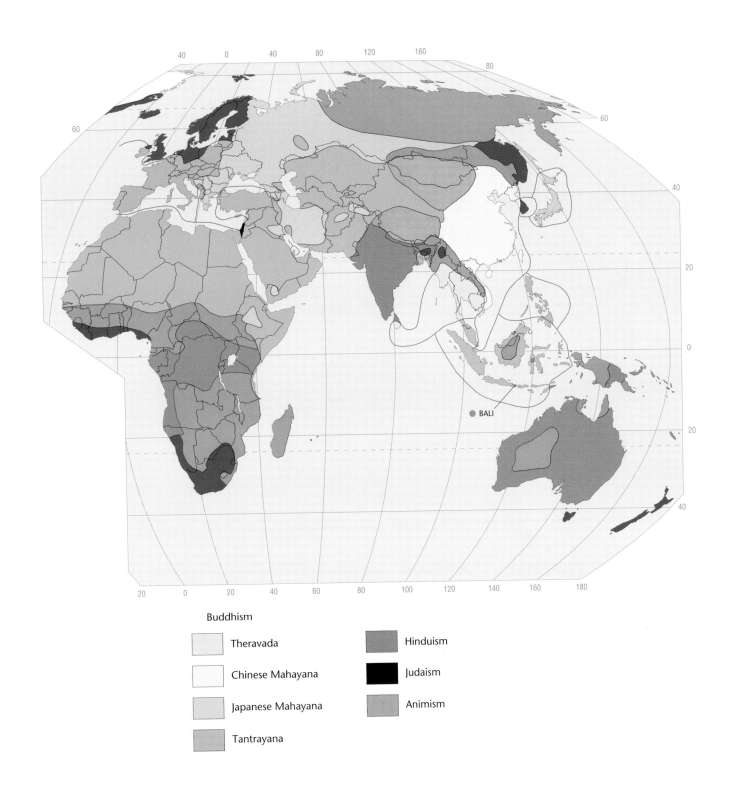

BALI

Buddhism

Theravada

Chinese Mahayana

Japanese Mahayana

Tantrayana

Hinduism

Judaism

Animism

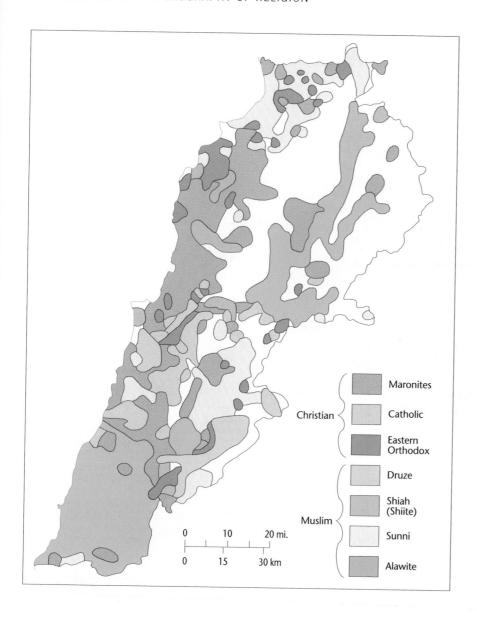

Figure 3.4 **Distribution of religious groups in Lebanon.** A land torn by sectarian warfare in recent times, Lebanon is one of the most religiously diverse parts of the world. Overall, Lebanon is today 37 percent Christian, 34 percent Shiite Muslim, 21 percent Sunni Muslim, and 7 percent Druze. Unshaded areas are largely unpopulated. *(Derived, with changes, from Klaer, 1996: 333; The Economist [February 24, 1996]. See also Stewart, 1996: 489–492.)*

Christianity, Islam, and Judaism are the world's three great monotheisms and share a common culture hearth in southwestern Asia (see Figure 3.14 on page 82). All three religions venerate the patriarch Abraham and are thus called *Abrahamic religions*. Because Christianity derived from Judaism, the two faiths share many elements, including the Old Testament (which forms part of the Christian Bible or holy book), prayer, and a clergy. This is the basis for the common term *Judeo-Christian*, used to describe beliefs and practices shared by the two faiths. Because Jesus was born into the Jewish faith, many Christians still accord Jews a special status as a chosen people and see Christianity as the natural continuation or fulfillment of Judaism.

Christianity has long been fragmented into separate churches (see Figure 3.3). The major division is threefold, made up of Catholics, Protestants, and the Eastern Christian

religions. Western Christianity, which now includes Catholics and Protestants, was initially identified with Rome and the Latin-speaking areas, whereas the Eastern Church dominated the Greek world from Constantinople (now the city of Istanbul, Turkey). Belonging to the Eastern group are the *Armenian* Church, reputedly the oldest in the Christian faith and today centered among a people of the Caucasus region; the *Coptic* Church, originally the nationalistic religion of Christian Egyptians and still today a minority faith there, as well as being the dominant church among the highland people of Ethiopia; the *Maronites*, Semitic descendants of seventh-century heretics who retreated to a mountain refuge in Lebanon (see Figure 3.4); the *Nestorians*, who live in the mountains of the Middle East and in India's Kerala state; and *Eastern Orthodoxy*, originally centered in Greek-speaking areas. After converting many Slavic groups, Eastern Ortho-

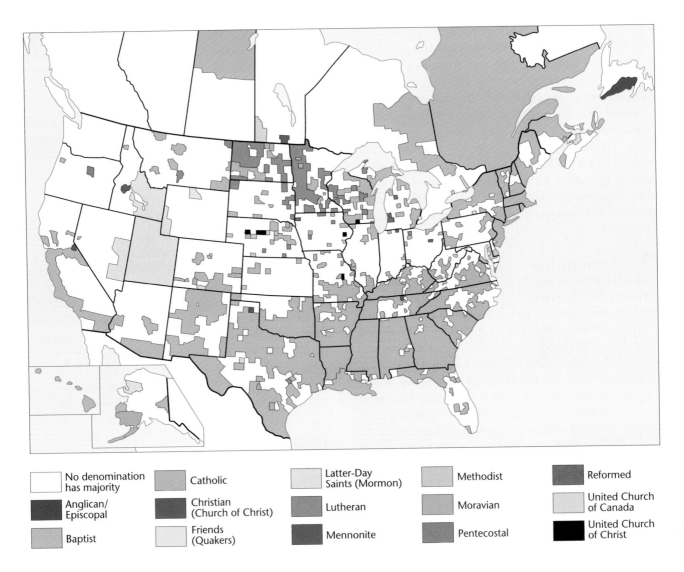

	No denomination has majority		Catholic		Latter-Day Saints (Mormon)		Methodist		Reformed
	Anglican/ Episcopal		Christian (Church of Christ)		Lutheran		Moravian		United Church of Canada
	Baptist		Friends (Quakers)		Mennonite		Pentecostal		United Church of Christ

Figure 3.5 **Leading Christian denominations in the United States and Canada,** shown by counties (for the United States) or census districts (for Canada). In the shaded areas, the church or denomination indicated claimed 50 percent or more of the total church membership. The most striking features of the map are the Baptist dominance through the South, a Lutheran zone in the upper Midwest, Mormon dominance in the interior West, and the zone of mixing in the American heartland.
(Simplified from Bradley et al., 1992; The National Atlas of Canada.)

doxy split into a variety of national churches, such as Russian, Greek, Ukrainian, and Serbian Orthodoxy, with a collective membership of some 214 million.

Western Christianity also splintered, most notably with the emergence of Protestantism in the 1400s and 1500s. Since then, the Roman Catholic Church, which alone includes 1.1 billion people, or more than one-sixth of humanity, has remained unified; but Protestantism, from its beginnings, tended to divide into a rich array of sects, which together have a total membership today of about 416 million. The denominational map of the United States and Canada vividly reflects the fragmentation of Western Chris-

tianity and the resulting complex pattern of religious culture regions (Figure 3.5). Numerous faiths imported from Europe were later augmented by Christian sects developed in America. The American frontier was a breeding ground for new religious groups, as individualistic pioneer sentiment found expression in splinter Protestant denominations. In many parts of the country, even a relatively small community may contain the churches of half a dozen religious groups. As a result, we find today about 2000 different religious denominations and cults in the United States alone. In a broad Bible Belt across the South, Baptist and other conservative fundamentalist denominations dominate, and Utah is at the core of a Mormon realm. A Lutheran belt stretches from Wisconsin westward through Minnesota and the Dakotas, and Roman Catholicism dominates southern Louisiana, the southwestern borderland, and the heavily industrialized areas of the Northeast. The Midwest is a thoroughly mixed zone, although Methodism is the largest single denomination.

Today, Christianity is geographically widespread and highly diverse in its local interpretation. Though it is not as fast-growing as Islam, intense missionary efforts strive to increase the number of adherents. Because of this work, Africa and Asia are the fastest-growing regions for Christianity.

Islam

Islam, another great proselytic faith, claims more than a billion followers, largely in the desert belt of Asia and northern Africa and in the humid tropics as far east as Indonesia and the Philippines (see Table 3.1 and Figure 3.3). Adherents of Islam, known as Muslims, are monotheists and worship one absolute God known as *Allah.* Islam was founded by Muhammad, considered to be the last and most important in a long line of prophets. The word of Allah is believed to have been revealed to Muhammad by the angel Gabriel (Jibrail) beginning in A.D. 610 of the Christian calendar in the Arabian city of Mecca (Figure 3.6). The *Qur'an,* Islam's holy book, is the text of these revelations and also serves as the basis of Islamic law, or *sharia.* Muslims consider both Jews and Christians to be, like themselves, "people of the Book," and all three religions share beliefs in heaven, hell, and the resurrection of the dead. Many biblical figures familiar to Christians, such as Moses, Abraham, Mary, and Jesus, are also venerated as prophets in Islam. Adherents to Islam are expected to pray five times daily at established times; give alms,

or *zakat,* to the poor; fast from dawn to sunset in the holy month of Ramadan; make at least one pilgrimage, if possible, to the sacred city of Mecca in Saudi Arabia; and profess belief in Allah, the one God whose prophet was Muhammad. These duties are known as the Five Pillars of the faith.

Although not as severely fragmented as Christianity, Islam, too, has split into separate groups. Two major sects prevail. *Shiite* Muslims, 16 percent of the Islamic total in diverse subgroups, form the majority in Iran and Iraq. *Sunni* Muslims, who represent the Islamic Orthodoxy, form the large majority worldwide (see Figure 3.3). Islam has not undergone a reformation parallel to that undergone by Christianity with Protestantism. However, liberal movements within Islam do have reformation as their goal.

Islam's strength is greatest in the Arabic-speaking lands, although the world's largest Islamic population is found in Indonesia. Other large clusters live in western China and in Bangladesh and Pakistan. Due to successful conversion efforts in non-Muslim areas and high birthrates in predominantly Muslim areas, Islam is the fastest-growing world religion. In the United States, more people convert to Islam than to any other religion, and Islam will soon surpass Judaism to become America's second-largest faith.

Hinduism

Hinduism, a religion closely tied to India and its ancient culture, claims about 800 million adherents (see Table 3.1 and Figure 3.3). Hinduism is a decidedly polytheistic religion. While Hindus recognize one supreme god, Brahman, it is his many manifestations that are worshipped directly. Some principal Hindu deities include Vishnu, Shiva, and the mother goddess Devi. Ganesha, the elephant-headed god depicted in Figure 3.7, is often revered by Hindu university

Figure 3.6 **Muslims at prayer in Mecca, Saudi Arabia.** *(Kazuyoshi Nomachi/Pacific Press Service.)*

Figure 3.7 **Ganesha.** The elephant-headed god of wisdom, intelligence, and education is revered by many Hindu university students. *(Punit Puranjpe/Reuters/Landov.)*

students, as Ganesha is the god of wisdom, intelligence, and education. Believing that no one faith has a monopoly on the truth, Hindus are notably tolerant of other religions.

Hindus strive to locate the harmonious and eternal truth, *dharma,* that is within each human being. Social divisions, or *castes,* separate Hindu society into four major categories, or *varna,* based on occupational categories: priests (Brahmins), warriors (Kshatriyas), merchants and craftsmen (Vaishyas), and workers (Shudras). Castes are related to dharma inasmuch as dharma implies a set of rules for each varna that regulate their behaviors with regard to eating, marriage, and use of space. All Hindus also share a be-

lief in *reincarnation,* the idea that though the physical body may die, the soul lives on and is reborn in another body. Related to this is the notion of *karma.* Karma can be viewed almost as a causal law, which holds that what an individual experiences in this life is a direct result of that individual's thoughts and deeds in a past life. Likewise, all thoughts and deeds, both good and bad, affect an individual's future lives. Ultimately *moksha,* or liberation of the soul from the cycle of death and rebirth, will occur once one's karma is cleared. *Ahimsa,* or the principle of nonviolence, involves veneration of all forms of life. This implies a principle of noninjury to all sentient creatures, which is why many Hindus are vegetarians.

Hinduism has splintered into diverse groups, some of which are so distinctive as to be regarded as separate religions. *Jainism,* for one, is an ancient outgrowth of Hinduism, claiming perhaps 4 million adherents, almost all in India, and tracing its roots back over 25 centuries. Although rejecting Hindu scriptures, rituals, and priesthood, the Jains share the Hindu belief in ahimsa and reincarnation. Jains adhere to a strict asceticism. For example, they practice veganism, a form of vegetarianism that prohibits the consumption of all animal-based products, including milk and eggs. *Sikhism,* by contrast, arose much later, in the 1500s, as an attempt to unify Hinduism and Islam. Centered in the Punjab state of northwestern India, where the Golden Temple at Amritsar serves as the principal shrine, Sikhism has about 23 million followers. Sikhs are monotheistic and have their own holy book, the *Adi Granth.*

No standard set of beliefs prevails, and the faith takes many local forms. Hinduism includes very diverse peoples. Once a proselytic religion, it is today a regional, national faith. A Hindu majority on the Indonesian island of Bali suggests the religion's former missionary activity (Figure 3.8).

Buddhism

Hinduism is the parent religion of Buddhism, which began 25 centuries ago as a reform movement based on the teachings of Prince Siddhartha Gautama, "the awakened one" (Figure 3.9). He promoted the four "noble truths": life is full of suffering; desire is the cause of this suffering; cessation of suffering comes with the quelling of desire; and an "Eight-Fold Path" of proper personal conduct and meditation permits the individual to overcome desire. The resultant state of enlightenment is known as *nirvana.* Those few individuals who achieve nirvana are known as *Buddhas.* The status of Buddha is open to anyone regardless of social status, gender, or age. Because Buddhism derives from Hinduism, the two religions share many beliefs, such as dharma, reincarnation, and ahimsa.

Today, Buddhism is the most widespread religion in Asia, dominating a culture region stretching from Sri Lanka

Figure 3.8 **Hindu temple in Bali, Indonesia.** Besakih, known as the "Mother Temple of Bali," is the largest Hindu temple complex on the island, occupying the slopes of Mount Agung. *(Courtesy of Patricia L. Price.)*

to Japan and from Mongolia to Vietnam. In the process of its proselytic spread, particularly in China and Japan, Buddhism fused with native ethnic religions such as Confucianism, Taoism, and Shintoism to form syncretic faiths that fall into the *Mahayana* division of Buddhism. Southern, or *Theravada*, Buddhism, dominant in Sri Lanka and mainland Southeast Asia, retains the greatest similarity to the religion's original form, whereas a variation known as *Tantrayana*, or *Lamaism*, prevails in Tibet and Mongolia (see Figure 3.3). Buddhism's tendency to merge with native religions, particularly in China, makes it difficult to determine the number of its adherents. Estimates range from 350 million to more than 500 million people (see Table 3.1). Although Buddhism in China has become mingled with local faiths to become part of a composite ethnic religion, elsewhere it remains one of the three great proselytic religions in the world, along with Christianity and Islam.

Animism/Shamanism

Peoples in diverse parts of the world often retain indigenous religions and are usually referred to collectively as **animists** (see Figure 3.3). Currently numbering perhaps 240 million, animists believe that certain inanimate objects possess spirits

Figure 3.9 **Buddhism is one of the religious faiths of South Korea.** Here an image of the Buddha is carved from a rocky bluff to create sacred space and a local pilgrimage shrine. *(Courtesy of Terry G. Jordan-Bychkov.)*

Figure 3.10 **Pet grave marker.** Pumpkin the cat was apparently baptized into the Christian faith and now lies at rest in Miami, Florida's, Pet Heaven Cemetery. *(Courtesy of Patricia L. Price.)*

tural forces are front and center, driving changes in politics, economics, and societies. A good example of how these arenas work together is provided by the contemporary religious landscape of Latin America and the Caribbean. In this region, Roman Catholicism has dominated the religious landscape since the time of the Iberian conquerors in the late 1400s. More Catholics live in this region than in any other on Earth, with three out of every five Catholics residing here. Brazil is the largest Catholic country in the world, with over 120 million adherents. However, the Catholic Church has been on the decline in Brazil and throughout the region in recent decades. Less than 80 percent of Brazilians are Catholics today, whereas 50 years ago that figure was over 95 percent. What has happened to the region's Catholics? Briefly, more and more Latin Americans feel that the Catholic Church has failed to keep in touch with the needs and concerns of modern urban societies. Birth control, divorce, and persistent poverty are issues that are simply not addressed by Roman Catholicism to the satisfaction of many Latin Americans. As a result, more and more are turning toward evangelical Protestant faiths, such as the Seventh-Day Adventist and Pentecostal churches (Figure 3.11). The focus of these churches on thrift, sobriety, and resolving problems directly rather than through the mediation of priests is

or souls. These spirits are believed to live in rocks and rivers, on mountain peaks and celestial bodies, in forests and swamps, and even in everyday objects. Wicca, a contemporary neopagan religion derived from ancient European practices of reverence for the mother goddess and the horned god, worships the god and the goddess who are thought to inhabit everything. Animistic elements can also pervade established religions. Japanese Shinto adherents worship *kami*, or spirits, that inhabit natural objects such as waterfalls and mountains. Even in places like the United States, where the majority of the inhabitants would not see themselves as animists, such beliefs are pervasive. For example, many people in the United States believe that their pets possess souls that ascend to heaven upon death (Figure 3.10). For some animists, the objects in question do not actually possess spirits but rather are valued because they have a particular potency to serve as a link between a person and the omnipresent god. A tribal religious figure, called by some a *shaman,* usually serves as an intermediary between the people and the spirits. We should not hastily classify such systems of belief as primitive or simple because they can be extraordinarily complex.

Changing Religious Profiles

As economic, social, and political changes occur in places, cultural forces such as religion must adapt. Sometimes cul-

Figure 3.11 **Protestant storefront church.** This Pentecostal church, Igreja o Brasil para Cristo, is one of the fastest-growing evangelical Protestant churches in Brazil. The garage-front arrangement shown here is located in the mining town of Lencois. Some of the 25 worshippers at this service went into a trance. *(Ponkawonka.)*

appealing to many. Others find their needs are best addressed by an array of African-based spiritist religions, which include Umbanda, Candomblé, and Santería. Whether Catholicism will ultimately reform from within to become more appealing to Latin Americans, or whether it will continue to lose out to rival religions, is one of the key questions concerning the Latin American and Caribbean religious landscape.

In the United States, geographer Roger Stump points to a twentieth-century trend toward regional religious divergence. Baptists in the South, Lutherans in the upper Midwest, Catholics in the Southwest, and Mormons in the West each dominate their respective regions more thoroughly today than at the turn of the century. Each of the four denominations is conservative and has a strong, long-standing infrastructure. Other experts, however, believe that American culture is becoming more religiously mixed, with weakening regional borders around religious core areas. Newer religious influences, too, are making an entrance onto the American religious stage. For example, if you have ever practiced yoga or meditation, you are engaging in Hindu and Buddhist practices (Figure 3.12). Many Americans do yoga or meditate as a means of physical or spiritual growth, for stress relief, or even to keep up with the latest trends, rather than as part of a religious

practice. Yet they are among the growing number of Americans who have found a blend of Eastern and Western religious practices to be compatible with their beliefs and lifestyles.

In some parts of the world, especially in much of Europe, religion has declined, giving way to *secularization* (Figure 3.13). The number of nonreligious, agnostic, and atheistic persons in the world is estimated at 913 million at present (see Table 3.1). The American Religious Identification Survey (see Geography of Religion on the Internet at the end of the chapter), compiled in 2001, found 30 million nonreligious adults in the United States, or about 14 percent of the population. In the state of Hawaii, for example, 51 percent of adults are unaffiliated with a church. Typically, secularization displays a marked regionalization on a variety of scales. Areas of surviving religious vitality lie alongside secularized districts in a disorderly jumble. Such patterns once again reveal the inherent spatial variety of humankind and invite analysis by the cultural geographer. In some instances, the retreat from organized religion has resulted from a government's active hostility toward a particular faith or toward religion in general. In other cases, we can attribute the decline to the failure of religions oriented to the needs of rural folk cultures to adapt to the urban scene.

Figure 3.12 **Yoga class in session.** Many people in the United States have incorporated Hindu and Buddhist spiritual practices into their lives. *(Ryan McVay/ Getty Images.)*

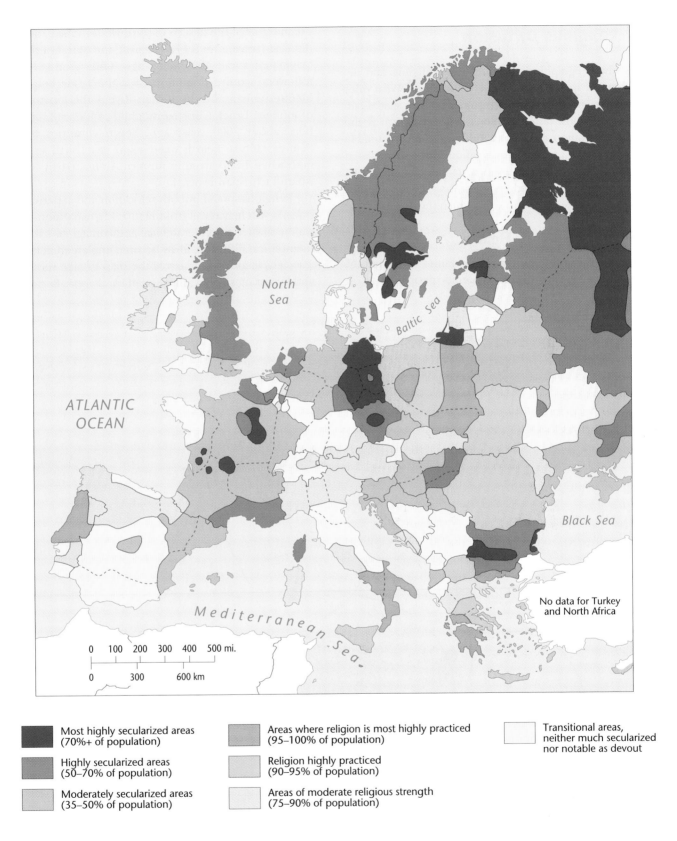

Most highly secularized areas
(70%+ of population)

Highly secularized areas
(50–70% of population)

Moderately secularized areas
(35–50% of population)

Areas where religion is most highly practiced
(95–100% of population)

Religion highly practiced
(90–95% of population)

Areas of moderate religious strength
(75–90% of population)

Transitional areas,
neither much secularized
nor notable as devout

Figure 3.13 Secularized areas in Europe. These areas, in which Christianity has ceased to be of much importance, occur in a complicated pattern. What causal forces might have been at work? In all of Europe, some 190 million people report no religious faith, amounting to 27 percent of the population. (*Source: Jordan-Bychkov and Jordan, 2002: 104.*)

Religious Diffusion

How did the geographical distribution of religions and denominations, of regions and places, come about? What roles did expansion and relocation diffusion play? The spatial patterning of religions, denominations, and secularism is the product of innovation and cultural diffusion. To a remarkable degree, the origin of the major religions was concentrated spatially in two principal culture hearth areas (Figure 3.14). A **culture hearth** is a focused geographic area where important innovations are born and from which they spread.

The Semitic Religious Hearth

All three of the great monotheistic faiths—Christianity, Judaism, and Islam—arose among Semitic peoples in or on the margins of the deserts of southwestern Asia, in the Middle East (see Figure 3.14). Judaism, the oldest of the three, originated some 4000 years ago. Only gradually did its followers acquire dominion over the lands between the Mediterranean and the Jordan River—the territorial base of modern Israel. Christianity, child of Judaism, originated here about 2000 years ago. Seven centuries later, the Semitic culture hearth once again gave birth to a major faith when Islam arose in western Arabia, partly from Jewish and Christian roots.

Religions spread by both relocation and expansion diffusion. As you may recall from Figure 1.9, expansion diffusion can be divided into hierarchical and contagious subtypes. In hierarchical diffusion, ideas become implanted at the top of a society, leapfrogging across the map to take root in cities and bypassing smaller villages and rural areas. Because their

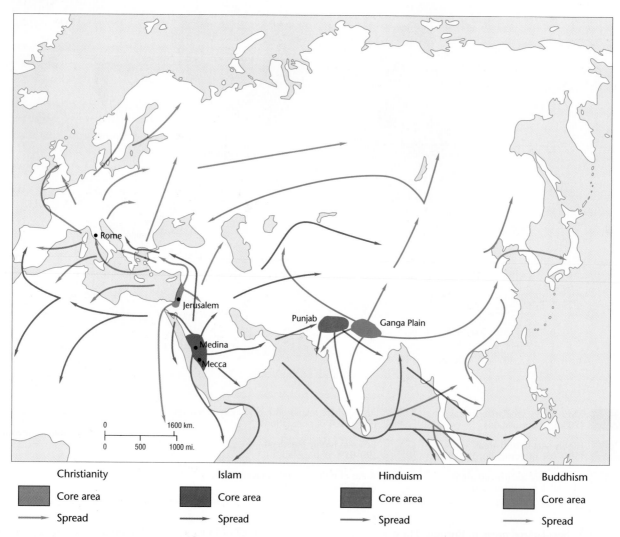

Christianity	Islam	Hinduism	Buddhism
Core area	Core area	Core area	Core area
Spread	Spread	Spread	Spread

Figure 3.14 The origin and diffusion of four major religions in Eurasia. Christianity and Islam, the two great proselytic monotheistic faiths, arose in Semitic southwestern Asia and spread widely through the Old World. Hinduism and Buddhism both originated in the northern reaches of the Indian subcontinent and spread throughout southeastern Eurasia.

main objective is to convert nonbelievers, proselytic faiths are more likely to diffuse than ethnic religions, and it is not surprising that the spread of monotheism was accomplished largely by Christianity and Islam, rather than Judaism. From Semitic southwestern Asia, both of the proselytic monotheistic faiths diffused widely.

Christians, observing the admonition in the Gospel of Matthew—"Go ye therefore and teach all nations, baptizing them in the name of the Father, and of the Son, and of the Holy Ghost, teaching them to observe all things whatsoever I have commanded you"—initially spread through the Roman Empire, using the splendid system of imperial roads to extend the faith. In its early centuries of expansion, Christianity displayed a spatial distribution that clearly reflected hierarchical diffusion (Figure 3.15). The early congregations were established in cities and towns, temporarily producing

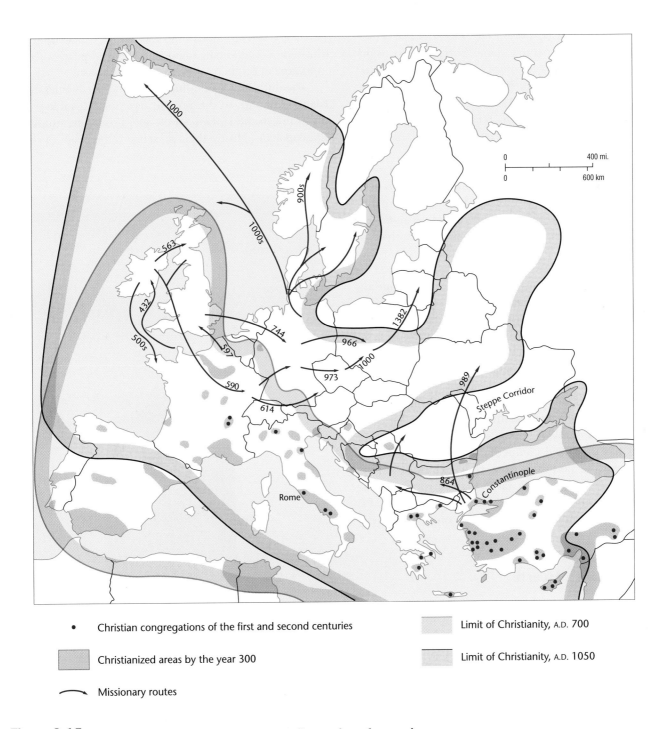

Figure 3.15 **The diffusion of Christianity in Europe, first to eleventh centuries.**

a pattern of Christianized urban centers and pagan rural areas. Indeed, traces of this process remain in our language. The Latin word *pagus,* "countryside," is the root of both *pagan* and *peasant,* suggesting the ancient heathen connotation of rurality.

The scattered urban clusters of early Christianity were created by such missionaries as the apostle Paul, who moved from town to town bearing the news of the emerging faith. In later centuries, Christian missionaries often used the technique of converting kings or tribal leaders, setting in motion additional hierarchical diffusion. The Russians and Poles were converted in this manner. Some Christian expansion was militaristic, as in the reconquest of Iberia from the Muslims and the invasion of Latin America. Once implanted in this manner, Christianity spread farther by means by contagious diffusion. When applied to religion, this method of spread is called **contact conversion** and is the result of everyday association between believers and nonbelievers.

Christian cultural diffusion has been so successful as to create some geographical oddities. For example, South Korea now has more Presbyterians than Scotland, where this denomination originated (Figure 3.16), and more members of the Church of England live in sub-Saharan Africa than in Great Britain.

The Islamic faith spread from its Semitic hearth area in a militaristic manner. Obeying the command in the Qur'an that they "do battle against them until there be no more seduction from the truth and the only worship be that of Allah," the Arabs expanded westward across North Africa in a wave of religious conquest. The Turks, once converted by the Arabs, carried out similar Islamic conquests. In a different sort of diffusion, Muslim missionaries followed trade routes eastward to implant Islam hierarchically in the Philippines, Indonesia, and the interior of China. Tropical Africa is the current major scene of Islamic expansion, an effort that has produced competition with Christians for the conversion of animists. As a result of diffusionary successes in sub-Saharan Africa and high birthrates in its older sphere of dominance, Islam has become the world's fastest-growing religion in terms of the number of new adherents.

The Indus-Ganga Hearth

The second great religious hearth area lay in the plains fringing the northern edge of the Indian subcontinent. This lowland, drained by the Ganga (Ganges) and Indus rivers, gave birth to Hinduism and Buddhism. Hinduism, which is at least 4000 years old, was the earliest faith to arise in this hearth. Its origin apparently lay in Punjab, from which it diffused to dominate the subcontinent, although some historians believe that the earliest form of Hinduism was in-

troduced from Iran by emigrating Indo-European tribes about 1500 B.C. Missionaries later carried the faith, in its proselytic phase, to overseas areas, but most of these converted regions were subsequently lost to other religions.

Branching off from Hinduism, Buddhism began in the foothills bordering the Ganga Plain about 500 B.C. (see Figure 3.14). For several centuries it remained confined to the Indian subcontinent, but missionaries later carried the religion to China (100 B.C. to A.D. 200), Korea and Japan (A.D. 300 to 500), Southeast Asia (A.D. 400 to 600), Tibet (A.D. 700), and Mongolia (A.D. 1500). Like Christianity, Buddhism developed many regional forms and nearly died out in its area of origin, reabsorbed into Hinduism.

The diffusion of Buddhism, like that of Christianity and Islam, continues to the present day. Some 2 million Buddhists live in the United States, about the same number as Episcopalians. Mostly, their presence is the result of reloca-

Figure 3.16 **Nearly half of all South Koreans are Christians.** Most of these are Protestants, and Presbyterianism is the leading denomination. *(Courtesy of Terry G. Jordan-Bychkov.)*

FOCUS ON

"When Jesus Came, the Corn Mothers Went Away"

Ramón Gutiérrez has written a beautiful book whose title is the same as the one for this box. In it, he describes the ancestral religion of the Pueblo Indians of New Mexico, which centered on the Corn Mothers, who gave life to people, plants, and animals alike. Infants received ears of maize (corn), which were kept throughout their entire lifetime. The maize ear symbolized the feminine fertility latent in seeds and the earth.

When Spanish Catholic missionaries converted the Pueblos, it seemed, superficially, as though the male deity Jesus had driven away the corn goddesses. Actually, the Virgin Mary assumed many of the roles of the Corn Mothers. After an unsuccessful rebellion, in which the Pueblos sought to evict the Spaniards and their religion, one of the Corn Mothers returned as "Our Lady of the Conquest."

In this way, two very different religions—one masculine, the other feminine—coalesced.

Adapted from Gutiérrez, 1991:13–14, 143, 161–163

tion diffusion by Asian immigrants to the United States, where immigrant Buddhists outnumber Buddhist converts by three to one.

REFLECTING ON GEOGRAPHY

Why, in the entire world, did only two hearths produce so many major religious faiths?

Barriers and Time-Distance Decay

Religious ideas move in the manner of all innovation waves. They weaken with increasing distance from their places of origin and with the passage of time. Barriers often delay or halt their spread. Most commonly, barriers are of the permeable type, allowing part of the innovation wave to diffuse but in the process weakening it, retarding its spread. An example is the partial acceptance of Christianity by various indigenous groups in Latin America and the western United States, which serves in some instances as a camouflage behind which many aspects of the tribal ethnic religions survive. In fact, permeable barriers are *normally* present in the expansion diffusion of religious faiths (see Focus On: "When Jesus Came, the Corn Mothers Went Away"). Most religions are modified by older local beliefs as they diffuse spatially. Rarely do new ideas, whether religious or not, gain unqualified acceptance in a region.

Absorbing barriers also exist in religious diffusion. The attempt to introduce Christianity into China provides a good example. When Catholic and Protestant missionaries reached China from Europe and the United States, they expected to find fertile ground for conversion—millions of people ready to receive the Word of God. However, they had crossed the boundaries of a culture region thousands of years old, in which some basic social ideas left little opening for Christianity and its doctrine of original sin. Long before, the Chinese had settled to their own satisfaction the question of what is basic human nature. As they saw the matter, humans are inherently good. Evil desires are merely a deviation from that natural state. People have only to shrug them off and they will return to their basic good nature. Consequently, the Chinese were baffled by the idea of original sin. The Christian image of humankind as flawed, of a gap between creator and created, of the Fall and the impossibility of returning to godliness, was culturally incomprehensible to the Chinese.

Other aspects of Christianity added to the cultural gap. How could the fall from grace come from too much knowledge, which is so highly prized in China? What is wrong with a snake in the Garden of Eden to a people whose art is filled with reptilian dragons, the imperial symbol? In short, many concepts of Christianity fell on rocky soil in China. Only in the early twentieth century, as China's social structure crumbled under Western assault, did a significant, though still small, number of Chinese convert to Christianity. Many of these were "rice Christians," poor Chinese willing to become Christians in exchange for the food that missionaries gave them.

In addition, religion itself can act as a barrier to the spread of nonreligious innovations. Religious taboos can even function as absorbing barriers, preventing diffusion of foods, drinks, and practices that violate the taboo. Mormons, who are forbidden to consume drinks containing caffeine, have not taken part in the American fascination with coffee. Sometimes these barriers are permeable. Certain Pennsylvania Dutch churches, for example, prohibit cigarette smoking but do not object to member farmers raising tobacco for sale in the commercial market.

Religious Ecology

What is the relationship between religion and the natural habitat? How does religion help guide our modification of the environment and shape our perception of nature? Does the habitat influence religion? All these questions, and more, fit into the theme of cultural ecology.

Appeasing the Forces of Nature

One of the main functions of many religions is the maintenance of a harmonious relationship between a people and their physical environment. That is, religion is at least perceived by its adherents to be part of the **adaptive strategy,** and for that reason physical environmental factors, particularly natural hazards and disasters, exert a powerful influence on the development of religions.

Environmental influence is most readily apparent in animistic faiths. In fact, an animistic religion's principal goal is to mediate between its people and the spirit-filled forces of nature. Animistic ceremonies and even the rites of great religions are often intended to bring rain, quiet earthquakes, end plagues, or in some other way manipulate environmental forces by placating the spirits believed responsible for these events. Sometimes the link between religion and natural hazard is visual. The great pre-Columbian temple pyramid at Cholula, near Puebla in central Mexico, strikingly mimics the shape of the awesome nearby volcano Popocatépetl, which towers to the menacing height of nearly 18,000 feet (5500 meters). Catholic missionaries retained the sacred status of the Cholula pyramid, although not its volcano-appeasing attribute, by erecting a church atop it.

Although the physical environment's influence on the major religions is less pronounced than it is on ani-

Figure 3.17 **The frequency of locust infestations and the number of "locust cults" in China.** These cults arose as an adaptive strategy in response to an environmental hazard. The worship of locusts was grafted onto the composite religion of China. (*Redrawn with permission from Hsu, 1969: 734, 745.*)

Figure 3.18 Condominium in Hong Kong. The square opening in this building is supposed to allow for the passage of the dragon who resides in the hill behind. *(Courtesy of Ari Dorfsman.)*

mistic faiths, it is still evident. Some adherents to the Judeo-Christian tradition feel that God uses plagues to punish sinners. An example is the belief that AIDS is a punishment from God on those guilty of the sin of homosexuality. Environmental stress can evoke a religious response not so different from that of animistic faiths. Local ministers and priests often attempt to alter unfavorable weather conditions with special services, and there are few churchgoing people in the Great Plains of the United States who have not prayed for rain in dry years. In northeastern China, repeated plagues of crop-destroying locusts gave rise over the centuries to a number of "locust cults," complete with temples. Almost 900 such temples were built, providing a place of worship for the locust and locust-gods (Figure 3.17). Suitable sacrifices and rituals were developed in an effort to avert the periodic infestations.

Animistic nature-spirits lie behind certain practices found in the great religions, such as feng shui. *Feng shui,* which literally means "wind and water," refers to the practice of harmoniously balancing the opposing forces of nature in the built environment. A Chinese and Korean Taoist-Buddhist fusion, it involved choosing environmentally auspicious sites for houses, villages, temples, and graves. The homes of the living and the resting places of the dead must be aligned with the cosmic forces of the world in order to assure good luck, health, and prosperity. Though the practice of feng shui dates back some 7000 years, contemporary people practice its principles. Figure 3.18 depicts a high-rise condominium in Hong Kong's Repulse Bay neighborhood. The square opening in the building's center is said to provide a passage for the dragon that dwells in the hill behind, allowing it to drink from the waters of the bay and return to its abode unencumbered. Many westerners have also adopted some of the principles of feng shui. Office spaces as well as homes are arranged according to its basic ideas. For example, artificial plants, broken articles, and paintings depicting wars are thought to bring negative energy into living spaces and so should be avoided.

Rivers, mountains, trees, forests, and rocks often achieve the status of sacred space, even in the great religions. The river Ganga and certain lesser streams such as the Bagmati in Nepal are holy to the Hindus (Figure 3.19), and the Jordan River has special meaning for Christians, who often transport its waters in containers to other continents for use in baptism. Most holy rivers are believed to possess soul-cleansing abilities. Hindu geographer Rana Singh speaks of the "liquid divine energy" of the Ganga "nourishing the inhabitants and purifying them."

Figure 3.19 **Bathing in the holy Ganga River at Varanasi, India.** The Hindu faithful come for ritual baths on the stair-stepped banks of the river. *(Porterfield/Chickering/Photo Research.)*

Mountains and other high places likewise often achieve sacred status among both animists and adherents of the great religions (Figure 3.20). Mount Fuji is sacred in Japanese Shintoism, and many high places are venerated in Christianity, including the Mount of Olives. Some mountains tower so impressively as to inspire sects devoted exclusively to them. Mount Shasta, a massive snowcapped volcano in northern California, near the Oregon border, serves as the focus of no fewer than 30 New Age cults, the largest of which is the "I Am" religion, founded in the 1930s (see Figure 3.20, right). Geographer Claude Curran, who studied the Shasta cults, found that, although few of the adherents live near the mountain, pilgrimages and festivals held during the summer swell the population of nearby towns and contribute to the local economy.

The Environment and Monotheism

On a grander scale, some geographers have sought to explain the origins of monotheism by environmental factors.

The three major monotheistic faiths—Christianity, Islam, and Judaism—all have their roots among the desert dwellers of the Middle East. Lamaism, the most nearly monotheistic form of Buddhism, flourishes in the deserts of Tibet and Mongolia. In all of these cases, the people involved (Hebrews, Arabs, Tibetans, and Mongols) were once nomadic herders (see Chapter 8), wandering from place to place in the desert with flocks and herds of livestock. Geographer Ellen Semple suggested in 1911 that such desert-dwelling peoples "receive from the immense monotony of their environment the impression of unity." Semple proposed that the unobstructed view of the stars and planets provided by the clear desert skies allowed the herders to see that the heavenly bodies moved across the sky in an orderly, repeated progression. This revelation supposedly suggested to the desert stargazers that a single guiding hand was responsible for the orderly system. Semple, in the classic style of environmental determinism, concluded that desert dwellers "gravitate inevitably into monotheism."

Other possibilistic rather than deterministic explanations have been proposed for the origins of monotheism. Some cultural geographers feel that we should look at the social structure of nomadic herding people for answers. Desert nomads are organized into tribes and clans ruled by a male chieftain or patriarch who has dictatorial powers over the members of the group. It is possible that the all-powerful male deity of Middle Eastern monotheism is simply a theological reflection of the all-powerful, secular, male patriarch. Other geographers have noted that these monotheistic nomads lived on the edges of larger, more established culture regions. New ideas, these scholars feel, tend to develop at the borders rather than at the core of regions, where older structures and ideas are firmly entrenched. The fact is, however, that we do not know enough about early monotheism to say with certainty why it arose. We are not even sure that the first monotheists were desert nomads, and we do know that some desert dwellers were polytheistic.

Ecotheology

Ecotheology is the name given to a rich and abundant body of literature studying the role of religion in habitat modification. More exactly, ecotheologists ask how the teachings and worldviews of religion are related to our attitudes about modifying the physical environment. In the words of Lynn White, "Human ecology is deeply conditioned by beliefs about our nature and destiny—that is, by religion." In some faiths, human power over natural forces is assumed. The Maori people of New Zealand, for example, believe that humans represent one of six aspects of

Figure 3.20 **Two high places that have evolved into sacred space.** The reddish sandstone Uluru, or Ayers Rock, in central Australia is sacred in Aboriginal animism and inspires awe from both near and afar. Snowy Mount Shasta in California is venerated by some 30 New Age cults, including the "I Am" religion. (See Huntsinger and Fernández-Giménez, 2000: 536–558.) Why do mountains so often inspire such worship? *(Left: Michael Fogden/Bruce Coleman; Right: Joel Sartore/National Geographic.)*

creation, the others being forest/animals, crops, wild food, sea/fish, and winds/storms. In the Maori worldview, people rule over all of these except winds/storms.

The Judeo-Christian tradition also teaches that humans have dominion over nature, but it goes further, promoting a teleological view. **Teleology** is the doctrine that the Earth was created especially for human beings, who are separate from and superior to the natural world (Figure 3.21). This view is implicit in God's message to Noah after the Flood, promising that "every moving thing that lives shall be food for you, and as I gave you the green plants, I give you everything" (see Focus On: The Color Green). The same theme is repeated in the Psalms, where Jews and Christians are told that "the heavens are the Lord's heavens, but the Earth he has given to the sons of men." Humans are not part of nature but separate, forming one member of a God-nature-human trinity.

Believing that the Earth was given to humans for their use, early Christian thinkers adopted the view that humans were God's helpers in finishing the task of creation, that human modifications of the environment were God's work. Small wonder, then, that the medieval period in Europe witnessed an unprecedented expansion of agricultural acreage, involving the large-scale destruction of woodlands and the drainage of marshes. Nor is it surprising that Christian monastic orders, such as the Cistercian and Benedictine monks, supervised many of these projects, directing the clearing of forests and the establishment of new agricultural colonies.

Subsequent scientific advances permitted the Judeo-Christian West to modify the environment at an unprecedented rate and on a massive scale. This marriage of technology and teleology is the root of our modern ecological crisis. The Judeo-Christian religious heritage, in short, has for millennia promoted an *instrumentalist view of nature* that is potentially far more damaging to the habitat than an *organic view of nature* in which humans and nature exist in balance. By contrast, the great religions of Asia and many animistic tribal faiths highlight teachings and beliefs that protect nature. In Hinduism, for example, geographer Deryck Lodrick found that the doctrine of ahimsa had resulted in the establishment of many animal homes, refuges, and hospitals, particularly in the northwestern part of India. The hospitals, or *pinjrapoles*, are maintained by the Jains. In this view of the world, people are part of and at harmony with nature. Such religions would presumably not threaten the ecological balance.

Geographer Yi-Fu Tuan disagrees. He points to a discrepancy between the stated ideals of religions and their real-world practices. Even though China enjoys an "old tradition of forest care" based on its composite religion, the Chinese woodlands have been systematically destroyed through the millennia. Nor are the Asian and tribal religions consistently protective of the environment. Buddhism, like Hinduism,

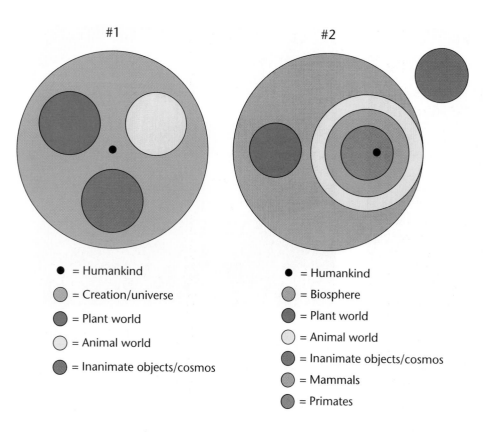

Figure 3.21 Models of the universe. Model 1 represents the traditional, Judeo-Christian, biblical/scriptural, teleological view, in which humankind is central to creation and autonomous from the natural world. Model 2 describes the modern scientific/elitist view, which rests on the findings of Darwin and others. Proponents of these two views will likely develop unique outlooks on environmental modification.

protects temple trees but demands huge quantities of wood for cremations (Figure 3.22). Animistic swidden agriculturalists (see Chapter 8) sometimes make offerings to appease the woodland spirits before destroying huge acreages of forest with machete and fire. The ancient earth goddesses demanded that fields be cleared from the forest for the land to be fruitful, and habitat destruction remains habitat destruction. Civilization itself, argues Tuan, is the exercise of human power over nature. Religion can resist but not overcome that exercise. Also, if people are assumed to be part of

Figure 3.22 Wood gathered for Hindu cremations at Pashupatinath, on the sacred river Bagmati in Nepal. These cremations contribute significantly to the ongoing deforestation of Nepal and reveal the underlying internal contradiction in Hinduism between conservation as reflected in the doctrine of ahimsa and sanctioned ecologically destructive practices. *(Courtesy of Terry G. Jordan-Bychkov.)*

The Color Green

Consider this image of a Muslim mosque in northern Nigeria. The color green is sacred in Islam and appears often on mosques and *minarets,* the tall circular towers from which Muslims are called to prayer. The prophet Muhammad declared his favorite color to be green, and his cloak and turban were green. In Christianity, green also has positive connotations, symbolizing fertility, freedom, hope, and renewal.

It is easy to understand how the color green, associated with the life-giving properties of well-watered vegetation, has become sacred to desert-born religions. In fact, all three of the great desert monotheisms—Islam, Christianity, and Judaism—consider water to have a special status in religious rituals. In general, all three religions view water as having the ability to purify and cleanse the body as well as purify and cleanse the soul of sins. Muslims use water in ablution, or washing, of the hands, face, or entire body before daily prayers and other rituals. Central to Christianity is baptism, where the newborn infant or adult convert is sprinkled with holy water or fully immersed, symbolizing the cleansing of original sin. Jews may engage in ritual baths, known as *mikveh,* before important events such as weddings (for women) or on Fridays, the day of the Jewish Sabbath (for men). The story of the Great Flood, found in the Book of Genesis in the Old Testament (common to both Jews and Christians), depicts the washing away of the sins of the world so that it could be born anew.

(Courtesy of Diane Rawson/Photo Researcher.)

---

nature, then one might conclude that no stewardship of the land by humankind seems logical, since we and all our works are "natural."

Godliness and Greenness

We should consider, too, that the Judeo-Christian tradition is not lacking in concern for environmental protection. In the Book of Leviticus, for example, farmers are instructed by God to let the land lie fallow one year in seven and not to gather food from wild plants in that "sabbath of the land." Robin Doughty, a humanistic cultural geographer, suggests that "Western Christian thought is too rich and complex to be characterized as hostile toward nature," although he feels that Protestantism, "in which worldly success symbolizes individual predestination," may be more conducive to "ecological intemperance." Beyond that, according to geographer Janel Curry-Roper, some fundamentalist Protestant sects herald ecological crisis and environmental deterioration as a sign of the coming Apocalypse, Christ's return, and the end of the present age. Thus they welcome ecological collapse and, obviously, are unlikely to be of much help in solving the problem of environmental degradation.

Some conservative, fundamentalist Protestants, however, have adopted conservationist views, citing biblical admonitions. The Flood story from the Old Testament, in which Noah saves diverse animals by bringing them onto the ark, is now viewed by many fundamentalists as a call to protect endangered species. An ecotheological focus underlies the multidenominational National Religious Partnership for the Environment, which includes many evangelical Protestant members. The hope is to mobilize the Christian Right against wanton environmental destruction in the same way that they oppose abortion.

Ecofeminists have also entered this debate. They point out that the rise of the all-powerful male sky-deity of Semitic monotheism came at the expense of earth goddesses of fertility and sustainability. Because the Judeo-Christian tradition elevated a sky-god remote from the Earth, the harmonious relationship between people and the habitat, male and female, was disrupted. Teleology was the inevitable result of the banishing of the Corn Mothers and all other female deities (refer again to Focus On: "When Jesus Came, the Corn Mothers Went Away"). The ancient holiness of ecosystems perished, endangering huge ecoregions. The **Gaia hypothesis** possesses an ecofeminist spirit, wherein the

Earth is seen as a mother figure that is able to react to humankind's environmental depredations through a variety of self-regulating mechanisms.

The idea of a link between godliness and Greenness has now spread worldwide. In the years following a conference in Italy in the mid-1980s—which brought together Greens and religious leaders representing Christianity, Islam, Judaism, Hinduism, and Buddhism—some 130,000 projects have arisen linking the Green teachings some see as inherent in these faiths to the ecology movement. For example, in Russia, the Orthodox Church is working to create wildlife preserves on monastery lands. The Patriarch of Constantinople, leader of Eastern Orthodox Christianity, has made the fight against pollution a church policy, and the Church of England has declared that abuse of nature is blasphemous. In Asia, a Buddhist Protection of Nature project emphasizes the teachings of that faith about nature. Leaders of nine major religions also met in 1995 to discuss environmental concerns, and in that same year the Eastern Orthodox Church announced that damaging the natural habitat constituted a sin against God. The Green teachings of long-dead saints such as Christianity's St. Francis of Assisi, who treasured birds and other wildlife, now receive heightened attention.

 Cultural Interaction in Religion

How does religion impact other aspects of culture? Can nonreligious elements within a culture help shape a faith?

Just as the interaction between religious belief and the environment can shape both religions and the land, religious faith is similarly intertwined with other aspects of culture. Spatial variations in religious belief influence and are influenced by social, economic, demographic, and political patterns in countless ways.

Religion and the Economy

In the economic sphere, religion can guide commerce, determine which crops and livestock are raised by farmers and what foods and beverages people consume, and even help decide which types of employment people engage in and in what neighborhood they reside (see Focus On: Sacred Cows). Every known religion expresses itself in food choices, to one degree or another. In some faiths, certain plants and livestock, as well as the products derived from them, are in great demand because of their roles in religious ceremonies and traditions. When this is the case, the plants or animals tend to spread with the faith.

For example, in some Christian sects in Europe and the United States, celebrants drink from a cup of wine that symbolizes the blood of Christ during the sacrament of Holy Communion. The demand for wine created by this ritual aided the diffusion of grape growing from the sunny lands of the Mediterranean to newly Christianized districts beyond the Alps in late Roman and early medieval times. The vineyards of the German Rhine were the creation of monks who arrived from the south between the sixth and ninth centuries. For the same reason, Catholic missionaries introduced the cultivated grape to California. In fact, wine was as-

FOCUS ON

Sacred Cows

Though only one out of every three of India's Hindus practices vegetarianism, most of India's Hindu population will not eat beef, and many will not use leather. Why, in a populous country such as India where many people are poor and where food shortages have plagued regions of the country in previous decades, do people refuse to consume beef? There are several quite legitimate reasons. First, the dairy products provided by cow's milk and its by-products, such as yogurt and *ghee* (clarified butter), are central to many regional Indian cuisines. If the cow is slaughtered it will no longer be able to provide milk. Second, in areas of the world that rely heavily on local agriculture for food production, such as India, cows provide valuable agricultural labor in tilling fields. Cows also provide free fertilizer in the form of dung. Finally, the value of the cow has been incorporated into

Indian Hindu beliefs and practices over many centuries and has become a part of culture. Krishna, an incarnation of the major Hindu deity Vishnu, is said to be both the herder and the protector of cows. Nandi, who is the deity Shiva's attendant, is represented as a bull.

Think for a moment about what you consider appropriate to eat. Perhaps beef is part of your diet, but would you eat horse meat? What is so different about a cow and a horse? Has the "mad cow" scare affected your consumption of beef? How about dog or cat meat? What makes certain animals pets in some cultures and dinner in others? Through this sort of questioning, you may come to realize that practices that seem second nature—like what you will and will not eat—are in fact the result of long histories that look very different from place to place.

sociated with religious worship even before Christianity arose. Vineyard keeping and wine making spread westward across the Mediterranean lands in ancient times in association with worship of the god Dionysus.

Religion also can often explain the absence of individual crops or domestic animals in an area. The environmentally similar lands of Spain and Morocco, separated only by the Strait of Gibraltar, show the agricultural impact of food taboos. On the Spanish, Roman Catholic side of the strait, pigs are common and pork a delicacy, but in Muslim Morocco on the African side, only about 12,000 swine can be found throughout the entire country. Muslims' avoidance of pork explains this contrast. Figure 3.23 maps the pork taboo. Judaism also imposes restrictions against pork and other meats, as is stated in the following passage from the Book of Leviticus:

These shall ye not eat, of them that chew the cud, or of them that divide the hoof: as the camel, because he cheweth the cud, but

divideth not the hoof; he is unclean unto you. And the coney, because he cheweth the cud, but divideth not the hoof; he is unclean unto you. And the hare, because he cheweth the cud, but divideth not the hoof; he is unclean unto you. And the swine, though he divide the hoof, and be cloven-footed, yet he cheweth not the cud; he is unclean unto you.

Scholars explain the Islamic and Judaic pork taboos in various ways. Some suggest that these two cultures were primarily concerned with the danger of parasites (which cause trichinosis) or that they considered pigs unclean. Others have suggested a theory based on economics and ecology, after observing that pork avoidance is characteristic of the monotheistic faiths that arose among desert nomads. The proponents of this view believe that nomadic herding originated on the borders of the great farming areas of the ancient Middle East, near the Tigris, Euphrates, Nile, and other rivers. Population pressures forced people to settle farther and farther from the riverbanks, so that eventually

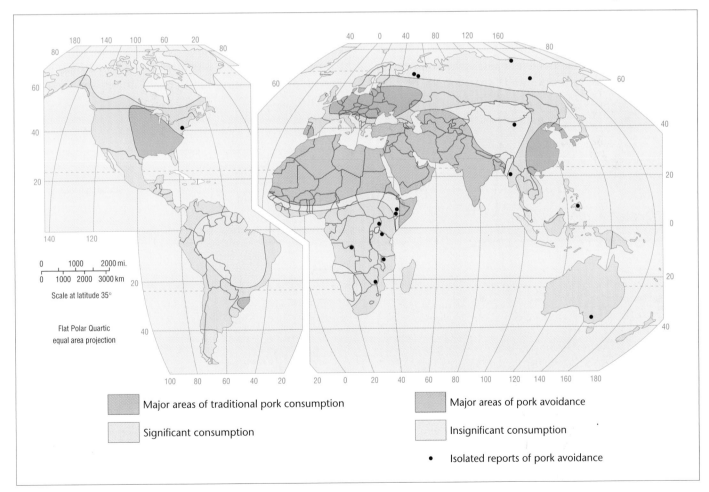

Figure 3.23 Consumption and avoidance of pork are influenced by religion. Some religions and churches—such as Islam, Judaism, and Seventh-Day Adventism—prohibit the eating of pork. Cultural groups with a traditional fondness for pork include central Europeans, Chinese, and Polynesians. *(Based in part on Simoons, 1994.)*

some groups lost access to irrigation waters and were forced to abandon most crop farming and turn to animal husbandry. The poor quality of the range required them to wander from place to place in the desert as nomads, seeking forage for their livestock. Pigs, valuable animals to the sedentary farmers of the river valleys, require shade, are poor travelers, and can find little to eat in the desert. As a result, the nomads relied instead on sheep, goats, horses, camels, and, in some areas, cattle. Because environmental conditions prevented the nomads from owning pigs, they declared pork undesirable in a "sour grapes" reaction. In time, this declaration found religious expression as a taboo. Ages later, as a final "revenge," Muslim nomads imposed their religion, complete with the pork taboo, on the farming people of the river valleys.

Because of prohibitions in the Qur'an, Muslims are also not permitted any alcoholic beverages. The Qur'an states: "O ye who have believed, wine, games of chance, idols, and divining arrows are nothing but an infamy of Satan's handiwork. Avoid them so that ye may succeed." Christians failed to reach a consensus on this taboo. Some Christian denominations prohibit all consumption of alcohol, in the belief that it is detrimental to health, welfare, and behavior, whereas others, as described above, use wine even in religious ceremonies. In the United States, such groups as the Baptists, Mormons, and Seventh-Day Adventists prohibit

alcohol; Roman Catholics, Lutherans, and several other denominations tolerate it. The economic imprint of these different attitudes can be seen in a map of "wet" and "dry" areas in the United States. Texas provides an excellent example because it is religiously diverse and by law allows each community to decide in local elections whether alcohol may be sold or served (Figure 3.24). Almost without exception, Catholic and Lutheran counties in Texas are "wet," whereas Baptist and Methodist counties are "dry."

Religious Pilgrimage

For many religious groups, journeys to sacred places, or **pilgrimages,** play an important role in the faith (Figure 3.25). Pilgrimages are typical of both ethnic and proselytic religions. They are particularly significant to followers of Islam, Hinduism, Shintoism, and Roman Catholicism.

The sacred places vary in character. Some have been the setting for miracles; a few are the source regions of the religions or areas where the founders of the faith lived and worked; others contain holy physical features such as rivers, caves, springs, and mountain peaks; and still others are believed to house gods or are religious administrative centers where leaders of the church reside. Examples include the Arabian cities of Mecca and Medina in Islam; Rome and the French town of Lourdes in Roman Catholicism; the Indian

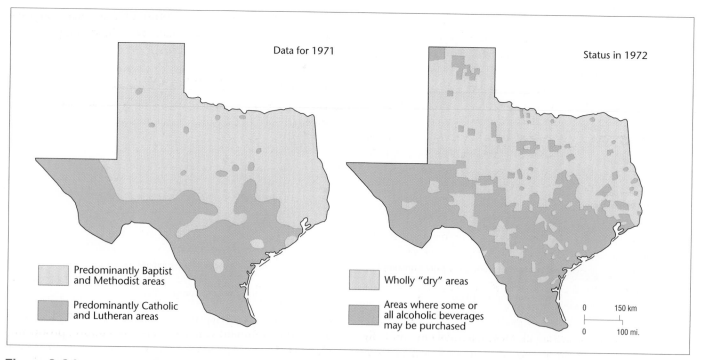

Figure 3.24 **The distribution of religion and alcohol sales in Texas.** Catholics and Lutherans generally choose to be "wet," whereas Baptists and Methodists favor prohibiting alcohol. *(Source: Jordan et al., 1984: 116, 148.)*

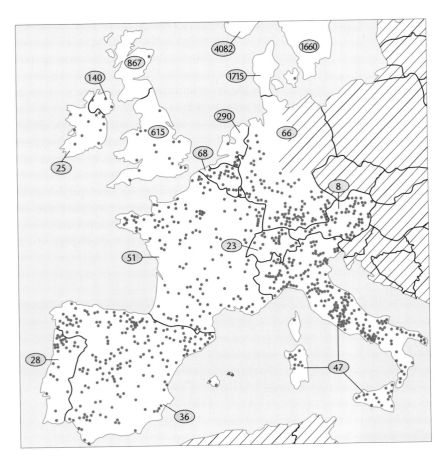

• One major pilgrimage shrine, 1990

Each circled number represents thousands
of inhabitants per religious pilgrimage
shrine (major and minor).
For example: (1660) equals 1,660,000 inhabitants.

⬚ No data

Figure 3.25 **Distribution of major
religious pilgrimage shrines in western
Europe.** These sites are most numerous
in Roman Catholic areas and in regions
of surviving religious vitality (compare
with Figure 3.13). Nineteen of these
shrines attract more than a million
pilgrims each year, massively affecting
the local economies. The numbers
indicate resident population per site by
country. *(Adapted from Nolan and Nolan,
1989: 31.)*

city of Varanasi on the holy Ganga River, a destination for
Hindu pilgrims; and Ise, the hearth of Shintoism in Japan.
Places of pilgrimage might be regarded as the *nodes* of func-
tional culture regions.

Religion provides the stimulus for pilgrimage by offering those who participate the reward of soul purification
or the attainment of some desired objective in their lives.
Pilgrims often journey great distances to visit major shrines.
Other sites, of lesser significance, draw pilgrims only from
local districts or provinces. Pilgrimages can have tremendous
economic impact because the influx of pilgrims amounts to
a form of tourism.

In some favored localities, the pilgrim trade provides
the only significant source of revenue for the community.
Lourdes, a town of about 16,000, attracts between 4 million
and 5 million pilgrims each year, many seeking miraculous
cures at the famous grotto where the Virgin Mary supposedly appeared. Not surprisingly, among French cities,
Lourdes ranks second only to Paris in number of hotels, although most of these are small. Mecca, a small city, annually
attracts hundreds of thousands of Muslim pilgrims from
every corner of the Islamic culture region. By land, by sea,
and (mainly) by air, the faithful come to this hearth of

Islam, a city closed to all non-Muslims. Such mass pilgrimages obviously have a major impact on the development of
transportation routes and carriers.

REFLECTING ON GEOGRAPHY

Does your religious faith influence the economic, social,
dietary, and political decisions you make?

 Religious Landscapes

**In what forms does religion appear in the cultural landscape?
Does the visibility of religion differ from one faith or denomination to another?** Because religion is so vital an aspect of
culture, its visible presence can be quite striking, reflecting
the role played by religious motives in the human transformation of the landscape. In some regions, the religious aspect is the dominant visible evidence of culture, producing
sacred landscapes. At the opposite extreme are areas almost
purely secular in appearance. Religions differ greatly in visibility, but even those least apparent to the eye usually leave

some subtle mark on the countryside. The content of religious landscapes is varied, ranging from houses of worship to cemeteries, wayside shrines, and place-names.

Religious Structures

The most obvious religious contributions to the landscape are the buildings erected to house divinities or to shelter worshippers. These structures vary greatly in size, function, architectural style, construction material, and degree of ornateness (Figure 3.26). To Roman Catholics, for example, the church building is literally the house of God, and the altar is the focus of key rituals. Partly for these reasons, Catholic churches are typically large, elaborately decorated,

and visually imposing. In many towns and villages, the Catholic house of worship is the focal point of the settlement, exceeding all other structures in size and grandeur. In medieval European towns, Christian cathedrals were the tallest buildings, representing the supremacy of religion over all other aspects of life.

To many Protestants—particularly the traditional Calvinistic chapel-goers of British background, including Methodists and Baptists—the church building is, by contrast, simply a place to assemble for worship. The result is an unsanctified, smaller, less ornate structure. The simpler church buildings of these Protestants appeal less to the senses and more to the personal faith. For this reason, their traditional structures are typically not designed for comfort, beauty, or high visibility,

Figure 3.26 **Traditional religious architecture takes varied forms.** St. Basil's Church on Red Square in Moscow (*upper left*) reflects a highly ornate Russian landscape presence, whereas the plain board chapel in the American South (*lower left*) demonstrates an opposite tendency favoring visual simplicity by British-derived Protestants. The ornate Hindu temple in Varanasi, India (*above*), offers still another sacred landscape. (*Source: Terry G. Jordan-Bychkov.*)

Figure 3.27 **In the Maori community of Tikitiki, on North Island, New Zealand,** a traditional Polynesian *marae,* or shrine (on the left), stands beside a Christian chapel (on the right). The religious landscape, in this odd juxtaposition, tells us much about the composite faith held by the modern Maori. *(Courtesy of Terry G. Jordan-Bychkov.)*

but instead appear deliberately humble (see Figure 3.26, bottom left). Similarly, the religious landscape of the Amish and Mennonites in rural North America, the "plain folk," is very subdued because they reject ostentation in any form. Some of their adherents meet in houses or barns, and the churches that do exist are very modest in appearance, much like those of the southern Calvinists.

Islamic mosques are usually the most imposing items in the landscape, whereas the visibility of Jewish synagogues varies greatly. Hinduism has produced large numbers of visually striking temples for its multiplicity of gods, but much worship is practiced in private households (see Figure 3.30). Houses of worship can also reveal subtler content and mes-

sages. In Polynesian Maori communities of New Zealand, for example, the *marae,* a structure linked to the pagan gods of the past, generally stands alongside the Christian chapel, which reflects the Maoris' conversion (Figure 3.27). The landscape thus reflects the blending of two faiths.

Nature religions such as animism generally place only a subtle mark on the landscape. Nature itself is sacred, and few shrines are needed. There are, not surprisingly, exceptions. In Korea, for example, where animism merged with Buddhism and the Chinese composite religion, animistic shrines survive in the landscape (Figure 3.28).

Paralleling this contrast in church styles are attitudes toward wayside shrines and similar manifestations of faith.

Figure 3.28 **Stacked stones at a pilgrimage site in South Korea,** perpetuating an ancient animistic/shamanistic practice. These stones had meaning in ancient times, a meaning since lost. *(Courtesy of Terry G. Jordan-Bychkov.)*

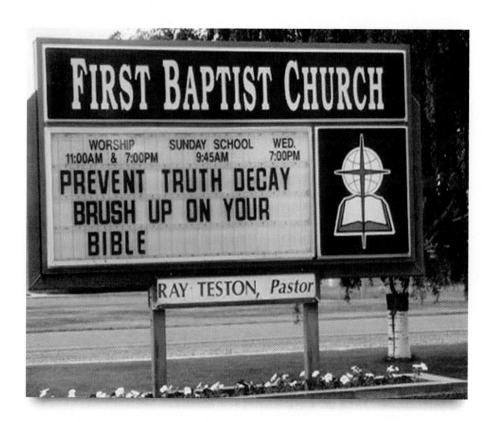

Figure 3.29 **Billboard in Three Forks, Montana.** Protestant billboards often use American-style advertising slogans to promote church attendance. *(Nancy H. Belcher.)*

Catholic culture regions typically abound with shrines, crucifixes, crosses, and other visual reminders of religion, as do some Eastern Orthodox Christian areas. Protestant areas, by contrast, are bare of such symbolism. Their landscapes, instead, display such features as signboards advising the traveler to "Get Right with God," a common sight in the southern United States (Figure 3.29).

The distinction between sacred and profane in the cultural landscape is not always easy for the outsider to discern. Along the Ganga River in Varanasi, India, steps—or *ghats*—lead down to the stream at many places (see Figure 3.19). To the uninitiated, these may seem intended for the convenience of fishers, swimmers, and people doing laundry. The more important role of the ghats, however, is to facilitate ritual bathing in the holy Ganga—the main goal of pilgrims coming to the city. Also, the ghats provide a place for funeral pyres in the cremation of the dead.

Landscapes of the Dead

Religions differ greatly in the type of tribute they award to the dead. This variation appears in the cultural landscape. The few remaining Zoroastrians, called Parsees, who preserve a once-widespread Middle Eastern faith now confined to parts of India, have traditionally left their dead exposed to be devoured by vultures. Thus, the Parsee dead leave no permanent mark on the landscape. Hindus cremate their

dead. Having no cemeteries, their dead, as with the Parsees, leave no obvious mark on the land. Yet on the island of Bali in Indonesia, Hinduism, animism, and reverence for ancestors exist in a syncretic blend. Temples to the family's ancestors occupy prominent places outside the houses of Balinese (Figure 3.30).

In Egypt, on the other hand, spectacular pyramids and other tombs were built to house dead leaders. These monuments, as well as the modern graves and tombs of the rural Islamic folk of Egypt, lie on desert land not suitable for farming (Figure 3.31). Muslim cemeteries are usually modest in appearance, but spectacular tombs are sometimes erected for aristocratic persons, giving us such sacred structures as the Taj Mahal in India (Figure 3.32), one of the architectural wonders of the world.

Chinese who practice their composite religion typically bury their dead, setting aside land for that purpose and erecting monuments to their deceased kin. In parts of pre-Communist China, as much as 10 percent of the land in some districts was covered by cemeteries and ancestral shrines, greatly reducing the acreage available for agriculture.

Christians also typically bury their dead in sacred places set aside for that purpose. These vary significantly from one Christian denomination to another. Some graveyards, particularly those of Mennonites and southern Calvinists, are very modest in appearance, reflecting the reluctance of these groups to use any symbolism that might be construed as idol-

Figure 3.30 **Temples dedicated to ancestors in Bali, Indonesia.** Bali's population practices a blend of Hinduism, animism, and ancestor worship. These temples to ancestors are a feature of every Balinese home, and offerings of incense, food, and flowers are made three times per day to show reverence. *(Courtesy of Ari Dorfsman.)*

atrous. Among certain other Christian groups, cemeteries are places of color and elaborate decoration (Figure 3.33).

Cemeteries often preserve truly ancient cultural traits, for people as a rule are reluctant to change their practices relating to the dead. The traditional rural cemetery of the southern United States provides a case in point. Fresh-water mussel shells are placed atop many of the elongated grave mounds, and rose bushes and cedars are planted throughout the cemetery. Recent research suggests that the use of roses may derive from the worship of an ancient, pre-Christian mother goddess of the Mediterranean lands. The rose was a symbol of this great goddess, who could

Figure 3.31 **Landscape of the dead, landscape of the living.** The Beni Hassan Islamic necropolis in central Egypt lies in the desert, just beyond the irrigable land, while the living make intensive use of every parcel watered by the Nile River. The mud brick structures are all tombs. Thus, the doubly dead landscape is sacred, whereas the realm of living plants and people is profane. *(Courtesy of Terry G. Jordan-Bychkov.)*

Figure 3.32 **The Taj Mahal in Agra, India.** Built as a Muslim tomb, it is perhaps the most impressive religious structure in the world. *(Pallava Bagla/Corbis.)*

restore life to the dead. Similarly, the cedar evergreen is an age-old pagan symbol of death and eternal life, and the use of shell decoration derives from an animistic custom in West Africa, the geographic origin of slaves in the American South. Although the present Christian population of the South is unaware of the origins of their cemetery symbolism, it seems likely that their landscape of the dead contains animistic elements thousands of years old, revealing truly ancient beliefs and cultural diffusions.

Religious Names on the Land

"St.-Jean," "St.-Aubert," "St.-Damase-des-Aulnaies," "Ste. Perpétue de L'Islet," "St.-Pamphile," "St.-Adalbert"—so read

Figure 3.33 **Two different Christian landscapes of the dead.** In the Yucatán Peninsula of Mexico, the dead rest in colorful, aboveground crypts, whereas in Amana, Iowa, communalistic

Germans prefer tidiness, order, and equality. *(Left: Macduff Everton/Corbis; Right: Courtesy of Terry G. Jordan-Bychkov.)*

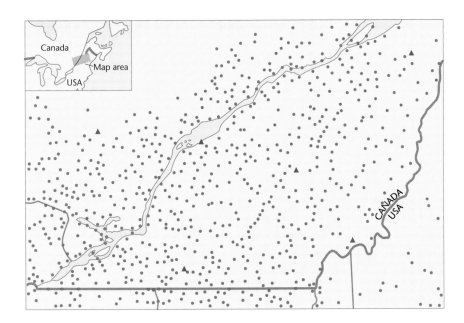

Names beginning with Notre Dame

Names beginning with Saint or Sainte

Other names

Figure 3.34 **Religious place-names dot the map of French Canada.** In the French-Canadian province of Québec, the dominant Roman Catholic religion finds an expression in the names given to towns and villages. Saints' names are dominant in the areas of purest French settlement. Nearer the U.S.-Canadian border, in townships settled by English-speaking people, religious place-names are rare.

the placards of town names as one drives from the St. Lawrence River south in Québec, paralleling the Maine border. All this saintliness has become a part of the French-Canadian landscape, demonstrating how religion often inspires the names that people place on the land (Figure 3.34). Within Christianity, the use of saints' names for settlements is very common in Roman Catholic and Greek Orthodox areas, especially in overseas colonial lands settled by Catholics, such as Latin America and French Canada. In areas of the Old World that were settled long before the advent of Christianity, saints' names were often grafted onto pre-Christian names, as in Alcazar de San Juan, in Spain, which combines Arabic and Christian elements.

REFLECTING ON GEOGRAPHY

What is the most visible element of the religious landscape where you live?

Toponyms in Protestant regions display less religious influence, but some imprint can usually be found. In the southern United States, for example, the word *chapel* as a part of the name, as in Chapel Hill and Ward's Chapel, is very common in the names of rural hamlets. Such names accurately convey the image of the humble, rural Protestant churches that are so common in the South.

Sacred Space

Sacred spaces consist of natural and/or human-made sites that possess special religious meaning, recognized as worthy of devotion, loyalty, fear, or esteem. By virtue of their sacred-

ness, these special places might be avoided by the faithful, sought out by pilgrims, or barred to members of other religions. Often sacred space includes the site of supposed supernatural events or is viewed as the abode of gods. Conflict can result if two religions venerate the same space (see Focus On: Conflict over Sacred Space). In Jerusalem, for example, the Muslim Dome of the Rock, on the site where Muhammad is believed to have ascended to heaven, stands above the Western Wall, the remnant of the ancient Jewish temple (Figure 3.35). Cemeteries are also generally regarded as a type of sacred space. So is Mount Sinai, described by geographer Joseph Hobbs as endowed "with special grace," where God instructed the Hebrews to "mark out the limits of the mountain and declare it sacred."

In his 1957 book *The Sacred and the Profane*, the renowned religious historian Mircea Eliade suggested that all societies, past and present, have sacred spaces. According to Eliade, sacred spaces are so important because they establish a geographic center on which society can be anchored. Through what he termed *hierophany*, a sacred space emerges from the profane, ordinary spaces surrounding it. A contemporary example of hierophany is provided by the appearance of an image of the Virgin of Guadalupe on a bank building in Clearwater, Florida, transforming the profane space of finance into a Catholic pilgrimage site (see Focus On: Our Lady of Clearwater). (For more information on another type of sacred space—sites originally marked by tragedy and violence—see Practicing Geography on page 104.)

Sacred space is receiving increased attention in the world. In the mid-1990s, the internationally funded Sacred Land Project began to identify and protect such sites, 5000 of which have been cataloged in the United Kingdom

FOCUS ON

Conflict over Sacred Space

When two or more religions claim the same sacred space, conflict is usually unavoidable. In 1992, in the town of Ayodhya in the state of Uttar Pradesh near the Nepal border in northern India, Hindus seized an Islamic mosque and destroyed it. They tore down the 450-year-old mosque in hopes of replacing it with a Hindu temple, claiming that the site is the precise birthplace of the pious god-king Rama, the "perfect Hindu" and protagonist of the epic tale *Ramayana*. Rama, whose very name became a synonym for the divine, is believed to have been an incarnation of the great god Vishnu, the most important solar deity, a preserver and restorer. To

Muslims, the destruction of the mosque was an affront to Allah that demanded retribution. Widespread religious rioting and violence plagued the country because of this desecration and conflict over sacred space, causing 2000 deaths. On the fifth anniversary of the mosque's destruction, bombs placed on trains by Muslim terrorists exploded in several parts of India, killing or injuring scores of people, and in December 2000, another 2000 people died in riots there. In March 2002, the Supreme Court of India forbade Hindu activists to perform ceremonies on the site and upheld a ban on building a new Hindu temple here.

alone. Included are such places as ancient stone circles, pilgrim routes, holy springs, and sites that convey mystery or great natural beauty. This last type falls into the category of *mystical places:* locations unconnected with established religion where, for whatever reason, some people believe that extraordinary, supernatural things can happen. The Bermuda Triangle in the western Atlantic, where airplanes and ships supposedly disappear, is a mystical place and, in

effect, a vernacular culture region. Some people find the expanses of the American Great Plains to be a mystical place, and writer Jonathan Raban spoke of them as "a landscape ideally suited to the staging of the millennium, open to the gaze of the Almighty." Sometimes the sacred space of vanished ancient religions never loses—or later regains—the functional status of mystical place, which has happened at Stonehenge in England.

Conclusion

Religion is firmly interwoven in the fabric of culture, a bright hue in the human mosaic, for religions vary greatly from one area to another, a regional diversity so profound as to give special significance to James Griffith's admonition that we should all "learn, respect, and walk softly." This religious spatial variation leads us to ask how these distributions came to be, a question best answered through the methods of cultural diffusion. Some religions, proselytic denominations, actively encourage their own diffusion. Other religions erect barriers to expansion diffusion by restricting membership to one particular ethnic group.

The theme of cultural ecology reveals some fundamental ties between religion and the physical environment. One

Figure 3.35 **Conflict over sacred space.** Jews pray at the Western Wall, the remnant of their great ancient temple in Jerusalem, in Israel. Standing above the wall, on the site of the vanished Jewish temple, is one of the holiest sites for Muslims—the golden-capped mosque called the Dome of the Rock, covering the place from which the Prophet Muhammad is believed to have ascended to heaven. Perhaps no other place on Earth is so heavily charged with religious meaning and conflict. *(Gary Cralle/Gettyone.)*

Our Lady of Clearwater

This 60-foot image appeared in December 1996 in the window of a bank building in Clearwater, Florida. A woman leaving the bank noticed that this iridescent image bore a striking resemblance to the Virgin of Guadalupe. Though some claim that the image is merely a coincidence caused by a sprinkler system, others believe this to be a miracle. The bank's parking lot quickly became a pilgrimage site, and Catholics from around the world gathered to behold the image. It is estimated that by the end of the 1996 holiday season, more than 400,000 people had visited the image. Rita Ring, an Ohio-based homemaker and visionary, claimed to have received a message from God that the image would appear. The Shepherds of Christ Ministries that Ring is associated with purchased the bank building in 2000. Mass is held daily at 6:21 P.M. in the parking lot.

Was this image a sign from God that the finance-driven world of the United States has forgotten about religion? Many believe so. Did the apparition's form as the Virgin of Guadalupe, a Mexican image, have anything to do with the large influx of Mexican immigrants to the Clearwater area in the 1990s?

In 2004, two of the glass panels were broken out. The news of the vandalism sent waves of shock and disbelief through the large community of devotees. An 18-year-old high school senior was charged with vandalizing the building by using a slingshot to fire ball bearings at the windows. The glass shards had to be hidden because so many people tried to take them as holy relics. The Shepherds of Christ plan to replace the broken panes with clear instead of mirrored glass.

(Courtesy of Patricia L. Price.)

major function of many religious systems, particularly the animistic faiths, is to appease and placate the forces of nature and to achieve harmony between humans and the physical environment. Religions differ in their outlook on environmental modification by humans. Religion is systemically related to politics and the economy, among other things. Everything from tourism to nationalism can have a religious component, reflecting the theme of cultural interaction.

The cultural landscape abounds with expressions of religious belief. Places of worship—temples, churches, and shrines—differ in appearance, distinctiveness, prominence, and frequency of occurrence from one religious culture region to another. These buildings provide a visual index to the various faiths. Cemeteries, religious place-names, and sacred spaces also add a special effect to the landscape that tells us about the religious character of the population. In all these ways, and more, the five themes of cultural geography prove relevant to the study of the world's religions.

The Making of Sacred Spaces

For this exercise, you will use Professor Foote's ideas about how spaces become sacred. In his book *Shadowed Ground: America's Landscapes of Violence and Tragedy,* Professor Foote argues that what a society chooses to forget about its past is at least as important as what it remembers in shaping an image of itself that it can present to the world. Professor Foote discusses how certain places in the United States have, or have not, become sacred sites. He notes, for example, that the battlefields of the Revolutionary and Civil Wars are well marked and visited by thousands every year. Yet the 1692 execution site of the supposed witches of Salem, Massachusetts, is unmarked. How could the exact site of such an infamous event in U.S. history be impossible to locate? Professor Foote realized that this was not limited to the United States, writing,

Kenneth Foote

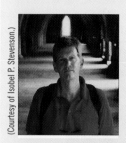

(Courtesy of Isobel P. Stevenson.)

Kenneth Foote came to geography the way many people do: he simply found it more interesting than anything else he'd studied before. He began college knowing he was interested in cities and thought he would become an architect or an urban planner.

However, at the University of Wisconsin, where he went to school, most of the classes on cities were offered by the geography department. Professor Foote says, "I soon found geography—particularly landscape studies and cultural and historical geography—more interesting than urban planning."

For the past decade, Professor Foote has focused on places and what happens to them in the aftermath of violent or tragic events. He has studied the sites of the Oklahoma City bombing and September 11, 2001, terrorist attacks in New York City, among others. "For me the question is why some of these places are transformed into powerful and evocative monuments while others disappear, or are actually effaced, from view entirely." His book *Shadowed Ground* (see Doing Geography at the end of the chapter) focuses on the United States, while his recent work concentrates on Europe. "Once I began to focus on the transformative effect of violence on people and place," he writes, "I realized there were many ways I could extend my work. For me, a good research question almost always suggests another and another and another." His current research looks at the very different ways in which European countries have interpreted places associated with the First and Second World Wars; the Holocaust; civil wars; and events of social, political, and economic violence in the twentieth and twenty-first centuries. Over the last few years he has become very interested in how national shrines and memorials are created, managed, and sometimes manipulated by certain groups. "I am becoming more and more interested in the way that the legacies of the Cold War will be remembered and commemorated throughout Europe."

Detailed case studies of places and events form the building blocks of Professor Foote's research. He uses photographs and maps to document what has happened at a place. He supplements this visual evidence by interviewing people about what happened as well as by searching through newspapers and other written documents to see what the written record says happened. Fieldwork—actually going to the place in question and consulting human, visual, and written sources in those places—is usually at the heart of how cultural geographers do their work, and Professor Foote is no exception. Because he enjoys traveling, meeting new people, and visiting libraries and archives, Professor Foote enjoys research more than any other part of his job. "I love to be on the road investigating interesting places, talking with people, or trying to locate good sources of local history. I try to be on the road at least one month a year, sometimes more."

"Indeed, soon after my first trip to Salem, I found myself in Berlin before the reunification of Germany. There I came across similar places—Nazi sites like the Gestapo headquarters and Reich chancellery—that have lain vacant since just after World War II and seem to be scarred permanently by shame" (p. 3).

Professor Foote suggests that sites of important events can be sanctified, obliterated, or fall somewhere in between. Sanctified sites are set apart from other sites, are carefully maintained, are often publicly owned, and attract annual visitors and ceremonies. On the other end of the spectrum, the sites of particularly shameful, stigmatized, or violent events may simply be obliterated from the landscape in an attempt to forget about them. When people are unsure of how an event fits into their history, the site where the event occurred may inhabit a sort of limbo, remaining unmarked until the society in question comes to terms with the event. This is the case with many sites of racially motivated violent or shameful acts in the United States, such as the Memphis, Tennessee, motel where Martin Luther King Jr. was assassinated in 1968 or the Manzanar, California, internment camp where Japanese-Americans were confined during World War II. Only recently have both sites become more prominently marked on the landscape after decades of neglect.

Think about a site in the place where you now live where a violent or tragic event occurred: a murder, a freak accident, a natural disaster, an assassination, an act of terrorism, a heinous crime. All places experience such events. If nothing comes readily to mind, inquire and inevitably you will come across them, even if you live in a rural area or a college town. Once you have identified a site, consider what status it now has. Is it sanctified, is it obliterated, or does it fall somewhere in between? Has the status of this site changed over time? How? What sort of debate, if any, occurred about what to do with this site? What sorts of signs, markers, and monuments exist in the landscape that tell you that the event occurred there? Does the site you're examining have a religious significance, or did it in the past? If not, can you connect the processes at work to set your site apart as special to similar processes that act to make some places holier than others in a religious sense?

Geography of Religion on the Internet

You can learn more about the geography of religion on the Internet at the following web sites:

American Religious Identification Survey 2001
http://www.gc.cuny.edu/faculty/research_studies/aris.pdf
This work by Barry A. Kosmin, Egon Mayer, and Ariela Keysar of the Graduate Center of the City University of New York contains the latest data on religious affiliations in the United States.

Glenmary Research Center
www.glenmary.org
Among other activities, the center conducts a census of religious denominations in the United States every 10 years; the 2000 census, listing membership by county, appeared late in 2001.

Global Mapping International
http://www.adherents.com/
This web site contains statistics on religious adherence worldwide.

Material History of American Religion Project, New York, N.Y.
www.materialreligion.org
Based at Columbia University, this site has information about religious material objects, including religious landscapes, in the United States.

World Council of Churches
www.wcc-coe.org
An interdenominational group, headquartered in Geneva, Switzerland, the World Council of Churches works for greater cooperation and understanding among different faiths.

Sources

Bradley, Martin B., et al. 1992. *Churches and Church Membership in the United States*. Atlanta: Glenmary Research Center.

Curran, Claude W. 1991. "Mt. Shasta, California, and the I Am Religion," in *Abstracts, The Association of American Geographers 1991 Annual Meeting, April 13–17, Miami, Florida*. Washington, D.C.: Association of American Geographers, 42.

Curry-Roper, Janel M. 1990. "Contemporary Christian Eschatologies and Their Relation to Environmental Stewardship." *Professional Geographer* 42: 157–169.

Doughty, Robin W. 1981. "Environmental Theology: Trends and Prospects in Christian Thought." *Progress in Human Geography* 5: 234–248.

The Economist. "Survey: Lebanon." February 24, 1996.

Eliade, Mircea. 1987 [1957]. *The Sacred and the Profane: The Nature of Religion*. Willard R. Trask (trans.). San Diego: Harcourt, Inc.

Foote, Kenneth E. 1997. *Shadowed Ground: America's Landscapes of Violence and Tragedy*. Austin: University of Texas Press.

Government of Canada. 1974. *The National Atlas of Canada*, 4th ed. Ottawa: Government of Canada, Surveys and Mapping Branch.

Griffith, James S. 1992. *Beliefs and Holy Places: A Spiritual Geography of the Pimería Alta*. Tucson: University of Arizona Press.

Gutiérrez, Ramón A. 1991. *When Jesus Came, the Corn Mothers Went Away*. Stanford, Calif.: Stanford University Press.

Hobbs, Joseph J. 1995. *Mount Sinai*. Austin: University of Texas Press.

Hsu, Shin-Yi. 1969. "The Cultural Ecology of the Locust Cult in Traditional China." *Annals of the Association of American Geographers* 59: 734, 745.

Huntsinger, Lynn, and María Fernández-Giménez. 2000. "Spiritual Pilgrims at Mount Shasta, California." *Geographical Review* 90: 536–558.

Johnstone, Patrick. 1986. *Operation World*, 4th ed. N.p.: S. T. L. Books.

Jordan, Terry G., et al. 1984. *Texas: A Geography*. Boulder, Colo.: Westview Press.

Jordan-Bychkov, Terry G., and Bella Bychkova Jordan. 2002. *The European Culture Area: A Systematic Geography*, 4th ed. Lanham, Md.: Rowman & Littlefield.

Lodrick, Deryck O. 1981. *Sacred Cows, Sacred Places: Origins and Survivals of Animal Homes in India*. Berkeley: University of California Press.

Nolan, Mary Lee, and Sidney Nolan. 1989. *Christian Pilgrimage in Modern Western Europe*. Chapel Hill: University of North Carolina Press.

Raban, Jonathan. 1996. *Bad Land: An American Romance*. New York: Pantheon Books.

Semple, Ellen Churchill. 1911. *Influences of Geographical Environment*. New York: Henry Holt.

Simoons, Frederick J. 1994. *Eat Not This Flesh: Food Avoidances in the Old World*, 2nd ed. Madison: University of Wisconsin Press.

Singh, Rana P. B. 1994. "Water Symbolism and Sacred Landscape in Hinduism." *Erdkunde* 48: 210–227.

Stewart, Dona J. 1996. "Economic Recovery and Reconstruction in Postwar Beirut." *Geographical Review* 86: 489–492.

Stump, Roger W. (ed.). 1986. "The Geography of Religion." Special issue, *Journal of Cultural Geography* 7: 1–140.

Tuan, Yi-Fu. 1968. "Discrepancies Between Environmental Attitude and Behavior: Examples from Europe and China." *Canadian Geographer* 12: 176–191.

White, Lynn, Jr. 1967. "The Historical Roots of Our Ecologic Crisis." *Science* 155: 1203–1207.

Ten Recommended Books
on the Geography of Religion

For additional suggested readings, see *The Human Mosaic* web site: www.whfreeman.com/jordan)

Al-Faruqi, Isma'il R., and David E. Sopher. 1974. *Historical Atlas of the Religions of the World*. New York: Macmillan. Pretty much what its title promises, this informative atlas allows you to see cultural diffusion in action over the centuries and millennia.

SEEING GEOGRAPHY

How can an ordinary landscape, such as a parking lot, become sacred space?

Parking lot shrine to the Virgin of Guadalupe, Self-Help Graphics and Art, East Los Angeles.

Parking Lot Shrine

This large statue of the Virgin of Guadalupe inhabits the corner of the parking lot of Self-Help Graphics and Art, an artists' cooperative in East Los Angeles. According to Michael Amezcua, neighborhood residents actively use this shrine, leaving offerings and petitions to the Virgin in this outdoor grotto. Every December 12, neighborhood residents gather here to celebrate the feast day of the Virgin of Guadalupe.

We could interpret this unique parking lot shrine to be a variation on the yard shrine, a common feature of the residential landscape of the southwestern United States. Throughout the Mexican-American homeland region of the Southwest, it is common to see a small shrine to the Virgin of Guadalupe in people's front yards. This, in turn, is a variation on the Mexican custom of maintaining elaborate shrines and altars to important religious figures. These are sometimes located inside the house in a space reserved especially for altars (called a *nicho*). Or they can be located outside the house, near the front door, as Mexican homes usually do not have a yard space in front of the house. On December 12, altars all over Mexico and Mexican-American areas in the United States are elaborately decorated with candles, ribbons, and flowers. Devotees of the Virgin of Guadalupe celebrate with family and neighbors throughout the night. Since turquoise blue is considered to be the favorite color of the Virgin of Guadalupe, this color abounds. Because the Virgin of Guadalupe is also the official patron saint of Mexico, the red, white, and green of the Mexican flag is also prevalent in altar decorations.

In Miami, another Latino population center in the United States, yard shrines are built to La Virgen de la Caridad de Cobre. Like the Virgin of Guadalupe, La Virgen de la Caridad is an American manifestation of the Virgin Mary. This Virgin hails from the copper mining village of Cobre, in Cuba. She is thought to protect seafarers and has been adopted by Cuban rafters as their patron saint. Yemayá, who is an *orisha*, or spirit, in the Afrocentric Cuban religious tradition of Santería, is often equated with La Virgen de la Caridad de Cobre, as both are associated with the sea.

What does the fact that this particular shrine is built in a parking lot rather than a yard say about what, and how, spaces become sacred? Can you think of a more mundane place than a parking lot for such a hallowed figure as the Virgin of Guadalupe? Perhaps the drive-through architecture of strip malls, highways, and parking lots that is so closely associated with the urban landscape of Los Angeles has something to do with it. Where else, other than in Los Angeles, can you find a sacred parking lot? ■

Gottlieb, Roger S. (ed.). 1995. *This Sacred Earth: Religion, Nature and Environment*. London: Routledge. A good introduction to ecotheology.

Halvorson, Peter L., and William M. Newman. 1994. *Atlas of Religious Change in America, 1952–1990*. Atlanta: Glenmary Research Center. This atlas shows the changing pattern of denominational membership in the United States in the last half of the twentieth century, revealing the strengthening of some religions and the weakening of others.

Harpur, James. 1994. *The Atlas of Sacred Places*. New York: Henry Holt. This volume is a useful depiction of the location of sacred places, or "sacred space," as we labeled it; you will be amazed by their number and diversity.

Jordan, Terry G. 1982. *Texas Graveyards: A Cultural Legacy*. Austin: University of Texas Press. The only book by a geographer on this aspect of the religious landscape, this volume is very revealing about a state possessing a wide array of ethnic groups.

Park, Chris. 1994. *Sacred Worlds: An Introduction to Geography and Religion*. London: Routledge. An introductory text on the geography of religion.

Pui-lan, Kwok (ed.). 1994. *Ecotheology: Voices from South and North*. New York: World Council of Churches Publications. A very readable sampling of recent ecotheological thought.

Sopher, David E. 1967. *The Geography of Religions*. Englewood Cliffs, N.J.: Prentice-Hall. The first introduction to the geography of religion to appear in English, it remains a classic.

Stoddard, Robert H., and Alan Morinis (eds.). 1997. *Sacred Places, Sacred Spaces: The Geography of Pilgrimages*. Baton Rouge: Geoscience Publications. Published by the Department of Geography and Anthropology at Louisiana State University, these 14 essays, each by a different author, draw attention to Christian, Muslim, Hindu, and lesser Asian pilgrimage traditions, as seen from the perspective of cultural geography.

Stump, Roger W. 2000. *Boundaries of Faith: Geographical Perspectives on Religious Fundamentalism*. Lanham, Md.: Rowman & Littlefield. After describing the background of fundamentalist movements within various world religions occurring in several countries, the author explains commonalities and clarifies political implications. One of the first examinations of the spatial strategies inherent in fundamentalism.

Aquí se habla Spanglish. What does this sign tell you about who uses the commercial space in this city?

Spanglish gas station sign in New York City. *(The Photo Works.)*

Turn to Seeing Geography on page 140 for an in-depth analysis of this scene.

SPEAKING 4 ABOUT PLACES
The Geography of Language

LANGUAGE IS ONE OF THE PRIMARY features that distinguishes humans from other animals. Many animals, including dolphins, whales, and birds, do indeed communicate with one another through patterned systems of sounds, scents and other chemicals, or movements. Furthermore, some nonhuman primates have been taught to use sign language to communicate with humans. However, the complexity of human language, its ability to convey nuanced emotions and ideas, and its importance for our existence as social animals set it apart from the communication systems used by other animals (see Focus On: Translating Animal Sounds). In many ways, language is the essence of culture. It provides the single most common variable by which different cultural groups are identified and by which groups assert their unique identity. Language not only facilitates the cultural diffusion of innovations, it also helps to shape the way we think about, perceive, and name our environment. A mutually agreed-upon system of symbolic communication, **language** offers the main means by which learned belief systems, customs, and skills pass from one generation to the next.

One of our first and most long-lasting ties to place is forged through language. The ability to name, or rename, a place is a key step in claiming a place as one's own, as shown, for example, by Figure 4.1, a political map of Antarctica. Notice how the claims of various nations are represented by straight lines drawn on the land. Notice, too, how many places are named after Antarctic explorers and monarchs of countries that claim portions of the continent: the Ross Sea and Ross Ice Shelf are named after James Clark Ross, the English explorer who charted much of Antarctica's coastline, while Queen Maud Land is named after Norway's Queen Maud. Interestingly, Roald Amundsen, the Norwegian explorer who gave Queen Maud Land its name in 1939, took part in an earlier trip that highlights the importance of language. In 1898 Amundsen was part of an ill-fated expedition to locate the magnetic south pole when

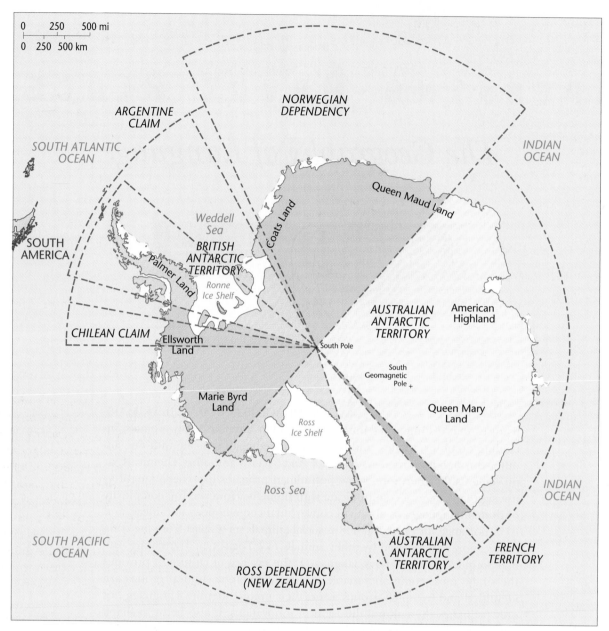

Figure 4.1 Naming place is closely related to claiming place.
This map shows the pie-shaped land claims of various nations.
Notice how place-names reflect the names of Antarctic
explorers or political rulers on the political map of this
continent. *(Adapted from Latrimer Clarke Corporation Pty Ltd.)*

his ship became stuck in the ice for more than one year. Several of Amundsen's shipmates, which included men from Poland, Romania, Norway, the United States, and Belgium, went insane. This was not just due to the long winter nights and the cold weather. In great part, language differences among the men became their biggest problem. They simply could not understand one another!

For all these reasons and more, cultural geographers study language. Most cultural groups have their own distinctive form of speech, either a separate language or a dialect. Because languages vary spatially and tend to form spatial groupings, they reinforce the sense of region and place through the linguistic *culture regions* they form. Different types of *cultural diffusion* have helped shape the contemporary linguistic map. Clearly, the specific physical habitats in which languages evolve shape their vocabularies. Moreover, the environment can guide the migrations of linguistic groups or provide refuges for languages in retreat. Thus, linguistic *ecology* is central to understanding the geography of language. Because language is so closely con-

FOCUS ON

Translating Animal Sounds

While a cat obviously sounds the same in any part of the world, the speakers of different human languages render that sound in diverse ways. The chart shows how the sounds of various animals "translate" into different human languages:

	English	Indonesian	Japanese	Greek
Dog	bow-wow	gonggong	wanwan	gav
Cat	meow	ngeong	nyaa	niaou
Bird	tweet-tweet	kicau	chunchun	tsiou tsiou
Rooster	cock-a-doodle-doo	kikeriku	kokekokkoo	ki-kiriki

This table was compiled using information from the web site "Sounds of the World's Animals," at http://www.georgetown.edu/faculty/ballc/animals/animals.html. This is a project of Dr. Catherine N. Ball in Georgetown University's Department of Linguistics. This fascinating web site has the translations of many more animal sounds into a diversity of human languages.

nected with every other aspect of culture, *cultural interaction* will be of great importance. Finally, the *cultural landscape* is literally shaped by such linguistic acts as naming, writing, and speaking.

 ## Linguistic Culture Regions

What is the geographical patterning of languages? Do the various languages provide the basis for formal and functional culture regions? The spatial variation of speech is remarkably complicated, adding intricate patterns to the human mosaic (Figure 4.2). Consequently, the logical place to begin our geographical study of language is with the theme of culture region.

Separate languages are those that cannot be mutually understood. In other words, a monolingual speaker of one language cannot comprehend the speaker of another. **Dialects,** by contrast, are variant forms of a language where mutual comprehension is possible. A speaker of English can generally understand that language's various dialects, regardless of whether the speaker comes from Australia, Scotland, or Mississippi. Nevertheless, a dialect is distinctive enough in vocabulary and pronunciation to label its speaker. About 6000 languages and many more dialects are spoken in the world today.

When different linguistic groups come into contact, a **pidgin** language, characterized by a very small vocabulary

derived from the languages of the groups in contact, often results. Pidgins primarily serve the purposes of trade and commerce. An example is Tok Pisin, meaning "talk business." Tok Pisin is a largely English-derived pidgin spoken in Papua New Guinea, where it has become the official national language in a country where many native Papuan tongues are spoken. Although New Guinea pidgin is not readily intelligible to a speaker of Standard English, certain common words like *gut bai* ("good-bye"), *tenkyu* ("thank you"), and *haumas* ("how much") reflect the influence of English. When pidgin languages acquire fuller vocabularies and become native languages of their speakers, they are called **creole** languages.

Another response to the need for speakers of different languages to communicate with each other is the elevation of one existing language to the status of a **lingua franca,** or a language of communication and commerce, over a wide area where it is not a mother tongue. The Swahili language enjoys lingua franca status in much of East Africa. English is fast becoming a global lingua franca (refer later to Culture in a Globalizing World on page 123). Finally, regions that have linguistically mixed populations may be characterized by **bilingualism,** which is the ability to speak two languages with fluency.

Language Families

One way in which geolinguists often simplify the mapping of languages is by grouping them into **language families:**

Languages

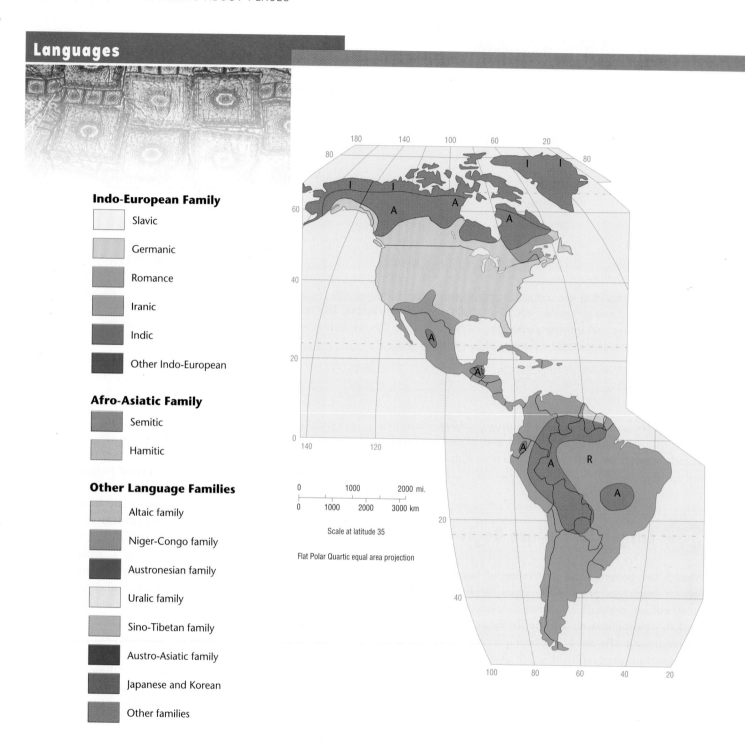

Indo-European Family

- Slavic
- Germanic
- Romance
- Iranic
- Indic
- Other Indo-European

Afro-Asiatic Family

- Semitic
- Hamitic

Other Language Families

- Altaic family
- Niger-Congo family
- Austronesian family
- Uralic family
- Sino-Tibetan family
- Austro-Asiatic family
- Japanese and Korean
- Other families

Scale at latitude 35

Flat Polar Quartic equal area projection

Figure 4.2 **The major linguistic formal culture regions of the world.** Although there are thousands of languages and dialects in the world, they can be grouped into a few linguistic families. The Indo-European language family represents around half of the world's population. It was spread throughout the world in part through Europe's empire-building efforts.

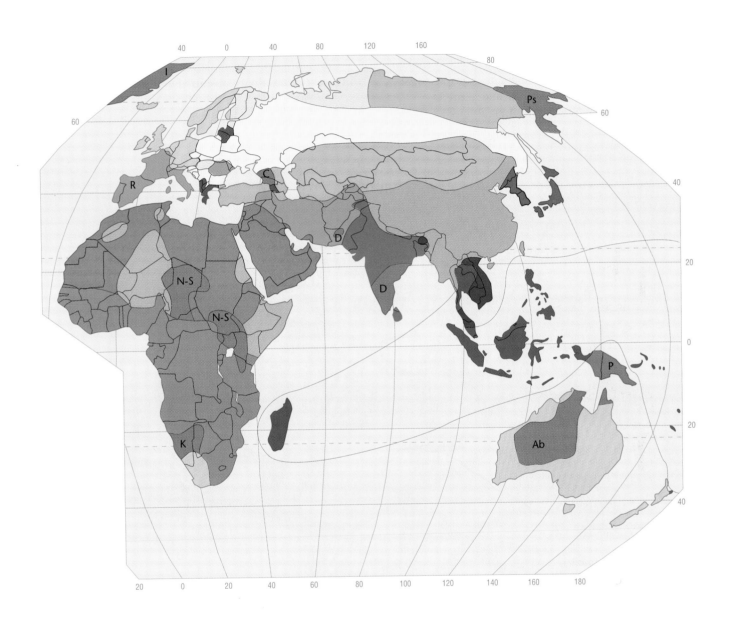

I = Inuktitut

A = Amerindian (several language families)

C = Caucasic

N-S = Nilo-Saharan

K = Khoisan

Ps = Paleosiberian

D = Dravidian

P = Papuan

Ab = Aborigine

R = Romance

tongues that are related and share a common ancestor. Languages and their interrelations can be graphically depicted as a tree with various branches (Figure 4.3). This classification makes the complicated linguistic mosaic a bit easier to comprehend.

Indo-European Language Family The largest and most widespread language family is the *Indo-European*, which is spoken on all the continents and is dominant in Europe, Russia, North and South America, Australia, and parts of southwestern Asia and India (see Figure 4.2). Romance, Slavic,

Germanic, Indic, Celtic, and Iranic are all Indo-European subfamilies. These subfamilies are in turn divided into individual languages. For example, English is a Germanic Indo-European language. Seven Indo-European tongues, including English, are among the 10 most spoken languages in the world as classified by number of native speakers (Table 4.1).

Comparing the vocabularies of various Indo-European tongues reveals their kinship. For example, the English word *mother* is similar to the Polish *matka*, the Greek *meter*, the Spanish *madre*, the Farsi *madar* in Iran, and the Sinhalese

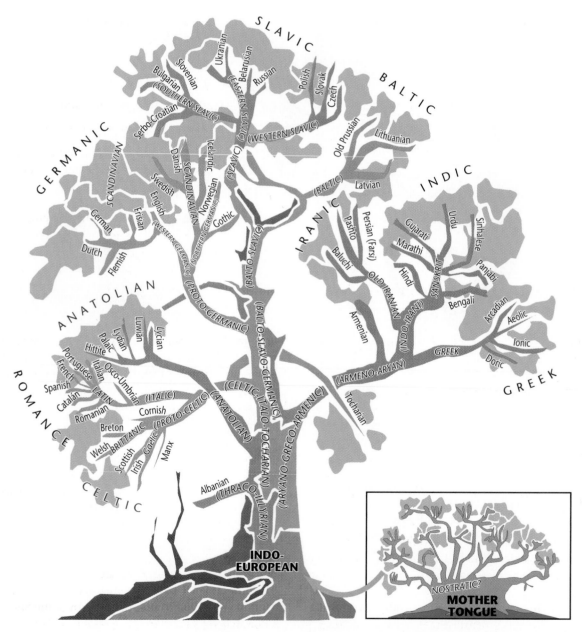

Figure 4.3 Linguistic family tree. Shown here are the relationship between the main "branches" of the linguistic family tree and a detailed image of one branch of that tree. (*Adapted from Clark Ford.*)

TABLE 4.1 The Ten Leading Languages in Numbers of Native Speakers*

Language	Family	Speakers (in millions)	Main Areas Where Spoken
Han Chinese (Mandarin)	Sino-Tibetan	885	China, Taiwan, Singapore
Hindi/Urdu	Indo-European	426	Northern India, Pakistan
Spanish	Indo-European	358	Spain, Latin America, Southwestern United States
English	Indo-European	343	British Isles, Anglo-America, Australia, New Zealand, South Africa, Philippines, former British colonies in tropical Asia and Africa
Arabic	Afro-Asiatic	235	Middle East, North Africa
Bengali	Indo-European	207	Bangladesh, eastern India
Portuguese	Indo-European	176	Portugal, Brazil, southern Africa
Russian	Indo-European	167	Russia, Kazakhstan, parts of Ukraine and other former Soviet republics
Japanese	Japanese and Korean	125	Japan
German	Indo-European	100	Germany, Austria, Switzerland, Luxembourg, eastern France, northern Italy

*"Native speakers" means mother tongue. (Sources: Encyclopaedia Britannica, 2000; World Almanac Books, 2001.)

---

mava in Sri Lanka. Such similarities demonstrate that these languages have a common ancestral tongue.

Afro-Asiatic Family A second language family is the *Afro-Asiatic*. It consists of two major divisions, Semitic and Hamitic. The Semitic languages cover the area from the Arabian Peninsula and the Tigris-Euphrates river valley of Iraq westward through Syria and North Africa to the Atlantic Ocean. Despite the considerable size of this region, there are fewer speakers of the Semitic languages than you might expect, as most of the areas that Semites inhabit are sparsely populated deserts. In addition to having the greatest number of native speakers, about 235 million, Arabic is also by far the most widespread Semitic language. Although many different dialects of Arabic are spoken, the written form is standard.

Hebrew, which is closely related to Arabic, is another Semitic tongue. For many centuries, Hebrew was a "dead" language, used only in religious ceremonies by millions of Jews throughout the world. With the creation of the state of Israel in 1948, a common language was needed to unite the immigrant Jews, who spoke the languages of their many different countries of origin. Hebrew was revived as the official national language of what otherwise would have been a **polyglot,** or multilanguage, state.

Amharic, a third major Semitic tongue, today claims 18 million speakers in the mountains of East Africa. Smaller numbers of people who speak Hamitic languages share North and East Africa with the speakers of Semitic languages. These tongues originated in Asia but today are spoken almost exclusively in Africa, by the Berbers of Morocco and Algeria, the Tuaregs of the Sahara, and the Cushites of East Africa.

Other Major Language Families Most of the rest of the world's population speak languages belonging to one of six remaining major families. Africa south of the Sahara Desert is dominated by the *Niger-Congo* language family, also called *Niger-Kordofanian,* which is spoken by about 325 million people. The greater part of the Niger-Congo culture region

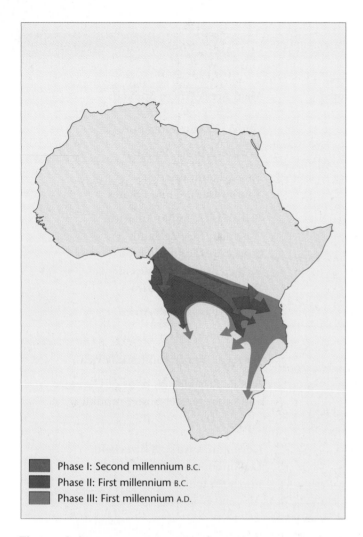

Figure 4.4 **Bantu expansionism.** The Bantu and their many languages spread from what is today southeastern Nigeria to the west and south, displacing Khoisan-speaking people who today exist in small linguistic islands. *(Adapted from Mark Dingemanse/ Wikipedia.)*

Phase I: Second millennium B.C.
Phase II: First millennium B.C.
Phase III: First millennium A.D.

belongs to the Bantu subgroup. Both Niger-Congo and its Bantu constituent are fragmented into a great many different languages and dialects, including Swahili. The Bantu and their many related languages spread from what is now southeastern Nigeria around 4000 years ago, first west and then south in response to climate change and new agricultural techniques (Figure 4.4). Around A.D. 1000, they established the ancient southern African urban center of Great Zimbabwe, which became a trading center for sub-Saharan African and Arab merchants.

Flanking the Slavic Indo-Europeans on the north and south in Asia are the speakers of the *Altaic* language family, including Turkic, Mongolic, and several other subgroups. The Altaic homeland lies largely in the inhospitable deserts, tundra, and coniferous forests of northern and central Asia.

Also occupying tundra and grassland areas adjacent to the Slavs is the *Uralic* family. Finnish and Hungarian are the two most important Uralic tongues, and both enjoy the status of official languages in their respective countries.

One of the most remarkable language families in terms of distribution is the *Austronesian*. Representatives of this group live mainly on tropical islands stretching from Madagascar, off the east coast of Africa, through Indonesia and the Pacific Islands, to Hawaii and Easter Island. This longitudinal span is more than half the distance around the world. The north-south, or latitudinal, range of this language area is bounded by Hawaii and Taiwan in the north and New Zealand in the south. The largest single language in this family is Malay-Indonesian, with 58 million native speakers, but the most widespread is Polynesian.

Sino-Tibetan is another of the major language families of the world. The Sino-Tibetan region extends throughout most of China and Southeast Asia. Han Chinese (Mandarin) is spoken in a variety of dialects as a mother tongue by 885 million people and serves as the official language of China. Burmese and Tibetan, which border the Chinese language region on the south and west, are among the other Sino-Tibetan languages. *Japanese and Korean*, with about 200 million speakers combined, probably form another Asian language family. The two perhaps have some link to the Altaic family, but even their kinship to each other remains controversial and unproven.

In Southeast Asia, the Vietnamese, Cambodians, Thais, and some tribal peoples of Malaya and parts of India speak languages that constitute the *Austro-Asiatic* family. They occupy a peripheral domain on which Sino-Tibetan, Indo-European, and Austronesian languages have all encroached.

The Shifting Boundaries of American English

Dialects as well as the language families explored above reveal a vivid geography. Geolinguists map dialects by using **isoglosses,** which indicate the borders of individual words or pronunciations. No two isoglosses are identical. Figure 4.5 provides an example of how isoglosses can crisscross one another. In most cases, however, multiple isoglosses parallel one another, in "bundles," and these serve as dialect boundaries. Even so, geolinguists often disagree about how many dialects are present in an area or exactly where isoglosses should be drawn.

The dialects of American English are a good example. At least three major dialects, corresponding to major culture regions, had developed in the eastern United States by the time of the American Revolution: the Northern, Midland, and Southern dialects (Figure 4.6). As the three subcultures expanded westward, their dialects spread and fragmented. Nevertheless, they retained much of their basic character even beyond the Mississippi River. Drawing the

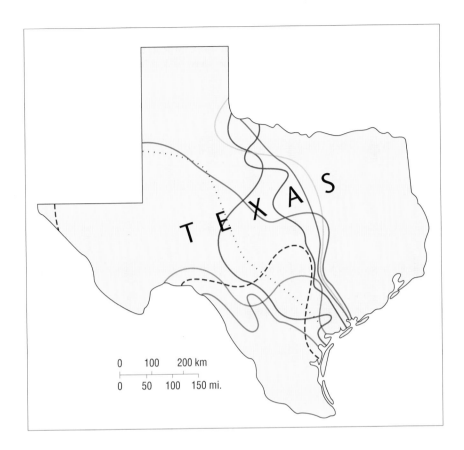

Eastern and Northern Borders of

——— Remuda (group of saddle horses)

——— Resaca (channel)

——— Vaquero (cowboy)

——— Arroyo (dry creek)

——— Pilón (something extra)

——— Mesa (flat-topped hill)

——— Frijoles (pinto beans)

· · · · · · Toro (bull)

– – – Acequia (irrigation ditch)

Figure 4.5 **Isoglosses cluster into "bundles."** At the time the data for this map were compiled, in the early 1960s, the Spanish language was making inroads into Texas from the South and the West, dividing it into two dialect regions. Though Spanish-speaking people have lived in Texas from the sixteenth century onward, it is likely that the predominance of Mexican-Americans in Texas today has made words like *frijoles* and *toro* almost universal throughout the state. (*Source: Atwood, 1962.*)

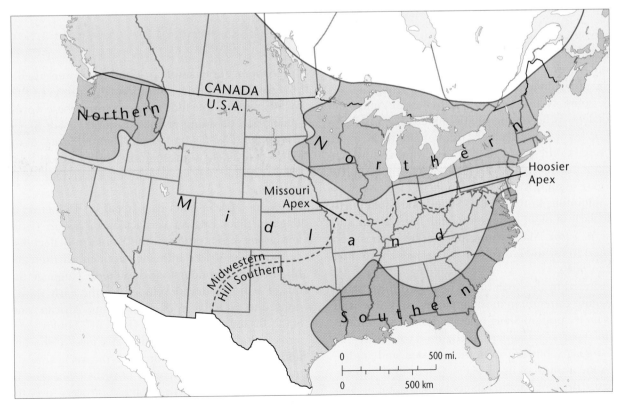

Figure 4.6 **Major dialects of North American English, with a few selected subdialects.** These dialects had developed by the time of the American Revolution. (*After Carver, 1986; Kurath, 1949.*)

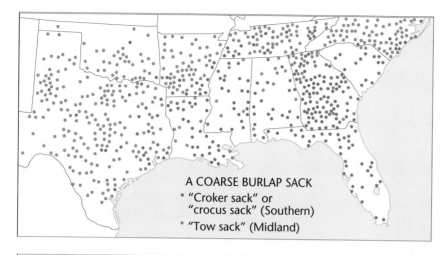

A COARSE BURLAP SACK
• "Croker sack" or
  "crocus sack" (Southern)
• "Tow sack" (Midland)

Figure 4.7 **Some Midland and Southern words in the American South.** Each dot represents one person interviewed who gave the response indicated. If you were drawing the isoglosses for these words, where exactly would you place them? If these two maps were your only evidence, where would you draw the Midland-Southern dialect border? These are common problems for the linguistic geographer, and they illustrate the artificiality of dialect maps and all formal culture regions. *(Sources: Atwood, 1962: 196, 199; Kurath, 1949; Wood, 1971: 325, 337–339.)*

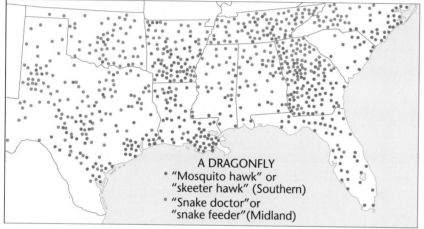

A DRAGONFLY
• "Mosquito hawk" or
  "skeeter hawk" (Southern)
• "Snake doctor"or
  "snake feeder"(Midland)

dialect boundaries is often difficult, and intelligent and reasonable disagreements are not uncommon (Figure 4.7).

Today, some of the unique vocabulary of American English dialects is becoming old-fashioned. For instance, the term *icebox* was used widely throughout the United States to refer to the precursor of the refrigerator, which was literally a wooden box with a compartment for ice that was used to cool food. Though the modern electric refrigerator is ubiquitous in the United States today, some people, particularly of older generations and in the South, still use the term *icebox*. Many young people, by contrast, no longer pause to say the entire word *refrigerator*, shortening it instead to *fridge*.

As illustrated by the birth of the new word *fridge*, slang terms are quite common in most languages, and American English is no exception. **Slang** refers to words and phrases that are not a part of a standard, recognized vocabulary for a given language, but are nonetheless used and understood by some or most of its speakers. Often subcultures—youth, drug dealers, nightclub-goers—have their own slang that is used within that community but is not readily understood by nonmembers. Slang words tend to be used for a period of time, then discarded, as newer terms re-

place them. For example, *cool* and *groovy* were used to refer to desirable, attractive, or fashionable things in the 1970s. While many people today still recognize these words, a new generation of young people are much more likely to use words like *sweet*, *tight*, and *phat*. Their children, in turn, will more than likely use yet another set of words. Slang illustrates another way in which American English changes over time.

Some African-Americans speak a distinctive form of English. Black English Vernacular, or *Ebonics* (from *ebony* and *phonics*), is a variety of the Southern dialect displaying considerable African influence in pitch, rhythm, and tone. Ebonics can be understood as a creole language that grew out of a pidgin that developed on the early slave plantations and is today spoken by some African-Americans. Some distinguishing characteristics of Ebonics speech patterns include the use of double negatives ("She don't like nothing"), omission of forms of the verb *to be* ("He my friend"), and nonconjugation of verbs ("She give him her paper yesterday"). There is some controversy over the place of Ebonics in the U.S. educational system. Does Ebonics constitute a distinctive language, rather than simply a dialect of English? Should it be taught—with its attendant grammar,

Imposing English

English-only laws are nothing new in the United States. Its history as a nation of immigrants has led to a population that at any one point in time speaks a variety of languages besides English. In its early days as a colony, one could hear German, Dutch, French, and a multitude of Native American languages spoken alongside English. This prompted both Benjamin Franklin and John Adams to propose enforcing English as the sole acceptable language, while Theodore Roosevelt once said that "the one absolutely certain way of bringing this nation to ruin or preventing all possibility of its continuing as a nation at all would be to permit it to become a tangle of squabbling nationalities. We have but one flag. We must also learn one language, and that

language is English." Citing concerns that providing official documents and services in multiple languages would be just too expensive, contemporary advocates of English-only legislation claim that mandating one language is one way to reduce the cost of government. Some proponents also feel that English-only laws encourage immigrants to assimilate through learning the official language of the United States. Opponents accuse the laws of being racist and suggest that supporters of English-only legislation are threatened by cultural diversity. Debates such as these bring up questions of the legal, social, and political status of minority groups and their languages, debates that exist in many countries besides the United States.

structure, and literature—to American schoolchildren? Are those who speak Ebonics and standard English technically bilingual?

In the United States today, many descendents of Spanish-speakers have adapted their speech to include words and variants of words in both Spanish and English, in a dialect known as "Spanglish" (see Seeing Geography at the end of the chapter). Though acceptance of Ebonics and Spanglish is hardly without conflict (see Focus On: Imposing English), they illustrate the fluidity of languages and how they are constantly evolving and changing as the needs and experiences of their users change. Although we are sometimes led to believe that Americans are becoming more alike, as a national culture overwhelms regional ones, the current status of American English dialects suggests otherwise. Linguistic divergence is still under way, and dialects continue to mutate on a regional level, just as they always have. Local variations in grammar and pronunciation proliferate, confounding the proponents of standardized speech and defying the homogenizing influence of the Internet, television, and other mass media.

Linguistic Diffusion

How did the mosaic of languages and dialects come to exist? Languages have diffused spatially since their inception. More often than not, the diffusion of some languages has come at the expense of many others. Ten thousand years ago, the human race consisted of only 1 million people, speaking an estimated 15,000 languages. Today, a population 6000 times larger speaks only 40 percent as many

tongues. Only 1 percent of all languages have as many as 500,000 speakers. Some experts feel that all but 300 languages will be extinct or dying by the year 2100. Clearly, cultural diffusion has worked to favor some languages and eliminate others. Each passing decade witnesses the extinction of more minor languages.

REFLECTING ON GEOGRAPHY

Can you think of reasons why the number of languages has declined so profoundly in the last 10,000 years?

Different types of cultural diffusion have helped shape the linguistic map. *Relocation diffusion* has been extremely important, for languages spread when groups, in whole or in part, migrated from one area to another. Some individual tongues or entire language families are no longer spoken in the regions where they originated, and in certain other cases the linguistic hearth is peripheral to the present distribution (compare Figures 4.2 and 4.8).

Indo-European Diffusion

The earliest speakers of Indo-European, according to a widely accepted new theory, lived in southern and southeastern Turkey, a region known as Anatolia, about 9000 years ago (Figure 4.8). The initial advance of these Indo-European speakers, then, apparently hinged on a major innovation—plant and animal domestication—and probably proceeded gradually and peacefully. As these people dispersed and lost contact with one another, different Indo-European groups gradually developed variant forms of the language, causing fragmentation of the language family.

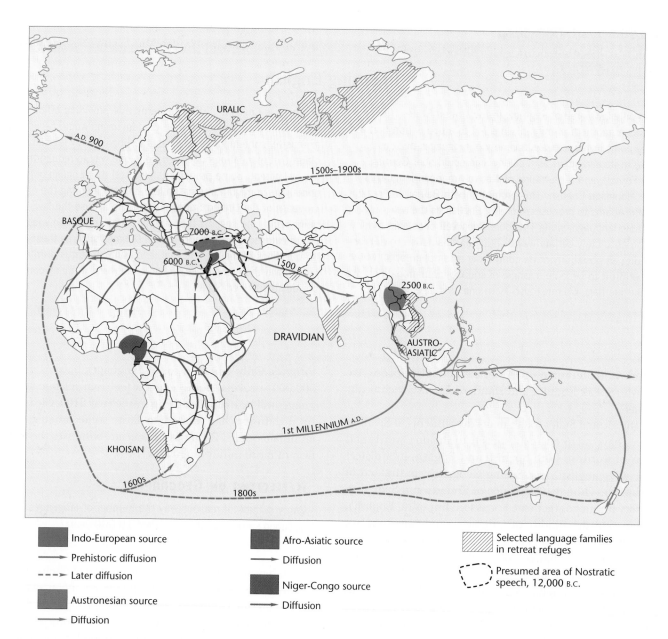

Figure 4.8 **Origin and diffusion of four major language families in the Eastern Hemisphere.** The early diffusion of Indo-European speech to the west and north probably occurred in conjunction with the diffusion of agriculture from the Middle Eastern center, as did the early spread of the Afro-Asiatic family. All such origins, lost in time, are speculative. As these and other groups advanced, certain linguistic families retreated to refuges in remote places, where they hold out to the present day. Sources, dates, and routes are mostly speculative. *(Sources: Krantz, 1988; Renfrew, 1989.)*

In later millennia, the diffusion of certain Indo-European languages—in particular Latin, English, and Russian—occurred in conjunction with the territorial spread of great political empires. In such cases of imperial conquest, relocation and expansion diffusion were not mutually exclusive. Relocation diffusion occurred as a small number of conquering elite came to rule an area. The language of the conqueror, implanted by relocation diffusion, often gained wider acceptance through expansion diffusion. Typically, the conqueror's language spread hierarchically—adopted first by the more important and influential persons and by city dwellers. The diffusion of Latin with Roman conquests, and Spanish with the conquest of Latin America, occurred in this manner.

Austronesian Diffusion

One of the most impressive examples of linguistic diffusion is that of the Austronesian languages, 5000 years ago, from a presumed hearth in the interior of Southeast Asia that was completely outside the present Austronesian culture region. From here, speakers of this language family first spread southward into the Malay Peninsula (see Figure 4.8). Then, in a process lasting perhaps several thousand years and requiring remarkable navigational skills, they migrated through the islands of Indonesia and sailed in tiny boats across vast, uncharted expanses of ocean to New Zealand, Easter Island, Hawaii, and Madagascar. If agriculture was the technology permitting Indo-European diffusion, sailing and navigation provided the key to the spread of the Austronesians.

Most remarkable of all was the diffusionary achievement of the Polynesian people, who form the eastern part of the Austronesian culture region. Polynesians occupy a triangular realm consisting of hundreds of Pacific islands, with New Zealand, Easter Island, and Hawaii at the three corners (Figure 4.9). The Polynesians' watery leap of 2500 miles

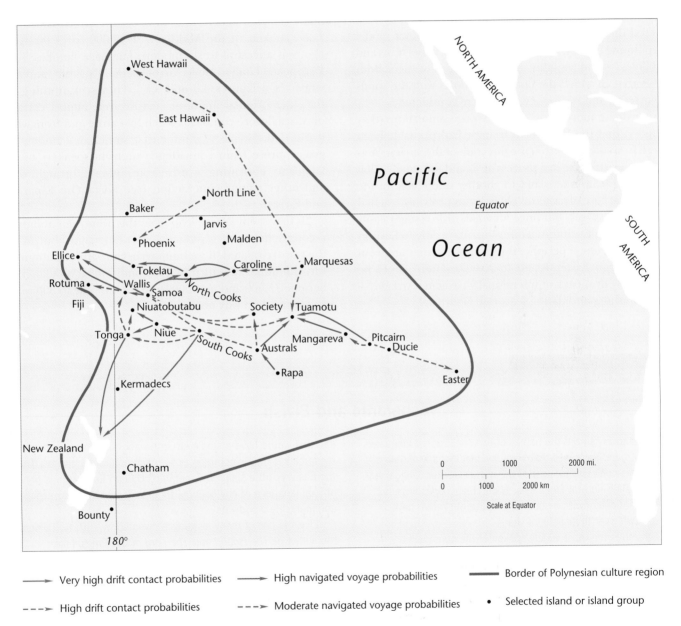

Figure 4.9 Probabilities of selected Polynesian drift and navigation voyages in the Pacific Ocean. According to a computer model, the outer arc of Polynesia, represented by Hawaii, Easter Island, and New Zealand, could have been reached only by navigated voyages. The earliest known Polynesian pottery shards were found in Tonga by archaeologists David Burley and William Dickinson, suggesting that the first distinctively Polynesian culture originated there. *(Adapted from Levison, Ward, and Webb, 1973: 5, 33, 35, 43, 61.)*

(4000 kilometers) from the South Pacific to Hawaii, a migration in outrigger canoes against prevailing winds into a new hemisphere with different navigational stars, must rank as one of the greatest achievements of seafaring. No humans had previously found the isolated Hawaiian Islands, and the Polynesian sailors had no way of knowing ahead of time that land existed in that quarter of the Pacific.

The relocation diffusion that produced the remarkable present distribution of the Polynesian languages has long been the subject of controversy. How, and by what means, could a traditional people have achieved the diffusion? Geolinguists Michael Levison, Gerard Ward, and John Webb answered these questions by developing a computer model incorporating data on winds, ocean currents, vessel traits and capabilities, island visibility, and duration of voyage. Both *drift* voyages, in which the boat simply floats with the winds and currents, and *navigated* voyages were considered.

After doing more than 100,000 voyage simulations, they concluded that the Polynesian triangle had probably been entered from the west, from the direction of the ancient Austronesian hearth area, in a process of "island hopping"—that is, migrating from one island to another one visible in the distance. The core of eastern Polynesia was probably reached in navigated voyages, but once attained, drift voyages easily explain much of the internal diffusion. According to Levison and his colleagues, a peripheral region, the "outer arc from Hawaii through Easter Island to New Zealand," could be reached only by means of intentionally navigated voyages—truly astonishing and daring feats (see Figure 4.9).

In carrying out their investigation, Levison and his colleagues employed the themes of culture region (present distribution of Polynesians) and cultural ecology (currents, winds, visibility of islands) to help describe and explain the workings of a third theme, cultural diffusion.

Linguistic Globalization

Using techniques that remain controversial, certain linguists are probing even more deeply into the origin and diffusion of languages, seeking still more elusive prehistoric tongues. Some scholars believe that an ancestral speech called *Nostratic,* spoken in the Middle East 12,000 to 20,000 years ago, was ancestral to six modern language families: Indo-European, Uralic, Altaic, Afro-Asiatic, Caucasic, and Dravidian (see Figures 4.3 and 4.8). They seek nothing less than the original linguistic hearth area, almost certainly in Africa, where complex speech first arose and from which it diffused. Skeptics counter that similarities among languages arose from coincidence or from speakers of one language borrowing words from others through trade and other cultural interaction (see Focus On: Esperanto and Elvish).

It may seem a large leap from the primordial tongue to a consideration of *globalization* and languages, but in fact the two are related. If we humans began with one language, why shouldn't we return to that condition? If one language became 15,000 and now 6000 and will dwindle to 300 within a century, then why not one?

FOCUS ON

Esperanto and Elvish

Esperanto and Elvish are the names of two constructed languages. That is, both are languages that were invented for a well-defined purpose. This contrasts to most of the world's spoken languages, which are called natural languages. Natural languages were not created intentionally with a specific purpose but rather have evolved slowly over thousands of years.

Esperanto is the most widely spoken of the constructed languages, with as many as 2 million speakers worldwide. Esperanto was invented by L. L. Zamenhof, a Polish oculist, in the 1880s. Zamenhof, who went by the pseudonym Dr. Esperanto (meaning "he who hopes"), wanted to create a language that would become a second language for everyone in the world. He based Esperanto on existing natural languages rather than inventing a completely new structure. Zamenhof wanted a language that is easily learned and easily understood as well as

one that would have a stable structure not open to the constant modification that is common to so many natural languages. Thus, there is very little slang in Esperanto. Though Esperanto is not an official language of any country, thousands of people do use it to communicate worldwide.

Elvish is one of many languages invented by J. R. R. Tolkien, the author of *The Hobbit* and *The Lord of the Rings.* Like Esperanto, Elvish is a constructed language invented for a specific purpose. It is one of several languages spoken by the Elvish inhabitants of Middle-Earth, the setting of Tolkien's novels. Unlike Esperanto, Elvish was never intended to supplement or replace any natural languages spoken in the human world, and its pronunciation and script are not easy to learn. However, there are several published dictionaries, language courses, and other resources available for those Tolkien aficionados who wish to learn Elvish.

Are the forces of modernization working to produce, through cultural diffusion, a single world language? And if so, what will that language be? English? Worldwide about 343 million people speak English as their mother tongue and perhaps another 350 million speak it well as a second, learned language. Adding other reasonably competent speakers who can "get by" in English, the world total reaches about 1.5 billion, more than for any other language. What's more, the Internet is one of the most potent agents of diffusion, and its language, overwhelmingly, is English (see Culture in a Globalizing World). English earlier diffused widely with the British Empire and U.S. colonialism, and today it has become the de facto language of globalization.

Consider the case of India, where the English language imposed by British rulers was retained after independence as the country's language of business, government, and education. It provided some linguistic unity for India, which had 800 indigenous languages and dialects. This is the reason that today many of India's nearly 1 billion people speak English well enough to provide customer support services over the telephone for clients in the United States. Even so, many people resent its use and "will not rest until English is driven out of the country," ridding India of a hated legacy of colonialism. Moreover, the spoken English of India has drifted away from standard British English. So has that of Singapore, a separate language now called Singlish. Many other regional, English-based languages have developed, languages that could not be readily understood in London or Chicago.

But is the diffusion of English to the entire world population likely? Will globalization and cultural diffusion produce one world language? Probably not. More likely, a situation similar to the one we found in religion will occur—the world divided largely among 5 to 10 major languages.

Despite the global dominance of English, in the United States fully 27 states have felt that the position of English is sufficiently insecure to require passage of English-only laws (Figure 4.10) (refer again to Focus On: Imposing English). Also troubling is the eclipse of local languages by these ever more dominant languages, such as English. Because language is the primary way of expressing culture, if a language

CULTURE IN A GLOBALIZING WORLD

Is English Taking Over the World, Virtually?

English is the second most widely spoken language on Earth, after Mandarin Chinese. And English is the most widely spoken second language in the world. It dominates the Internet as well. Here are the 10 most prevalent languages on the Internet as of early 2005, measured as a percent of total Internet users:

English	34.7%	Italian	3.5%
Chinese	13.8%	Portuguese	2.7%
Japanese	8.3%	Dutch	1.7%
Spanish	6.8%		
German	6.5%		
French	4.5%	Top 10 languages	86.4%
Korean	3.9%	Rest of languages	13.6%

However, much of what comes across our computer and cell phone screens isn't a readily recognizable form of English. As with the diffusion of spoken English to far-flung regions of the British Empire, the English language that is spread via electronic correspondence is subject to significant modification. Phonetic, rather than stylistically correct, spelling of words is common. In addition, e-mail, instant messaging on the Internet, and text messaging on cell phones require a lot of typing and are notoriously deficient in conveying emotions. For these reasons, users often use abbreviations and symbols to shorten the number of keystrokes used, to add emotional punctuation to their correspondence, and to make electronic communication hard to monitor by those who don't understand the language (particularly parents!). *POS* (parent over shoulder), *AFK* (away from keyboard), *VBG* (very big grin), *LOL* (laughing out loud), and *GMTA* (great minds think alike) are some examples, as are the symbol combinations depicting different emotions on sideways faces: :-) (user is smiling or joking), :-@ (user is screaming or cursing), and :-# (well, shut my mouth!). Spoken and written English are quickly picking up these cyberspeech patterns with expressions like *PITA*, used to indicate that someone is a "pain in the ass" without actually saying so! As your instructor for this class will likely confirm, such abbreviations and symbols have even worked their way into term papers at the college level, much to the consternation or delight of language scholars.

Percentages from http://www.internetworldstats.com/stats7.htm.

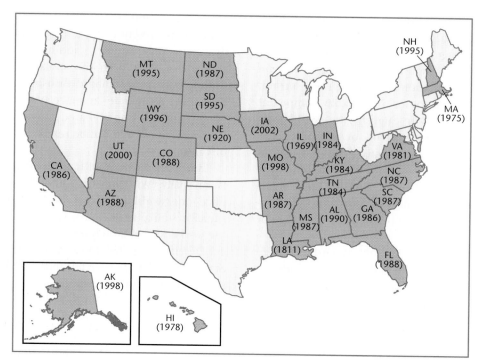

Figure 4.10 States of the United States that have some form of official English-only laws. Dates show the year enacted. In the 1980s, the influx of immigrants to the United States from Asia and Latin America prompted many of these laws. Iowa, a state that passed an English-only law in 2002, has received a relatively large number of Mexican immigrants who have come to the United States in recent years on the heels of Mexico's monetary devaluation. Typically, English-only laws require that state documents be published in English. Some states' laws, however, prohibit the state from doing business in a language other than English or providing services like multilingual emergency medical hotlines. *(Source: Adapted from U.S. English, Inc.)*

dies out there is a good chance that the culture of its speakers will, too (see Focus On: Language and Cultural Survival). Languages, like animal species, are classified as endangered or extinct. Endangered languages are those that are not being taught to children by their parents and are not being used actively in everyday matters. Some linguists feel that more than half of the world's roughly 6800 languages are endangered. Ethnologue, an online language resource (see Linguistic Geography on the Internet at the end of the chapter for this web site address), considers 417 world languages to be nearly extinct. Languages that have only a few elderly speakers still living fall into this category. The Americas and the Pacific regions together account for over three-quarters of the world's current nearly extinct languages (Figure 4.11). In Argentina, for example, only five families speak Vilela, while only seven or eight speakers of Tuscarora remain in Canada. When these speakers die, it is likely that their language will die out with them.

Related to linguistic extinction is the existence of so-called remnant languages that survive, typically in small *linguistic islands* that are surrounded by the dominant language. One example is *Khoisan*, found in the Kalahari Desert of southwestern Africa and characterized by distinctive clicking sounds. The pockets of Khoisan seen in Figure 4.2 survived

after the expansion of the Bantu, discussed earlier (see Figure 4.4). Other remnant languages include *Dravidian*, spoken by hundreds of millions of people in southern India,

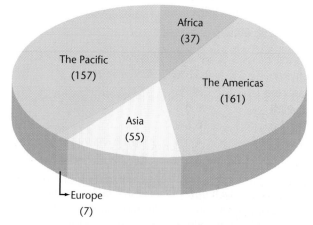

Figure 4.11 Distribution of the world's nearly extinct languages. This chart shows the regional distribution of the world's nearly extinct languages, or those languages that have only a few elderly speakers still living. Nearly extinct languages account for 6 percent of the world's total existing languages. *(Source: Adapted from Ethnologue, "Nearly Extinct Languages," http://www.ethnologue.com/nearly_extinct.asp.)*

Language and Cultural Survival

As Figure 4.11 shows, almost 40 percent of the world's nearly extinct languages are found in the Americas. They represent a wealth of Native American languages that are slowly becoming suffocated by English, Spanish, and Portuguese. Keith Basso, an anthropologist who has written an intriguing book titled *Wisdom Sits in Places,* discusses the landscape of distinctive place-names used by the Western Apache of New Mexico. The people Basso studied use place-names to invoke stories that help the Western Apache remember their collective history. According to Nick Thompson, one of Basso's interviewees, "White men need paper maps. . . . We have maps in our minds" (p. 43). Thompson goes on to assert that calling up the names of places can guard against forgetting the correct way of living, or adopting the bad habits of white men, once Western Apaches move to other areas. "The names of all these places are good. They make you remember how to live right, so you want to replace yourself again" (p. 59).

One of the places Basso heard about is called Shades of Shit. Here is what he was told:

It happened here at Shades of Shit.

They had much corn, those people who lived here, and their relatives had only a little. They refused to share it. Their relatives begged them but still they refused to share it.

Then their relatives got angry and forced them to stay at home. They wouldn't let them go anywhere, not even to defecate. So they had to do it at home. Their shades [shelters] filled up with it. There was more and more of it! It was very bad! Those people got sick and nearly died.

Then their relatives said, "You have brought this on yourselves. Now you live in shades of shit!" Finally, they agreed to share their corn.

It happened at Shades of Shit. (p. 24)

Today, merely standing at this place or speaking its graphic name reminds Western Apache that stinginess is a vice that can threaten the survival of the entire community.

adjacent northern Sri Lanka, and a part of Pakistan, as well as Australian *Aborigine, Papuan, Caucasic, Nilo-Saharan, Paleo-siberian, Inuktitut,* and a variety of *Native American* language families. In a few cases, individual minor languages represent the sole survivors of former families. *Basque,* spoken in the borderland between Spain and France, is such a survivor, unrelated to any other language in the world.

Linguistic Ecology

Language interacts with the environment in two basic ways. First, the specific physical habitats in which languages evolve help shape their vocabularies. Second, the environment can guide the migrations of linguistic groups or provide refuges for languages in retreat. The following section, from the viewpoint of possibilism, suggests some ways in which the physical environment influences vocabulary and the distribution of language.

Habitat and Vocabulary

Humankind's relationship to the land played a strong role in the emergence of linguistic differences, even at the level of vocabulary. For example, the Spanish language—which originated in Castile, a dry and relatively barren land rimmed by hills and high mountains—is especially rich in words describing rough terrain, allowing speakers of this tongue to distinguish even subtle differences in the shape and configuration of mountains, as Table 4.2 reveals. Similarly, Scottish Gaelic possesses a rich vocabulary to describe types of topography—a common attribute of the Celtic languages spoken by hill peoples. In the Romanian tongue, also born of a rugged landscape, words relating to mountainous features tend to be keyed to use of that terrain for livestock herding. English, by contrast, which developed in the temperate wet coastal plains of northern Europe, is relatively deficient in words describing mountainous terrain (Figure 4.12). However, English abounds with words describing flowing streams and wetlands. In the rural American South alone, one finds *river, creek, branch, fork, prong, run, bayou,* and *slough.* This vocabulary indicates that the area is a well-watered land with a dense network of streams.

Clearly, then, language serves an *adaptive strategy.* Vocabularies are highly developed for those features of the environment that involve livelihood. Without such detailed vocabularies, it would be difficult to communicate sophisticated information relevant to the community's livelihood.

The Habitat Provides Refuge

The environment also influences language insofar as inhospitable areas provide protection and isolation. Such areas

TABLE 4.2	Some Spanish Words Describing Mountains and Hills

Spanish Word	English Meaning
candelas	Literally "candles"; a collection of *peñas*
ceja	Steep-sided breaks or escarpment separating two plains of different elevation
cejita	A low escarpment
cerrillo or *cerrito*	A small *cerro;* a hill
cerro	A single eminence, intermediate in size between English *hill* and *mountain*
chiquito	Literally "small," describing minor secondary fringing elevations at the base of and parallel to a *sierra* or *cordillera*
cordillera	A mass of mountains, as distinguished from a single mountain summit
cuchilla	Literally "knife"; the comblike secondary crests that project at right angles from the sides of a *sierra*
cumbre	The highest elevation or peak within a *sierra* or *cordillera;* a summit
eminencia	A mountainous or hilly protuberance
loma	A hill in the midst of a plain
lomita	A small hill in the midst of a plain
mesa	Literally "table"; a flat-topped eminence
montaña	Equivalent to English *mountain*
pelado	A barren, treeless mountain
pelon	A bare conical eminence
peloncilla	A small *pelon*
peña	A needlelike eminence
picacho	A peaked or pointed eminence
pico	A summit point; English *peak*
sandia	Literally "watermelon"; an oblong, rounded eminence
sierra	An elongated mountain mass with a serrated crest
tinaja	A solitary, hemispheric mountain shaped like an inverted bowl

(Source: Hill, 1896.)

Figure 4.12 **A scene in the desert of the western United States.** "Mountains," yes, but what kind of mountains? (See Table 4.2.) The English language cannot describe such a place adequately, because it is the product of a very different, humid and cool, physical landscape. As a result, the ability of English speakers to name dryland environmental features will be less precise in such places. Does this limitation of English mean that it would be a less-than-satisfactory world language? *(David Muench/Corbis.)*

often provide minority linguistic groups refuge from aggressive neighbors and are, accordingly, referred to as **linguistic refuge areas.** Rugged hill and mountain areas, excessively cold or dry climates, dense forests, remote islands, and extensive marshes and swamps can all offer protection to minority language groups. For one thing, unpleasant environments rarely attract conquerors. Also, mountains tend to isolate the inhabitants of one valley from those in adjacent ones, discouraging contact that might lead to linguistic diffusion.

Examples of these linguistic refuge areas are numerous. The rugged Caucasus Mountains and nearby ranges in central Eurasia are populated by a large variety of peoples and languages (Figure 4.13). Similarly, the Alps, the Himalayas, and the highlands of Mexico are linguistic **shatter belts—** areas where diverse languages are spoken. Mountains provide isolation and are natural shatter belts. In the Rocky Mountains of northern New Mexico, an archaic form of Spanish survives, largely as a result of isolation that ended only in the early 1900s. The Dhofar, a mountain tribe in Oman, preserves Hamitic speech, a language family otherwise vanished from all of Asia. Bitterly cold tundra climates of the far north have sheltered Uralic and Inuktitut speakers, and a desert has shielded Khoisan speakers from Bantu invaders. On the Sea Islands, off the coast of South Carolina and Georgia, some remnants of African languages can still be heard, protected for centuries by insularity (see Focus On: Gullah Culture). In short, hostile or isolated environments protect linguistic groups that might otherwise be eclipsed by more dominant languages.

Still, environmental isolation is no longer the vital linguistic force it once was. Fewer and fewer places are so isolated that they remain little touched by outside influences.

Today, inhospitable lands may offer linguistic refuge, but it is no longer certain that they will in the future. Even an island situated in the middle of the vast Pacific Ocean does not offer reliable refuge in an age of airplanes, satellite-transmitted communications, and global tourism. Similarly, marshes and forests provide refuge only if they are not drained and cleared by those who wish to use the land more intensively. The reality of the world is no longer isolation, but contact.

The Habitat Helps Shape Language Areas

Environmental barriers and natural routes have often guided linguistic groups onto certain paths. The wide distribution of the Austronesian language group, as we have seen, cannot be fully understood without knowledge of prevailing winds and water currents in the Pacific and Indian oceans. Migrating Indo-Europeans entering the Indian subcontinent through low mountain passes in the northwest were deflected by the Himalayas and the barren Deccan Plateau into the rich Ganga-Indus river plain. Even today in parts of India, according to Charles Bennett, the Indo-European/Dravidian "language boundary seems to approximate an ecological boundary" between the water-retentive black soils of the plains and the thinner, reddish Deccan soils.

Because such physical barriers as mountain ridges can discourage groups from migrating from one area to another, they often serve as linguistic borders as well. In parts of the Alps, speakers of German and Italian live on opposite sides of a major ridge. Portions of the mountain rim along the northern edge of the Fertile Crescent in the Middle East form the border between Semitic and Indo-European tongues. Linguistic borders that follow such physical features

---

FOCUS ON

Gullah Culture

The Gullah, or Geechee, people are descendants of African slaves brought to the United States in the eighteenth and nineteenth centuries to work on plantations. Many of their nearly 10,000 descendants today inhabit coastal islands of South Carolina, Georgia, and North Florida. Because the original African cultural roots have been so extensively preserved, the Gullah are sometimes called the most African-American community in the United States. Gullah cuisine incorporates African foodstuffs such as okra. Gullah language, too, is a distinctive combination of Elizabethan English and African tongues. It is the only surviving example of an English-based creole language in North

America. This is an example of a Gullah phrase: "Da' buckruh' hogmeat flabuh me mout' 'tell uh done fuhgit uh hab sin fuhkill'um". It translates to Standard English as: "That white man's pork flavored my mouth so that I forgot the sin I committed in killing the hog." This and other words and phrases can be found in the Gullah glossary online at http://www.gullahtours.com/gullah_dictionary.html.

The development of Gullah coastal islands for tourism and housing for wealthy nonlocals has threatened the survival of Gullah culture. So has the out-migration of Gullah youth in search of better economic opportunities.

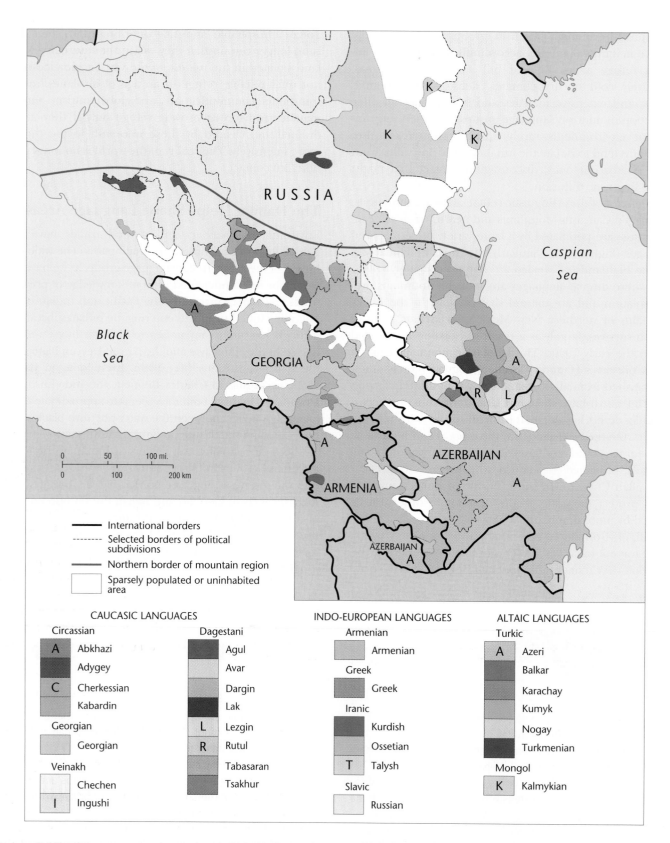

Figure 4.13 **The environment is a linguistic refuge in the Caucasus Mountains.** The rugged mountainous region between the Black and Caspian seas—including parts of Armenia, Russia, Georgia, and Azerbaijan— is peopled by a great variety of linguistic groups, representing three major language families. Mountain areas are often linguistic shatter belts because the rough terrain provides refuge and isolation. For more information about this fascinating and diverse region, see Wixman, 1980.

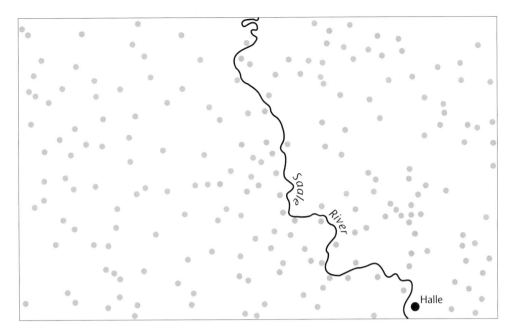

Figure 4.14 **Long ago—about 1200 years ago, to be exact—the German-Slavic language border on the plains of northern Europe paralleled the Saale River.** This fact is revealed by the names of villages and towns. Many Slavic place-names survive east of the river, but the modern language border lies much farther east, and no Slavic speakers remain here. *(Source: Jordan-Bychkov and Jordan, 2002.)*

generally tend to be stable, and they often endure for thousands of years. By contrast, language borders that cross plains and major routes of communication—the Germanic-Slavic boundary on the northern European plain for example—are often unstable (Figure 4.14).

 ## Culturo-Linguistic Interaction

How do languages and dialects interact with other facets of culture? Language is intertwined with all aspects of culture. The theme of cultural interaction allows us to probe some of these complex links between speech and other cultural phenomena. Complex linguistic maps, such as that in Figure 4.13, cannot be understood without reference to the social, demographic, political, and technological characteristics of the groups in question. At root, linguistic cultural interaction often reflects or reinforces the dominance of one group over another, a dominance based partly in culture.

Technology and Linguistic Dominance

Particular language groups achieve cultural dominance over neighboring groups in a variety of ways, often with profound results for the linguistic map of the world. Technological superiority is usually involved. Earlier, we saw how plant and animal domestication—the technology of the "agricultural revolution"—aided the early diffusion of the Indo-European language family.

An even more basic technology was the invention of writing, which appears to have developed as early as 5300 years ago in several hearth areas, including in Egypt, among the Sumerians in what is today Iraq, and in China. Writing helped civilizations develop and spread, giving written languages a major advantage over those that remained spoken only. Written languages can be published and distributed widely, and they carry with them the figurative as well as literal status of standard, official, and legal communication.

Transportation technology also profoundly affects the geography of languages. Ships, railroads, and highways all serve to spread the languages of the cultural groups that build them, sometimes spelling doom for the speech of less technologically advanced peoples whose lands are suddenly opened to outside contacts. The Trans-Siberian Railroad, built about a century ago, spread the Russian language eastward to the Pacific Ocean. The Alaska Highway, which runs through Canada, carried English into Native American refuges. The construction of highways in Brazil's remote Amazonian interior threatens the native languages of that region. Another example is the predominance of English on the Internet, which can be understood as a contemporary information highway (Figure 4.15).

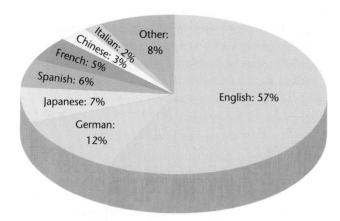

Figure 4.15 Languages used to access Google, the Internet search engine, in January 2002. The prevalence of English as the lingua franca of the Internet is clear. (*Source: Adapted from http://www.netz-tipp.de/sprachen.html.*)

REFLECTING ON GEOGRAPHY

Can we view the Internet as a principal transportation route responsible for spreading English throughout the world today? If so, what does the spread of Internet access to areas formerly isolated by their physical landscape mean for the survival of linguistic minorities?

Language and Empire

Written language facilitates record keeping, allowing governments and bureaucracies to develop. Thus, the languages of conquerors tend to spread with imperial expansion. Highly organized, literate empires represent simply another technological advantage for the territorial growth of some groups at the expense of others. The imperial expansion of Britain, France, the Netherlands, Belgium, Portugal, Spain, and the United States across the globe altered the linguistic practices of millions of people (Figure 4.16). This empire building superimposed Indo-European tongues on the map of the tropics and subtropics. The areas most affected were Asia, Africa, and the Austronesian island world. A parallel case from the ancient world is China, also a formidable imperial power that spread its language to those it conquered. During the Tang dynasty (A.D. 618–907), Chinese control extended to Tibet, Mongolia, Manchuria (in contemporary northeastern China), and Korea. The 4000-year-old written Chinese language proved essential for the cohesion and maintenance of its far-flung empire. Though people throughout the empire spoke different dialects or even different languages, a common writing system lent a measure of mutual intelligibility at the level of the written word.

Even though imperial nations have, for the most part, given up their colonial empires, the languages they transplanted overseas survive (see Practicing Geography). As a result, English still has a foothold in much of Africa, South Asia, the Philippines, and the Pacific islands. French persists in former French and Belgian colonies, especially in northern, western, and central Africa; Madagascar; and Polynesia (Figure 4.17). In most of these areas, English and French function as the languages of the educated elite, often holding official legal status. They are also used as a lingua franca of government, commerce, and higher education, helping hold together states with multiple native languages.

The Social Morale Model

Once a language diffuses spatially as a result of technological advantage or imperial conquest, the replacement of the indigenous languages typically begins. Geographer Charles Withers proposed the *social morale model* to explain the process that, over time, places the conquered group in a lower social class and sees it lose pride in its language and

Figure 4.16 The mesh of language and empire in South America. The Treaty of Tordesillas, signed by Spain and Portugal in 1494, established the political basis for the present linguistic pattern in South America. Portugal was awarded the eastern part of the continent and Spain, the rest. (*Courtesy of Terry G. Jordan-Bychkov.*)

ILE PROPRE - VIE PROPRE

Bora - Bora, Ile propre, c'est notre affaire à tous.
Bora - Bora, Fenua ma, E ohipa ia na te Taatoaraa.

Ensemble, gardons notre Ile propre.
Tatou paatoa, ia vai ma noa to tatou Fenua.

IA VAI MA NOA
BORA - BORA

Figure 4.17 French, the colonial language of the empire, shares this sign on the isle of Bora Bora in French Polynesia with the native variant of the Polynesian tongue. Until recently, French rulers allowed no public display of the Polynesian language and tried to make the natives adopt French. *(Courtesy of Terry G. Jordan-Bychkov.)*

culture, which leads to the eventual abandonment of both. An educational system based solely on the socially dominant language produces bilingualism, and the number of **monoglots,** or persons able to speak only one language, declines (Figure 4.18). If the conquered group had been literate, they usually lapse at this stage into illiteracy in their traditional language. Often, no official status is accorded to the conquered language, conveying the message of social inferiority—the old way of speech is primitive and its use is socially degrading. One of the first acts of the new republican government of France in 1793 was to mandate the elimination of regional languages and dialects, using the apparatus of government to achieve that goal. In the modern world, where communications media are so pervasive, denying the oppressed language groups access to broadcast facilities can hasten the process of decline.

In Great Britain, the plight of the Welsh language (a Celtic Indo-European tongue), one of the most thoroughly studied cases of linguistic decline, illustrates Withers's social morale model (see Figure 4.18). The retreat of Welsh be-

fore English in the twentieth century was nearly catastrophic. Its speakers were long denigrated. Moreover, the British educational system promoted English. Urbanization and industrialization prompted a massive rural emigration directed to the English-speaking towns and factories. Geographer Keith Buchanan referred to the decline of Welsh and other Celtic languages as a "liquidation" carried out by the ruling English. All of this made it seem likely that the inhabitants of Wales would soon no longer know what the names of the towns, rivers, and mountains of their native land meant, nor would they even be able to understand their family names. However, in a policy reversal, the British government extended educational and media rights to Welsh, and Wales attained political autonomy within the United Kingdom. As a result, a modest revival of the Welsh language is under way today.

The history of the linguistic geography of the United States likewise reveals the profound decline of languages other than English, also following the social morale model. Almost up to the present day, the languages of Native Americans in both the United States and Canada have been greatly marginalized by the dominant culture. Large numbers of Native American children were taken from their families and placed in special boarding schools, often hundreds of miles from their homes. In these schools, run by the white-controlled Bureau of Indian Affairs, the children were forbidden on pain of punishment to speak their own languages. These and other assaults reduced the number of Native American languages in the territory of the United States from about 300 in the year 1500 to 175 today, only 20 of which will be passed on to the next generation. Fifty-five of these languages are spoken by fewer than 10 people and thus run the risk of becoming extinguished when their speakers die out. The Navajo tongue, which had 148,000 speakers in 1990, is known to only one in three Navajo first-graders today.

A similar process led most immigrants to the United States to abandon their native languages. As late as 1910, one out of every four Americans could speak some language other than English with the skill of a native (as compared to 14 percent in 1990). This was a result of the mass immigrations from Germany, Poland, Italy, Russia, China, and many other foreign lands. Much of this linguistic diversity has given way to English, partly because these other languages lacked legal status, partly because of the monolingual educational system in the United States, and partly because of social pressures.

The success of Spanish-speakers in preserving, and indeed in some areas of the United States in actively promoting, the Spanish language raises questions for the social morale model. In Miami, Florida, for example, many local government and business transactions are conducted in

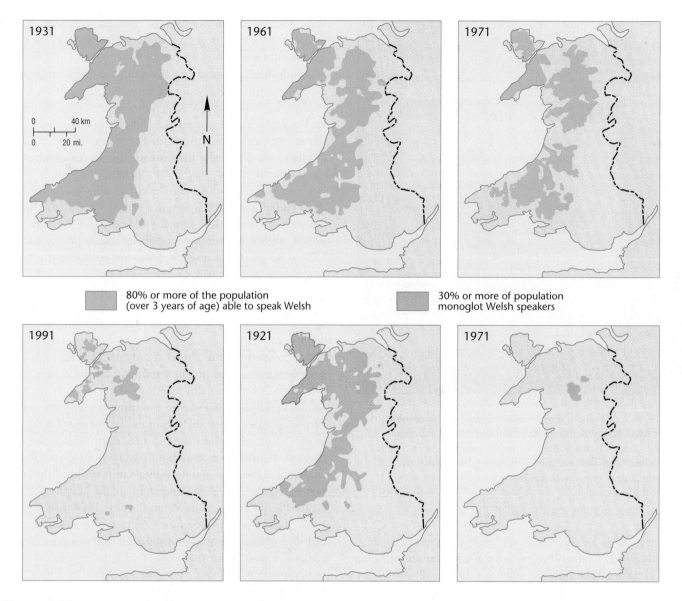

Figure 4.18 **Retreat of the Welsh language in the twentieth century.** For centuries, the Welsh have been dominated by English-speaking people in the United Kingdom. As a result, the language has declined. Between 1931 and 1991, the number of Welsh speakers fell from 909,000 to 497,000. Meanwhile, the district known as the Bro Gymraeg, where Welsh is spoken, shrank and began to fragment. English penetrated along the coast and valleys, causing Welsh to retreat into the hilliest terrain. Monoglots are people who are able to speak only one language, in this case Welsh. Note how their retreat has been far more profound than that of the bilingual Welsh speakers. Bilingualism is often a transitional phase in the extinction of minority languages. *(After Aitchinson and Carter, 1994; Bowen and Carter, 1975; Jones and Griffiths, 1963; Williams, 1937.)*

Spanish. The ability to speak Spanish is an explicit or at least a tacit job requirement for many seeking employment in Miami. Street signs, radio stations, and daily conversations in Spanish abound. Across the United States, legal challenges to monolingual education practices are being raised by those who believe that bilingual education should be offered in public schools. Far from experiencing a morale problem, many Spanish speakers are actively asserting pride in their language.

REFLECTING ON GEOGRAPHY

Should English be made the official language of the United States? Why or why not?

Language and Religion

Cultural interaction creates situations in which language is linked to a particular religious faith or denomination, a link-

PRACTICING GEOGRAPHY

Allan Pred

(Courtesy of Michele Pred.)

Like other geographers profiled in this book, Allan Pred engaged in all sorts of geographic activities as a child. "I can recall, as a child, perhaps five or six years old, spending my time on a street corner in the North Bronx. It was a major thoroughfare and there was a lot of long-distance traffic. And I'd just stand there looking for out-of-state license places and see how many I could count." Later, with a friend, he invented a fantasy baseball league. He still remembers the large map he drew for the fictional "Idaho-Montana league." Professor Pred is reluctant to speculate on whether this was indicative of an early interest in geography, a deep wish to escape elsewhere, or just creativity in the face of childhood boredom.

More specifically, Professor Pred recounts how desperation drove him to majoring in geography in college. As an undergraduate, he attended Antioch University in Ohio, which he describes as "a real intellectual hotbed" in those days. "I stumbled around in my first year. I'd started chemistry because that's what my parents thought I should do." Though he did well in chemistry, he soon became convinced that he wanted to study social sciences. He finally decided on geography after "I had worked my way through the catalog and the requirements of various majors. I chose geography because it had the smallest number of requirements and would give me the greatest freedom in choosing classes. So it was a pragmatic means to satisfy my general curiosity."

When it came time to graduate from Antioch, he thought he would continue his studies at the Fletcher School of Diplomacy at Tufts University in Massachusetts, where he had been accepted. Like all seniors at Antioch, before graduating he had to write a long introspective essay on his goals and where he wanted to go in life. In the process of writing that essay, "It became clear to me that I was much too much of a person who made a practice of going against the grain to have any chance of survival in the State Department. It was April and I was in a state of panic. I happened to pick up the latest issue of the *Annals* [*of American Geographers,* the main geography journal]." He read it and decided, "I'm going into geography because I don't know what else to do, and this looks interesting."

Apparently this was a wise choice. Professor Pred has built a distinguished career as a practicing geographer at the University of California, Berkeley. His research focuses on modernity, racism, and Sweden. He has published about 20 books, including *Even in Sweden: Racisms, Racialized Spaces, and the Popular Geographical Imagination* in 2000 and *The Past Is Not Dead: Facts, Fictions, and Enduring Racial Stereotypes* in 2004. His latest work is a book he is compiling with another geographer, Derek Gregory, titled *Inhuman Geographies.* His project in this book involves "reworking my discontents and outrage over the Bush administration's handling of Iraq and the 'war on terror.'"

Though he is not a linguistic geographer in the classic sense that we have presented in this chapter, Professor Pred's focus has always been on how we write and how our writing is connected with how, and what, we know. Professor Pred's writing often reads like poetry. He uses innovative writing strategies not typically seen in academic texts, such as using different fonts and superimposing words on pictures.

Professor Pred seeks to view simultaneously "the visible geographies that geographers have always been preoccupied with and the invisible geographies of power relations and the world of knowing, meaning, and discourse." He finds it difficult to separate what he does as a scholar from what he does in his everyday life, saying "everything is grist for my mill. In recent years the research issues have come to me. I haven't gone out looking for them."

Professor Pred goes to Sweden every year. "Since the mid-1980s I'd been seeing and hearing and reading things in the everyday media. I'd take ethnographic notes on conversations and things I'd seen happen on the street. Without any specific intent in mind, I built up an extensive archive of newspaper clippings and other items. There came a point in about 1990–1991 where I just had the sense that things had gone painfully far in Sweden and that I was reading what was going on in a way that my Swedish colleagues could not or would not see. I felt a moral obligation to start writing about this."

age that greatly heightens cultural identity. Perhaps Arabic provides the best example of this cultural link. It spread from a core area on the Arabian Peninsula with the expansion of Islam. Had it not been for the evangelical success of the Muslims, Arabic would not have diffused so widely. The other Semitic languages also correspond to particular religious groups. Hebrew-speaking people are of the Jewish faith, and the Amharic speakers in Ethiopia tend to be Coptic, or Eastern, Christians. Indeed, we can attribute the preservation and recent revival of Hebrew to its active promotion by Jewish nationalists who feel that teaching and promoting Hebrew to diasporic Jews facilitates unity.

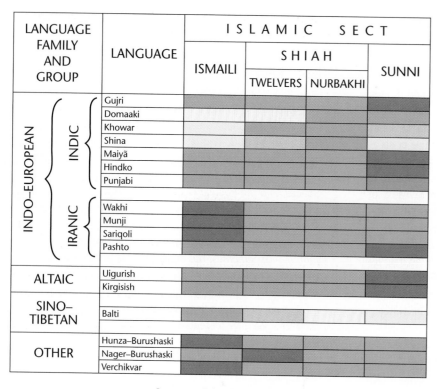

Figure 4.19 **The correlation between language and religion in the Hindu Kush and Himalaya Mountains of northern Pakistan.** Correlations do not prove cause-and-effect relationships, so the evidence of linkages between religion and language is more complex than that. For more information about the Muslim sects shown, look back to Chapter 3. *(Source: Kreutzmann, 1995: 109, 117.)*

The link between language and religion can often be seen even within very small areas. German geographer Hermann Kreutzmann, who studied the cultures of isolated mountain valleys in northernmost Pakistan, found that over 90 percent of the speakers of 12 of the 17 languages he studied in that region belonged to one or another of the four local Muslim sects (Figure 4.19). In other words, the language spoken by mountain people usually helps to determine their religious denomination.

Certain languages have even acquired a religious status. Latin survived mainly as the ceremonial language of the Roman Catholic Church and Vatican City. In non-Arabic Muslim lands, such as Iran, where people consider themselves Persians and speak Farsi, Arabic is still used in religious ceremonies. Great religious books can also shape languages by providing them with a standard form. Martin Luther's translation of the Bible led to the standardization of the German language, and the Koran is the model for written Arabic. The early appearance of a hymnal and the Bible in the Welsh language aided the survival of that Celtic tongue, and Christian missionaries in diverse countries have translated the Bible into local languages, helping to preserve them. In Fiji, the appearance of the Bible in one of the 15 local dialects elevated it to the dominant native language of the islands.

Sometimes the influence of religion on language is far more subtle. For example, as Indo-European-speaking farmers spread northward into the boreal forests of Europe thousands of years ago, they mixed with peoples who worshipped bears, as part of the so-called *bear cults*. These natives would not even utter the word *bear*, for fear of offending the sacred animal. The invading Indo-Europeans implanted their language but adopted the bear-worship cult of the forest peoples. No longer wanting to use their ancient Indo-European word for bear, *arksos*, for fear of offending the bear-god, they created new words—cautious euphemisms—such as the English *bear* ("the brown one") or the Russian *medved* ("he who knows how to find honey")!

 # Linguistic Landscapes

In what ways are languages visible and, as a result, part of the cultural landscape? Road signs, billboards, graffiti, placards, and other publicly displayed writings not only reveal the locally dominant language but also can be a visual index to bilingualism, linguistic oppression of minorities, and other facets of linguistic geography (Figure 4.20). Further-

Figure 4.20 **Samoan, a Polynesian language belonging to the Austronesian family,** becomes part of the linguistic landscape of Apia, the capital of independent Western Samoa in the Pacific Ocean. When this area was still a British colony, such a visual display of the native language would not have been permitted. *(Courtesy of Terry G. Jordan-Bychkov.)*

is particular to a subculture and transmitted through symbols or a highly stylized script.

Toponyms

Language and culture also intersect in the names that people place on the land, whether they are given to settlements, terrain features, streams, or various other aspects of their surroundings. These place-names, or **toponyms,** often directly reflect the spatial patterns of language, dialect, and ethnicity (see Figure 4.14). Toponyms become part of the cultural landscape when they appear on signs and placards. Look again at our example of religious toponyms (see Figure 3.34). Toponyms can be very revealing, for as geographer Stephen Jett said, they often provide insights into "linguistic origins, diffusion, habitat, and environmental perception." Many place-names consist of two parts—the *generic* and the *specific.* For example, in the American place-names Huntsville, Harrisburg, Ohio River, Newfound Gap, and Cape Hatteras, the specific segments are *Hunts-, Harris-,*

more, differences in writing systems render some linguistic landscapes illegible to those not familiar with other ways of writing (Figure 4.21).

Messages

Linguistic landscapes send messages, both friendly and hostile. Often these messages have a political content and deal with power, domination, subjugation, or freedom. In Turkey, for example, until recently Kurdish-speaking minorities were not allowed to broadcast music or television programs in Kurdish, to publish books in Kurdish, or even to give their children Kurdish names. Because Turkey wishes to join the European Union, these minority language restrictions have come under intense outside scrutiny. In 2002, Turkey reformed its legal restrictions to allow Kurdish in daily life, but not in public education. The Canadian province of Québec, similarly, has tried to eliminate English-language signs. In Ireland, there is a movement to replace English-language place-name signs with signs depicting the original Gaelic place-names. The suppression of minority languages, and moves to reinstate them in the landscape, offers an indication of the social and political status of minority populations more generally.

Other types of writing, such as gang-related graffiti, can denote ownership of territory or send messages to others that they are not welcome (Figure 4.22). Only those who understand the specific gang symbols used will be able to decipher the message. Misreading such writing can have deadly consequences for those who stray into unfriendly territory. In this way gang symbols can be understood as a dialect that

Figure 4.21 **Linguistic landscapes can be hard to read** for those who are not familiar with the script used for writing. For many English-speaking monoglots, who are visually accustomed to the Latin alphabet, the linguistic landscape of countries such as Korea appears illegible. *(Courtesy of Terry G. Jordan-Bychkov.)*

Figure 4.22 Graffiti is used to mark gang territory. This wall in the Polanco neighborhood of Guadalajara, Mexico, is covered with graffiti. Gangs use stylized scripts that are often unintelligible to nonmembers to mark their territory. *(Courtesy of Patricia L. Price.)*

Ohio, Newfound, and *Hatteras.* The generic parts, which tell what *kind* of place is being described, are *-ville, -burg, River, Gap,* and *Cape.*

Generic toponyms are of greater potential value to the cultural geographer than specific names because they appear again and again throughout a culture region. There are literally thousands of generic place-names, and every culture or subculture has its own distinctive set of them. They are particularly valuable both in tracing the spread of a culture and in reconstructing culture regions of the past. Sometimes generic toponyms provide information about changes people wrought long ago in their physical surroundings.

Generic Toponyms of the United States

The three dialects of the eastern United States (see Figure 4.6)—Northern, Midland, and Southern—illustrate the value of generic toponyms in cultural geographical detective work. For example, New Englanders, speakers of the Northern dialect, often used the terms *Center* and *Corners* in the names of the towns or hamlets. Outlying settlements frequently bear the prefix *East, West, North,* or *South,* with the specific name of the township as the suffix. Thus, in Randolph Township, Orange County, Vermont, we find settlements named Randolph Center, South Randolph, East Randolph, and North Randolph. A few miles away lies Hewetts Corners.

These generic usages and duplications are peculiar to New England, and we can locate areas settled by New Englanders as they migrated westward by looking for such place-

names in other parts of the country. A trail of "Centers" and name duplications extending westward from New England through upstate New York and Ontario and into the upper Midwest clearly indicates their path of migration and settlement (Figure 4.23). Toponymic evidence of New England exists in areas as far afield as Walworth County, Wisconsin, where Troy, Troy Center, East Troy, and Abels Corners are clustered; in Dufferin County, Ontario, where one finds places such as Mono Centre; and even in distant Alberta, near Edmonton, where the toponym Michigan Centre doubly suggests a particular cultural diffusion. Similarly, we can identify Midland American areas by such terms as *Gap, Cove, Hollow, Knob* (a low, rounded hill), and *-burg,* as in Stone Gap, Cades Cove, Stillhouse Hollow, Bald Knob, and Fredericksburg. We can recognize Southern speech by such names as *Bayou, Gully,* and *Store* (for rural hamlets), as in Cypress Bayou, Gum Gully, and Halls Store.

Toponyms and Cultures of the Past

Place-names often survive long after the culture that produced them vanishes from an area, thereby preserving traces of the past. Australia abounds in Aborigine toponyms, even in areas from which the native peoples disappeared long ago (Figure 4.24). No toponyms are more permanently established than those identifying physical geographical features, such as rivers and mountains. Even the most absolute conquest, exterminating an aboriginal people, usually does not entirely destroy such names. Quite the contrary, in fact. Geographer R.D.K. Herman speaks of *anticonquest,* in which the defeated people finds its toponyms venerated and perpetuated by the conqueror, who at the same time denies the people any real power or cultural influence. The abundance of Native American toponyms in the United States provides an example (see Doing Geography at the end of the chapter).

In Spain and Portugal, seven centuries of Moorish rule left behind a great many Arabic place-names (Figure 4.25). An example is the prefix *guada-* on river names (as in Guadalquivir and Guadalupejo). The prefix is a corruption of the Arabic *wadi,* meaning "river" or "stream." Thus, Guadalquivir, corrupted from Wadi-al-Kabir, means "the great river." The frequent occurrence of Arabic names in any particular region or province of Spain reveals the remnants of Moorish cultural influence in that area, rather than anticonquest. Many such names were brought to the Americas through Iberian conquest, so that Guadalajara, for example, appears on the map as an important Mexican city.

New Zealand, too, offers some intriguing examples of the subtle messages that can be conveyed by archaic toponyms. The native Polynesian people of New Zealand are the Maori. As cultural geographer Hong-key Yoon has observed, the

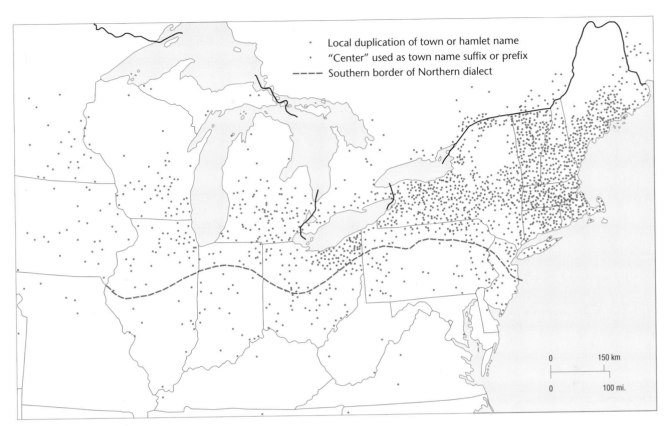

· Local duplication of town or hamlet name
· "Center" used as town name suffix or prefix
--- Southern border of Northern dialect

0   150 km
0   100 mi.

Figure 4.23   Generic place-names reveal the migration of Yankee New Englanders and the spread of the Northern dialect. Two of the most typical place-name characteristics in New England are the use of *Center* in the names of the principal settlements in a political subdivision and the tendency to duplicate the names of local towns and villages by adding the prefixes *East, West, North,* and *South* to the subdivision's name. As the concentration of such place-names suggests, these two Yankee traits originated in Massachusetts, the first New England colony. Note how these toponyms moved westward with New England settlers but thinned out rapidly to the south, in areas not colonized by New Englanders. Compare this illustration with Figure 4.6.

Figure 4.24   An Australian Aborigine specific toponym joined to an English generic name, near Omeo in Victoria state, Australia. Such signs give a special, distinctive look to the linguistic landscape and speak of a now-vanished culture region. *(Courtesy of Terry G. Jordan-Bychkov.)*

survival rate of Maori names for towns varies according to the size of its population. The four largest New Zealand cities all have European names, but of the 20 regional centers, with populations of 10,000 to 100,000, 40 percent have Maori names. Almost 60 percent of the small towns, with fewer than 10,000 inhabitants, bear Maori toponyms. Similarly, while only 20 percent of New Zealand's provinces have Maori names, 56 percent of the counties do. Nearly all streams, hills, and mountains retain Maori names. The implication is that British settlement of New Zealand was largely an urban phenomenon.

These Maori toponyms, which are heard and seen as one drives across New Zealand, help make the country a unique place. What is the mental impact of such names, visually displayed on signs, on New Zealanders of European origin? One might imagine responses ranging from discomfort, even hostility, on the part of those faced with a linguistically alien landscape, to a sense of comfort, homecoming, and belonging for those to whom this landscape is familiar terrain. Linguistic landscapes not only bear

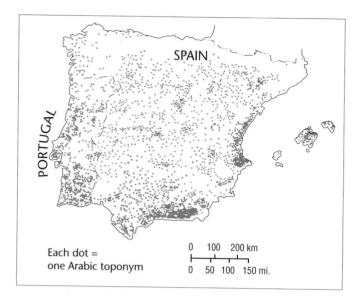

Figure 4.25 **Arabic toponyms in Iberia.** Arabic, a Semitic language, spread into Spain and Portugal with the Moors over a thousand years ago. A reconquest by Romance Indo-European speakers subsequently rooted out the Arabic-speaking North Africans in Iberia, but today one out of four Spanish words has an Arabic root. A reminder of the Semitic language also survives in Iberian toponyms, or place-names. Using this map, you can easily speculate about the direction of the Moorish invasion and retreat, the duration of Moorish rule in different parts of Iberia, and the main centers of former Moorish power. *(Source: Houston, 1967.)*

meaningful messages but also help shape the very character of places, as well as senses of belonging and exclusion for those who inhabit them.

Conclusion

Language, then, is an essential part of culture that can be studied using the five themes of cultural geography. Language is firmly enmeshed in the cultural whole. Its families, dialects, vocabulary, pronunciation, and toponyms display distinct spatial variations that are shown on maps of linguistic culture regions. Languages ebb and flow across geographical areas through the processes of diffusion. Relocation and expansion diffusion, both hierarchical and contagious, are apparent in the movement of language.

Language and physical environment interact in a linguistic ecology, with the physical environment helping to shape linguistic elements such as vocabulary, while language can also shape our use and perception of the environment. The study of cultural interaction shows that language is related to other elements of culture. In fact, language is the basis for the expression of all elements of culture, so the geography of languages is closely bound to the geographies of religion, politics, technology, economy, and much else. Finally, we can see language in the landscapes created by literate societies. The visible alphabet, public signs, and generic toponyms together create a linguistic landscape that can be read using one's "geographic eyes."

Language and religion, the subjects of this chapter and Chapter 3, both provide the building blocks for understanding *ethnicity*, to which we turn in Chapter 5.

DOING GEOGRAPHY

Toponyms and Roots of Place

As you recall from this chapter, toponyms can give us important clues about the historical, social, political, and physical geography of a place. One example of this is the prevalence of indigenous place-names throughout the Americas, from Canada to Chile. You may say a place-name on a daily basis without being aware of its roots in an indigenous language. According to Charles Cutler, European settlers simply appropriated many of the Native American words for plants, animals, foods, and places with little or no modification in their pronunciation. These words are known as *loanwords*. For example, *Milwaukee* comes from an Algonquin word meaning "good spot or place," while *Chicago* is also Algonquin in origin and probably means "garlic field." The commonly used derogatory place-name *Podunk* is also indigenous in origin, from the Natick word for "swampy place." In fact, more than half of the states in the United States have names of Native American origin.

For this exercise you will explore the theme of toponyms in more detail. You need to choose, or be assigned by your instructor, a state in the United States or a province in Canada to focus on. Your first task is to find a map of your assigned state or province. It should be a map that is detailed enough to show the names of political and physical features, such as cities, towns, counties or parishes, rivers, mountains, lakes, and so on. You can find such maps in the reference section of your library, in printed or CD-ROM atlases, and online at sites such as the University of Texas's Perry-Castañeda map collection, located at http://www.lib.utexas.edu/maps/. Many maps in atlases also have an index of place-names that can be useful to you.

Now you will need to examine your map with an eye to the different categories of toponyms. Make a list of at least five place names for each category:

- Historical people or events
- Non-English place-names (excluding Native American names)
- Native American place-names
- Place-names transplanted from elsewhere (e.g., "New" York)
- Descriptions of physical features (landforms, elevation, etc.)
- Descriptions of natural resources

Did you find at least five examples for each category? If not, why do you think you didn't? For which category of toponyms did you find the most examples? Why? Were toponyms of one or more categories clustered spatially on the map? If so, where and why? What do the names say about the history, culture, and physical geography of the state or province you examined?

Linguistic Geography on the Internet

You can learn more about linguistic geography on the Internet at the following web sites:

Atlas of North American English

http://www.ling.upenn.edu/phono_atlas/home.html

Explore the TELSUR project web site from the University of Pennsylvania, which provides updates on a major ongoing study designed to produce a phonological atlas of North America.

Dictionary of American Regional English

http://polyglot.lss.wisc.edu/dare/dare.html

Discover a reference web site that describes regional vocabulary contrasts of the English language in the United States and includes numerous maps.

Ethnologue

http://www.ethnologue.com

This site provides information on how languages change over time as well as on endangered and nearly extinct languages

The Museum of Human Language

http://www.geocities.com/agihard/mohl/mohl.html#LANGUAGES

Visit this "virtual museum," where you can find information on world languages—including the birth, modification, and death of languages—and how people acquire language.

Sources

Aitchison, John, and Harold Carter. 1994. *A Geography of the Welsh Language, 1961–1991*. Cardiff, U.K.: University of Wales Press.

Atwood, Elmer B. 1962. *The Regional Vocabulary of Texas*. Austin: University of Texas Press.

Basso, Keith H. 1996. *Wisdom Sits in Places: Landscape and Language Among the Western Apache*. Albuquerque: University of New Mexico Press.

Bennett, Charles J. 1980. "The Morphology of Language Boundaries: Indo-Aryan and Dravidian in Peninsular India," in David E. Sopher (ed.), *An Exploration of India: Geographical Perspectives on Society and Culture*. Ithaca, N.Y.: Cornell University Press, 234–251.

Bomhard, Allan R., and John C. Kerns. 1994. *The Nostratic Macrofamily*. Berlin: Mouton de Gruyter.

Bowen, E. G., and Harold Carter. 1975. "The Distribution of the Welsh Language in 1971." *Geography* 60: 1–5.

Buchanan, Keith. 1977. "Economic Growth and Cultural Liquidation: The Case of the Celtic Nations," in Richard Peet (ed.), *Radical Geography: Alternative Viewpoints on Contemporary Social Issues*. Chicago: Maaroufa Press, 125–143.

Cutler, Charles. 1994. *O Brave New Words! Native American Loanwords in Current English*. Norman: University of Oklahoma Press.

Dingemanse, Mark. Wikipedia. http://en.wikipedia.org/wiki/Image:Bantu_expansion.png

Drucker, Johanna. 1984. "Language in the Landscape." *Landscape* 28(1): 7–13.

Encyclopaedia Britannica. 2000. *2000 Britannica Book of the Year*. Chicago: Encyclopaedia Britannica.

Ford, Clark. http://www.public.iastate.edu/~cfford/342worldhistoryearly.html

Herman, R. D. K. 1999. "The Aloha State: Place Names and the Anti-Conquest of Hawaii." *Annals of the Association of American Geographers* 89: 76–102.

Hill, Robert T. 1896. "Descriptive Topographic Terms of Spanish America." *National Geographic* 7: 292–297.

Houston, James M. 1967. *The Western Mediterranean World*. New York: Praeger.

Jett, Stephen C. 1997. "Place-Naming, Environment, and Perception Among the Canyon de Chelly Navajo of Arizona." *Professional Geographer* 49: 481–493.

Jones, Emrys, and Ieuan Griffiths. 1963. "A Linguistic Map of Wales, 1961." *Geographical Journal* 129: 192–196.

Jordan-Bychkov, Terry G., and Bella Bychkova Jordan. 2002. *The European Culture Area: A Systematic Geography*. Lanham, Md.: Rowman & Littlefield, Chapter 4.

Kreutzmann, Hermann. 1995. "Linguistic Diversity and Regional Differentiation of Denominational Groups in the Hindukush-Karakoram." *Erdkunde* 49: 109–117.

Latrimer Clarke Corporation Pty Ltd. http://www.altapedia.com

Levison, Michael, R. Gerard Ward, and John W. Webb. 1973. *The Settlement of Polynesia: A Computer Simulation*. Minneapolis: University of Minnesota Press.

Marckwardt, Albert H., and J. L. Dillard. 1980. *American English*, 2nd ed. New York: Oxford University Press.

Renfrew, Colin. 1989. "The Origins of Indo-European Languages." *Scientific American* 261(4): 106–114.

Stavans, Ilan. 2003. *Spanglish: The Making of a New American Language*. New York: Rayo

Tuan, Yi-Fu. 1991. "Language and the Making of Place." *Annals of the Association of American Geographers* 81: 684–696.

U.S. English, Inc. http://www.us-english.org/inc/official/states.asp

Williams, Trevor. 1937. "A Linguistic Map of Wales." *Geographical Journal* 89: 146–151.

Wood, Gordon R. 1971. *Vocabulary Change: A Study of Variation in Eight of the Southern States*. Carbondale: Southern Illinois University Press.

World Almanac Books. 2001. *World Almanac and Book of Facts 2001*. New York: World Almanac Books.

Yoon, Hong-key. 1986. "Maori and Pakeha Place Names for Cultural Features in New Zealand," in *Maori Mind, Maori Land: Essays on the Cultural Geography of the Maori People from an Outsider's Perspective*. Bern, Switzerland: Peter Lang, 98–122.

Ten Recommended Books and Special Issues on the Geography of Language

For additional suggested readings, see *The Human Mosaic* web site: www.whfreeman.com/jordan)

SEEING GEOGRAPHY

What does this sign tell you about who uses the commercial spaces in this city?

Street scene in New York City.

Aquí se habla Spanglish

Languages are fluid, always being altered and reinvented as the needs and experiences of their users change. Thanks to relocation diffusion upon conquest of the East Coast of North America by the British in the seventeenth century, the primary language of the United States is English. The language then expanded westward as English-speaking peoples conquered more and more of the continent's territory. But the English spoken in Britain's overseas colonies has never been "the Queen's English." Rather, British colonies in North America, Australia, the Caribbean, Africa, and eastern and southern Asia have all developed their own distinctive dialects. Indigenous words have been incorporated into English vocabularies, as the sections on toponyms in this chapter show. Pidgins, creoles, and distinctive dialects have resulted in places of high multilingual exposure, such as Singapore and the Anglophone Caribbean islands. Waves of immigrants have added further to the linguistic richness of English-speaking areas.

In 2002, Hispanics surpassed African-Americans as the nation's numerically most significant minority group. In some U.S. cities, Hispanics constitute more than half of the population, a fact that brings into question the designation "minority." For example, the population of Miami, Florida, is two-thirds Hispanic, and more than three-fourths of the residents of El Paso and San Antonio, Texas, are Hispanic. In the United States today, Spanish-speaking peoples from Latin America provide the largest flow of immigrants into the United States. Even midsize and smaller towns in the midwestern and southern United States are becoming destinations for Spanish-speaking immigrants, sharply changing the ethnic composition of cities like Shelbyville, Tennessee; Dubuque, Iowa; and Siler City, North Carolina.

It is logical to assume that the Spanish language spoken by these new immigrants, and by the families of Hispanic-Americans, will have a growing impact on American English. As the opening photograph for this chapter illustrates, Spanish words have become common sights in U.S. cities, appearing frequently on street signs. But Spanish and English have combined in a rich, complex fashion as well, to produce a hybrid language called Spanglish. The phrase "Vámonos al downtown a tomar una bironga after work hoy" is an excellent example. It translates into Standard English as "Let's go downtown and have a beer after work today." *Vámonos* ("let's go"), *tomar* ("to drink"), and *hoy* ("today") are Spanish words that are combined in the same sentence with the English words *downtown* and *after work*. This is referred to by linguists as code-switching. But the noun *bironga*, which means "beer" in English, is a Spanglish invention: it exists in neither English nor Spanish. This is quite common in Spanglish, and neologisms like *hanguear* ("to hang out"), *deioff* ("day off"), and *parquear* ("to park" a vehicle) abound. The term *gasetería* in the photo shown here is also an invented Spanglish word.

Spanglish reflects the growing Spanish-English bilingualism of many U.S. residents, the flexibility of language, and the enduring creativity of human beings as we attempt to communicate with one another. Ilan Stavans, author of *Spanglish: The Making of a New American Language*, likens Spanglish to jazz. "Yes," Stavans writes, "it is the tongue of the uneducated. Yes, it's a hodgepodge. . . . But its creativity astonished me. In many ways, I see in it the beauties and achievements of jazz, a musical style that sprung up [sic] among African-Americans as a result of improvisation and lack of education. Eventually, though, it became a major force in America, a state of mind breaching out of the ghetto into the middle class and beyond. Will Spanglish follow a similar route?" (p. 3) ∎

Carver, Craig M. 1986. *American Regional Dialects: Word Geography.* Ann Arbor: University of Michigan Press. One of the best overall presentations of American English dialects from the standpoint of vocabulary.

Cassidy, Frederic C. (ed.). 1985–2002. *Dictionary of American Regional English.* 4 vols. Cambridge, Mass.: Harvard University Press. A massive compilation of words used only regionally within the United States, with maps showing distributions.

Desforges, Luke, and Rhys Jones (eds.). 2001. "Geographies of Languages/Languages of Geography." Special issue, *Social and Cultural Geography* 2(3): 261–346. The manifold ways in which geographers have examined the spaces and places of various languages.

Krantz, Grover S. 1988. *Geographical Development of European Languages.* New York: Peter Lang. Presents a new theory and model of how the Indo-European languages fragmented as linguistic diffusion occurred in prehistoric Europe.

Kurath, Hans. 1949. *Word Geography of the Eastern United States.* Ann Arbor: University of Michigan Press. The classic study that gave rise to the geographical study of American English dialects.

Laponce, J. A. 1987. *Languages and Their Territories.* Anthony Martin-Sperry (trans.). Toronto: University of Toronto Press. Treats the themes that (1) languages protect themselves by territoriality and (2) the modern political state typically acts overtly to destroy minority languages.

Moseley, Christopher, and R. E. Asher (eds.). 1994. *Atlas of the World's Languages.* London: Routledge. A wonderfully detailed color map portrait of the world's complex linguistic mosaic; thumb through it at your library and you will come to appreciate how complicated the patterns and spatial distributions of languages remain, even in the age of globalization.

Williams, Colin H. (ed.). 1988. *Language in Geographical Context.* Clevedon, U.K., and Philadelphia: Multilingual Matters. Eight geolinguists provide an introduction to the field, with examples drawn mainly from Europe, especially the British Isles.

Withers, Charles W. J. 1988. *Gaelic Scotland: The Transformation of a Culture Region.* London: Routledge. A geographer analyzes one of the dying Celtic languages within the framework of the models presented in this chapter.

Wixman, Ronald. 1980. *Language Aspects of Ethnic Patterns and Processes in the North Caucasus.* Research Paper No. 191. University of Chicago, Department of Geography. A cultural geographer surveys a part of the most complex linguistic maze in the entire world—the Caucasus Mountains.

A Journal

in the Geography of Language

World Englishes. Published by the International Association for World Englishes, the journal documents the fragmentation of English into separate languages around the world. Edited by Larry E. Smith.

When does cuisine cease to be ethnic and become simply "American"?
What role does cultural diffusion play in the process?

**Neon signs collected from ethnic restaurants in the United States by the Smithsonian
Institution in Washington, D.C.** *(Courtesy of Terry G. Jordan-Bychkov.)*

Turn to Seeing Geography on page 174 for an in-depth analysis of the above question.

ETHNIC 5 GEOGRAPHY

Homelands and Islands

A STATUE OF THE AMERICAN national hero Paul Revere, mounted on his horse, towers over a pedestrian mall near the Old North Church in Boston. Close by is the Revere home, lovingly preserved. A scene as American as apple pie, you may say. But what language are the elderly women speaking as they sit on benches near the statue and go about their knitting? By the sound of it, certainly not English. Closer inspection reveals Italian family names, such as Giuffre's Fish Market, on almost every business establishment in Revere's neighborhood; Italian pizzerias; a predominantly Italian outdoor vegetable market; a Sons of Italy lodge hall; and Italian-American women leaning out of upper-story windows on opposite sides of the narrow streets to converse, Naples-style. Revere, himself of French ethnic extraction, would be astounded. Boston's North End is now Italian! A pilgrimage to the site where the American Revolution began has also become a trip to Little Italy.

Half a continent away, the midwestern town of Wilber, settled by Bohemian immigrants beginning about 1865, bills itself as "The Czech Capital of Nebraska" and annually invites visitors to attend a "National Czech Festival." Celebrants are promised Czech foods such as *koláce, jaternice,* poppyseed cake, and *jelita;* Czech folk dancing; "colored Czech postcards and souvenirs" imported from Europe; and handicraft items made by Nebraska Czechs (bearing an official seal and trademark to prove authenticity). Thousands of visitors attend the festival each year. Without leaving Nebraska, these tourists can move on to "Norwegian Days" at Newman Grove, the "Greek Festival" at Bridgeport, the Danish "Grundlovs Fest" in Dannebrog, "German Heritage Days" at McCook, the "Swedish Festival" at Stromsburg, the "St. Patrick's Day Celebration" at O'Neill, several Native American powwows, and assorted other ethnic celebrations (Figure 5.1).

Figure 5.1 **The town of Stromsburg, Nebraska.** Proud of its Swedish heritage, Stromsburg holds a "Swedish Festival" each year in June.

Nebraska is still a magnet for immigrants, but since the 1990s, they have been overwhelmingly non-European. In particular, Mexican immigrants employed in Nebraska's meat-processing industry find nontraditional destinations

such as Nebraska and other upper midwestern states attractive. In general, immigrants to the United States today are more likely to come from Asia or Latin America than from Europe, and they are changing the face of ethnicity in the United States (Figure 5.2). Indeed, ethnicity is a central aspect of the cultural geography of most countries, forming one of the brightest motifs in the human mosaic.

Race is often used interchangeably with *ethnicity,* but the two have very different meanings, and one must be careful in choosing between the two terms. **Race** can be understood as a genetically significant difference among human populations. A few biologists today support the view that human populations do form racially distinct groupings, arguing that race explains phenomena such as the susceptibility to certain diseases. In contrast, many social scientists have noted the fluidity of definitions of *race* across time and space, suggesting that race is a social construct rather than a biological fact (Figure 5.3). In the United States, for example, the so-called one-drop rule meant that anyone with any African-American ancestry at all was considered black. This rule was intended to prevent interracial marriage. It also meant that moving out of the category "black" was, and still is today, extremely difficult, since one's racial status is determined by ancestry. In Brazil, by contrast, physiognomic features such as skin pigmentation, eye color, and hair texture are used to identify a person racially, with the result that many racial categories exist in Brazil. Siblings are frequently classified in quite different racial terms depending on their appearance, the same person can be put into multiple racial categories by different people, and individuals' own racial self-designations can depend on such variables as their mood at the time they are asked. Increased economic or educational status can "whiten" people formerly classified as black. However, one must keep in mind that Brazil was also the last country in the Americas to abolish slavery, and discrimination against darker-skinned Brazilians is common today.

Studies of genetic variation have demonstrated that there is far more variability within so-called racial groups than between them, which has led most scholars to believe that all human beings are, genetically speaking, members of just one race: *Homo sapiens sapiens.* In fact, many social scientists have dropped the term *race* altogether in favor of *ethnicity.* Throughout this chapter, we will use the term *ethnicity* to signal differences among groups. This is not to say, however, that **racism,** the belief that human capabilities are determined by racial classification and that some races are superior to others, does not exist.

What exactly is an ethnic group? The word *ethnic* is derived from the Greek word *ethnos,* meaning a "people" or "nation," but that definition is too broad. For our purposes, an **ethnic group** consists of people of common ancestry and

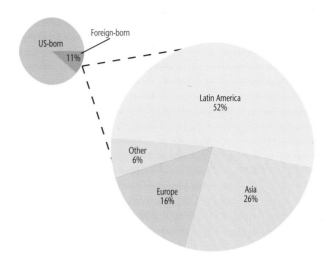

Figure 5.2 **The foreign-born population of the United States.** The smaller chart shows that 11 percent, or 31.1 million of the total U.S. population of 281.4 million, was born abroad. The larger chart shows that the majority of these people came from Latin America and Asia. *(Source: U.S. Census, 2000.)*

cultural tradition, often living as a minority in a larger society or host culture. A strong feeling of group identity, of belonging, characterizes ethnicity. Membership in an ethnic group is largely involuntary, in the sense that a person cannot simply decide to join; instead, he or she must be born into the group. In some cases, outsiders can join an ethnic group by marriage or adoption.

Different ethnic groups may base their identities on different traits. For some, such as the Jews, ethnicity primarily means religion; for the Amish, it is both folk culture and religion; for Swiss-Americans, it is national origin; for German-Americans, it is ancestral language. Religion, language, folk culture, and place of origin can all help provide the basis of the sense of "we-ness" that underlies ethnicity.

Making a definition of *ethnic* still more difficult is the distinction between *immigrant* and *aboriginal* groups. Many if not most ethnic groups around the world originated when they migrated from their native lands and settled in a new country. In their old home, they often belonged to the host culture and were not ethnic; but, transplanted by relocation diffusion to a foreign land, they simultaneously became a minority and ethnic. Chinese are not ethnic in China, but if they come to America they are. Indigenous ethnic groups that continue to live in their ancient homes become ethnic when absorbed into larger political states. The Navajo, for example, reside on their traditional and ancient lands and became ethnic only when the United States annexed their territory.

This is not to say that ethnic minorities remain unchanged by their host culture. **Acculturation** often occurs,

meaning that the ethnic group adopts enough of the ways of the host society to be able to function economically and socially. Stronger still is **assimilation,** which implies a complete blending with the host culture and may involve the loss of many distinctive ethnic traits. Intermarriage is perhaps the most effective way of encouraging assimilation. Many students of American culture have long assumed that all ethnic groups would eventually be assimilated into the American melting pot, but relatively few have been, instead using acculturation as their way of survival. The past three decades, in fact, have witnessed a resurgence of ethnic identity in the United States, Canada, Europe, and elsewhere.

Ethnic geography is the study of the spatial aspects of ethnicity. Ethnic groups are the keepers of distinctive cultural traditions and the focal points of various kinds of social interaction. They are the basis not only of group identity but also of friendships, marriage partners, recreational outlets, business success, and political power bases. These interactions can offer cultural security and reinforcement of tradition. Ethnic groups often practice unique adaptive strategies and usually occupy clearly defined areas, whether rural or urban. In other words, the study of ethnicity has built-in geographical dimensions.

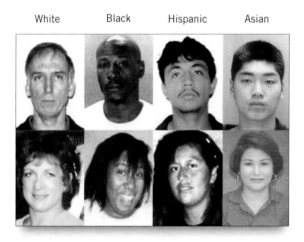

Figure 5.3 **Mugshots of people from different races.** Phenotype variations—visible bodily differences such as facial features, skin color, and hair texture—are considered indicative of "race" by the U.S. Federal Bureau of Investigation (FBI). "Race" is one of several visible characteristics—including tattoos, scars, height, and weight—often used by law enforcement to identify suspects. These are photos from the FBI's Most Wanted list. How is this idea of race as defined by visible differences different from race as it is commonly understood in the United States? *(Courtesy of Federal Bureau of Investigation.)*

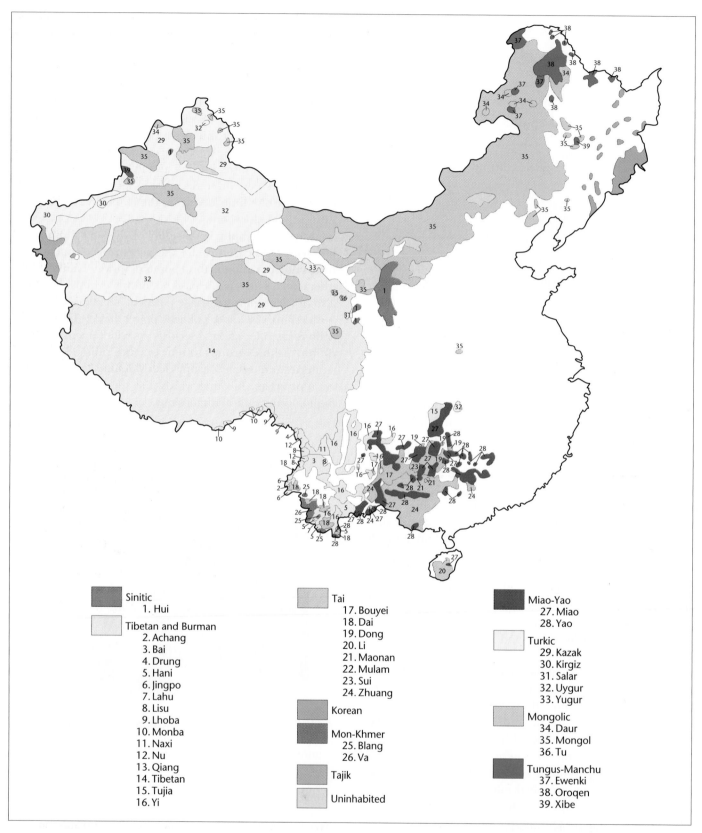

Sinitic
1. Hui

Tibetan and Burman
2. Achang
3. Bai
4. Drung
5. Hani
6. Jingpo
7. Lahu
8. Lisu
9. Lhoba
10. Monba
11. Naxi
12. Nu
13. Qiang
14. Tibetan
15. Tujia
16. Yi

Tai
17. Bouyei
18. Dai
19. Dong
20. Li
21. Maonan
22. Mulam
23. Sui
24. Zhuang

Korean

Mon-Khmer
25. Blang
26. Va

Tajik

Uninhabited

Miao-Yao
27. Miao
28. Yao

Turkic
29. Kazak
30. Kirgiz
31. Salar
32. Uygur
33. Yugur

Mongolic
34. Daur
35. Mongol
36. Tu

Tungus-Manchu
37. Ewenki
38. Oroqen
39. Xibe

Figure 5.4 Ethnic minorities in China. Most ethnic groups are Turkic, Mongolic, Tai, Tibetan, or Burman in speech, but the rich diversity extends even to the Tajiks of the Indo-European language family. Unshaded areas are Han (Mandarin) Chinese, the host culture. Which of these ethnic regions are homelands and which islands? Why are China's ethnic groups concentrated in sparsely populated peripheries of the country? *(Source: Adapted and simplified from Carter et al., 1980.)*

Ethnic Regions

How are ethnic groups distributed geographically? Do ethnic culture regions have a special spatial character? Formal ethnic culture regions exist in most countries (Figure 5.4). To map these regions, geographers rely on data as diverse as surnames in telephone directories and census totals for national origin. Given the cultural complexity of the real world, each method produces a slightly different map (Figure 5.5). Regardless of the mapping method, ethnic culture regions reveal a vivid mosaic of minorities in most countries of the world.

Ethnic Homelands and Islands

There are four types of ethnic culture regions: the rural ethnic homelands and islands, and the urban ethnic neighborhoods and ghettos. The difference between ethnic homelands and islands is their size, in terms of both area and population. **Ethnic homelands** cover large areas, often overlapping state and provincial borders, and have sizable populations. Because of their size, age, and geographical segregation, they tend to reinforce ethnicity. The residents of homelands typically seek or enjoy some measure of political autonomy or self-rule. By contrast, **ethnic islands** are small dots in the rural countryside, usually occupying an area smaller than a county and serving as home to several hundred to several thousand people (at most). Homeland populations usually exhibit a strong sense of attachment to the region. Most homelands belong to indigenous ethnic groups and include special, venerated places that serve to symbolize and celebrate the region—shrines to the special identity of the ethnic group. In its fully developed form, the homeland represents that most powerful of geographical entities, one combining the attributes of both *formal* and *functional* culture regions.

North America houses a number of viable ethnic homelands (Figure 5.6), including Acadiana, the Louisiana French homeland now increasingly identified with the Cajun people and also recognized as a vernacular region; the Hispano or Spanish-American homeland of highland New Mexico and Colorado; the Tejano homeland of south Texas; the Navajo Reservation homeland in Arizona and

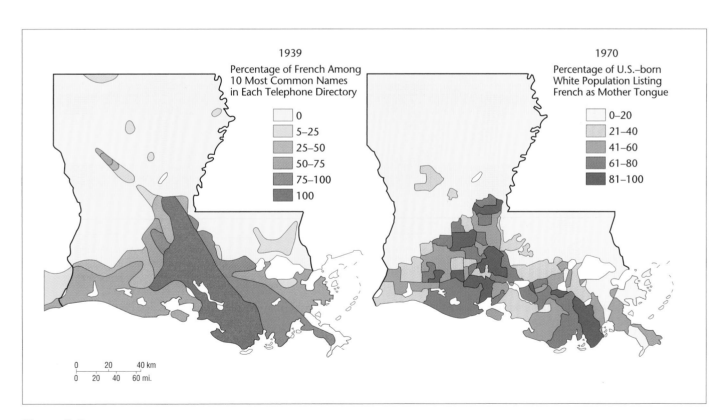

Figure 5.5 **Acadiana, the Louisiana French homeland, as mapped by two different methods.** The 1939 map was compiled by sampling the surnames in telephone directories. The 10 most common names in each directory were determined, and the percentage of these 10 that were of French origin was recorded. When no telephone directories were available, surnames on mailboxes were used. The 1970 map is based on census data for the Caucasian population's "mother tongue," defined by the Bureau of the Census as the language spoken in the home during the respondent's childhood. *(After Allen, 1978; Meigs, 1941: 245.)*

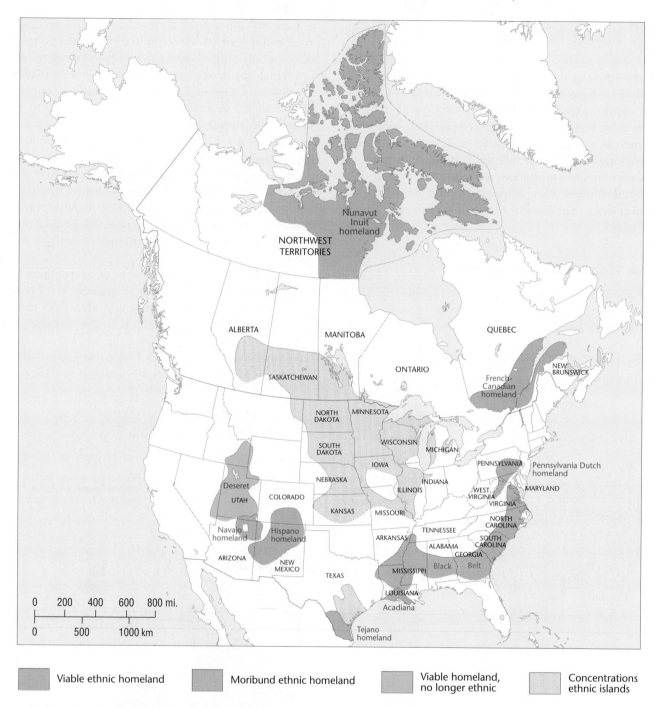

Viable ethnic homeland   Moribund ethnic homeland   Viable homeland, no longer ethnic   Concentrations ethnic islands

Figure 5.6 Selected ethnic homelands in North America, past and present, and concentrations of rural ethnic islands. The Hispano homeland is also referred to as the Spanish-American homeland. With the return migration of African-Americans from northern industrial cities such as Chicago to rural southern areas, the moribund Black Belt homeland might soon be enjoying a second life. Note: Nunavut became a functioning political unit within Canada in 1999. *(Sources: Arreola, 2002; Carlson, 1990; Meinig, 1965; Nostrand and Estaville, 2001.)*

New Mexico; and the French-Canadian homeland centered on the valley of the lower St. Lawrence River in Québec. Some geographers would also include Deseret, a Mormon homeland in the Great Basin of the intermontane West.

Some ethnic homelands have experienced decline and decay. These include the Pennsylvania Dutch homeland, weakened to the point of extinction by assimilation, and the southern Black Belt, diminished by the collapse of the plantation-sharecrop system and the resulting African-American relocation to urban areas. Mormon absorption into the American cultural mainstream has largely negated Mormon ethnic status, whereas nonethnic immigration has diluted the Hispano homeland. At present, the most vigorous ethnic homelands are those of the French-Canadians and south Texas Mexican-Americans.

If ethnic homelands succumb to assimilation and their people are absorbed into the host culture, then a geographical residue, or **ethnic substrate,** remains. The resulting culture region, though no longer ethnic, nevertheless retains some distinctiveness. It differs from surrounding regions in

a variety of ways. In seeking to explain its distinctiveness, geographers often discover an ancient, vanished ethnicity. For example, the Italian province of Tuscany owes both its name and some of its uniqueness to the Etruscan people, who ceased to be an ethnic group 2000 years ago, when they were absorbed into the Latin-speaking Roman Empire. More recently, the massive German presence in the American heartland (Figure 5.7), now largely nonethnic, helped shape the cultural character of the Midwest, which can be said to have a German ethnic substrate.

Ethnic islands are much more numerous than homelands or substrates, peppering large areas of rural North

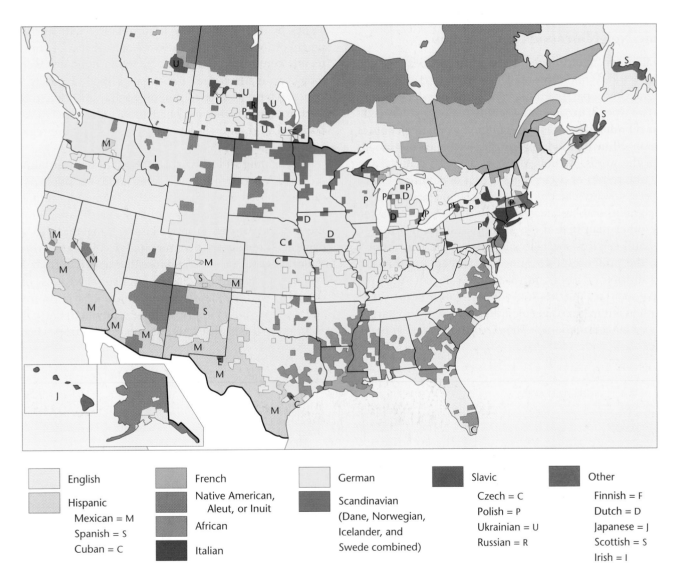

Figure 5.7 **Ethnic and national-origin groups in North America.** Notice how the border between Canada and the United States generally also forms a cultural boundary. Several ethnic homelands appear on this map, as do many ethnic islands. Areas shown as "Scandinavian" are those where the total of all Scandinavian origins combined exceeds the origins of any other group. *(Sources: Allen and Turner, 1987: 210; Census of Canada, 1991; Dawson, 1936: iv.; U.S. Census, 1990.)*

America, as Figure 5.6 suggests. Ethnic islands develop because, in the words of geographer Alice Rechlin, "a minority group will tend to utilize space in such a way as to minimize the interaction distance between group members," facilitating contacts within the ethnic community and minimizing exposure to the outside world. People are drawn to rural places where others of the same ethnic background are found. Ethnic islands survive from one generation to the next because most land is inherited. Moreover, land is typically sold within the ethnic group, which helps to preserve the identity of the island. Social stigma is often attached to those who sell land to outsiders. Even so, the smaller size of ethnic islands makes their populations more susceptible to acculturation and assimilation.

Ethnic Neighborhoods and Ghettos

Formal ethnic culture regions also occur in cities throughout the world, as minority populations initially create, or are consigned to, separate ethnic residential quarters (Figure 5.8). Two types of urban ethnic culture regions exist. An **ethnic neighborhood** is a voluntary community where people of common ethnicity reside by choice. Such neighborhoods are, in the words of Peter Matwijiw, an Australian geographer, "the results of preferences shown by different ethnic groups . . . toward maintaining group cohesiveness." An ethnic neighborhood has many benefits: common use of a language other than that of the majority culture, nearby kin, stores and services specially tailored to a certain group's tastes, the presence of factories that rely on an ethnically based division of labor, and institutions important to the group—such as churches and lodges—that remain viable only when a number of people live close enough to participate in their activities often. Miami's orthodox Jewish population clusters in the Miami Beach neighborhood in part because the proximity of synagogues and kosher food establishments makes religious observance far easier than it would be in a neighborhood that did not have a sizable orthodox Jewish population.

The second type of urban ethnic region is a **ghetto.** The term has traditionally been used to describe an area within the city where a certain ethnic group lives. Historically, the term dates from thirteenth-century medieval Europe, when Jews lived in segregated, walled communities called ghettos. Ethnic residential quarters have, in fact, long been a part of urban cultural geography. In ancient times, conquerors often forced the vanquished native people to live in ghettos. Religious minorities usually received similar treatment. Islamic cities, for example, had Christian districts. If one abides by the origin of the term, relatively affluent Jewish neighborhoods, such as the Venetian ghetto of the fourteenth century or the Miami neighborhood of Aventura today, are neither black nor impoverished. Typically, however, the term *ghetto* is commonly used in the United States today to signal an impoverished, urban, black enclave neighborhood. A ghetto is as much a functional culture region as a formal one.

Coinciding with the urbanization and industrialization of North America, ethnic neighborhoods became typical in the northern United States and in Canada around 1840. Instead of dispersing throughout the residential areas of the city, immigrant groups clustered together. To some degree, ethnic groups that migrated to cities came from different parts of Europe than those that settled in rural areas. Whereas Germany and Scandinavia supplied most of the rural settlers, the cities drew much more heavily on Ireland and eastern and southern Europe. Catholic Irish, Italians, and Poles, along with Jews from eastern Europe, became

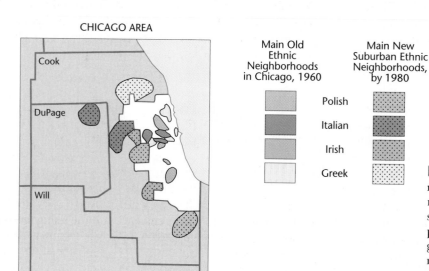

CHICAGO AREA

Main Old Ethnic Neighborhoods in Chicago, 1960

Main New Suburban Ethnic Neighborhoods, by 1980

Polish

Italian

Irish

Greek

Figure 5.8 **The changing location of ethnic neighborhoods in Chicago.** Central-city ethnic neighborhoods are often relocated to the suburbs as acculturation progresses or as processes such as gentrification displace ethnic groups. Relatively affluent suburban ethnic neighborhoods are called *ethnoburbs*. (*Source: Adapted from Winsberg, 1986: 142–143.*)

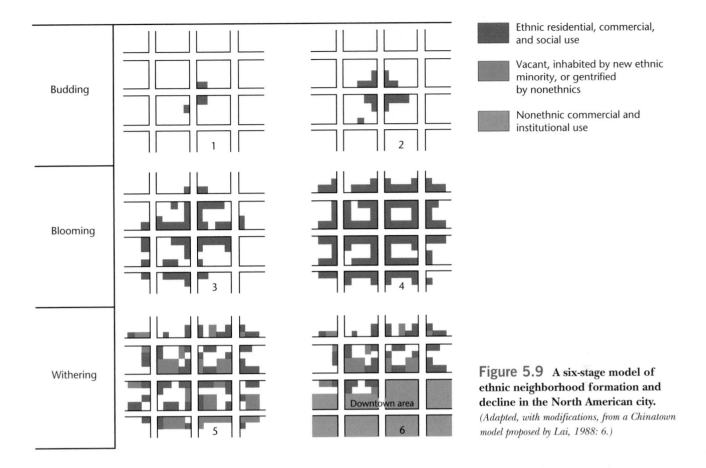

Figure 5.9 **A six-stage model of ethnic neighborhood formation and decline in the North American city.** *(Adapted, with modifications, from a Chinatown model proposed by Lai, 1988: 6.)*

Legend:
- Ethnic residential, commercial, and social use
- Vacant, inhabited by new ethnic minority, or gentrified by nonethnics
- Nonethnic commercial and institutional use

Budding — 1, 2
Blooming — 3, 4
Withering — 5, 6 (Downtown area)

the main urban ethnic groups, although lesser numbers of virtually every nationality in Europe came to the cities of North America (see Figure 5.8). These groups were later joined by French-Canadians, southern blacks, Puerto Ricans, Appalachian whites, Native Americans, Asians, and other non-European groups.

Regardless of their particular history, the neighborhoods created by ethnic migrants tend to be transitory. As a rule, urban ethnic groups remain in neighborhoods while undergoing acculturation. As a result, their central-city ethnic neighborhoods experience a life cycle (Figure 5.9) in which one group is replaced by another, later-arriving one. We can see this process in action in the succession of groups that resided in certain neighborhoods and then moved on to more desirable areas. The list of groups that passed through one Chicago neighborhood from the nineteenth century to the present provides an almost complete history of American migratory patterns. First came the Germans and Irish, who were succeeded by the Greeks, Poles, French-Canadians, Czechs, and Russian Jews, who were soon hard-pressed by the Italians. The Italians, in turn, were challenged by Chicanos and a small group of Puerto Ricans. As this succession occurred, the established groups

had often attained enough economic and cultural capital to move to new areas of the city. In many cities, established ethnic groups moved to the suburbs. Even when ethnic groups relocated from inner-city neighborhoods to the suburbs, residential clustering survived. The San Gabriel Valley, about 20 miles (32 kilometers) from downtown Los Angeles, has developed as a major Chinese suburb. These suburban ethnic neighborhoods can house relatively affluent immigrant populations and are called *ethnoburbs*. Ethnic neighborhoods will receive additional attention in Chapter 11.

Recent Ethnic Migrants

In the United States, immigration laws have changed over the past 40 years, shifting in 1965 from the quota system based on national origins to one that allowed a certain number of immigrants from the Eastern and Western hemispheres, as well as giving preference to certain categories of migrants, such as family members of those already residing in the United States. These changes, and the rising levels of undocumented immigration, have led to a growing ethnic variety in North American cities. Asia, rather than Europe, is now the principal source of immigrants for both Canada and the United States, with Chinese, Koreans, Filipinos, Indians, and Vietnamese constituting the most numerous immigrant groups. Asia supplied 37 percent of all legal immigrants to the United States in the mid-1990s, and Asians are projected to grow from just 4 percent of the U.S. population today to 9 percent by 2050. People of Japanese ancestry form the largest national-origin group in Hawaii, and Washington State elected the first Chinese-American governor in the country's history in 1996. Many West Coast cities, from Vancouver to San Diego, have acquired very sizable Asian populations. Vancouver, already 11 percent Asian by 1981, has since absorbed many more Asian immigrants, particularly from Hong Kong, which again became part of China in 1997. The 2001 Canadian census shows Chinese as the third-largest ethnic-origin group in Vancouver, after British and French, accounting for more than 17 percent of that city's population. In the United States, the West Coast is home to about 40 percent of the Asian population, mostly in California, while the urban corridor that stretches from New York City to Boston houses another concentration (Figure 5.10).

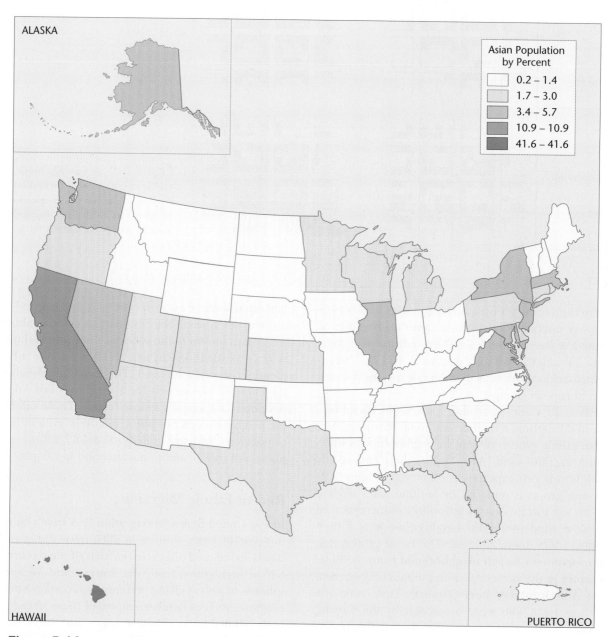

Figure 5.10 **Asian population by state.** People indicating "Asian" alone as a percent of the total population by state. *(Source: U.S. Census, 2000.)*

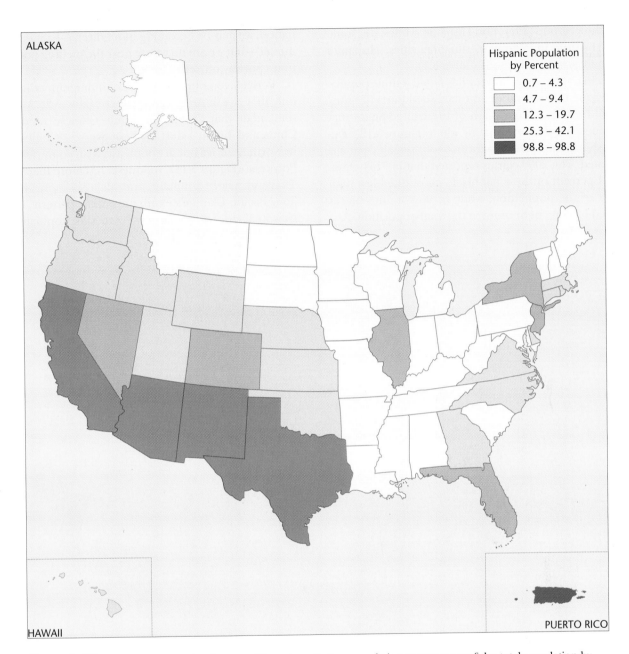

Figure 5.11 **Hispanic population by state.** Hispanic or Latino population as a percent of the total population by state. "Hispanic" is an ethnic category and can encompass one or several racial designations. *(Source: U.S. Census, 2000.)*

Spatially speaking, Asians are less segregated than African-American or Hispanic populations.

Latin America, including the Caribbean countries, has also surpassed Europe as a source of immigrants to North America (Figure 5.11). The three largest national-origin groups of Hispanic immigrants—Mexicans, Cubans, and Puerto Ricans—are still the most prevalent, but they have been supplemented since the 1980s by waves of Central American and, increasingly, South American arrivals. Miami has become home to Hispanic immigrants from across the continent (see Focus On: Calle Ocho on page 157) and is often called "the capital of the Americas." East Coast cities have absorbed large numbers of immigrants from the West Indies. The two largest national-origin groups coming to New York City as early as the 1970s were from the Dominican Republic and Jamaica, displacing Italy as the leading source of immigrants. For the United States as a whole, Latinos have narrowly surpassed African-Americans as the largest ethnic group after non-Hispanic whites. In some popular Hispanic immigrant destination cities, Hispanics constitute majority populations (Table 5.1).

As demographer William Frey has noted, ethnic populations continue to concentrate in established ports of entry. There still remains a large swath of the United States that has remained largely non-Hispanic white (Figure 5.12). Figure 5.13 shows that black Americans, too, remain spatially concentrated. The 2000 census reported that in 3141 counties, or 64 percent of the total, blacks constituted less than 6 percent of the population, while in 96 counties blacks constituted 50 percent or more of the total population. As a nation, we may be becoming more diverse—a more colorful mosaic—but we are no where near the melting pot we sometimes portray ourselves to be.

Perhaps too often, we think of immigrant ethnic groups only in a North American context (Table 5.2). We need to remember that 28 million ethnic Chinese reside outside China and Taiwan. Most of these overseas Chinese live not in North America but in Southeast Asian countries and even Polynesia (Figure 5.14). Indonesia has more than 7 million, Thailand nearly 6 million, and Malaysia more than 5 million. Pacific Islanders exhibit a similar pattern. Auckland, New Zealand, has the largest Polynesian population of any

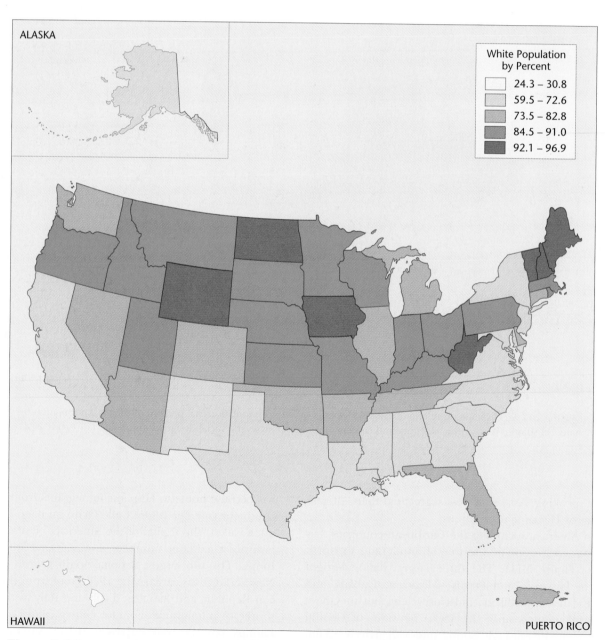

Figure 5.12 **White population by state.** People indicating "white" alone as a percent of the total population by state. (*Source: U.S. Census, 2000.*)

TABLE 5.1	U.S. Cities of 100,000 or More with the Highest Ethnic Concentrations		
	Largest Concentration	**Second-Largest Concentration**	**Third-Largest Concentration**
Black	Gary, Indiana (84%)	Detroit, Michigan (81.6%)	Birmingham, Alabama (73.5%)
White	Livonia, Michigan (95.5%)	Cape Coral, Florida (93%)	Boise, Idaho (92.2%)
Hispanic	East Los Angeles, California (96.8%)	Laredo, Texas (94.1%)	Brownsville, Texas (91.3%)
Asian	Honolulu, Hawaii (55.9%)	Daly City, California (50.7%)	Fremont, California (37%)

The figures for black, white, and Asian are for that category alone, not in combination with other races. The figures for Hispanic can include any racial designation. (Source: U.S. Census of 2000.)

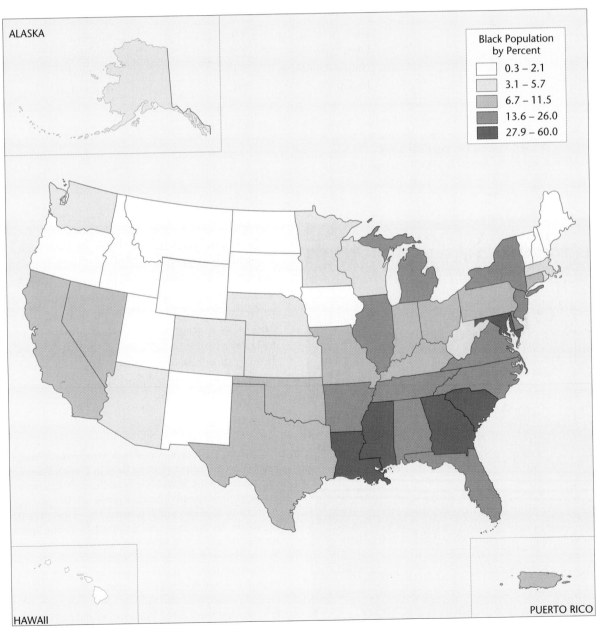

Figure 5.13 **Black population by state.** People indicating "black or African-American" alone as a percentage of the total population by state. *(Source: U.S. Census, 2000.)*

TABLE 5.2 The Ten Largest National-Origin/Ethnic Groups in Three Multinational Countries

UNITED STATES		CANADA		RUSSIA	
Ancestry Group	Percentage of Total Population	Ancestry Group	Percentage of Total Population	Ancestry Group	Percentage of Total Population
German	13.8	French	33.8	Russian	80.8
Hispanic	12.6	English	26.3	Tatar	3.9
African	12.6	German	5.0	Ukrainian	2.3
Irish	8.6	Asian	4.8	Chuvash	1.2
English/British	8.3	Scottish	4.8	Bashkir	1.0
U.S./American	8.2	Italian	3.9	Belarussian	0.7
Italian	5.3	Irish	3.9	Mordva	0.6
Asian	4.0	Ukrainian	2.3	Chechen	0.6
French	3.1	Native American	2.1	Udmurt	0.5
Scottish	3.0	Jewish	1.4	Armenian	0.5

The U.S. figures are for the first-reported ancestry of all respondents, though many of these people also reported another ancestry, which is not reflected in the figures. Seven million people, or 3 percent of the total, reported their first ancestry as mixed racial. (Sources: Demographic Yearbook of Russia, *2000; Government of Canada; U.S. Census of 2000. U.S. and Russia data are for 2000, Canada for 1991.)*

city in the world. Australia, Argentina, and Brazil also have large ethnic populations. Parts of East Africa have long been home to relatively affluent South Asian Indian populations, while Lebanese populations in West Africa enjoy a similarly privileged position. Even European countries such as Germany, the United Kingdom, Italy, and Spain—long known as sources rather than destinations of migrants—today are home to millions of Africans, Turks, and Asians. Immigration-based ethnicity is far from being a phenomenon limited to North America.

Figure 5.14 **Store owned by a prosperous ethnic Chinese retailer on the island of Bora Bora in French Polynesia. The** population of the island is overwhelmingly Polynesian. Only 0.8 percent of the people are Europeans, 6.6 percent are "Demis" (a mixture of white and Polynesian), and less than 0.5 percent are Asian. Yet this store and many others in the archipelagoes of the Pacific are owned by persons of Chinese heritage. Why don't Polynesians own such stores? Because (1) they have no tradition of retailing and (2) theirs is a communal society that shares wealth. If a Polynesian were to open a store, all of his or her relatives would have the right to come and take merchandise for free, sharing the wealth. The store would fail within a month. And so the way was left open for the Chinese, who have a very different culture. *(Courtesy of Terry G. Jordan-Bychkov.)*

Calle Ocho

For many of Miami's Cuban-Americans, Calle Ocho, or Southwest Eighth Street, is sacred space. In fact, it is a long thoroughfare that connects Miami in Florida's southeast corner with Tampa on the state's northwest coast. So for most of its route across Florida it is called the Tamiami Trail, and only the small portion of the street that runs through Miami's Little Havana neighborhood is referred to as Calle Ocho. But Calle Ocho is the name that locals and outsiders alike are most familiar with. In the early 1960s, the first wave of Cuban refugees came to the United States on the heels of Castro's communist revolution on the island. Some went north, to places like Union City, New Jersey, where today there is a sizable Cuban-American population. Others, however, came (or eventually relocated) to Miami. Once a predominantly Jewish neighborhood called Riverside, this neighborhood became the heart of early Cuban immigration and was renamed Little Havana. Shops along Calle Ocho reflect the Cuban origins of the residents: grocers such as Sedanos and La Roca cater to the Spanish-inspired culinary traditions of Cuba; cafés selling small cups of strong, sweet *café Cubano* exist on every block; and famed restaurants like Versailles are social gathering points for Cuban-Americans.

Because ethnicity and its expression on the landscape are fluid and ever-changing, the landscape of Calle Ocho reflects the current demographic changes under way in Little Havana. While the neighborhood is still a Latino enclave, with a Hispanic population in excess of 95 percent, not even half of its population identified as "Cuban" in the 2000 census. More than one-quarter of Little Havana's residents are recent arrivals from Central American countries, particularly Nicaragua and Honduras, while more and more Argentineans and Colombians are arriving—like the Cubans before them—on the heels of political and economic chaos in their home countries. Today you are just as likely to see a Nicaraguan *fritanga* restaurant as a Cuban coffee shop along Calle Ocho. This has prompted some to suggest that the neighborhood's name be changed from Little Havana to The Latin Quarter.

Cultural Diffusion and Ethnicity

How do the various types of cultural diffusion—relocation, hierarchical, and contagious—help us understand the complicated geographical patterns of ethnicity? Do ethnic homelands, islands, ghettos, and neighborhoods result from different types of diffusion?

Migration and Ethnicity

Much of the ethnic pattern in many parts of the world—including North America, Australia, and virtually all urban neighborhoods on every continent—is the result of *relocation diffusion*. In fact, ethnicity is often created by the migration process itself, as people leave countries where they belonged to a nonethnic majority and become a minority in a new home. Voluntary migration has accounted for much of the ethnic diversity in the United States and Canada, while the involuntary migration of political and economic refugees has always been an important factor in ethnicity worldwide and is becoming ever more so in North America.

Chain migration may be involved in relocation diffusion. In chain migration, an individual or small group decides to migrate to a foreign country. This decision typically arises from negative conditions in the home area, such as political persecution or lack of employment, and the perception of better conditions in the receiving country. Often ties between the sending and receiving areas are preexisting, such as those formed when military bases of receiving countries are established in sending countries. The first emigrants, or "innovators," may be natural leaders who influence others, particularly friends and relatives, to accompany them in the migration. The word spreads to nearby communities, and soon a sizable migration is under way from a fairly small district in the source country to a comparably small area or neighborhood in the destination country (Figures 5.15 and 5.16). In village after village, the first emigrants often rank high in the local social order, so that *hierarchical diffusion* also occurs. That is, the *decision* to migrate spreads by a mixture of hierarchical and contagious diffusion, whereas the actual migration itself represents relocation diffusion.

Chain migration causes the movement of people to become *channelized*, a process in which a specific source region becomes linked to a particular destination, so that neighbors in the old country became neighbors in the new country as well. This process was at work three centuries ago and still operates today. The recent mass migration of Latin Americans to the United States provides an example.

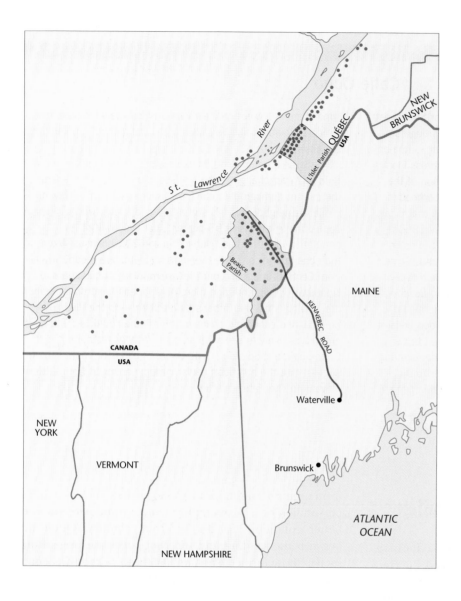

- Birthplace of 10 immigrants to Brunswick, Maine, 1880–1900

- Birthplace of one immigrant to Waterville, Maine, 1890–1925

Figure 5.15 **Ethnic chain migration from French Canada to the United States.** Ethnic islands and urban neighborhoods typically result from chain migration. One of the more significant ethnic migrations of the late nineteenth and early twentieth centuries was the movement of French-Canadians to the factory towns of New England, a migration accomplished by many small clusters of people. This map shows the clustered sources of French-Canadians who migrated to the towns of Brunswick and Waterville in Maine between 1880 and 1925. The parish of Beauce supplied most of the Waterville French, whereas L'Islet Parish was the leading source of Brunswick French. *(After Allen, 1972: 377; see also Allen, 1974.)*

Research by geographer Richard Jones revealed that different parts of the southwestern United States draw upon different source regions in Mexico (Figure 5.17).

Involuntary migration also contributes to ethnic diffusion and the formation of ethnic culture regions. Refugees from Cambodia and Vietnam created ethnic groups in North America, as did Guatemalans and Salvadorans fleeing political repression in Central America. Often such forced migrations may result from policies of *ethnic cleansing*, in which countries expel or massacre minorities outright to produce cultural homogeneity in their populations. In Europe, the newly independent country of Croatia has systematically expelled its Serb minority in a campaign of ethnic cleansing. Following forced migration, the relocated group often engages in voluntary migration to concentrate in some new locality. Cuban political refugees, scattered widely throughout the United States in the 1960s, reconvened in south Florida, and Vietnamese refugees continue to gather in Southern California and Texas (see Focus On: Re-Creating Vietnamese Landscapes).

Return migration represents another type of ethnic diffusion and involves the voluntary movement of a group back to its ancestral homeland or native country. The large-scale return since 1975 of African-Americans from the cities of the northern and western United States to the Black Belt ethnic homeland in the South is one of the most notable such movements now under way. This type of ethnic migration is also channelized. For example, geographers James Johnson and Curtis Roseman found that 7 percent of African-Americans in Los Angeles County, California,

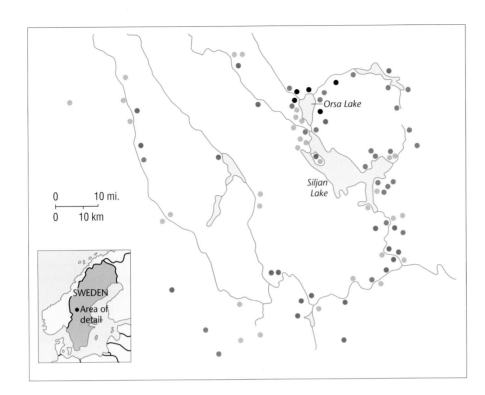

—— River

● Community sending earliest emigrants, 1860–1863

● Emigration began, 1864–1867

● Emigration began 1868

● Emigration began 1869–1875

Figure 5.16 **Contagious diffusion of the decision to emigrate in a portion of Dalarna Province, Sweden, 1860–1875.** Many Swedes left for the American Midwest in the latter half of the nineteenth century, and the decision to emigrate spread through the countryside, passing from one settlement to the next. This particular emigration peaked during a famine from 1868 to 1870. Notice the leap far south, to the two 1864–1867 communities at the bottom of the map. *(Adapted and simplified from Ostergren, 1988: 116.)*

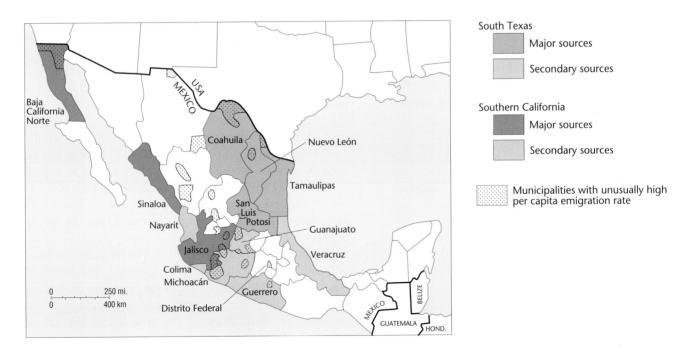

South Texas
▨ Major sources
▨ Secondary sources

Southern California
▨ Major sources
▨ Secondary sources

▦ Municipalities with unusually high per capita emigration rate

Figure 5.17 **Sources by state and county of undocumented Mexican nationals apprehended by the Immigration and Naturalization Service in south Texas and Southern California.** A weighted index was employed to assign values to the different Mexican states. The clustered or channelized migration sources have influenced the ethnic cultures in the two extremities of the Hispanic borderland. This has led to striking cultural contrasts between Southern California's and south Texas's Mexican-American populations. *(Derived from Jones, 1982: 165–166; Jones, 1988: 17.)*

FOCUS ON

Re-Creating Vietnamese Landscapes

Geographer Christopher Airriess has studied Vietnamese refugees in the United States. These refugees were initially brought to one of four reception centers, then further dispersed to rural and urban locations throughout the country on the theory that spatial dispersal would hasten their assimilation into mainstream U.S. society. Airriess's work reveals that a process of secondary, *chain migration* later led many of them to cluster in selected urban areas that offer warm weather and proximity to other Vietnamese friends and relatives. Focusing on the Versailles neighborhood of New Orleans, Airriess found that the fact that the neighborhood is surrounded by swamps, canals, or bayous on three sides affords a degree of cultural isolation from other ethnic groups in the city. This has led to Versailles becoming an *ethnic neighborhood* where Vietnamese refugees can re-create elements of their home

landscape in the United States. The most prominent *landscape signature* of the Vietnamese in Versailles is the vegetable gardens found on the perimeter of the neighborhood. *Cultural preadaptation* has led to the reproduction of Vietnamese rural landscapes here, sometimes with plants sent directly from Vietnam. It is the older Vietnamese who plant and tend the gardens. Such gardening provides a therapeutic activity, allows them to retain traditional dietary habits, enables them to produce folk medicines from plants, and reduces household food expenditures. Airriess notes that "the image of conical-hat-wearing gardeners leaning over plants within a multitextured and moisture-soaked, vibrant green agricultural scene, coupled with frequent flyovers of military helicopters, is an eerie scene of wartime Vietnam reproduced" (2002, pp. 244–245).

---

moved away between 1985 and 1990, including many who went to the American South. Indeed, the 1990s witnessed the largest return migration of blacks to the American South ever, from all parts of the United States. This acts to revitalize the southeastern black homeland depicted in Figure 5.6.

Similarly, many of the 200,000 or so expatriate Estonians, Latvians, and Lithuanians left Russia and other former Soviet republics to return to their newly independent Baltic home countries in the 1990s, losing their ethnic status in the process. Clearly, migration of all kinds turns the ethnic mosaic into an ever-changing kaleidoscope.

REFLECTING ON GEOGRAPHY

Why might African-Americans have begun return migration to the South after 1975, and why did this movement accelerate in the 1990s?

Simplification and Isolation

When groups migrate and become ethnic in a new land, they have, in theory at least, the potential to introduce the totality of their culture by relocation diffusion. Conceivably, they could reestablish every facet of their traditional way of life in the area where they settle. However, ethnic immigrants never successfully introduce the totality of their culture. Rather, profound **cultural simplification** occurs. As geographer Cole Harris noted, "Europeans established overseas drastically simplified versions of European society."

This happens, in part, because of chain migration: only fragments of a culture diffuse overseas, borne by groups from particular places migrating in particular eras. In other words, some simplification occurs at the point of departure. Moreover, far more cultural traits are implanted in the new home than actually survive. Only selected traits are successfully introduced, and others undergo considerable modification before becoming established in the new homeland. In other words, *absorbing barriers* prevent the diffusion of many traits, and *permeable barriers* cause changes in many other traits, greatly simplifying the migrant cultures. In addition, choices that did not exist in the old home become available to immigrant ethnic groups. They can borrow alien ways from groups they encounter in the new land, invent new techniques better suited to the adopted place, or modify traditional or alien ways as they see fit. Most immigrant ethnic groups resort to all these devices, in varying degrees.

The displacement of a group and its relocation in a new homeland can have widely differing results. The degree of isolation an ethnic group experiences in the new home helps determine whether traditional traits will be retained, modified, or abandoned. If the new settlement area is remote and contacts with outsiders are few, diffusion of traits from the sending area is more likely. Because contacts with groups in the receiving area are rare, little borrowing of traits can occur. Isolated ethnic groups often preserve in archaic form cultural elements that disappear from their ancestral country. That is, they may, in some respects, change less than their kinfolk back in the mother country.

Language and dialects offer some good examples of this preservation of the archaic. Germans living in ethnic islands in the Balkan region of southeastern Europe preserve archaic South German dialects better than do Germans living in Germany itself, and some medieval elements survive in the Spanish spoken in the Hispano homeland of New Mexico. The highland location of Taiwanese aboriginal peoples helped maintain their archaic Formosan language, belonging to the Austronesian family, despite attempts by Chinese conquerors to acculturate them to the Han Chinese culture and language.

 Ethnic Ecology

How do ethnic groups interact with their habitat? Is there a special bond between ethnic groups and the land they inhabit that helps to form their self-identity? Ethnicity is very closely linked to cultural ecology. The *possibilistic* interplay between people and physical environment is often evident in the pattern of ethnic culture regions, in ethnic migration, and in ethnic persistence or survival.

Cultural Preadaptation

For those ethnic groups created by migration or relocation diffusion, the cultural ecological concept of cultural preadaptation provides an interesting approach. **Cultural preadaptation** involves a complex of adaptive traits possessed by a group in advance of migration that gives them the ability to survive and a competitive advantage in colonizing the new environment. Most often, preadaptation occurs in groups migrating to a place environmentally similar to the one they left behind. The adaptive strategy they had pursued before migration works reasonably well in the new home.

The preadaptation may be accidental, but in some cases the immigrant ethnic group deliberately chooses a colonization area that physically resembles its former home. The state of Wisconsin, dotted with scores of ethnic islands, provides some fine examples of preadapted immigrant groups that sought environments resembling their homelands. Particularly revealing are the choices of settlement sites made by Finns, Icelanders, English, and Cornish who came to Wisconsin (Figure 5.18). The Finns—coming from a cold, thin-soiled, glaciated, lake-studded, coniferous forest zone in Europe—settled the North Woods of Wisconsin, a land similar in almost every respect to the one from which they had

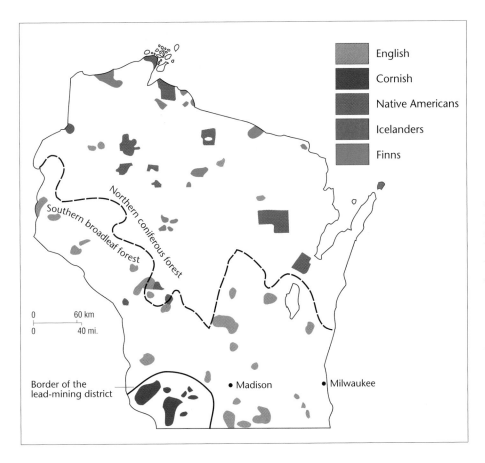

Figure 5.18 The ecology of selected ethnic islands in Wisconsin. Notice that Finnish settlements are concentrated in the infertile North Woods section, as are the Native American reservations. The Finns went there by choice, and the Native Americans survived there because few white people were interested in such land. The English, by contrast, are found more often in the better farmland south of the border of the North Woods. Some of the English were miners from Cornwall, and they were drawn to the lead-mining country of southwestern Wisconsin, where they could practice the profession already known to them. Icelanders, an island people, chose an island as their settlement site in Wisconsin. *(After Hill, 1942.)*

migrated. Icelanders, from a bleak, remote island in the North Atlantic, located their only Wisconsin colony on Washington Island, an isolated outpost surrounded by the waters of Lake Michigan. The English, accustomed to good farmland, generally founded ethnic islands in the better agricultural districts of southern and southwestern Wisconsin. Cornish miners from the Celtic highlands of Cornwall in southwestern England sought out the lead-mining communities of southwestern Wisconsin, where they continued their traditional occupation. The Bantu expansion mentioned in Chapter 4 was probably initially driven by climate change and expansion of the Sahara (see Figure 4.4). The Bantu spread south and west in search of forested lands similar to those they had previously inhabited. But their progress southward was finally inhibited because their agricultural techniques and cattle were not adapted to the drier Mediterranean climate of southern Africa.

Elsewhere in the American heartland, thousands of ethnic Germans from wheat-growing communities on the open steppe grasslands of southern Russia, the so-called Russian-Germans, settled the prairies of the Great Plains. There they established thriving wheat farms like those of their eastern European source area, using varieties of grain brought from their semiarid homeland. Ukrainians in Canada chose the *aspen belt*—a transitional area of prairie, marsh, and scrub forest—as their settlement zone in Manitoba, Saskatchewan, and Alberta because it resembled their former European home (Figure 5.19).

Such ethnic niche-filling has continued to the present day. Cubans have clustered in southernmost Florida, the only part of the United States mainland to have a *tropical savanna* climate identical to that in Cuba; and many Vietnamese have settled as fishers on the Gulf of Mexico, especially in Texas, where they could continue their traditional livelihood (refer again to Focus On: Re-Creating Vietnamese Landscapes). Yet historical and political patterns, as well as the factors driving chain migration discussed earlier, are also at work in these contemporary patterns of ethnic clustering. They act to temper the influence of the physical environment on ethnic residential selection, making it only one of many considerations.

Ethnic Environmental Perception

This deliberate site selection by ethnic immigrants represents rather accurate environmental perception of the new land. As a rule, however, immigrants tend to perceive the *ecosystem* of their new home as more like that of their abandoned native land than is actually the case. Their perceptions of the new country emphasize the similarities and minimize the differences. Perhaps the search for similarity results from homesickness or an unwillingness to admit that migration has brought them to a largely alien land. Perhaps growing to adulthood in a particular kind of physical environment inhibits one's ability to perceive a different ecosystem accurately. Whatever the reason, the distorted perception occasionally caused problems for ethnic farming groups. A period of trial and error was often necessary to come to terms with the New World environment. Sometimes crops that thrived in the old homeland proved poorly suited to the particular American setting. In such cases, **cultural maladaptation** is said to occur.

REFLECTING ON GEOGRAPHY

Can you think of examples where cultures were particularly maladapted to their new surroundings and experienced spectacular ecological failures as a result?

Figure 5.19 **In a Ukrainian ethnic island near Edmonton, Alberta, an ethnic church shines in the sunlight as a storm approaches.** Ukrainians settled particularly in the transition zone between prairie and woodland in western Canada, an ecological setting similar to their European homeland. *(Courtesy of Terry G. Jordan-Bychkov.)*

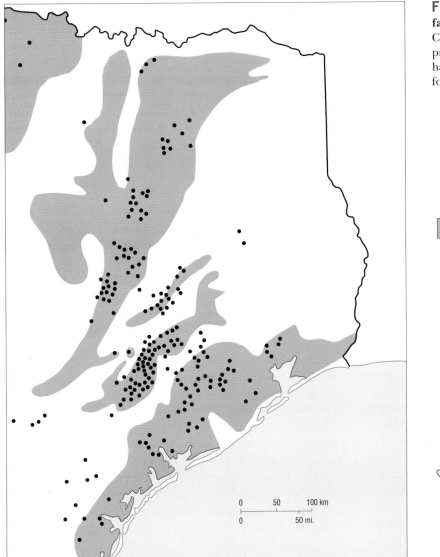

Figure 5.20 **The cultural ecology of Czech farm settlements in Texas.** Note the tendency of Czechs to settle in tallgrass prairie regions. The prairie grasses were underlaid by rich soils that have supported a prosperous Czech farming class for well over a century. *(After Maresh, 1946–1947.)*

 Tallgrass prairie areas

• Czech farm settlement

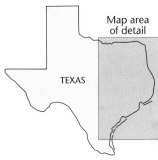

Map area of detail

TEXAS

Even if the colonization area differed in some important respect from the mother country, ethnic immigrants often used their skills as farmers to choose a settlement site wisely, thereby furthering their economic success and aiding in the survival of their culture. In the colonization of rural North America, for example, Germans and Czechs consistently chose the best farmland, a choice that helped them to become prosperous and superior farmers. Geographer Russel Gerlach, researching the German communities of the Ozark highlands in southern Missouri, found that whereas Appalachian southern settlers in that region chose easy-to-work sandy and bottomland soils, Germans often located superior soils that were harder to work. In Lawrence County, Missouri, for example, the Germans were relative latecomers but still obtained some of the best land when they selected dark-soiled prairie lands that earlier Anglo-American settlers had avoided. In Gerlach's words, "A map showing the distribution of Germans in the Ozarks can also be a map of the better soils in the region." A similar ability to select choice soils can be detected among the Czechs in Texas, the state containing the largest rural population of that ethnic group in the United States. Figure 5.20 reveals the remarkable degree to which the Czech farming communities in Texas are concentrated in tallgrass prairie regions underlaid by dark, fertile soils. By contrast, Anglo-Texans tended to avoid open prairies as farming sites, and no other group was as drawn to this ecological niche as the Czechs.

Ethnic Cultural Interaction

How is ethnic identity linked to other aspects of culture? To *place?* If ethnicity possesses a vital link to ecology, it is also firmly integrated into the fabric of culture. The very concept of ethnicity can find a basis in the theme of cultural interaction. The particular combination and interaction of traits that fuse to form an ethnic identity become, in a sense, something greater than the sum of its parts. This interaction never happens exactly the same way in any two groups, and the resulting uniqueness underlies ethnic distinctiveness.

For example, ethnicity plays a role in shaping what members of an ethnic group eat, what religious faith they practice, whom they marry, how they earn a living, and in what ways they spend their leisure time. In the process, an identity emerges. The complicated pattern of ethnic homelands, ghettos, and neighborhoods influences the spatial distribution of diverse cultural phenomena.

Ethnicity and Livelihood

In many urban ethnic neighborhoods, specific groups gravitated early to particular kinds of jobs. In some cases, the identification of ethnic groups and job types is strong enough to produce stereotyped images in the popular imagination. The Irish police, Chinese launderers, Korean grocers, Italian restaurant owners, and Jewish retailers provide examples from the United States.

Even within the same occupation, different ethnic groups often retain distinctiveness. For example, a once-popular belief in the United States held that farmers of German origin were superior to British-Americans as tillers of the soil. As early as 1789, Benjamin Rush, describing the Pennsylvania Germans, enumerated 16 ways "in which they differ from most of the other farmers" of that state. Germans in the South still retained their agricultural superiority in the 1930s, according to a study by Walter Kollmorgen, a pioneer in the field of ethnic geography. His research on a German ethnic island in Alabama revealed that German-Americans practiced a more diversified agriculture, had higher incomes, and owned land more often than did Anglos. Today, such claims of superiority rooted in German ethnicity would be viewed as verging on ethnic supremacism, and a more nuanced historical analysis of landholding and wealth would be in order.

This is not to say that ethnicity has no bearing on issues such as land use and crop selection. As geographer Jennifer Helzer discovered, some recently arrived Asian immigrant groups introduced distinctive intensive gardening techniques to the United States. The Hmong people from Laos, 50,000 of whom now live in California, cultivate their distinctive ethnic gardens in and around such cities as Chico and Redding, using interstate highway easements and other odd parcels of land that most American farmers would never think of using. A typical Hmong garden includes mustard greens, bitter melon, chili peppers, and other special crops needed in their traditional cuisine. These intensively cultivated Hmong gardens stand in marked contrast to the nearby monotonous almond groves of Sacramento Valley agribusiness (refer again to Focus On: Re-Creating Vietnamese Landscapes).

Ethnic Foodways

"Tell me what you eat, and I'll tell you who you are." This oft-quoted phrase arises from the connections between identity and **foodways,** or the customary behaviors associated with food preparation and consumption that vary from place to place and from ethnic group to ethnic group. As geographers Barbara and James Shortridge point out, "Food is a sensitive indicator of identity and change." Immigration, intermarriage, technological innovation, and the availability or unavailability of certain ingredients mean that modifications and simplifications of traditional culinary traditions are inevitable over time.

Though Singapore occupies the southern tip of the Malaysian Peninsula in extreme Southeast Asia, its cuisine draws heavily from southern Chinese cooking. This is because three-quarters of Singapore's multiethnic population is of Chinese ancestry. Intermarriage between Chinese men, who came to Singapore as traders and settled there, and local Malay women resulted in a distinctive, spicy cuisine called *nonya.*

Though the corn tortilla remains a staple of central Mexican foodways and is consumed at every meal by some families, many middle-class urban women in Mexico no longer have the time to soak, hull, and grind corn by hand to make tortillas. Rather, children are often sent every afternoon to the corner *tortillería* to purchase *masa,* or corn dough, or even hot stacks of the finished product. Convenience notwithstanding, old-timers complain that the uniform machine-made tortillas will never come close to the flavor and texture of a handmade tortilla. In some regions, notably in the northern part of Mexico and southern Texas, the labor-intensive corn tortilla was replaced by wheat tortillas, which are much easier to make. Geographer Daniel Arreola has plotted the Taco-Burrito and the Taco-Barbeque isoglosses in southwestern Texas (Figure 5.21). These lines show the transition between different Mexican culinary influences (tacos versus burritos) and between Mexican and European foodways (tacos versus barbeque), with the barbeque sandwich preferred by the German, Czech, Scandinavian, Anglo, and black Texan populations to the north and

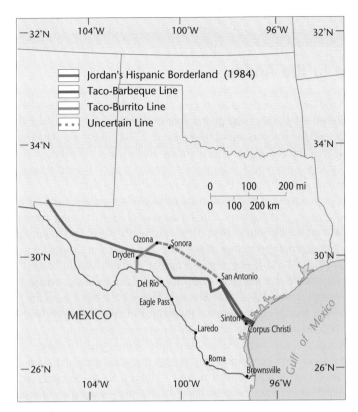

Figure 5.21 **The Taco-Burrito and Taco-Barbeque lines.** The transition between different styles of Mexican, and Mexican and European, foodways is depicted on this map of Texas. Note that the lines coincide with the borders of the Hispanic homeland as defined by Jordan. *(Sources: After Arreola, 2002: 175; Jordan, 1984.)*

east of the line. Note the similarity between this and the isoglosses depicted in Figure 4.5.

In the rural, mountainous Appalachian region of the eastern United States, distinct foodways persist and literally flavor this region. Geographer John Rehder observed that during and after World War II, Appalachians maintained their cultural distinctiveness in the face of migration to northern cities in part through "care packages" of lard, dried beans, grits, cornmeal, and other foods unavailable in the North. Grocery stores in the Little Appalachia ethnic neighborhoods that formed in cities like Detroit, Cleveland, and Chicago soon began to cater to the distinct food preferences of the population. Thus, Appalachian foodways were maintained as Appalachians moved north.

Rehder tells of sending students on a scavenger hunt during a class field trip to Pikeville, Tennessee. To one young man, he handed a card that read "What are cat head biscuits and sawmill gravy?"

About a half an hour later, my "biscuit man" returned with a scared look on his face and tears welling up in his eyes. I asked,

"Where did you go and what happened?" He replied, "Well, . . . I . . . went to the feed store and asked an old man there, 'What are cat head biscuits and sawmill gravy?' just like you told me to do. Only the old man just growled at me and said, 'Son, if you don't know, HELL, I ain't goin' to tell you!' And with that our lad left the feed store dejected and thoroughly upset. To calm him down, I said, "Why don't you just go on down to the café. Get a little something to drink and maybe calmly run your question by them down there." After a sufficient amount of time, I decided to go check on him. He was sitting on a red upholstered stool at the counter. As I drew closer, he looked up and, with fresh and quite different tears in his eyes, pointed to his plate: "This," he said proudly, "is cat head biscuits and sawmill gravy!" (2004, p. 208)

Rehder explains that cat head biscuits are flour biscuits made in the exact size and shape of a cat's head and baked golden in a wood stove. Sawmill gravy is a southern-style white gravy made in a cast-iron skillet. Legend has it that the cook at the Little River Lumber Company logging camp ran out of flour for the gravy and substituted cornmeal. The loggers complained about the texture, referring to it as "sawmill gravy." For further discussion of ethnicity and food, see Doing Geography and Seeing Geography at the end of the chapter.

Ethnicity and Globalization

What is the future of ethnicity? Will the potent forces of *globalization* wipe it out? For a century or more, the demise of ethnic groups has been predicted. The idea of capitalist America as a *melting pot* has been used to describe the process wherein the mixing of diverse peoples would eventually absorb everyone into American mainstream culture. In communist lands, Marxist doctrine preached that ethnic groups would vanish in the golden age of socialist egalitarianism.

Such a change did not happen, under either capitalism or communism. Michael Novak was among the first to note the remarkable persistence of ethnicity, writing of *The Rise of the Unmeltable Ethnics.* Then, late in the twentieth century, an *ethnic resurgence,* especially among indigenous groups, became evident in many countries around the world. In a very real way, many ethnic groups and their geographical territories have become bulwarks of resistance to globalization (see Focus On: Dress and Tradition in the Andes). As Libia Grueso, Carlos Rosero, and Arturo Escobar observe, Colombia's black population organized in the 1990s to resist modern development strategies that have long seen the rain-forest areas of Colombia's Pacific coast merely as a source of raw materials. Blacks as well as indigenous peoples, who have historically occupied these areas, organized around ethnicity to oppose the destruction of their biodiverse lands. Interestingly, their efforts coincided with a shift

Dress and Tradition in the Andes

The Andes are a long, high mountain range that runs parallel to South America's Pacific coast. Their highland valleys, called *altiplano,* have been home to dense indigenous populations for millennia. Lynn Meisch describes the preservation of traditional forms of dress among the highland peoples of central Ecuador's Otavalo Valley. Upon conquest, the indigenous men were quickly put to work by the Spaniards in weaving workshops. Because they no longer had time to weave their family's clothing on traditional backstrap looms, and because they were legally prohibited from dressing like whites, they developed a distinctive style of dress in the sixteenth century. Though these garments are produced on European-style treadle looms rather than by traditional methods, their form and color mark those who wear them as *indígenas,* or natives, of the Otavalo Valley region.

Dress styles, like all other things cultural, change and evolve over time through conquest, diffusion of new techniques, and the whims of fashion. For Ecuador's indigenous highlanders, conquest by the Incas in 1495 meant a shift from the *manta,* or wrap, for men to the *camiseta,* or shirt. For women, typical dress has evolved from the *anaco,* a square cotton wrap held closed at the

shoulders by copper or silver pins and bound at the waist by a belt called a *faja,* described by the Spaniard Sancho Paz Ponce just after Spanish conquest of the region in 1582. Today, women dress quite conservatively and retain many pre-Hispanic elements, including the red backstrap-woven *mama chumbi,* or mother belt, which is held shut by the *wawa chumbi,* or baby belt.

Meisch notes that community pressure discourages drastic change in styles of dress. "In the summer of 1989 a young woman wearing a green *anaku* [wrap skirt] was met by stares and murmurs of disapproval from other *indígenas* as she walked in Otavalo" (1991, p. 151). Young men who appear in public without poncho and hat are referred to by older men as *lluchu,* meaning "naked." Meisch quotes 19-year-old Breenan Conteron: "When I leave my village to visit other cities in my country of Ecuador I always wear this costume because in this way I value and respect my ancestors, who fought to maintain their culture, traditions and customs. And I am proud that through my inheritance and in my blood I am a bearer of this culture" (1991, p. 156). So much for globalization eradicating tradition! In this case, wearing traditional clothing has become a visible marker of ethnic pride.

away from Colombia's long-standing official policy of creating at least the image of a racially homogeneous society and toward the government's recognition of the country's rich multiethnic and multicultural composition. (For an example of an opposite trend—the melding of ethnic persistence with globalization rather than resistance to it—see Culture in a Globalizing World.)

Ethnic Landscapes

What is the *visible* aspect of ethnicity? Ethnicity is often, or perhaps usually, visible on the land, and we can properly speak of ethnic landscapes. Ethnic landscapes often differ from mainstream landscapes in the styles of traditional architecture, in the patterns of surveying the land, in the distribution of houses and other buildings, and in the degree to which they "humanize" the land. In particular, many rural areas bear an ethnic imprint on the cultural landscape (Figure 5.22). Often the imprint is subtle, discernible only to those who pause and look closely. Sometimes it is quite striking, flaunted as an "ethnic flag" and immediately visible, even to the untrained eye (Figure 5.23). Persistence, change,

and degree of subtlety in the ethnic landscape can provide valuable evidence of the degree of acculturation and the level of group pride.

Finnish Landscapes in America

A good example of ethnicity in the cultural landscape of rural America is provided by the *sauna.* In Finland, these small steam bathhouses, usually built of logs, are seen at almost every farmstead. The Finns find it refreshing in cold weather to take a steam bath in the superheated sauna. The sauna is an important element in the cultural landscape of Finland. When Finns came to America, they brought the sauna with them. In the early 1960s, geographers Cotton Mather and Matti Kaups made a study of this Finnish landscape feature in Minnesota and Michigan. They found the sauna to be an excellent visual indicator of Finnish-American ethnic islands. In one sample area, an almost purely Finnish rural district in the Upper Peninsula of Michigan, 88 percent of all Finnish-American residences had a sauna out back. In an area of greater ethnic mixture in northern Minnesota, 77 percent of Finnish houses had adjacent saunas, as contrasted with only 6 percent of non-Finnish residences in the same district.

Figure 5.22 **Oldenburg, a German Catholic town in Indiana,** announces its ethnic landscape to the arriving visitor. *(Courtesy of Terry G. Jordan-Bychkov.)*

Cultural landscapes, though, can lie, or at least distort reality. "White" Finns—those on the conservative side of the political spectrum—fostered and promoted the image of upper midwestern Finns as a colorful rural folk living in log cabins and bathing in saunas. Professor Kaups examined this Finnish-American ethnic landscape more closely and discovered something rather startling. A sizable element, the "Red" Finns—those with leftist political affiliations—were essentially invisible. Although very numerous in the mining and logging towns of upper Michigan, Wisconsin, and Minnesota, these socialist Finns left almost no trace on

the landscape—understandable, given the cultural context of cold war America at the time. Kaups had to look in cemeteries to find evidence of these socialist Finns, such as the communist hammer and sickle carved on gravestones. The quaint cultural landscape, such as that of saunas and log cabins, can greatly mislead the casual observer. You should always look for the subtle as well as the obvious in cultural landscapes.

Ethnic Settlement Patterns

Even within the constraints of a government-imposed land-survey system, some ethnic groups created their own distinctive settlement patterns. Often this was accomplished even where a rigid rectangular survey existed.

In the Missouri Ozarks, for example, Germans and non-Germans alike settled a region of rectangular survey. In a close look at present-day settlement maps, we can see that rather different patterns developed. German-American farmsteads lie on public roads much less often than do non-German houses (Figure 5.24). In many instances, the Germans built their farmhouses well away from the nearest public road.

The Mescalero Apaches of New Mexico also make an ethnic statement in their settlement pattern, as geographer Martha Henderson discovered. Despite a century of efforts by the federal government to disperse these eastern Apaches throughout their reservation, in the Anglo-American manner, they persist in clustering in villages *matrilocally* (that is, near the maternal clan home). In the process, the Apaches "continue to display vestiges of the precontact heritage" in the landscape.

When Brazil's capital was moved from Rio de Janeiro to Brasília in 1960, very few pedestrian-friendly public spaces were incorporated into the urban plan of architects Lúcio

Figure 5.23 **An "ethnic flag" in the cultural landscape.** This maize granary, called a *cuezcomatl*, is unique to the Indian population of Tlaxcala state, Mexico. The structure holds shelled maize. In Mexico, even the cultivation of maize long remained an Indian trait, as the Spaniards preferred wheat. *(Courtesy of Terry G. Jordan-Bychkov.)*

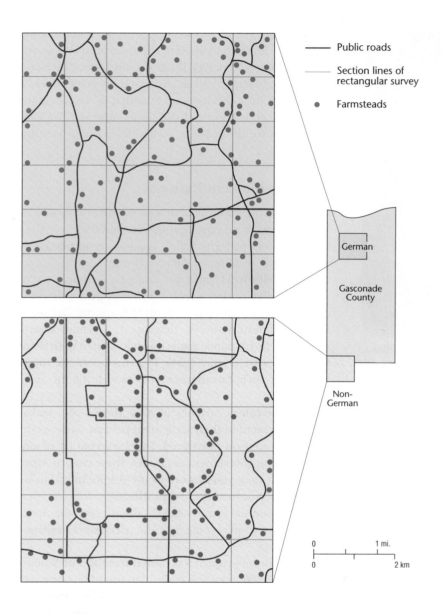

— Public roads

⋯⋯ Section lines of rectangular survey

• Farmsteads

German

Gasconade County

Non-German

0   1 mi.

0   2 km

Figure 5.24 **Distribution of farmsteads in German and non-German rural parts of Gasconade County, Missouri, 1970.** Both areas have identical survey systems and similar road patterns, yet the German farmers generally situate their houses farther from the public roads than do non-Germans. *(After Gerlach, 1976: 71.)*

Costa and Oscar Niemeyer. Rather, residences were concentrated in high-rise apartments called *superquadra;* streets were designed for high-speed motor traffic only; and no smaller plazas, cafés, or sidewalks were included—all of which discouraged informal socialization. Indeed, as historian James C. Scott notes in his discussion of Brasília, the lack of human-scale public gathering places was intentional. "Brasília was to be an exemplary city, a center that would transform the lives of the Brazilians who lived there—from their personal habits and household organization to their social lives, leisure, and work. The goal of making over Brazil and Brazilians necessarily implied a disdain for what Brazil had been." But because the housing needs of those building the city and serving the government workers had not been planned, Brasília soon developed surrounding slums that did not fol-

low an orderly layout. And because the desires of wealthier residents were not met by the uniform *superquadra* apartments, unplanned but luxurious residences and private clubs were also built. By 1980, 75 percent of Brasília's population lived in unanticipated settlements. And because, as previously mentioned, Brazil's social structure is in part based on skin pigmentation, it is the poorer and darker-skinned workers who live in the peripheral slums, while the wealthier and lighter-skinned residents tend to live in isolated enclaves for the rich.

Urban Ethnic Landscapes

Ethnic cultural landscapes also appear in the urban setting, in both neighborhoods and ghettos. A fine example is the

CULTURE IN A GLOBALIZING WORLD

Selena: Crossing the Line

In July 2002, the U.S. Census Bureau announced that Hispanics had surpassed blacks as the largest minority ethnic population of the United States. The cultural influences of the country's diverse Hispanic populations are myriad. The increasing buying power of Hispanics is also of growing interest for marketers. So when it comes to the powerful combination of music and money, it's hard to find a hotter segment than the Latin music market.

In 1999, the Recording Industry Association of America estimated that 4.9 percent of the $6-billion-per-year U.S. music industry was captured by the Latin music segment, representing an 11 percent increase in sales from the previous year. Latin music includes tropical styles such as salsa, merengue, and cumbia; the accordion-influenced Tejano genre; conjuntos such as Los Tigres del Norte and Los Tucanes de Tijuana; and styles that appeals to younger tastes, such as alternative, hip-hop, electronic, and Christian-inspired pop. And whether you like their music or not, it's hard to be unaware of megawatt pop stars who appeal to both Spanish- and English-speaking audiences in the United States, Latin America, and Europe. Gloria Estefan, Ricky Martin, Enrique Iglesias, and Shakira provide just a few examples.

In March 1995, the life of the potentially biggest crossover pop sensation ever was cut tragically short when Selena Quintanilla-Pérez, just 23 years old, was shot by her fan-club manager, Yolanda Saldívar. Born in 1971 in Lake Jackson, Texas, Selena's first performance was at the age of 8 in her father's Mexican restaurant. After the restaurant failed, the family moved to the East Texas coastal town of Corpus Christi, where Selena continued to perform and to tour the state playing weddings, local festivals, and *quinceñeras* (15th-birthday celebrations for girls) with her band, Los Dinos.

Selena signed with the Capitol EMI label in 1989. She realized early that in order to succeed, she would have to develop a global sound that went beyond the accordion-based Tejano music that sold well locally in the Texas Valley, to urban-influenced hip-hop and ballads that played better to a national Latino audience. From there, her music moved south of the border, to an international listenership in Mexico and South America. Though her first language was English, she performed most of her music in Spanish. At first, she had to be taught to sing the lyrics phonetically because she did not speak or read Spanish. She needed an interpreter to speak to the media in those Latin American countries where her first

(Celene Reno/Corbis Sygma.)

hits took off. But she soon learned Spanish and was easily able to sing and interview in both languages.

In February 1995, a month before her death, Selena performed to a record 61,000 fans in the Houston Astrodome. Her album *Dreaming of You* was not released until after her death. It would be the last border that Selena crossed, as it represented a crossover from a Spanish- to an English-speaking public.

Interestingly, her personal geography remained local even as her fame took her further across so many literal and figurative borders. Just shy of her 21st birthday, she married the guitarist in her band, Chris Pérez. They bought a house in Corpus Christi, next door to her parents. Selena was able to maintain the family ties that were so important to her while at the same time breaking ethnic and gender stereotypes and crossing cultural divides. Longtime Latino media personality Johnny Canales compared Selena to Whitney Houston and Janet Jackson, only "I'd say she's like those people, but better. Those people never sang *tejano*. She could do what they could do, but it would be hard for them to do what she does" (quoted in Mitchell, 1995).

Figure 5.25 **Mexican-American exterior mural, Barrio Logan, San Diego, California.** This mural bears an obvious ideological-political message and helps create a sense of this place as a Mexican-American neighborhood. See also Arreola, 1984. *(Courtesy of Terry G. Jordan-Bychkov.)*

brightly colored exterior mural typically found in Mexican-American ethnic neighborhoods in the southwestern United States (Figure 5.25). These began to appear in the 1960s in Southern California, and they exhibit influences rooted in both the Spanish and the indigenous cultures of Mexico, according to geographer Daniel Arreola (see Practicing Geography). A wide variety of wall surfaces, from apartment house and store exteriors to bridge abutments, provide the space for this ethnic expression. The subjects portrayed are also wide ranging, from religious motifs to political ideology, from statements about historical wrongs to ones about urban zoning disputes. Often they are specific

to the site, incorporating well-known elements of the local landscape and thus heightening the sense of place and ethnic "turf." Inscriptions can be in either Spanish or English, but many Mexican murals do not contain a written message, relying instead on the sharpness of image and vividness of color to make an impression.

Usually the visual ethnic expression is more subtle. Color alone can connote and reveal ethnicity to the trained eye. Red, for example, is a venerated and auspicious color to the Chinese, and when they established Chinatowns in Canadian and American cities, red surfaces proliferated (Figure 5.26). Light blue is a Greek ethnic color, derived from the flag of

Figure 5.26 **Two urban ethnic landscapes.** Houses painted red reveal the addition of a Toronto residential block to the local Chinatown. The use of light blue trim, the Greek color, coupled with the planting of a grape arbor at the front door of a dwelling in the Astoria district of Queens, New York City, marks the neighborhood as Greek. *(Courtesy of Terry G. Jordan-Bychkov.)*

PRACTICING GEOGRAPHY

Daniel Arreola

(Courtesy of Daniel Arreola.)

For Daniel Arreola, practicing geography is a family affair. He traces his interest in cultural geography to his grandfathers. His paternal grandfather owned a ranch outside of Escondido, California, where Professor Arreola spent several summers during his youth. "The trip to this part of Southern California from my hometown in Santa Monica was always an adventure and surely imprinted my later desire to travel. The experience of the out-of-doors in the San Diego backcountry was a wonderland of nature during the 1950s and helped cultivate my attraction to ranch living Mexican style." His grandfather on his mother's side took him on frequent walks through the neighborhood and to the beach. "As part of those wanderings, he would tell me stories about the people and places we passed through, and this experience no doubt branded me as an observer and cemented my passion for walking as exploration."

Professor Arreola has written a number of books, including the award-winning *Tejano South Texas: A Mexican American Cultural Province*. In this book, he examines the physical, historical, and social aspects of south Texas that make it an ethnic homeland distinct from other areas of Mexican-American population in the United States. Professor Arreola's concern with illuminating the diverse cultural geographic patterns within Latino communities in the United States is taken up again in his newest edited collection, titled *Hispanic Places, Latino Places*.

For Professor Arreola, research is actually a two-step process involving re-search *and* search. "To do any type of investigation, one must first re-search—in other words, examine and come to some understanding of what others have written about a subject." Typically this involves reading materials in the library and in archives where written or visual records are stored. The most interesting part of the project—the search—comes next. "Search as opposed to re-search means discovery of new information, and the best way to discover is to go into the field. Geographers, since ancient times, have been entrusted with the responsibility to describe the surface of the Earth." Typically, he uses the case study method, which he describes as "an empirical inquiry that enables me to examine a contemporary place in its real-life context, and where the boundaries between the place I am studying and its geographical context are not clearly evident. As part of my case study method, I depend on diachronic inquiry, or understanding of past situations relevant to the place I am studying, because to understand a contemporary place almost always necessitates an appreciation of a past for that place." Professor Arreola does interviews, draws maps, and takes photographs of the places where he works.

His interest in the way places look and how places change over time has shaped Professor Arreola's current project. He began to collect historical postcards of the borderlands region between Mexico and the United States about 15 years ago and now has thousands of them. He recently visited the places where these pictures were originally taken and rephotographed about 100 of them from the same spot. He will assess how these border places have changed over three separate time periods: the1920s, the 1930s/1940s, and the 1950s/1960s. As part of the fieldwork for this project, he interviewed local residents of different generations to understand how residents remember place. He says, "I hope to combine my understanding of landscape change through my visual documentation with the oral histories of place residents to tell the story of changing border communities."

their ancestral country. Not only that, but Greeks also avoid red, which is perceived as the color of their ancient enemy, the Turks. Green, an Irish Catholic color, also finds favor in Muslim ethnic neighborhoods in countries as far-flung as France and China, because it is the sacred color of Islam (see also Focus On: The Color Green in Chapter 3 on page 91).

REFLECTING ON GEOGRAPHY

Can you give additional examples of urban ethnic landscapes from the town or city where you live?

Conclusion

The five themes of cultural geography have provided new perspectives on ethnicity. Ethnicity helps shape the layout of cities and rural areas. Ethnic traditions lend distinctiveness to the foodways, politics, business activities, and leisure activities of places. The fate of ethnic distinctiveness in the face of globalization is one of the most interesting topics in contemporary cultural geography.

By now, we hope you are beginning to think and see as geographers do. The world is patterned in terms of culture.

What these patterns are, why they change, how they change, and how these changes affect people living in various places is the basic focus of cultural geography. As we will see in Chapter 6, ethnicity, along with language and religion, is at the heart of many of today's most pressing political geography questions.

DOING GEOGRAPHY

Tracing Ethnic Foodways Through Recipes

At some point in our family histories, we all trace our roots back to migrants. Perhaps your ancestors walked here some 30,000 years ago. Perhaps they arrived on slave ships in the seventeenth century. Perhaps they were traders who settled and married locals. Were they part of the waves of Europeans in the eighteenth, nineteenth, and early twentieth centuries, or have you yourself only recently immigrated? More than likely, your ethnic inheritance results from a combination of different immigrant groups. As the geographer Doreen Massey wrote, "In one sense or another most places have been 'meeting places'; even their 'original inhabitants' usually came from somewhere else" (1994, p. 171). In other words, if you dig into the history of any place, you'll find layers upon layers of people coming in from other places and bringing their cultural baggage— recipes and all—with them.

In this exercise, you will be analyzing one of the most commonplace, yet revealing, items of ethnic geography: a recipe. Certainly, you are what you eat, but you also eat where you are, and the foodways in which you take an active part are very revealing of both who you are and where you are. Even though you may not be conscious of it, the simple act of cooking a meal sets into motion all sorts of cultural geography elements: regional identity, ethnic heritage, place-specific agricultural traditions, and so on. Together these form important components of identity and place.

Identify a recipe to analyze. Most of you grew up, or are now living, in households where meals are cooked on site at least some of the time. You should choose a recipe that is used often and has been around for a while. The best candidate is a favorite family recipe that has been passed down through the generations (see note, below). If you don't have a copy of the recipe, you will need to interview a person who does—if necessary, by phone or e-mail. With a written recipe now in front of you, think about the following questions. Remember to ask your interviewee these questions, too.

- Where does this recipe come from? What country, or region, is it identified with?
- Do any of the recipe's ingredients give clues about the origins of the recipe? Do the ingredients draw on

particular animal or plant ingredients that are, or were, produced where the recipe originated?

- Has the recipe been modified to substitute ingredients that are no longer available, either because the person who used the recipe migrated or because the ingredients went out of production?
- Are there ingredients used that are identified with particular ethnic groups and perhaps aren't consumed by others living in the same place?
- Do elements of the recipe's preparation give additional clues about the foodways of the people who developed the recipe?
- Are there special occasions, like holidays, when this recipe is always used?
- Do any of the ingredients or methods of preparation have symbolic meanings or stories associated with them?
- How many terms from this chapter can you make use of in your recipe analysis?

In sharing the results of the recipe analysis, the class can list the various places and ethnicities that together comprise the foodways of the students. Do you come up with mostly local traditions, or are students in the class literally coming from all over the map when it comes to eating traditions? The class might want to make up a cookbook of various recipes and map the places they come from.

Note: If you are attending school in a foreign country, use a family recipe from your native homeland. E-mail or call a family member to discuss this recipe using the guidelines for this exercise. Also, some of you may have grown up in an institutional setting, where you consumed food prepared in a cafeteria. Institutional foods can be very revealing of local ethnic influences, so choose a commonly prepared evening meal dish for the exercise.

Ethnic Geography
on the Internet

You can learn more about ethnic geography on the Internet at the following web sites:

2000 Census of the United States
http://www.census.gov
Go to the American FactFinder section of the web page. Here you will find a wonderful selection of maps that show themes (thematic maps) generated from census data. Some of the maps used in this chapter were found here.

Ethnic Geography Specialty Group, Washington, D.C.
http://www.unl.edu/ag/geography/ethnic
This web site provides information about a specialty group within the Association of American Geographers, whose membership includes nearly all U.S. specialists in the study of ethnic geography.

Food: Past and Present
http://www.teacheroz.com/food.htm
Here you will find a list of links to hundreds of web pages that deal with all aspects of food: diets of historical and contemporary cultures, recipes, and foodways of regions and ethnic groups in the United States.

Sources

Achenbach, Hermann. 1835. *Tagebuch meiner Reise nach den Nord-amerikanischen Freistaaten* [Diary of my trip to the North American free states]. Düsseldorf: Beyer and Wolf.

Airriess, Christopher. 2002. "Creating Vietnamese Landscapes and Place in New Orleans," in Kate A. Berry and Martha L. Henderson (eds.), *Geographical Identities of Ethnic America: Race, Space, and Place.* Reno: University of Nevada Press, 228–254.

Allen, James P. 1972. "Migration Fields of French Canadian Immigrants to Southern Maine." *Geographical Review* 62: 366–383.

Allen, James P. 1974. "Franco-Americans in Maine: A Geographical Perspective." *Acadiensis* 4: 32–66.

Allen, James P. 1978. Map of Louisiana French, based on the U.S. Census of 1970, distributed at the annual meeting of the Association of American Geographers, New Orleans.

Arreola, Daniel D. 1984. "Mexican-American Exterior Murals." *Geographical Review* 74: 409–424.

Arreola, Daniel D. 2002. *Tejano South Texas: A Mexican American Cultural Province.* Austin: University of Texas Press.

Carlson, Alvar W. 1990. *The Spanish American Homeland: Four Centuries in New Mexico's Río Arriba.* Baltimore: Johns Hopkins University Press.

Carter, Timothy J., et al. 1980. "The Peoples of China." Map supplement, *National Geographic* (July): 158.

Dawson, C. A. 1936. *Group Settlement: Ethnic Communities in Western Canada.* Toronto: Macmillan.

Demographic Yearbook of Russia. 2000. Moscow: Goskomstat Rossii.

Frey, William H. 2001. "Micro Melting Pots." *American Demographics* (June): 20–23.

Gerlach, Russel L. 1976. *Immigrants in the Ozarks: A Study in Ethnic Geography.* Columbia: University of Missouri Press.

Grueso, Libia, Carlos Rosero, and Arturo Escobar. 1998. "The Process of Black Community Organizing in the Southern Pacific Coast Region of Colombia," in Sonia Alvarez, Evelina Dagnino, and Arturo Escobar (eds.), *Cultures of Politics, Politics of Culture: Re-Visioning Latin American Social Movements.* Boulder, Colo.: Westview Press, 196–219.

Harris, R. Colebrook. 1977. "The Simplification of Europe Overseas." *Annals of the Association of American Geographers* 67: 469–483.

Helzer, Jennifer J. 1994. "Continuity and Change: Hmong Settlement in California's Sacramento Valley." *Journal of Cultural Geography* 14(2): 51–64.

Henderson, Martha L. 1990. "Settlement Patterns on the Mescalero Apache Reservation Since 1883." *Geographical Review* 80: 226–238.

Hill, G.W. 1942. "The People of Wisconsin According to Ethnic Stocks, 1940." *Wisconsin's Changing Population.* Bulletin, Serial 2642. Madison: University of Wisconsin.

Hoelscher, Steven D. 1998. *Heritage on Stage: The Invention of Ethnic Place in America's Little Switzerland.* Madison: University of Wisconsin Press.

Isajiw, Wsevolod W. 1994. "Definitions of Ethnicity: New Approaches." *Ethnic Forum* 14(1): 9–16.

Johnson, James H., Jr., and Curtis C. Roseman. 1990. "Recent Black Outmigration from Los Angeles: The Role of Household Dynamics and Kinship Systems." *Annals of the Association of American Geographers* 80: 205–222.

Jones, Richard C. 1982. "Channelization of Undocumented Mexican Migrants to the U.S." *Economic Geography* 58: 156–176.

Jones, Richard C. 1988. "Micro Source Regions of Mexican Undocumented Migration." *National Geographic Research* 4: 11–22.

Jordan, Terry G., with John L. Bean Jr. and William M. Holmes. 1984. *Texas: A Geography.* Boulder, Colo.: Westview Press.

Kaups, Matti E. 1995. "Cultural Landscape—Log Structures as Symbols of Ethnic Identity." *Material Culture* 27(2): 1–19.

Kollmorgen, Walter M. 1941–1943. "A Reconnaissance of Some Cultural-Agricultural Islands in the South." *Economic Geography* 17: 409–430; 19: 109–117.

Lai, David C. 1988. *Chinatowns: Towns Within Cities in Canada.* Vancouver: University of British Columbia Press.

Maresh, Henry R. 1946–1947. "The Czechs in Texas." *Southwestern Historical Quarterly* 50: 236–240.

Massey, Doreen. 1994. *Space, Place, and Gender.* Minneapolis: University of Minnesota Press.

Mather, Cotton, and Matti E. Kaups. 1963. "The Finnish Sauna: A Cultural Index to Settlement." *Annals of the Association of American Geographers* 53: 494–504.

Matwijiw, Peter. 1979. "Ethnicity and Urban Residence: Winnipeg, 1941–71." *Canadian Geographer* 23: 45–61.

Meigs, Peveril, III. 1941. "An Ethno-Telephonic Survey of French Louisiana." *Annals of the Association of American Geographers* 31: 243–250.

Meinig, Donald W. 1965. "The Mormon Culture Region." *Annals of the Association of American Geographers* 55: 191–220.

Meisch, Lynn A. 1991. "We Are Sons of Atahualpa and We Will Win: Traditional Dress in Otavalo and Saraguro, Ecuador," in Margot Blum Schevill, Janet Catherine Berlo, and Edward B. Dwyer (eds.), *Textile Traditions of Mesoamerica and the Andes: An Anthology.* New York: Garland Publishing, 145–177.

Mitchell, Rick. 1995. "Selena: In Life, She Was the Queen of *Tejano* Music. In Death, the 23-Year-Old Singer Is Becoming a Legend." *Houston Chronicle,* May 21, http://www.chron.com/content/chronicle/metropolitan/selena/95/05/21/legend.html.

Novak, Michael. 1972. *The Rise of the Unmeltable Ethnics.* New York: Macmillan.

Ostergren, Robert. 1988. *Community Transplanted: The Trans-Atlantic Experience of a Swedish Immigrant Settlement in the Upper Middle West, 1835–1915.* Madison: University of Wisconsin Press.

Pillsbury, Richard. 1998. *No Foreign Food: American Diet in Time and Place.* Boulder, Colo.: Westview Press.

Rechlin, Alice. 1976. *Spatial Behavior of the Old Order Amish of Nappanee, Indiana.* Geographical Publication No. 18. Ann Arbor: University of Michigan.

Rehder, John B. 2004. *Appalachian Folkways.* Baltimore: Johns Hopkins University Press.

Rush, Benjamin. 1875. *An Account of the Manners of the German Inhabitants of Pennsylvania.* Philadelphia: Samuel P. Town.

Scott, James C. 1998. *Seeing Like a State: How Certain Schemes to Improve the Human Condition Have Failed.* New Haven, Conn.: Yale University Press.

SEEING GEOGRAPHY

When does cuisine cease to be ethnic and become simply "American"? What role does cultural diffusion play in the process?

Neon signs collected from ethnic restaurants in the United States by the Smithsonian Institution in Washington, D.C.

American Restaurant Neon Signs

This remarkable image comes not from a cultural landscape but from a montage of neon signs collected for an exhibit some years ago at the Smithsonian Institution in Washington, D.C. The exhibit represented a small sampling of the kinds of ethnic foods available commercially in the United States. It showed how ethnically diverse America had become.

What, more precisely, can these diverse, artificially assembled fragments from many cultural landscapes tell us? That we are a multiethnic society? Of course. As cultural geographer Richard Pillsbury recently said, America has "no foreign food" because we have accepted every possible foreign cuisine and made it our own.

Cultural interaction is also revealed here. Massive changes in U.S. immigration laws in the 1960s had the effect of greatly diversifying the immigrant stream, allowing such a food diversity to become established.

Implicit in the photo, too, are culture regions—in the form of ethnic neighborhoods. Each of these signs comes from an ethnic neighborhood, and the further regional implication is that such neighborhoods are proliferating.

Cultural diffusion is also obvious. How could these different cuisines have reached our shores other than by relocation diffusion?

So, in this manner, landscape images demand cultural interactive explanations, imply cultural regions, and require cultural diffusion. The various themes of cultural geography work together, are inseparable, and constitute a functioning whole. ■

Shannon, Gary W., and Gerald F. Pyle. 1992. *Disease and Medical Care in the United States: A Medical Atlas of the Twentieth Century.* New York: Macmillan.

Shortridge, Barbara G., and James R. Shortridge (eds.). 1998. *The Taste of American Place: A Reader on Regional and Ethnic Foods.* Lanham, Md.: Rowman & Littlefield.

Winsberg, Morton D. 1986. "Ethnic Segregation and Concentration in Chicago Suburbs." *Urban Geography* 7: 135–145.

Ten Recommended Books
on Ethnic Geography

(For additional suggested readings, see *The Human Mosaic* web site: www.whfreeman.com/jordan)

Allen, James P., and Eugene J. Turner. 1987. *We the People: An Atlas of America's Ethnic Diversity.* New York: Macmillan. A superb, award-winning atlas of color maps showing each national-origin and ethnic group in the United States, by county, and accompanied by a highly informative text.

Berry, Kate A., and Martha L. Henderson (eds.). 2002. *Geographical Identities of Ethnic America: Race, Space, and Place.* Reno: University of Nevada Press. Eighteen different experts on American ethnic geography explain how place shapes ethnic/racial identities and, in turn, how these groups create distinctive spatial patterns and ethnic landscapes.

Gumilev, Leo. 1990. *Ethnogenesis and the Biosphere.* Moscow: Progress Publishers. The classic study of the relationship between ethnogenesis and the habitat, or ethnic ecology, by a distinguished Russian geographer who was persecuted by communist authorities for his beliefs.

Jordan, Terry G., and Matti E. Kaups. 1989. *The American Backwoods Frontier: An Ethnic and Ecological Interpretation.* Baltimore: Johns Hopkins University Press. The authors use the concepts of cultural preadaptation and ethnic substrate to reveal how the forest colonization culture of the American eastern woodlands developed and helped shape half a continent.

Louder, Dean R., and Eric Waddell (eds.). 1993. *French America: Mobility, Identity, and Minority Experience Across the Continent.* Baton Rouge: Louisiana State University Press. A comprehensive geographical study of the Franco-American and French-Canadian peoples in their North American diaspora.

McKee, Jesse O. (ed.). 2000. *Ethnicity in Contemporary America: A Geographical Appraisal,* 2nd ed. Lanham, Md.: Rowman & Littlefield. This clear and thoughtful text offers a geographical analysis of U.S. immigration patterns and the development of selected ethnic minority groups, focusing especially on their origin, diffusion, socioeconomic characteristics, and settlement patterns within the United States; many well-known geographers contributed chapters.

Noble, Allen G. (ed.). 1992. *To Build in a New Land: Ethnic Landscapes in North America.* Baltimore: Johns Hopkins University Press. A superb study of widely differing traditional ethnic cultural landscapes in the United States and Canada, revealing what diverse countries we inhabit.

Nostrand, Richard L., and Lawrence E. Estaville, Jr. (eds.). 2001. *Homelands: A Geography of Culture and Place Across America.* Baltimore: Johns Hopkins University Press. A collection of essays on an array of North American ethnic homelands, together with in-depth treatment of the geographical concept of homeland.

Rehder, John B. 2004. *Appalachian Folkways.* Baltimore: Johns Hopkins University Press. An exploration of the folk culture of the Appalachian region of the United States, including the distinctive settlement history, folk architecture, cuisine, speech, and belief systems.

Yoon, Hong-key. 1986. *Maori Mind, Maori Land: Essays on the Cultural Geography of the Maori People.* Bern, Switzerland: Peter Lang. A highly readable study of the indigenous Polynesian ethnic group in New Zealand; also useful as a comparison to the situation in North America.

Why are some parts of the world fragmented into many small states and homelands?

PALESTINIAN NATIONAL
AUTHORITY
DEPARTURE

BON VOYAGE

The border between Israel and the Gaza Strip, part of the Palestinian Arab homeland.

(Agence France Presse/Corbis.)

Turn to Seeing Geography on page 210 for an in-depth analysis of the above question.

POLITICAL GEOGRAPHY

A Divided World

ROM THE BREAKUP OF EMPIRES TO
regional differences in voting patterns, from the drawing of international
boundaries to congressional redistricting in the U.S. system of democracy,
from the resurgence of nationalism to separatist violence, human political
behavior is inherently geographical. National policies about environmental
protection, guerrillas seeking a secure base for their operations, and the natural defense provided for an independent country by a surrounding sea all
reveal an intertwining of ecology and politics. These spatial and environmental connections provide the basis for political geography. As geographer
Gearóid Ó Tuathail has said, **political geography** "is about power, an ever-
changing map revealing the struggle over borders, space, and authority."

 ## Political Culture Regions

How is political geography revealed in culture regions? The theme of culture
region is essential to the study of political geography because an array of both
formal and functional political regions exists. Among these, the most important and influential is the **state.**

A World of States

The fundamental political geographical fact is that the Earth is divided into
nearly 200 independent countries or states, creating a diverse mosaic of *functional culture regions* (Figure 6.1). The state is a political institution that has

Independent Countries

Abbreviations

A	AUSTRIA
AL	ALBANIA
B	BELGIUM
BA	BOSNIA-HERZEGOVINA
BF	BURKINA FASO
BG	BULGARIA
BOTS	BOTSWANA
BY	BELARUS
CH	SWITZERLAND
CZ	CZECHIA
D	GERMANY
EG	EQUATORIAL GUINEA
EST	ESTONIA
ET	EAST TIMOR
GBI	GUINEA BISSAU
H	HUNGARY
HR	CROATIA
IC	IVORY COAST
L	LUXEMBOURG
LT	LITHUANIA
LV	LATVIA
MK	MACEDONIA
NL	NETHERLANDS
RCA	CENTRAL AFRICAN REPUBLIC
RL	LEBANON
RO	ROMANIA
RU	RUSSIA
SK	SLOVAKIA
SLO	SLOVENIA
SM	SERBIA & MONTENEGRO
TC	TURKISH CYPRUS
TM	TURKMENISTAN
UAE	UNITED ARAB EMIRATES
WAG	THE GAMBIA
WAL	SIERRA LEONE
ZW	ZIMBABWE

Most of the countries on this map have homepages on the Worldwide Web. Visit The Human Mosaic *online to learn more about them.*

0 1000 2000 mi.

0 1000 2000 3000 km

Scale at latitude 35°

Flat Polar Quartic
equal area projection

taken a variety of forms over the centuries, ranging from Greek city-states, to Chinese dynastic states, to European feudal states. When we talk about states today, however, we mean something very specific and historically recent. States are independent political units, with a centralized authority that makes claims to sole jurisdiction over a bounded terri- tory. Within that territory, the central authority controls and enforces a single system of political and legal institutions. Importantly, in the modern international system states rec- ognize each other's **sovereignty.** That is, every state recog- nizes every other state's right to exist and control its own affairs within its territorial boundaries. While exceptions

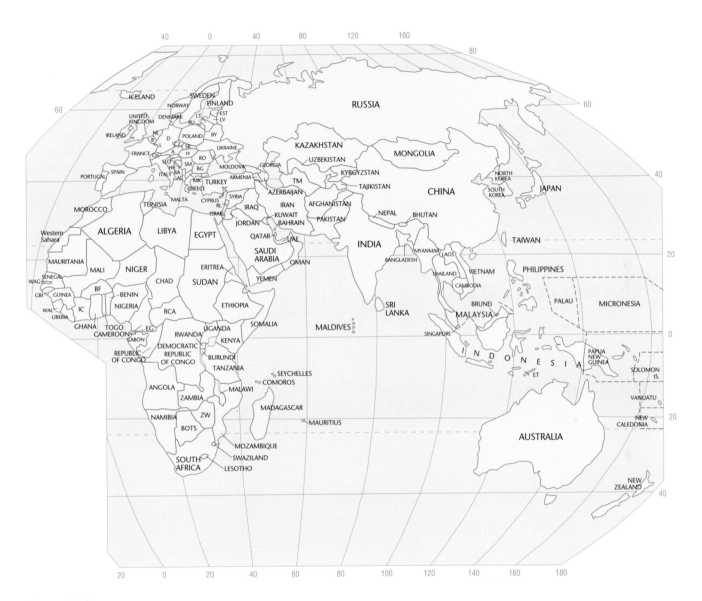

Figure 6.1 **The independent countries of the world.** In the twentieth century, the map was in rapid flux, with a proliferation of countries. This process began after World War I with the breakup of such empires as those of Austria-Hungary and Turkey, then intensified after World War II when the overseas empires of the British, French, Italians, Dutch, Americans, and Belgians collapsed. More recently, the Russian-Soviet Empire disintegrated.

can be found, these defining characteristics hold generally around the world.

Closer inspection reveals that some parts of the world are fragmented into many different states, whereas others exhibit much greater unity. The United States occupies about the same amount of territory as Europe, but the lat-ter is divided into 46 independent countries. The continent of Australia is politically united, whereas South America has 12 independent entities and the African mainland has 47.

The modern state is a tangible geographical expression of one of the most common human tendencies: the need to belong to a larger group that controls its own piece of the

Earth, its own territory. So universal is this trait that scholars coined the term **territoriality** to describe it. Most geographers view territoriality as a *learned* cultural response. Robert Sack, for example, regards territoriality as a cultural strategy that uses power to control area and communicate that control, thereby subjugating the inhabitants and acquiring resources. He argues, for example, that the precise marking of borders is a practice originally unique to modern Western culture. The modern territorial state, he claims, emerged rather recently in sixteenth-century Europe and diffused around the globe through European *colonialism*.

Political territoriality, then, is a thoroughly cultural-geographical phenomenon. The sense of collective identity

that we call *nationalism* springs from a learned or acquired attachment to region and place. Geography and national identity cannot be separated.

Distribution of National Territory   One of the most important geographical aspects of the modern state is the shape and configuration of the national territory. As a rule, the more compact the territory, the easier is national governance. Theoretically, the most desirable shape for a country is circular or hexagonal. These two geometric forms maximize compactness, allow short communication lines, and minimize the amount of border to be defended. Of course, no country actually enjoys this ideal degree of compactness,

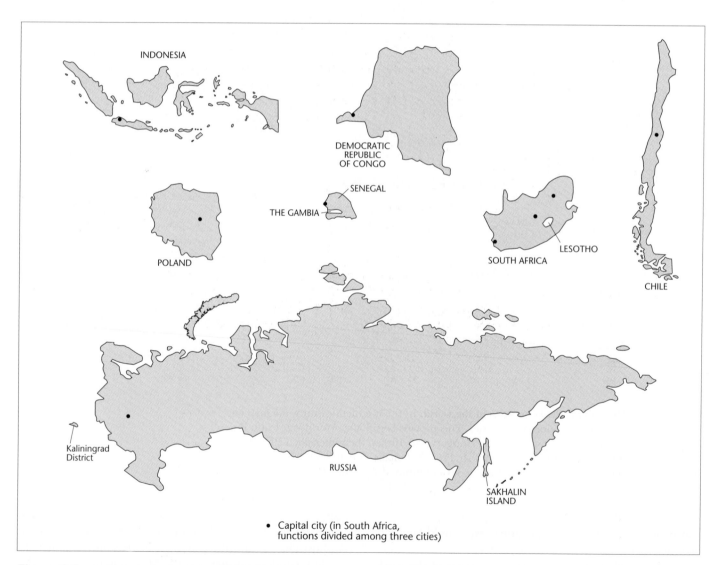

Figure 6.2 **Differences in the distribution of national territory.** The map, drawn from Eurasia, Africa, and South America, shows wide contrasts in territorial shape. Poland and, to a lesser extent, Congo (Kinshasa) approach the ideal hexagonal shape, but Russia is elongated and has an exclave in the Kaliningrad District, whereas Indonesia is fragmented into a myriad of islands. The Gambia intrudes as a pene-enclave into the heart of Senegal, and South Africa has a foreign enclave, Lesotho. Chile must overcome extreme elongation. What problems can arise from elongation, enclaves, fragmentation, and exclaves?

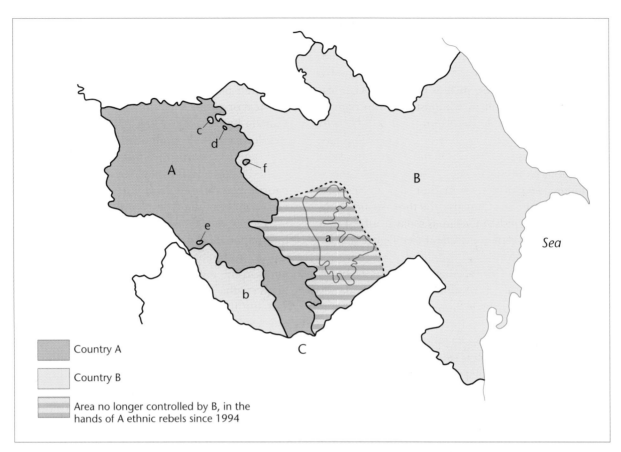

Country A

Country B

Area no longer controlled by B, in the
hands of A ethnic rebels since 1994

Figure 6.3 **Two independent countries, A and B.** A seeks to
liberate region a, where a population speaking the same language
and adhering to the same religion as the people of A live. In a war
lasting from 1990 to 1994, the people of region a seceded from B,
and a tenuous ceasefire was arranged. B, meanwhile, has an
exclave, b, on the opposite, western side of A, and the people of
region b form another ethnic minority, unrelated to B. Country B
also possesses several much smaller enclaves—c, d, and e, the last

of which is regarded as part of b (an exclave of an exclave!). A
also has a tiny exclave, f. In other words, the distribution of
national territories is troublesome to both A and B, particularly
given the hostile relations between them. These are real countries.
Using an atlas, try to identify them. If you fail, you can find the
answer at the end of this chapter. Have any recent events occurred
here? *(Sources: Office of the Geographer, U.S. Department of State, personal
communication, 1997; Smith et al., 1997: 37.)*

although some—such as France, Poland, Democratic Republic of Congo, and Brazil—come close (Figure 6.2).

Any one of several unfavorable territorial distributions
can inhibit national cohesiveness. Potentially most damaging to a country's stability are enclaves and exclaves. An
enclave is a district surrounded by a country but not ruled
by it. Enclaves can be either self-governing (Lesotho in Figure 6.2) or an exclave of another country. In either case, its
presence can pose problems for the surrounding country.
Potentially just as disruptive is the *pene-enclave,* an intrusive
piece of territory with only the smallest of outlets (The Gambia in Figure 6.2).

Exclaves are parts of national territory separated from
the main body of the country to which they belong by the
territory of another (Kaliningrad District in Figure 6.2; Figure 6.3). Alaska, for instance, is an exclave of the United

States. Exclaves are particularly undesirable if a hostile power
holds the intervening territory, for defense of such an isolated area is difficult and makes substantial demands on
national resources. Moreover, an exclave's inhabitants, isolated from their fellow countrymen, may develop separatist
feelings, thereby causing additional problems. Pakistan provides a good example of the national instability created by
exclaves. Pakistan was created in 1947 as two main bodies of
territory separated from each other by almost 1000 miles
(1600 kilometers) of territory in northern India. West Pakistan had the capital and most of the territory, but East Pakistan was home to most of the people. West Pakistan hoarded
the country's wealth, exploiting East Pakistan's resources but
giving little in return. Ethnic differences between the peoples of the two sectors further complicated matters. In 1971,
a quarter of a century after its founding, Pakistan broke

apart. The distant exclave seceded and became the independent country of Bangladesh (see Figure 6.1).

Even when a national territory is geographically united, instability can develop if the shape of the state is awkward. Narrow, enlongated countries, such as Chile, The Gambia, and Norway, can be difficult to administer, as can nations consisting of separate islands (see Figures 6.1 and 6.2). In these situations, transportation and communications are difficult, causing administrative problems. The multi-island country of Indonesia is threatened by several major secession movements; one of these—in East Timor—recently succeeded (see Figure 6.1). Similarly, the three-island country of Comoros, in the Indian Ocean, is today troubled by a separatist movement on Anjouan Island (see Figure 6.1).

Boundaries Political territories have different types of boundaries. Until fairly recent times, many boundaries were not sharp, clearly defined lines, but instead zones called **marchlands.** Today, the nearest equivalent to the marchland is the **buffer state,** an independent but small and weak country lying between two powerful, potentially belligerent countries. Mongolia, for example, is a buffer state between Russia and China; Nepal occupies a similar position between India and China (see Figure 6.1). If one of the neighboring countries assumes control of the buffer state, it loses much of its independence and becomes a **satellite state.**

Most modern boundaries are lines rather than zones, and we can distinguish several types. **Natural boundaries** fol-

low some feature of the natural landscape, such as a river or mountain ridge. **Ethnographic boundaries** are drawn on the basis of some cultural trait, usually a particular language used or religion practiced. **Geometric boundaries** are regular, often perfectly straight lines drawn without regard for physical or cultural features of the area. The United States-Canada border west of the Lake of the Woods (about 93° west longitude) is a geometric boundary, as are most county and state (or province) borders in the central and western United States and Canada. Not all boundaries are easily categorized; some boundaries are of mixed type, composites of two or more of the types listed.

Finally, **relic boundaries** are those that no longer exist as international borders. Nevertheless, they often leave behind a trace in the local cultures. With the reunification of Germany in the autumn of 1990, the old Iron Curtain border between the former German Democratic Republic in the east and the Federal Republic of Germany in the west was quickly dismantled (Figure 6.4). In a remarkably short time span, measured in weeks, the Germans reopened severed transport lines and created new ones, knitting the enlarged country together. Even so, remnants and reminders of the old border remained, as it continued to function as provincial boundaries within Germany. Furthermore, it still separated two parts of the country with strikingly different levels of prosperity. One of the most remarkable geographical aspects of international borders is their divisive character. As Germans unified a country long cut in two by an international boundary, other recently independent countries in

Figure 6.4 A boundary disappears. In Berlin, the view toward the Brandenburg Gate changed radically between 1989 and 1991, when the Berlin Wall was destroyed and Germany reunited. *(Courtesy of Terry G. Jordan-Bychkov.)*

FOCUS ON

Political Boundaries in Cyberspace

What happens to political boundaries in cyberspace? E-mail, the Internet, and the World Wide Web can cross borders in ways not previously possible, although radio, telephone, and fax machines possess some of the same border-defying qualities. In Germany, for example, Nazi and neo-Nazi propaganda is prohibited, yet the dissemination of this material is protected in the United States by the First Amendment as freedom of speech. What happens when this propaganda originates in the United States and is posted electronically to online bulletin boards worldwide? Can the German government prosecute the originator of the message— an American—for violating a German law?

How can countries impose their laws and boundaries on the computer age? Only by restricting access to computers and phone lines, both of which require a totalitarian regime. The computer age is eroding political boundaries by allowing information and ideas to diffuse more rapidly and completely. As a result, political barriers to cultural diffusion have become very fragile.

Europe, such as Estonia and Latvia, enforced their new borders by blocking some existing roads that had once served to unite the territory.

(For a brief look at a very recent issue affecting boundaries, see Focus On: Political Boundaries in Cyberspace.)

Spatial Organization of Territory   States differ greatly in the way their territory is organized for purposes of administration. Political geographers recognize two basic types of spatial organization: **unitary** and **federal.** In unitary countries, power is concentrated centrally, with little or no provincial authority. All major decisions come from the central government, and policies are applied uniformly throughout the national territory. France and China are unitary in structure, even though one is democratic and the other totalitarian. A federal government, by contrast, is a more geographically expressive political system. That is, it acknowledges the existence of regional cultural differences and provides the mechanism by which the various regions can perpetuate their individual characters. Power is diffused, and the central government surrenders much authority to the individual provinces. The United States, Canada, Germany, Australia, and Switzerland, though exhibiting varying degrees of federalism, provide examples. The trend in the United States has been toward a more unitary, less federal government, with fewer states' rights. By contrast, federalism remains vital in Canada, representing an effort to counteract French-Canadian demands for Québec's independence. That is, by emphasizing federalism, the central government allows more latitude for provincial self-rule, thus lessening public support for the more radical option of secession.

Whether federal or unitary, a country functions through some system of political subdivisions. In federal systems, these subdivisions sometimes overlap in authority, with confusing results. For example, the Native American reservation in the United States occupies a unique and ambiguous place in the federal system of political subdivisions. These semi-autonomous enclaves are legally sanctioned political territories that only indigenous Americans can possess. Although not sovereign, they do have certain rights to self-government that conflict with other local authorities. Reservations do not fit neatly into the American political system of states, counties, townships, precincts, and incorporated municipalities.

Centrifugal and Centripetal Forces   While the spatial organization of territory, degree of compactness, and type of boundaries can influence an independent country's stability, other forces are also at work. Cultural factors often make or break a country. The most viable independent countries, those least troubled by internal discord, have a strong feeling of group solidarity among their population. Group identity is the key.

In the case of the modern state, the primary source of group identity is **nationalism.** Nationalism is the idea that the individual derives a significant part of his or her social identity from a sense of belonging to a nation. We can trace the origins of modern nationalism to the late eighteenth century and the emergence of the modern nation-state. Political geographer John Agnew cautions us, however, that the meaning and form of nationalism are unstable, making it difficult to generalize. One version is state nationalism, wherein the nation-state is exalted and individuals are called to sacrifice for the good of the greater whole. The twentieth-century history of state nationalism in Europe is marked by two horrific world wars in which millions of lives were sacrificed. Referring to the First World War, Agnew points out that the "war itself was also the outcome of a mentality in which the individual person had to sacrifice for the good of the greater whole: the nation-state" (1998, p. 95). Another form is substate nationalism, in which ethnic or linguistic minority populations seek to secede from the state or to alter state territorial boundaries to promote cultural homogeneity and political autonomy.

Geographers refer to factors that promote national unity and solidarity as **centripetal forces.** By contrast, anything that disrupts internal order and furthers the destruction of the country is called a **centrifugal force.** Many states encourage centripetal forces that help fuel nationalistic sentiment. Such things as an official national language, national history museums, national parks and monuments, and sometimes even a national religion are actively promoted and supported by the state. We consider an array of centripetal and centrifugal forces later, in the sections on political ecology and politico-cultural interaction.

Supranational Political Bodies

In addition to independent countries and their governmental subdivisions, the third major type of political functional culture region is the **supranational organization** (Figure 6.5). **Supranationalism** exists when countries voluntarily give up some portion of their sovereignty to gain the advantages of a closer political, economic, and cultural association with their neighbors. Sometimes supranational organizations take the form of **regional trading blocs,** such as the North American Free Trade Agreement (NAFTA, comprised of the Canada, the United States, and Mexico), which promote the freer flow of goods and services across international borders.

In the twentieth century, supranational organizations grew in number and importance, coincident with and counterbalancing the proliferation of independent countries. Some represent the vestiges of collapsed empires, such as the British Commonwealth, French Community, and Commonwealth of Independent States (CIS)—the latter a shadow of the former Soviet Union. Most supranationals, such as the Arab League or the Association of Southeast Asian Nations (ASEAN), possess little cohesion.

The *European Union,* or EU, is by far the most powerful, ambitious, and successful supranational organization in the world (see Figure 6.5). It grew from a central core area of six countries in the 1950s to a present membership of 25. At first the EU was merely a customs union whose purpose was to lower or remove tariffs that hindered trade, but it gradually took on more and more of a political and cultural role. An underlying motivation was to weaken the power of its member countries to the point that they could never again wage war against one another—a response to the devastation of Europe in two world wars.

The member countries have all sacrificed some of their sovereign powers to the EU administration. A single monetary currency, the *euro,* has been adopted by most EU members. Most international borders within the EU are now completely open, requiring no passport checks. More importantly for citizenship and national identity, the EU is standardizing a range of social norms related to the tolerance of religious and ethnic difference, human rights, and gender relations. In effect the EU is pushing supranationalism to its logical conclusion. That is, at some future date nationalism as a focus of identity will be obsolete and people will think of themselves as European rather than as, say, Italian, or Latvian, or Polish. We will have to wait to learn whether centripetal or centrifugal forces will win out in the EU's grand experiment.

REFLECTING ON GEOGRAPHY

What will motivate the existing and prospective member countries of the European Union to continue to sacrifice aspects of their independence to create a stronger union?

Electoral Geographical Regions

Voting in elections creates another set of political culture regions. A free vote of the people on some controversial issue provides one of the purest expressions of culture, revealing attitudes on religion, ethnicity, and ideology. Geographers can devise *formal culture regions* based on voting patterns, giving rise to the subspecialty known as **electoral geography.**

Mapping voting tendencies over many decades shows deep-rooted, formal electoral behavior regions. In Europe, for example, some districts and provinces have a long record of rightist sentiment, and many of these lie toward the center of Europe. Peripheral areas, especially in the east, are often leftist strongholds (Figure 6.6). Every country where free elections are permitted has a similarly varied electoral geography. In other words, cumulative voting patterns typically reveal sharp and pronounced regional contrasts. Electoral geographers refer to these borders as *cleavages.*

Electoral geographers also concern themselves with *functional* culture regions, in this case the voting district or precinct. Their interests are both scholarly and practical. For example, following each census, political redistricting takes place in the United States. In redistricting, new boundaries are drawn for congressional districts to reflect the population changes since the previous census. The goal is to establish voting areas of more or less equal population and to increase or reduce the number of districts depending on the amount and direction of change in total popu-

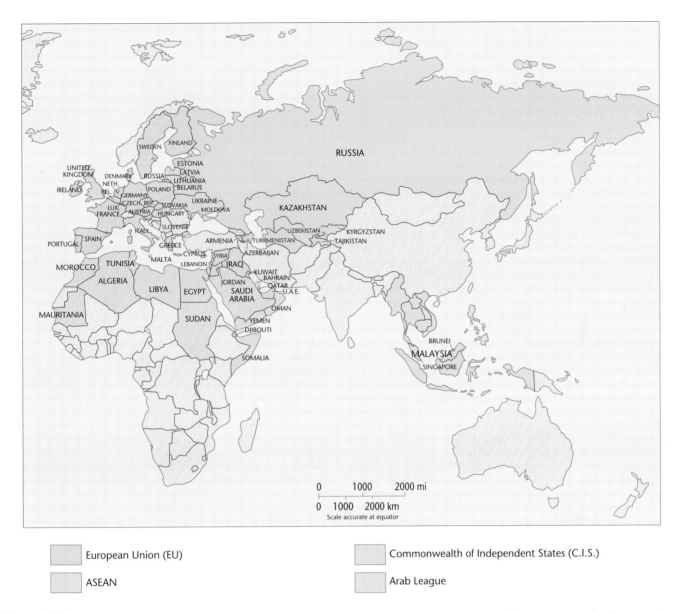

European Union (EU)

ASEAN

Commonwealth of Independent States (C.I.S.)

Arab League

Figure 6.5 **Some supranational political organizations in the Eastern Hemisphere.** These organizations vary greatly in purpose and cohesion. ASEAN stands for the Association of Southeast Asian Nations, and its purposes are both economic and political. What might this map indicate about globalization?

lation. These form the electoral basis for the U.S. House of Representatives. State legislatures are based on similar districts. Geographers often assist in the redistricting process. Richard Morrill of the University of Washington directed the redrawing of both congressional and legislative district boundaries in his state following one of the recent censuses.

The pattern of voting precincts or districts can influence election results. If redistricting remains in the hands of legislators, instead of impartial experts such as Morrill, then the majority political group or party will often try to arrange the voting districts geographically in such a way as to maxi-

mize and perpetuate its power. Cleavage lines will be crossed to create districts that have a majority of voters favoring the party in power or some politically important ethnic group. This practice is called **gerrymandering** (Figure 6.7), and the resultant voting districts often have awkward, elongated shapes. Gerrymandering can be accomplished by one of two methods. One is to draw district boundaries so as to concentrate all of the opposition party into one district, thereby creating an unnecessarily large majority while also ensuring that it cannot win elsewhere. A second is to draw the district boundaries so as to dilute the opposition's vote so that it does not form a simple majority in any district.

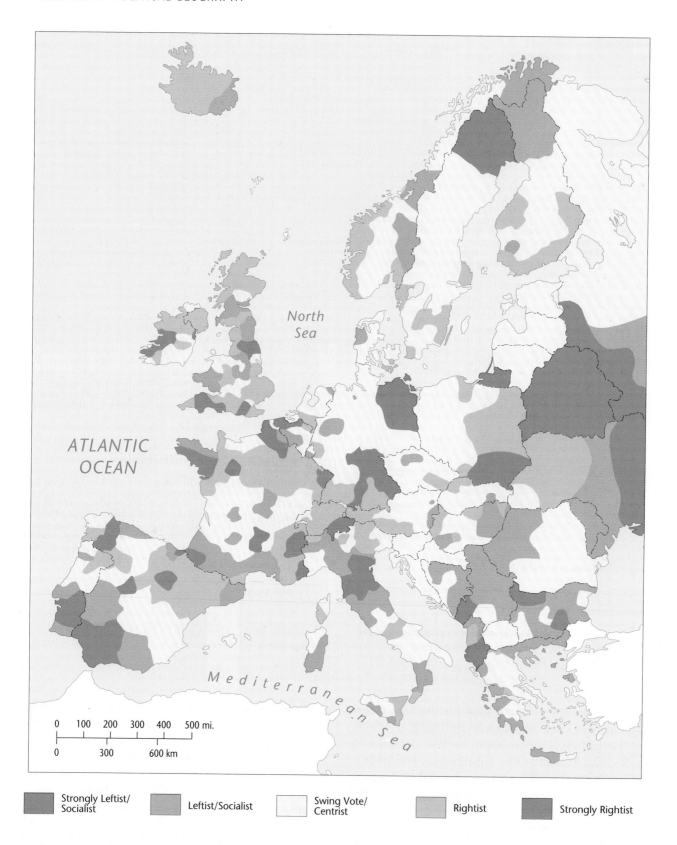

	Strongly Leftist/ Socialist		Leftist/Socialist		Swing Vote/ Centrist		Rightist		Strongly Rightist

Figure 6.6 **The electoral geography of Europe.** A conservative-rightist core contrasts with a socialist-leftist periphery. Data are based on elections held in the period 1950 to 1995. In the formerly communist countries, the record of free elections began only in 1990. *(Source: Jordan-Bychkov and Jordan, 2002: 226.)*

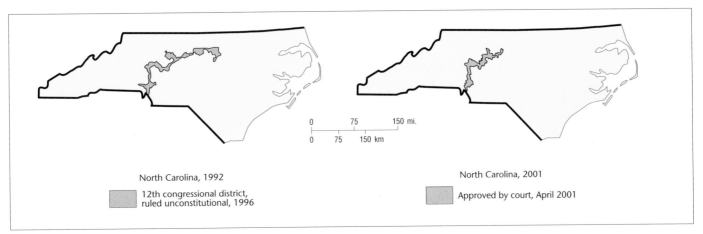

North Carolina, 1992

12th congressional district, ruled unconstitutional, 1996

North Carolina, 2001

Approved by court, April 2001

Figure 6.7 **Gerrymandering of a congressional district in North Carolina.** The North Carolina Twelfth District was created in 1992 to ensure an African-American majority so that an additional minority candidate could be elected to Congress. Note the awkward shape of these districts, often a sign of gerrymandering. In 1996, the North Carolina district and others gerrymandered for racial purposes were declared unconstitutional. The lines were redrawn, but although the district still looks very much gerrymandered, the courts approved the revised version. *(Source: New York Times.)*

 Political Diffusion

Do political ideas, institutions, and countries expand and spread by means of cultural diffusion? Yes. Moreover, political boundaries can act as barriers to the spread of ideas or knowledge, thereby slowing or preventing diffusion (see Focus On: Political Boundaries as Barriers to Cultural Diffusion). Beyond that, political events and developments can trigger human migration, or relocation diffusion. Clearly, the concepts of diffusion outlined in Chapter 1 apply to political geography.

Country Building as Diffusion

Some independent countries sprang full grown into the world, but most diffused outward from a small nucleus called a **core area,** annexing adjacent lands, often over many centuries. Generally, core areas possess a particularly attractive set of resources for human life and culture. Larger

FOCUS ON

Political Boundaries as Barriers to Cultural Diffusion

Political boundaries can strongly affect how we look at the world. For instance, geographers have shown that a political boundary can be a strong barrier against cultural diffusion, against the flow of information from one area to another. A study of schoolchildren in Dals Ed, in Sweden, and Halden, just across the border in Norway, shows that the children can easily recall place-names in their own country but not those in the neighboring country. Although language differences between Sweden and Norway are slight, the border puts a powerful barrier between schoolchildren only miles apart.

When the children of Dals Ed and Halden drew mental maps of both countries, each group showed a marked preference for its own national locations. On the Swedish maps, areas of desirability sloped gently away from Swedish places that the children knew. The nearby Norwegian border looked like a geological fault line. Preference suddenly dropped away.

A partial explanation for this phenomenon is that the children on each side of the border are open to quite different sources of information. The Swedish geographer T. Lundén has analyzed textbooks on both sides of the border and demonstrated clearly how the geographical content in them differs, always offering the readers more information about "us" than about "them."

Adapted from Gould and White, 1974: 143–146

numbers of people cluster there than in surrounding districts, especially if the area has some measure of natural defense against aggressive neighboring political entities. This denser population, in turn, may produce enough wealth to support a large army, which then provides the base for further expansion and relocation diffusion from the core area.

During this expansion, the core area typically remains the country's single most important district, housing the capital city and the cultural and economic heart of the nation. The core area is the *node* of a functional culture region. France expanded to its present size from a small core area around the capital city of Paris. China diffused from a nucleus in the northeast, and Russia originated in the small principality of Moscow (Figure 6.8). The United States grew westward from a core between Massachusetts and Virginia on the Atlantic coastal plain, an area that still has the national capital and the densest population in the country.

The diffusion of independent countries in this manner produces the *core-periphery* configuration, described in Chapter 1 as typical of both functional and formal culture re-

gions. Although the core dominates the periphery, a certain amount of friction exists between the two. Peripheral areas generally display pronounced, self-conscious regionality and occasionally provide the settings for secession movements. Even so, countries that diffused from core areas are, as a rule, more stable than those created all at once to fill a political void. The absence of a core area can blur or weaken citizens' national identity and makes it easier for various provinces to develop strong local or even foreign allegiances. Belgium and Democratic Republic of Congo offer examples of countries without political core areas. In the case of Congo, this situation partly accounts for the history of secessionist conflicts and internecine wars since the country gained independence from colonial rule in 1960.

Countries with multiple, competing core areas are potentially the least stable of all. This situation often develops when two or more independent countries are united. The main threat is that one of the competing cores will form the center of a separatist movement and break apart the country. In Spain, Castile and Aragon united in 1479, but

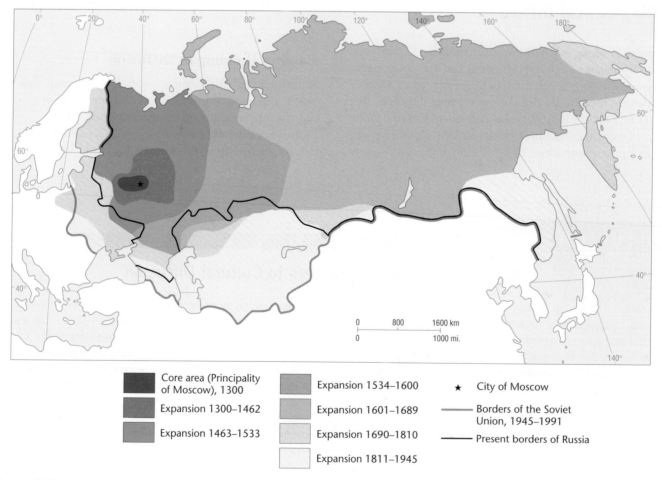

Figure 6.8 **Russia developed from a core area.** Can you think of reasons why expansion to the east was greater than expansion to the west? What environmental goals might have motivated Russian expansion?

the union remains shaky more than five centuries later—in part because the old core areas of the two former countries, represented by the cities of Madrid and Barcelona, continue to compete for political control and cultural influence. That these two cities symbolize two language-based cultures, Castilian and Catalan, compounds the division.

Diffusion of Independence and Innovations

The principles of cultural diffusion also help explain a great variety of other political phenomena. Contagious expansion diffusion, for example, often operates in the political sphere. It can be seen in the spread of political independence in Africa. In 1914, only two African countries—Liberia and Ethiopia—were fully independent of European colonial or white minority rule and even Ethiopia later fell temporarily under Italian control. Influenced by developments in India and Pakistan, the Arabs of North Africa began a movement for independence. Their movement gained momentum in the 1950s and swept southward across most

of the continent between 1960 and 1965. By 1994, independence had spread into all remaining parts of the continent, eventually reaching the Republic of South Africa, formerly under white minority rule (Figure 6.9).

Despite its rapid spread, diffusion of African self-rule occasionally encountered barriers. Portugal, for example, clung tenaciously to its African colonies until 1975, when a change in government in Lisbon reversed a 500-year-old policy, allowing the colonies to become independent. In colonies where there were large populations of European settlers, independence came slowly and usually with bloodshed. France, for example, sought to hold on to Algeria because many European colonists had settled there. The country nonetheless achieved independence in 1962, but only after years of violence. In Zimbabwe, a large population of European settlers refused London's orders to move toward majority rule, resulting in a bloody civil war and delaying the country's independence until 1979.

On a quite different scale, political innovations also spread within independent countries. American politics

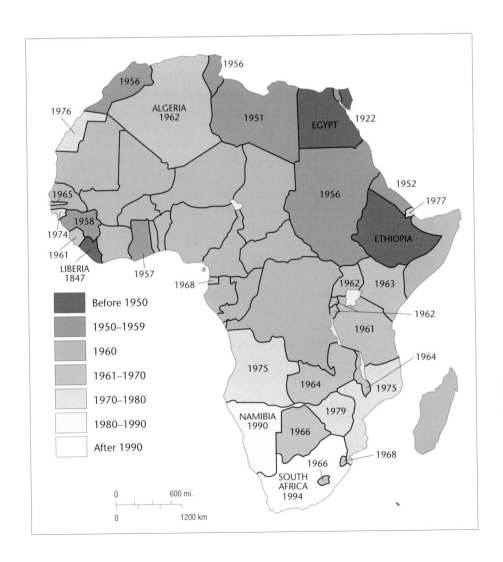

Figure 6.9 Independence from European colonial or white minority rule diffused through Africa. Prior to the 1950s, there were only three independent countries in Africa. Between 1951 and 1994, self-rule and independence spread from the Mediterranean to the Cape of Good Hope. What barriers might have slowed this diffusion, so that 43 years were required for it to run its course?

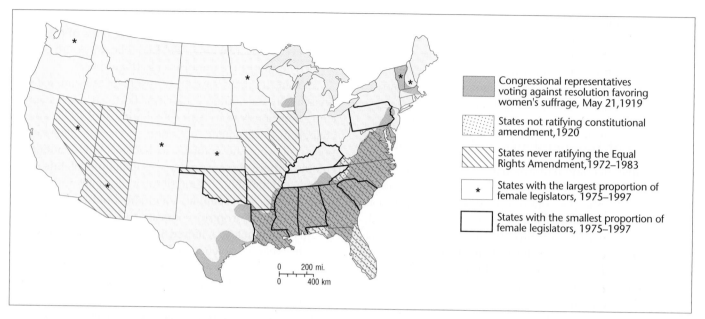

▨	Congressional representatives voting against resolution favoring women's suffrage, May 21,1919
▦	States not ratifying constitutional amendment,1920
▨	States never ratifying the Equal Rights Amendment,1972–1983
✱	States with the largest proportion of female legislators, 1975–1997
☐	States with the smallest proportion of female legislators, 1975–1997

0   200 mi.
0   400 km

Figure 6.10 **The diffusion of suffrage for women in the United States and of the Equal Rights Amendment.** The suffrage movement achieved victory through a constitutional amendment in 1920. Both the suffrage movement and the campaign for an Equal Rights Amendment (ERA) for women failed to gain approval in the Deep South, an area that also lags behind most of the remainder of the country in the election of women to public office. What might be the barriers to diffusion in the Deep South? The states failing to ratify the ERA lay mostly in the same area. The ERA movement did not succeed, in contrast to the earlier suffrage movement. *(Adapted in part from Paulin and Wright, 1932.)*

abounds with examples of cultural diffusion. A classic case is the spread of suffrage for women, a movement that culminated in 1920 with the ratification of a constitutional amendment (Figure 6.10). Opposition to women's suffrage was strongest in the Deep South, a region that later exhibited the greatest resistance to ratification of the Equal Rights Amendment and displayed the most reluctance to elect women to public office.

Federal statutes permit, to some degree, laws to be adopted in the individual functional subdivisions. In the United States and Canada, for example, each state and province enjoys broad lawmaking powers, vested in the legislative bodies of these subdivisions. The result is often a patchwork legal pattern that reveals the processes of cultural diffusion at work. A good example is the clean air movement, which began in California with the initiation of state legislation regulating automotive and industrial emissions. It later spread to other states and provided the model for clean air legislation at the federal level.

Politics and Migration

Very often political events provide the motivation for migration, both voluntary and forced. An excellent example is provided by the breakup of the Soviet Union into 15 independent countries in 1991. During the long period of Soviet unity, the country's various national groups migrated into one another's territories in large numbers. Ethnic Russians, for instance, settled in all parts of the Soviet Union, even though only one of the 15 constituent republics was Russian by identity. Likewise, many members of the other 14 major ethnic groups had relocated outside their republics.

When the Soviet Union dissolved, a profound reverse migration set in almost immediately. Ethnic Russians returned to Russia, Estonians to Estonia, Azeris to Azerbaijan, and so on. By 1995, about 2 million ethnic Russians had migrated to Russia. Fully half a million of these came from recently independent Kazakhstan in central Asia. In that same period, 150,000 ethnic Kazakhs returned to Kazakhstan from Russia and other former Soviet republics. This process continues to the present day, though the flow of migrants has slowed. (For yet another result of migration, see Culture in a Globalizing World.)

 ## Political Ecology

What is the relationship between politics and ecology? When we look carefully we find that people's use of the land and natural resources is profoundly influenced by politics. Whether a particular habitat is conserved or degraded often has much to do with the structures of a country's land laws, tax codes, and agricultural policies. On the other hand,

CULTURE IN A GLOBALIZING WORLD

The Condition of Transnationality

Transnationalism and *transnationality* are terms that are increasingly being heard in the halls of academia as well as in popular discourse and the media. Among other things, these terms suggest that the processes of globalization are raising new questions about cultural identities. Nationality and ethnicity may continue to be important under globalization, but what should one make of the increasing number of people who live, work, and play in a way that is neither rooted in a tightly knit ethnic community nor territorially grounded in the traditional nation-state? What sorts of cultural identities do these people create and defend? Is there a culture of transnationalism emerging?

Geographer Katharyne Mitchell (see Practicing Geography on page 195) suggests that we might think about some of the cultural implications of globalization in terms of a "condition of transnationality." She points out that the restructuring of the world economy under globalization has produced a great increase in the movement of people across borders. One of the key ways in which this movement is different from other historical migrations is that it tends not to be unidirectional and permanent. With the aid of new transportation and communications technologies, people are able to maintain social networks and move bodily in ways that transcend political boundaries. The experience of cultural "in-betweenness"—of living in and being linked to multiple places around the globe, while being rooted in no single place—has become fundamental to the identity of a growing group of people.

Mitchell's study of Hong Kong Chinese immigrants in Vancouver, British Columbia, illustrates the idea of transnationalism. In the 1980s, the Canadian government created a new category of immigration designed to attract business investment. Immigrants entering the country under this law had to establish businesses based in Canada. The main immigrants taking advantage of this law were Hong Kong Chinese businesspeople leaving the colony in anticipation of its handover to the People's Republic of China.

As it happened, these immigrants maintained business and social ties in both Hong Kong and Canada, moving freely and frequently between them. In the process, a whole set of cultural conflicts were ignited between longtime Vancouver residents and the transnational Chinese. Neighborhoods were transformed as the transnationals attempted to establish themselves economically and culturally. They rapidly bought up real estate, demolished old houses, built houses in uncharacteristic architectural styles, and redesigned residential landscaping. Their mobility—a culturally defining characteristic of transnationals—made them appear transient and rootless in the eyes of longer-term residents and weakened the legitimacy of their claims and practices. This case shows us that the cultural aspects of transnationalism are bound up with the economic and political processes of globalization.

From Mitchell, 1998, 2003

---

increasingly politics is being defined by changing ecological conditions. How governments respond to ecological crises like the loss of biodiversity, pollution, and climate change has become an important political issue. Let's examine this complex two-way interaction of politics and ecology.

Chain of Explanation

When geographers Piers Blaikie and Harold Brookfield coined the term *political ecology*, they were interested in trying to understand how political and economic forces affect people's relationships to the land. They suggested that focusing on proximate or immediate causes—the farmer dumping pesticides in a river, the poor peasant cutting a patch of tropical forest—provided an inadequate and misleading explanation of human-environment relations. As an alternative, they developed the idea of a "chain of explana-

tion" as a method for identifying ultimate causes. The chain of explanation begins with the individual "land manager," the person with direct responsibility for land-use decisions—the farmers, timber cutters, firewood gatherers, or livestock keepers. The chain of explanation then moves up in spatial scale, tracing the land mangers' economic, cultural, and political relationships from the local to the national and, ultimately, the global scale.

One of the primary areas that the chain-of-explanation approach addresses is the character of the state, particularly regarding the way that national land laws, natural resource policies, tax codes, and credit policies influence land-use decision making. For example, if a state assesses high taxes on land improvements, such as terracing and channeling, its tax policies actually create disincentives for land managers to implement soil conservation measures. Conversely, if a state provides cheap loans to land managers to build such structures, its credit policies encourage soil conservation. There are many such examples of state influences on individual land-use decisions, leading Blaikie and Brookfield to argue that one cannot fully explain the causes of environmental problems without analyzing the role of the state.

Geopolitics

Spatial variations in politics and the spread of political phenomena are often linked to terrain, soils, climate, natural resources, and other aspects of the physical environment. The term **geopolitics** was originally coined to describe the influence of geography and the environment on political entities. Conversely, established political authority can be a powerful instrument of environmental modification, providing the framework for organized alteration of the landscape and for environmental protection.

Before modern air and missile warfare, a country's survival was aided by some sort of natural protection, such as surrounding mountain ranges, deserts, or seas; bordering marshes or dense forests; or outward-facing escarpments. Political geographers named such natural strongholds **folk fortresses.** The folk fortress might shield an entire country or only its core area. In either case, it is a valuable asset. Surrounding seas have helped protect the British Isles from invasion for the last 900 years. In Egypt, desert wastelands on the east and west insulated the fertile, well-watered Nile Valley core. In the same way, Russia's core area was shielded by dense forests, expansive marshes, bitter winters, and vast expanses of sparsely inhabited lands. France—centered on the plains of the Paris Basin and flanked by mountains and hills such as the Alps, Pyrenees, Ardennes, and Jura along its borders—provides another good example (Figure 6.11).

Expanding countries often regard coastlines as the logical limits to their territorial growth, even if those areas belong to other peoples, as the drive of the United States to the Pacific Ocean in the first half of the nineteenth century makes clear. U.S. expansion was justified by the doctrine of *manifest destiny,* based on the belief that the Pacific shoreline offered the logical and predestined western border for the country. A similar doctrine led Russia to expand in the directions of the Mediterranean and Baltic seas and the Pacific and Indian oceans.

The Heartland Theory

Discussions of environmental influence, manifest destiny, and Russian expansionism lead naturally to the **heartland theory** of Halford Mackinder. Propounded in the early twentieth century and based on environmental determinism, the heartland theory addresses the balance of power in the world and, in particular, the possibility of world conquest based on natural habitat advantage. It held that the

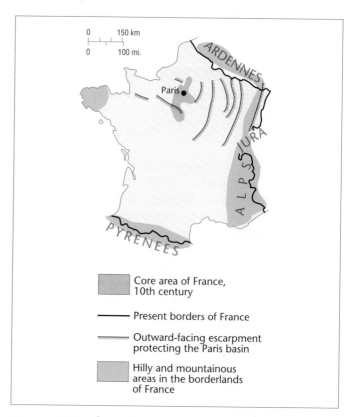

Figure 6.11 **The distribution of landforms in France.** Terrain features such as ridges, hills, and mountains offer protection. Outward-facing escarpments form a folk fortress that protected the core area and capital of France until as recently as World War I. Hill districts and mountain ranges lend stability to French boundaries in the south and southeast.

Eurasian continent was the most likely base from which to launch a successful campaign for world conquest.

In examining this huge landmass, Mackinder discerned two environmental regions: the **heartland,** which lies remote from the ice-free seas, and the **rimland,** the densely populated coastal fringes of Eurasia in the east, south, and west (see Chapter 7) (Figure 6.12). Far from the sea, the heartland was invulnerable to the naval power of rimland empires, but the cavalry and infantry of the heartland could spill out through diverse natural gateways and invade the rimland region. Mackinder thus reasoned that a unified heartland power could conquer the maritime countries with relative ease. He believed that the East European Plain would be the likely base for unification. As Russia had already unified this region at the time, Mackinder, in effect, predicted that the Russians would pursue world conquest

Following Russia's communist revolution in 1917, the leaders of rimland empires and the United States employed a policy of containment. This policy, in no small measure, found its origin in Mackinder's theory and resulted in numerous wars to contain what was then considered a Russian-inspired conspiracy of communist expansion. Overlooked all the while were the fallacies of the heartland theory, particularly its reliance on the discredited doctrine

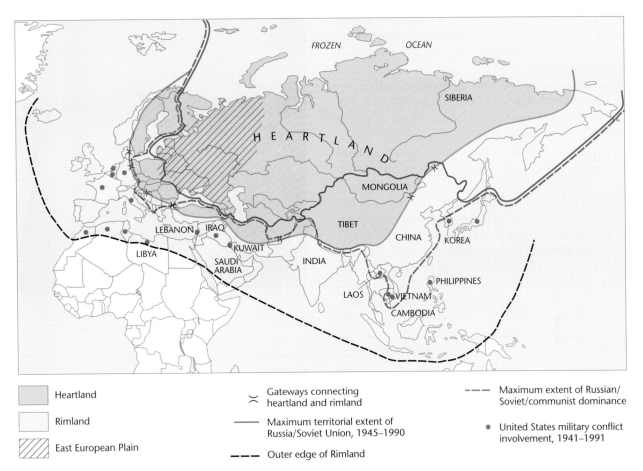

Figure 6.12 **Heartland versus rimland in Eurasia.** For most of the twentieth century, the heartland, epitomized by the Soviet Union and communism, was seen as a threat to America and the rest of the world, a notion based originally on the environmental deterministic theory of the political geographer Halford Mackinder. Control of the East European Plain would permit rule of the entire heartland, which, in turn, would be the territorial base for world conquest. In the cold war, 1945 to 1990, the United States and its rimland allies sought to counter this perceived menace by a policy of containment—resisting every expansionist attempt by the heartland powers. *(After Mackinder, 1904; Spykman, 1944.)*

of environmental determinism. In the end, Russia proved unable to hold together its own heartland empire, much less conquer the rimland and the world.

Geopolitics Today

In the post–cold war period, geopolitics has reemerged as a dynamic field of political-geographic thought. As geographers Gerard Toal and John Agnew explain, the meaning of political geography is now reversed. Instead of focusing on the question of the influence of geography and the environment on politics, "it now becomes the study of how geography is informed by politics." By this they mean the way in which political goals and ideologies, based on preconceived notions of cultural identities, regional stereotypes, and regional development hierarchies, influence the ordering of the world. How does the geopolitical culture of a state structure the world into places of crisis or stability, regions of opportunity or danger, and states of allies or enemies? Many geographers distinguish this new focus on culture by labeling their approach "critical geopolitics."

One of the important aspects of critical geopolitics is a concern with how geopolitics influences our understanding of human-environment relations and affects the way we transform the environment. Consider, for example, the current scientific and policy debates over global climate change caused by greenhouse gas emissions. Worldwide debates must be placed in the historical geopolitical context of the global North's political and economic domination of the global South. From the South's perspective, according to Simon Dalby, "the North got rich by using fossil fuels for generations. Why should those in the South forego the same possibilities just because they come on the development scene a little later?" According to advocates of the South, the North's ideas about restricting future emissions of greenhouse gases globally will have a disadvantageous effect on the South's economic development. Thus, questions of global environmental management are not restricted to the realm of science and technology; they also fall squarely in the realm of geopolitics.

Another illustration of how geopolitics influences human-environment relations is seen in the debates concerning global biodiversity conservation. Current global conservation policy suggests that the most effective way to save the world's biodiversity is by creating protected areas such as national parks and reserves. However, Roderick Neumann has demonstrated that these protected areas, whether in the North or the South, were created in the historical context of European conquest and colonization. In the British Empire, protected areas were part of a grand economic development strategy to spatially reorder colonies into separate spheres of nature and culture. In the United States, park creation was conducted in the context of *manifest destiny* and the removal of Native Americans from their homelands and their placement in reservations. In both cases, the environmental management strategies of native cultures were denigrated as immoral and irrational, providing the justification for discarding local land and resource claims and practices. Today, those who have lost their land to protected areas argue bitterly that they bear the main costs of conservation (Figure 6.13). Thus, as with the case of global climate change, the North-South debates over strategies for global biodiversity conservation fall under the domain of geopolitics.

Warfare and Environmental Destruction

Of course many political actions have an ecological impact, but perhaps none are as devastating as warfare. "Scorched

Figure 6.13 **Two visions of the landscape.** Johnson Holy Rock looks out over Bear Butte State Park in the Black Hills near Sturgis, South Dakota. The Oglala Sioux Tribe of Pine Ridge Indian Reservation, of which Holy Rock is a member, considers the park area to be sacred ground. What kinds of conflicts arise between conservation goals and indigenous peoples' rights and how might we resolve them? *(Ann Heisenfelt/AP Photo.)*

earth," the systematic destruction of resources, has been a favored practice of retreating armies for millennia. Even military exercises and tests can be devastating. Certain islands in the Pacific were rendered uninhabitable, perhaps forever, by American hydrogen bomb testing in the 1950s. Actions during the Persian Gulf War of 1991 included an oil spill of 294 million gallons (1.1 billion liters) covering 400 square

Figure 6.14 **A Kuwaiti oil field ablaze during the Persian Gulf War, 1991,** giving a new meaning to "scorched earth." Severe ecological damage almost invariably accompanies warfare. Could modern war be waged without such damage? *(Noel Quidu/Gamma Liaison.)*

PRACTICING GEOGRAPHY

Katharyne Mitchell

(Courtesy of Katharyne Mitchell.)

Professor Katharyne Mitchell spent her undergraduate years studying literature, music, and art, all but oblivious to the discipline of geography. It was not until graduate school, working toward a degree in architecture, that she discovered the discipline. "I think I hardly even knew what geography was until Manuel Castells told me that all of the questions I had been pestering him with concerning space and power were questions then being pursued by geographers." She switched majors, earned her doctorate in geography, and never looked back. "It was like coming home." Professor Mitchell is now in the Department of Geography at the University of Washington, specializing in the study of cultural identity, citizenship, and transnationalism related to immigration.

Research for her sometimes "feels like detective work," where one painstakingly gathers evidence and "suddenly all of the different kinds of data click together." Professor Mitchell is convinced that "the more types of methods one can bring to bear on answering a research question, the better." If, for example, she is addressing macroeconomic and political questions, she concentrates on examining statistics and quantitative data of various kinds. If, on the other hand, the questions are cultural and social, her methods are more qualitative. "I examine newspapers, photographs, flyers, advertisements, journals, postcards, and other documents from the time period I'm analyzing," she explains, "and I always interview people and read what they have to say in letters to the editor and other media." Part of her methodology is spending time walking through the relevant spaces and taking photographs.

She is currently studying how immigrants and second-generation children are educated to become "cultural" citizens of a particular nation. "By this I mean how do kids come to form a particular kind of allegiance to a particular country—especially in the contemporary time period when so much migration is transnational and there are so many global pressures on immigrant individuals and families." She was led to this research through her interests in differing explanations of immigrant integration, from multiculturalism to assimilation. One of the ways through which she approaches the question is to focus on national education systems. According to Professor Mitchell, national systems of education are important sites "in which to study the ways in which individuals are constituted or 'made' into certain kinds of national subjects or 'citizens.'"

miles (1000 square kilometers) in the Gulf waters, with attendant loss of flora and fauna; the burning of oil fields; the mass bulldozing of sand by the Iraqis to make defensive berms, with consequent wind erosion and loss of vegetation; and the solid-waste pollution produced by 500,000 coalition forces in the Arabian Desert, including 6 million plastic bags discarded weekly by American forces alone (Figure 6.14).

Clearly, warfare—especially modern high-tech warfare—is environmentally catastrophic. From an ecological standpoint, it does not matter who started or won a war. Everyone loses when such destruction occurs, given the worldwide interconnectedness of the life-supporting ecosystem.

Politico-Cultural Interaction

How is politics intertwined with other diverse aspects of culture? The increasing number of independent countries, voting patterns, and other topics that interest political geographers are partly explained by cultural phenomena. In addition, political decisions often have far-reaching effects on culture. Indeed, the political organization of territory, both past and present, is revealed to some degree in almost every facet of culture.

The Nation-State

The link between political and cultural patterns is epitomized by the **nation-state,** created when a *nation*—a people of common heritage, memories, myths, homeland, and culture, speaking the same language and/or sharing a particular religious faith—achieves independence as a separate country. Nationality is *culturally* based in the nation-state, and the country's raison d'être lies in that cultural identity. The more the people have in common culturally, the more stable and potent is the resultant nationalism. Examples of modern nation-states include Germany, Sweden, Japan, Greece, South Korea, Armenia, and Finland (Figure 6.15). Each of these countries has a culturally homogeneous population, with only small minority groups. Their homogeneity represents a *centripetal force.* Many other independent

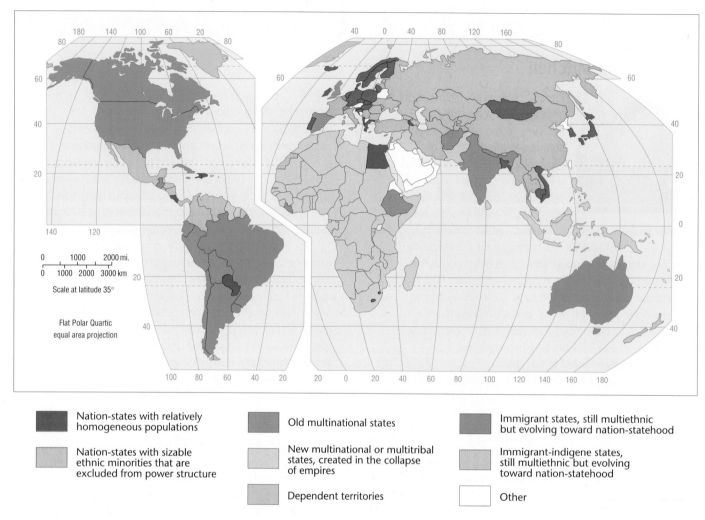

Nation-states with relatively homogeneous populations

Nation-states with sizable ethnic minorities that are excluded from power structure

Old multinational states

New multinational or multitribal states, created in the collapse of empires

Dependent territories

Immigrant states, still multiethnic but evolving toward nation-statehood

Immigrant-indigene states, still multiethnic but evolving toward nation-statehood

Other

Figure 6.15 **Nation-states, multinational countries, and other types.** This classification, as is true of all classifications, is arbitrary and debatable. How would you change it, and why?

countries also function as nation-states because the political power rests in the hands of a dominant, nationalistic cultural group, while sizable ethnic minorities reside in the national territory as second-class citizens. This creates a *centrifugal force* disrupting the country's unity. Many of the new nation-states carved out of the defunct Soviet Union and Yugoslavia, such as Estonia, Georgia, and Russia, contain large, territorially compact ethnic minorities, as do some much older nation-states, including France and China. A nation-state, then, is an independent country that exists as the result of the efforts and desires of a culturally homogeneous and powerful majority.

Cultural Contradictions of State Borders

Many independent countries—the large majority, in fact— are not nation-states but instead contain multiple national, ethnic, and religious groups within their boundaries. India,

Indonesia, the United Kingdom, and South Africa provide examples of older multinational countries (Figure 6.16). A much larger number arose in the second half of the twentieth century with the collapse of European colonialism, particularly in Africa, South Asia, and Southeast Asia. Political boundaries drawn in colonial times without regard to the cultures of indigenous ethnic or tribal groups carried over to the newly independent countries. While these states are often culturally diverse, they are sometimes plagued by internal ethnic conflict. What's more, members of a single, territorially homogeneous ethnic group may find themselves divided among different states by culturally arbitrary international borders.

Ethnic Separatism

Ethnic groups and indigenous peoples are cultural minorities living in a state dominated by a culturally distinct major-

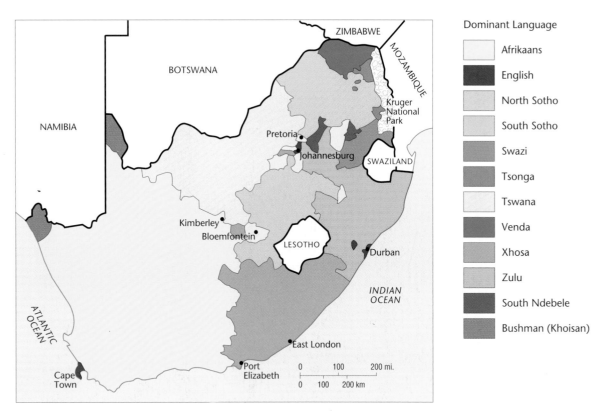

Figure 6.16 **Languages of the Republic of South Africa, a multinational state.** The mixture includes ten native tribal tongues and two languages introduced by settlers from Europe.

ity. Those that inhabit ethnic *homelands* (see Chapter 5) often seek greater autonomy or even full independence as nation-states (Figure 6.17). Even some old and traditionally stable multinational countries have felt the effects of separatist movements, including Canada and the United Kingdom. Some countries, such as the Soviet Union, Yugoslavia, and Czechoslovakia, collapsed under the pressure, splintering into multiple nation-states. Certain other countries discarded the *unitary* form of government and adopted an ethnic-based *federalism,* in hopes of preserving the territorial boundaries of the state. The expression of ethnic nationalism ranges from public displays of cultural identity to organized protests and armed insurgencies. Often the ethnic group or political party in control of the country's military responds with forced deportations and even attempted genocides. Occasionally successful secessions occur, resulting in the birth of a new nation-state.

Francophones in Canada represent a cultural-linguistic minority group seeking secession. Approximately 7 million French-Canadians, concentrated in the province of Québec, form a large part of that country's total population of 31.6 million. Descended from French colonists who immigrated in the 1600s and 1700s, these Canadians lived under English or Anglo-Canadian rule and domination from 1760 until well into the twentieth century. Even the provincial government of Québec long remained in the hands of the English. A political awakening eventually allowed the French to gain control of their own homeland province, and as a result Québec differs in many respects from the rest of Canada. The laws of Québec retain a predominantly French influence, whereas the remainder of Canada adheres to English common law. French is the primary language of Québec and is heavily favored over English in provincial law, education, and government. In several elections, a sizable minority among the French-speaking population favored independence for Québec, and many Anglo-Canadians emigrated from the province. In 1995, more than half of the French-speaking electorate voted for independence, but the non-French minority in the province tipped the vote narrowly in favor of continued union with Canada. More recently, however, the campaign for independence seems to have weakened.

REFLECTING ON GEOGRAPHY

Should Canada split into two independent countries? What would the advantages and disadvantages be for an independent Québec if this split occurred?

Ethnic Separation

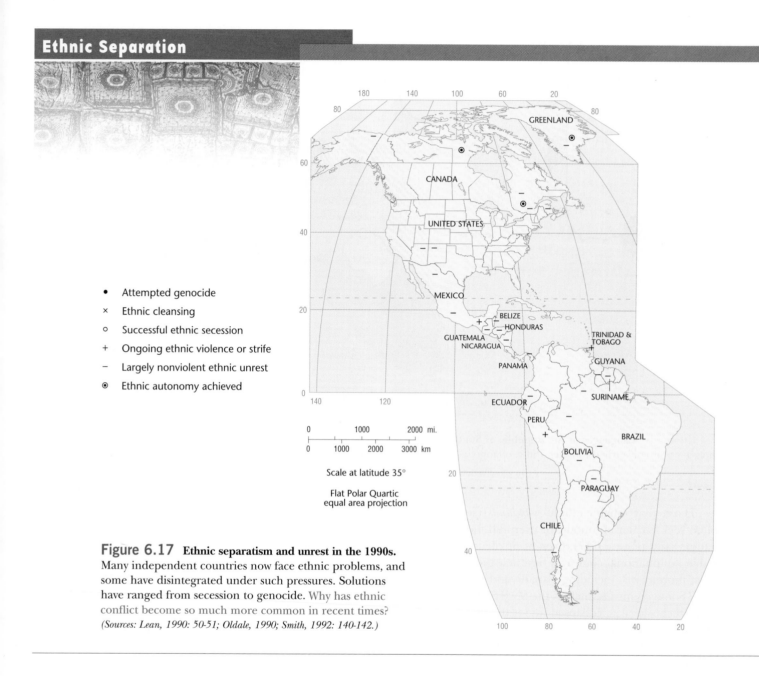

- • Attempted genocide
- × Ethnic cleansing
- ○ Successful ethnic secession
- + Ongoing ethnic violence or strife
- – Largely nonviolent ethnic unrest
- ◉ Ethnic autonomy achieved

Figure 6.17 **Ethnic separatism and unrest in the 1990s.**
Many independent countries now face ethnic problems, and
some have disintegrated under such pressures. Solutions
have ranged from secession to genocide. Why has ethnic
conflict become so much more common in recent times?
(Sources: Lean, 1990: 50-51; Oldale, 1990; Smith, 1992: 140-142.)

On a more general level, one result of such unrest and
separatist desires is that the international political map
reflects a strong linguistic-religious character. Nevertheless,
the distribution of cultural groups is so confoundingly complicated and peoples are so thoroughly mixed in many
regions that ethnographic political boundaries can rarely be
drawn to everybody's satisfaction.

The Cleavage Model

Why do so many cultural minorities seek political autonomy
or independence? The **cleavage model,** originally developed

by Seymour Martin Lipset and Stein Rokkan to explain voting patterns in electoral geography, also sheds light on this
phenomenon. It proposes to explain persistent regional patterns in voting behavior (which, in extreme cases, can
presage separatism) in terms of tensions pitting the national
core area against peripheral districts, urban against rural,
capitalists against workers, and the dominant culture against
minority ethnic cultures. Not infrequently, these tensions
coincide geographically: an urban core area monopolizes
wealth and cultural and political power while ethnic minorities, excluded from the power structure, reside in peripheral,
largely rural, and less affluent areas.

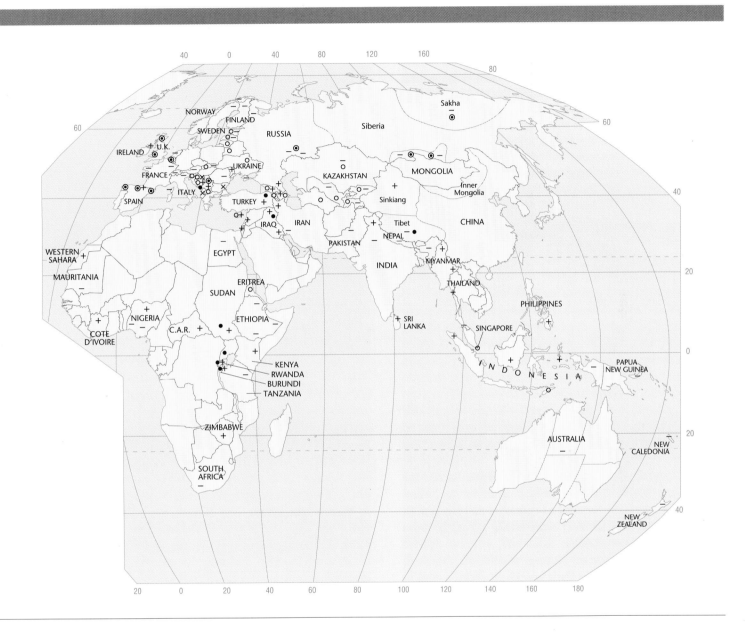

The great majority of ethnic separatist movements shown in Figure 6.17, particularly those that have moved beyond unrest to violence or secession, are comprised of peoples living in national peripheries, away from the core area of the country. Every republic that seceded from the defunct, Russian-dominated Soviet Union lay on the borders of that former country. Similarly, the Slovenes and Croats, who withdrew from the former Yugoslavia, occupied border territories peripheral to Serbia, which contained the former national capital of Belgrade. Northern Ireland lies on the periphery of the United Kingdom, as does rebellious Kurdistan, which is made up of peripheral areas of Iraq, Iran, Syria, and Turkey—the countries that currently rule the Kurdish lands (Figure 6.18). Restive Tibet is on the margins of China, and the Arab West Bank-Gaza districts under Israeli rule are likewise peripheral in location (see Figure 6.17). Slovakia, long poorer and more rural than the Czechia and remote from the center of power at Prague, became another secessionist ethnic periphery. In a few cases, the secessionist peripheries were actually more prosperous than the political core area, and the separatists resented the confiscation of their taxes to support the less affluent core. Slovenia and Croatia both occupied such a position in the former Yugoslavia.

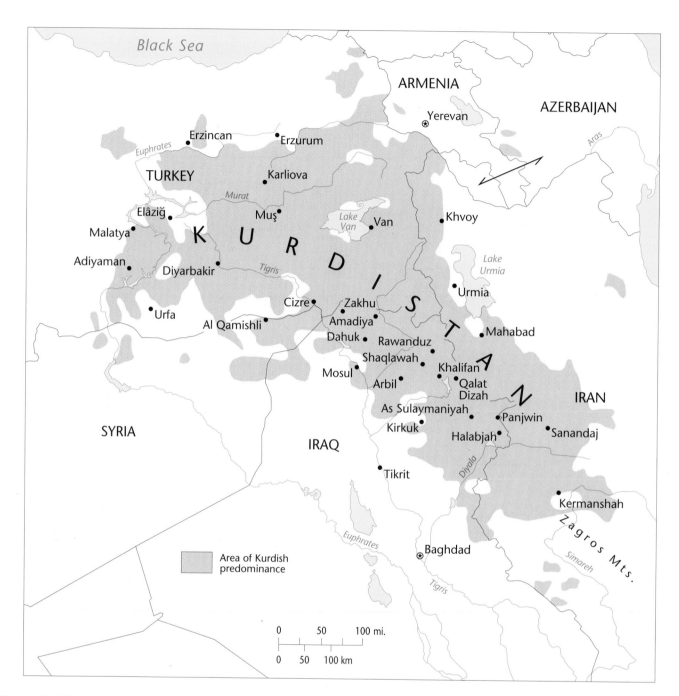

Figure 6.18 **Kurdistan.** This mountainous homeland of the Kurds now lies divided among several countries. The Kurds, numbering 25 million, have lived in this region for millennia. They seek independence and have waged guerrilla war against Iran, Iraq, and Turkey, but, so far, independence has eluded them. What might cause so large and populous a nation to fail to achieve independence? *(Source: Office of the Geographer, U.S. Department of State.)*

By distributing power, *federalist* government reduces such *core-periphery* tensions and decreases the appeal of separatist movements. Switzerland epitomizes such a country and as a result has been able to join Germans, French, Italians, and speakers of Raeto-Romansh into a single, stable independent country. Canada developed under Francophone pressure toward a Swiss-type system, extending con-siderable self-rule privileges even to the Inuit and Native American groups of the north. Russia, too, has adopted a more federalist structure to accommodate the demands of ethnic minorities, and 31 ethnic republics within Russia have achieved considerable autonomy. One of these, Chechnya (called Ichkeria by its inhabitants), has been fighting for independence.

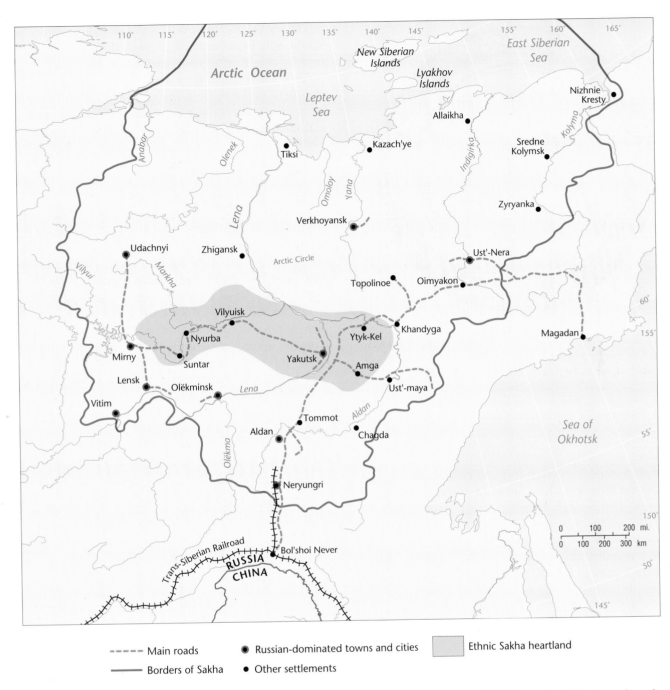

Figure 6.19 **The Republic of Sakha, a part of Russia, has achieved considerable autonomy as a result of ethnic considerations.** For its location in Russia, see Figure 6.17. What would hinder the republic if it sought full independence? *(Source: Jordan and Jordan-Bychkov, 2001: 4.)*

An Example: The Sakha Republic

The Sakha Republic (also called Yakutia), in the huge Russian province of Siberia, provides a useful example of rising ethnic demands (Figure 6.19). The peripheral republic is enormous, forming one-fifth of Russia's land area, and is two and a half times the size of Alaska. Roughly 35 percent of its population of 1 million consists of ethnic Sakha, or Yakuts, a people of Turkic origin (see Chapter 4). Russians, who outnumber the Sakha in the republic, are concentrated in 10 urban areas, while the Sakha are dominant in the rural/small-town core of the republic.

The demands of the Sakha led to a declaration of "state sovereignty" in 1990. The republic now has its own elected

Figure 6.20 **Coat of arms of the ethnic Republic of Sakha in Russia.** The inscription is bilingual—Sakhan and Russian—and the picture of the horse rider is taken from ancient primitive rock art. Why might this ancient image have been used in the coat of arms of a republic seeking increased autonomy? *(Source: Courtesy of the government of the Republic of Sakha.)*

president and parliament, a flag and coat of arms, and a constitution (Figure 6.20). It has attained some measure of economic independence from Russia, especially with regard to authority over mineral rights. The republic can also prohibit nuclear testing on its territory. A survey in 1995 revealed that 72 percent of all ethnic Yakuts felt more loyalty to Sakha than to Russia. Surprisingly, a third of all Russians living in the republic expressed this same loyalty.

The Sakha Republic does not seek independence from Russia. Still, its autonomy represents the embryo of a country. Ongoing Russian emigration from Sakha further complicates the matter. It is increasingly difficult, here as elsewhere in the modern world, to determine exactly what an independent country is. Words such as *sovereignty* have become blurred in meaning.

Political Imprint on Economic Geography

The core-periphery economic differences implicit in the *cleavage model* clearly reveal that the internal spatial arrangement of an independent country influences economic patterns, presenting a cultural interaction of politics and the economy. Moreover, laws differ from one country to another, which affects economic land use. As a result, political boundaries can take on an economic character as well.

For example, the U.S.-Canadian border in the Great Plains crosses an area of environmental and cultural similarity. Yet the presence of the border, representing the limits of jurisdiction of two different bodies of law and regulations, fostered differences in agricultural practices. In the United States, an act passed in the 1950s encouraged sheep raising by guaranteeing an incentive price for wool. No such law was passed in Canada. Consequently, sheep became far more numerous on the American side of the border, while Canadian farmers devoted more attention to swine (Figure 6.21).

Islamic Law in Nigerian Politics

As we saw in Chapter 3, politics is often intertwined with religion. Some countries function as *theocracies*. In many others, internal religious divisions are expressed politically. A good example is Nigeria, divided between a Muslim north and a Christian/animist south (Figure 6.22). In recent years, all of

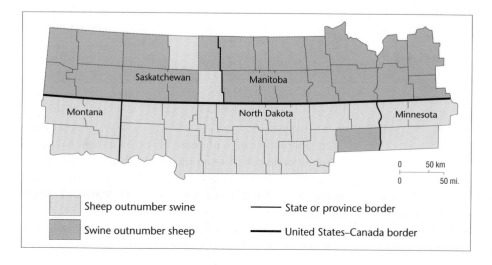

Sheep outnumber swine   State or province border

Swine outnumber sheep   United States–Canada border

Figure 6.21 **The political impact on the economy.** Government intervention can be seen in the choice of livestock in the border area between the United States and Canada. Sheep are more numerous than swine on the U.S. side of the boundary, partly because of government-backed price incentives for wool. The map reflects conditions in the 1960s. Since then, the contrast has essentially disappeared. Why might that have happened? *(Source: Reitsma, 1971: 220-221. See also Reitsma, 1988.)*

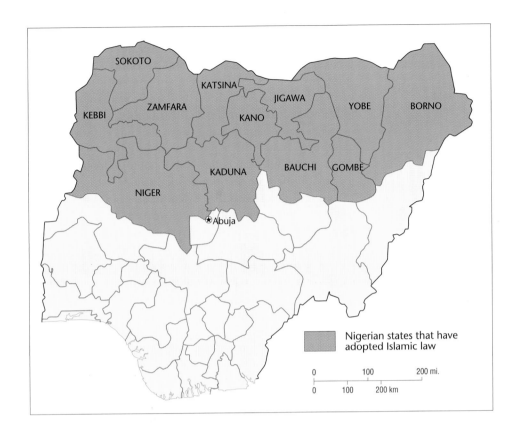

Figure 6.22 **States within Nigeria that have adopted Islamic law as of January 1, 2002.** The religious tension within this African country was already intense before the regional imposition of a religion-based legal system. Can Nigeria hold together? *(Source: Embassy of Nigeria, Washington, D.C.)*

the states of northern Nigeria added criminal law to the jurisdiction of sharia courts. Sharia is Islamic law, which is detailed in the Qur'an and has long been applied in personal and civil law in northern Nigeria, where the majority of the population is Muslim. While Muslims welcomed the change, it has caused tensions between the Muslim majority and local non-Muslim minorities. Non-Muslims are not tried in sharia courts, but they have complained that their political and economic marginalization has increased since the change. There has been an increase in religious violence in the northern states and even reports that some Christian populations have chosen to flee the region. The biggest concern is that the country might fragment along this new politico-religious border, though that is not likely. At the very least, this movement strengthens the centrifugal forces at work in this troubled country, which has already experienced one bloody, but unsuccessful, secessionist war.

 ## Landscape and Politics

How does politics influence landscape? How are landscapes politicized? The world over, national politics is literally written on the landscape. State-driven initiatives for frontier settlement, economic development, and territorial control have profound effects on the landscape. Conversely, politi-

cal writers and policy makers look to landscape as a source of imagery to support or discredit political ideologies.

Imprint of the Legal Code

Many laws affect the cultural landscape. Among the most noticeable are those that regulate the land-survey system, because they often require that land be divided in specific geometric patterns. As a result, political boundaries can become highly visible (Figure 6.23). In Canada, the laws of the French-speaking province of Québec encourage land survey in long, narrow parcels, but most English-speaking provinces, such as Ontario, use a rectangular system. Thus, the political border between Québec and Ontario can be spotted easily from the air.

Legal imprints can also be seen in the cultural landscape of urban areas. In Rio de Janeiro, height restrictions on buildings have been enforced for a long time. The result is a waterfront lined with buildings of uniform height (Figure 6.24). By contrast, most American cities have no height restrictions, allowing skyscrapers to dominate the central city. The consequence is a jagged skyline, like that of San Francisco or New York City. Many other cities around the world lack height restrictions, such as Malaysia's Kuala Lumpur, which has the world's tallest skyscrapers.

Perhaps the best example of how political philosophy and the legal code are written on the landscape is the

Figure 6.23 **Can you find the United States–Mexico border in this picture?** The scene is near Mexicali, the capital of Baja California Norte. Why does the cultural landscape so vividly reveal the political border? *(Courtesy of Terry G. Jordan-Bychkov.)*

so-called township and range system of the United States. The system is the brainchild of Thomas Jefferson—an early U.S. president and one of the authors of the country's constitution—who chaired a national committee on land surveying that resulted in the U.S. Land Ordinance of 1785. Jefferson's ideas for surveying, distributing, and settling the western frontier lands as they were cleared of Native Americans were based on a political philosophy of "agrarian democracy." Jefferson believed that political democracy had to be founded on economic democracy, which in turn required a national pattern of equitable land ownership by small-scale independent farmers. In order to achieve this agrarian democracy, the western lands would need to be surveyed into parcels that could then be sold at prices within reach of family farmers of modest means.

Jefferson's solution was the township and range system, which established a grid of square-shaped "townships" with 6-mile (9.6-kilometer) sides across the Midwest and West. Each of these was then divided into 36 sections of 1 square mile (2.6 square kilometers), which were in turn divided into quarter-sections, and so on. Sections were to be the basic landholding unit for a class of independent farmers. Townships were to provide the structure for self-governing communities responsible for public schools, policing, and tax collection. With the exception of the 13 original colonies

Figure 6.24 **Legal height restrictions, or their absence, can greatly influence urban landscapes.** Kuala Lumpur *(left)*, a city in Malaysia, lacks such controls, and its skyline is punctuated by spectacular skyscrapers, the tallest in the world. In Rio de Janeiro *(above)*, by contrast, height restrictions allow the natural environment to provide the "high-rises." *(Left: S. Thinakaran/ AP Photo; Right: Martin Wendler/Peter Arnold, Inc.)*

Figure 6.25 Imposing order on the land. This aerial view of Canyon County, Idaho, farmland reveals a landscape grid pattern. This pattern was imposed on the landscape across much of the United States following the passage of the 1785 Land Ordinance. *(David Frazier/Image Works.)*

and a few other states or portions of states, a gridlike landscape was imposed on the entire country as a result of Jefferson's political philosophy and accompanying land-survey system (Figure 6.25).

Physical Properties of Boundaries

Demarcated political boundaries can also be strikingly visible, forming *border landscapes*. Political borders are usually most visible where tight restrictions limit the movement of people between neighboring countries. Sometimes such boundaries are even lined with cleared strips, barriers, pillboxes, tank traps, and other obvious defensive installations. At the opposite end of the spectrum are international borders, such as that between Tanzania and Kenya in East Africa, that are unfortified, thinly policed, and in many places very nearly invisible. Even so, undefended borders of this type are usually marked by regularly spaced boundary pillars or cairns, customhouses, and guardhouses at crossing points (Figure 6.26).

The visible aspect of international borders is surprisingly durable, sometimes persisting centuries or even millennia after the boundary becomes obsolete. Ruins of boundary defenses, some dating from ancient times, are common in certain areas. The Great Wall of China is probably the best-known reminder of past boundaries (Figure 6.27). Hadrian's Wall in England, which marks the northern border during one stage of Roman occupation and parallels the modern border between England and Scotland, is a similar reminder.

A quite different type of boundary, marking the territorial limits of urban street gangs, is evident in the central areas of many American cities. The principal device used by these gangs to mark their turf is spray-paint graffiti. Geographers David Ley and Roman Cybriwsky studied this phenomenon in Philadelphia. They found borders marked by externally directed, aggressive epithets, taunts, and obscenities, placed there to warn neighboring gangs. A street gang

Figure 6.26 Even peaceful, unpoliced international borders often appear vividly in the landscape. Sweden and Norway insist on cutting a swath through the forest to mark their common boundary. Why would they do this? *(Courtesy of Terry G. Jordan-Bychkov.)*

Figure 6.27 **The Great Wall of China** is probably the most spectacular political landscape feature ever created and one of the few made by humans that is visible from outer space. The wall, which is 1500 miles (2400 kilometers) long, was constructed over many centuries by the Chinese in an ultimately unsuccessful attempt to protect their northern boundary from adjacent tribes of nomadic herders. Can you think of comparable modern structures? *(Courtesy of Terry G. Jordan-Bychkov.)*

The visibility of provincial borders within a country also reflects the central government's strength and stability. Stable, secure countries, such as the United States, often permit considerable display of provincial borders. Displays aside, such borders are easily crossed. Most state boundaries within the United States are marked with signboards or other features announcing the crossing. By contrast, unstable countries, where separatism threatens national unity, often suppress such visible signs of provincial borders. Also in contrast, such "invisible" borders may be exceedingly difficult to cross when a separatist effort involves armed conflict.

REFLECTING ON GEOGRAPHY

What visible imprints of the Washington, D.C.-based central government can be seen in the political landscape of the United States?

National Iconography on the Landscape

The cultural landscape is rich in symbolism and visual metaphor, and political messages are often conveyed through such means. Statues of national heroes or heroines and of symbolic figures such as the goddess Liberty or Mother Russia form important parts of the political landscape, as do assorted monuments (Figure 6.28). The elabo-

of white youths, for example, plastered its border with a black gang's neighborhood with slogans such as "White Power" and "Do Not Enter [District] 21-W, _____." The gang's core area, its "home corner," contains internally supportive graffiti, such as "Fairmount Rules" or a roster of gang members. Thus, a perceptive observer can map gang territories on the basis of these political landscape features.

The Impress of Central Authority

Attempts to impose centralized government appear in many facets of the landscape (see Focus On: Politics, Religion, and Cultural Landscape). Railroad and highway patterns focused on the national core area, and radiating outward like the spokes of a wheel to reach the hinterlands of the country, provide good indicators of central authority. In Germany, the rail network developed largely before unification of the country in 1871. As a result, no focal point stands out. On the other hand, the superhighway system of autobahns, encouraged by Hitler as a symbol of national unity and power, tied the various parts of the Reich to such focal points as Berlin or the Ruhr industrial district.

Figure 6.28 **Mount Rushmore,** in the Black Hills of South Dakota, presents a highly visible expression of American nationalism, an element of the political landscape. If political landscapes are created by an elite, in an effort to legitimize and justify their control over territory, then who might disapprove of this monument? *(Brownie Harris/The Stock Market.)*

Politics, Religion, and Cultural Landscape

Political reshaping of the cultural landscape can take many forms. Consider a remarkable event in Afghanistan in the year 2001, before the collapse of the ruling Taliban government. A fundamentalist Islamic group ruling in a theocracy, the Taliban declared that several ancient Buddhist images, carved into cliffs and dating from the era before Islam originated, were sacrilegious idols. Said the mullah Muhammad Omar, a Taliban official, "These false idols have been gods of the infidels."

The Taliban decided to destroy these huge statues, as much as 2000 years old, which represented the world's most significant Buddhist statuary heritage and dominated the cultural landscape in one valley of Bamiyan Province. Despite worldwide protests, the demolition was carried out as planned, bringing the cultural landscape into visual compliance with extremist Muslim fundamentalism but destroying one of the world's great art treasures. The photo on the left shows the statuary before the destruction; the photo on the right, after.

(Paul Almasy/Corbis.)

(Reuters/Corbis.)

rate use of national colors can be visually very powerful as well. Landscape symbols such as the Rising Sun flag of Japan, the Statue of Liberty in New York harbor, and the Latvian independence pillar in Riga (which stood untouched throughout half a century of Russian-Soviet rule) evoke deep patriotic emotions. The sites of heroic (if often futile) resistance against invaders, as at Masada in Israel, prompt similar feelings of nationalism.

Some geographers feel that the political iconography of landscape derives from an elite, dominant group in a country's population and that the purpose is to legitimize or justify its power and control over an area. The dominant group seeks both to rally emotional support and to arouse fear in

potential or real enemies. As a result, the iconographic political landscape is often controversial or contested, representing only one side of an issue. Look again at Figure 6.28. The area in which Mount Rushmore stands, the Black Hills, is sacred to the Native Americans who controlled the land before whites seized it. How might these Native Americans, the Lakota Sioux, perceive this monument? Are any other political biases contained in it? Cultural landscapes are always complicated and subject to differing interpretations and meanings, and political landscapes are no exception.

Cultural geographic studies of the political iconography of landscape have greatly enriched our understanding of political geography. Stephen Daniels, for example, demonstrated the importance of woodland landscapes for "naturalizing" ideas about the political and social order in late-eighteenth- and early-nineteenth-century England. Oak woodlands were imagined to embody the traditional conservative values associated with the economic and political dominance of the landed aristocracy. Newly planted coniferous woodlands of pine and fir were seen as a threat to the traditional order and a sign of the disruptive influence of the emerging class of industrial capitalists. Thus, debates over competing political ideologies were blended with debates over competing landscape aesthetics.

In a more contemporary study, geographer Gail Hollander has demonstrated the important symbolic role that the landscape and environment of the Florida Everglades have played in U.S. presidential elections. The symbolic role of the Everglades changed over time, from the 1928 to the 2004 presidential campaigns. In 1928, it was presented as worthless swampland. As such, it played a key role in the election of Herbert Hoover, who promised to drain it for agricultural development. By the 1970s, it was seen as an endangered wetland in need of protection and ecological restoration. Thus, in the 1996, 2000, and 2004 presidential campaigns the candidates' positions on the Everglades were seen as indicators of their commitment to the environment. When George W. Bush posed with pruning shears in the Everglades in May 2004, it offered him a chance to symbolically link his presidential campaign to the ecological restoration of what has come to be viewed as a national treasure (Figure 6.29).

Figure 6.29 **President Bush visits Everglades National Park in Florida.** Such visits to iconic national parks and protected landscapes are common in U.S. political campaigns and are meant to symbolize a candidate's commitment to protecting the environment. *(Joe Raedle/Getty News.)*

diverse imprints on the cultural landscape, while landscapes often provide the symbolism and visual metaphors to support or refute political ideologies. Political geography is clearly important to understanding the human mosaic.

Conclusion

Political spatial variations—from local voting patterns to the spatial arrangement of international power blocs—add yet another dimension to the complex human mosaic. In particular, independent countries operate as vital functional culture regions, which help shape many other aspects of culture. Political culture regions constantly change as political innovations ebb and flow across their surfaces. Political phenomena as varied as the nation-state, separatist movements, women's suffrage, and the territorial expansion of countries move along the paths of diffusion.

Political ecology helps us understand the links between systems of power and the physical environment. Countries do not exist in an environmental vacuum. The spatial patterns of landforms often find reflection in boundaries, core areas, folk fortresses, and global strategies. Likewise, political culture very much influences our ideas and judgments about landscape and environment.

Cultural interaction underscores the relationships between politics and other facets of culture. Harmony and stability within countries often depend on the relative cultural homogeneity of the population. Finally, politics leaves

DOING GEOGRAPHY

The Complex Geography of Congressional Redistricting

Congressional redistricting normally happens every 10 years in the United States, following each national census. In some cases, such as Texas in 2002, redistricting occurs between censuses. Newspaper reports suggest that as a result of the 2002 congressional redistricting in Texas, the U.S. Congress will remain in the hands of a Republican Party majority for the foreseeable future. Does this mid-census redistricting fall under the category of Republican gerrymandering, as some claim, or is it, as the Texas Republican Party argues, a case of necessary adjustments in response to population shifts? Either way, the case of Texas demonstrates how critically important the drawing of congressional district boundaries is to democratic governance.

Your assignment in this exercise is to try to identify cases of possible gerrymandering in your home state or an adjacent state. The first thing you will need to do is obtain a map of congressional district boundaries in your chosen state. Once you have done so, see if you can visually identify districts that may have been gerrymandered. Figure 6.7 and the discussion on pages 184–185 should be helpful to you in identifying such districts.

Having identified your candidate(s) for gerrymandering, there are a few questions that you need to address. First, what was it about the configuration of the boundaries that made you think the district(s) may have been gerrymandered? When were the boundaries drawn? Can you identify which of the major political parties were in power when the boundaries were drawn? Which party do these boundaries favor and why? That is, what are the racial, economic, religious, and ethnic characteristics of the district(s) that may suggest a particular party affiliation? Finally, look at the proportion of major party registration in nearby districts to see if you can determine whether the boundary lines were drawn in order to dilute or to concentrate opposition votes.

Political Geography
on the Internet

You can learn more about political geography on the Internet at the following web sites:

European Union
http://www.europa.eu.int
Here you can find information about the 25-member supranational organization that is, increasingly, reshaping the internal political geography of Europe.

International Boundary News Archive
http://www-ibru.dur.ac.uk/resources/newsarchive.html
This database contains more than 10,000 boundary-related reports from a wide range of news sources around the world dating from 1991 to March 2001.

International Geographical Union (IGU): Commission on Political Geography
http://www.cla.sc.edu/geog/wpm/
The objective of the commission is to study the main theoretical issues of political geography, including questions of the rise and fall of empires, the emergence of new geopolitical models, and contemporary challenges to the state. The site features the commission's newsletters.

Political Geography Specialty Group, Association of American Geographers
http://www.politicalgeography.org/
This site provides details about the activities and meetings of specialists in political geography and includes useful links to other sites featuring political geography and geopolitics.

United Nations
http://www.un.org
Search the worldwide organization with a membership that includes the large majority of independent countries. The site contains politically diverse information about such ventures as peacekeeping and conflict resolution.

Sources

Agnew, John. 1998. *Geopolitics: Re-Visioning World Politics*. London: Routledge.

Agnew, John. 2002. *Making Political Geography*. London: Arnold.

Blaikie, Piers, and Harold Brookfield. 1987. *Land Degradation and Society*. London, Methuen.

Blouet, Brian W. 1987. *Halford Mackinder: A Biography*. College Station: Texas A & M University Press.

Brunn, Stanley D. 1974. *Geography and Politics in America*. New York: Harper & Row.

Dalby, Simon. 2002. "Environmental Governance," in R. Johnston, P. Taylor, and M. Watts (eds.), *Geographies of Global Change: Remapping the World*. London: Routledge, 427–440.

Daniels, Stephen. 1988. "The Political Iconography of Woodland in Later Georgian England," in D. Cosgrove and S. Daniels (eds.), *The Iconography of Landscape*. Cambridge: Cambridge University Press, 43–82

Elazar, Daniel J. 1994. *The American Mosaic: The Impact of Space, Time, and Culture on American Politics*. Boulder, Colo: Westview Press.

Gould, Peter, and Rodney White. 1974. *Mental Maps*. Baltimore: Penguin.

Hollander, Gail. 2005. "The Material and Symbolic Role of the Everglades in National Politics." *Political Geography* 24 (4): 449–475.

Jordan, Bella Bychkova, and Terry G. Jordan-Bychkov. 2001. *Siberian Village: Land and Life in the Sakha Republic*. Minneapolis: University of Minnesota Press.

Jordan-Bychkov, Terry G., and Bella Bychkova Jordan. 2002. *The European Culture Area: A Systematic Geography*, 4th ed., Lanham, Md.: Rowman & Littlefield, Chapter 7.

Lean, Geoffrey, et al. 1990. *Atlas of the Environment*. New York: Prentice-Hall.

Ley, David, and Roman Cybriwsky. 1974. "Urban Graffiti as Territorial Markers." *Annals of the Association of American Geographers* 64: 491–505.

Lipset, Seymour Martin, and Stein Rokkan (eds.). 1967. *Party Systems and Voter Alignments: Cross-National Perspectives*. New York: Free Press.

Mackinder, Halford J. 1904. "The Geographical Pivot of History." *Geographical Journal* 23: 421–437.

Mitchell, Katharyne. 1998. "Fast Capital, Race, and the Monster House," in R. George (ed.), *Burning Down the House: Recycling Domesticity*. Boulder, Colo.: Westview Press, 187–212.

Mitchell, Katharyne. 2002. "Cultural Geographies of Transnationality," in K. Anderson, M. Domosh, S. Pile, and N. Thrift (eds.), *Handbook of Cultural Geography*. London: Sage, 74–87.

Morrill, Richard L. 1981. *Political Redistricting and Geographic Theory*. Washington, D.C.: Association of American Geographers, Resource Publications.

Neumann, Roderick P. 1995. "Local Challenges to Global Agendas: Conservation, Economic Liberalization, and the Pastoralists' Rights Movement in Tanzania." *Antipode* 27(4): 363–382.

Neumann, Roderick P. 2002. "The Postwar Conservation Boom in British Colonial Africa." *Environmental History* 7(1): 22–47.

Neumann, Roderick P. 2004. "Nature-State-Territory: Toward a Critical Theorization of Conservation Enclosures," in R. Peet and M. Watts (eds.), *Liberation Ecologies*, 2nd ed. London: Routlege, 195–217.

Oldale, John. 1990. "Government-Sanctioned Murder." *Geographical Magazine* 62: 20–21.

SEEING GEOGRAPHY

Why are some parts of the world fragmented into many small states and homelands?

The border between Israel and the Gaza Strip, part of the Palestinian Arab homeland.

Israel–Gaza Strip Border

Are you a "border enthusiast"? Do approaching and crossing a political border—particularly one that divides countries hostile or unfriendly to each other—raise your pulse level and get your adrenaline flowing? Does the sight of gun-toting border guards, the prospect of a search of your vehicle, and the presence of barriers at once alarm and fascinate you? Then you are a border enthusiast. Here you stand at the border crossing of Erez between Israel and the Palestinian Arab–controlled Gaza Strip. It is a dangerous place where the ever-present guards are ready for anything. So, in this manner, landscape images demand cultural interactive explanations and imply culture regions. The various themes of cultural geography work together, are inseparable, and constitute a functioning whole.

Various geographically based emotions cause your border enthusiasm. You are about to enter a different functional culture region. The people on the other side are different religiously, linguistically, and in standard of living. The cultural interactions that produced this border are numerous, complex, and in some measure ancient. The political landscape leaves no doubt of the existence of the border or culture region. It is a very special place, indeed, where two nations claim the same land. ∎

O'Reilly, Kathleen, and Gerald R. Webster. 1998. "A Sociodemographic and Partisan Analysis of Voting in Three Anti-Gay Rights Referenda in Oregon." *Professional Geographer* 50: 498–515.

Ó Tuathail, Gearóid. 1996. *Critical Geopolitics.* Minneapolis: University of Minnesota Press.

Paulin, C., and John K. Wright. 1932. *Atlas of the Historical Geography of the United States.* New York: American Geographical Society and the Carnegie Institute.

Reitsma, Hendrik J. 1971. "Crop and Livestock Production in the Vicinity of the United States–Canada Border." *Professional Geographer* 23: 216–223.

Reitsma, Hendrik J. 1988. "Agricultural Changes in the American-Canadian Border Zone, 1954–1978." *Political Geography Quarterly* 7: 23–38.

Rumley, Dennis, and Julian V. Minghi (eds.). 1991. *The Geography of Border Landscapes.* London: Routledge.

Sack, Robert D. 1986. *Human Territoriality: Its Theory and History.* Studies in Historical Geography, No. 7. Cambridge: Cambridge University Press.

Smith, Dan. 1992. "The Sixth Boomerang: Conflict and War," in Susan George (ed.), *The Debt Boomerang.* London: Pluto Press.

Smith, Dan, et al. 1997. *The State of War and Peace Atlas,* 3rd ed. New York: Penguin.

Smith, Graham. 1999. "Russia, Geopolitical Shifts and the New Eurasianism." *Transactions of the Institute of British Geographers* 24: 481–500.

Spykman, Nicholas J. 1944. *The Geography of the Peace.* New York: Harcourt Brace.

Toal, Gerard, and Agnew, John. 2002. "Introduction: Political Geographies, Geopolitics and Culture," in K. Anderson, M. Domosh, S. Pile, and N. Thrift (eds.), *Handbook of Cultural Geogarphy.* London: Sage.

Ten Recommended Books
on Political Geography

(For additional suggested readings, see *The Human Mosaic* web site: www.whfreeman.com/jordan)

Agnew, John. 1998. *Geopolitics: Re-Visioning World Politics.* London: Routledge. A leading political geographer critically examines the historical European perspective on world politics and shows how that vision of world order continues to influence geopolitical thinking.

Agnew, John. 2002. *Making Political Geography*. London: Arnold. This book provides an excellent overview of the field of political geography, highlighting the contributions of key thinkers from the nineteenth century to the present.

Dalby, Simon, and Gearóid Ó Tuathail (eds.). 1998. *Rethinking Geopolitics*. London: Routledge. Fifteen contributors to this postmodernist collection address questions of political identity and popular culture, state violence and genocide, militarism, gender and resistance, cyberwar, and the mass media. They suggest that political geography needs to be reconceptualized for the twenty-first century.

Herb, Guntram H., and David H. Kaplan (eds.). 1999. *Nested Identities: Nationalism, Territory, and Scale*. Lanham, Md.: Rowman & Littlefield. This collection of essays by 14 leading political geographers focuses on the geographical issue of territoriality, through the device of case studies of troubled countries and regions at different scales.

Hooson, David (ed.). 1994. *Geography and National Identity*. Oxford: Blackwell. Essays examine the connection between identity and homeland in a wide variety of settings and argue that the globalization of culture has strengthened the bonds between place and identity.

O'Loughlin, John (ed.). 1994. *Dictionary of Geopolitics*. Westport, Conn.: Greenwood Press. A basic reference book on political geography.

Olwig, Kenneth. 2002. *Landscape, Nature, and the Body Politic: From Britain's Renaissance to America's New World*. Madison: University of Wisconsin Press. This is an impressively researched historical study of the importance of landscape in shaping ideas of nation and national identity in England and the United States.

Shelley, Fred M., J. Clark Archer, Fiona M. Davidson, and Stanley D. Brunn. 1996. *Political Geography of the United States*. New York: Guilford Press. A historical survey of the role of U.S. regionalism in shaping the American political system.

Wallerstein, Immanuel. 1991. *Geopolitics and Geoculture: Essays on the Changing World-System*. Cambridge: Cambridge University Press. A collection of Wallerstein's essays that link the collapse of the Soviet Union to the end of U.S. hegemony around the world.

Williams, Colin H. (ed.). 1993. *The Political Geography of the New World Order*. London: Belhaven. A collection of essays that explore the geopolitical consequences of the collapse of the Soviet Union and the rising importance of Europe and Japan.

Political-Geographical Journals

Geopolitics. This journal explores contemporary geopolitics and geopolitical change with particular reference to territorial problems and issues of state sovereignty. Published by Frank Cass. Volume 1 appeared in 1996.

Political Geography. This is a journal devoted exclusively to political geography. Formerly titled *Political Geography Quarterly*, the journal changed its name in 1992. Published by Elsevier. Volume 1 appeared in 1982.

Space and Polity. This journal is dedicated to understanding the changing relationships between the state and regional/local forms of governance. It highlights the work of scholars whose research interests lie in studying the relationships among space, place, and politics. Published by Carfax Publishing. Volume 1 appeared in 1997.

Answers

Figure 6.3 A, Armenia; B, Azerbaijan; C, Iran; a, Nagorno-Karabakh; b, the Nakhichevan Autonomous Republic; c, the Okhair Eskipara enclave; d, Sofulu enclave; e, Kyarki enclave; f, Bashkend enclave.

Would you feel comfortable walking here? If not, why not?

A street scene in the large city of Kolkata, India. *(Jayanta Shaw/Reuters.)*

Turn to Seeing Geography on page 256 for an in-depth analysis of the above questions.

GEODEMOGRAPHY

Peopling the Earth

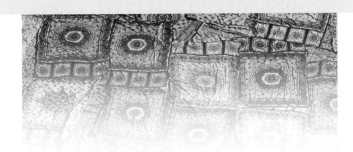

POPULATION GEOGRAPHY, OR **geodemography,** is the study of the spatial and ecological aspects of population, including density, distribution, fertility, gender, living standard, health, age, nutrition, mortality, and mobility. All these demographic characteristics vary from one place to another, helping shape the mosaiclike pattern of the world.

The most essential demographic fact is that well over 6 billion people inhabit the Earth today. Throughout the history of humankind, populations have become very diverse in a great variety of spacial ways. This diversity provides the subject matter of geodemography. As always, we will approach our study using the five themes of cultural geography.

 Demographic Regions

In what ways do demographic traits vary regionally? How is the theme of culture region expressed in terms of population characteristics?

Population Distribution and Density

If the 6,400,000,000 inhabitants of the Earth were evenly distributed across the land area, the **population density** would be about 108 persons per square mile (42 per square kilometer). However, people are very unevenly distributed, creating huge disparities in density. Greenland, for example,

Population Density

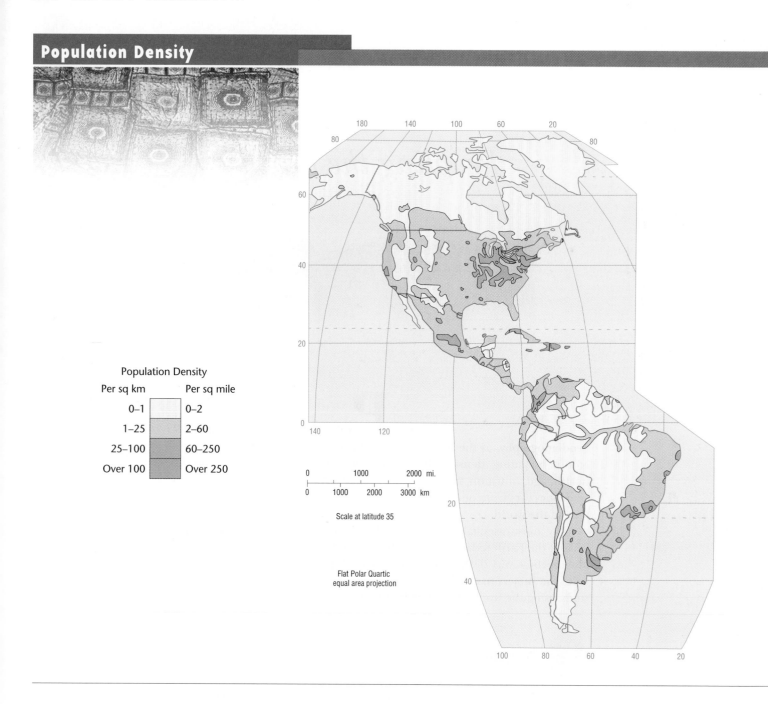

Population Density

Per sq km	Per sq mile
0–1	0–2
1–25	2–60
25–100	60–250
Over 100	Over 250

Scale at latitude 35

Flat Polar Quartic
equal area projection

Figure 7.1 **Population density in the world.** Try to imagine the diverse causal forces—physical, environmental, and cultural—that have been at work over the centuries to produce this complicated spatial pattern. It represents the most basic cultural geographical distribution of all. *(Sources: Population Reference Bureau;* Statistical Abstract of the United States; *United Nations Population Information Network; World Population Data Sheet.)*

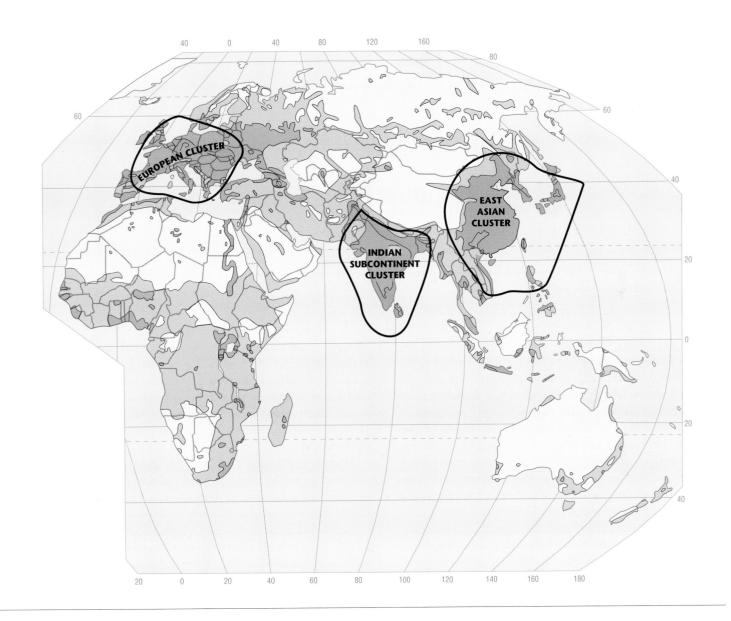

has 0.1 person per square mile (0.04 per square kilometer), whereas Bangladesh has 2300 persons per square mile (890 per square kilometer) (Figure 7.1).

If we consider the distribution of people by continents, we find that 72.7 percent of the human race lives in Eurasia—Europe and Asia. The continent of North America is home to only 7.9 percent of all people, Africa to 13.2 percent, South America to 5.7 percent, and Australia and the Pacific islands to 0.5 percent. If we consider population distribution by country, we find that 21 percent of all humans reside in China, 17 percent in India, and only 4.6 percent in the third-largest nation in the world, the United States (Table 7.1). In fact, one out of every 50 humans lives in just one valley of one province of China: the Red Basin of Sichuan.

Population density can be divided into categories. On one end of the spectrum, thickly settled areas have 250 or more persons per square mile (100 or more per square kilometer); on the other end, largely unpopulated areas have fewer than 2 persons per square mile (fewer than 1 per square kilometer). Moderately settled areas, with 60 to 250 persons per square mile (25 to 100 per square kilometer) and thinly settled areas inhabited by 2 to 60 persons per square mile

TABLE 7.1 The World's Ten Most Populous Countries, 2004 and 2005			
Largest Countries in 2004	**Population in 2004 (in millions)**	**Largest Countries in 2050**	**Population in 2050 (estimated, in millions)**
China	1,300	India	1,628
India	1,087	China	1,437
United States	294	United States	420
Indonesia	219	Indonesia	308
Brazil	179	Nigeria	307
Pakistan	159	Pakistan	295
Russia	144	Bangladesh	280
Bangladesh	141	Brazil	221
Japan	137	Democratic Republic of Congo	181
Nigeria	128	Ethiopia	173

(Source: World Population Data Sheet, 2004.)

(1 to 25 per square kilometer), fall between these two extremes. These categories create formal demographic regions based on the single trait of population density. As Figure 7.1 shows, a fragmented crescent of densely settled areas stretches along the western, southern, and eastern edges of the huge Eurasian continent. Two-thirds of the human race is concentrated in this crescent, which contains three major population clusters: eastern Asia, the Indian subcontinent, and Europe. Outside of Eurasia, only scattered districts are so densely settled. Despite the image of a crowded world, thinly settled regions are much more extensive than thickly settled ones and they appear on every continent. Thin settlement characterizes the northern sections of Eurasia and North America, the interior of South America, most of Australia, and a desert belt through North Africa and the Arabian Peninsula into the heart of Eurasia.

Although population density describes the distribution of people, it does not say anything about their standard of living, overpopulation, or underpopulation. Some of the most densely populated areas in the world have the highest standards of living—and even suffer from labor shortages (for example, the major industrial areas of western Europe). In certain other cases, regions designated as thinly settled may actually be severely overpopulated, marginal agricultural lands. Although 1000 persons per square mile (400 per square kilometer) is a "sparse" population for an industrial district, it is "dense" for a rural area. For this reason, *physiological density*—the density beyond which people cease to be nutritionally self-sufficient using their particular *adaptive*

strategy—provides a far more meaningful index of overpopulation. Unfortunately, physiological density is difficult to measure. Americans, for example, consume far more food and other resources than do most other people in the world. Our physiological density would be at the breaking point if we did not annex the resources of much of the rest of the world.

Population densities, whether absolute or physiological, shift over time. To gain a dynamic perspective, we need to consider the geography of demographic change. Births and deaths can be thought of as additions to and subtractions from the population of a place (see Focus On: The Rule of 72). They provide what demographers refer to as *natural increases* and *natural decreases* to a population. This contrasts with the population changes caused by immigration and outmigration, which we will consider later in this chapter. Usually, data on births and deaths are provided at the national level, because that is the scale at which most statistics on births and deaths are gathered through national censuses.

Patterns of Natality

Births can be measured by several geodemographic methods. The older way was simply to calculate the **birthrate:** the number of births per year per thousand population.

More revealing is the **total fertility rate,** or **TFR,** which is measured as the average number of children born per woman during her reproductive lifetime, considered to be from 15 to 44 years of age. The TFR is a more useful measure than the birthrate, because it focuses on the female segment of the population, reveals average family size, and gives an indication of future changes in the population structure. A TFR of 2.1 is needed to produce an eventually stabilized population, one that does not increase or decrease. Once achieved, this condition is called **zero population growth.**

The TFR varies markedly from one part of the world to another, revealing a vivid geography (Figure 7.2). In southern and eastern Europe, the average TFR is only 1.3. Every country with a TFR of 2.0 or lower will eventually experience population decline. Bulgaria, for example, has a TFR of 1.2 and is expected to lose 38 percent of its population by 2050. Interestingly, the Chinese Special Administrative Regions of Hong Kong and Macao report TFRs of only 0.9 and 0.8, respectively, the lowest in the world as of 2004.

By contrast, sub-Saharan Africa has the highest TFR (5.6) of any sizable part of the world, led by Niger with 8.0, Somalia and Guinea-Bissau with 7.1 each, and Mali with 7.0. Elsewhere in the world, only Yemen, on the Arabian Peninsula, can rival the African rate with its TFR of 7.0.

The Geography of Mortality

Another way to assess demographic change is to analyze **death rates:** the number of deaths per year per 1000 people. Of course, death is a natural part of the life cycle, and there is no way to achieve a death rate of zero. But death comes in different forms geographically. In the developed world, most people die of age-induced degenerative conditions, such as heart disease, or from maladies caused by industrial pollution of the environment. Many types of cancer fall in the latter category. By contrast, contagious diseases such as malaria, HIV/AIDS, and diarrhea are a leading cause of death in poorer countries. Civil warfare, inadequate health services, and the age structure of a country's population will also affect its death rate.

The highest death rates occur in sub-Saharan Africa, the poorest world region and most afflicted by life-threatening diseases and civil strife (Figure 7.3 on pages 220–221 illustrates the geography of HIV/AIDS). In general, death rates of more than 25 per 1000 are uncommon today. Sierra Leone, however, has a death rate of 29, which reflects the political turbulence in that country. By contrast, the American tropics generally have rather low death rates, as does the desert belt across North Africa, the Middle East, and central Asia. In these regions, the predominantly young population depresses the death rate. Compared to Sierra Leone, Ecuador's death rate of only 4 per 1000 seems quite low. Because of its much older population, most of Europe—including Russia—displays a somewhat higher death rate. Belgium's death rate in 2004 was 10, a higher number than Ecuador's 4 in large part because of its much more elderly population

FOCUS ON

The Rule of 72

A handy tool you can use to figure out the doubling time of a population is called the Rule of 72. To use it, you take a country's rate of annual increase, expressed as a percent, and divide it into the number 72. The result is the number of years a population growing at a given rate will take to double.

For example, the natural annual growth of the United States expressed as a percent in 2004 was 0.6 percent. If you divide 72 by 0.6, you get 120. That means that the population of the United States will double every 120 years. This doesn't factor in the relatively high levels of immigration experienced by the United States, which in reality will cause its population to double faster than every 120 years.

What about other countries with faster rates of growth? Consider Guatemala, which is growing at 2.8 percent per year. When we do the math, we find that Guatemala's population is doubling every 25.7 years—much faster than every 120 years!

0.6 percent, 2.8 percent—these don't sound like such high rates. And if we were discussing your bank account rather than the populations of countries, you would be less than impressed to see your money double only every 25 years! (Incidentally, you can apply the Rule of 72 to your bank account or to any other figure that grows at an annual rate.) You may be tempted to say, "Look, there are only 12 million people in Guatemala, so it doesn't really matter if its population is doubling quickly. What really matters is the fact that at an annual increase of 1.7 percent, India's 1 billion people will double to 2 billion in 42 years, or China's 1.3 billion will double as fast as the U.S. population—every 120 years—but that will add another 1.3 billion to the world's population, more than four times what the United States will add by doubling!" You will be partly right and partly wrong in your assessment. Viewed at the global scale, it does indeed make a significant difference when China's or India's population doubles. But if you are a resident of Guatemala, or the Guatemalan government, a doubling of your country's population every 25 years means health care, education, jobs, fresh water, and housing must be supplied to twice as many people every 25 years.

Fertility Rate

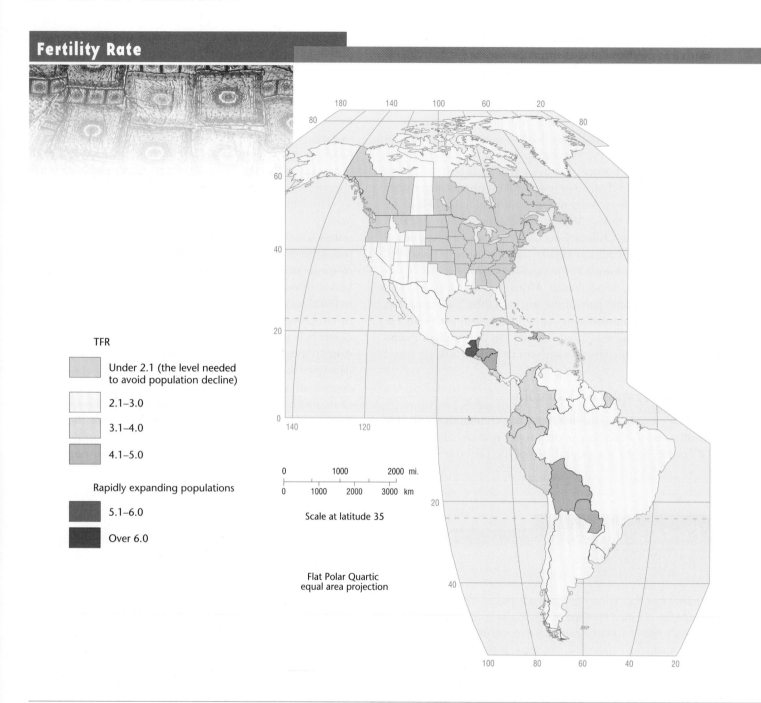

TFR

Under 2.1 (the level needed to avoid population decline)

2.1–3.0

3.1–4.0

4.1–5.0

Rapidly expanding populations

5.1–6.0

Over 6.0

0   1000   2000 mi.
0   1000   2000   3000 km

Scale at latitude 35

Flat Polar Quartic
equal area projection

Figure 7.2 **The total fertility rate (TFR) in the world.** The TFR indicates the average number of children born to women over their lifetimes. A rate of 2.1 is needed to produce a stable population over the long run; below that, population will decline. Fast growth is associated with a TFR of 5.0 or higher. *(Sources: Population Reference Bureau;* Statistical Abstract of the United States; *United Nations Population Information Network; World Population Data Sheet; United Nations Population Division.)*

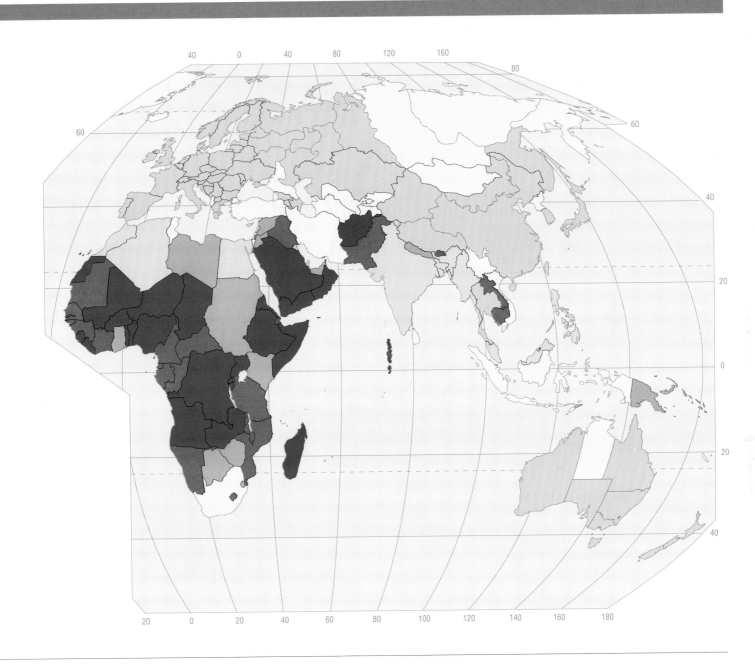

structure. Australia, Canada, and the United States, which continue to attract mostly young immigrants, have lower death rates than most of Europe. Canada's death rate, for instance, is 7 per 1000.

Population Explosion

When considered together, the spatial patterns of population density, TFR, and mortality create one of the fundamental problems of the modern age: the **population explosion**—a dramatic increase in world population since 1900 (Figure 7.4 on page 222). The crucial element triggering this explosion has been a dramatic decrease in the death rate, particularly for infants and children, in most of the world, without an accompanying universal decline in the TFR. At one time, in traditional cultures, only two or three offspring in a family of six to eight children might live to adulthood, but when improved health conditions allowed more of the children to survive, the cultural norm encouraging large families persisted.

Adult HIV/AIDS Cases

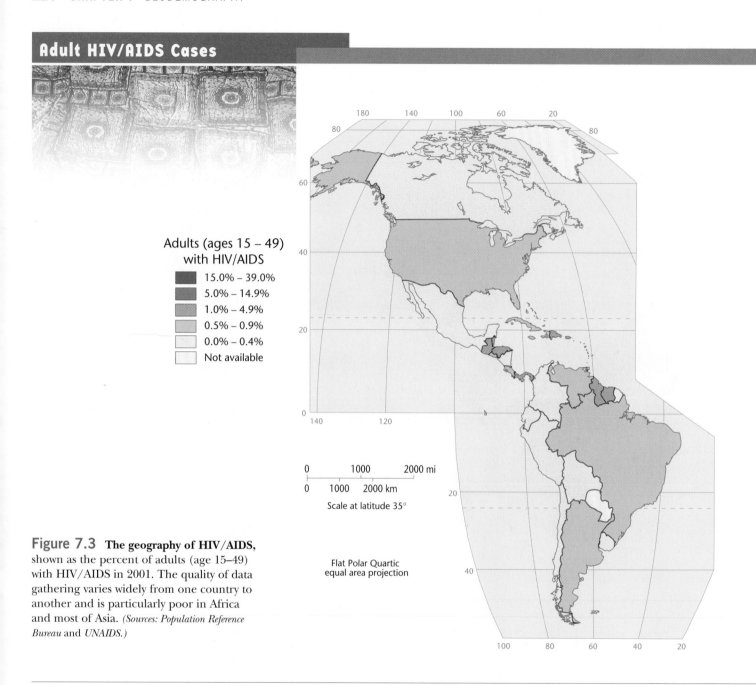

Adults (ages 15 – 49)
with HIV/AIDS

- 15.0% – 39.0%
- 5.0% – 14.9%
- 1.0% – 4.9%
- 0.5% – 0.9%
- 0.0% – 0.4%
- Not available

Flat Polar Quartic
equal area projection

Scale at latitude 35°

Figure 7.3 **The geography of HIV/AIDS,** shown as the percent of adults (age 15–49) with HIV/AIDS in 2001. The quality of data gathering varies widely from one country to another and is particularly poor in Africa and most of Asia. *(Sources: Population Reference Bureau and UNAIDS.)*

The population crisis is simple to describe on a global scale. Until very recently, the number of people in the world has been increasing geometrically, doubling in shorter and shorter periods of time. Consider that it took from the beginning of human history until A.D. 1800 for the Earth's population to grow to 1 billion, from 1800 to 1930 to grow to 2 billion, and only 45 more years to double again by 1975. The overall effect of even a few population doublings is astonishing. An example of geometric progression is provided by the legend of the king who was willing to grant any

wish to the person who could supply a grain of wheat for the first square of his chessboard, two grains for the second square, four for the third, and so on. To cover all 64 squares and win, the candidate would have had to present a cache of wheat larger than today's worldwide wheat crop. Looked at another way, it is estimated that 61 billion humans have lived in the entire 200,000-year period since the species *Homo sapiens* originated. Of these, 6.4 billion (roughly 10 percent) are alive today. One of every 10 humans who ever lived on Earth is alive today. If we were to consider only those

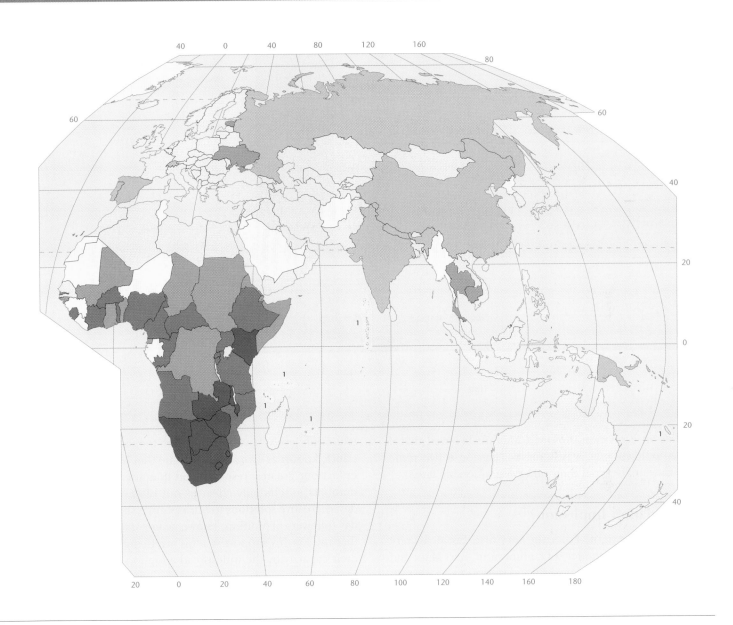

humans who survived into adulthood, the proportion alive today would come closer to 20 percent!

Some scholars foresaw long ago that an ever-increasing population would eventually present difficulties. The most famous pioneer observer of population growth, the English economist and cleric Thomas Malthus, published *An Essay on the Principle of Population*—known as the "dismal essay"—in 1798. He believed that the human ability to multiply far exceeds our ability to increase food production. Consequently, Malthus maintained that "a strong and constantly operating check on population" will necessarily act as a natural control on numbers. Malthus regarded famine, disease, and war as the inevitable outcome of the human population's outstripping the food supply (Figure 7.5). He wrote, "Population, when unchecked, increases in a geometrical ratio. Subsistence only increases in an arithmetical ratio. A slight acquaintance with numbers will show the immensity of the first power in comparison of the second."

The adjective *Malthusian* entered the English language to describe the dismal future Malthus foresaw. Being a cleric

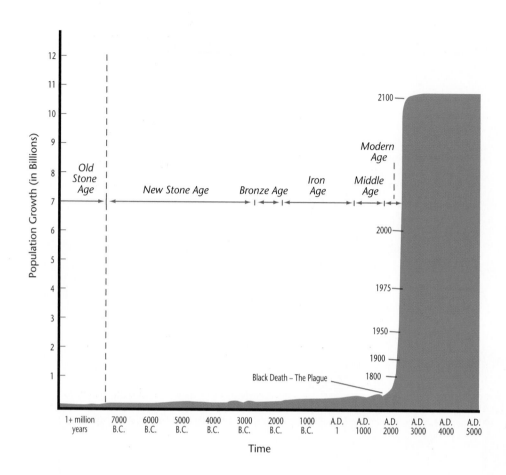

Figure 7.4 **S-shaped world population curve.** Is the global population explosion nearing its end? If this graph is right, the world's population will stabilize at nearly 11 billion by the year 2100. *(Adapted from Population Reference Bureau and United Nations,* World Population Projections 2100, *1998.)*

as well as an economist, however, Malthus believed that if humans could voluntarily restrain the "passion between the sexes," they might avoid their otherwise miserable fate.

Or Population Implosion?

But was Malthus right? From the very first, his ideas were controversial. The founders of communism, Karl Marx and Friedrich Engels, blamed poverty and starvation on the evils of society but suggested that when times are especially hard, the poor find ways to achieve birth control. Taking this view of things might lead one to believe that the miseries of starvation, warfare, and disease are more the result of a maldistribution of the world's wealth than of overpopulation.

Malthus also forgot to factor into his predictions the notion that human beings, when faced with conundrums such as scarce food supplies, are highly creative. This has led critics of Malthus and his modern-day followers to point out that while population has doubled three times since Malthus wrote his essay, food supplies have doubled five times over. Scientific innovations such as the green revolution have led to food increases that have far outpaced population growth (see Chapter 8). And other measures of well-being, including life expectancy, air quality, and average

education levels, have all improved, too. Some of Malthus's critics, known as *cornucopians,* argue that human beings are in fact our greatest resource and that attempts to curb our numbers misguidedly cheat us out of geniuses who could devise creative solutions to our resource shortages. Modern-day followers of Malthus, known as *neo-Malthusians,* counter that the Earth's support systems are being strained beyond their capacity by the widespread adoption of wasteful Western lifestyles.

At the beginning of the new millennium, the fact is that the world's population is growing more slowly than before. The world's TFR has fallen to 2.8. One demographer has gone so far as to declare that "the population explosion is over." Others use such terms as *demographic collapse* and *population implosion.* All this leads us to the phenomenon known as the demographic transition.

Demographic Transition

All industrialized, technologically advanced countries have achieved low fertility rates and stabilized or declining populations, having passed through what is called the **demographic transition** (Figure 7.6). In preindustrial societies, birth and death rates were both high, leading to almost no

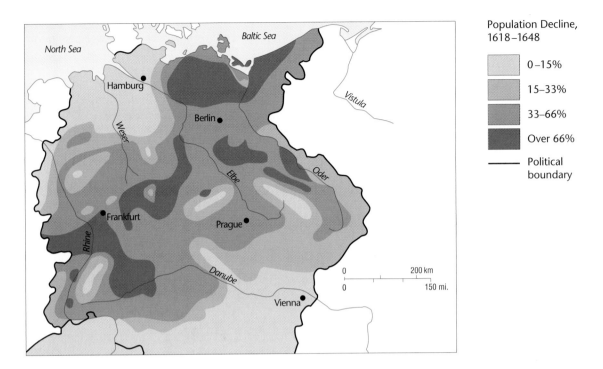

Figure 7.5 War as a device for population control in central Europe, 1618–1648. Thomas Malthus regarded war as inevitable to help control population growth. He would understand this map, which reveals how effective war can be in destroying people.

The Thirty Years' War, with its attendant killing, starvation, and disease, drastically reduced the population in some central European provinces. Population density was greatly altered.
(*After* Westermanns Grosser Atlas, *1956: 107.*)

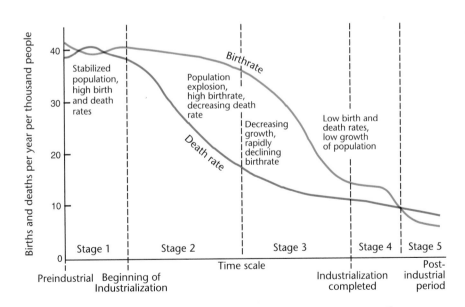

Figure 7.6 The demographic transition as a graph. The "transition" occurs in several steps, as the industrialization of a country progresses. In stage 2, the death rate declines rapidly, causing a population explosion as the gap between the number of births and deaths widens. Then, in stage 3, the birthrate begins a sharp decline. The transition ends when, in stage 4, both birth and death rates have reached low levels, by which time the total population is many times greater than at the beginning of the transformation. In the postindustrial phase, population decline eventually begins.

Annual Population Change

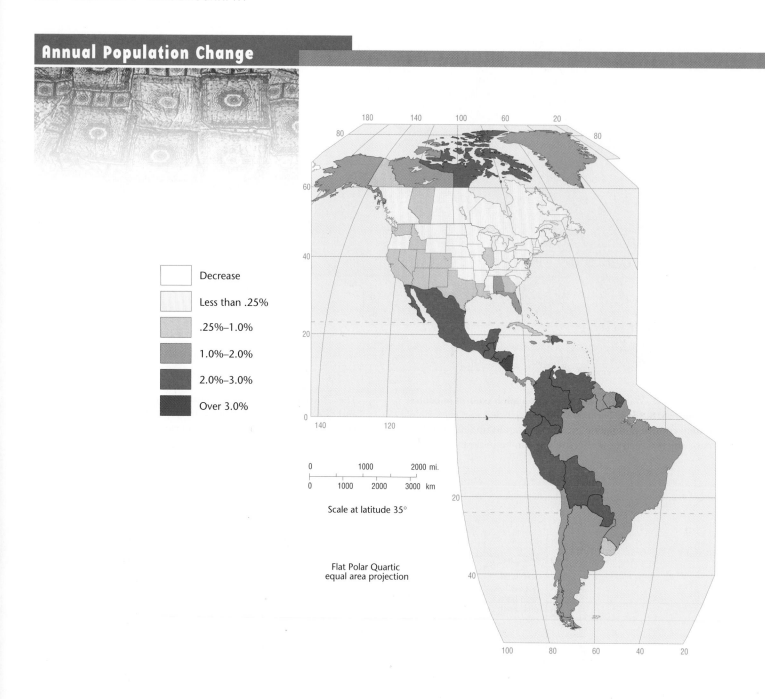

Figure 7.7 **Annual population increase.** The change is calculated as the difference between the number of births and deaths in a year, taken as a percentage of total population. Migration is not considered. Note the contrast between tropical areas and the middle and upper latitudes. In several places, countries with a very slow increase border areas with extremely high growth. *(Sources: Population Reference Bureau; Statistical Abstract of the United States; United Nations Population Information Network; World Population Data Sheet.)*

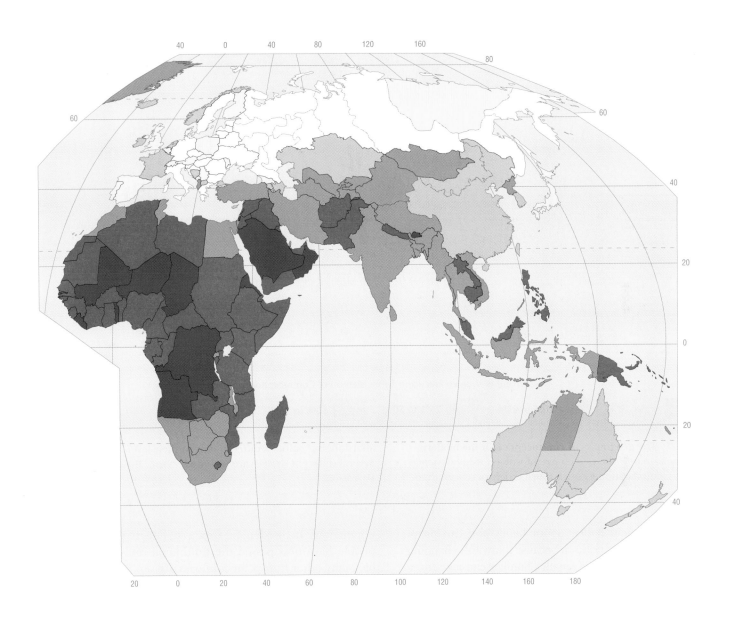

population growth. With the coming of the industrial era, medical advances and improvements in diet set the stage for a drop in death rates. Human life expectancy in the industrialized countries soared from an average of 35 years in the eighteenth century to 75 years or more at present. Yet birthrates did not fall so quickly, leading to a population explosion as fertility outpaced mortality. In Figure 7.6, this is shown in late stage 2 and early stage 3 of the model. Eventually, a decline in the birthrate followed the decline in the death rate, slowing population growth. Finally, in the postindustrial period (see Chapter 9), the demographic transition produced zero population growth or actual decline (Figure 7.7).

Achieving lower death rates is relatively cost effective, historically requiring little more than the provision of safe drinking water and vaccinations against common infectious disease. Less death tends to be uncontroversial and fast acting, demographically speaking. Getting birthrates to fall, however, can be far more difficult, especially for a government that needs to be reelected. Birth control, abortion, and

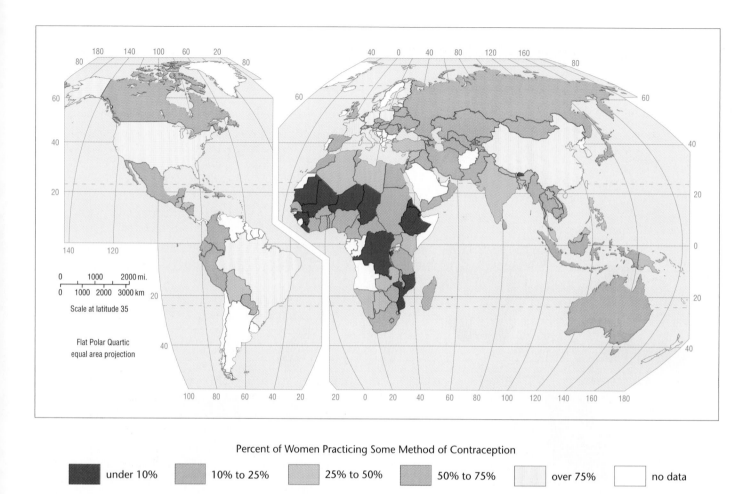

Percent of Women Practicing Some Method of Contraception

| | under 10% | | 10% to 25% | | 25% to 50% | | 50% to 75% | | over 75% | | no data |

Figure 7.8   The geography of contraception in the modern world, as measured by the percentage of women using devices of any sort. Contraception is much more widely practiced than abortion, but cultures differ greatly in their level of acceptance. Several different devices are included. *(Source: World Population Data Sheet.)*

challenging long-held beliefs about family size can prove quite controversial. In addition, because it involves changing a cultural norm, the idea of smaller families can take three or four generations to take hold. Increasing educational levels for women is closely associated with falling fertility levels, as is access to various contraceptive devices (Figure 7.8).

Age Distributions

Some countries have overwhelmingly young populations, with close to half the population under 15 years of age. Uganda is such a country, with 51 percent in that age category, as are some countries in Latin America, Africa, and tropical Asia (Figure 7.9). In sub-Saharan Africa, 44 percent of all people are younger than 15. Others, generally countries that industrialized early, have a great preponderance of middle-aged people in the over 15–under 65 age bracket. A growing number of affluent countries have remarkably aged populations. In Sweden, for example, fully 17 percent of the people have now passed the traditional retirement age of 65. Many other European countries are not far behind (see Focus On: Rent-a-Grandpa). A sharp contrast emerges when Europe is compared with Africa, Latin America, or parts of Asia, where the average person never even lives to age 65. In Mauritania, Niger, Afghanistan, Guatemala, and many other countries, only 2 to 3 percent of the people have reached that age. Very different cultures result in populations that have disproportionate numbers of young or aged people, adding another component to the human mosaic.

Age structure also differs spatially within individual countries. For example, rural populations in the United States and many other countries are usually older than those in urban areas. The flight of young people to the cities has left some rural counties in the midsection of the United States with populations whose median age is 45 or older. Some warm areas of the United States have become retire-

Rent-a-Grandpa

Italy has one of the lowest birth rates in the world. With a TFR of just 1.3, Italy is projected to have its population shrink by 10 percent between 2004 and 2050. Partially responsible for this low level of growth is the fact that Italy's population is also one of the oldest in the world, with 18.6 percent of its population age 65 or older. Combined with these demographic changes is the fact that more Italian women than ever work outside the home for an income.

Given that the Italian culture does not embrace the institutionalization of the growing ranks of their elderly, and faced with the reality that there are few women willing or able to stay at home full time to care for them, Italians have gotten creative. Elderly men and women can apply for adoption by families in need of grandfathers or grandmothers. One such man, Giorgio Angelozzi, recently moved in with the Rivas, a Roman family with two teenagers. Angelozzi said that Marlena Riva's voice reminded him of his deceased wife, Lucia, and this is what convinced him to choose the Riva family. Dagmara Riva, the family's teenage daughter, says that Mr. Angelozzi has helped her with Latin studies and that "Grandpa is a person of great experience, an affectionate person. We're very happy we invited him to live with us."

Adapted from D'Emilio, 2004

ment havens for the elderly; parts of Arizona and Florida, for example, have populations far above the average age. Communities such as Sun City near Phoenix, Arizona, legally restrict residence to the elderly. In Great Britain, coastal districts have a much higher proportion of elderly than does the interior, causing the map to resemble a hollow shell and suggesting that the aged often migrate to seaside locations when they retire.

A very useful graphic device for comparing age characteristics is the **population pyramid** (Figure 7.10 on page 230). Careful study of such pyramids not only reveals the past progress of birth control but also allows geographers to predict future population trends. Youth-weighted pyramids, those that are broad at the base, suggest the rapid growth typical of the population explosion. Those that have more of a cylindrical shape represent countries approaching population stability or in demographic decline.

Geography of Gender

Although the human race is divided almost evenly between females and males, geographical differences do occur in the **sex ratio:** the ratio between men and women in a population (Figure 7.11 on pages 232–233). Slightly more boys than girls are born, but infant boys have slightly higher mortality rates than infant girls. Recently settled areas typically have more males than females, as is evident in parts of Alaska, northern Canada, and tropical Australia. At the latest census, males constituted 53 percent of Alaska's inhabitants. By contrast, Mississippi's population was 52 percent female, reflecting in part the emigration of young males in search of better economic opportunity elsewhere. Some poverty-stricken parts of South Africa are as much as 59 percent female. Prolonged wars reduce the male population. And, in general, women tend to outlive men. The population pyramid is also useful in showing gender ratios. Note, for instance, the larger female populations in the upper bars for both the United States and Sun City, Arizona, in Figure 7.10.

Beyond such patterns, gender often influences demographic traits in specific ways. Often *gender roles*—culturally specific notions of what it means to be a man and what it means to be a woman—are closely tied to how many children are produced by couples. In many cultures, women are considered more womanly when they produce many offspring. By the same token, men are seen as more manly when they father many children. Because the raising of children often falls to women, the spaces that many cultures associate with women tend to be the private family spaces of the home. Public spaces such as streets, plazas, and the workplace, by contrast, are often associated with men (see Chapter 10). Some cultures go so far as to restrict where women and men may and may not go, resulting in a distinctive geography of gender. Falling fertility levels that coincide with higher levels of education for women, however, have resulted in numerous challenges to these cultural ideas of male and female spaces. As more and more women enter the workplace, for instance, ideas of where women should and should not go slowly become modified (see Culture in a Globalizing World on page 231).

Other forces also influence the geography of gender. A disturbing tendency exists in certain countries, most

Youth and Old Age Populations

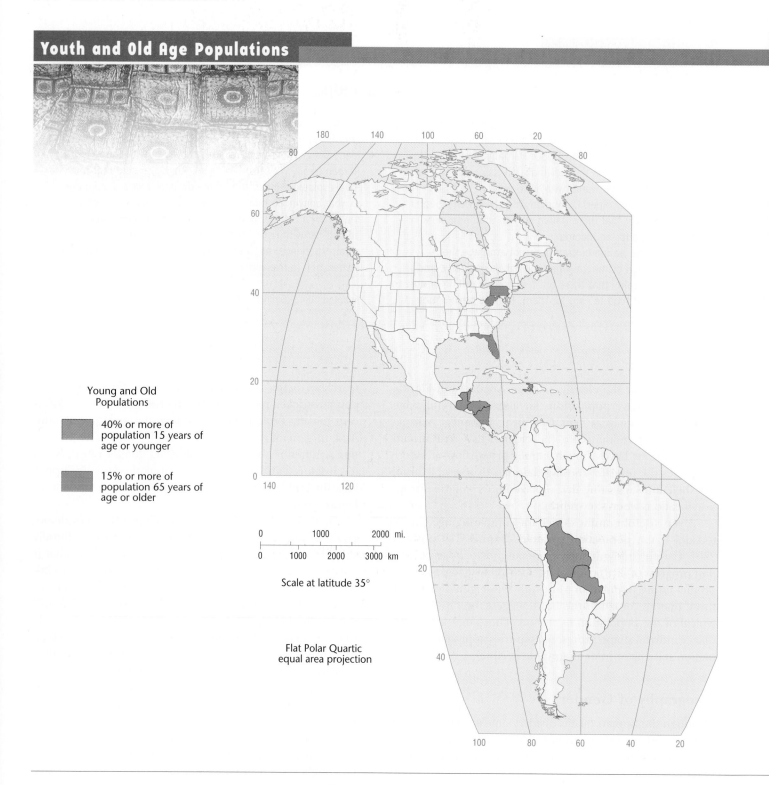

Young and Old
Populations

40% or more of
population 15 years of
age or younger

15% or more of
population 65 years of
age or older

0   1000   2000 mi.

0   1000   2000   3000 km

Scale at latitude 35°

Flat Polar Quartic
equal area projection

Figure 7.9 **The world pattern of youth and old age.** Some countries have populations with unusually large numbers of elderly people; others have preponderantly young populations. What issues might be associated with either situation? *(Sources: Population Reference Bureau; Statistical Abstract of the United States; United Nations Population Information Network; World Population Data Sheet.)*

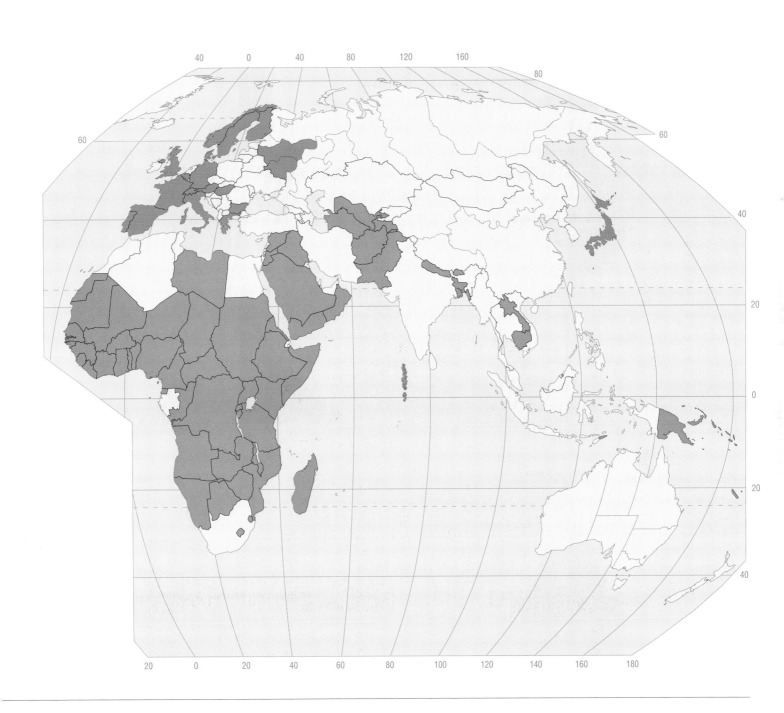

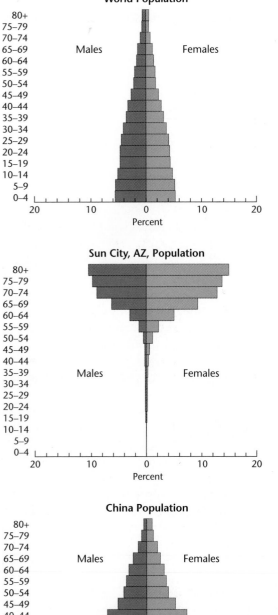

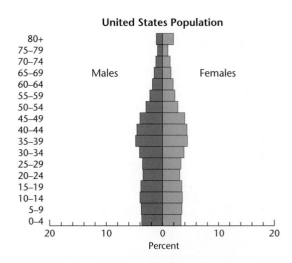

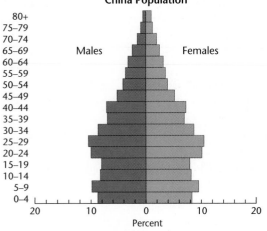

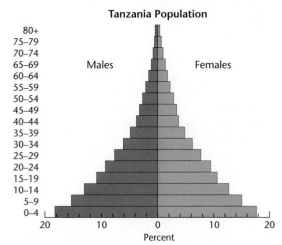

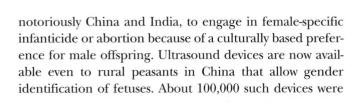

Figure 7.10 **Population pyramids for the world and selected countries and communities.** Tanzania displays the classic stepped pyramid of a rapidly expanding population, whereas the U.S. pyramid looks more like a precariously balanced pillar. China's population pyramid reflects the lowered numbers of young people as a result of that country's one-child policy. How do these pyramids help predict future population growth? *(Source: Population Reference Bureau.)*

notoriously China and India, to engage in female-specific infanticide or abortion because of a culturally based preference for male offspring. Ultrasound devices are now available even to rural peasants in China that allow gender identification of fetuses. About 100,000 such devices were in use as early as 1990 in China; and by the middle of that decade there were 121 males for every 100 females among children two years of age or younger. The sex ratio in China is being radically changed, and a profound gender imbalance already exists there. In India, too, there were only

The Missing Women of Ciudad Juárez

Ciudad Juárez is Mexico's fifth-largest city, located just across the border from El Paso, Texas. The long-standing close relationship, both geographically and economically, between the two cities has led many to refer to El Paso and Ciudad Juárez as "twin cities." Such twin cities exist along the length of the 2000-mile-long (3200-kilometer-long) border between the United States and Mexico, including San Diego and Tijuana, Brownsville and Matamoros, and Calexico and Mexicali.

One important aspect of the recent history of twin cities is the establishment of offshore factories, known as *maquiladoras* (from the Spanish verb *maquilar,* which translates loosely as "to process using a machine," "to mill [grain]," or "to assemble"). U.S. producers of goods with high labor costs, such as electronics, clothing, and automobiles, moved the labor-intensive parts of their production process to plants in Mexico in order to take advantage of the much lower wages they could pay to Mexican workers, which allows them to keep the price of their goods low. Maquiladoras have been in existence since the 1960s, and today there are around 4000 such factories throughout Mexico that together employ more than 1 million people.

Many of those employed on the assembly lines of these plants are women. In fact, maquiladoras prefer to hire women. It is argued that their smaller hands can perform assembly tasks more rapidly and that women have more patience with the repetitive nature of the work. In general, corporations believe that women provide a more docile workforce than men would: they are willing to work for lower pay, are easier to fire, and are less likely to form unions.

However, the rise in jobs for women comes at a time when Mexican men are facing high levels of unemployment. As a result, many wives and daughters have become the main breadwinners for families. This challenges societal norms that define men as responsible for supporting their families economically, while women are expected not to work outside the home for wages. Some men, of course, have taken this in stride and now play a major role in caring for their children and homes while their wives bring home the paycheck. Many men, however, have migrated to the United States in search of work, sometimes abandoning their families in Mexico. Others have resorted to alcoholism and violence to deal with the frustration of unemployment. Some men view women at work and on the streets as little more than prostitutes, definitely "out of place."

Ciudad Juárez has the highest reported level in Mexico of domestic violence against women. In addition, more than 300 women have disappeared in Ciudad Juárez since 1993. Many, but not all, of them were maquiladora workers. Roughly one-third of them appear to have been victims of a serial killer or a string of copycat killers. There are many theories about the identity of the killer or killers. They include suggestions that the responsible party is an Egyptian chemist who worked in a maquiladora and now manipulates a gang of killers using a cell phone from jail, a gang of maquiladora bus drivers, a psychopath from El Paso, members of a satanic cult who use the bodies for rituals, producers of snuff films, or organ traffickers. Yet no definitive arrests have been made, and the killings continue to occur.

As with many areas of the world, Mexico has experienced profound cultural shifts, including those surrounding gender roles, as its economy has incorporated offshore factory production as a central part of its development plan.

Relatives of women who have been murdered in Ciudad Juárez protest with photos of their daughters during a demonstration on November 25, 2003, in Mexico City. The first formal meeting between a Mexican president and the mothers of women killed in a decade-long string of murders in Ciudad Juárez marked what some called a high point in the women's fight for justice. *(AP Photo/Jose Luis Magana.)*

Gender Ratio

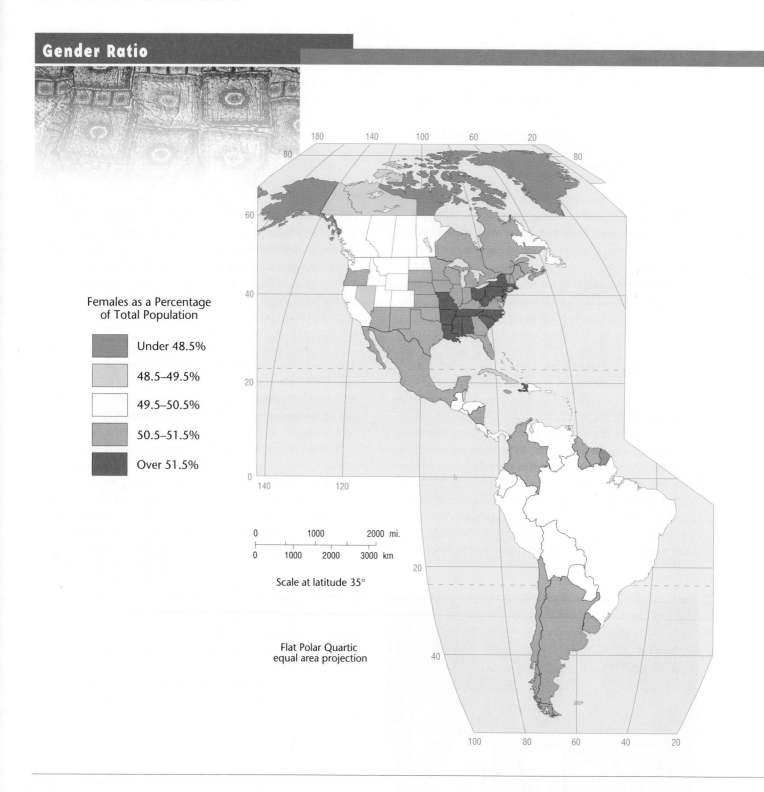

Females as a Percentage of Total Population

- Under 48.5%
- 48.5–49.5%
- 49.5–50.5%
- 50.5–51.5%
- Over 51.5%

0   1000   2000 mi.

0   1000   2000   3000 km

Scale at latitude 35°

Flat Polar Quartic
equal area projection

Figure 7.11 **Females as a percentage of total population.** *(Sources: Population Reference Bureau;* Statistical Abstract of the United States; *United Nations Population Information Network;* World Population Data Sheet.*)*

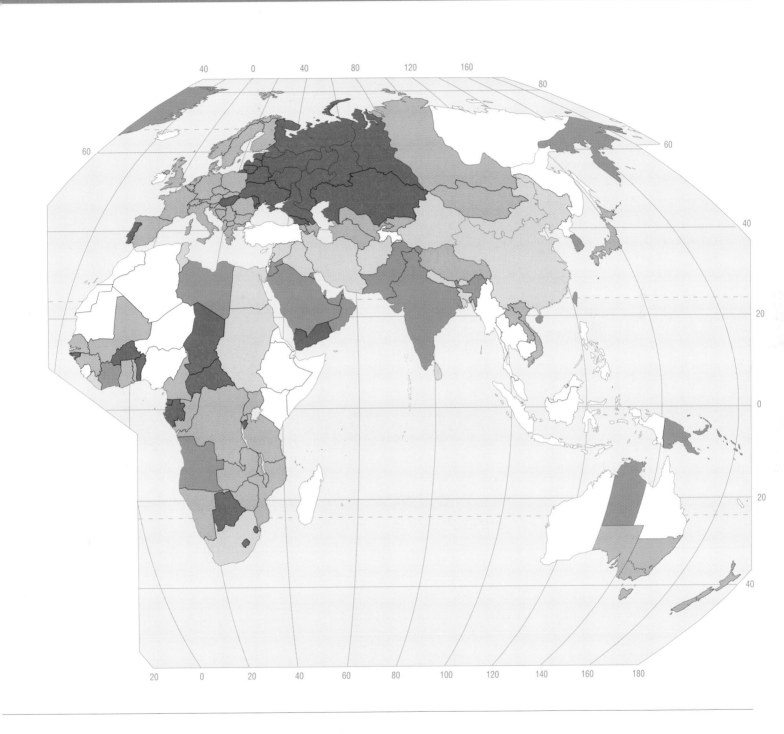

Infant Mortality Rate

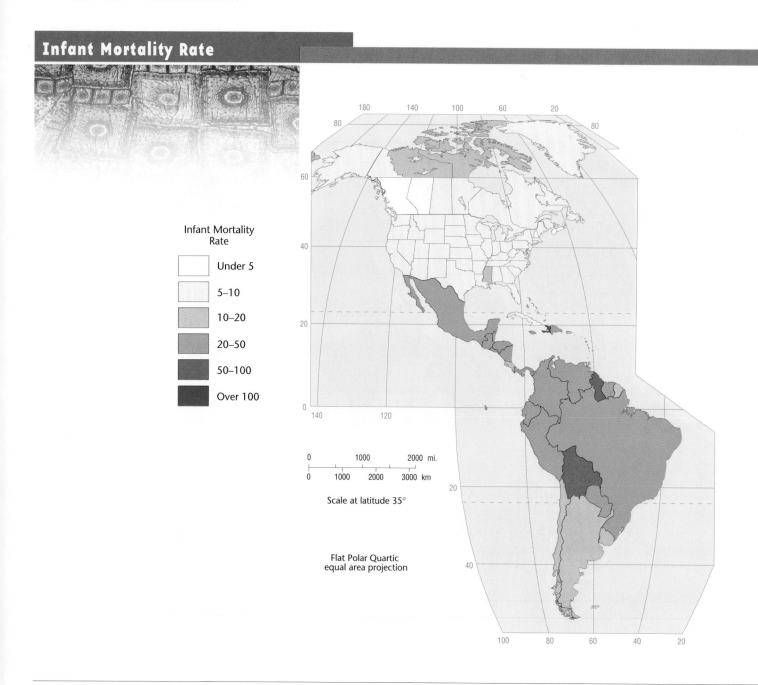

Infant Mortality Rate

- Under 5
- 5–10
- 10–20
- 20–50
- 50–100
- Over 100

0   1000   2000 mi.
0   1000   2000   3000 km

Scale at latitude 35°

Flat Polar Quartic
equal area projection

Figure 7.12 **The present world pattern of infant mortality rate.** The numbers indicate the number of children, per 1000 born, who die before reaching one year of age. The world's infant mortality rate is 57. Experts believe that this rate is the best single measure of living standards. *(Sources: Population Reference Bureau; Statistical Abstract of the United States; United Nations Population Information Network; World Population Data Sheet.)*

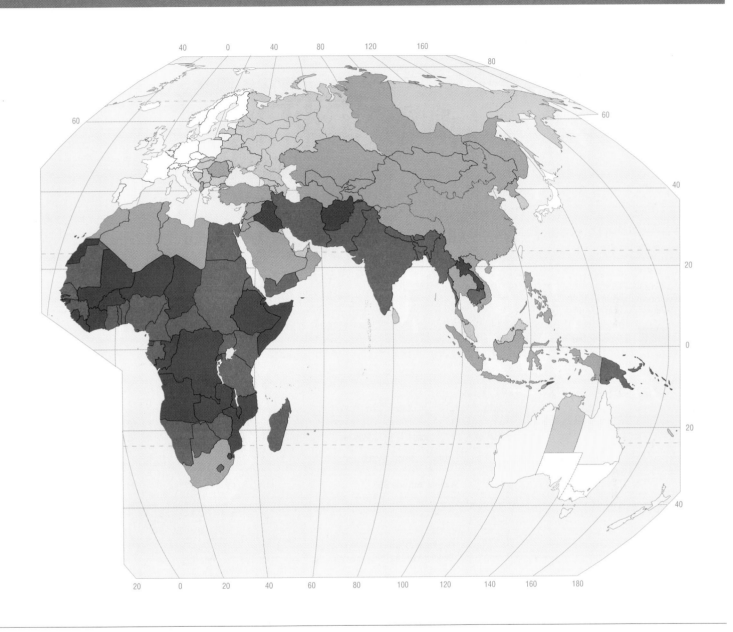

927 girls for each 1000 boys in 2001. That ratio had earlier dropped from 962 in 1981 to 945 in 1991, a trend that is obviously continuing. The use of ultrasound techniques in gender-specific abortion is most prevalent in northern India—where, for example, the 2001 census found only 793 girls for each 1000 boys in Punjab state.

Standard of Living

Various demographic traits can be used to assess *standard of living* and analyze it geographically. Figure 7.12 is a simple attempt to map living standards using the **infant mortality rate:** a measure of how many children per 1000 die before reaching one year of age. Many experts believe that the infant mortality rate is the best single index of living standards because it is affected by many different factors: health, nutrition, sanitation, access to doctors, availability of clinics, education, ability to obtain medicines, and adequacy of housing. A vivid geographical pattern is revealed by the infant mortality rate. Nowadays, we often hear of "North versus South" to refer to the gap in well-being between the prosperous, developed countries and poor, underdeveloped tropical nations.

Human Development

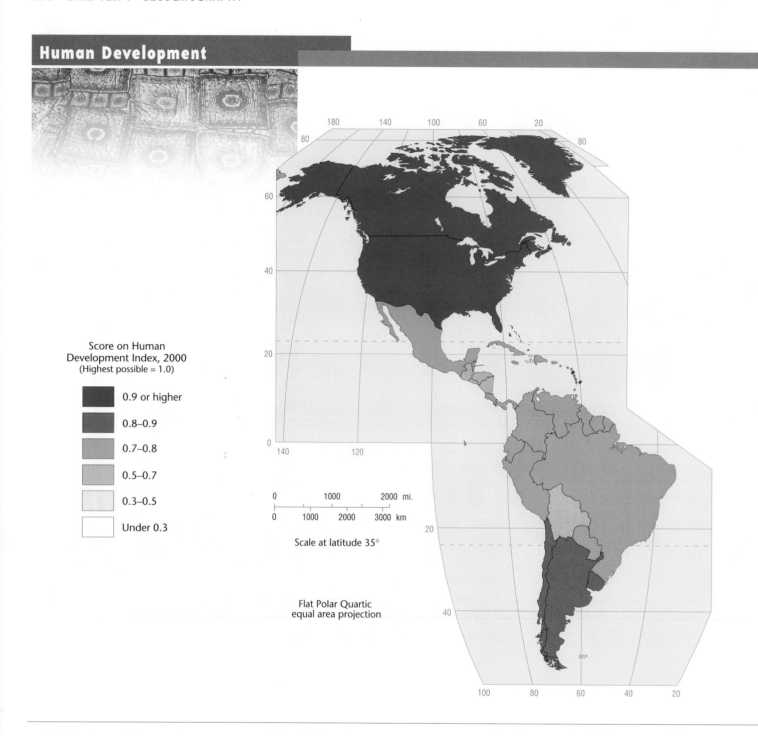

Score on Human
Development Index, 2000
(Highest possible = 1.0)

- 0.9 or higher
- 0.8–0.9
- 0.7–0.8
- 0.5–0.7
- 0.3–0.5
- Under 0.3

Scale at latitude 35°

Flat Polar Quartic
equal area projection

Figure 7.13 **Rankings of the Human Development Index,** which uses multiple criteria to measure standard of living or quality of life. (*Source:* Human Development Report 2000.)

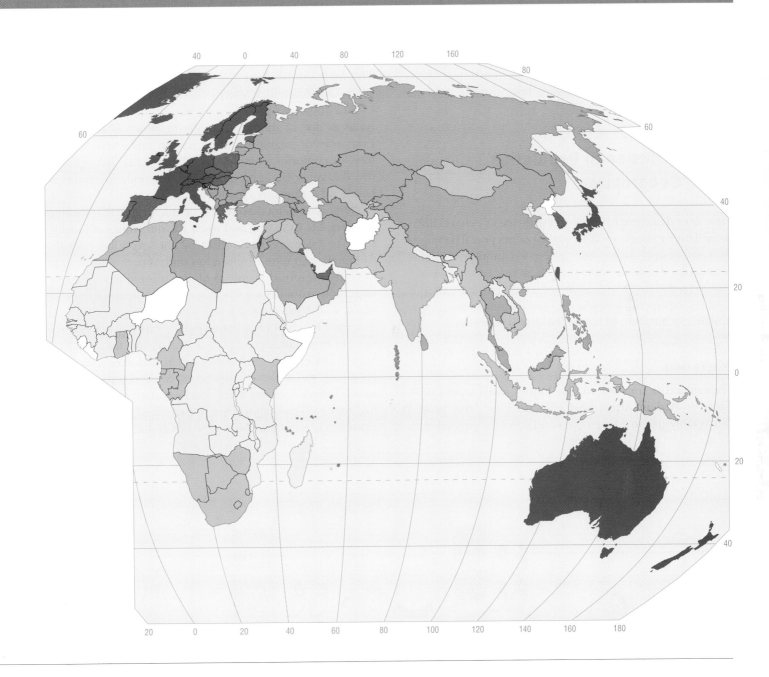

An even better measure of quality of life is the United Nations HDI, or *Human Development Index*, which combines measures of literacy, life expectancy, education, and wealth (Figure 7.13). The highest possible score is 1.000, and the two top-ranked countries are Norway and Sweden. All 25 of the lowest-ranked countries are in Africa.

Examination of the HDI reveals some surprises. If all countries spent equally on those things that improve their HDI rankings, such as education and health care, then we would expect the wealthiest countries to place first on the list. The United States ranked 4th among 177 nations in wealth as measured by the gross domestic product, or GDP, in 2002. Yet it ranked 8th in the world on the HDI. Compare this to Barbados, which ranked 40th by GDP but came in much higher on the HDI at 29th. Why did Barbados rank much higher than its monetary wealth would indicate, while the United States ranked lower? We would have to conclude that the government of Barbados places a relative priority on spending for education and health care, while the government of the United States does not.

Even more striking is the low standing of the United States when the Human Poverty Index, or HPI, is used. The HPI measures social and economic deprivation. Among the world's high-income countries, the United States ranks last when it comes to the percentage of its population living below the poverty line, which in 2000 was 17 percent.

Diffusion in Population Geography

How does demography relate to the theme of cultural diffusion? Three examples will show the connection. The migration of people from one place to another, altering population densities, offers the purest type of *relocation diffusion*. Epidemic diseases, which of course influence mortality rates, represent *contagious diffusion* in its most basic form. Finally, the diffusion of fertility control is considered.

Migration

Humankind is not tied to one locale. *Homo sapiens* most likely evolved in Africa, and ever since we have proved remarkably able to adapt to new and different physical environments. We have made ourselves at home in all but the most inhospitable climates, shunning only such places as ice-sheathed Antarctica and the shifting sands of the Arabian Peninsula's "Empty Quarter." Our permanent habitat extends from the edge of the ice sheets to the seashores, from desert valleys below sea level to high mountain slopes. This far-flung distribution is the product of migration (see Focus On: Kennewick Man).

For those people who migrate, the process generally ranks as one of the most significant events of their lives. Even ancient migrations often remain embedded in folklore for centuries or millennia (Figure 7.14). Recognizing the fundamental importance of migration, geographers have long devoted much attention to it.

Migration takes place when people decide that moving is preferable to staying and when the difficulties of moving seem to be more than offset by the expected rewards. Although migration is relocation diffusion, the decision to migrate can spread by means of expansion diffusion. Every migration, from the ancient dispersal of humankind out of Africa to the present-day movement toward urban areas, is governed by a host of **push-and-pull factors** that act to make the old home unattractive or unlivable and the new land attractive. Generally, push factors are the most central. After all, a basic dissatisfaction with the homeland is prerequisite to voluntary migration. The most important factor prompting migration throughout the thousands of years of human existence is economic. More often than not, migrating peo-

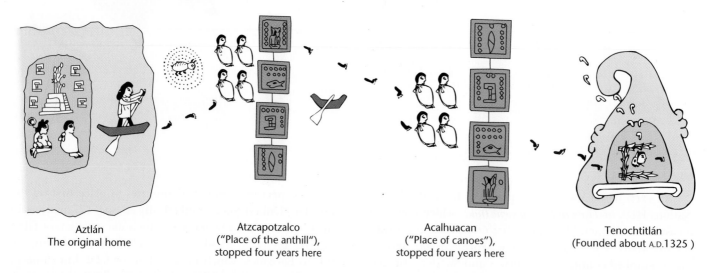

Figure 7.14 **Segments of an Aztec codex,** depicting the prehistoric migration of the ancient Aztecs from an island, possibly in northwestern Mexico, to another island in a lake at the site of present-day Mexico City, where they founded their capital, Tenochtitlán. Clearly, the epic migration was a central event in their collective memory. (*After de Macgregor, 1984: 217.*)

FOCUS ON

Kennewick Man

In 1996, two college students were watching the annual hydroplane races from the banks of the Columbia River in eastern Washington when they stumbled across a skull. Thinking it might be evidence from a murder, they called the police. Investigation uncovered the skeletal remains of a man, but he was no recent murder victim. Instead, forensic tests revealed that he had lived some 9300 years ago. The students had found the oldest and most complete human remains in North America.

He was dubbed Kennewick Man because he had been discovered in the vicinity of the city of Kennewick, Washington. But where did he come from? U.S. law says that human remains found before the time of Christopher Columbus's arrival in 1492 are automatically assumed to be of Native American origin, even if no direct link to modern peoples can be established. But reconstruction of the remains suggested that Kennewick man was much taller and thinner than most Native Americans at that time. Furthermore, his rounded skull and high-bridged, large nose gave him a distinctly European look when the reconstruction of his facial features was completed.

Could Europeans have had a presence in North America long before the arrival of Columbus? Many scholars think so. Certainly

Viking explorers, among them Leif Eriksson, probably came ashore at Newfoundland (in present-day Canada) around A.D. 1000. But claiming a European origin for Kennewick Man has proved far from uncontroversial. If Kennewick Man were indeed not of Native American origin, the legal basis for Native American claims to land might be challenged. Yet the Umatilla tribe's account of their creation says that the Umatilla have always lived in the tri-cities area of eastern Washington, where Kennewick Man was found. Local Native Americans have invoked NAGPRA, the Native American Graves Protection and Repatriation Act of 1990, which would allow the remains to be handed over to them for reburial. Scientists, on the other hand, wish to study the remains of Kennewick Man further for clues to the early settlement of the Americas.

As of 2004, courts had decided in favor of the scientists, though the Umatilla and three other tribes may choose to appeal the ruling. Today, the remains of Kennewick Man are housed in the Burke Museum on the University of Washington campus in Seattle. Clearly, much more than the fate of some old bones is at stake.

---

ple seek greater prosperity through better access to resources, especially land.

In the nineteenth century, more than 50 million European emigrants, seeking better lives outside their native lands, changed the distribution of racial and ethnic groups across much of the Earth. Today, migration patterns are very different (Figure 7.15). Europe, for example, now receives immigrants rather than sending out emigrants. International migration stands at an all-time high, much of it labor migration associated with the process of *globalization*.

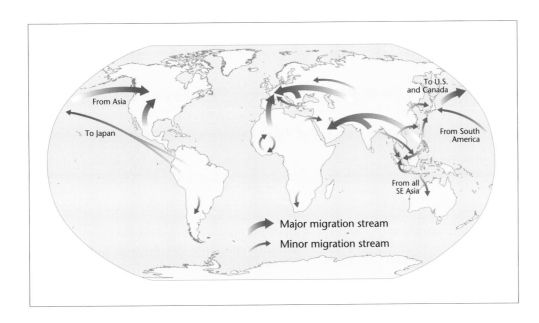

Figure 7.15 **Major and minor migration flows today.** Why have these flows changed so profoundly in the past hundred years? (*Source: Population Reference Bureau.*)

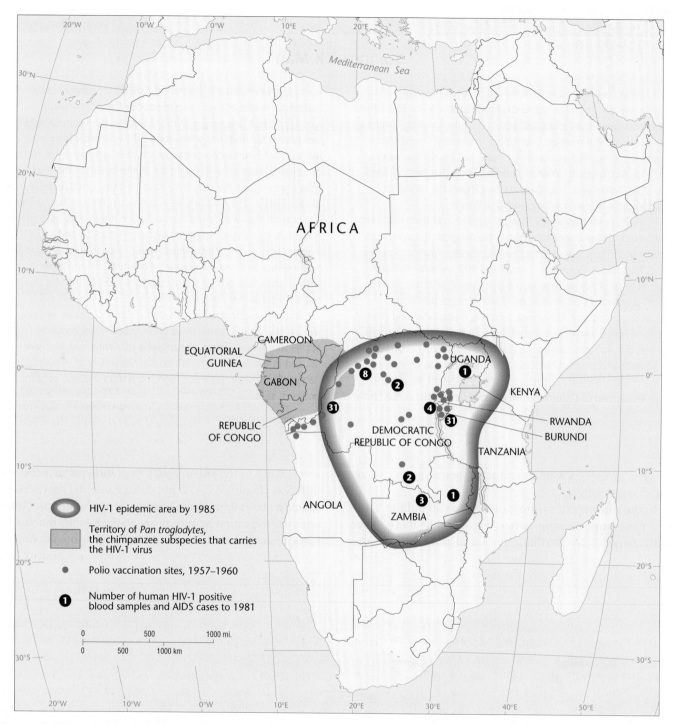

Figure 7.16 **Early diffusion of the HIV-1 virus that causes AIDS,** involving an infected chimpanzee subspecies. *(Sources:* *Gould, 1993; Hooper, 1999; Paul, 1994; Shannon, Pyle, and Bashshur, 1991: 49, 68, 73.)*

About 160 million people today live outside the country of their birth.

Forced migration also often occurs. The westward displacement of the Native American population of the United States, the dispersal of the Jews from Palestine in Roman times and from Europe in the mid-twentieth century, the export of Africans to the Americas as slaves, and the "clearances" of Scottish farmers by landlords to make way for large-scale sheep raising provide depressing examples. Today, refugee movements are all too common, prompted mainly by despotism, war, ethnic persecution, and famine. Recent decades have witnessed a flood of refugees. Perhaps as many as one-tenth of those people who today live outside their native country are refugees. Both forced migrations and refugee movements challenge the basic assumption of the push-and-pull model, which posits that human movement is the result of choices.

Disease Diffusion

A new depth of meaning is given to the term *contagious diffusion* when we consider the spread of diseases. The global pattern of HIV/AIDS has been the focus of some medical geographers' research.

Several theories exist to explain the origin of HIV in humans and its subsequent diffusion. Today there is still a fair amount of controversy surrounding the subject. Edward Hooper's theory is intriguing. He claims that an experimental polio vaccine was made using chimpanzee tissue and widely administered by health officials between 1957 and 1960 in what was then the Belgian-ruled part of tropical Africa—today the Democratic Republic of Congo (formerly Zaire), Burundi, and Rwanda. The earliest recorded cases of AIDS all occurred in or near places where the vaccine had been given (Figure 7.16).

Most experts reject Hooper's idea, believing instead that the transferal of HIV-1 from chimpanzees may have occurred as early as 1930. The earliest documented case, in 1959, was contracted by a man living in Kinshasa on the Congo River. In 1999, an international team of researchers funded by the National Institute of Allergy and Infectious Diseases reported their belief that HIV-1 was introduced into the human population when hunters became exposed to the infected blood of chimpanzees. The chimpanzee subspecies is found in Gabon and surrounding countries (see Figure 7.16). The researchers believe that there have been at least three independent occurrences of cross-species transmission from chimpanzees to humans. The researchers caution that further incidences of cross-species transmission are possible because the trade in bushmeat—chimpanzees and other animals that are hunted and consumed by humans—continues in western equatorial Africa.

The disease then apparently diffused throughout central and western Africa, following transport routes and greatly facilitated by rapid urbanization of the region. Among those infected, it seems, were Haitians who came from the West Indies to the newly independent Republic of Congo (later renamed Zaire, now called the Democratic Republic of Congo) to fill civil service posts in the early 1960s. Those who became infected probably took HIV back with them to their Caribbean nation. Europeans visiting central Africa also became infected and then brought the disease to their homelands. The first AIDS cases in the United States were documented in the early 1980s among male homosexuals, initially leading the disease to be erroneously labeled GRID, or Gay-Related Immuno Deficiency. However, the majority of HIV infections worldwide are transmitted heterosexually. As of 2003, women accounted for nearly 50 percent of those living with HIV/AIDS worldwide, while constituting 57 percent of cases in sub-Saharan Africa.

Although one might expect all diseases to spread exclusively by contagious diffusion, in fact they spread through all types of diffusion. Relocation diffusion—in the forms of tourism, long-distance truck transportation in Africa, and the temporary migration of Haitian civil servants to the Congo—apparently played a role in the spread of HIV. Hierarchical diffusion is implicit in the tendency of HIV to gain footholds in urban areas and to be spread by people affluent enough to participate in international tourism.

Diffusion of Fertility Control

Cultural diffusion in population geography involves more than migration and contagious diseases. For example, the final two stages of the demographic transition depend on both the successful cultural diffusion of effective methods of birth control and the widespread acceptance of the notion that small families are preferable to large ones. Sustained fertility decline arose as an innovation in Europe in the first half of the 1800s. France was the place of origin (Figure 7.17). The idea spread slowly at first but eventually diffused through most of Europe. As a rule, fertility decline became accepted as countries industrialized, largely because children were no longer needed to help with farmwork.

In some largely rural countries, resistance to fertility control persisted, thus partially causing the population explosion. Faced with the unwillingness of people to reduce the birthrate voluntarily, a few countries—most notably China—adopted a policy of enforced fertility control. Chinese authorities sought not merely to halt population growth but, ultimately, to decrease the number of people. All over China today, one sees billboards and posters admonishing the citizens that "one couple, one child" is the ideal family (Figure 7.18). Violators face huge monetary fines, cannot request new housing, lose the rather generous benefits provided to the elderly by the government, forfeit their children's access to higher education, and may even lose their jobs. Late marriages are encouraged. In response, between 1970 and 1980, the TFR in China plummeted from 5.9 births per woman to only 2.7, then to 2.2 by 1990, 2.0 by 1994, and 1.7 in 2004 (see Figure 7.2). China achieved one of the greatest short-term reductions of birthrates ever

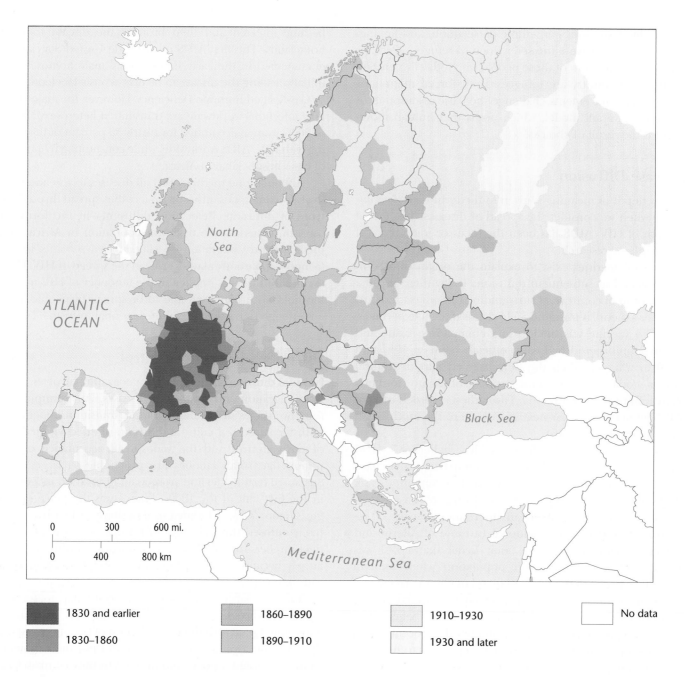

	1830 and earlier		1860–1890		1910–1930		No data
	1830–1860		1890–1910		1930 and later		

Figure 7.17 **Onset of sustained fertility decline in Europe.** The movement began in France and slowly diffused through the various other European countries. What specific type or types of cultural diffusion were probably at work? *(Adapted from Coale and Watkins, 1986: 484ff.)*

recorded, thus proving that cultural diffusion can be imposed. In recent years, the Chinese population control program has been less rigidly enforced, as economic growth eroded the government's control over the people. This relaxation has allowed more couples to have two children instead of one; however, the rise of economic opportunity and migration to cities has led other couples voluntarily to have smaller families. China, through a combination of coercive policies and economic growth, has completed the demographic transition.

REFLECTING ON GEOGRAPHY

Are the governments of overpopulated countries justified in legally requiring small families? In requiring involuntary sterilization?

Figure 7.18 **Population control in the People's Republic of China.** China has aggressively promoted a policy of "one couple, one child" in an attempt to relieve the pressures of over-population. These billboards convey the government's message. Violators—those with more than one child—are subject to fines, loss of job and old-age benefits, loss of access to better housing, and other penalties. *How effective would such billboards be in influencing people's decisions? Why is one of the signs in English?* *(Courtesy of Terry G. Jordan-Bychkov.)*

 Population Ecology

How is the theme of cultural ecology relevant to the study of population geography?
At the most basic level, a successful adaptive strategy permits a people to exist and reproduce in a given ecosystem. Cultural ecologists believe that population size and growth are indicators of successful adaptation, while maladaptive strategies lead to the dwindling of a people's numbers or even to their extinction. Similarly, when groups migrate to new places as settlers, their success or failure will depend in part on *preadaptation:* the extent to which a group's ways of life, their adaptive strategies in their old home, preconditioned them for success in the new land (see Chapter 5). Preadaptation is often a matter of chance, particularly when prior knowledge of the new land is limited or when migrants have little control over their destinations.

Environmental Influence

Regardless of adaptive strategy, population is often influenced in a possibilistic manner by the local availability of resources. In the middle latitudes, population densities tend to be greatest where the terrain is level, the climate is mild and humid, the soil is fertile, mineral resources are abundant, and the sea is accessible. Conversely, population tends to thin out with excessive elevation, aridity, coldness, ruggedness of terrain, and distance from the coast (Figure 7.19).

Climatic factors influence where people settle. Most of the sparsely populated zones in the world have, in some respect, "defective" climates from the human viewpoint (see Figure 7.1). The thinly populated northern edges of Eurasia and North America are excessively cold, and the belt from North Africa into the heart of Eurasia matches the major desert zones of the Eastern Hemisphere. Humans remain creatures of the humid and subhumid tropics, subtropics, or midlatitudes and have not fared well in excessively cold or dry areas. Small populations of Inuit (Eskimo), Sami (Lapps), and other peoples live in some of the less hospitable areas of the Earth, but these regions do not support large populations. Humans have proved remarkably adaptable, and our cultures contain adaptive strategies that allow us to live in many different physical environments; but perhaps, as a species, we have not entirely moved beyond the adaptive strategies that suited us so well to the climatic features of sub-Saharan Africa, where we began.

Humankind's preference for lower elevations is especially true for the middle and higher latitudes. Indeed, most mountain ranges in those latitudes stand out as regions of sparse population. By contrast, inhabitants of the tropics often prefer to live at higher elevations, concentrating in dense clusters in mountain valleys and basins (see Figure 7.1). By doing so, they escape the humid, hot climate and diseases of the tropic lowlands. For example, in tropical portions of South America, more people live in the Andes Mountains than in the nearby Amazon lowlands. The capital

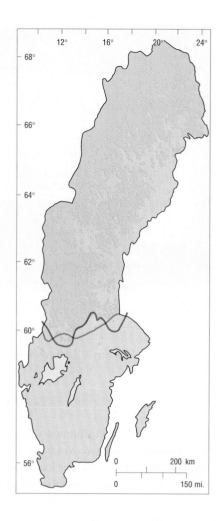

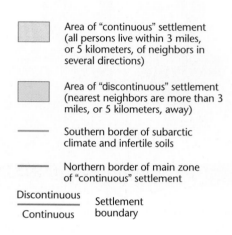

Figure 7.19 **Environment and population distribution in Sweden.** The northern boundary of the thickly settled area corresponds closely to the southern limit of the bitterly cold subarctic climate and the infertile, acidic soils of the coniferous forests. Does a similar boundary exist in North America? *(Adapted from Stone, 1962: 379.)*

cities of many tropical and subtropical nations lie in mountain areas above about 3000 feet (900 meters) in elevation. This is also the result of the fertile volcanic soils of these mountain valleys and basins, which were needed to support larger populations in agrarian societies.

The tendency to live on or near the seacoast exists, for a variety of reasons. The continents of Eurasia, Australia, and South America resemble hollow shells, with the majority of the population clustered around the rim of each continent (see Figure 7.1). In Australia, half the total population lives in just five port cities, and most of the remainder is spread out over nearby coastal areas. This preference for living by the sea stems partly from the trade and fishing opportunities the sea offers. At the same time, continental interiors tend to be regions of climatic extremes. For example, Australians speak of the "dead heart" of their continent, an interior land of excessive dryness and heat. People also seek places where fresh water is available. In desert regions, population clusters reflect the locations of scattered oases and occasional rivers, such as the Nile, that rise from sources outside the desert (Figure 7.20).

Still another environmental factor that affects population distribution is disease. Some diseases attack valuable domestic animals, depriving people of food and clothing resources. Such diseases have an indirect effect on population density. For example, in parts of East Africa, livestock is attacked by a form of sleeping sickness. This particular disease is almost invariably fatal to cattle but not to humans. The people in this part of East Africa depend heavily on cattle, which provide food, represent wealth, and serve a religious function in some tribes. The spread of a disease fatal to cattle has caused entire tribes to migrate away from infested areas, leaving those areas unpopulated (Figure 7.21).

Environmental Perception and Population Distribution

Perception of the physical environment plays a major role in a group's decision about where to settle and live. Different cultural groups often "see" the same physical environment in different ways. These varied responses to a single

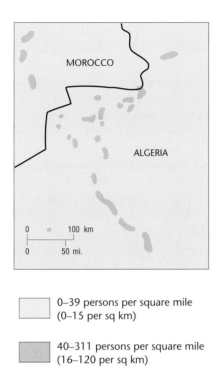

Figure 7.20 Population distribution reveals the availability of water in a desert. These scattered clusters of people live in the Sahara Desert of North Africa, and the pattern is typical of many arid regions. Dot clusters indicate the presence of oases; lines reveal stream courses. *(After Mattingly and Schmidt, 1971.)*

0–39 persons per square mile
(0–15 per sq km)

40–311 persons per square mile
(16–120 per sq km)

environment influence the distribution of people. A good example appears in a part of the European Alps shared by German- and Italian-speaking peoples. The mountain ridges in that area—near the point where Switzerland, Italy, and Austria join—run in an east-west direction, so that each ridge has a sunny, south-facing slope and a shady, north-facing one. German-speaking people, who rely on dairy farming, long ago established permanent settlements some 650 feet (200 meters) higher on the *shady* slopes than the settlements of Italians, who are culturally tied to warmth-loving crops, on the *sunny* slopes. This example demonstrates how contrasting cultural attitudes toward the physical environment and land use affect settlement patterns.

Sometimes the same cultural group changes its perception of an environment over time, with a resulting redistribution of its population. The coalfields of western Europe provide a good case in point. Before the industrial age, many coal-rich areas—such as the Midlands of England, southern Wales, and the lands between the headwaters of the Oder (or Odra) and Vistula rivers in Poland—were only sparsely or moderately settled. The development of steam-powered engines and the increased use of coal in the iron-smelting process, however, created a tremendous demand. Industries grew up near the European coalfields, and people flocked to these areas to take advantage of the new jobs. In other words, once a technological development gave a new cultural value to coal, many sparsely populated areas containing that resource acquired large concentrations of people.

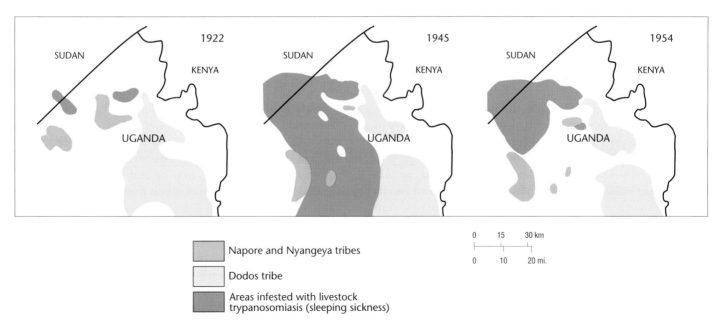

Napore and Nyangeya tribes

Dodos tribe

Areas infested with livestock trypanosomiasis (sleeping sickness)

Figure 7.21 Disease can influence settlement. The effect is apparent in this example in northeastern Uganda, East Africa. Note in particular the changing distribution of the Napore and Nyangeya groups based on the spread and eradication of sleeping sickness. *(Adapted from Deshler, 1960: 549.)*

Recent studies indicate that much of the interregional migration in the United States today is prompted by a desire for a pleasant climate and other desirable physical environmental traits, such as beautiful scenery. Surveys of immigrants to Arizona revealed that its sunny, warm climate is a major reason for migration. An attractive environment provided the dominant factor in the growth of the population and economy of Florida. The most desirable environmental traits that serve as stimulants for American migration include (1) mild winter climate and mountainous terrain, (2) a diverse natural vegetation that includes forests and a mild summer climate with low humidity, (3) the presence of lakes and rivers, and (4) nearness to the seacoast. Different age and cultural groups often express different preferences, but all are influenced by their perceptions of the physical environment in making decisions about migration.

REFLECTING ON GEOGRAPHY

What is your ideal climate? Do you now live in a place with such a climate? If not, do you intend to migrate for this reason?

Population Density and Environmental Alteration

People modify their habitats through their adaptive strategies. Particularly in areas where population density is high, radical alterations often occur. This can happen in fragile environments even at relatively low population densities, because the Earth's **carrying capacity,** or the maximum number of people that can be supported in a given area, varies greatly from one place to another and from one culture to another.

A worldwide ecological crisis exists in part because, at present densities, many of our adaptive strategies are not sustainable. The population explosion and the ecological crisis are closely related. For example, in Haiti, where rural population pressures have become particularly severe, the trees in previously forested areas have been stripped for fuel, leaving the surrounding fields and pastures increasingly denuded and vulnerable to erosion. In short, overpopulation can precipitate environmental destruction—which, in turn, results in a downward cycle of worsening poverty, with an eventual catastrophe that is both ecological and demographic. Thus, many cultural ecologists believe that attempts to restore the balance of nature will not succeed until we halt or even reverse population growth, although they recognize that other causes are at work in ecological crises. Adaptive strategy is as crucial as density and, in some cases, population pressure leads to better conservation techniques of land use.

The worldwide ecological crisis is not strictly a function of overpopulation. A relatively small percentage of the Earth's population controls much of the industrial technology and consumes a disproportionate percentage of the world's resources each year. Americans, who make up less than 5 percent of the global population, account for about 25 percent of the resources consumed globally each year. New houses built in the United States in 2002 were, on average, 38 percent bigger than those built in 1975, despite a shrinking average household size. If everyone in the world had an average American standard of living, the Earth could support only about 500 million people—only 8 percent of the present population. As the economies of large countries such as India and China continue to surge, the resource consumption of their populations is likely to rise as well, since the human desire to consume appears to be limited only by the ability to pay for it.

Cultural-Demographic Interaction

Can we gain additional understanding of demographic patterns by using the theme of cultural interaction? Are culture and demography intertwined? Culture influences population density, migration, population growth, and numerous other demographic traits, such as inheritance laws, food preferences, politics, and differing attitudes toward migration.

Cultural Factors

Many of the forces that influence the distribution of people are basic characteristics of a group's culture. For example, we must understand the preference of people living in Southeast Asia for rice as opposed to other grains before we can try to interpret the dense concentrations of people in rural areas there. The population in the humid lands of tropical and subtropical Asia expanded as this highly prolific, labor-intensive grain was domesticated and widely adopted. Environmentally similar rural zones elsewhere in the world, where rice is not the staple of the inhabitants' diet, never developed such great population densities. Similarly, the introduction of the potato into Ireland in the 1700s allowed a great increase in rural population because it yielded much more food per acre than did traditional Irish crops. Failure of the potato harvests in the 1840s greatly reduced the Irish population, through both starvation and emigration.

Cultural groups also differ in their tendency to migrate. For instance, religious ties bind some groups to their traditional homelands. In China, religious duties—in particular, the responsibilities to tend ancestral graves and perform rites at parental death—kept many in their native land. The Navajo of the American Southwest practice the custom of burying the umbilical cord in the floor of the hogan (house) at birth. Psychologically, this seems to strengthen the Navajo attachment to the home and discourage migration. Other religious cultures place no stigma on emigration. In fact, some groups consider migration a way of life. The Irish, unwilling to accept the poverty of their native land, proved so prone to migration that the population of Ireland today is only about half what it was in 1840.

Culture can also condition a people to accept or reject crowding. **Personal space**—the amount of space that individuals feel "belongs" to them as they move about their everyday business—varies from one cultural group to another (see Doing Geography and Seeing Geography at the end of the chapter). When Americans talk with one another, they typically stand farther apart than, say, Italians. The large personal space demanded by the American may well come from a heritage of sparse settlement. Early pioneers felt uncomfortable when they first saw smoke from the chimneys of neighboring cabins. As a result, American cities sprawl across large areas, with huge suburbs dominated by separate houses surrounded by private yards. Most European cities are compact, and their residential areas consist largely of row houses or apartments.

Political Factors

The political mosaic of the world is linked to population geography in many ways. Governmental policies often influence the fertility rate, as we have seen in the case of China. Forced or *involuntary migration*, too, is usually the result of political forces. These have become particularly common in the past century or so, usually to achieve *ethnic cleansing*—the removal of unwanted minorities in *nation-states*. Ethnic cleansing it is an age-old practice. It has happened most recently in the Balkans (in southeastern Europe) and in the African nation of Sudan's Darfur region. In Darfur, the Sudanese government has backed Arab militias known as Janjaweed. When the Fur, Masalit, and Zaghawa ethnic groups, who have historically farmed in Darfur, organized to demand more representation in the Sudanese government, and when Arab pastoralists were driven into their lands because of drought and desertification in their own lands, this historic conflict escalated in 2003. The Janjaweed have systematically exterminated thousands and forced millions more into refugee camps or to flee to nearby Chad.

Governments also restrict voluntary migration. Most countries, in fact, have laws restricting immigration into their countries. Two independent countries, Haiti and the Dominican Republic, share the tropical Caribbean island of Hispaniola in the West Indies. Haiti, which supports 638 persons per square mile (246 per square kilometer), is far more densely settled than the Dominican Republic, which has only 450 persons per square mile (174 per square kilometer) (Figure 7.22). Haiti is also poorer and has experienced

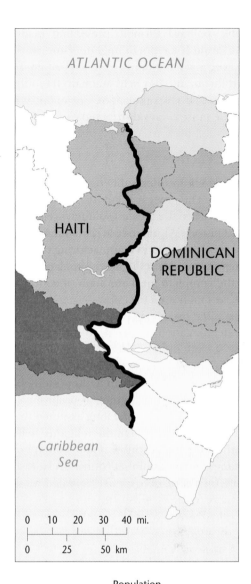

Population	
Per sq mile	Per sq km
Under 100	Under 25
100–150	25–50
150–200	50–75
300–500	125–200
500–1000	200–400
Over 1000	Over 400

Figure 7.22 **Population density contrast along the Haiti–Dominican Republic boundary.** Migration across this political frontier on the island of Hispaniola in the Caribbean has been restricted, causing the boundary to become a demographic border as well. What other factors might have helped create this pattern? *(Source: United Nations Population Information Network.)*

considerable political turmoil, presenting many Haitians with powerful push factors to migrate. Government restrictions, however, make migration from Haiti to the Dominican Republic difficult and also help maintain the different population densities. If Hispaniola were one country, its population would be more evenly distributed over the island.

Economic Factors

Economic conditions often influence population density in profound ways. The process of industrialization over the past 200 years has caused the greatest voluntary relocation of people in world history. Within industrial nations, people moved from rural areas to cluster in manufacturing regions. Agricultural changes have also influenced population density. For example, the complete mechanization of cotton and wheat cultivation in mid-twentieth-century America allowed those crops to be raised by a much smaller labor force. As a result, profound depopulation occurred, to the extent that many small towns serving these rural inhabitants ceased to exist.

When geographers apply the theme of cultural interaction in their demographic research, they often obtain negative results that are as enlightening as positive correlations. For example, many experts had long assumed that vegetarianism in India, based in Hindu religious belief, led to protein deficiency, malnutrition, and resultant health problems in many rural areas of that country. A study by Aninda Chakravarti, a cultural geographer, revealed no spatial cor-

relation between vegetarians and the consumption of animal protein (Figure 7.23). That is, nonvegetarians also eat little or no meat. Instead, the greatest protein deficiency occurs in areas where rice, rather than wheat bread, accounts for the greater part of grain consumption. Chakravarti found that meat was too expensive even for those who had no taboo against it and that the custom of "polishing" rice, to make it pure white in color, removed most of its nutritive value.

Gender and Geodemography

Gender often interacts with other factors to influence geodemographic patterns and migrations (see Practicing Geography on page 252). For example, together gender, race, and nationality can create situations in which women from specific countries are viewed as desirable immigrants. In nineteenth-century America, Irish female immigrants were considered to be highly reliable employees and often found work as domestic servants.

For several decades, women from the Philippines have migrated to Hong Kong to be domestic servants, doing chores for and looking after the children of the families who hire them (Figure 7.24). Wages in Hong Kong are much higher than back home in the Philippines, prompting the migration. However, working conditions can be far from ideal, involving hard physical labor and long hours. Reports of abuse of Filipina servants by their employers are numer-

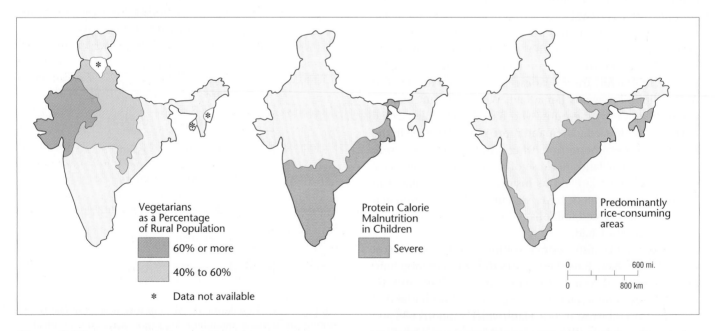

Figure 7.23 **Protein malnutrition, vegetarianism, and rice consumption in India.** In studying cultural integration, the geographer sometimes finds that the obvious answers are wrong.

The disease and death that can result from protein deficiency are apparently unrelated to vegetarianism; instead, a link to rice consumption is suggested. *(After Chakravarti, 1982.)*

Figure 7.24 **Filipina domestic servants in Hong Kong.** On Sunday, their day off, these women congregate in covered walkways and other public spaces. They exchange gossip, play cards, cut each other's hair, and relax. *(Courtesy of Patricia L. Price.)*

ous. If a servant is fired, she will be deported if she cannot find another job quickly. The stress of long separations from husbands and children back in the Philippines has led to the breakup of families.

Some of these women become coerced into Asia's booming sex industry, as well. Geographer James Tyner has studied migration from the Philippines to Japan. Incredibly, 93 percent of this migration consists of female "entertainers." In part, poverty in the Philippines provided the push factor in this movement, but Tyner also points to more complex pull factors, such as the stereotypical view held by Japanese men in which Filipinas are seen as highly desirable, exotic sex objects but also culturally inferior and thus "willing victims" who gladly become prostitutes.

 The Settlement Landscape

How is the distribution of people reflected in the cultural landscape? Differing densities and arrangements of population are revealed, at the largest scale, by maps showing the distribution of dwellings. These differences in the cultural landscape can be illustrated by using the example of *rural* settlement types. Farm people differ from one culture to another, one place to another, in how they situate their dwellings, producing greatly varied rural cultural land-

scapes. They range from tightly *clustered* villages on the one extreme to fully *dispersed* farmsteads on the other, as shown in Figure 7.25.

Farm Villages

In many parts of the world, farming people group themselves together in clustered settlements called **farm villages.** These tightly bunched settlements vary in size from a few dozen inhabitants to several thousand. Contained in the village **farmstead** are the house, barn, sheds, pens, and garden. The fields, pastures, and meadows lie out in the country beyond the limits of the village, and farmers must journey out from the village each day to work the land.

Farm villages are the most common form of agricultural settlement in much of Europe, in many parts of Latin America, in the densely settled farming regions of Asia (including much of India, China, and Japan), and among the sedentary farming peoples of Africa and the Middle East. These compact villages come in many forms. Most are irregular clusterings—a maze of winding, narrow streets and a jumble of farmsteads (see Figures 7.25a and 7.26). Such *irregular clustered* farm villages developed organically over centuries, without any orderly plan to direct their growth. Other types of farm villages are very regular in their layout, revealing the imprint of planned design. The *street village,* the simplest of these planned types, consists of farmsteads grouped along both sides of a single, central street, producing an elongated settlement (see Figures 7.25b and 7.27). Street villages are particularly common in eastern Europe and much of Russia. Another type, the *green village,* consists of farmsteads grouped around a central open place, or green, which forms a commons (see Figure 7.25c). Green villages occur throughout most of the plains areas of northern and northwestern Europe, and English immigrants laid out some such settlements in colonial New England. Also regular in layout is the *checkerboard village,* based on a gridiron pattern of streets meeting at right angles (see Figure 7.25g). Mormon farm villages in Utah are of this type, and checkerboard villages also dominate most of rural Latin America and northeastern China.

Why do so many farm people settle together in villages? Traditionally, the countryside was unsafe, threatened by roving bands of outlaws and raiders. Farmers could better defend themselves against such dangers by grouping together in villages. In many parts of the world, the populations of villages have grown larger during periods of insecurity and shrunk again when peace returned. Many farm villages occupy the most easily defended sites in their vicinity, what geographers call *strong-point* settlements.

In addition to defense, the quality of the environment helps determine whether people settle in villages. In deserts

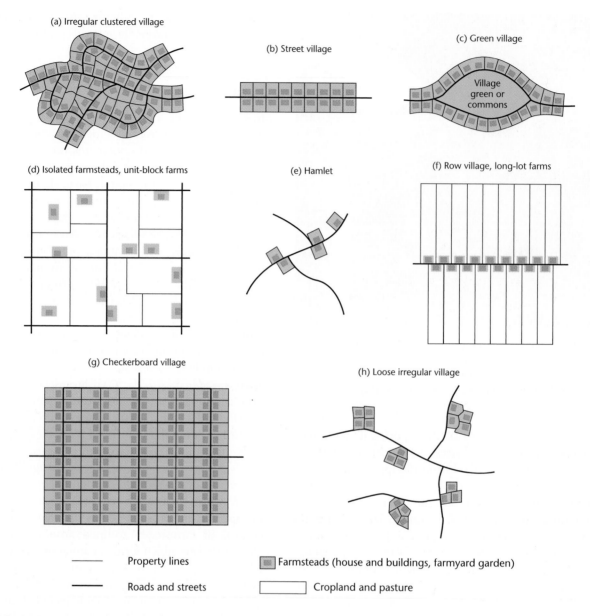

(a) Irregular clustered village

(b) Street village

(c) Green village

Village green or commons

(d) Isolated farmsteads, unit-block farms

(e) Hamlet

(f) Row village, long-lot farms

(g) Checkerboard village

(h) Loose irregular village

——— Property lines

———— Roads and streets

▦ Farmsteads (house and buildings, farmyard garden)

▭ Cropland and pasture

Figure 7.25 **Rural settlement landscapes.** The way individual farmers choose to locate their farmsteads leads to a general settlement pattern on the land. In some areas, farmsteads are scattered and isolated. In areas where farmsteads are grouped, there are several possible patterns of clustering.

and in limestone areas where the ground absorbs moisture quickly, farmsteads are built around the few sources of water. Such *wet-point* villages cluster around oases or deep wells. Conversely, a superabundance of water—in marshes, swamps, and areas subject to floods—often prompts people to settle in villages on available *dry points* of higher elevation.

Various communal ties strongly bind villagers together. Groups of farmers linked to one another by blood relationships, religious customs, communal landownership, or other similar bonds usually form clustered villages. Mormon farm villages in the United States provide an excellent example of the clustering force of religion. Communal or state ownership of the land—as in China and parts of Israel—encourages the formation of farm villages.

Isolated Farmsteads

In many other parts of the world, the rural population lives in dispersed, isolated farmsteads, often some distance from their nearest neighbors (see Figure 7.25d). These dispersed rural settlements grew up mainly in Anglo-America, Australia, New Zealand, and South Africa—that is, in the lands colonized by

Figure 7.26 **Two irregular clustered villages.** The village on the left with adjacent irrigated grain fields is near Gonggar in southeastern Tibet. The village nestles against a hill, and much of it is built on land unfit for cultivation. The village shown on the right is in northern Switzerland. Although halfway around the world from the village in Tibet, it also shows the irregular plan. *(Courtesy of Terry G. Jordan-Bychkov.)*

emigrating Europeans. But even in areas dominated by village settlements—such as Japan, Europe, and parts of India—some isolated farmsteads appear (Figure 7.28).

The conditions encouraging dispersed settlement are precisely the opposite of those favoring village development. These include peace and security in the countryside, removing the need for defense; colonization by individual pioneer families rather than by socially cohesive groups; agricultural private enterprise, as opposed to some form of communalism; and well-drained land where water is readily available. Most dispersed farmsteads originated rather recently, dating primarily from the colonization of new farmland in the last two or three centuries.

REFLECTING ON GEOGRAPHY

What disadvantages might a settlement pattern of isolated farmsteads present for the people who live there?

In between the clustered farm villages and the isolated farmsteads are *semiclustered* rural settlements. These consist of three types. The most common is the *hamlet*, consisting of a small number of farmsteads grouped loosely together (see Figures 7.25e and 7.29). Loose, irregular villages involve several hamlets located close to one another, sometimes sharing a common name (see Figure 7.25h). Finally, the *row village* is a third common type of semiclustered settlement, consisting of a loose chain of farmsteads spaced at intervals along a road, river, or canal and often extending for many miles (see Figure 7.25f).

Reading the Cultural Landscape

The rural settlement forms described above provide a chance to "read" the cultural landscape. In doing so, we must always be cautious, looking for the subtle as well as the overt and not forming conclusions too quickly.

Figure 7.27 **Street village beside the great Siberian river Lena in the Sakha Republic (Yakutia), part of Russia.** Farmsteads lie along a single street, creating an elongated settlement. One can distinguish Russian ethnic villages in Sakha by this form, whereas the native Yakut villages have a checkerboard pattern. In this way, the cultural landscape reveals the ethnicity of the inhabitants. *(Courtesy of Terry G. Jordan-Bychkov.)*

PRACTICING GEOGRAPHY

Rachel Silvey

(Courtesy of Rachel Silvey.)

By now, you have probably noticed that many of the geographers profiled in the Practicing Geography sections chose geography after considering a number of other possibilities. Rachel Silvey, a geodemographer at the University of Colorado in Boulder, Colorado, is certainly no exception. "I came to geography somewhat circuitously," she says. In fact, her story combines the process of choosing a major with the love of travel that seems to be so common for our profiled geographers. "As an undergraduate student, I chose geography as a field when I realized it would permit long-term international research projects and when it became clear that my research couldn't be squeezed into the compartments of other disciplinary homes."

Professor Silvey's research focuses on Indonesia. She has interviewed women who work in the multinational factories that exist throughout the developing world, where labor costs are low. She was particularly interested in how these women's relationships with their families were reshaped as they migrated for work reasons and left their villages behind.

Today, Professor Silvey is working on two related projects. The first is an analysis of the role of religion in the lives of people who shift their homes between Jakarta and Los Angeles. Such people are crafters of transnational landscapes and identities. Professor Silvey is particularly interested in finding out more about how the Islamic identities of these people helps to shape, and at the same time challenge, some of the gender rules established in transnational migrant communities. Her second project brings Bangladesh into the picture. Both Indonesia and Bangladesh are Muslim countries with relatively large and dense populations. In this project, Professor Silvey is exploring inequalities in people's social networks, especially those inequalities that have to do with gender and economic standing, in order to understand how these are reflected in the health of people in rural areas who do not migrate. Professor Silvey says, "Geography allows me to make connections among the wide range of social and political issues that other disciplines seem to divide up into arbitrary disciplinary pieces. As a geographer, I'm able to continue to spend time doing fieldwork in Indonesia, and this allows me to deepen my relationships with people in the migrant communities to which I've returned every couple years since 1995."

Most of Professor Silvey's time in the field involves interviewing people at length about their own perceptions of migration, gender, and development. These in-depth ethnographic portraits of people living their lives in places provide a complement, and sometimes a corrective, to what Professor Silvey sees as the "lower-resolution analyses of migration that are produced by spatial demographers." A mainstay of ethnographic research methods is participant observation, whereby the researcher shares the day-to-day lives of those he or she is researching. "I live with migrants and factory workers and involve myself in their everyday activities. These grounded experiences give me a sense of the meanings of particular positioned migrant subjectivities." Professor Silvey also uses large-scale demographic data sets, among them the Indonesian census and the Indonesian Family Life Survey, to provide background information and a context for her micro-level work.

Not surprisingly, Professor Silvey identifies doing international fieldwork as one of the most enjoyable parts of her job as a practicing geographer. "I enjoy spending time in Indonesia, speaking the language there, and learning about people's conceptions of gender, history, culture, and geographic change." She also points to teaching as an exciting part of her job. Professor Silvey notes that what she learns as a participant observer in the field not only forms the backbone of her scholarly research; it also provides her teaching with great firsthand material. "The narratives and images that I collect during my fieldwork also allow me to effectively teach students about the place- and person-specific dimensions of migration process." Professor Silvey feels that one of the best parts of teaching human geography is that "the subject matter encourages students' active engagement with contemporary global issues."

For example, the Mayas of the Yucatán Peninsula in Mexico reside in checkerboard villages, a rural settlement landscape that is both suggestive and potentially misleading (Figure 7.30). Before the Spanish conquest in the late 1400s, Mayas lived in wet-point villages of the irregular clus-tered type, situated alongside *cenotes*—natural sinkholes that provided water in a land with no surface streams. The Spaniards destroyed these settlements, replacing them with checkerboard villages. Wide, straight streets accommodated the wheeled vehicles of the European conquerors.

Figure 7.28 **A truly isolated farmstead, in the Vestfjörds district of northwestern Iceland.** This type of rural settlement dominates almost all lands colonized by Europeans migrating overseas. Iceland was settled by Norse Vikings a thousand years ago. *(Courtesy of Terry G. Jordan-Bychkov.)*

Superficially, the checkerboard landscape suggests the cultural victory of the Spaniards. Looking more closely, however, shows that, in fact, Mayan culture prevailed. Even today, many Mayas make little use of wheeled vehicles in village life, and many of the Spaniards' "streets" merely make way for Mayan footpaths that wind among boulders and outcroppings of bedrock. Irregularities in the checkerboard, coupled with a casual distribution of dwellings, suggest Mayan resistance to the new geometry. Spanish-influenced architecture—flat-roofed houses of stone, the town hall, a church, and a hacienda mansion—remain largely confined to the area near the central plaza. The Catholic church stands on the very place where an ancient Mayan temple had been. A block away, the traditional Mayan pole huts with thatched, hipped roofs prevail, echoed by cookhouses of the same design. Indian influence increases markedly with distance from the plaza.

The dooryard gardens surrounding each hut are full of traditional native plants—such as papayas, bananas, chili peppers, nuts, yucca, and maize—with only a few citrus trees to reveal Spanish influence. In the same yards, each carefully ringed with dry rock walls, as in pre-Columbian times, pigs descended from those introduced by the conquerors share the ground with the traditional turkeys of the Maya and apiaries for indigenous stingless bees. Occasionally the Mayan language is heard, although Spanish prevails. So does Catholicism, but the absence of huts around the once-sacred cenote suggests a lingering pagan influence.

Sometimes, then, the overt aspects of a cultural landscape are merely one element of the story. We should always look deeper and become sensitive to subtle visual clues.

Conclusion

In our study of population geography, we have seen that humankind is unevenly distributed over the Earth. Spatial variations in fertility, death rates, rates of population change, age groups, gender ratios, and standards of living also exist: these patterns can be depicted as culture regions. The principles of cultural diffusion prove useful in analyzing human migration and also help explain the spread of birth control and diseases.

Cultural ecology shows how the environment and people's perception of it influence the distribution of people and sometimes help guide migrations. We also found that population density is linked to the level of environmental alteration and that overpopulation can have a destructive impact on the environment.

Cultural interaction suggests how demography and mobility are linked to such elements of culture as food preferences, migration taboos, politics, and economic opportunity. Cultural attitudes can encourage people to be mobile or sedentary and can lead them to accept crowding or to feel uncomfortable without plenty of personal space. In many ways, then, spatial variations in demographic traits are enmeshed in the fabric of culture.

Figure 7.29 **A seaside hamlet on the Olafsfjörd in northern Iceland.** The inhabitants pursue both dairying and fishing. *(Courtesy of Terry G. Jordan-Bychkov.)*

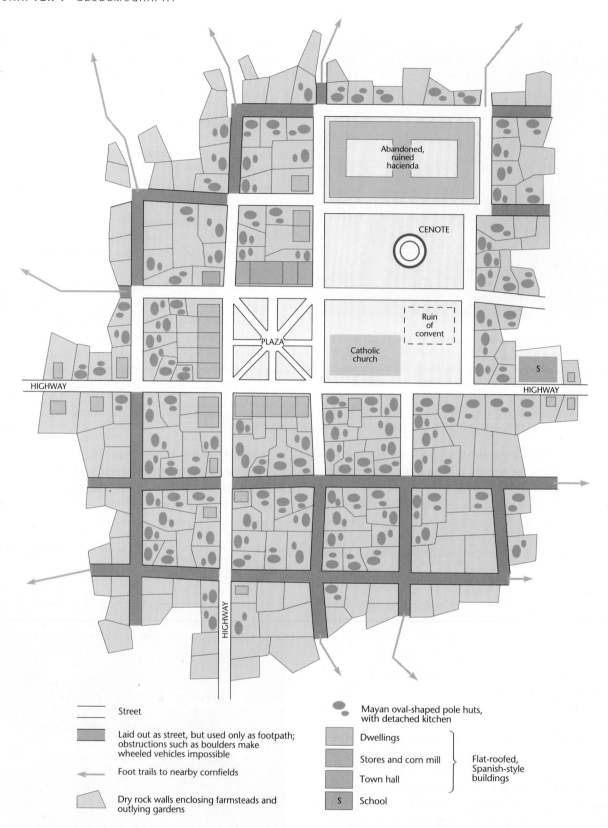

Street

Laid out as street, but used only as footpath; obstructions such as boulders make wheeled vehicles impossible

Foot trails to nearby cornfields

Dry rock walls enclosing farmsteads and outlying gardens

Mayan oval-shaped pole huts, with detached kitchen

Dwellings

Stores and corn mill

Town hall

S School

Flat-roofed, Spanish-style buildings

Figure 7.30 A hypothetical modern Mayan checkerboard farm village in Yucatán Province, Mexico. Spanish influence— seen in the grid pattern, plaza, church, hacienda, and flat-roofed buildings—weakens with distance from the center, and the rigid checkerboard masks a certain irregularity of farmstead layout. A *cenote* is a large, deep sinkhole filled with water, and these natural pools served a major religious function among the Mayas before Christianity came. (*Source: Composite of 1987 field observations by Terry G. Jordan-Bychkov in some 15 villages east and southeast of Mérida.*)

How people distribute themselves over the Earth's surface finds a vivid expression in the cultural landscape. Using the example of the rural landscape, we have seen how different cultures developed distinctive settlement forms, each of which reflects a unique distribution of population on the local level.

DOING GEOGRAPHY

Public Space, Personal Space: Too Close for Comfort?

As the Seeing Geography section for this chapter notes, different people seem to require different amounts of personal space. The size of one's comfort zone varies with social class, gender, ethnicity, the situation at hand, and what one has grown accustomed to over one's life. Some Arabs, for example, consider it appropriate and even polite to be close enough for another to smell his or her breath during conversation. Those from cultures that have not developed a high tolerance for personal contact might experience such closeness as intrusive or even disgusting. Americans conducting business in Japan are often surprised at the level of physical closeness expected in their dealings. Such closeness might well be interpreted as overstepping one's bounds, literally, in the United States!

In this exercise, you will gather some data on the size of the personal space needed by those around you. Observe and record your findings, and discuss them in class as a group.

The first part of this exercise involves observing your professors as they lecture in class. Is your class a large one that meets in a lecture hall? If so, where does your professor sit or stand in relation to the students? Does the professor have his or her own designated space in the classroom? Where is it located, and how big is it? Does the professor ever step outside of it? How does this professor's use of space compare to that of other professors you have, and why do you think this is so? If you have a smaller class, compare the use of space by that professor. Is it different from the behavior of the professors in large lecture halls? Under what circumstances, if any, do your professors get close to students, and how close do they get?

The second part of this exercise involves noting how close you can get to same-gender friends. Strike up a conversation with a friend standing next to you. Discreetly move closer and closer to your friend until he or she moves away or says something about your proximity. How much space separated you when this happened? What do you think would happen if you tried this with a stranger? With a friend or a stranger of a different gender? With a friend or a stranger from a different culture?

Did all your classmates have similar experiences, or were your findings notably different? Are all students in your class from similar economic or ethnic backgrounds? If not, that may explain some of the differences that emerge. In what ways do planners and architects take personal space preferences into account when they design cities, streets, buildings, homes, and classrooms?

Population Geography
on the Internet

You can learn more about population geography on the Internet at the following web sites:

Population Reference Bureau, Inc., Washington, D.C.
http://www.prb.org/
This organization is concerned principally with the issues of overpopulation and standard of living. The graphics bank in the "PRB Library" section has a wealth of images on all aspects of global population for use in presentations and reports. Some of the maps in this chapter were adapted from PRB maps.

United Nations High Commissioner for Refugees
http://www.unhcr.ch/
This United Nations web site provides basic information about refugee situations worldwide. The site includes regularly updated maps showing refugee locations and populations and photos of refugee life.

U.S Census Bureau Population Clocks
http://www.census.gov/main/www/popclock.html
Check real-time figures here for the population of the United States. and the population of the world.

U.S. Centers for Disease Control and Prevention (CDC), Atlanta, Georgia
http://www.cdc.gov/
Part of the U.S. government's Department of Health and Human Services, the Centers for Disease Control and Prevention maintains this web site, which provides a plethora of information on the health of the nation. The "Data and Statistics" section provides an especially rich resource for those seeking numbers on demographic and health-related topics.

World Health Organization, Geneva, Switzerland
http://www.who.int/home-page/
Learn about the group that distributes information on health, mortality, and epidemics as it seeks to improve health conditions around the globe. The "Global Atlas of Infectious Diseases" allows you to create detailed maps from WHO data.

Worldwatch Institute, Washington, D.C.
http://www.worldwatch.org
This organization is concerned with the ecological consequences of overpopulation and the wasteful use of resources. It seeks sustainable ways to support the world's population and brings attention to ecological crises. Free online registration allows you to access the "Research Library" and its thousands of full-text Worldwatch Institute reports, papers, and press releases.

SEEING GEOGRAPHY

Would you feel comfortable walking here? If not, why not?

A street scene in the large city of Kolkata, India.

Street in Kolkata, India

Do you need your "personal space"? Most Americans and Canadians do. If so, Kolkata (formerly Calcutta), India, is a place you might want to avoid. The photo was taken in March 2001, on the day the Indian government announced that the country's population had well exceeded 1 billion and that 181 million had been added to India's population between the censuses of 1991 and 2001. West Bengal state, where Kolkata is located, has the highest population density in the country.

Why do people form such dense clusters? The theme of cultural interaction would tell us of *push factors* that encourage people to leave their farms and move to the city. Some can no longer make a living or feed their families with the food provided by the tiny plots of land they work. Others are forced off the land by landlords who want to convert to mechanized Western methods of agriculture that use far less labor (see Chapter 8). But cultural interaction also tells us of *pull factors* exerted by cities such as Kolkata—the hope or promise of better-paying jobs, the encouragement of friends and relatives who had come to the city earlier, or the greater availability of government services. And so, pushed and pulled, they come to the teeming, overcrowded city, to jostle and elbow their way through the streets.

But it is not only cities in the developing world that become so dense. If you have ever visited, or lived in, Manhattan, New York, you are all too familiar with dense crowds of people. In fact, there are some who grow up in these environments and find the relative solitude of rural areas to verge on terrifying. They prefer the bustle of activity and the sounds of the city, and they feel at home in a crowd.

Being a woman is another reason that you might feel uncomfortable in this Kolkata street environment. Notice the nearly complete lack of women in this crowd. Many societies have strict norms that dictate where women, and men, may and may not go. Harassment or even violence may be the result of violating these norms (refer again to Culture in a Globalizing World on page 231).

The study of the size and shape of people's envelopes of personal space is called *proxemics*. Anthropologist Edward T. Hall, whose book *The Hidden Dimension* is listed in Ten Recommended Books on Population Geography at the end of the chapter, is the founder of this science. Urban planners, architects, psychologists, and sociologists, as well as geographers, use proxemics to explain why some people need more space than others and how this varies culturally. ■

Sources

Chakravarti, Aninda K. 1982. "Diet and Disease: Some Cultural Aspects of Food Use in India," in Allen G. Noble and Ashok K. Dutt (eds.), *India: Cultural Patterns and Processes*. Boulder, Colo.: Westview Press, 301–323.

Coale, Ansley J., and Susan C. Watkins. 1986. *The Decline of Fertility in Europe*. Princeton, N.J.: Princeton University Press.

de Macgregor, María T. de Gutiérrez. 1984. "Population Geography in Mexico," in John J. Clarke (ed.), *Geography and Population*. Oxford: Pergamon.

D'Emilio, Frances. 2004. "Italy's Seniors Finding Comfort with Strangers," *Miami Herald*, 30 October, pp. 1A, 2A.

Deshler, Walter. 1960. "Livestock Trypanosomiasis and Human Settlement in Northeastern Uganda." *Geographical Review* 50: 541–554.

Gould, Peter. 1993. *The Slow Plague: A Geography of the AIDS Pandemic.* Oxford: Blackwell.

Hooper, Edward. 1999. *The River: A Journey to the Source of HIV and AIDS.* Boston: Little, Brown.

Hooson, David J. M. 1960. "The Distribution of Population as the Essential Geographical Expression." *Canadian Geographer* 4: 10–20.

Human Development Report 2000. 2000. New York: United Nations Publications.

Jordan, Terry G. 1973. *The European Culture Area: A Systematic Geography.* New York: Harper & Row.

Malthus, Thomas R. 1989 [1798]. *An Essay on the Principle of Population.* Patricia James (ed.). Cambridge: Cambridge University Press.

Mattingly, Paul F., and Elsa Schmidt. 1971. "The Maghreb: Population Density." *Annals of the Association of American Geographers* 61 (Map Supplement No. 15).

Paul, Bimal K. 1994. "AIDS in Asia." *Geographical Review* 84: 367–379.

Shannon, Gary W., Gerald F. Pyle, and Rashid L. Bashshur. 1991. *The Geography of AIDS: Origins and Course of an Epidemic.* New York: Guilford.

Stone, Kirk H. 1962. "Swedish Fringes of Settlement." *Annals of the Association of American Geographers* 52: 373–393.

Tyner, James A. 1996. "Filipina Migrant Entertainers." *Gender, Place and Culture* 3: 77–93.

Westermanns Grosser Atlas zur Weltgeschichte. 1956. Braunschweig, Germany: Georg Westermann.

World Population Data Sheet. 2002. Washington, D.C.: Population Reference Bureau.

Ten Recommended Books
on Population Geography

(For additional suggested readings, see *The Human Mosaic* web site: www.whfreeman.com/jordan)

Castles, Stephen, and Mark J. Miller. 1998. *The Age of Migration: International Population Movements in the Modern World,* 2nd ed. New York: Guilford. A global perspective on migrations, why they occur, and the effects they have on different countries, in an age of unprecedented volume of migration. Explores how migration has led to the formation of ethnic minorities in numerous countries as well as its impact on domestic politics and economics.

Coleman, David, and Roger Schofield (eds.). 1986. *The State of Population Theory: Forward from Malthus.* New York: Blackwell. A collection of essays aimed at improving existing population theory originating from a 1984 demography symposium. Topics range from hunter-gatherer populations to sub-Saharan systems of reproduction to religion and reproduction in contemporary Europe.

Gesler, Wilbert M. 1991. *The Cultural Geography of Health Care.* Pittsburgh: University of Pittsburgh Press. Examines health and disease in their cultural context with examples from the Appalachians, India, and China. Attention is given to the role culture plays in the development of different health care delivery systems.

Hall, Edward T. 1966. *The Hidden Dimension.* Garden City, N.Y.: Doubleday. This is the classic study of proxemics conducted by an anthropologist. Hall argued that culture, above all else, shapes our criteria for defining, organizing, and using space.

Mackay, Judith. 1993. *The State of Health Atlas.* New York: Simon & Schuster. A collection of 35 color maps of current health conditions around the world, including population control, fertility, and life expectancy.

Meade, Melinda S., and Robert J. Earickson. 1999. *Medical Geography,* 2nd ed. New York: Guilford. Surveys the perspectives, theories, and methodologies that geographers use in studying human health; a primary text that undergraduates can readily understand.

Newman, James L. 1995. *The Peopling of Africa: A Geographic Interpretation.* New Haven, Conn.: Yale University Press. Explores the role of genetic background, language, occupation, and religion as well as differing natural and human environmental circumstances in the peopling of Africa before the arrival of European colonialists.

Roberts, Brian K. 1996. *Landscapes of Settlement.* London: Routledge. Discusses the role and significance of rural settlements, drawing from global case studies. Outlines the formation of different spatial arrangements at the farmstead, hamlet, and village scales.

Seager, Joni, and Mona Domosh. 2001. *Putting Women in Place: Feminist Geographers Make Sense of the World.* New York: Guilford. A highly readable account of why paying attention to gender is crucial to understanding the spaces we live and work in.

Tone, Andrea. 2002. *Devices and Desires: A History of Contraceptives in America.* New York: Hill & Wang. This social history of birth control in the United States details the fascinating relationship between the state and the long-standing attempts of men and women to limit their fertility.

Journals
in Population Geography

Gender, Place and Culture: A Journal of Feminist Geography. Published by the Carfax Publishing Co., P.O. Box 2025, Dunnellon, Fla. 34430. Volume 1 appeared in 1994.

Population and Environment: A Journal of Interdisciplinary Studies. Volume 1 was published in 1996.

Population Bulletin. Published quarterly by the Population Reference Bureau, 1875 Connecticut Ave. NW, Suite 520, Washington, D.C. 20009.

What differences can you "read" in these landscapes and how do you explain them? How accurately can you determine their locations?

Two types of contemporary agricultural landscapes. *(Left: Jim Wark/AirPhoto; Right: Michael Busselle/Corbis.)*

Turn to Seeing Geography on page 294 for an in-depth analysis of the above question.

AGRICULTURAL GEOGRAPHY

Food from the Good Earth

T HE WORLD'S POPULATION SEEKS
its livelihood in various ways but depends, either directly or indirectly, on
agriculture for the daily food necessary for survival. We can too easily forget
that the entire urban-industrial society rests, none too securely, on the base
of the food surplus generated by farmers and herders and that without agriculture there could be no cities or universities, no factories or offices.

Agriculture, the tilling of crops and rearing of domesticated animals to
produce food, feed, drink, and fiber, has been the principal enterprise of
humankind through all of recorded history. Even today, agriculture remains
by far the most important economic activity in the world, occupying the
greater part of the land area and employing about 40 percent of the working
population. In some parts of Asia and Africa, more than three-quarters of the
labor force is devoted to agriculture. North Americans, on the other hand,
live in an urban society in which less than 2 percent of the population work
as agriculturists. As recently as 1880, 44 percent of all Americans were farmers, but since then an ever smaller segment of our population has produced
the food and fiber needed. Likewise, Europe's labor force is as thoroughly
nonagricultural as North America's. Most of the rest of the world's population, however, continue to live in farm villages, like those described at the
end of Chapter 7.

 **Agro-Regions**

How is the theme of culture region relevant to agriculture? Over the course
of thousands of years, farmers adapted to different habitats, creating an array

Agricultural Regions

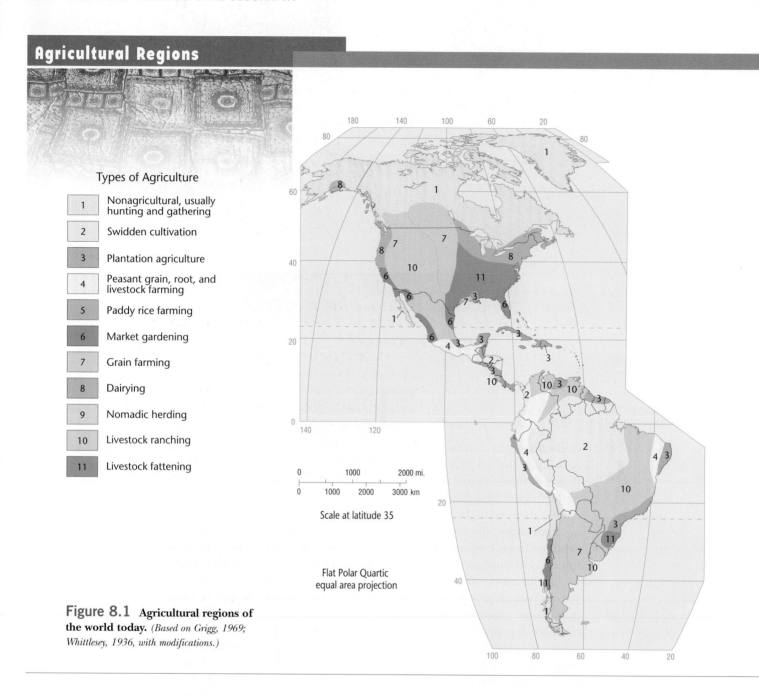

Types of Agriculture

1   Nonagricultural, usually hunting and gathering

2   Swidden cultivation

3   Plantation agriculture

4   Peasant grain, root, and livestock farming

5   Paddy rice farming

6   Market gardening

7   Grain farming

8   Dairying

9   Nomadic herding

10   Livestock ranching

11   Livestock fattening

0   1000   2000 mi.

0   1000   2000   3000 km

Scale at latitude 35

Flat Polar Quartic
equal area projection

Figure 8.1 **Agricultural regions of the world today.** *(Based on Grigg, 1969; Whittlesey, 1936, with modifications.)*

of different types of agriculture, each of which occupies a formal **agro-region** (Figure 8.1).

Swidden Cultivation

Many of the peoples of tropical lowlands and hills in the Americas, Africa, and Southeast Asia practice a land-rotation agricultural system known as **swidden cultivation.** The term *swidden* is derived from an old English term meaning "burned clearing." Using machetes or other bladed instruments, swidden cultivators chop away the undergrowth from

small patches of land and kill the trees by removing a strip of bark completely around the trunk. After the dead vegetation dries out, the farmers set it on fire to clear the land. Because of these clearing techniques, swidden cultivation is also called *slash-and-burn* agriculture. Working with digging sticks or hoes, the farmers then plant a variety of crops in the ash-covered clearings, varying from the maize (corn), beans, bananas, and manioc of Native Americans to the yams and nonirrigated rice grown by hill tribes in Southeast Asia (Figure 8.2). Different crops typically share the same clearing, a practice called **intercropping.** This technique allows taller,

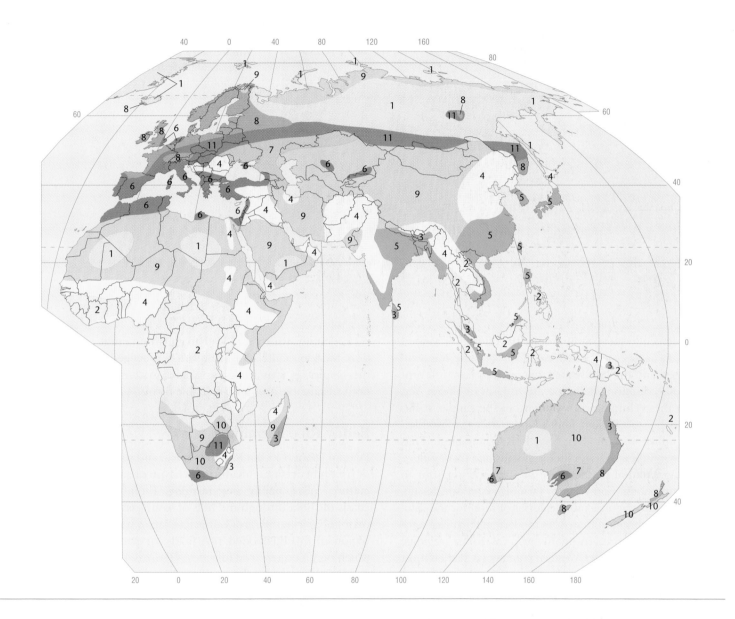

stronger crops to shelter lower, more fragile ones; reduces the chance of total crop losses from disease or pests; and provides the farmer with a varied diet. The complexity of many intercropping systems reveals the depth of knowledge acquired by swidden cultivators over many centuries. Relatively little tending of the plants is necessary until harvest time, and no fertilizer is applied to the fields because the ashes from the fire are a sufficient source of nutrients.

The planting and harvesting cycle is repeated in the same clearings for perhaps four or five years, until soil fertility and crop yields decline. These fields are then aban-

doned, and new clearings are prepared to replace them. Because the farmers periodically shift their cultivation plots, another commonly used term for the system is *shifting cultivation.* The abandoned cropland lies fallow, often returning to bush or forest, for 10 to 20 years before farmers return to clear and start the cycle again. Swidden cultivation represents one form of **subsistence agriculture:** food production mainly for the family and local community rather than for market. Farm animals play only a small role in swidden cultivation; that is, farmers keep few if any livestock, often relying on hunting and fishing for much of their protein supply.

Figure 8.2 **Swidden cultivation.**
This Indian woman in the Amazon Basin of Brazil tends a typical field. Note the intercropping, which includes bananas, and the ashes from the burning of the clearing at the base of the tree stump. Women were the first farmers and domesticated perhaps all crops. Are low-technology methods necessarily inferior? (*Helen Trembly/Families of the World.*)

Swidden cultivation in the tropics has often been viewed by outsiders as destructive and inefficient because the techniques used and the landscapes that result are so different from those common in temperate-zone agriculture. Yet, although the technology of swidden may be simple, it has proved to be an efficient and adaptive strategy. Swidden farming, unlike some modern systems, is sustainable and has endured for millennia. One should not assume that modern Western agricultural methods are in every way superior to those of traditional non-Western farming systems. After all, swidden farming returns more calories of food for the calories spent on cultivation than does modern mechanized agriculture. Furthermore, in many tropical forest regions, swidden cultivation, unlike Western plantations, has left most of the forest intact over centuries of continuous use.

Nonetheless, swidden cultivation can be destructive and unsustainable under certain conditions. In poor countries with large landless populations, one often finds a front of pioneer swidden farmers advancing on the forests. These are people desperately trying to make a living by opening up new lands. As the soil's productivity declines, however, they are forced to move on and clear another patch of forest, and a cycle of environmental destruction is created. Another condition that may diminish the sustainability of swidden cultivation occurs when a population experiences a sudden increase in its rate of growth. Often, improved health conditions have caused a drop in death rates, causing the population to pass from the first to the second stage of the demographic transformation (see Chapter 7). As a result, farmers must shorten the period during which the land is

recuperating, which can lead to environmental deterioration. Swidden cultivation, still widely practiced throughout the tropics, is thus a highly variable system, occurring in both sustainable and unsustainable forms.

Paddy Rice Farming

Peasant farmers in the humid tropical and subtropical parts of Asia practice a highly distinctive type of subsistence agriculture called **paddy rice farming.** From the monsoon coasts of India through the hills of southeastern China and on to the warmer parts of Korea and Japan stretches a broad region of diked, flooded rice fields, or paddies, many of which perch on terraced hillsides (Figure 8.3). The terraced paddy fields form a striking cultural landscape. These fields must be drained and repaired each year. (see Figure 1.16).

Rice, the dominant paddy crop, forms the basis of "vegetable civilizations," in which almost all the caloric intake is of plant origin. Many paddy farmers also raise a cash crop for market, such as tea, sugarcane, mulberry bushes for silkworm production, or the fiber crop jute. Asian farmers also raise pigs, water buffalo, poultry, and shrimp in the irrigation reservoirs, although they remain basically vegetarians. Farmers in India use draft animals, such as the water buffalo, to a greater extent than do other paddy farmers.

Most paddy rice farms are tiny. A landholding of 3 acres (about 1 hectare) is considered adequate to support a farm family. Such a small amount of land is sufficient for survival partly because irrigated rice provides a very large output of food per unit of land. Still, the paddy farmers must till their

Figure 8.3 **Cultivation of rice on the island of Bali, Indonesia.** Paddy rice farming traditionally entails enormous amounts of human labor and yields very high productivity per unit of land. What are the disadvantages of such a system? *(Denis Waugh/Tony Stone Images.)*

small patches intensively to harvest enough food. They must carefully transplant the small rice sprouts from seedbeds to the paddy. People from Western cultures can scarcely imagine the magnitude of tedious hand labor involved. Irrigation is key and requires a complex set of coordinated tasks to deliver water when and where it is needed. Often paddy farmers also plant and harvest the same parcel of land two times each year—a practice known as **double-cropping**—while applying large amounts of organic fertilizer to the land. So productive is this system that per-acre yields exceed those of American agriculture.

The modern era has witnessed a restructuring of paddy rice farming in the more developed countries such as Japan, Korea, and Taiwan. In some cases, the entire terrace structure has been reengineered to produce larger fields that can be worked with machines. In addition, dams, electric pumps, and reservoirs now provide a more reliable water supply, and high-yielding seeds, pesticides, and chemical fertilizers boost production further. Most paddy rice farmers now produce mainly for urban markets.

Peasant Grain, Root, and Livestock Farming

In colder, drier Asian farming regions that are climatically unsuited to paddy rice farming—as well as in the river valleys of the Middle East, in parts of Europe, in Africa, and in the mountain highlands of Latin America and New Guinea—farmers practice a diverse system of agriculture

based on bread grains, root crops, and herd livestock (Figures 8.4 and 8.5). Many geographers refer to these farmers as **peasants,** recognizing that they often represent a distinctive *folk culture* strongly rooted in the land. Peasants are generally small-scale farmers who own their fields and produce both for their own subsistence and for sale in the market. The dominant grain crops in these regions are, variously, wheat, barley, sorghum, millet, oats, and maize. Common cash crops—some of them raised for export—are cotton, flax, hemp, coffee, and tobacco.

These farmers also raise herds of cattle, pigs, sheep, and, in South America, llamas and alpacas. The livestock pull the plow; provide milk, meat, and wool; serve as beasts of burden; and produce manure for the fields. They also consume a portion of the grain harvest. In some areas, such as the Middle Eastern river valleys, the use of irrigation helps support this peasant system. In general, however, most modern agricultural technologies are beyond the financial reach of most peasants.

Plantation Agriculture

In certain tropical and subtropical areas, Europeans and Americans introduced a commercial agricultural system called **plantation agriculture.** A **plantation** is a huge landholding devoted to capital-intensive, large-scale, specialized production of one tropical or subtropical crop for the global market. Plantation agriculture long relied on large amounts of manual labor, initially in the form of slave labor and later as wage labor. The plantation system originated in

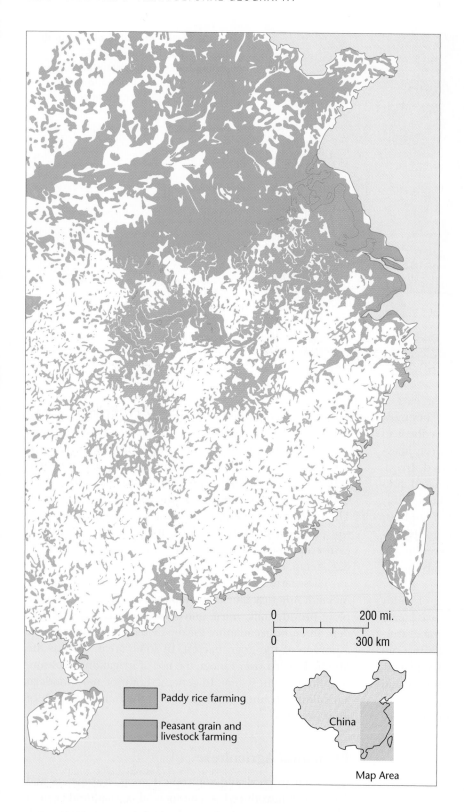

Figure 8.4 **Two agricultural regions in China.** The intricacies of culture region boundaries are suggested by the distribution of two types of agriculture in Taiwan and the eastern part of China. What might account for the more fragmented distribution of paddy rice farming, as contrasted with peasant grain, root, and livestock farming? Where would you draw the cultural boundary between the two types of agriculture? All such cultural geographical borders are difficult to draw. *(Source: Chuan-jun, 1979.)*

0 200 mi.
0 300 km

Paddy rice farming

Peasant grain and livestock farming

China

Map Area

the 1400s on Portuguese-owned sugarcane-producing islands off the coast of tropical West Africa—São Tomé and Principe—but the greatest concentration is now in the American tropics. Most plantations lie near the seacoast, close to the shipping lanes that carry their produce to nontropical lands such as Europe, the United States, and Japan.

Workers usually live right on the plantation, where a rigid social and economic segregation of labor and management produces a two-class society of the wealthy and the poor. As a result of the concentration of ownership and production, a handful of multinational corporations (MNCs), such as Chiquita and Dole, control the largest share of plan-

Figure 8.5 **Peasant grain, root, and livestock agriculture in highland New Guinea.** Distinctive "raised fields" with sweet potato mounds are found here among the farmers of highland New Guinea. These people raise diverse crops but give the greatest importance to sweet potatoes, together with pigs. Why might they go to the trouble of creating these small mounds? *(Courtesy of Terry G. Jordan-Bychkov.)*

Figure 8.6 **Plantation agriculture.** This sign was erected by the management at the entrance to a banana plantation in Costa Rica. "Welcome to Freehold Plantation, a workplace where labor harmony reigns; in mutual respect and understanding, we united workers produce and export quality goods in peace and harmony." How does this message suggest that, in fact, not all is harmonious here and that the tension of the two-class plantation system might simmer below the surface? *(Courtesy of Terry G. Jordan-Bychkov.)*

tations globally. Tension between labor and management is not uncommon, and the societal ills of the plantation system remain far from cured (Figure 8.6).

Plantations provided the base for European and American economic expansion into tropical Asia, Africa, and Latin America. They maximize the production of luxury crops for Europeans and Americans: sugarcane, bananas, coffee, coconuts, spices, tea, cacao, and tobacco (Figure 8.7). Similarly, Western textile factories require cotton, sisal, jute, hemp, and other fiber crops from the plantation areas. Much of the profit from these plantations is exported, along with the crops themselves, to Europe and North America, another source of political friction between countries of the global North and South.

Figure 8.7 **Tea plantation in the highlands of Papua New Guinea.** Although profitable for the owners and providing employment for a small labor force, the plantation recently displaced a much larger population of peasant grain, root, and livestock farmers. This is one result of globalization. Should the government have prevented such a displacement? *(Courtesy of Terry G. Jordan-Bychkov.)*

Each plantation district in the tropical and subtropical zones tends to specialize in one crop. Coffee and tea, for instance, grow in the tropical highlands, with coffee most prevalent in the upland plantations of tropical America and tea confined mainly to the hill slopes of India and Sri Lanka. Today, coffee remains the economic lifeblood of many less developed countries, whereas sugarcane and bananas are the major lowland plantation crops of tropical America. In most cases, plantation workers process the crop at least partially before sending it to the distant market. For example, sugar is generally milled and cotton ginned on the plantation. This combination of raising and partially processing the crop is a major distinguishing trait of the plantation system.

Globalization has brought major changes to plantation agriculture. Beyond the concentration of ownership among a small number of MNCs, machines have increasingly replaced hand labor, and the former workers, unemployed, flock to the cities of the Third World countries. The mechanized, modernized system is called *neoplantation*.

Market Gardening

The growth of urban markets in the last few centuries also gave rise to other commercial forms of agriculture, including **market gardening,** also known as truck farming. Unlike plantations, truck farms are located in developed countries and specialize in intensively cultivated nontropical fruits, vegetables, and vines. They raise no livestock. Many districts concentrate on a single product such as wine, table grapes, raisins, olives, oranges, apples, lettuce, or potatoes, and the entire farm output is raised for sale, rather than for consumption on the farm. Many truck farmers participate in cooperative marketing arrangements and depend on migratory seasonal farm laborers to harvest their crops. Market garden districts appear in most industrialized countries. In the United States, a broken belt of market gardens extends from California eastward through the Gulf and Atlantic coast states, with scattered districts in other parts of the country. The lands around the Mediterranean Sea are dominated by market gardens. In regions of mild climates, winter vegetables are a common market crop raised for sale in colder regions.

Livestock Fattening

In **livestock fattening,** farmers raise and fatten cattle and hogs for slaughter. One of the most highly developed fattening areas is the famous Corn Belt of the U.S. Midwest, where farmers raise corn and soybeans to feed cattle and hogs. A similar system prevails over much of western and central Europe, though the feed crops there are more commonly oats and potatoes. Smaller zones of commercial livestock fattening appear in overseas European settlement zones such as southern Brazil and South Africa.

One of the central traditional characteristics of livestock fattening is the combination of crop and animal raising. Farmers breed many of the animals they fatten, especially hogs. In the last half of the twentieth century, livestock fatteners began to specialize their activities; some concentrated on breeding animals, others on preparing them for market. In the factory-like **feedlot,** farmers raise imported cattle and hogs on purchased feed (Figure 8.8). Such feed-

Figure 8.8 **Cattle feedlot for beef production.** This feedlot, in Colorado, is reputedly the world's largest. What ecological problems might such an enterprise cause? *(William Strode/Woodfin Camp.)*

lots are most common in the U.S. West and South, partly because winters are less severe there.

Although commercial livestock fattening is often organized with assembly-line precision and has proved profitable, the specter of famine in recent years has brought its nutritional efficiency into question. In the 1900s, world grain production rose significantly faster than world population growth, and cereals provide most of the protein intake of the world's people. But in the same century, meat eating soared in the Western world, particularly in the United States, wiping out most of these gains. At least one-half of America's harvested agricultural land is planted with feed crops for livestock, and more than 70 percent of the grain raised in the United States goes for livestock fattening, but livestock are not an efficient method of protein production. A cow, for instance, must eat 21 pounds (9.5 kilograms) of protein to produce 1 pound (0.5 kilogram) of edible protein. Plants are far more efficient protein converters. By some estimates, protein lost through conversion from plant to meat could make up almost all of the world's present protein deficiencies. This basic inefficiency has spread to some poorer nations, such as Costa Rica and Brazil, where rain forest is being destroyed and swidden cultivators displaced to make way for cattle pasture to fatten beef for the global fast-food market.

Grain Farming

Grain farming is a type of specialized agriculture in which farmers grow wheat or, less often, rice or corn for commercial markets. The United States is the world's leading wheat and corn exporter. The United States, Canada, Australia, the European Union (EU), and Argentina together account for more than 85 percent of all wheat exports, while the United States alone accounts for about 70 percent of world corn exports. Wheat belts stretch through Australia, the Great Plains of interior North America, the steppes of Russia and Ukraine, and the pampas of Argentina. Farms in these areas are generally very large, ranging from family-run wheat farms to giant corporate operations (Figure 8.9). Extensive rice farms, operated under the same commercial system, occupy small areas of the Texas-Louisiana coastal plain and lowlands in Arkansas and California.

Widespread use of machinery, chemical fertilizers, pesticides, and improved seed varieties enables grain farmers to operate on this large scale. The planting and harvesting of grain is more completely mechanized than any other form of agriculture. Commercial rice farmers employ such techniques as sowing grain from airplanes. Harvesting is usually done by hired migratory crews using corporation-owned machines (Figure 8.10). Perhaps grain farming's ultimate development is the **suitcase farm,** which is found in the Wheat Belt of the northern Great Plains of the United States. The people who own and operate these farms do not live on the land. Most of them own several suitcase farms, lined up in a south-to-north row through the Plains states. They keep fleets of farm machinery, which they send north with crews of laborers along the string of suitcase farms to plant, fertilize, and harvest the wheat. The progressively later ripening of the grain as one moves north allows these farmers to maintain and harvest crops on all their farms with the same crew and the same machinery. Except for visits by migratory crews, the suitcase farms are uninhabited.

Figure 8.9 **A "wheat landscape" in the Palouse,** a grain farming region on the borders of Washington and Oregon. Grain elevators are a typical part of such agricultural landscapes. The raising of one crop such as wheat over entire regions is called *monoculture.* What problems might be linked to monoculture? *(Courtesy of Terry G. Jordan-Bychkov.)*

Figure 8.10 **Mechanized wheat harvest on the Great Plains of the United States.** North American grain farmers operate in a capital-intensive manner, investing in machines, chemical fertilizers, and pesticides. What long-term problems might such methods cause? What benefits are realized in such a system? *(Roger Du Buisson/The Stock Market.)*

Such highly mechanized, absentee-owned, large-scale operations, or **agribusinesses,** are rapidly replacing the traditional American family farm, an important part of the U.S. rural heritage. Geographer Ingolf Vogeler documented the decline of family farms in the American countryside and argued that U.S. governmental policies, prompted by the forces of globalization, have consistently favored the interests of agribusiness, thereby hastening the decline. The American family farm, though still celebrated as a myth and icon, no longer plays much of a role in the grain lands.

Dairying

In many ways, the specialized production of dairy goods closely resembles livestock fattening (see Focus On: Thomas Hardy on the Geography of Dairying). In the large dairy belts of the northern United States from New England to the upper Midwest, western and northern Europe, southeastern Australia, and northern New Zealand, the keeping of dairy cows depends on the large-scale use of pastures. In colder areas, some acreage must be devoted to winter feed crops, especially hay. Dairy products vary from region to region, depending in part on how close the farmers are to their markets. Dairy belts near large urban centers usually produce milk, which is more perishable, while those farther away specialize in butter, cheese, or processed milk. An extreme case is New Zealand, which, because of its remote location from world markets, produces much butter.

REFLECTING ON GEOGRAPHY

Why is *dairying* confined to northern Europe and the overseas lands settled by northern Europeans? (See Figure 8.1.)

As with livestock fattening, in recent decades a rapidly increasing number of dairy farmers have adopted the feedlot system and now raise their cattle on feed purchased from other sources. Feedlots are especially common in the southern United States. Often situated on the suburban fringes of large cities for quick access to market, the dairy feedlots are factory farms. Farmers buy feed and livestock replacements, instead of breeding and raising them on the farm. In these large-scale, automated operations, the number of cows is far greater than on family-operated dairy farms. Like industrial factory owners, feedlot dairy owners rely on hired laborers to help maintain their herds. Less pleasing to the eye and nose than traditional dairy farms, the feedlots are another indicator of the rise of globalization-induced agribusiness and the decline of the family farm. By easing trade barriers, globalization compels U.S. dairy farmers to compete with producers in other parts of the world. Huge feedlots, a factory-style organization of production, automation, and the concentration of ownership and increasing size of dairy farms are responses to this intense competition.

Nomadic Herding

In the dry or cold lands of the Eastern Hemisphere, particularly in the deserts, prairies, and *savannas*—tropical grasslands lightly strewn with trees—of Africa, the Arabian Peninsula, and the interior of Eurasia, **nomadic livestock herders** graze cattle, sheep, goats, and camels. North of the tree line in Eurasia, the cold *tundra*—a region covered with mosses, sedges, grass, and lichens—forms another zone of nomadic herders, who raise reindeer. The common characteristic of all nomadic herding is mobility. Herders must move with their livestock in search of forage for the animals

Thomas Hardy on the Geography of Dairying

Farming culture regions are readily observable, and you need not be a professional geographer to observe them. Some of the finest "geography" has been written by regional novelists. Among these writers, none surpass Thomas Hardy, who penned beautiful descriptions of the countryside of his native southern England. Here is his word picture of a late-nineteenth-century commercial dairy region, the Vale of Frome:

> She found herself on a summit commanding the . . . Valley of the Great Dairies, the valley in which milk and butter grew to rankness. . . . It was intrinsically different from the Vale of Little Dairies, Blackmoor Vale, which . . . she had exclusively known till now. The world was drawn to a larger pattern here. The enclosures numbered fifty acres instead of ten, the farmsteads were more extended, the groups of cattle formed tribes hereabout; there only families. These myriads of cows stretching under her eyes from the far east to the far west outnumbered any she had ever seen at one glance before. The green lea was speckled as thickly with them as a canvas by Van Alsloot or Sallaert with burghers. . . .

> Suddenly there arose from all parts of the lowland a prolonged and repeated call—Waow waow waow. It was . . . the ordinary announcement of milking-time—half-past four o'clock, when the dairymen set about getting in the cows. The red and white herd nearest at hand, which had been phlegmatically waiting for the call, now trooped towards the steading in the background, their great bags of milk swinging under them as they walked. . . .

> Long thatched sheds stretched round the enclosure, . . . their eaves supported by wooden posts rubbed to a glossy smoothness by the flanks of infinite cows and calves of bygone years. . . . Between the posts were ranged the milchers. . . . The dairy-maids and men had flocked down from their cottages and out of the dairyhouse with the arrival of the cows from the meads. . . . Each girl sat down on her three-legged stool, her face sideways, her right cheek resting against the cow. . . .

From Hardy, 1891

---

as seasons and range conditions change. Some nomads migrate from lowlands in winter to mountains in summer; others shift from desert areas during the rainy season to adjacent semiarid plains in the dry season, or from tundra in summer to nearby forests in winter. Some nomads herd while mounted on horses, such as the Mongols of East Asia, or on camels, such as the Bedouin of the Arabian Peninsula. Others, such as the Rendile of East Africa, herd cattle, goats, and sheep on foot.

The need for mobility dictates that the few material possessions the nomads have be portable, including the tents used for housing (Figure 8.11). The mobile lifestyle also

Figure 8.11 Nomadic pastoralists in West Africa. This Fulbe-Waila pastoralist household in Chad is moving their livestock to new pastures. Mobility is key to their successful use of the variable and unpredictable environment of this region of Africa. They are taking with them all of their possessions, including their shelter—a hut, which they have packed on top of one of their cows. *(Frank Kroenke/Peter Arnold, Inc.)*

The Future of the Nomadic Maasai of East Africa

With land-use change, population growth, and the demands of the global economy, the survival of nomadic herding cultures is in doubt worldwide. Here Tepilit Ole Saitoti, a Maasai born in Tanzania and holder of an MS degree from the University of Michigan, reflects on his people's past and future:

Our ancestors led our people beyond their farthest horizons. Their strength and might may be seen in our legends as well as in the size of our land. With their gleaming spearpoints and broad shields, they acquired the best grazing land in East Africa, the pride of any herder. They played their parts well, and we are proud for them. If this noble race of men must now be humble and destitute because of the passage of time, we do not have to accept disgrace and the disappearance of

our race. We must adapt to new situations in order to survive. I do not underestimate the challenges ahead, be we must stand up to them in the way we conquered Endikir Ekerio, our legendary escarpment, and the many famines and wars of the past. Our spearpoints are now like the teeth of infants and it seems the wisdom of the elders no longer counts, but we must survive. We must not follow the way of those races of men who have vanished from the surface of the earth. We have our culture and our governments behind us and our courage, pride, and noble truth. All we need now is determination, and jointly with all other African peoples we will not only survive but multiply and prosper.

From Saitoti, 1980

means that wealth is typically measured in nomadic cultures by the size of livestock holdings, rather than in the accumulation of property and personal possessions. Usually, the nomads obtain nearly all of life's necessities from livestock products or by bartering with the sedentary farmers of adjacent river valleys and oases. For centuries, nomads presented a periodic military threat to even the greatest farming civilizations—for example, the Mongols, who attacked China, could not be held back even by the Great Wall.

Nomadic herding everywhere was in decline for most of the twentieth century (see Focus On: The Future of the Nomadic Maasai of East Africa). A number of national governments have established policies encouraging nomads to practice **sedentary cultivation** of the land. A practice begun in the nineteenth century by British and French colonial administrators in North Africa, the settling of nomadic tribes, allows greater control by the central governments. Moreover, many nomads are voluntarily abandoning their traditional life to seek jobs in urban areas or in the Middle Eastern oil fields. Further impetus to abandon nomadic life recently came from severe drought in sub-Saharan Africa's *Sahel* region, which decimated livestock herds.

In recent decades, research conducted by geographers and anthropologists in Africa's semiarid environments has revealed the sound logic of nomadic herding practices. These studies demonstrate that nomadic cultures' pasture and livestock management strategies are rational responses to an erratic and unpredictable environment. Rainfall is

highly irregular in time and space, and herding practices must adjust. The most important of nomadic strategies is mobility, which allows herders to take fullest advantage of the resulting variations in range productivity. These findings have led to a new appreciation of nomadic herding cultures, which may cause governments to reconsider sedentarization programs and postpone the demise of herding cultures.

Livestock Ranching

Superficially, **ranching** might seem similar to nomadic herding. It is, however, a fundamentally different livestock-raising system. Although both nomadic herders and livestock ranchers specialize in animal husbandry to the exclusion of crop raising and both live in arid or semiarid regions, livestock ranchers have fixed places of residence and operate as individuals rather than within a communal or tribal organization. In addition, ranchers raise livestock for market on a large scale, not for their own subsistence, and they are typically of European ancestry rather than being an indigenous people.

Livestock ranchers are found worldwide in areas with environmental conditions too harsh for crop production. There they raise only two kinds of animals in large numbers: cattle and sheep. Ranchers in the United States and Canada, tropical and subtropical Latin America, and the warmer parts of Australia specialize in cattle raising. Midlatitude ranchers in the Southern Hemisphere specialize in sheep.

The extent of their production is such that New Zealand and Argentina produce 65 percent of the world's export wool. Sheep outnumber people by 6 to 1 in Australia and 13 to 1 in New Zealand.

Urban Agriculture

In recent decades, yet another type of agriculture has arisen, as people have migrated to cities. We might best call this **urban agriculture.** Millions of city dwellers, especially in Third World countries, now produce enough vegetables, fruit, meat, and milk from tiny urban or suburban plots to provide most of their food, often with a surplus to sell. In China, urban agriculture now provides 90 percent or more of all vegetables consumed, and in African metropolises such as Nairobi and Kampala, 20 percent of all food comes from urban lands. Even a developed country such as Russia derives nearly half of its food from such operations. Similarly, neighborhood gardens can also be found in inner-city areas of North America.

Geographer Susanne Freidberg has conducted research demonstrating the importance of urban agriculture to family income and food security in West Africa. Focusing on the city of Bobo-Dioulasso in Burkina Faso, Freidberg showed that though plots were small, urban agriculture offered residents "a culturally meaningful way to fulfill their roles as food producers and family providers." In its heyday in the 1970s and 1980s, urban farming provided substantial incomes from vegetable sales in both the domestic and export markets. Since then, collapsing demand and the deterioration of environmental conditions have threatened the enterprise and undermined cooperation and trust within the urban agricultural communities.

Nonagricultural Areas

Areas of extreme climate, particularly deserts and subarctic forests, do not support any form of agriculture. Such lands are found in much of Canada, Australia, and Siberia. Often these areas are inhabited by **hunting-and-gathering** groups of native peoples, such as the Inuit and Australian Aborigines, who gain a livelihood by hunting game, fishing where possible, and gathering edible and medicinal wild plants. At one time all humans lived as hunter-gatherers. Today, fewer than 1 percent of humans do. Given the various inroads of the modern world, even these people rarely depend entirely on hunting and gathering. In most hunting-and-gathering societies, a division of labor by gender occurs. Males perform most of the hunting and fishing, whereas females carry out the equally important task of gathering harvests from wild plants. Hunter-gatherers generally rely on a great variety of animals and plants for their food.

REFLECTING ON GEOGRAPHY

What types of agriculture occur in the three main densely populated areas of the world? (Compare Figures 7.1 and 8.1.) Are these two characteristics—type of agriculture and population density—linked?

Agricultural Diffusion

How does the theme of cultural diffusion help us understand the map of agro-regions? The various agro-regions we've discussed result from *cultural diffusion*. Agriculture and its many components are inventions; they arose as innovations in certain source areas and diffused to other parts of the world.

Origins and Diffusion of Plant Domestication

Agriculture probably began with the domestication of plants rather than animals. A **domesticated plant** is one deliberately planted, protected, cared for, and used by humans. Such plants are also genetically distinct from their wild ancestors because they are a result of deliberate improvement through selective breeding by agriculturists. Accordingly, they tend to be bigger than wild species, bearing larger, more abundant fruit or grain. For example, the original wild Indian maize grew on a cob only 0.75 inch (2 centimeters) long, which is one-tenth to one-twentieth the size of the cobs of domesticated maize.

Plant domestication and improvement constituted a process, not an event. It began as the gradual culmination of hundreds, or even thousands, of years of close association between humans and the natural vegetation. The first step in domestication was perceiving that a certain plant was useful, which led initially to its protection and eventually to deliberate planting.

Cultural geographer Carl Johannessen suggests that the domestication process can still be observed today. He believes that by studying current techniques used by native subsistence farmers in places such as Central America, we can gain insight into the methods of the first farmers of prehistoric antiquity. Johannessen points out that two steps are typically required to develop and improve plant varieties: (1) selection of seeds or shoots only from superior plants; and (2) genetic isolation from other, inferior plants to prevent cross-pollination. Johannessen's study of the present-day cultivation of the *pejibaye* palm tree in Costa Rica revealed that native cultivators actively engage in seed selection. All choose the seed of fresh fruit from superior trees, ones that bear particularly desirable fruit, as determined by size, flavor, texture, and color. Such trees are often given personal names, an indication of the value placed on them. Superior seed stocks are built up gradually over the years, with the result that elderly farmers generally have the best selections. Seeds are shared freely within family and clan groups, allowing rapid diffusion of desirable traits.

Johannessen also reported that some Indian groups clearly knew of the need for genetic isolation to reduce contamination from cross-pollination in maize plants. In Panama, for example, one native tribe of swidden cultivators raised 14 varieties of maize, each in a field separated from all the others by intervening forest.

The widespread association of female deities with agriculture suggests that it was women who first worked the land. Recall the almost universal division of labor in hunting-gathering-fishing societies. Because women had day-to-day contact with wild plants and stayed closer to home, they probably initiated plant domestication.

Locating Centers of Domestication

When, where, and how did these processes of plant domestication develop? Most experts now believe that the process of domestication was independently invented at many different times and locations. Geographer Carl Sauer, who conducted pioneering research on the origins and dispersal of plant and animal domestication, was one of the first to propose this explanation.

Sauer believed that domestication did not develop in response to hunger. He maintained that necessity was not the mother of agricultural invention, because starving people must spend every waking hour searching for food and have no time to devote to the centuries of leisurely experimentation required to domesticate plants. Instead, he suggested this invention was accomplished by peoples who had enough food to remain settled in one place and devote considerable time to plant care. The first farmers were probably sedentary folk, rather than migratory hunter-gatherers. He reasoned that domestication did not occur in grasslands or large river floodplains because primitive cultures would have had difficulty coping with the thick sod and periodic floodwaters. Sauer also believed that the hearth areas of domestication must have been in regions of great *biodiversity* where many different kinds of wild plants grew, thus providing abundant vegetative raw material for experimentation and crossbreeding. Such areas typically occur in hilly districts, where climates change with differing sun exposure and elevation above sea level.

Geographers and archaeologists continue to investigate the geographic origins of domestication. Most agree that agriculture arose independently in at least three, and possibly more, regions of biodiversity (Figure 8.12). Archaeolog-

ical evidence indicates that the oldest among these primary centers is the Fertile Crescent in the Middle East, where the great bread grains—wheat, barley, rye, and oats—as well as grapes, apples, olives, and many other crops were first domesticated roughly 10,000 years ago. When diffusion from the Fertile Crescent brought agriculture to northern and eastern Africa, a secondary center of domestication developed through *stimulus diffusion*, adding crops such as sorghum, peanuts, yams, coffee, and okra.

Southeast Asia—and possibly some lands now submerged by shallow seas—was the second great center of agricultural innovation. Rice, citrus, taro, bananas, and sugarcane, among other crops, were all developed there. There, too, stimulus diffusion apparently yielded a secondary center, in northeastern China, where millet was domesticated.

Later, about 5000 or more years ago, Native Americans in Mesoamerica achieved the third great independent invention of agriculture, from which came crops such as maize, tomatoes, chili peppers, beans, and squash. Sauer was among the first scholars to argue that Native Americans had independently invented agriculture, rather than acquiring it as the result of stimulus diffusion from the Eastern Hemisphere. As the Mesoamerican crop complex spread southward, it, too, produced a secondary center of stimulus diffusion, in northwestern South America, which first produced the white potato, sweet potato, and manioc.

Overall, the Native Americans domesticated an array of crops far superior in nutritional value to those of the two Eastern Hemisphere centers combined. To exclude all Native American domesticates from your diet for just a single day, you would have to go without not only those foods just listed but also pineapples, sunflower seeds and oil, vanilla, chocolate, pumpkins, papayas, various other foods, and tobacco.

In *Guns, Germs, and Steel*, biogeographer Jared Diamond suggests a different set of geographic centers of domestication. He identifies five regions of definite independent invention: Southwest Asia (Fertile Crescent), China, Mesoamerica, the Andes, and the eastern United States. In addition, there is inconclusive evidence that in another four regions—the African Sahel, West Africa, Ethiopia, and New Guinea—domestication arose through independent invention. These uncertainties continue to be investigated, and researchers are making new discoveries that will lead to a better understanding of the origins and dispersal of domesticates.

Pets or Meat? Tracing Animal Domestication

A **domesticated animal** is one that depends on people for food and shelter and that differs from wild species in physical appearance and behavior as a result of controlled breeding and frequent contact with humans. Animal domestication apparently occurred later in prehistory than did the first planting of crops—with the probable exception of the dog, whose companionship with humans appears to be much more ancient. Typically, people value domesticated animals and take care of them for some utilitarian purpose. Certain domesticated animals, such as the pig and the dog, probably attached themselves voluntarily to human settlements to feast on garbage. At first, perhaps, humans merely tolerated these animals, later adopting them as pets or as sources of meat.

The early farmers of the Middle East in the Fertile Crescent deserve credit for the first great animal domestications, most notably that of herd animals. The wild ancestors of major herd animals—such as cattle, pigs, horses, sheep, and goats—lived primarily in a belt running from Syria and southeastern Turkey eastward across Iraq and Iran to central Asia. Most animal domestication seems to have taken place in that general region or in adjacent areas. Farmers in the Middle East were the first to combine domesticated plants and animals in an integrated system, the antecedent of the peasant grain, root, and livestock farming described earlier. These people began using cattle to pull the plow, a revolutionary invention that greatly increased the acreage under cultivation.

Farmers of the ancient crop hearth in southern Asia apparently did not excel as domesticators of animals. The taming of certain kinds of poultry may be attributed to them, but probably little else. Similarly, the Native American, who made superior contributions to plant domestication, remained rather unsuccessful in taming animals, perhaps in part because suitable wild animals were less numerous. The llama, alpaca, guinea pig, Muscovy duck, and turkey were among the few American domesticates.

Modern Diffusions

Cultural diffusion did not end with the original spread of farming and herding (see Focus On: Cultural Diffusion: The Potato in Germany). During the succeeding millennia, new ideas arose, were transformed, and spread. Over the past 500 years, European exploration and colonialism were instrumental in redistributing a wide variety of crops on a global scale: maize and potatoes from North America to Eurasia and Africa, wheat and grapes from the Fertile Crescent to the Americas, and West African rice to the Carolinas and Brazil.

Even today, the farming of specific crops continues to spread in areas such as the Amazon Basin, extending the diffusion begun many millennia ago. Introduction of the

FOCUS ON

Cultural Diffusion: The Potato in Germany

How does a domestic plant spread into new areas and gain wider acceptance? The progress is often slow and not without resistance, as the following eyewitness account from the province of Pomerania, Kingdom of Prussia, shows.

In 1743, through the goodness of King Frederick the Great, the people of Kolberg district received a present completely unknown to us. A large freight wagon full of potatoes arrived at the market square, and, by a beating of drums, the announcement was made that all farmers and gardeners were to assemble before the town hall. The town councilors then showed the new fruit to the assembled crowd. Detailed instructions were read aloud concerning the planting, cultivation, and cooking of the potato. However, few of the people paid attention to the oral instructions, choosing instead to take the highly praised tubers in their hands, smelling, licking, and tasting them. Shaking their heads, they passed them around, eventually throwing them to the dogs, who also sniffed and rejected them. "These things," they said, "have

no smell or taste. What good are they to us?" Hardly anyone understood the instructions for planting. Quite general was the belief that potatoes would grow into trees from which you could gather like fruit in due time. Those who did not throw the potatoes on the rubbish heap, but instead planted them, did so incorrectly.

The town councilors learned that some skeptics had not entrusted their tuberous treasures to the earth. For that reason they instituted a strict potato inspection during the summer months and levied a small monetary fine on those found to be obstinate.

The next year the king renewed his benevolent gift, but this time the authorities sent along a man familiar with raising potatoes, and he helped the people plant and cultivate. In this manner, the new product first came to my district, and ever since has spread rapidly. Now a general famine can never again devastate the province.

Translated and condensed from Nettelbeck, 1910: 8–10

Diffusion of Agriculture

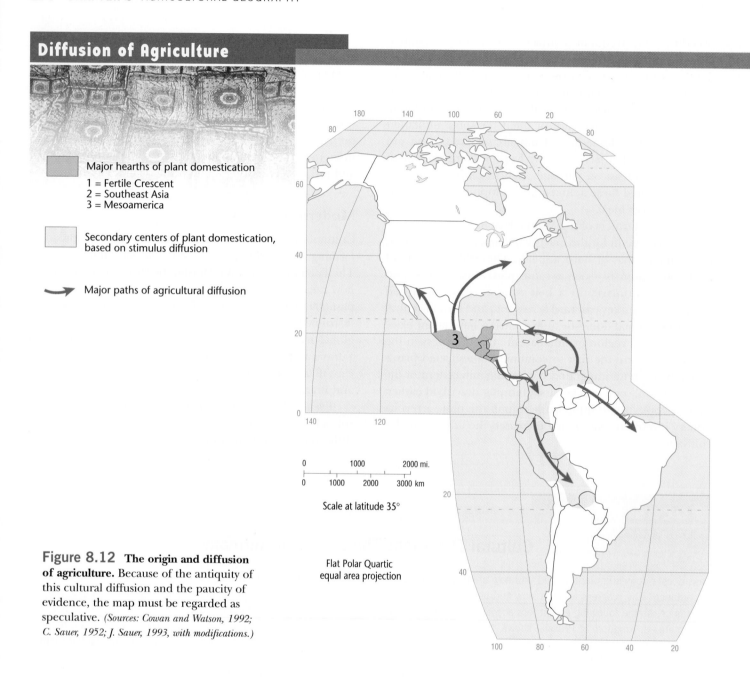

Major hearths of plant domestication
1 = Fertile Crescent
2 = Southeast Asia
3 = Mesoamerica

Secondary centers of plant domestication, based on stimulus diffusion

Major paths of agricultural diffusion

0   1000   2000 mi.
0 1000 2000 3000 km

Scale at latitude 35°

Flat Polar Quartic
equal area projection

Figure 8.12 **The origin and diffusion of agriculture.** Because of the antiquity of this cultural diffusion and the paucity of evidence, the map must be regarded as speculative. *(Sources: Cowan and Watson, 1992; C. Sauer, 1952; J. Sauer, 1993, with modifications.)*

lemon, orange, grape, and date palm by Spanish missionaries in eighteenth-century California, where no agriculture existed in the Native American era, provides a recent example of *relocation diffusion*. This was part of a larger process of multidirectional diffusion. Eastern Hemisphere crops were introduced to the Americas, Australia, New Zealand, and South Africa through the mass emigrations from Europe over the past 500 years. Crops from the Americas diffused in the opposite direction. For example, chili peppers and maize, carried by the Portuguese to their colonies in South Asia, became basic elements of the diet all across that region

(Figure 8.13). One could not imagine southern Asian cuisine today devoid of chili pepper seasoning.

In cultural geography, our understanding of agricultural diffusion is not narrowly focused on the crops alone; it also includes an analysis of the cultures and *indigenous knowledge* systems in which they are embedded. For example, geographer Judith Carney's study of the diffusion of African rice (*Oryza glaberrima*), which was domesticated independently in the inland delta area of West Africa's Niger River, shows the importance of indigenous knowledge. European planters and slave owners did not simply carry seeds across the

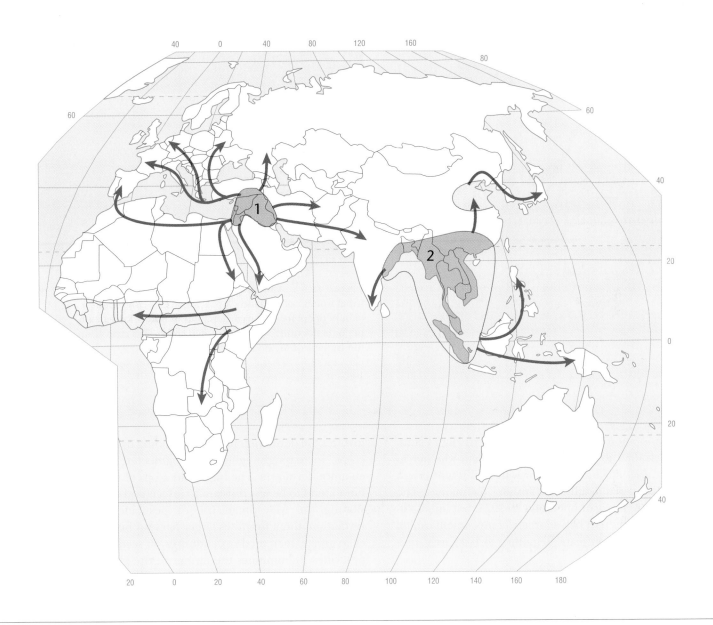

Atlantic from Africa to cultivate in the Americas. Rather, the Africans who were taken into slavery, particularly women from the Gambia River region, alone had the knowledge and skill to cultivate rice. Slave owners actively sought slaves from specific ethnic groups and geographic locations in the West African rice-producing zone, suggesting that they knew about and needed Africans' skills and knowledge. Carney argues that the "association of agricultural skills with certain African ethnicities within a specific geographic region" means that research on agricultural diffusion must address the relation of culture to technology and the environment.

In the twentieth century the world witnessed many farming innovations and diffusions. The spread of hybrid maize through the United States provides a good example of *expansion diffusion* (Figure 8.14). Such innovations often gain initial acceptance by wealthier, large-scale farmers before being adopted by smaller-scale operations, providing a good example of *hierarchical diffusion*.

One of the major innovation diffusions in twentieth-century American agriculture involved the spread of pump irrigation through many parts of the western Great Plains. Geographer Leonard Bowden made a detailed study of this

Figure 8.13 **Chili peppers in Nepal and Korea.** A Tharu tribal woman of lowland Nepal prepares a condiment made of chili peppers from her garden, and in South Korea chili peppers dry under a plastic-roofed shed. This crop comes from the Indians of Mexico. How might it have diffused so far and become so important in Asia? For the answer, see Andrews, 1993. *(Courtesy of Terry G. Jordan-Bychkov.)*

irrigation innovation in the Colorado northern High Plains. Farmers there had to decide much more than whether to irrigate, because irrigation brought with it different crops, different markets, and different farming techniques. The first irrigation well began operation by 1935, but initial diffusion was slowed in part by a shortage of investment capital in the Great Depression years. Beginning in 1948, irrigation spread quite rapidly.

In studying the spread of pump irrigation, Bowden observed *contagious diffusion* from the core area of initial acceptance. The closer a potential irrigation site lay to an already irrigated farm, the more likely its owner was to accept the innovation—an example of the *neighborhood effect.* Initial barriers to the diffusion of irrigation weakened over time. At first, banks and other moneylending institutions were reluctant to lend money to farmers for investment in irrigation. Once the technique proved to be economically successful, however, loans were easier to obtain and interest rates fell.

Not all innovations involve expansion diffusion and spread wavelike across the land in the manner of pump irrigation and hybrid maize. A much less orderly pattern is more typical. The **green revolution** in Asia provides an example. The green revolution is a product of modern agricultural science and has accompanied globalization. It involves the development of high-yielding hybrid varieties of crops, increasingly genetically engineered, coupled with chemical fertilizers. The high-yield crops of the green revolution tend to be less resistant to insects and diseases, necessitating the widespread use of pesticides. The green revolution, then, promises larger harvests but ties the farmer to greatly increased expenditures on seed, fertilizer, and pesticides. It enmeshes the farmer in the global corporate economy. In some countries, most notably India, the green revolution diffused rapidly in the latter half of the twentieth century. By contrast, countries such as Myanmar resisted the revolution, favoring traditional methods. An uneven pattern of acceptance still characterizes the paddy rice areas today.

The green revolution illustrates how cultural and economic factors influence patterns of diffusion.. In India, for example, new hybrid rice and wheat seeds first appeared in 1966. Although requiring chemical fertilizers and protection by pesticides, the new hybrids allowed India's 1970 grain production to double in output from its 1950 level. However, poorer farmers—the great majority of agriculturists—could not afford the capital expenditures for chemical fertilizer and pesticides, and the gap between rich and poor farmers widened. Many of the poor became displaced from the land and flocked to the overcrowded cities of India,

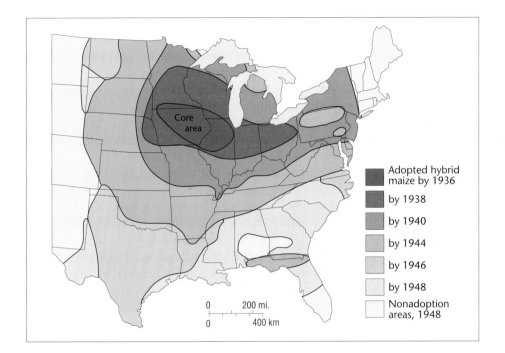

Figure 8.14 **The diffusion of hybrid maize in the United States.** Hybrid maize spread from a core area of initial acceptance in Iowa and Illinois through expansion diffusion, reaching most of the eastern United States in little over a decade. What type of diffusion does the pattern suggest? *(After Griliches, 1960: 277.)*

Legend:
- Adopted hybrid maize by 1936
- by 1938
- by 1940
- by 1944
- by 1946
- by 1948
- Nonadoption areas, 1948

aggravating urban problems. To make matters worse, the use of chemicals and poisons on the land heightened environmental damage.

The widespread adoption of hybrid seeds has created another problem: the loss of plant diversity, or genetic variety. Before hybrid seeds diffused around the world, each farm developed its own distinctive seed types through the annual harvest-time practice of saving seeds from the better plants for the next season's sowing. Enormous *genetic diversity* vanished almost instantly when farmers began purchasing hybrids rather than saving seed from the last harvest. "Gene banks" have belatedly been set up to preserve what remains of domesticated plant variety, not just in the areas affected by the green revolution but also in the American Corn Belt and many other agricultural regions where hybrids are now dominant. In sum, the green revolution proved at best to be a mixed blessing.

 Agro-Ecology

How are agriculture and ecology interrelated? How does the theme of cultural ecology help us understand types of agriculture? Agriculture is related to the physical environment at the most basic level, for farming involves direct use of the land and is directly influenced by the local climate. Because farmers and herders work and live on the land, a very close relationship exists between agriculture and the physical environment. In many ways, the map of agricultural regions reflects adaptation to environmental influences. At the same time, thousands of years of agricultural use of the land have led to massive alterations in our natural environment.

Markets and Cultural Ecological Change

Historically, climate and the physical environment have exerted perhaps the greatest influence on the different forms of agriculture. People had to adjust their subsistence strategies and techniques to prevailing regional climate conditions. In addition, soils play an influential role in both agricultural practices and food provisioning. Swidden cultivation, in part, reflects an adaptation to poor tropical soils, which rapidly lose their fertility when farmed. Peasant agriculture, by contrast, often owes its high productivity to the fertility of local volcanic soils, which are not so quickly exhausted. Terrain is also an influence, with farmers tending to cultivate relatively level areas (Figure 8.15). In sum, the constraints of climate, soil, and terrain historically limited the types of crops and cultivation practices possible.

For most of human history, people obtained their provisions locally and had locally distinct dietary cultures. The development of global markets over the past 500 years has shifted cultural food preferences and altered the ecology of vast areas of the planet. A multitude of crops have diffused around the globe, creating new regional cuisines (imagine Italian cuisine without tomatoes!) while at the same time simplifying the global diet to a disproportionate reliance on only three grains: wheat, rice, and maize. The expansion of European empires in the seventeenth and eighteenth

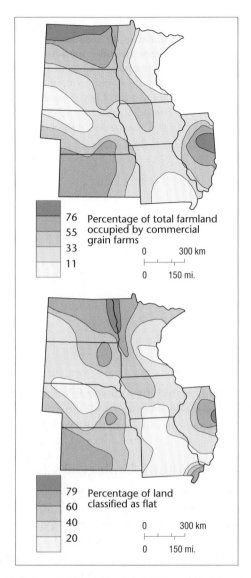

Figure 8.15 The influence of terrain on agriculture. The spatial relationship of commercial grain farming and flat terrain appears in the American Midwest, about 1960. "Flat" terrain is defined as any land with a slope of 3 degrees or less. Commercial grain farming is completely mechanized, and flat land permits more efficient machine operation. The result is this striking correlation between a type of agriculture and a type of terrain. What other factors might attract mechanized grain farming to level land? *(After Hidore, 1963: 86, 87.)*

centuries was inseparable from the expansion of tropical plantation agriculture. Plantations in warm climates produced what were then luxury foods for markets in the global North, which had developed seemingly insatiable appetites for sugar, tea, coffee, and other tropical crops. The expansion of plantation agriculture had profound effects on local ecology, all but obliterating, for example, the forests of the Caribbean and the tropical coasts of the Americas (Figure 8.16).

In short, we have witnessed the development of a global food system, which, for better or worse, has freed the affluent regions of the world from the constraints of local ecologies. Fresh strawberries, bananas, pears, avocados, pineapples, and many, many other types of temperate, subtropical, and tropical produce are available in our urban supermarkets any day, any time of the year. The emphasis on a relatively small number of crops desired by northern consumers can mean the abandonment of local crop varieties and a decline in the associated biological diversity. Meanwhile, imported refined wheat from the North enters poor tropical countries by the shipload, altering local dietary cultures and undercutting the ability of local farmers to sell their crops at a profitable price.

These are the general patterns, but the globalization of food and agriculture has complex effects on culture and ecology that vary from location to location and by spatial scale. These complexities are best illustrated through a case study from the Peruvian Andes. Geographer Karl Zimmerer (see Practicing Geography) conducted extensive fieldwork among Quichua peasant farmers in the Paucartambo Andes in order to determine the effects of economic change on indigenous agricultural practices and the genetic diversity of local crops. He wanted to test the general hypothesis that as globalization and national economic policies integrate indigenous farmers into market production, the diversity of crops declines, ultimately resulting in *genetic erosion* (i.e., a decline in the genetic diversity of cultivars).

Zimmerer's study produced surprising findings on the complex relationships among culture, economy, and the environment. On the question of whether farmers must abandon crop diversity in order to adopt new, commercially oriented high-yielding varieties, he found there was no simple answer. In fact, it was the more well-off peasants, heavily involved in commercial farming, who had the resources and land to cultivate diverse crops and "enjoy their agronomic, culinary, cultural, and ritual values." Among these values was the use of diverse, noncommercial potato varieties in local bartering. The ability to use noncommercial varieties in this way is valued in the local culture because it is a traditional way to cement interpersonal bonds. Such uses emphasize the cultural importance of crop diversity. Zimmerer discovered that the cultural relevance of crops was a strong motivation for planting by well-off farmers. At least 90 percent of the genetically diverse crops had been conserved, even as the Quichua were further integrated into commercial production for the market.

A number of lessons can be drawn from Zimmerer's study, chief among them the need to carefully examine the effects of globalization on culture and environment, rather than simply assuming that local agricultural practices will give way to the demands of the marketplace. The Quichua farmers who benefited most from their participation in the

Figure 8.16 **An oil palm plantation in Malaysia.** Plantation agriculture continues to expand in many Third World countries. While plantation-grown export commodities can be important to national economies, the accompanying destruction of tropical rain forests is a high ecological price to pay. *(Stuart Franklin/Magnum.)*

market were those best able to cultivate traditional varieties, which functioned as an expression of cultural identity and their sense of place. Cultural values, and not merely a strict economic or ecological calculus, critically influenced farming decisions.

Sustainable Agriculture

As Zimmerer's and many other cultural geography studies have shown, local and indigenous knowledge about ecological conditions can be a foundation for sustainable agriculture. Sustainability—the survival of a land-use system for centuries or millennia without destruction of the environmental base—is the central agricultural ecological issue. The case of the Quichua peasants offers an optimistic assessment of indigenous knowledge as the basis for long-term sustainability. Their response to contemporary market pressures suggests that development and conservation can be compatible. Their knowledge of complex and variable ecological conditions in the Andes has allowed them to farm a range of highly diverse crop varieties, a practice that in some cases has been strengthened by economic development.

Another example of sustainable indigenous agriculture is the paddy areas near the margins of the Asian wet-rice region, where the unreliability of rainfall causes harvests to vary greatly from one year to the next. Farmers developed complex cultivation strategies to avert periodic famine, including the use of many varieties of rice. Such farmers, including those in parts of Thailand, almost universally rejected the green revolution. The simplistic advice given to them by agricultural experts working for the Thai government was not appropriate for their marginal lands. Based on

generations of experimentation, the local farmers knew that the traditional diversified adaptive strategy was superior. A similarly subtle adaptation to environmental influence can be observed in West Africa, where peasant grain, root, and livestock farmers raise a multiplicity of crops in the more humid lands near the coast. These crops fall away one by one toward the drier interior of the continent, where the careful observer finds instead numerous drought-resistant varieties of only a few basic crops flourishing. Most geographers, having observed many other such cases where local practices have proved effective and sustainable, now agree that agricultural experts need to consider indigenous knowledge in their development plans.

The Desertification Debate

Over the millennia, as dependence on agriculture grew and as population increased, humans made ever larger demands on the forests. With the rise of urban civilization and conquering empires, the human transformation of forests to fields accelerated and expanded. In many parts of China, India, and the Mediterranean lands, forests virtually vanished. In transalpine Europe, the United States, and some other areas, they were greatly reduced (Figure 8.17).

Grasslands suffered similar modifications. Farmers occasionally plowed grasslands too dry for sustainable crop production, and herders sometimes damaged semiarid pastures through overgrazing. The result could be **desertification,** a process first studied half a century ago by geographer Rhoads Murphey. He argued that farmers caused substantial parts of North Africa to be added to the margins of the Sahara Desert (Figure 8.18). He noted the

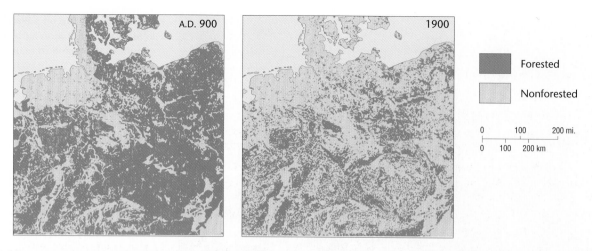

Figure 8.17 **The agricultural impact on the forest cover of central Europe from A.D. 900 to 1900.** Extensive clearing of the forests, mostly before 1350, was tied largely to expansion of farmland. The distribution of forests in 1900 closely resembles that of hills and mountain ranges. Why might this pattern have developed? *(Redrawn from Darby, 1956: 202–203.)*

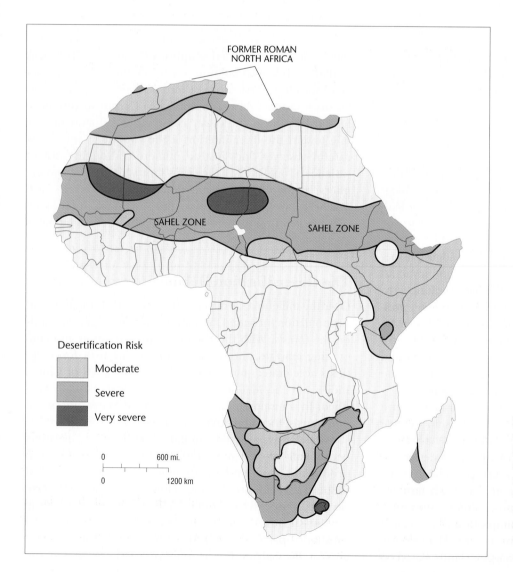

Figure 8.18 **Risk of desertification in Africa.** Are the deserts of the world expanding because of agricultural land use? Or do desert boundaries advance and retreat primarily in response to climate fluctuations? Geographer Rhoads Murphey began this debate half a century ago, and it still rages. Africa has been the center of the debate. *(Murphey, 1951; Thomas, 1993: 320.)*

Karl Zimmerer

(Courtesy of Karl Zimmerer.)

University of Wisconsin geography professor Karl Zimmerer discovered the discipline of geography through his interests in agriculture. As an undergraduate, he was a student intern at the Land Institute in Salina, Kansas, where research was focused on developing alternatives to conventional agriculture and the food supply. As Zimmerer recalls, "Its director, Wes Jackson, suggested that I consider the field of geography for graduate school. I read books, visited departments, talked to students and listened to faculty lectures, and recognized that this was the discipline for me." Geography offered him the ideal disciplinary setting for pursuing his broad interests in agriculture and food, which range from environmental to political issues.

Professor Zimmerer finds three aspects of practicing geography particularly compelling and exciting. "First is the challenge of understanding the multifaceted changes of agriculture in Latin America and the United States. . . . Part of my interest is the fusion of the human world and the natural world that takes place in agriculture." In particular, he is interested in the new changes in the areas of biotechnology and corporate agribusiness.

"Second is the excitement and intellectual engagement of fieldwork [and] working closely with the diverse people in farming sites. When in the Andean countries, most often Bolivia and Peru, I speak Quechua as well as Spanish. Using these languages is not only exciting and engaging, but it also continually reinforces for me the importance of languages in addition to English."

The third area of practicing geography that appeals to Professor Zimmerer is communicating his knowledge through teaching, speaking, and writing. "Often I find myself faced with new and welcome challenges in understanding,

interpreting, and telling the stories of the changes in agriculture." As an example, through the feedback that he has received from his teaching and public speaking, Zimmerer "became increasingly aware of this diverse, expanding, and possibly hopeful (although potentially explosive) interface of agriculture and conservation." The agriculture-conservation interface has subsequently become an important part of his research and writing.

His work in the field typically involves a variety of methods and techniques, including a lot of interviewing and related qualitative ethnographic methods. "I also do a fair amount of archival research," he explains, "since many of my projects on agriculture have a historical dimension and since they are often located in places where archival research is the main way of gaining information and awareness about the past." Professor Zimmerer is no stranger to quantitative methods, which are important for studying the environmental aspects of agriculture, such as biodiversity and soil properties. "In the latter sort of research I often use biogeography and ecology field methods and have also used laboratory techniques."

As this edition of *Human Mosaic* goes to press, Professor Zimmerer is enjoying a year-long sabbatical as a fellow of the Agrarian Studies Program at Yale University. There he is studying "the development of geographical ideas of sustainable use that have taken shape through the influence of natural historians and scientists in Latin America, Europe, and the United States." Part of the research, which covers a 500-year period of change, focuses "on the changes that were taking place in the environments themselves—especially mountain areas." As Professor Zimmerer's current research bears fruit, we can look forward to the informative findings and fascinating insights about the human mosaic that we've grown to expect from his work.

catastrophic decline of countries such as Libya and Tunisia in the 1500 years since the time of Roman rule, when North Africa served as the "granary of the Empire," yielding huge wheat harvests.

More recent research on desertification has centered on the *Sahel,* a region just south of the Sahara Desert in Africa (see Figure 8.18). In the Sahel, a series of droughts in the 1970s and 1980s raised concern over the issue, as demonstrated by the 1976 United Nations Conference on Deserti-

fication. One theory advanced at the conference was that farmers and pastoralists were overusing the land. The resulting destruction of vegetation could pass a critical threshold, beyond which the plant life could not regenerate. Soon lands that had been covered with pastures and fields could become permanently joined to the dunes of the adjacent Sahara. In sum, researchers theorized that Africans were overgrazing rangelands and using poor cultivation practices, causing the desert to spread southward.

In the intervening years, substantial evidence, much of it obtained through satellite remote sensing, has raised questions about this theorized link between land use and the advancing Sahara Desert. Satellite imagery suggests to many researchers that the semiarid lands possess more resiliency than was once thought. Since 1960, they claim, the Sahara-Sahel boundary has not migrated steadily south but merely fluctuated as it always has, responding to wetter and drier years. New research by geographers and anthropologists also challenges the generalized claim that Africans were misusing the land. These findings suggest that African land-use practices in the region are highly adapted to the variable and unpredictable environments of the Sahel. A great deal of careful research is needed to distinguish the fluctuations caused by climate variability from permanent ecological damage caused by human misuse.

One might asume that irrigation would provide a solution for desertification. However, irrigation has had unintentional impacts on the land. For example, well-and-pump irrigation has drastically lowered the water table in parts of the American Great Plains, particularly Texas, causing ancient springs to go dry and promising an early end to intensive agriculture there. Irrigation, in other words, may ultimately spread rather than diminish desertification. Another area where desertification is the consequence of irrigation lies on the borderland between Kazakhstan and Uzbekistan in central Asia. The once-huge *Aral Sea* became so diminished by the diversion of irrigation water from the rivers flowing into it that large areas of dry lakebed now lie exposed. Not only was the local fishing industry destroyed, but noxious, chemical-laden dust storms now blow from the barren lakebed onto nearby settlements, causing assorted health problems. Irrigation water diverted to huge cotton fields, then, destroyed an *ecosystem* and produced another desert.

REFLECTING ON GEOGRAPHY

What might be some ecological consequences of expanding cropland to meet the world's rising food needs?

Equally as serious as desertification is the increasing chemical contamination of the land through both fertilizers and pesticides, used mainly by commercial farmers in Western cultures. Chemicals first became important as agricultural fertilizers in Germany in the mid-1800s, and central Europeans remain some of the most chemical-dependent farmers to this day. The chemicals diffused widely, spreading in conjunction with the green revolution and neoplantation. Together with the use of large machines, chemicals allowed drastic reductions in the amount of labor needed in agriculture. However, the ecological consequences could well be devastating, and in some areas serious contamination problems have appeared.

Environmental Perception by Agriculturists

People perceive the physical environment through the lenses of their culture. Each person's agricultural heritage can be influential in shaping these perceptions. This is not surprising, because human survival depends on how successfully people can adjust their ways of making a living to environmental conditions.

The American Great Plains provide a good example of how an agricultural experience in one environment influenced farmers' environmental perceptions and subsequent behavior in another environment. Plains farmers came from the humid eastern United States, and they consistently underestimated the problem of drought in their new home. In the 1960s, geographer Thomas Saarinen revealed that although the oldest and most experienced Great Plains farmers had the most accurate perception of drought, almost every farmer still underestimated the actual frequency of such dry periods. By contrast, *culturally preadapted* German immigrants from the steppes of Russia and Ukraine, an area very much like the American Great Plains, accurately perceived the new land and experienced fewer problems.

Above all, farmers rely on climatic stability. A sudden spell of unusual weather events can change agriculturists' environmental perceptions. Geographer John Cross studied Wisconsin agriculture, following a series of floods, droughts, and other anomalies. He found that two-thirds of all Wisconsin dairy farmers now believe the climate is changing, for the worse, and fully one-third told him that continued climatic variability threatened their continued operation. Perhaps they perceive the environmental hazard to be greater than it really is, but they make decisions based on their perceptions.

 Agro-Cultural Interaction

How does agriculture interact with other facets of culture? Let us next observe some of the ways other cultural forces influence agricultural activities. Religious taboos, politically based tariff restrictions, rural land-use zoning policies, government subsidies, population density, and many other factors affect the type and distribution of agricultural activities. Among some peoples, the system of crop and livestock raising becomes so firmly enmeshed in the culture that both society and religion are greatly influenced (see Focus On: Cultural Interaction: The Example of Cattle Among the Dasanetch).

FOCUS ON

Cultural Interaction: The Example of Cattle Among the Dasanetch

The Dasanetch are a herding people living close to Lake Rudolf in East Africa, where the borders of Ethiopia, Kenya, and Sudan meet. For them, cattle are more than mere domestic animals from which they derive milk, meat, blood, and skins. Cattle occupy a central position in their society, serving religious and social roles in addition to their economic function. Dasanetch men identify closely with their cattle and sometimes even assume the personal name of a favorite ox. Cattle themes appear

often in the song, dance, myth, and ritual of the Dasanetch. Cattle are also an essential aspect of the unmarried woman's dowry and serve as a medium of exchange. "Cattle are therefore central in the organization and functioning of Dasanetch society," bearing utilitarian, subjective, and monetary values. In this way, agriculture, religion, and society are thoroughly integrated.

Derived from Carr, 1977: 99–100

Intensity of Land Use

A great spatial variation exists in the intensity of rural land use. **Intensive agriculture** means that a large amount of human labor or investment capital, or both, is put into each acre or hectare of land, with the goal of obtaining the greatest output of produce. One can calculate intensity by measuring either energy input or the level of productivity. In much of the world, especially the paddy rice areas of Asia, high intensity is achieved through prodigious application of human labor, which results in a rice output per unit of land that is the highest in the world. In Western countries, high intensity is achieved through the use of massive amounts of investment capital for machines, fertilizers, and pesticides, resulting in the highest agricultural productivity per capita found anywhere.

Many geographers support the theory that increased land-use intensity is a common response to population growth. As demographic pressure mounts, farmers systematically discard the more geographically extensive adaptive strategies to focus on those that provide greater yield per unit of land. In this manner, the population increase is accommodated. The resultant farming system may be riskier, because it offers fewer options and possesses greater potential for environmental modification, but it does yield more food—at least in the short run. Other geographers reject this theory, arguing instead that population density increases following innovations, such as the introduction of new high-calorie crops, that lead to greater land-use intensity.

The von Thünen Model

Economic determinists, another type of geographer, look to market forces and transportation costs as keys to explaining

the level of land-use intensity. They use the *core-periphery model* developed in the nineteenth century by the German scholar-farmer Johann Heinrich von Thünen. In his model, von Thünen proposed an "isolated state" that had no trade connections with the outside world; possessed only one market, located centrally in the state; and had uniform soil, climate, and level terrain throughout. He further assumed that all farmers located the same distance from the market had equal access to it and that all farmers sought to maximize their profits and produced solely for market. Von Thünen created this model to study the influence of distance from market and the concurrent transport costs on the type and intensity of agriculture.

Figure 8.19 presents a modified version of von Thünen's isolated-state model, which reflects the effects of improvements in transportation since the 1820s, when von Thünen proposed his theory. The model's fundamental feature is a series of concentric zones, each occupied by a different type of agriculture, located at progressively greater distances from the central market.

REFLECTING ON GEOGRAPHY

Why should we study spatial models, such as von Thünen's, when they do not depict reality?

For any given crop, the intensity of cultivation declines with increasing distance from the market. Farmers near the market have minimal transportation costs and can invest most of their resources in labor, equipment, and supplies to augment production. Indeed, because their land is more valuable and subject to higher taxes, they have to farm intensively to make a bigger profit. With increasing distance from the market, farmers invest progressively less in production per unit of land because they have to spend

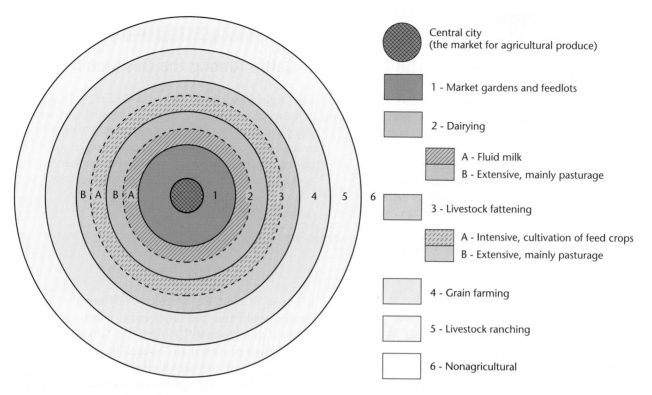

Figure 8.19 **Von Thünen's isolated-state model.** The model is modified to fit the modern world better, showing the hypothetical distribution of types of commercial agriculture. Other causal factors are held constant to illustrate the effect of transportation costs and differing distances from the market. The more intensive forms of agriculture, such as market gardening, are located nearest the market, whereas the least intensive form (livestock ranching) is most remote. Why does the model have the configuration of concentric circles? Compare this model to the real-world pattern of agricultural types in Uruguay, South America, shown in Figure 8.20.

progressively more on transporting produce to market. The effect of distance means that highly perishable products such as milk, fresh fruit, and garden vegetables need to be produced near the market, whereas peripheral farmers have to produce nonperishable products or convert perishable items into a more durable form, such as cheese or dried fruit.

The concentric-zone model describes a situation in which highly capital-intensive forms of commercial agriculture, such as market gardening and feedlots, lie nearest to market. The increasingly distant, successive concentric belts are occupied by progressively less intensive types of agriculture, represented by dairying, livestock fattening, grain farming, and ranching.

How well does this modified model describe reality? As we would expect, the real world is far more complicated. Still, on a world scale, we can see that intensive commercial types of agriculture tend to occur most commonly near the huge urban markets of northwestern Europe and the eastern United States (see Figure 8.1). An even closer match can be observed in smaller areas, such as in the South American nation of Uruguay (Figure 8.20).

The value of von Thünen's model can also be seen in the underdeveloped countries of the world. Geographer Ronald Horvath made a detailed study of the African region centering on the Ethiopian capital city of Addis Ababa. Although noting disruptions caused by ethnic and environmental differences, Horvath found "remarkable parallels between von Thünen's crop theory and the agriculture around Addis Ababa." Similarly, German geographer Ursula Ewald applied the model to the farming patterns of colonial Mexico during the period of Spanish rule, concluding that even this culturally and environmentally diverse land provided "an excellent illustration of von Thünen's principles on spatial zonation in agriculture."

Can the World Be Fed?

Are starvation and recurrent famine inevitable as the world's population grows, as Thomas Malthus predicted (see Chapter 7)? Or can our agricultural systems successfully feed more than 6 billion people?

In trying to answer these questions, we face a paradox. Today, some 850 million people are malnourished, some

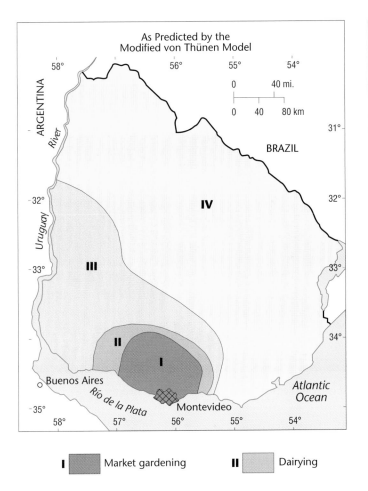

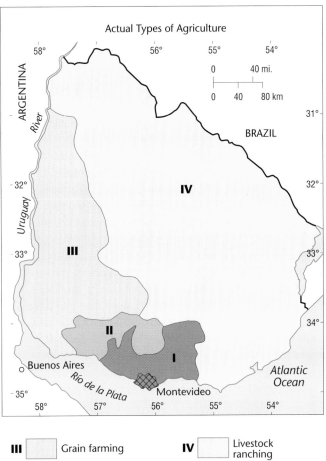

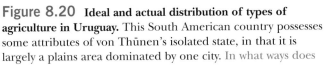

Figure 8.20 **Ideal and actual distribution of types of agriculture in Uruguay.** This South American country possesses some attributes of von Thünen's isolated state, in that it is largely a plains area dominated by one city. In what ways does the spatial pattern of Uruguayan agriculture conform to von Thünen's model? How is it different? What might cause the anomalies? (For the answers, see Griffin, 1973.)

to the point of starvation. Almost every year we read of famines, usually in an African country. Yet—and this would astound Malthus—food production has grown more rapidly than the world population over the past 40 or 50 years. Per capita, more food is available today than in 1950, when only about half as many people lived on Earth.

Cultural interaction helps explain these startling facts. If the world food supply is sufficient to feed everyone and yet hunger afflicts one of every six or seven persons, then some cultural or social factors must be responsible. Ultimately poverty and politics, not food shortage, cause hunger. Many Third World countries do not grow enough food to feed their populations, and they cannot afford to purchase enough imported food to make up the difference. As a result, famines can occur even when plenty of food is available. Irish starved by the millions in the 1840s while adjacent Britain possessed enough surplus food to have prevented this catastrophe. Bangladesh suffered a major famine in 1974, a year of record agricultural surpluses in the world.

Even when major efforts are made to send food from wealthy countries to famine-stricken areas, the poor transportation infrastructure of Third World countries often prevents effective distribution. Political instability can disrupt food shipments, and the donated food often falls into the hands of corrupt local officials. So while the immediate causes of famine may be environmental, the failure to relieve hunger has a political and cultural explanation.

Globalization

The process of *globalization* and its impact on agriculture has been referred to throughout this chapter. Such references have frequently been accompanied by the term *agribusiness* (see Culture in a Globalizing World). The theme of cultural interaction allows us to draw these references together.

Globalization, you will recall, involves the restructuring of the world economy by multinational corporations thriving in an era of free-trade capitalism, rapid communications,

CULTURE IN A GLOBALIZING WORLD

The Global Chicken

American dietary culture underwent fundamental changes during the post–World War II period, none more dramatic than the shift from beef to poultry as the preferred protein source. From 1945 to 1995, per capita consumption of chicken in the United States rose from 5 to 70 pounds (2.25 to 31.5 kilograms) and by 1990 surpassed that of beef. This is a startling development in American culture, where the myth of the cowboy herding cattle on the open range has been so central to an imaged national identity. Since the 1990s, the per capita consumption of chicken has continued to grow as that of beef continues to decline, especially since the rise in publicity about mad cow disease

Where does all this new poultry production come from, and where are the sites of consumption? Advances in U.S. agrotechnologies for the breeding, nutrition, housing, and processing of chickens largely account for increases in production efficiency. This has allowed the U.S. poultry industry, largely centered in the South, to become the world's single largest supplier of broilers. As the taste for chicken spread worldwide, U.S. producers were positioned to gain increasing shares of an expanding market. From 1980 to 2002, world trade in broilers grew nearly 500 percent, while the U.S. share of that trade rose from 22.2 to 46.1 percent. China has been the hottest import market because rising affluence there has led to increasing per capita consumption. At the same time, China is increasing its production *and* its exports of poultry. It is likely to become a major competitor with the United States for access to other Asian markets.

The story of the global chicken gets more interesting if we look more closely at cultural food preferences. There is a peculiarity and a particularity to the culture of chicken consumption in the United States—an overwhelming preference for breast meat. This cultural predilection greatly influences what the importing countries eat, since the remainder of the chicken cannot simply be thrown away. Hence 87 percent of U.S. exports in 2000 were in the form of frozen cuts, 40 percent of which were leg quarters.

(Robert Nickelsburg/Time Life Pictures/Getty Images.)

The growing power and reach of multinational corporations is a hallmark of globalization, no less so in food production and consumption than for other economic sectors. Farmers who produce a single commodity, such as poultry, must produce far more than the local market can consume in order to be profitable. Thus, they must sell in national and global markets, access to which requires a dependence on multinational agribusinesses. So pervasive is the reach of agribusiness that many poultry farmers no longer own the chickens they produce; multinational corporations do. Farmers contract with multinationals to receive chicks, feed, transport, and other inputs. When the chickens mature, they are trucked to the contracting corporation's processing plant, where they are weighed and the cost of inputs deducted from the farmers' shares. The farmers take their earnings to pay the mortgages on their lands and buildings, and the chickens are processed for the global food system.

From Boyd and Watts, 1997; Norberg-Hodge, Merrifield, and Gorelick, 2002; U.S. Department of Agriculture.

---

improved transport, and computer-based information systems. When applied to agriculture, the globalization process tends to produce *agribusiness*—the totally commercial, large-scale, mechanized, chemical-dependent, hybrid-using, genetically engineered, and **monocultural** (raising a single specialty crop on vast tracts) modern farming system. The green revolution is part of agricultural globalization, as are countless "rural development" projects in Third World countries, usually funded by the World Bank or the International Monetary Fund. These projects typically displace *peasant* farmers to make way for agribusinesses. The family-run farm is one victim of agricultural globalization.

Multinational corporations are largely responsible. The five biggest hybrid vegetable seed suppliers control 75 percent of the global market, and the ten largest agrochemical manufacturers command 85 percent of the world supply. Four corporations supply more than two-thirds of the U.S. consumption of hybrid seed maize. Sometimes single companies—Monsanto, for example—both supply the seeds and manufacture the pesticides. What's more, the genetic engineering of seed is also often done in-house. This arrangement allows Monsanto to genetically engineer "Roundup Ready" seed varieties. Roundup is an herbicide manufactured by Monsanto, and their Roundup Ready gene builds in greater tolerance to higher doses. The seeds essentially became vehicles to sell more herbicide.

Genetically modified (GM) crops, the products of biotechnology, are seen by many as another aspect of globalization. Genetic engineering produces new organisms through gene splicing. Pieces of DNA are recombined with the DNA of other organisms to produce new properties, such as pesticide tolerance or disease resistance. DNA can be transferred not only between species but also between plants and animals, which makes this technology truly revolutionary and unlike any other developments since the beginning of domestication. Agribusinesses are able to patent the processes and resulting genetically engineered organisms and thus claim legal ownership of new life-forms.

Commercial production of GM crops began in the United States in 1996. The technology has now spread around the globe, but the United States still dominates, accounting for two-thirds of the world's production. Two crops, soybeans and corn, account for the rapid growth of GM food production in the United States. By 2004, 85 percent of all soybeans and 45 percent of all corn produced in the United States were genetically modified. A glance at a world map of consumption and production of GM crops verifies their rapid spread (Figure 8.21).

If you provision your household from a U.S. supermarket, you have undoubtedly ingested GM foods. Whether or

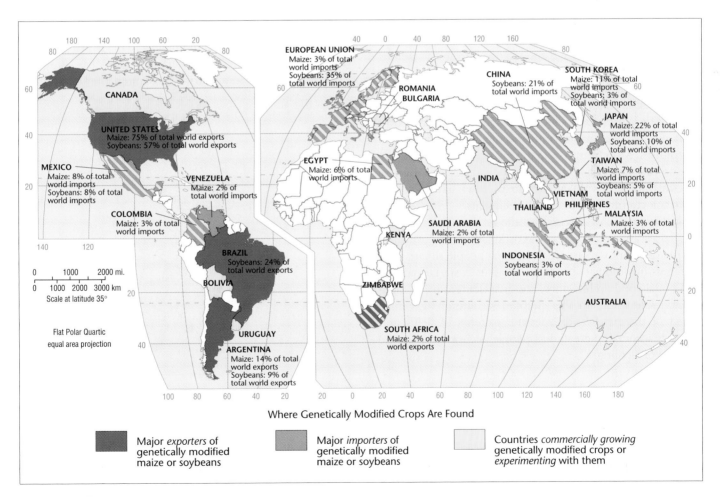

Figure 8.21 **Worldwide use of genetically altered crop plants, especially maize and soybeans.** This diffusion has occurred despite warnings from many ecologists and geneticists. What problems might arise? *(Sources: National Corn Growers Association; U.S. Department of Agriculture.)*

not one finds this troubling is strongly related to the strength of certain cultural norms and values that vary from region to region and country to country. The public's response to GM foods has differed considerably depending on the cultural context. In England and western Europe, where national identities are strongly linked to the countryside and its agrarian culture, there has been a great deal of activism against biotechnology in agriculture. In response to public pressure, major supermarket chains, such as Sainsbury's in England, have refused to sell GM foods since 1998. In the United States, the response has been far more muted, so much so that the expansion of GM crop planting has proceeded virtually without public debate. These cultural differences are now coming to the fore of globalization debates as the European Union challenges the United States over international trade in GM seeds and foods.

 Agricultural Landscapes

What is the agricultural component of the cultural landscape? What might we learn about agriculture by examining its unique landscape? A great part of the world's land area is cultivated or pastured. In this huge area, the visible imprint of humankind might best be called the **agricultural landscape**. The agricultural landscape often varies even over short distances, telling us much about local cultures and subcultures. Moreover, it remains in many respects a window on the past, and archaic features abound. For this reason, the traditional rural landscape can teach us a great deal about the cultural heritage of its occupants.

In Chapter 7, we discussed some aspects of the agricultural landscape, in particular the rural settlement forms. We saw the different ways in which farming people situate their dwellings in various cultures. In Chapter 2, we considered traditional rural architecture, another element in the agricultural landscape. In this chapter, we attend to a third aspect of the rural landscape: the patterns of fields and property ownership created as people occupy land for the purpose of farming.

Survey, Cadastral, and Field Patterns

A **cadastral pattern** is one that describes property-ownership lines, whereas a *field pattern* reflects the way that a farmer subdivides land for agricultural use. Both can be greatly influenced by **survey patterns,** the lines laid out by surveyors prior to the settlement of an area. Major regional contrasts exist in survey, cadastral, and field patterns, for example, *unit-block*

versus *fragmented landholding* and regular, geometric survey lines versus irregular or unsurveyed property lines.

Fragmented farms are the rule rather than the exception in the Eastern Hemisphere. Under this system, farmers live in farm villages or smaller **hamlets.** Their landholdings lie splintered into many separate fields situated at varying distances and lying in various directions from the settlement. One farm can consist of 100 or more separate, tiny parcels of land (Figure 8.22). The individual plots may be roughly rectangular in shape, as in Asia and southern Europe, or they may lie in narrow strips. The latter pattern is most common in Europe, where farmers traditionally worked with a bulky plow that was difficult to turn. The origins of the fragmented farm system go back to an early period of peasant communalism. One of its initial justifications was a desire for peasant equality. Each farmer in the village needed land of varying soil composition and terrain. Travel distance from the village was to be equalized. From the rice paddies of Japan and India to the fields of western Europe, the fragmented holding remains a prominent feature of the cultural landscape.

Unit-block farms, by contrast, are those in which all of the farmer's property is contained in a single, contiguous piece of land. Such forms are found mainly in the overseas area of European settlement, particularly the Americas, Australia, New Zealand, and South Africa. Most often, they reveal a reg-

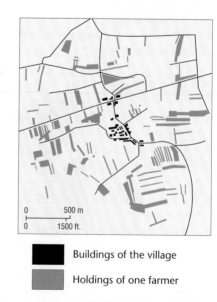

Buildings of the village

Holdings of one farmer

Figure 8.22 Fragmented landholdings surround a French farm village. The numerous fields and plots belonging to one individual farmer are shaded. Such fragmented farms remain common in many parts of Europe and Asia. What are the advantages and disadvantages of this system? *(After Demangeon, 1946.)*

The American *township and range system*, discussed in Chapter 6, first appeared after the Revolutionary War as an orderly method for parceling out federally owned land for sale to pioneers. It imposed a rigid, square, graph-paper pattern on much of the American countryside; geometry triumphed over physical geography. Similarly, roads follow section and township lines, adding to the checkerboard character of the American agricultural landscape. Canada adopted an almost identical survey system, which is particularly evident in the Prairie Provinces (Figure 8.24).

REFLECTING ON GEOGRAPHY

What advantages does the checkerboarded North American rural landscape offer? What disadvantages?

Equally striking in appearance are *long-lot* farms, where the landholding consists of a long, narrow unit-block stretching back from a road, river, or canal (Figure 8.25). Rather than occurring singly, long-lots lie grouped in rows, allowing this cadastral survey pattern to dominate entire districts. Long-lots occur widely in the hills and marshes of central and western Europe, in parts of Brazil and Argentina, along the rivers of French-settled Québec and southern Louisiana, and in parts of Texas and northern New Mexico.

Figure 8.23 **American township and range survey creates a checkerboard** in the Imperial Valley of California, a human mosaic indeed. *(Courtesy of Terry G. Jordan-Bychkov.)*

ular, geometric land survey. The checkerboard of farm fields in the rectangular survey areas of the United States provides a good example of this cadastral pattern (Figure 8.23).

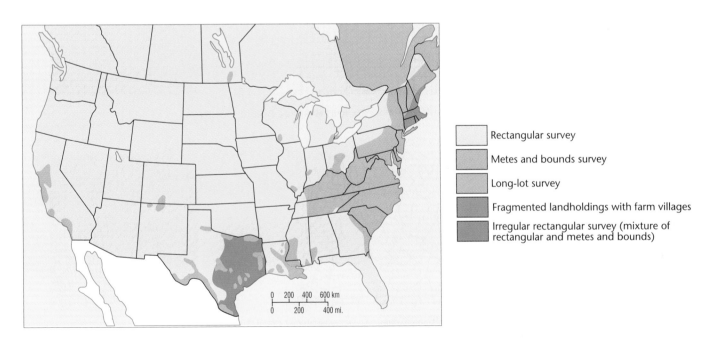

Figure 8.24 **Original land-survey patterns in the United States and southern Canada.** The cadastral patterns still retain the imprint of the various original survey types. What impact on rural life might the different patterns have? The map is necessarily generalized, and many local exceptions exist.

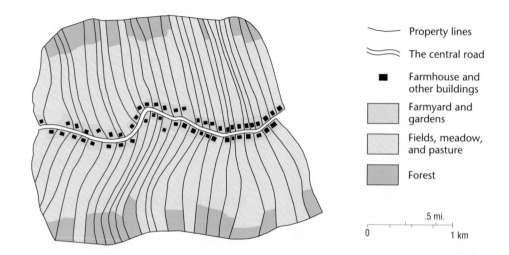

Legend:
— Property lines
≋ The central road
■ Farmhouse and other buildings
▢ Farmyard and gardens
▢ Fields, meadow, and pasture
▨ Forest

.5 mi.
0   1 km

Figure 8.25 **A long-lot settlement in the hills of central Germany.** Each property consists of an elongated unit-block of land stretching back from the road in the valley to an adjacent ridgecrest, part of which remains wooded.

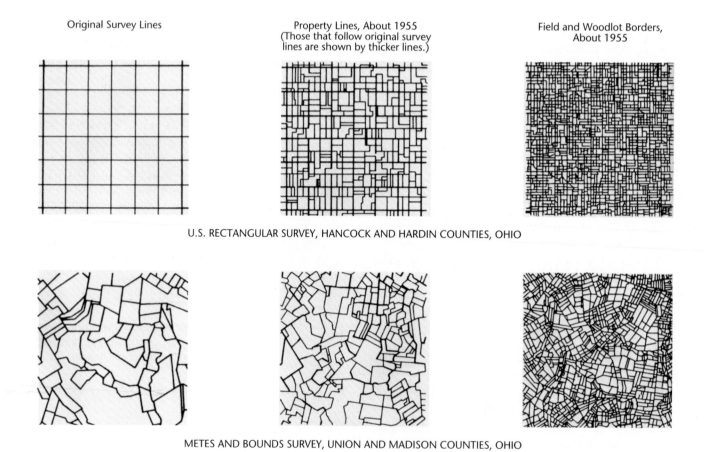

Original Survey Lines

Property Lines, About 1955 (Those that follow original survey lines are shown by thicker lines.)

Field and Woodlot Borders, About 1955

U.S. RECTANGULAR SURVEY, HANCOCK AND HARDIN COUNTIES, OHIO

METES AND BOUNDS SURVEY, UNION AND MADISON COUNTIES, OHIO

Figure 8.26 **Two contrasting land-survey patterns, rectangular and metes and bounds.** Both types were used in an area of west-central Ohio. Note the impact these survey patterns had on modern cadastral and field patterns. What other features of the cultural landscape might be influenced by these patterns? *(After Thrower, 1966: 40, 63, 84.)*

Figure 8.27 Traditional fence in the mountains of Papua New Guinea. The fence is designed to keep pigs out of sweet potato gardens. The modern age has had an impact, as revealed in the use of tin cans to decorate and stabilize the fence. Each culture has its own fence types, adding another distinctive element to the agricultural landscape. *(Courtesy of Terry G. Jordan-Bychkov.)*

These unit-block farms are elongated because such a layout provides each farmer with fertile valley land, water, and access to transportation facilities, either roads or rivers. In French America, long-lots appear in rows along streams because waterways provided the chief means of transport in colonial times. In the hill lands of central Europe, a road along the valley floor provides the focus, and long-lots reach back from the road to the adjacent ridgecrests.

Some unit-block farms have irregular shapes rather than the rectangular or long-lot patterns. Most of these result from *metes and bounds* surveying, which makes much use of natural features such as trees, boulders, and streams. Parts of the eastern United States were surveyed under the metes and bounds system, with the result that farms there are much less regular in outline than those where rectangular survey was used. The juncture of the two survey systems is quite apparent from an airplane (Figure 8.26).

Fencing and Hedging

Property and field borders are often marked by fences or hedges, heightening the visibility of these lines in the agricultural landscape. Open-field areas, where the dominance of crop raising and the careful tending of livestock make fences unnecessary, still prevail in much of western Europe, India, Japan, and some other parts of the Eastern Hemisphere, but much of the remainder of the world's agricultural lands is enclosed.

Fences and hedges add a distinctive touch to the cultural landscape (Figure 8.27). Different cultures have their own methods and ways of enclosing land, so that types of fences and hedges can be linked to particular groups. Fences in different parts of the world are made of substances as diverse as steel wire, logs, poles, split rails, brush, rock, and earth. Those who visit rural New England, western Ireland, or Yucatán may retain a visual memory of the mile upon mile of stone fence that typifies those landscapes. Barbed-wire fences swept across the American countryside a century ago, but some remnants of older types can still be seen. In Appalachia, the traditional split-rail zigzag fence of pioneer times survives here and there. As do most visible features of culture, fence types can serve as indicators of cultural diffusion.

The hedge is a living fence. Few who have visited the mazelike hedgerow country of Brittany and Normandy in France or large areas of Great Britain and Ireland fail to perceive these living fences as a major aspect of the rural landscape. To walk or drive the roads of hedgerow country is to experience a unique feeling of confinement quite different from the openness of barbed wire or unenclosed landscapes.

Conclusion

We have seen that the ancient and honored form of livelihood called agriculture varies markedly from region to region, reflected in formal agro-regions, and that we can better understand this complicated pattern through the themes of agro-ecology, diffusion, cultural interaction, and agricultural landscape. Once again we have seen the interwoven character of the five themes of cultural geography. In many fundamental ways, the agricultural revolution changed humankind. In equally dramatic fashion, the industrial revolution sparked further changes. We will use the five themes to guide an exploration of the industrial world in the next chapter.

DOING GEOGRAPHY

The Global Geography of Food

For most of history, people obtained the food they needed either by growing it themselves or by procuring it directly from farmers who lived nearby. The choice and availability of food were limited and changed seasonally. About 100 years ago, this situation began to change dramatically as the pace of urbanization and industrialization accelerated. Today, very few people in developed countries know where the food they eat was produced or who produced it. Fewer still grow any of the food that they consume. Yet one can walk into a supermarket and find aisles full of fresh produce, meat, fish, and a variety of grain-based products any day of the year, regardless of the season or proximity to farms.

Where does this food come from? Who produces and sells it? Your task for this exercise is to find out. This exercise can be organized as a group or individual project. As a group project, people can be assigned to research particular categories of food, such as meat and poultry, cereals and grains, fruits and vegetables, and dairy products. As an individual project, you should begin with a typical day's meals and identify all the ingredients (don't forget the seasonings and cooking oils used in preparation).

The project starts at the food markets where you usually shop. For much of the information you will need, you can refer to the labels on the food items. For some items, such as fish, poultry, and meat, you may need to speak to the butcher or store manager. Find out, as specifically as possible, where the food item was produced. Find out the name of the company that marketed the product and, if available, the name of the parent company.

Once you have this basic information, you will need to head to the library and perhaps log on to the Internet to do further research. The first task is to organize a list of companies and the food products they market. The second is to locate the geographic origins of the food products. Now look for patterns. Which and how many companies are involved? What proportion of the food supply does each control? What proportion and which kinds of food are produced in other countries? Can you trace the movement of particular food commodities from the field to the dining table? Do certain kinds of foods tend to be produced closer to the market than others? Do certain kinds of food tend more than others to be marketed by large corporations? Can you think of explanations for the patterns you identify?

Finally, you can take this investigation to a greater depth. Can you determine from your research what the conditions are where the food is produced? For example, what landscape changes occur when regions begin producing for the global food system? How is production structured? Is it organized into large corporate plantations or small peasant farm plots? Are there ethical dilemmas involved in the production, processing, or transportation of some food commodities? For example, what are the conditions for workers? Have concerns over the treatment of animals been raised? These are just a few of the many questions we can investigate to help us understand how our cultural food preferences are linked to agricultural landscapes and culture regions around the world.

Agricultural Geography
on the Internet

You can learn more about agricultural geography in the Internet at the following web sites:

Agriculture, Food, and Human Values (AFHVS)
http://web.clas.ufl.edu/users/rhaynes/afhvs/
Founded in 1987, AFHVS promotes interdisciplinary research and scholarship in the broad areas of agriculture and rural studies. The organization sponsors an annual meeting and publishes a journal by the same name.

Food First
http://www.foodfirst.org/
Founded in 1975 by author-activist Francis Moore Lappé, Food First is a nonprofit, "people's" think tank and clearinghouse for information and political action. Formally named the Institute for Food and Development Policy, the organization highlights root causes and value-based solutions to hunger and poverty around the world, with a commitment to establishing food as a fundamental human right.

International Food Policy Research Institute, Washington, D.C.
http://www.ifpri.cgiar.org
Learn about strategies for more efficient planning for world food supplies and enhanced food production from a group concerned with hunger and malnutrition. Part of this site deals with domesticated plant biodiversity.

United Nations Food and Agriculture Organization (FAO), Rome, Italy
http://www.fao.org/
Discover an agency that focuses on expanding world food production and spreading new techniques for improving agriculture as it strives to predict, avert, or minimize famines.

United States Department of Agriculture, Washington, D.C.
http://www.usda.gov/
Look up a wealth of statistics about American farming from the principal federal regulatory and planning agency dealing with agriculture.

Urban Agriculture Notes
http://www.cityfarmer.org
This is the site of Canada's Office of Urban Agriculture. Urban agriculture is a new and growing field that is not yet completely defined even by those closest to it. It concerns itself with all manner of subjects from rooftop gardens to composting toilets to air pollution and community development. It encompasses mental and physical health, entertainment, building codes, rats, fruit trees, herbs, recipes, and much more.

World Bank Group, Washington, D.C.
http://www.worldbank.org
Read about an agency that provides development funds to countries, particularly economically distressed regions. It is a driving force behind globalization and agribusiness.

Worldwatch Institute
http://www.worldwatch.org/
Learn about a privately financed organization focused on long-range trends, particularly food supply, population growth, and ecological deterioration.

Sources

Andrews, Jean. 1993. "Diffusion of Mesoamerican Food Complex to Southeastern Europe." *Geographical Review* 83: 194–204.

Binns, T. 1990. "Is Desertification a Myth?" *Geography* 75: 106–113.

Bowden, Leonard W. 1965. *Diffusion of the Decision to Irrigate.* Department of Geography, Research Paper No. 97. Chicago: University of Chicago.

Boyd, William, and Michael Watts. 1997. "Agroindustrial Just-In-Time: The Chicken Industry and Postwar American Capitalism," in Watts, M. and D. Goodman (eds.), *Globalizing Food: Agrarian Questions and Global Restructuring.* London: Routledge, 192–225.

Carney, Judith. 2001. *Black Rice: The African Origins of Rice Cultivation in the Americas.* Cambridge, Mass.: Harvard University Press.

Carr, Claudia J. 1977. *Pastoralism in Crisis: The Dasanetch and Their Ethiopian Lands.* Department of Geography, Research Paper No. 180. Chicago: University of Chicago.

Chakravarti, A. K. 1973. "Green Revolution in India." *Annals of the Association of American Geographers* 63: 319–330.

Chuan-jun, Wu (ed.). 1979. "China Land Utilization." Map. Beijing: Institute of Geography of the Academica Sinica.

Cowan, C. Wesley, and Patty J. Watson (eds.). 1992. *The Origins of Agriculture: An International Perspective.* Washington, D.C.: Smithsonian Institution Press.

Cross, John A. 1994. "Agroclimatic Hazards and Farming in Wisconsin." *Geographical Review* 84: 277–289.

Darby, H. Clifford. 1956. "The Clearing of the Woodland in Europe," in William L. Thomas, Jr. (ed.), *Man's Role in Changing the Face of the Earth.* Chicago: University of Chicago Press, 183–216.

Demangeon, Albert. 1946. *La France.* Paris: Armand Colin.

Diamond, J. 1999. *Guns, Germs, and Steel: The Fates of Human Societies.* New York: W.W. Norton.

Ewald, Ursula. 1977. "The von Thünen Principle and Agricultural Zonation in Colonial Mexico." *Journal of Historical Geography* 3: 123–133.

Freidberg, S. 2001. "Gardening on the Edge: The Conditions of Unsustainability on an African Urban Periphery." *Annals of the Association of American Geographers* 91(2): 349–369.

Griffin, Ernst. 1973. "Testing the von Thünen Theory in Uruguay." *Geographical Review* 63: 500–516.

Grigg, David B. 1969. "The Agricultural Regions of the World: Review and Reflections." *Economic Geography* 45: 95–132.

Griliches, Zvi. 1960. "Hybrid Corn and the Economics of Innovation." *Science* 132 (July 26): 275–280.

Hardy, Thomas. 1891. *Tess of the d'Urbervilles.* New York: Harper & Brothers.

Hewes, Lewlie. 1973. *The Suitcase Farming Frontier: A Study in the Historical Geography of the Central Great Plains.* Lincoln: University of Nebraska Press.

Hidore, John J. 1963. "Relationship Between Cash Grain Farming and Landforms." *Economic Geography* 39: 84–89.

Horvath, Ronald J. 1969. "Von Thünen's Isolated State and the Area Around Addis Ababa, Ethiopia." *Annals of the Association of American Geographers* 59: 308–323.

Johannessen, Carl L. 1966. "The Domestication Processes in Trees Reproduced by Seed: The Pejibaye Palm in Costa Rica." *Geographical Review* 56: 363–376.

Kenzer, Martin S. (ed.). 1987. *Carl O. Sauer: A Tribute.* Corvallis: Oregon State University.

Leighly, John. 1987. "Ecology as Metaphor: Carl Sauer and Human Ecology." *Professional Geographer* 39: 405–412.

Meitzen, August. 1895. *Siedelung und Agrarwesen der Westgermanen und Ostgermanen, der Kelten, Römer, Finnen und Slawen.* 3 vols. plus atlas. Berlin: Wilhelm Hertz.

Murphey, Rhoads. 1951. "The Decline of North Africa Since the Roman Occupation: Climatic or Human?" *Annals of the Association of American Geographers* 41: 116–131.

Nettelbeck, Joachim. 1910. *Ein Mann: Des Seefahrers und aufrechten Bürgers Joachim Nettelbeck Lebensgeschichte von ihm selbsterzählt.* Ebenhausen bei Munich: Wilhelm Langewiesche-Brandt.

Norberg-Hodge, Helena, Todd Merrifield, and Steven Gorelick. 2002. *Bringing the Food Economy Home: Local Alternatives to Global Agribusiness.* London: Zed.

Popper, Deborah E., and Frank Popper. 1987. "The Great Plains: From Dust to Dust." *Planning* 53(12): 12–18.

Saarinen, Thomas F. 1966. *Perception of Drought Hazard on the Great Plains.* Department of Geography, Research Paper No. 106. Chicago: University of Chicago.

Saitoti, T. O. 1980. *Maasai.* New York: Abrams.

Sauer, Carl O. 1952. *Agricultural Origins and Dispersals.* New York: American Geographical Society.

Sauer, Jonathan D. 1993. *Historical Geography of Crop Plants.* Boca Raton, Fla.: CRC Press.

Thomas, David S. G. 1993. "Sandstorm in a Teacup? Understanding Desertification." *Geographical Journal* 159(3): 318–331.

Thomas, David S. G., and Nicholas J. Middleton. 1994. *Desertification: Exploding the Myth.* New York: John Wiley.

Thrower, Norman J. W. 1966. *Original Survey and Land Subdivision.* Chicago: Rand McNally.

SEEING GEOGRAPHY

What differences can you "read" in these landscapes and how do you explain them? How accurately can you determine their locations?

Reading Agricultural Landscapes

Let us take a careful look at each photo and systemically identify the differences in each, beginning with the one on the left. The most striking aspect of this aerial landscape shot is the abrupt division between the cultivated land at the top and the noncultivated land at the bottom. Looking closely, we see that an irrigation channel forms the boundary between the two. A second prominent feature of the landscape is the checkerboard pattern of the fields and the straight roads forming their boundaries. Other details emerge as you look more closely. For example,

Two types of contemporary agricultural landscapes.

the settlement pattern consists of isolated, sparsely arranged farmsteads separated by large expanses of cultivated fields. You might also note that the uncultivated land is brown and treeless and that trees in the cultivated portion are found only along the watercourses.

The landscape features in the photo on the right are nearly the opposite of those in the one on the left. Here settlement is clustered in a densely populated village centered on a church and town square. The fields are of irregular size and shape and form a band of cultivated land around the concentrations of houses, some of which are built of stone. There is no clear evidence of irrigation. Trees and shrubs are concentrated in the outermost band but also occur throughout the landscape, which overall appears verdant.

Putting all these visual clues together leads us to conclude that the landscape on the left must be somewhere in the western United States. We know this region was surveyed and settled under the township and range system, which explains the isolated farmsteads and checkerboard pattern. We also know that much of the western United States is arid or semiarid, which explains the need for irrigation and the general lack of trees and green vegetation in the bottom half of the photo. In fact, it is in Mack, Colorado, where irrigation meets the desert. The landscape on the right is probably located in Europe. The large church in the center and dense cluster of houses suggest the settlement pattern of a historical market town. The irregular fields and their close proximity to the town are explained by deep historical patterns of land ownership and the reliance on foot travel in preindustrial agriculture. The verdant landscape and absence of irrigation suggest the temperate climate characteristic of western Europe. In fact it is the vineyard region of Saône-et-Loire, France. ∎

Vogeler, Ingolf. 1981. *The Myth of the Family Farm: Agribusiness Dominance of United States Agriculture.* Boulder, Colo.: Westview Press.

von Thünen, Johann Heinrich. 1966. *Von Thünen's Isolierte Staat: An English Edition of Der Isolierte Staat.* Carla M. Wartenberg (trans.). Elmsford, N.Y.: Pergamon Press.

Walsh, Richard J. (ed.). 1948. *The Adventures of Marco Polo, as Dictated in Prison to a Scribe in the Year 1298; What He Experienced and Heard During His Twenty-Four Years Spent in Travel Through Asia and at the Court of Kublai-Khan.* New York: John Day.

Whittlesey, Derwent S. 1936. "Major Agricultural Regions of the Earth." *Annals of the Association of American Geographers* 26: 199–240.

Wilken, Gene C. 1987. *Good Farmers: Traditional Agricultural and Resource Management in Mexico and Central America.* Berkeley: University of California Press.

Zimmerer, Karl. 1996. *Changing Fortunes: Biodiversity and Peasant Livelihood in the Peruvian Andes.* Berkeley: University of California Press.

Ten Recommended Books
on Agricultural Geography

(For additional suggested readings, see *The Human Mosaic* web site: www.whfreeman.com/jordan)

Galaty, John G., and Douglas L. Johnson (eds.). 1990. *The World of Pastoralism: Herding Systems in Comparative Perspective.* New York: Guilford Press. A multidisciplinary collection of essays spanning five continents that analyzes the productivity of different animal herding practices and their contributions to herding societies.

Grigg, David B. 1995. *An Introduction to Agricultural Geography,* 2nd ed. London: Routledge. A comprehensive introduction to the human and environmental factors that influence how agriculture and agricultural practices differ from place to place.

Hart, John Fraser. 1998. *The Rural Landscape.* Baltimore: Johns Hopkins University Press. A synthesis of Hart's work on America's rural landscape that illustrates and explains a wide array of rural landscape elements, including coal mines, fences, barns, and resort towns.

Ilbery, Brian, Quentin Chiotti, and Timothy Rickard (eds.). 1997. *Agricultural Restructuring and Sustainability: A Geographical Perspective.* Wallingford, U.K.: C. A. B. International. A selection of papers dealing with agricultural restructuring and sustainability delivered at a conference of rural geographers from Canada, the United Kingdom, the United States, and New Zealand.

Jordan, Bella Bychkova, and Terry G. Jordan-Bychkov. 2001. *Siberian Village: Land and Life in the Sakha Republic.* Minneapolis: University of Minnesota Press. An account of an agricultural way of life in the far north, on the very outermost limits of the farming world near the Arctic Circle, among a remarkable Turkic people.

Middleton, Nick, and David S. G. Thomas (eds.). 1997. *World Atlas of Desertification,* 2nd ed. London: Arnold. Look at the cartographic evidence and decide for yourself whether the deserts of the world are enlarging at the expense of agricultural lands.

Sachs, Carolyn E. 1996. *Gendered Fields: Rural Women, Agriculture, and Environment.* Boulder, Colo.: Westview Press. An exploration of the commonalities and differences in rural women's experiences and their strategies for dealing with the challenges and opportunities of rural living.

Sauer, Carl O. 1969. *Seeds, Spades, Hearths, and Herds.* Cambridge, Mass.: MIT Press. The renowned American cultural geographer presents his theories on the origins of plant and animal domestication—the beginnings of agriculture.

Turner, B. L., II, and Stephen B. Brush (eds.). 1987. *Comparative Farming Systems.* New York: Guilford Press. An interdisciplinary collection of essays that integrates socioeconomic, political, environmental, and technical elements of farming systems in Latin America, Anglo-America, Africa, Asia, and Europe.

Watts, M., and D. Goodman (eds). 1997. *Globalizing Food: Agrarian Questions and Global Restructuring.* London: Routledge. This edited volume, containing primarily the work of geographers, analyzes globalization and the biotechnological revolution in agriculture.

Journals
in Agricultural Geography

Agriculture and Human Values. An interdisciplinary journal dedicated to the study of ethical questions surrounding agricultural practices and food. Published by Kluwer. Volume 1 appeared in 1984. Visit the home page of the journal at http://www.kluweronline.com/issn/0889–048X/current.

Journal of Rural Studies. An international interdisciplinary journal ranked as the best of its kind. Published by Pergamon, an imprint of Elsevier Science, Amsterdam, the Netherlands. Volume 1 appeared in 1985. Visit the home page of the journal at http://www.elsevier.nl/locate/jrurstud.

*How is this Chinese landscape connected to the Wal-Mart
located in your neighborhood?*

Buildings that house a set of shoe factories in Guangdong Province, China.
(Courtesy of Charles Cowles Gallery, New York, & Robert Koch Gallery, San Francisco.)
Turn to Seeing Geography on page 328 for an in-depth analysis of the above question.

9 INDUSTRIES
A Faustian Bargain

Faust was a sorcerer/scholar who lived some 500 years ago. His life has been immortalized in numerous dramas, operas, legends, and biographies—most famously by the great German writer Goethe. Faust sought both an understanding of the universe and the pleasures of the flesh. Frustrated by his own limitations, he made a pact with the devil, selling his soul for knowledge and pleasure.

Modern society long ago made its own Faustian bargain: to give up both the difficulties and the advantages of the ancient rural way of life to achieve, at what turned out to be at great cost, the benefits of the industrial age. In effect, we laid waste to much of the Earth in order to live better. This Faustian bargain was made possible by the second of two great economic revolutions that have occurred in the development of culture. The first of these, the domestication of plants and animals, occurred in our prehistory. This agricultural revolution, discussed in Chapter 8, ultimately resulted in a large increase in human population, a greatly accelerated modification of the physical environment, and major cultural readjustments. The second of these upheavals, the **industrial revolution,** is still taking place. It involves a series of interrelated inventions that led to the use of machines and inanimate power in the manufacturing process and transportation. The industrial revolution, which began in the eighteenth century, released undreamed-of productive powers. Suddenly, whole societies could engage in the seemingly limitless multiplication of goods and services. Rapid bursts of human inventiveness followed, as did gigantic population increases and a massive, often unsettling, remodeling of the environment. The industrial revolution is still running its course today, though it is perhaps more accurate to speak of many industrial revolutions, since its effects are felt differently in different places around the world. Few lands remain untouched by its machines, factories, transportation devices, and communication techniques.

Almost every facet of our lives is affected in some way by industrial activity. On a Friday night out, you might drive in a car to a single outlet in a nationwide chain of restaurants, where you order fried chicken raised indoors several states away on special enriched grain, brought by refrigerated truck to a deep freeze, and cooked in an electric deepfryer. Later, at a movie, you buy a candy bar manufactured halfway across the country. Then you enjoy a series of machine-produced pictures that flash in front of your eyes so rapidly that they seem to be moving. Just about every object and event in your life is affected, if not actually created, by the industrial revolution. In this chapter, we examine and explain the cultural geographies of industrialization and its cultural ramifications.

 ## Industrial Regions

How can the theme of culture region be applied to industrial activity? Three types of industrial activity can be distinguished, with each occupying a distinct culture region. **Primary industries** involve extracting natural resources from the Earth. Fishing, hunting, lumbering, oil extraction, farming, and mining provide examples of primary industries (Figure 9.1). **Secondary industry** is the processing stage, commonly called manufacturing. Secondary industries process the raw materials extracted by primary industries, transforming them into more usable forms. Ore is converted into steel; logs are milled into lumber; fish are processed and canned. As a rule, several steps occur in manufacturing,

and each of these steps comprises its own industry. Many factories turn out products that serve as raw materials for other secondary industries. For example, steel mills provide steel for automobile factories, and lumber mills make building materials for construction companies, also a secondary industry. The third type of industrial activity involves **services** of some sort rather than the extraction or production of commodities. So wide is the range of services that some geographers find it useful to distinguish three different types: *transportation/communication services, producer services,* and *consumer services.*

Each of the three types of industrial activity displays unique spatial patterns. Applying the theme of culture region, geographers refer to these as industrial regions. Figure 9.2 reveals some of these patterns on a global scale.

Primary Industry

Primary industries extract both renewable and nonrenewable resources. **Renewable resources** are those that, with conscientious management, can be used without being permanently depleted. Examples include forests, water, fishing grounds, and agricultural land. Unfortunately, as the demand for the products of primary industries increases, overexploitation of renewable resources frequently causes their depletion or even elimination. The 1990s, for example, witnessed the beginning of a worldwide crisis in the oceanic fishing industry, as a result of overfishing. **Nonrenewable resources**—minerals and petroleum, for example—are those that are depleted when used. Most petroleum exports come from the Persian Gulf countries of southwestern Asia.

Figure 9.1 Oil field at sunset. Primary industries extract natural resources from the Earth. *(Bill Ross/Corbis.)*

Saudi Arabia and neighboring Persian Gulf states produce about 30 percent of the world's oil and possess an even larger share of the known petroleum reserves.

Secondary Industry

Until fairly recently, most of the world's manufacturing plants were clustered together in pockets within several regions, particularly Anglo-America, Europe, Russia, and Japan. In the United States, secondary industries once clustered mainly in the northeastern part of the country, a region referred to as the American Manufacturing Belt (Figure 9.3 on page 302). Across the Atlantic, manufacturing occupied the central core of Europe, which was surrounded by a less industrialized periphery (Figure 9.4 on page 303). Japan's industrial complex was located along the shore of the Inland Sea and throughout the southern part of the country.

Secondary industrial regions usually consist of several zones, each dominated by a particular kind of industry. This pronounced regional specialization occurs because different types of manufacturing activities find different locations more or less advantageous. For example, iron- and steel-processing plants tend to locate close to their mining source, given that transporting these primary materials is very expensive, while textile mills, which are heavily dependent on labor, tend to locate in areas that can supply inexpensive workers (for more on this topic, see the section on industrial cultural interaction). Over time, this development of specialized manufacturing regions led to a core-periphery pattern, where several regions contained the major industries, each drawing on the resources of the peripheral areas surrounding it to continue its industrial activity. Historically, this created the pattern described above, with manufacturing dominated by several key countries. Resources extracted from the peripheries flowed to the core, leading to the impoverishment of these peripheral areas. The resultant geographical pattern—one of the fundamental realities of our age—is often referred to as **uneven development** or regional disparity.

Although the manufacturing dominance of the developed countries persists, a major global geographical shift is currently under way. In virtually every core country, much of the secondary sector is in marked decline, especially traditional mass-production industries, such as steel making, that require a minimally skilled, blue-collar workforce. This decline was greatly accelerated by the oil shortages of the 1970s. In such districts, factories are closing and blue-collar unemployment rates are at the highest level since the Great Depression of the 1930s. In the United States, for example, where manufacturing employment began a relative decline around 1950, nine out of every ten new jobs in recent years have been low-paying service positions. The manufacturing industries surviving and now booming in the core countries

are mainly those requiring a highly skilled or artisanal workforce, such as high-tech firms and companies producing high-quality consumer goods. Because the blue-collar workforce has proved largely unable to acquire the new skills needed in such industries, many old manufacturing districts lapse into deep economic depression. Moreover, high-tech manufacturers employ far fewer workers than heavy industries and tend to be geographically concentrated in very small districts, sometimes called **technopoles** (see Figures 9.2, 9.3, and 9.4).

The word **deindustrialization** describes the decline and fall of once-prosperous factory and mining areas, such as the American Manufacturing Belt, now often called the Rust Belt (see Figure 9.3). Manufacturing industries lost by the core countries relocate to newly industrializing lands that were once the periphery. South Korea, Taiwan, Singapore, Brazil, Mexico, coastal China, and parts of India, among others, have experienced a major expansion of manufacturing. Companies move to these areas for many different reasons, including cheaper labor costs, lower environmental standards, and the relative proximity of these plants to their expanding markets outside the traditional core. This ongoing locational shift in manufacturing regions is largely the work of **transnational corporations.** One can no longer think of decisions about market location, labor supply, or other aspects of industrial planning within the framework of a single plant controlled by a single owner. Instead, we now deal with a highly complex international corporate structure that is able to coordinate spatially diffuse production, marketing, and management facilities. In other words, transnational corporations, many of which are headquartered in places like New York or London, locate their manufacturing plants in the most cost-efficient place, wherever that is around the world, and then ship their products to the places where they can be sold for the most profit.

An example is the automobile industry, one of the most multinational in sales and production. According to geographer Peter Dicken, both Ford and General Motors produce almost two-thirds of their cars (63.9 percent and 61.8 percent, respectively) outside the United States—most often in Europe but also in Canada, Mexico, and Brazil (Figure 9.5 on page 304). In comparison, the manufacturing facilities of the textile and garment industries are disproportionately located in China, which has a large pool of relatively low-wage workers and a government eager to offer incentives. Nearly 6 million workers in China are employed in the textile and garment industries, making it the country with the largest concentration of this type of employment, followed distantly by India, a country that employs about 1.5 million such workers. However, these aggregate statistics mask many of the differences in where and how certain types of garments are produced within the world markets. Much high-end, designer clothing tends to be produced in different

Industry Types

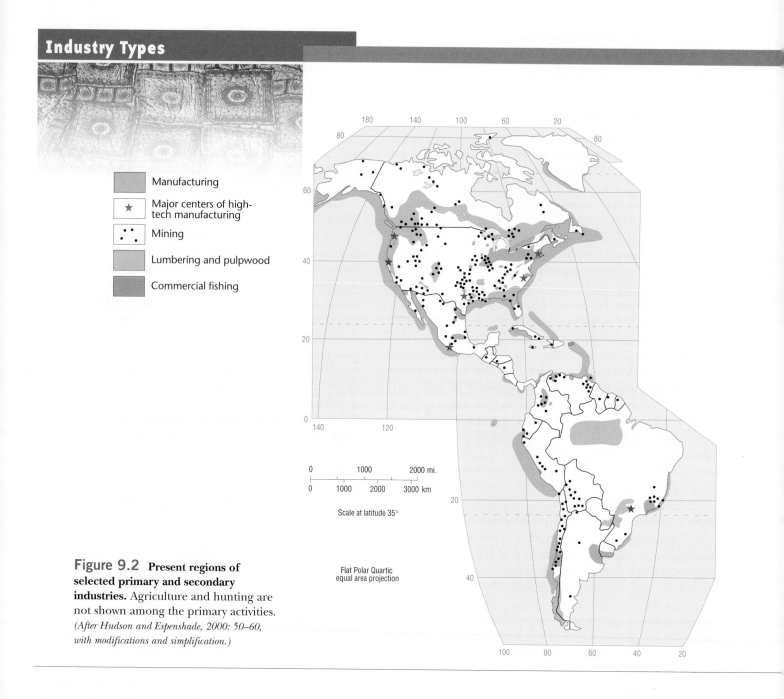

Manufacturing

★ Major centers of high-
tech manufacturing

Mining

Lumbering and pulpwood

Commercial fishing

0   1000   2000 mi.

0   1000   2000   3000 km

Scale at latitude 35°

Flat Polar Quartic
equal area projection

Figure 9.2 **Present regions of
selected primary and secondary
industries.** Agriculture and hunting are
not shown among the primary activities.
*(After Hudson and Espenshade, 2000: 50–60,
with modifications and simplification.)*

places and under different conditions from cheaper, mass-produced garments. The activity described in Doing Geography will help clarify and explain some of these distinctions within the complex global textile and garment industry. This is all part of the process of *globalization,* to which we have alluded frequently.

Service Industries

The decline of primary and secondary industries in the older developed core, or *deindustrialization,* has ushered in an era widely referred to as the **postindustrial phase.** Both

the United States and Canada are in the postindustrial era, as is most of Europe and Japan. In this postindustrial phase, service industries are most prevalent.

Transportation/communication services, part of both the industrial and postindustrial phases, include transportation, communication, and utility services. Highways, railroads, airlines, pipelines, telephones, radio, television, and the Internet are all referred to as "transportation/communication services." All facilitate the distribution of goods, services, and information. Modern industries require well-developed transport systems, and every industrial district is served by a network of such facilities. As one measure of the

importance of transport, Figure 9.6 on pages 304–305 maps the number of persons per automobile by country.

Major regional differences exist in the relative importance of the various modes of transport. In Russia and Ukraine, for example, highways have below-average industrial significance; instead, railroads—and to a lesser extent waterways—carry much of the transport load. Indeed, Russia still lacks a paved transcontinental highway. In the United States, by contrast, highways reign supreme, while the railroad system has declined. Western European nations rely heavily on a greater balance among rail, highway, and waterway transport. Meanwhile, electronic transfers of funds and telecom-

munications between computers continents apart add a new dimension and speed to the exchange of data and ideas.

Producer services are services required by producers of goods, such as insurance, legal services, banking, advertising, wholesaling, retailing, consulting, information generation, and real estate transactions. Such businesses represent one of the major growth sectors in postindustrial economies, and a geographical segregation has developed, in which manufacturing is increasingly shunted to the peripheries while corporate headquarters and the producer-related service activities remain, for the most part, in the core. Some of these producer service activities, however, are

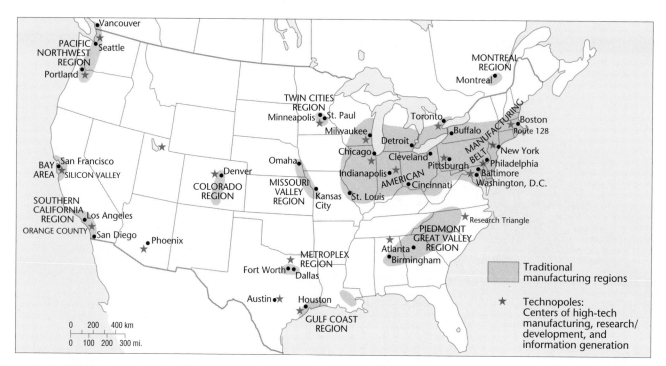

Figure 9.3 **Major regions of industry in Anglo-America.**
The largest and most important region is still the American Manufacturing Belt, the traditional industrial core of the United States. Dispersal of manufacturing to other regions occurred after World War II and now involves mainly high-tech and information-based enterprises, or technopoles. Why do high-tech industries have a distribution different from that of more traditional manufacturing?

now moving offshore, to such places as the Caribbean and India, to take advantage of educated but low-wage workers (see Culture in a Globalizing World on page 322). Nevertheless, the main control centers for these large companies are still located within the major cities of the West.

An inherent problem with this spatial arrangement is that it leads to more uneven development: global corporations invest in secondary industry in the peripheries, but profits flow back to the core, where the corporate headquarters are located. As early as 1965, American-based corporations took, on average, about four-fifths of their net profits out of Latin America in this way. As a result, the industrialization of less developed countries actually increases the power of the world's established industrial nations. Consequently, although industrial technology has spread everywhere, the basic industrial power of the planet is more centralized today than ever before. As we said earlier, global corporations are based mainly in several large cities in the older industrial regions—places like New York, Tokyo, and London (see section on world/global/globalizing cities in Chapter 10). Similarly, loans for industrial development come from banking institutions in Europe, Japan, and the United States, with the result that interest payments drain away from poor to rich countries.

Increasingly important in the producer service industries are the collection, generation, storage, retrieval, and process-ing of computerized knowledge and information, including research, publishing, consulting, and forecasting. The impact of computers is changing the world dramatically, a process that has accelerated since about 1970, with implications for the spatial organization of all human activities and each of the three industrial sectors. Many producer service businesses depend on a highly skilled, intelligent, creative, and imaginative labor force. Although information-generating activity is focused geographically in the old industrial core, the distribution of this activity, if viewed on a more local scale, can be seen to coalesce in technopoles around major universities and research centers. The presence of Stanford and the University of California at Berkeley, for example, helped make the San Francisco Bay Area a major center of such industry. Similar technopoles have developed near Harvard and MIT in New England and near the Raleigh–Durham–Chapel Hill "Research Triangle" of North Carolina (see Figure 9.3). These **high-tech corridors** (see section on new urban landscapes in Chapter 11)—or "silicon landscapes," as some have dubbed them—occupy relatively little area. In other words, the information economy is highly focused geographically, contributing to and heightening uneven development spatially. In Europe, for example, the emerging core of producer service industries is even more confined geographically than the earlier concentration of manufacturing (see Figure 9.4).

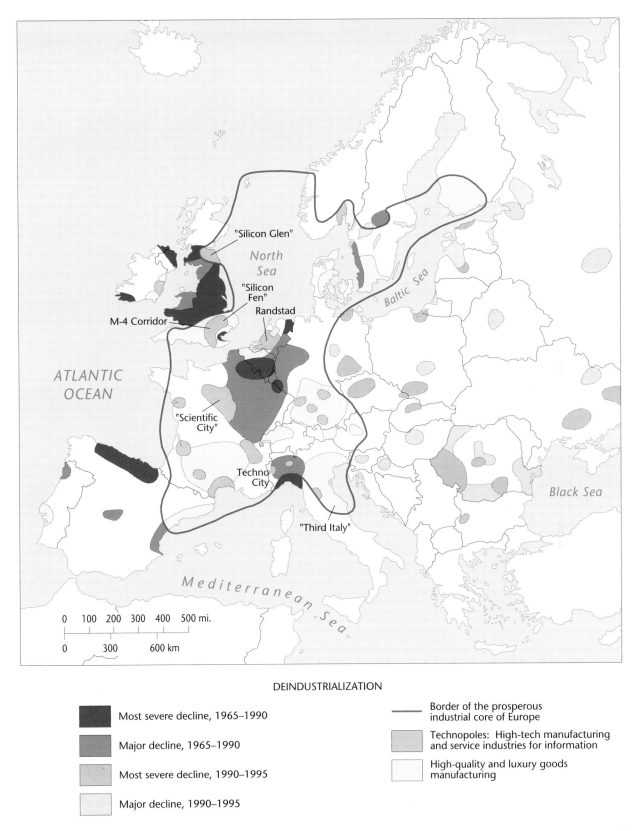

DEINDUSTRIALIZATION

Most severe decline, 1965–1990

Major decline, 1965–1990

Most severe decline, 1990–1995

Major decline, 1990–1995

—— Border of the prosperous industrial core of Europe

Technopoles: High-tech manufacturing and service industries for information

High-quality and luxury goods manufacturing

Figure 9.4 Industrial regions and deindustrialization in Europe. New, prosperous centers of industry specializing in high-quality goods, luxury items, and high-tech manufacture have surpassed older centers of heavy industry—both primary and secondary. The regions in decline were earlier centers of the industrial revolution. Why might the industrial districts in decline not have shared the new prosperity? Why did eastern Europe fall so far behind? *(Source: Jordan-Bychkov and Jordan, 2002: 300.)*

Number of Persons per Car

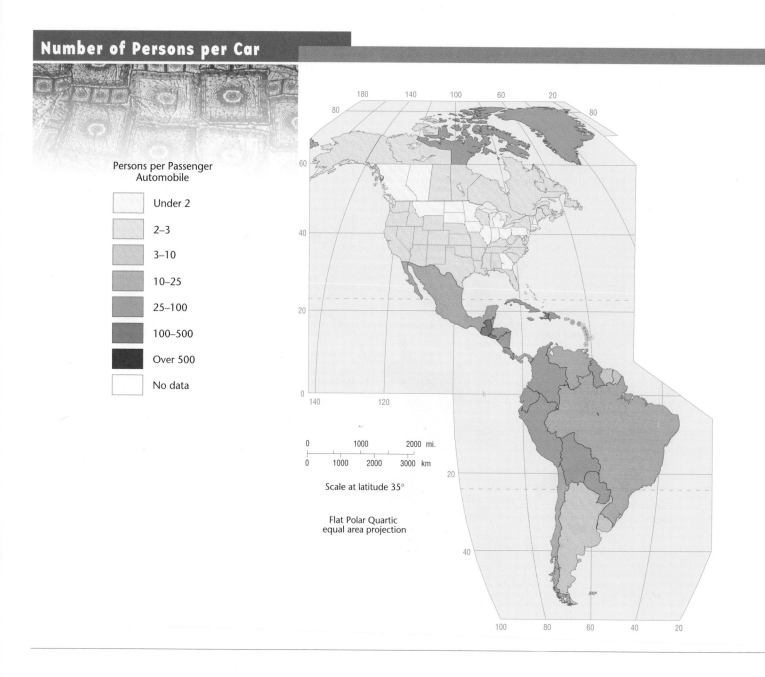

Persons per Passenger Automobile

- Under 2
- 2–3
- 3–10
- 10–25
- 25–100
- 100–500
- Over 500
- No data

0   1000   2000 mi.
0   1000   2000   3000 km

Scale at latitude 35°

Flat Polar Quartic
equal area projection

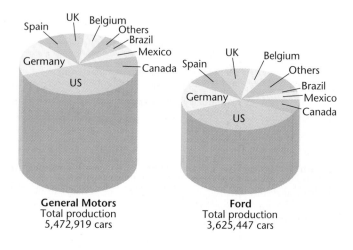

General Motors
Total production
5,472,919 cars

Ford
Total production
3,625,447 cars

Figure 9.5 **The global geography of General Motors and Ford.** As you can see from these diagrams, automobiles are produced in a range of countries around the world. Do you think you would find a similar global pattern of production for Japanese automobile manufacturers? *(Adapted from Dicken, 2003.)*

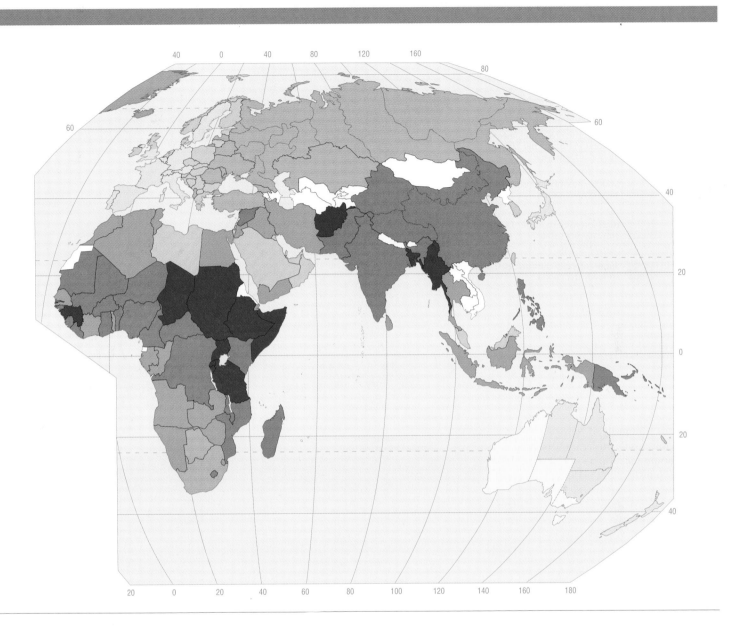

Figure 9.6 **The number of persons per automobile today.** The most highly industrialized nations have the lowest number of persons per car. Is this a valid measure of prosperity? *(United Nations, 2000: 572–587.)*

Consumer services include education, government, recreation/tourism, and health/medicine. One of the most rapidly expanding activities included under consumer services is *tourism*. By 1990, this industry already accounted for 5.5 percent of the world's economy, generated $2.5 trillion in income, and employed 112 million workers—more than any other single industrial activity and amounting to 1 of every 15 workers in the world. Just a decade later, the total income generated had risen to $4.5 trillion and tourism employed 1 of every 12 workers. This trend toward the increased importance of tourism has continued, often in spite of terrorist attacks directed against tourists, as in Egypt during the fall of 1997 and Bali in 2002. Like all other forms of industry, tourism varies greatly in importance from one region or country to another (Figure 9.7), with some countries, particularly those in tropical island locations, depending principally on tourism to support their national economies (Figure 9.8).

Tourism

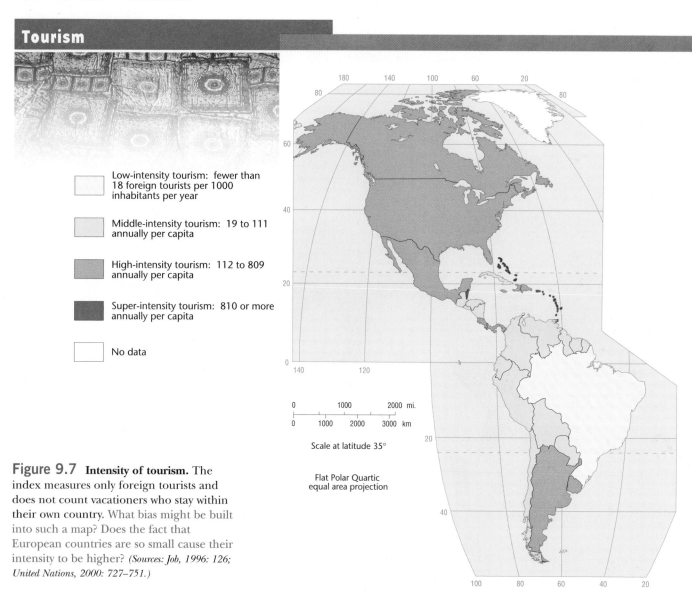

Low-intensity tourism: fewer than 18 foreign tourists per 1000 inhabitants per year

Middle-intensity tourism: 19 to 111 annually per capita

High-intensity tourism: 112 to 809 annually per capita

Super-intensity tourism: 810 or more annually per capita

No data

Scale at latitude 35°

Flat Polar Quartic equal area projection

Figure 9.7 **Intensity of tourism. The** index measures only foreign tourists and does not count vacationers who stay within their own country. What bias might be built into such a map? Does the fact that European countries are so small cause their intensity to be higher? *(Sources: Job, 1996: 126; United Nations, 2000: 727–751.)*

Figure 9.8 **Tourism, often on a primitive level, reaches even into remote areas.** Small charter buses now deliver climbers to a thatched tourist hut, which lacks running water, at the foot of Mount Wilhelm in highland Papua New Guinea— an area totally unknown to the outside world as late as 1930. Increasing numbers of tourists from Europe, North America, and Japan seek out such places. How might these places change as a result of tourism? *(Courtesy of Terry G. Jordan-Bychkov.)*

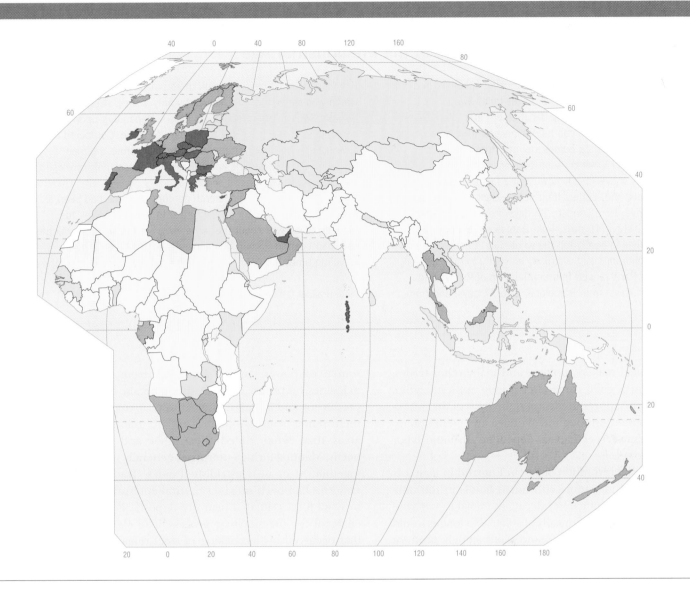

 **Industrial Diffusion**

How do industrial regionalization, uneven development, and core-periphery patterns come to exist? The theme of cultural diffusion permits us to begin to answer such questions. Perhaps the most basic issue is the diffusion of the industrial revolution itself.

Origins of the Industrial Revolution

Until the industrial revolution, society and culture remained overwhelmingly rural and agricultural. To be sure, industry already existed in this setting. For as long as our biological species has existed, we have fashioned tools, weapons, utensils, clothing, and other objects, but tradition-

ally these items were made by hand, laboriously and slowly. Before about 1700, most such manufacturing was carried on in two rather distinct systems: cottage industry and guild industry.

Cottage industry, by far the more common system, was practiced in farm homes and rural villages, usually as a sideline to agriculture. Objects for family use were made in each household, usually by women. Additionally, most villages had a cobbler, miller, weaver, and smith, all of whom worked part-time at these trades in their homes. Skills passed from parents to children with little formality.

By contrast, the **guild industry** consisted of professional organizations of highly skilled, specialized artisans engaged full-time in their trades and based in towns and cities. A guild was a fraternal organization of artisans skilled in a particular craft. Guilds existed for weavers, glassblowers,

FOCUS ON

Distance in the Preindustrial Age

Our lives are a constant adventure in shrinking space. With a car, we're just minutes from a friend who lives miles away. The airplane has put us within jet-lag distance of Paris, Moscow, and Beijing. In such an age, we can hardly imagine what an obstacle distance often proved to be before the industrial revolution.

A record of 10,000 letters sent to Venice, Italy, in the early sixteenth century shows clearly how great a factor distance was in the preindustrial world. Letters from nearby Genoa took an average of 6 days to arrive; from London, 27 days; from Constantinople, 37 days; from Lisbon, 46 days; from Damascus, 80 days. But these average figures hardly tell the whole tale. Changing human and climatic conditions lent a striking elasticity to mail delivery. Deliveries from Paris ranged from a minimum of 7 days to a maximum of 34 days; from Barcelona, 8 to 77 days; and from

Florence, 1 to 13 days—to pick three places at random. Zara, which was separated from Venice by only a short stretch of the Adriatic Sea, held the record. Its letters, depending upon sailing conditions, took from 1 day to 25 days to arrive. Compared to other goods, however, letters moved briskly across the map. Sixteenth-century Italians knew that it took even their privileged goods 3 months to reach London.

In fact, before the eighteenth century, distance had been a relatively constant factor for centuries. In terms of travel, the Mediterranean was about the same "size" in the sixteenth century as it had been in Roman times more than 1000 years earlier. Traveling times did not change much until the nineteenth century.

From Braudel, 1972, vol. I: 356

---

silversmiths, steel makers, potters, and many other trades. Membership in a guild came after a long apprenticeship, during which the apprentice learned the skills of the profession from a master. Although the cottage and guild systems differed in many respects, both depended on hand labor and human power.

The industrial revolution began in England in the early 1700s. First, machines replaced human hands in the fashioning of finished products, rendering the word *manufacturing* ("made by hand") technically obsolete. No longer would the weaver sit at a hand loom and painstakingly produce each piece of cloth. Instead, large mechanical looms were invented to do the job faster and cheaper. Second, human power gave way to various forms of inanimate power. Water power, the burning of fossil fuels, and later electricity and the energy of the atom fueled the machines. Men and women, once the producers of handmade goods, became tenders of machines.

The initial breakthrough came in the secondary, or manufacturing, sector. More specifically, it occurred in the British *cotton textile cottage industry*, centered at that time in the district of Lancashire in northwestern England. At first the changes were modest and on a small scale. Mechanical spinners and looms were invented, and flowing water—long used as a source of power by local grain millers—was harnessed to drive the looms. During this stage, manufacturing industries were still largely rural and dispersed. Sites where rushing streams could be found, especially those with waterfalls and rapids, were ideal locations. Later in the eighteenth century, the invention of the steam engine provided a better

source of power, and a shift away from water-powered machines occurred. The steam engine also allowed textile producers and other manufacturers to move away from their power sources—water—and to relocate instead in areas that better suited their labor and transportation needs. Manufacturing enterprises generally began to cluster together, in or near established cities. Traditionally, *metal industries* had been small-scale, rural enterprises, carried on in small forges situated near ore deposits. Forests provided charcoal for the smelting process. The chemical changes that occurred in the making of steel remained mysterious even to the craftspeople whose job it was, and much ritual, superstition, and ceremony were associated with steel making. Techniques had changed little since the beginning of the Iron Age, 2500 years before.

The industrial revolution radically altered all this. In the eighteenth century, a series of inventions by iron makers living in Coalbrookdale, in the English Midlands, allowed the old traditions, techniques, and rituals of steel making to be swept away and replaced by a scientific, large-scale industry. *Coke*, nearly pure carbon derived from high-grade coal, was substituted for charcoal in the smelting process. Large blast furnaces replaced the forge, and efficient rolling mills took the place of hammer and anvil. Mass production of steel resulted, and the new industrial order was built of steel. Other manufacturing industries made similar transitions, and entirely new types arose, such as machine making.

Primary industries were also revolutionized. Coal mining was the first to feel the effects of the new technology. The adoption of the steam engine required huge amounts of coal to fire the boilers, and the conversion to coke in the smelting process further increased the demand for coal. New mining techniques and tools were invented, and coal mining became a large-scale, mechanized industry. However, coal, heavy and bulky, was difficult to transport. As a result, manufacturing industries began flocking to the coalfields to be near the supply. Similar modernization occurred in the mining of iron ore, copper, and other metals needed by rapidly growing industries.

The industrial revolution also affected the service industries, most notably in the development of new forms of transportation. Traditional wooden sailing ships gave way to steel vessels driven by steam engines, canals were built, and later railroads became more prevalent. The need to move raw materials and finished products from one place to another both cheaply and quickly was the main stimulus that led to these transportation breakthroughs. Without them, the impact of the industrial revolution would have been minimized (see Focus On: Distance in the Preindustrial Age).

Once in place, the railroads and other innovative modes of transport associated with the industrial revolution fostered

additional cultural diffusion. Ideas spread more rapidly and easily because of this efficient transportation network. Nor has this process yet ended. As geographer Chris Airriess has noted, transnational corporations linked by globalization created worldwide containerized shipping based in megaports such as Singapore, and then further revolutionized the shipping industry by adopting new information technologies to speed the movement of goods even more.

Diffusion of the Industrial Revolution

Great Britain maintained a virtual monopoly on the industrial revolution well into the 1800s. Indeed, the British government actively tried to prevent the diffusion of the various inventions and innovations that made up the industrial revolution. After all, they gave Britain an enormous economic advantage and contributed greatly to the growth and strength of the British Empire. Nevertheless, this technology finally diffused beyond the bounds of the British Isles (Figure 9.9), with continental Europe being impacted first. In the last half of the nineteenth century, the industrial revolution took firm root hierarchically in the coalfields of

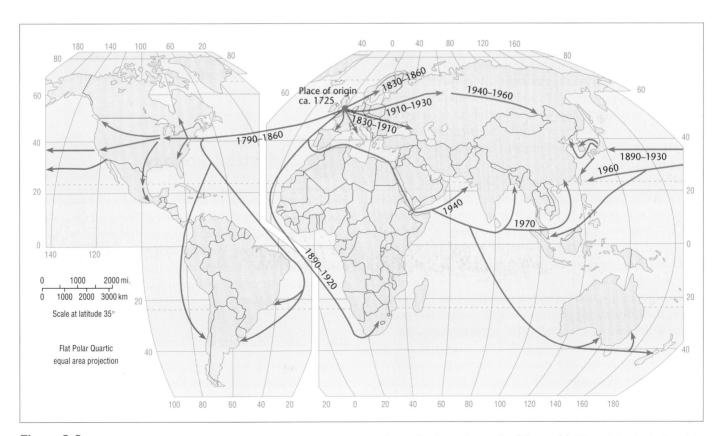

Figure 9.9 **The diffusion of the industrial revolution.** By diffusion from Great Britain, the industrial revolution has changed cultures in much of the world. Why might the industrial revolution have originated in so small and peripheral a country?

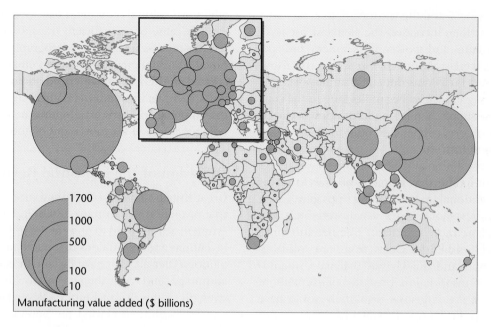

Figure 9.10 **Map of world manufacturing production.** Notice that the "old" industrial regions of the United States, Europe, and Japan still dominate much of the world's manufacturing, although countries like China and Brazil are important new centers of manufacturing. Identify several factors that have contributed to this uneven distribution of industrialization. *(Adapted from Dicken, 2003.)*

Germany, Belgium, and other nations of northwestern and central Europe. The diffusion of railroads in Europe provides a good index of the spread of the industrial revolution there. The United States began rapid adoption of this new technology about 1850, followed half a century later by Japan, the first major non-Western nation to undergo full industrialization. In the first third of the twentieth century, the diffusion of industry and modern transport spilled over into Russia and Ukraine.

More recently, countries such as Taiwan, South Korea, China, India, Indonesia and Malaysia—countries geographers and others refer to as newly industrializing countries (NICs)—have become centers of manufacturing. Much of the manufacturing in these countries is destined for the export market—part of the globalizing processes we have been talking about. Instead of exporting raw materials, these countries are now exporting such things as DVDs and Barbie dolls. Indonesia estimates that manufactured goods now comprise more than half of its exports, compared to only 2 percent in 1980. Yet even with this massive diffusion of industry, the geographic pattern of the world's manufacturing sites remains quite uneven (Figure 9.10). The United States, Japan, and Germany still account for almost 60 percent of the world's manufacturing output, with such "new" countries as South Korea accounting for almost 3 percent and China for 2.7 percent. (See Seeing Geography at the end of the chapter.)

REFLECTING ON GEOGRAPHY

Identify and discuss some of the reasons that the "old" manufacturing core still retains its dominance in the global manufacturing system.

 Industrial Ecology

How might the theme of cultural ecology best be applied to the geographical study of industries? The general answer is clear: it is precisely industrial ecology that lies at the heart of our Faustian bargain. We have tacitly agreed to the ongoing destruction of the planet in exchange for living comfortably today, for all three types of industrial activity create serious ecological problems.

Renewable Resource Crises

At first glance, it might seem that only finite resources are affected by industrialization, but even renewable resources such as forests and fisheries are endangered. So, while *deforestation* is an ongoing process that began at least 3000 years ago, the industrial revolution drastically increased the magnitude of the problem. In just the last half-century, a third of the world's forest cover has been lost. Lumber use tripled between 1950 and 2000, and the demand for paper increased fivefold. Today, we witness the rapid destruction of one of the last surviving great woodland ecosystems: the tropical rain forest (Figure 9.11). The most intensive rainforest clearing is occurring in the East Indies and Brazil, and commercial lumber interests are largely responsible (Figure 9.12). Although trees represent a renewable resource when properly managed, too many countries are in effect mining their forests. Canadians and Americans can only hypocritically chastise countries such as Brazil and Indonesia for not protecting their tropical rain forests, because their own west coast midlatitude rain forests in the Pacific Northwest, British Columbia, and Alaska continue to suffer severe damage as a result of unwise lumbering practices. In any case, *foreign* rather than Brazilian interests now hold logging rights to nearly 30 million acres (12 million hectares) of Amazonian rain forest. Even when forests are converted into scientifically managed "tree farms," as is true in most of the developed world, ecosystems are often destroyed. Natural ecosystems have plant and animal diversity that cannot be sustained under the monoculture of commercial forestry.

Similarly, *overfishing* has brought a crisis to many ocean fisheries, a problem compounded by pollution of many of the world's seas. The total fish catch of all countries combined rose from 84 million metric tons in 1984 to more than 122 million metric tons by the late 1990s, causing some species to decline. Salmon in Pacific coastal North America and cod in the Maritime Provinces of Canada can be said to have reached a "marine biological crisis." Overfishing caused a catastrophic recession in the Newfoundland cod industry, and some experts forecast a collapse of the world's fisheries in the near future.

Acid Rain

Secondary and service industries pollute the air, water, and land with chemicals and other toxic substances. **Acid rain** is one example. Known to researchers for a century and a half, acid rain received widespread publicity beginning in the early 1980s. The burning of fossil fuels by power plants, factories, and automobiles releases acidic sulfur oxides and nitrogen oxides into the air; these chemicals are then flushed from the atmosphere by precipitation. The resultant rainfall has a much higher acidity than normal. Overall, 84 percent of the world's energy is generated by burning fossil fuels, making acid rain a prevalent phenomenon.

Acid rain can poison fish, damage plants, and diminish soil fertility. Such problems have been studied intensively in Germany, one of the most completely industrialized nations in the world. German scholars have been impressed by the dramatic suddenness with which the catastrophic effects of acid rain arrived. In 1982, only 8 percent of forests in western Germany showed damage, but by 1990 the proportion had risen to more than half. Now only a crash program of pollution control and energy conservation can save the country's woodlands. The neighboring Czech Republic faces a comparable problem.

In North America, the effects of acid rain have accumulated, but not yet with the catastrophic speed seen in central Europe. More than 90 lakes in the seemingly pristine Adirondack Mountains of New York were "dead," devoid of fish life, by 1980, and 50,000 lakes in eastern Canada face a similar fate. Since about 1990, the acid-rain problem has become less severe in many parts of the world, especially Europe, but the situation in the Adirondacks has not improved. Recent studies suggest that acid rain now causes

Figure 9.11 Destruction of tropical rain forest near Madang in Papua New Guinea by Japanese lumbering interests. The entire forest is leveled to extract a relatively small number of desired trees. Why are overtly destructive policies employed? *(Courtesy of Terry G. Jordan-Bychkov.)*

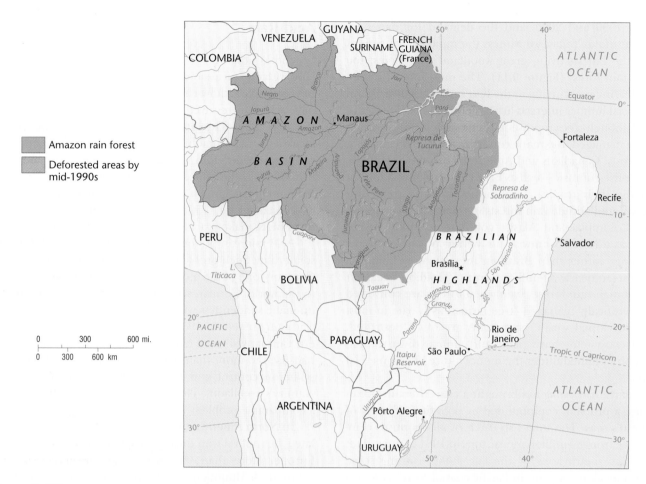

Figure 9.12 **The tropical rain forest of the Amazon Basin.** In Brazil, the rain forest is under attack by settlers, ranchers, and commercial loggers. Its removal will intensify the impact of the greenhouse gases, especially carbon dioxide, because the forest acts to convert those gases into benign forms. About 10,000 square miles (26,000 square kilometers) of Brazil's tropical rain forest is cleared each year. (*Source: Worldwatch Institute web site.*)

mass killings of marine life along the northeastern coast of the United States and in the forests in the Appalachians (Figure 9.13). Oxides of nitrogen seem to be the principal culprit in the coastal waters, and the impact has been noted in Chesapeake, Delaware, and Narragansett bays, as well as in Long Island Sound. For years, the government of Canada urged U.S. officials to take stringent action to help alleviate acid-rain damage, because much of the problem on the Canadian side of the border derives from American pollution, but their pleas had little effect. Despite countermeasures, the acid-rain problem is not improving.

Global Warming

Most scientists now agree that we have entered a phase of **global warming** caused by industrial activity and, most particularly, by the greatly increased amount of carbon dioxide (CO_2) produced by burning fossil fuels. Some scientists warn against unquestioned acceptance of this theory, but the circumstantial evidence seems overwhelming (Figure 9.14). The eight hottest years on record all occurred in the period 1990–2001, based on records compiled at more than 14,000 locations. In 2002, a huge ice mass the size of Rhode Island broke off from Antarctica and fragmented into icebergs in the ocean. This ice mass, before it shattered as a result of warming temperatures, measured 1260 square miles (3264 square kilometers) in area and 650 feet (226 meters) in thickness.

At issue is the so-called **greenhouse effect.** Every year billions of tons of CO_2 are produced worldwide by fossil-fuel burning, at a level 75 percent greater than in 1860. By some estimates, the atmospheric concentration of CO_2 has climbed to the highest level in 180,000 years (see Figure 9.14). In addition, the ongoing destruction of the world's rain forests adds huge additional amounts of CO_2 to the atmosphere. Although CO_2 is a natural component of the

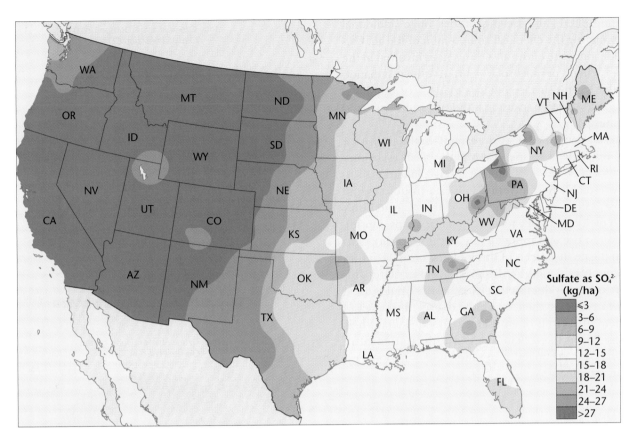

Figure 9.13 **Distribution of acid rain in the United States.**
Measurements are taken from the annual sulfate deposition,
derived from airborne sulfur oxides (SO₂). Deposition levels of
18 pounds per acre (20 kilograms per hectare) are generally
regarded as threatening to some aquatic and terrestrial
ecosystems. Nitrate components of acid rain are not shown. Might
this distribution cause Canada and the United States to engage in
a dispute? *(Source: National Atmospheric Deposition Program web site.)*

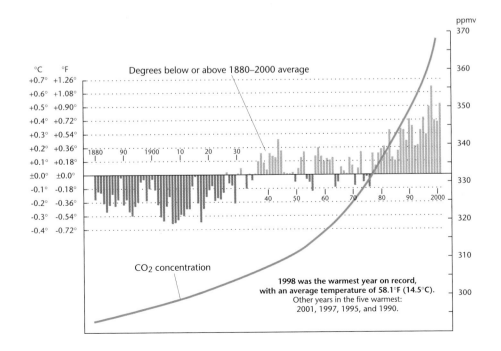

Figure 9.14 **The correlation
between rising globally averaged
temperatures and increasing carbon
dioxide emissions.** Correlations prove
nothing, but the evidence seems
compelling. *(Sources: O'Hare, 2000: 358;
Worldwatch Institute web site.)*

Earth's atmosphere, the freeing of this huge additional amount is altering the chemical composition of the air. Carbon dioxide, only one of the absorbing gases involved in the greenhouse effect, permits solar short-wave heat radiation to reach the Earth's surface but acts to block or trap long-wave outgoing radiation, causing a thermal imbalance and global heating.

The result could be, at worst, a rapid buildup of solar heat that would lead to the evaporation of all water and make any form of life impossible, causing planet Earth to eventually resemble hostile Venus. Less catastrophically, the greenhouse effect could warm the global climate only enough to melt or partially melt the polar ice caps, causing the sea level to rise and inundate the world's coastlines. To begin to mitigate the effects of this looming crisis, 38 industrialized countries signed the Kyoto Protocol in 2001. This document, originally discussed in Kyoto in 1997, binds these countries to reducing their emissions of greenhouse gases so that their 2012 levels of emissions will be less than their 1990 levels. The United States agreed to this protocol in 1997 but has since changed its position and is no longer a part of the agreement.

Ozone Depletion

Potentially even more serious is the depletion of the upper-atmosphere *ozone layer*, which acts to shield humans and all other forms of life from the most harmful types of solar radiation. Several manufactured chemicals, including the freon used in refrigeration and air conditioning, are almost certainly the main culprits.. Most of the industrialized countries of the world contribute large amounts of these chemicals, and they signed the Montreal Protocol in 1989 aimed at reducing the ozone-damaging substances.

REFLECTING ON GEOGRAPHY

If we cannot be certain that global warming and upper-level ozone depletion are caused by industrial activity rather than being natural fluctuations or cycles, should we take action or simply wait and see what happens?

Little progress has been made, however, and recent research suggests that the problem may be far worse than previously believed. In 2001, winter ozone levels in the Arctic high latitudes fell to 20 to 25 percent of normal. The ozone decrease in the Arctic was first noticed in the early 1990s, with the observation of an ozone hole in that region comparable to the one first detected in the Antarctic during the 1980s. The problem continues today (Figure 9.15). The activist organization Greenpeace, among others, warns that

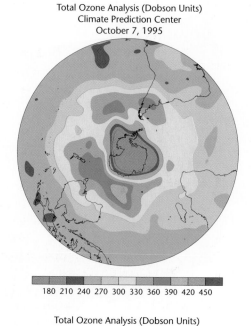

Total Ozone Analysis (Dobson Units)
Climate Prediction Center
October 7, 1995

180 210 240 270 300 330 360 390 420 450

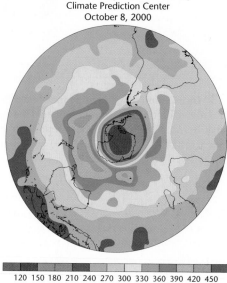

Total Ozone Analysis (Dobson Units)
Climate Prediction Center
October 8, 2000

120 150 180 210 240 270 300 330 360 390 420 450

Figure 9.15 **Ozone depletion zone over the Southern Hemisphere, centered on Antarctica.** After rapid growth for decades, the size of the ozone hole has begun to stabilize, though some deterioration is evident. The atmospheric concentrations of chlorofluorocarbons, which cause the problem, have declined in recent years, but it will require decades for the ozone hole to be "mended." *(Source: U.S. National Oceanic and Atmospheric Administration.)*

ozone depletion now threatens the future of all forms of life on Earth. Perhaps in the end we will find that industrialization, which has become so integral a part of our culture over the previous two centuries, is simply ecologically untenable and cannot be maintained. In short, our modern industrial way of life may prove a maladaptive strategy in terms of cultural ecology.

Radioactive Pollution

Like acid rain, *radioactive pollution* is invisible. It comes from nuclear power plants and waste storage facilities. The catastrophe at Chernobyl in Ukraine on April 26, 1986, clearly demonstrated the danger inherent in the Faustian bargain that has led Japan, much of Europe, and many other parts of the world to depend heavily on nuclear power.

When the Chernobyl nuclear reactor core melted down, causing two explosions, a sizable area around Chernobyl in Ukraine and Belarus became heavily contaminated with deadly radiation; everyone within an 18-mile (30-kilometer) radius of the destroyed reactor had to be evacuated. This area remains uninhabited today, save for a few elderly people who refused to leave. Beyond this zone, sizable swaths across Europe were bombarded with various radioactive isotopes, such as cesium-137, a long-term hazard because it has a *half-life* (the time required for its radioactivity to decrease by half) of 30 years and attacks the entire human body. Another major component of the Chernobyl pollution was iodine-131, with a half-life of 8.1 days, which collects in the thyroid gland. Some estimates place the amount of cesium-137 released as equivalent to at least 750 Hiroshima atomic bombs. Ultimately, a sizable part of both Ukraine and Belarus may be declared unfit for human habitation, and additional tens of thousands of people could die from exposure to radiation caused by this single catastrophe. Strontium-90, another radioactive contaminant, continues to leak into the groundwater table at Chernobyl. The ominous term *national sacrifice area* is now heard in governmental circles in various countries as a potential euphemism for districts rendered permanently uninhabitable by radiation pollution. Some geographers speak of "hazardscapes" to describe such places.

Environmental Sustainability

The key issue in all these industry-related ecological problems is sustainability. Can our present industrial-based way of life continue without causing ecological collapse?

The Environmental Sustainability Index (ESI) has been devised to measure, country by country, the level of progress toward sustainability. The highest possible score on the ESI is 100, the lowest 0. No fewer than 21 "core indicators" involving 67 different variables are considered (Figure 9.16). These include air and water quality, biodiversity, population pressures, private business sector responsiveness, level of governmental intervention, and so on. In 2005, the highest-ranked country was Finland, at 75.1; the lowest was North Korea, at 29.2. Although far from being a perfect measure, the ESI clearly points to the regions of the world where ecosystems are most highly stressed. These lie mainly in the tropics and subtropics.

Developing new sources of energy is one of the keys to environmental sustainability. For example, genuine progress is being made in the use of wind power to generate electricity. In the United States alone, wind power produced over 6200 megawatts of electricity by the end of 2003, about 1 percent of the total generated. This represents a significant increase over previous years, although the United States lags far behind such countries as Denmark, Spain, and Germany. California, Texas, Iowa, and Minnesota are the leading wind-power states.

Another development fostering sustainability is **ecotourism,** defined as responsible travel that does not harm ecosystems or the well-being of local people. Ecotourism arose when it was recognized that even seemingly benign industries such as tourism can create ecological problems. Ecotourists tend to visit out-of-the-way places with exotic, healthy ecosystems. They disdain the comforts of large hotels and resorts, preferring more spartan conditions. Revenues from ecotourism helped rescue Uganda's mountain gorillas from extinction, especially when the government realized that the wildlife served as a valuable tourist attraction.

Also notable has been the rise of the **Greens,** political activists who advocate an emphasis on environmental issues. Many countries now have Green political parties. Also active in environmental advocacy are groups such as the Sierra Club, Greenpeace, and the Nature Conservancy.

 Industrial Cultural Interaction

Can our understanding of the industrialized world be aided by the theme of cultural interaction? Yes, but in a very different way from cultural ecology. Cultural interaction allows us to understand, among other things, the location of industries. Industrial location theory seeks to explain the spatial distribution of industry by referring mainly to other aspects of society. One of the major theorists of industrial location was Alfred Weber, a German geographer active in the first half of the twentieth century. He devised a model of how to understand industrial locations in regard to several factors, including labor supply, markets, resource location, and transportation. The discussion that follows is based on many of his ideas.

Labor Supply

Labor-intensive industries are those industries in which labor costs form a large part of total production costs. Examples

Environmental Sustainability

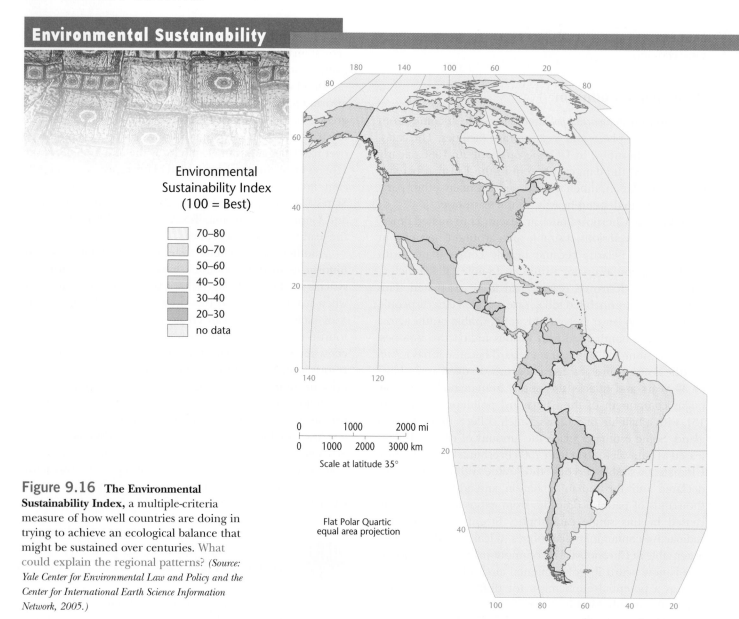

Environmental
Sustainability Index
(100 = Best)

- 70–80
- 60–70
- 50–60
- 40–50
- 30–40
- 20–30
- no data

Flat Polar Quartic
equal area projection

Figure 9.16 **The Environmental
Sustainability Index,** a multiple-criteria
measure of how well countries are doing in
trying to achieve an ecological balance that
might be sustained over centuries. What
could explain the regional patterns? *(Source:
Yale Center for Environmental Law and Policy and the
Center for International Earth Science Information
Network, 2005.)*

include industries that depend on skilled workers producing small objects of high value, such as computers, cameras, and watches, and/or industries that require large numbers of semiskilled workers, such as the textile and garment industries. Manufacturers consider several characteristics of labor in deciding where to locate factories: availability of workers, average wages, necessary skills, and worker productivity. Workers with certain skills tend to live and work in a small number of places, partly as a result of the need for higher education or for person-to-person training in handing down such skills. Consequently, manufacturers often seek locations where these skilled workers live. Geographer Amy Glasmeier (see Practicing Geography) has traced the history and contemporary conditions of the watchmaking

industry in four countries (Great Britain, the United States, Switzerland, and Japan), showing how the availability of a pool of skilled labor, and the maintenance of that pool through different forms of education and training, was critical to the success of these businesses.

In recent decades, with the increasing effects of globalization, two trends have been evident in terms of the relationship between the location of industry and labor supply. On the one hand, the increased mobility of people has in some ways lessened the locational influence of the labor force. Migration of labor accelerated after 1950, especially in Europe and the United States. Large numbers of workers in Europe migrated from south to north, leaving their homes in Spain, Italy, Greece, Turkey, and the Balkan states to find

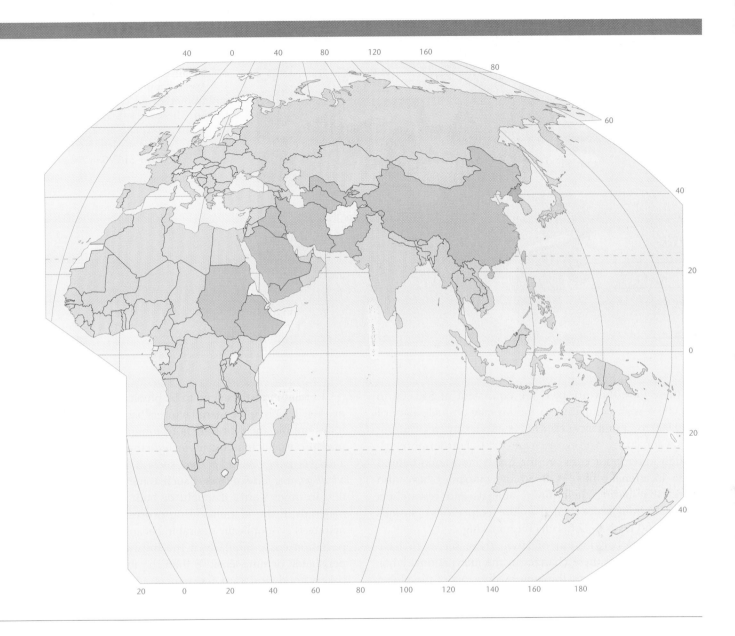

employment in the main European manufacturing belt. Today, labor migration is at an all-time high, lessening labor's influence on industrial location. On the other hand, particularly for industries that are reliant on large pools of labor and that are transnational in structure, the location of labor has become even more important. These industries are often referred to as "**footloose**"—in the sense that they shift the location of their facilities in search of cheap labor. We discussed this earlier in regard to the textile and garment industries (see the section on secondary industry), but here we can see how globalization is enabling more industries to locate their production facilities close to labor supply.

Some companies are even locating their producer service activities in places where they can take advantage of cheaper labor costs. In the 1990s, many companies began to move what we typically called secretarial jobs—filing, typing, document formatting, and so on—out of their corporate headquarters and into places and spaces that were cheaper, both in terms of rental of office space and, especially, in terms of labor costs. More recently, some types of businesses, such as accounting firms, Wall Street investment houses, advertising agencies, and insurance companies, have found it cost effective to **outsource** other white-collar jobs that are generally considered more skilled, such as legal research, financial analysis, and accounting. Chennai (formerly known as Madras), India, for example, is a primary site of these more skilled outsourced activities (Figure 9.17). Here, educated and highly skilled workers are trained to

Figure 9.17 **Back-office workers in New Delhi, India.** This photo was taken inside the Wipro Spectramind call center, a company that serves customers of a U.S.-based computer manufacturer and an Internet service provider in Great Britain. There are still many call centers located in the United States, but increasingly these services are being outsourced. Why? *(AFP/Getty Images.)*

do these jobs; they are paid the equivalent of $10,000 to $20,000 a year, compared to the average annual salary of $100,000 for a similar worker in New York City (see Culture in a Globalizing World on page 322). Furthermore, although lower labor costs are the major motivation behind these locational shifts, Wall Street companies have also found that having their junior analysts and researchers located in India keeps them from the temptations of insider trading and leads to better decision making.

A new global division of labor, then, seems to have emerged. Behind these changes in the international labor market lies the strategic thinking by directors of the global corporations. According to a U.S. Department of Commerce study, as early as the mid-1970s, 298 American-based global corporations employed as many as 25 percent of their workers outside the United States. Since then, as we have seen, the practice has become even more common. Such factories and offices, despite relocation costs, quickly drive up corporate profit margins. In addition, the ability of these corporations to plan on an international scale and to shift the production of a given product to faraway lands has a weakening effect on organized labor inside the United States.

Markets

Geographically, a **market** includes the area in which a product may be sold in a volume and at a price profitable to the manufacturer. The size and distribution of markets are generally the most important factors in determining the spatial distribution of industries.

Certain industries need to be physically located near the market. That is, some manufacturers have to situate their factories among their customers to minimize costs and maximize profits. Such industries include those that manufacture a *weight-gaining finished product,* such as bottled beverages, or a *bulk-gaining finished product,* such as metal containers or bottles. In other words, if weight or bulk is added to the raw materials in the manufacturing process, location near the market is economically desirable because of the high transportation costs. Similarly, if the finished product is more perishable or time-sensitive than the raw materials, as with bakery goods and local newspapers, a location near the market is also required. In addition, if the product is more fragile than the raw materials that go into its manufacture, as with glass items, the industry will be attracted to locations near its market. In each of these cases—gain in weight or bulk, perishability, or fragility—transportation costs of the finished product are much higher than those of the raw materials. On the other hand, items that become easier to transport after manufacturing are often produced in locations close to the site of the raw materials.

As a rule, we can say that in industrial cultures, the greatest market potential exists where the largest numbers of people live. Once an industry locates in a particular place, it provides additional jobs, attracting laborers into the area. This additional population in turn enlarges the local market, thereby attracting other industries. In the same way, the industries arriving later attract still more people and still more industries, creating an **agglomeration.** Industrial districts develop in this manner, through a snowballing increase

Amy Glasmeier

(Courtesy of Amy Glasmeier.)

Part teacher, part researcher, part activist, economic geographer Amy Glasmeier of Penn State says that the most exciting part of her job is "engaging people at all spatial scales from the smallest community to the level of large international organizations." For Glasmeier, "practicing" geography means real-world problem solving. "I never study a problem that is purely theoretical, but rather I am interested in real-world problems. I like being able to solve social problems through understanding the role geography plays in economic activity."

And she's taken on an incredible array of problems, from industrial restructuring and regional development (in places like Switzerland, Silicon Valley, and Appalachia), to telecommunications policy, to the political economy of the environment. What unites these various issues is a passion for solving problems of inequality, whether that relates to unequal access to the Internet or to environmental health. Tackling such seemingly intractable problems might overwhelm some, but not Glasmeier. Her diverse educational

background and work experiences help. Trained as an urban and regional planner, and now teaching in a geography department, Glasmeier has worked for and with federal agencies, international organizations, and private foundations. Also helpful is her willingness to engage in numerous research methods. "I always use multiple methods and always check what I find statistically with history and real-world ground truthing. I like to talk to policy audiences, and I like to train activists to use statistics and analytical thinking to challenge the status quo. I always start from a historical perspective."

For now, she's focusing much of her attention on a large project called *One Nation, Pulling Apart,* funded by the Ford Foundation, whose goal is to better understand the expansion, persistence, and geography of poverty in the United States. Working with student collaborators and using her full toolbox of methods, Glasmeier is exploring the real, lived effects of industrial restructuring on individuals and communities. "I'm rethinking poverty policy in the United States since 1960, hoping to enliven a new debate about the importance of space in the construction and perpetuation of poverty and economic inequality."

in people, infrastructure, and industries. China presents a compelling recent case study of industrial agglomeration, given its large population base (close to 1.5 billion people) that serves as both a great source of labor and an expanding consumer market. Because China has more than 40 cities with populations exceeding a million (Figure 9.18) and also has a stable government that encourages foreign investment, transnational companies find the opportunities for low-cost production and expanding consumption there appealing. And once these centers of industry are established, more people, particularly from the rural areas, move in to provide even more labor and a larger market base, leading to a new cycle of agglomeration.

State Policies

Political influence on the spatial distribution of industry is common. Governments often intervene directly in decisions about industrial location. Such intervention typically results from a desire to encourage foreign investment; to create national self-sufficiency by diversifying industries; to

bring industrial development and a higher standard of living to poverty-stricken provinces; to establish strategic, militarily important industries that would otherwise not develop; or to halt agglomeration in existing industrial areas. Such governmental influence becomes most pronounced in highly planned economic systems, particularly in certain socialist countries such as China, but it works to some extent in almost every industrial nation.

The scattering of industry in Russia, motivated partly by a desire to lessen the catastrophic effect of a military attack, provides an example. A major industrial complex in the Ural Mountains, deep in the interior of Russia, was developed partly in response to the German military advance in 1941. For similar strategic reasons, the U.S. government during World War II encouraged the development of an iron and steel industry in Utah, an economically inefficient location that would not have attracted such industry without government intervention. The American aircraft industry similarly became dispersed as a result of government policy. The Italian government has deliberately forced industries to establish factories in the impoverished southern part of that

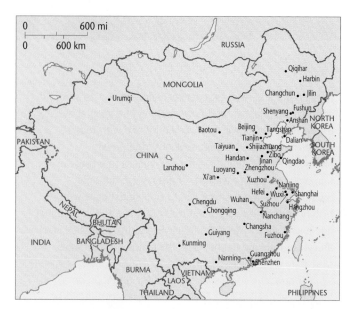

Figure 9.18 **Chinese cities with a population over 1 million.** As you can see from this map, there are more than 40 cities in China with populations that exceed 1 million. Each of these agglomerations represents a large consumer market and source of labor. Why do you think most of these cities are increasing in population? *(Source: Thomas Brinkhoff: City Population, http://www.citypopulation.de.)*

country in an effort to improve the standard of living. Similarly, the American government encouraged new industrial development in economically depressed Appalachia. The United Kingdom, with some limited success, has attempted to retard further industrial development in existing population centers, causing many new factories to be situated in rural areas or small towns.

Local and state governments, not just national governments, often directly influence industrial locations. Action by such governments sometimes takes the form of tax concessions, such as those granted by a number of states, counties, and cities in the United States. These concessions commonly last for a specified period of time, often 10 years or less, and are designed to persuade industries to locate in areas under the local or state jurisdiction. Conversely, governments can act to prevent the establishment of industries viewed as undesirable. A brewery, for example, could be kept out of an area where influential local church leaders hold prohibitionist views and bring their influence to bear on government officials. Some American municipalities have refused to allow development of particularly pollution-prone industries such as copper smelters, waste disposal, and paper mills.

Other types of government influence come in the form of tariffs, import-export quotas, political obstacles to the free movement of labor and capital, and various methods of

hindering transportation across borders. Tariffs, in effect, reduce the size of a market area proportional to the amount of tariff imposed. A similar effect is produced when the number of border-crossing points is restricted. In some parts of the world, especially Europe, the impact of tariffs and borders on industrial location has been greatly reduced by the establishment of free-trade blocs—groups of nations that have banded together economically and abolished most tariffs. Of these associations, the European Union (EU) is perhaps the most famous. Composed of 25 nations, the EU has succeeded in abolishing tariffs within its area. The North American Free Trade Agreement (NAFTA) among the United States, Canada, and Mexico—with future expansion to include other countries—is a similar achievement in the Western Hemisphere. At a much larger spatial scale, the World Trade Organization (WTO) administers trade agreements and settles trade disputes, including those over tariffs, throughout much of the world. With nearly 150 member countries, the WTO regulates approximately 97 percent of world trade. The WTO was formed in 1995, replacing the international organization known as GATT (General Agreement on Tariffs and Trade) that had been established after World War II.

Transnational corporations, which scatter their holdings across international borders, would seem to suffer from such political regulations. In reality, however, multinational enterprises are well placed to take advantage of some government policies. Various countries act differently to encourage or discourage foreign investment, creating major spatial discontinuities in opportunities for the global corporations. Areas where foreign investment is encouraged are often called **export processing zones** (EPZs), although in China they are called special economic zones (SEZs). In general, these zones are designated areas of countries where governments create conditions conducive to export-oriented production, including trade concessions, exemptions from certain type of legislation, provision of physical infrastructure and services, and waivers of restrictions on foreign ownership. According to Peter Dicken, about 90 percent of these zones are located in Latin America, the Caribbean, Mexico, and Asia (Figure 9.19). Those located along the U.S.-Mexican border are populated by American-owned assembly plants called *maquiladoras* (Figure 9.20), most of which utilize Mexican low-wage labor, predominantly women, to produce textiles, clothing, and electronics for the export market (see Focus On: Women, Men, and Work in the Maquiladoras on page 324).

Industrialization and Cultural Change

In these various ways, different aspects of culture are integrated with industrial location, but equally pronounced are

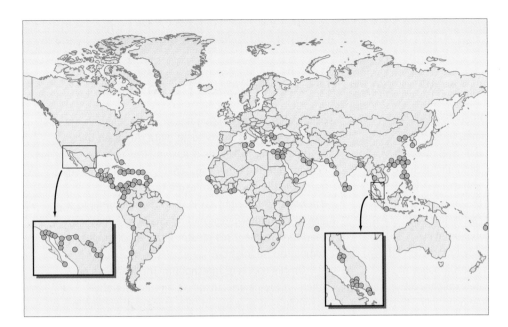

Figure 9.19 **Global sites of export processing zones.** Notice the concentration of these zones along the U.S.-Mexican border. What explains this phenomenon? *(Adapted from Dicken, 2003.)*

Figure 9.20 **Maquiladora in Nuevo Laredo, Mexico.** In this maquiladora, Mexican workers are completing telephone repairs for AT&T. Why are many of these workers women? *(Bob Daemmrich/The Image Works.)*

the effects of industry on culture. Indeed, industrialization is the most potent and effective agent of cultural change in modern times. Entire cultures have been reshaped as a consequence of the industrial revolution. Traditions thousands of years old have been discarded almost overnight.

Further, the changes wrought by industrialization include increased interregional trade and intercultural contact, basic alterations in employment patterns, a shift from rural to urban residence for vast numbers of people, the release of women from the home, the ultimate disappearance of child labor, an initial increase in the rate of population growth followed by a drop to unprecedented low birthrates, greatly increased individual mobility and mass migrations of people, the dispersal of the multigeneration family, greatly increased educational opportunities for the nonwealthy, and an increase in government influence and functions. Focus On: Women, Men, and Work in Maquiladoras provides an interesting case study of the complex changes wrought by industrialization in the Mexican border zone.

Industrial Landscapes

In what ways has industrialization altered the cultural landscape? The change has been profound, and we can properly speak of an **industrial landscape.** It forms part of daily life, a prominent and often disturbing visible feature of our surroundings. Industry creates a landscape not normally

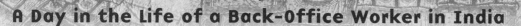

CULTURE IN A GLOBALIZING WORLD

A Day in the Life of a Back-Office Worker in India

Harish Kuman trains new employees for Office Tiger, an American-owned company located in Chennai, India, that provides services such as equity analysis and legal research for a variety of predominantly American companies such as Wall Street firms, accounting companies, and insurance conglomerates. His job includes teaching business skills that range from American slang to PowerPoint, skills that will enable his trainees to make it past the probation of six months and become full-fledged Tigers, ready to move up into more skilled jobs of analysis and research. With a policy of rewarding good and hard work and a climate explicitly set up as a meritocracy, Office Tiger thrives on employees like Harish who work long hours, often 80 a week. In turn, Harish gains money, experience, and exposure to another way of life and an alternative future. He also finds that his position with this American company has changed him in fundamental ways. Here is a snapshot from a typical day in his life:

> The neighborhood where Harish has lived all his life is named Triplicane, and was once an ancient fishermen's village. It is today so densely populated that some travel guides mistake it for a slum. Harish's house is off the main road, in an alley of jasmine peddlers, Muslim shop workers, and Hindu priests. He rises around 5:30 A.M., mounts his rusted bike, and rides to work. His passage doesn't rouse the beggar children, who have learned his recently acquired belief that direct handouts to the poor encourage sloth. At work, he trains his

candidates, takes ten minutes or so for lunch in the office pantry, and trains some more. At seven-thirty in the evening, when it's 9 A.M. in New York, he confers with the American banking clients for whom he tailors his training, to insure that he is emphasizing the right skills. And then he turns to a slew of computer-programming challenges that may show management his greater gifts. He often goes home after midnight.

On his concrete threshold in Triplicane, as on others in the neighborhood, is an intricate chalk design known as a kolam. His grandmother, who is seventy-nine, draws it there each morning, in the Hindu hope of keeping catastrophe safely out in the streets. At night, from her mat, she listens for her grandson, sometimes cupping a hand around an elaborately bejeweled ear. The ear adornment was the custom in the village where she was born, a place where the tigers were real and said to devour boys in one go, not bit by bit each workday. She is the first at the door when her grandson rings the bell. He leaves his new square-toed lace-ups at the threshold, swallows a few spoonfuls of rice to silence protests about his declining weight, and joins his extended family on the floor. It is then that his grandmother, if not Harish, can sleep.

From Boo, Katherine. 2004. "The Best Job in Town." *The New Yorker* (July 5).

designed for beauty, charm, or aesthetic appeal, but rather for profit and utility. Often, by almost anyone's standards, ugly industrial landscapes are poor places for humans to spend their lives.

Each level of industrial activity produces its own distinctive landscape. Primary industries exert perhaps the most drastic impact on the land. The resulting landscapes contain slag heaps, clear-cut commercial forests, massive strip-mining scars, gaping open-pit mines, and "forests" of oil derricks. Some industrial landscapes take on a bizarre, otherworldly character, at once horrible and fascinating (Figure 9.21). Certain other primary industrial landscapes, in contrast, please the eye and complement the beauty of nature. The

fishing villages of Portugal or Newfoundland even attract tourists (Figure 9.22). In still other cases, efforts are made to restore the preindustrial landscape. Examples include the establishment of artificial grasslands in old strip-mining areas of the American Midwest and the creation of recreational ponds in old mine pits along interstate highways in the same region. The most obvious features of the landscapes of secondary industry, or manufacturing, are factory buildings. Early- to mid-nineteenth-century industrial landscapes are easy to identify because the technologies that ran these factories were reliant on water power. Hence, the mill buildings that housed the machinery were designed in linear form to take full advantage of the turbines that were connected to

Figure 9.21 **Three primary industrial landscapes.** *Upper left:* This bizarrely colored "industrial mosaic" is on the margins of the Great Salt Lake in Utah, where chemicals and minerals such as metallic magnesium, potassium, and sodium chloride are derived from the water by solar evaporation. *Upper right:* This open-pit mine is Bingham Canyon in Utah, the second largest in the world. *Bottom:* This mind-boggling, artificial "Alp" is the result of potash mining near Kassel in Germany. *(Courtesy of Terry G. Jordan-Bychkov.)*

waterwheels. What's more, given this locational requirement, these mill complexes were most often built in rural areas. Entire communities, most often with housing for the workers, were thus constructed along with the mills. These mill towns dotted the landscape of England, Scotland, and New England, the site of the first industrial developments in the United States (Figure 9.23). Later—as water power was supplanted by steam, coal, and then electric power—factories were located near urban areas, taking advantage of the housing supply already there and the proximity to a large consumer base. These industrial landscapes were often located at the edge of downtowns, lining the railroad routes into the city, and were surrounded by working-class housing (see the

section on class, "race," and gender in the industrial city in Chapter 10). In the second half of the twentieth century—with the development of the interstate highway system and the trucking industry, as well as the switch to high-tech industries such as electronics—industrial landscapes took on a different shape. Factories began to move to industrial parks at interstate exchanges, and their architecture became less conspicuous, looking more like "box" stores than traditional factories (Figure 9.24).

Given the degree of deindustrialization in certain parts of the old core industrial regions, it is not surprising that many of these factory complexes, particularly those that date from the nineteenth and early twentieth centuries, are

Figure 9.22 **A fishing village in Newfoundland.** Primary industrial landscapes can be pleasing to the eye. What problems might such a landscape also suggest? *(Courtesy of Terry G. Jordan-Bychkov.)*

derelict or are being retrofitted into housing or commercial uses. Others now house historical museums depicting past industrial technologies and ways of life. Lowell, Massachusetts, an early (mid-nineteenth-century) planned industrial town that produced textiles, is now the site of a national park. A good percentage of its factories, canals, and housing complexes have been preserved and can be toured by visitors. In Great Britain, many sites of industrial history are now preserved as museums. New Lanark, located outside of Glasgow in Scotland, is now a World Heritage Site and provides a particularly interesting example of an industrial landscape, given that it was originally estab-

FOCUS ON

Women, Men, and Work in the Maquiladoras

Young women constitute a large percentage of the labor force in the maquiladora factories along the U.S.-Mexican border. For the American-owned companies that employ them, they are considered the cheapest and most reliable pool of labor. Many of these women leave their homes and villages in other parts of Mexico to work in these plants, living in company or state-owned dormitories, while others live with their families close by, frequently in squatter settlements. Though often considered hazardous and back-breaking, these jobs provide a much-needed source of capital for many of these women and their families. They also disrupt the gender division of labor within their own homes. Geographer Altha Cravey analyzed such effects on the lives of women and men working in maquiladora plants in Nogales, Mexico, pointing out the connections between domestic work arrangements and factory work, and, for some, the potentially liberating disruptions caused by women working away from home:

As individual Nogales households adapt to change, such as fluctuations in income and household composition, household members devise new arrangements for meeting daily and long-term needs. Overall, males contribute domestic labor to approximately 60% of Nogales households, and it is common to find men who *regularly* assume responsibility for some domestic tasks. Negotiations over the simple tasks of child care, cleaning, shopping, and cooking are less simple than they might seem at first glance. The result may challenge long-standing gender norms, amounting even to a renegotiation of the social meaning of gender itself. For instance, one male informant who regularly cares for his children during his wife's hours at the factory seemed to downplay his sustained domestic labor, as if it contradicted his ideal self-image. He and his partner had settled on this arrangement after a long period of fighting over the expense of paying a neighbor for child care. . . . His struggles and those of others like him result in the invention of new male (and female) identities.

Adapted from Cravey, 1998

Figure 9.23 **Mill buildings in central Massachusetts.** Most textile mills in New England were abandoned by the mid-twentieth century, as textile production moved to southern states and then later to countries outside the United States. What accounts for the footloose nature of the textile industry? *(Courtesy of Mona Domosh.)*

lished by Robert Owen as a utopian community. He included in his planning good schools, housing, and even a co-operative food store in order to create a benevolent community of workers (Figure 9.25).

Yet in other parts of the world, as we've learned in this chapter, industrial landscapes are far from derelict; they are, in fact, being built anew. In Southeast Asia, China, and Mexico large industrial landscapes are under construction. Some, like the maquiladoras (refer again to Focus On: Women, Men, and Work in the Maquiladoras), are similar to the early mill towns in that they, too, are being constructed in nonurban sites without housing or other infra-

structure. In the maquiladoras, as well as in many industrial regions of China, housing comes either in the form of dormitories or in informal squatter settlements (Figure 9.26).

Service industries, too, produce a cultural landscape. Its visual content includes elements as diverse as high-rise bank buildings, hamburger stands, "silicon landscapes," gasoline stations, and the concrete and steel webs of highways and railroads. Some highway interchanges can best be described as a modern art form, but perhaps the aesthetic high point of the industrial landscape is found in bridges, which are often graceful and beautiful structures. The massive investment in these transportation systems has even changed the

Figure 9.24 **Footwear factory in Picardie, France.** This factory is located right along the highway, providing easy access for its employees and for the trucks that transport its products. Are there any visual clues here that this structure is a factory rather than a "box" store? *(ForestierYves/Corbis Sygma.)*

Figure 9.25 **New Lanark, Scotland.** Robert Owens's planned industrial town is now a World Heritage Site. Compare these buildings to the workers' dormitory in Figure 9.26, and consider the changes that have occurred (or haven't occurred) in the provision of housing for industrial workers. *(Courtesy of Mona Domosh.)*

way we view the landscape. As geographer Yi-Fu Tuan commented, "In the early decades of the twentieth century vehicles began to displace walking as the prevalent form of locomotion, and street scenes were perceived increasingly from the interior of automobiles moving staccato-fashion

through regularly spaced traffic lights." Los Angeles, the ultimate automobile city, provides perhaps the best example of the new viewpoints provided by the industrial age. Its freeway system allows individual motorists to observe their surroundings at nonstop speeds. It also allows the driver to look *down* on the world. The pedestrian, on the other hand, is slighted. The view from the street is not encouraged. In some areas of Los Angeles, streets actually have no sidewalks at all, so that the pedestrian viewpoint is functionally impractical. In other areas, the layout of the main avenues has been planned with the car in mind, and the pedestrian feels ill at ease amid the nonhuman surroundings—noise, traffic jams, drive-in banks, and parking lots. The shopping street is no longer scaled to the pedestrian—Los Angeles's Ventura Boulevard extends for 15 miles (24 kilometers).

Producer services related to financial activities, such as legal services, trade, insurance, and banking, were traditionally located in high-rise buildings in urban centers, but with suburbanization they, too, have taken on a nonurban form. Many are now located in five- or six-story buildings, along the interstates surrounding cities, in what we've called high-tech corridors (Figure 9.27). Other producer service industries choose to maintain their downtown location for symbolic reasons. Some consumer services, particularly retailing, have created distinctive and, within the American context at least, socially important landscapes. Shopping malls are now dominant features of the North American suburb and often serve as catalysts to suburban land development, in effect creating entirely new landscapes, all geared toward consumption. Chapter 11 provides more details about these new and emerging landscape elements.

Figure 9.26 **Workers' dormitory in Dongguan, China.** Notice the similarity in clothing hanging on each worker's balcony. Compare this image to Figure 9.25. *(Courtesy of Charles Cowles Gallery, New York, & Robert Koch Gallery, San Francisco.)*

Figure 9.27 **Office buildings in suburban Florida.** Most of the activities that take place in these offices are related to banking. Why are these buildings set back off the road? *(Courtesy of Mona Domosh.)*

Conclusion

As we have seen, then, one of the most significant events of our age is the diffusion of industrialization, which has brought a host of far-reaching cultural changes. Already the industrial revolution has modified the regions, habitats, cultures, and landscapes of some lands so greatly that people who lived there in the past would be bewildered by the modern setting. As it turns out, much of the process of industrialization has been carried out in cities. Indeed, industrialization is the principal cause of urbanization. It is time, in the following two chapters, for us to turn our attention to the *city* as a cultural phenomenon.

DOING GEOGRAPHY

What You Wear, Where?

As we've pointed out in this chapter, the textile and garment industries have historically been very footloose, able to move production facilities to locations that suit manufacturers, often because of the low cost of labor. In today's global world, that tendency is even more pronounced, with manufacturers of clothing and other garment-related materials outsourcing many aspects of production and often subcontracting with other companies to complete different tasks in different parts of the world. It's possible, then, that the clothes and shoes you are wearing right now were designed in one place, woven into fabric in another place, and assembled in yet another.

This exercise is about tracing the "origins" of the clothes and shoes you are wearing right now and about asking "Why?" The cost of labor, as we've learned, is important, but it certainly isn't the only factor in determining where garments and shoes are made. In manufacturing in general, other locational factors include the locations of markets as well as state and international policies, such as NAFTA. For clothing and shoes, another important factor is fashion. Styles change often, and there might be a need for manufacturers to be able to change their production quickly. This would lead companies to locate manufacturing facilities close to their main markets, which might mean in the United States or Canada.

Start this exercise by locating as many of the labels as you can on the shoes and all the pieces of clothing you are wearing right now. Read them carefully and create a list and a map of the places mentioned on the labels. This alone should give you a good sense of the global nature of this industry! Now, ask "Why?" Why are certain items manufactured in particular places? Is there a pattern to these places? What are the similarities in these countries? What are the differences? Consider each of the locational factors we've mentioned—labor, markets, state policies, consumer trends—and try to generalize the why of what you wear.

Industrial Geography on the Internet

You can learn more about industrial geography on the Internet at the following web sites:

Greenpeace
http://www.greenpeace.org
This is the site for information about an activist group that uses both orthodox and illegal methods in its attempts to bring attention to environmental crises.

Sierra Club
http://www.sierraclub.org
See this site for information about an established, mainstream organization of environmental activists.

United Nations Industrial Development Organization
http://www.unido.org
This specialist agency of the United Nations is devoted to promoting sustainable industrial development in countries with developing and/or transition economies. The site contains industrial statistics and information on women in industrial development, and it allows you to access data and maps of the least developed countries in the world.

Worldwatch Institute, Washington, D.C.
http://www.worldwatch.org
This nongovernmental watchdog and research institute compiles and analyzes the latest information about such ecological problems as global warming, industrial pollution, and deforestation. It also seeks sustainable alternatives.

SEEING GEOGRAPHY

How is this Chinese landscape connected to the Wal-Mart located in your neighborhood?

Buildings that house a set of shoe factories in Guangdong Province, China.

Factories in Guangdong Province, China

The buildings depicted in this image house a set of factories in Guangdong Province, China, that produce different types of shoes (Nike, New Balance, Reebok), some of which are contracted to be sold in the United States. Given that Wal-Mart accounts for 12 percent of China's exports to the United States, it's not difficult to surmise that some of the shoes produced here, in southeastern China, will make their way to the shoe racks at your local store. China manufactures almost half of all the shoes in the world, and this particular manufacturing site, employing approximately 50,000 workers, is said to be the world's largest shoe production site.

The shoe industry is a particularly good example of the worldwide scale of contemporary economic globalization and of how this globalization is changing lives and landscapes in complex ways. The group of shoe factories shown here—called the Yu Yuan manufacturing plant—is actually owned by the Bao Cheng Group, a large corporation controlled by Taiwanese investors and entrepreneurs. With labor costs rising in Taiwan, these entrepreneurs began to invest heavily in China in the late 1980s and early 1990s. Most of the workers shown in this image have moved to this new urban center from surrounding rural areas, where it was difficult to make a living as farmers. This rural-to-urban migration promises to be the largest human migration in history, and it is estimated that by the year 2010, almost half of China's population (approximately 1.5 billion) will live in urban centers. Almost 70 percent of the workers at the Yu Yuan factories are women, leading to transformations in family structure and domestic arrangements similar to what is happening in the border region in Mexico (refer again to Focus On: Women, Men, and Work in the Maquiladoras).

Even more changes are on the horizon. The Chinese economy is booming, bringing with it higher economic standards and therefore rising labor costs. As a result, the Taiwanese entrepreneurs who own the Bao Cheng Group have begun to look elsewhere for cheaper labor and have already moved a number of their factories to Vietnam. It may be only a matter of time before some of the factory buildings shown in this photograph are transformed to house other types of commercial activities or are torn down to make way for different land uses altogether. ■

Sources

Airriess, Christopher A. 2001. "Regional Production, Information-Communication Technology, and the Developmental State: The Rise of Singapore as a Global Container Hub." *Geoforum* 32: 235–254.

Alfrey, Judith, and Catherine Clark. 1993. *The Landscape of Industry.* London: Routledge.

Boo, Katherine. 2004. "The Best Job in Town." *The New Yorker* (July 5).

Braudel, Fernand. 1972. *The Mediterranean and the Mediterranean World in the Age of Phillip II.* New York: Harper & Row.

Brown, Laurie, Martha Ronk, and Charles E. Little. 2000. *Recent Terrains: Terraforming the American West.* Baltimore: Johns Hopkins University Press.

Dicken, Peter. 2003. *Global Shift: Reshaping the Global Economic Map in the 21st Century.* New York: Guilford Press.

Francaviglia, Richard V. 1991. *Hard Places: Reading the Landscape of America's Historic Mining Districts.* Iowa City: University of Iowa Press.

Goethe, Johann W. von. 1957. *Faust.* George M. Priest (trans. and ed.). New York: Alfred A. Knopf.

Holden, Andrew. 2000. *Environment and Tourism.* New York: Routledge.

Hudson, John C., and Edward B. Espenshade Jr. (eds.). 2000. *Goode's World Atlas,* 20th ed. Chicago: Rand McNally.

Jakle, John A., and Keith A. Sculle. 1994. *The Gas Station in America.* Baltimore: Johns Hopkins University Press.

Job, Hubert. 1996. "Modell zur Evaluation der Nachhaltigkeit Tourismus." *Erdkunde* 50: 112–132.

Jordan-Bychkov, Terry G., and Bella Bychkova Jordan. 2002. *The European Culture Area,* 4th ed. Lanham, Md.: Rowman & Littlefield.

National Atmospheric Deposition Program web site. http://nadp.sws.uiuc.edu

O'Hare, Greg. 2000. "Reviewing the Uncertainties in Climate Change Science." *Area* 32: 357–368.

Park, Chris C. 1989. *Chernobyl: The Long Shadow.* London: Routledge.

Power, Thomas M. 1996. *Lost Landscapes and Failed Economies: The Search for the Value of Place.* Washington, D.C.: Island Press.

Thompson, John H., and Michihiro Miyazaki. 1959. "A Map of Japan's Manufacturing." *Geographical Review* 49: 1–17.

Tuan, Yi-Fu. 1989. "Cultural Pluralism and Technology." *Geographical Review* 79: 269–279.

United Nations. 2000. *Statistical Yearbook.* New York: United Nations.

Warrick, Richard, and Graham Farmer. 1990. "The Greenhouse Effect, Climatic Change and Rising Sea Level: Implications for Development." *Transactions of the Institute of British Geographers* 15: 5–20.

Weber, Alfred. 1929. *Theory of the Location of Industries.* Carl J. Friedrich (trans. and ed.). Chicago: University of Chicago Press.

"Wind Power: Maybe This Time." 2001. *The Economist* (March 10): 30–31.

Yale Center for Environmental Law and Policy and the Center for International Earth Science Information Network. 2005. *2005 Environmental Sustainability Index.* New Haven: Yale University.

Ten Recommended Books
on Industrial Geography

(For additional suggested readings, see *The Human Mosaic* web site: www.whfreeman.com/jordan)

Cater, Erlet, and Gwen Lowman (eds.). 1994. *Ecotourism: A Sustainable Option?* Chichester, U.K.: John Wiley and the Royal Geographical Society. An excellent analysis of ecotourism, assessing whether it is as ecologically benign as the name suggests.

Cravey, Altha. 1998. *Women and Work in Mexico's Maquiladoras.* Lanham, Md.: Rowman & Littlefield. A detailed analysis of the relationships between gender and work in two different places along the U.S.-Mexican border.

Dicken, Peter. 2003. *Global Shift: Reshaping the Global Economic Map in the 21st Century.* New York: Guilford Press. An incredibly comprehensive look at the causes and effects of the increasingly global and interlinked industries of the world.

Drake, Frances. 2000. *Global Warming: The Science of Climate Change.* London: Arnold. A British geographer presents the complicated issue of global warming in terms intelligible to the undergraduate student, stripping away the jargon of science while retaining the essential message of climate change.

Glasmeier, Amy. 2000. *Manufacturing Time: Global Competition in the Watch Industry, 1795–2000.* New York: Guilford Press. A detailed case study chronicling the historical and spatial changes of the watch industry in Japan, Switzerland, and the United States.

Hall, Colin M., and Stephen J. Page. 1999. *The Geography of Tourism and Recreation: Environment, Place and Space.* New York: Routledge. An excellent comprehensive introduction to the topic, containing case studies from North America, Europe, China, Australia, and the Pacific islands.

Harrington, James W., and Barney Warf. 1995. *Industrial Location: Principles and Practice.* New York: Routledge. A useful basic primer on industrial location written for nonexperts.

McDowell, Linda. 1997. *Capital Culture: Gender at Work in the City.* 1997. Oxford: Blackwell. An interesting look at the importance of gender identity to the functioning of the financial sector.

Peck, Jamie. 1996. *Work-Place: The Social Regulation of Labor Markets.* New York: Guilford Press. A detailed analysis of the relationships among labor, place, and state policies.

Seager, Joni. 1995. *The State of the Earth Atlas,* 2nd ed. New York: Simon & Schuster. A basic source for anyone concerned about environmental problems. A collection of truly sobering maps.

Journals in Industrial Geography

Economic Geography, published by Clark University. Volume 1 appeared in 1925.

Journal of Transport Geography, published by Elsevier Science. Volume 1 was published in 1993.

What are some of the major environmental and social impacts of an increasingly urbanized world?

View of Rio de Janeiro from Sugarloaf Mountain. *(Blaine Harrington III/The Stock Market.)*
Turn to Seeing Geography on page 372 for an in-depth analysis of the above question.

URBANIZATION

The City in Time and Space

10

IMAGINE THE 2 MILLION YEARS THAT humankind has spent on Earth as a 24-hour day. In this framework, settlements of more than a hundred people came about only in the last half-hour. Towns and cities emerged only a few minutes ago, and large-scale urbanization began less than 60 seconds ago. Yet it is during these "minutes" that we see the rise of civilization. *Civitas,* the Latin root word for *civilization,* was first applied to settled areas of the Roman Empire. Later it came to mean a specific town or city. *To civilize* meant literally "to citify."

Urbanization over the past 200 years has strengthened the links among culture, society, and the city. An urban explosion has gone hand in hand with the industrial revolution. According to United Nations estimates, the world's urban population has more than tripled since 1950 (733 million in 1950 versus 3.17 billion in 2005) and will reach 4.94 billion by the year 2030. At that time, over 60 percent of the Earth's population will live in cities. The cultural geography of the world will change dramatically as we become a predominantly urban people and the ways of the countryside are increasingly replaced by urban lifestyles.

In this chapter, we consider the overall patterns of urbanization, learn how urbanization began and developed, and discuss the differing forms of cities in the developing and developed worlds. In addition, we examine some of the external factors influencing city location. In Chapter 11, we look at the internal aspects of the city, seen through the five themes of cultural geography.

Urbanized Population

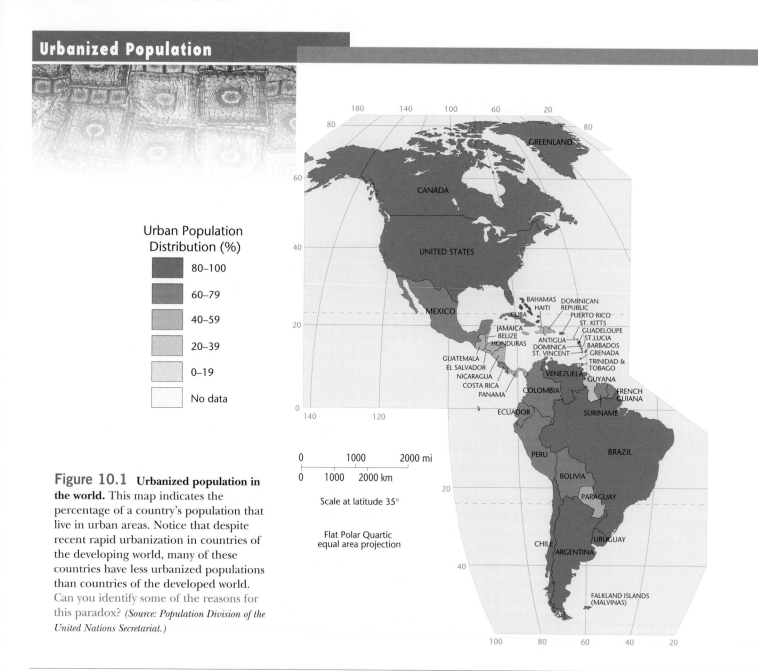

Urban Population Distribution (%)

- 80–100
- 60–79
- 40–59
- 20–39
- 0–19
- No data

0   1000   2000 mi
0   1000 2000 km

Scale at latitude 35°

Flat Polar Quartic
equal area projection

Figure 10.1 **Urbanized population in the world.** This map indicates the percentage of a country's population that live in urban areas. Notice that despite recent rapid urbanization in countries of the developing world, many of these countries have less urbanized populations than countries of the developed world. Can you identify some of the reasons for this paradox? (*Source: Population Division of the United Nations Secretariat.*)

Culture Region

How are urban areas and urban populations spatially arranged? A quick look at Figure 10.1 reveals differing patterns of **urbanized population**—the percentage of a nation's population living in towns and cities—around the world. For example, the countries of Europe, North America, Latin America, and the Caribbean have relatively high levels of urbanization, with approximately 75 percent of each coun-

try's population living in urban areas. The nations of Africa and Asia, on the other hand, are less urbanized, with approximately 38 percent of each country's population residing in urban areas. What one cannot detect from this map is the spatial arrangement of urban areas within countries. The urban populations of some countries—Mexico, for example—are concentrated in a few small sections; others, such as France, have a fairly even distribution of urban and rural areas. How do geographers explain these varying regional patterns of urbanization?

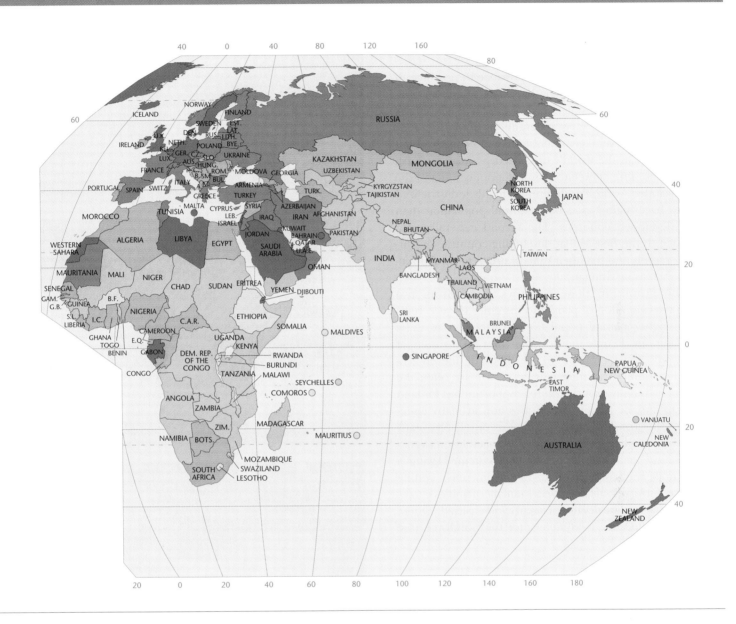

Patterns and Processes of Urbanization

According to United Nations estimates, almost all the worldwide population growth in the next 30 years will be concentrated in urban areas, with the cities of the less developed regions responsible for most of that increase. The reasons for this explosion in urban population growth and its uneven distribution around the world vary, as each country's unique history and society present a slightly different narrative of urban and economic development. Mak-

ing matters more complex is the lack of a standard definition of what constitutes a city. Consequently, the criteria used to calculate a country's urbanized population differ from nation to nation. Using data based on these varying criteria would result in misleading conclusions. For example, the Indian government defines an urban center as an area having 5000 inhabitants, with an adult male population employed predominantly in nonagricultural work. In contrast, the U.S. Census Bureau defines a city as a densely populated area of 2500 people or more, and South Africa counts as a city any settlement of 500 or more people. Furthermore, some countries revise their definitions of urban settlements to suit specific purposes. China-watchers were baffled in 1983 when that country's urban population swelled by 13 percent in one year, only to learn that China had simply revised its census definitions for urban settlements, with criteria that vary from province to province. It is important to remember, then, that an international comparison of urbanized population data can be made only by taking into account the varying definitions of what a city is.

Nonetheless, several generalizations can be made about the differences in the world's urbanized population. First, there is a close link between urbanized population and the more developed world. Put differently, highly industrialized countries have higher rates of urbanized population than do less developed countries. The second generalization, closely tied to the first, is that developing countries are urbanizing rapidly and that their ratio of urban to rural population is increasing dramatically.

Urban growth in these countries comes from two sources: the migration of people to the cities (Figure 10.2) and the higher natural population growth rates of these recent migrants. People move to the cities for a variety of reasons, most of which relate to the effects of uneven economic development in their country. Cities are often the centers of economic growth, whereas opportunities for land ownership and/or farming-based jobs are, in many countries, rare. Because urban employment is unreliable, many migrants continue to have large numbers of children to construct a more extensive family support system. Having a larger family increases the chances of someone's getting work. The demographic transition to smaller families comes later, when a certain degree of security is ensured. Often, this transition occurs as women enter the workforce (see Chapter 7).

Impacts of Urbanization

Although rural-to-urban migration affects nearly all cities in the developing world, the most visible cases are the extraordinarily large settlements we call **world cities**—those having populations of over 10 million. Table 10.1 shows the world's 20 largest cities, over half of which are in the developing world. This is a major change from 30 years ago, when the list would have been dominated by Western, industrialized cities, a trend that most expect to continue. Projections for future growth, however, must be qualified by two considerations. First, cities of the developing world will continue to explode in size only if economic development expands. If it stagnates because of political or resource problems, city growth will probably slow (although urban migration might increase if rural economies deteriorate). For example, Mexico City's growth is linked to that country's economic growth

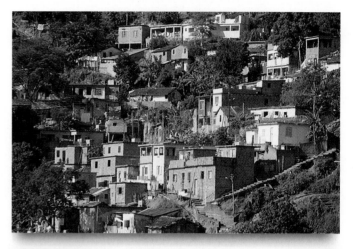

Figure 10.2 **Urbanization.** Shown here are scenes from a squatter settlement in Rio de Janeiro (*top*), the business district in Kolkata (Calcutta) (*middle*), and a residential district of Manila (*bottom*). For more information about the growth of such cities, see the section on globalizing cities in the developing world. As is evident from this scene in Kolkata, the downtowns of cities in the developing world are often more vibrant than those of the developed world. Can you think of some reasons for this? (*Top: Najilah Feaney/Saba; Middle: Earl Young/Tony Stone Images; Bottom: Bruno Zehnder/Peter Arnold, Inc.*)

TABLE 10.1 The World's 20 Largest Metropolitan Areas*

Rank	Metropolitan Area	Country	Population (thousands)	Average Annual Percent Change
1	Tokyo/Yokohama	Japan	32,800	0.68
2	New York	United States	21,800	0.56
3	Mexico City	Mexico	20,900	1.51
4	Seoul	Korea, South	20,850	1.07
5	Mumbai (Bombay)	India	20,000	2.60
6	Jakarta	Indonesia	19,850	1.03
7	Delhi/New Delhi	India	19,750	3.91
8	São Paulo	Brazil	19,350	1.63
9	Osaka/Kobe/Kyoto	Japan	17,400	0.14
10	Shanghai	China, P.R. of	17,200	2.10
11	Manila	Philippines	16,600	2.40
12	Hong Kong/Shenzhen	China, P.R. of	16,500	4.50
13	Kolkata (Calcutta)	India	15,500	1.74
14	Los Angeles	United States	15,350	1.08
15	Moscow	Russia	14,800	0.96
16	Cairo	Egypt	14,750	1.79
17	Buenos Aires	Argentina	13,300	0.62
18	Beijing	China, P.R. of	13,000	2.53
19	London	United Kingdom	12,850	0.24
20	Karachi	Pakistan	12,400	3.40

*Populations estimated as of January 1, 2005, and annual rates of change for 2000–2005. (Source: Prepared by Richard L. Forstall. Used by permission.)

and, more specifically, to Mexico's oil industry, which fluctuates according to the world market for oil. Second, because these world cities are plagued by transportation, housing, employment, and ecological problems—such as an inadequate water supply, in the case of Mexico City—some countries are trying to control urban migration. The success or failure of these policies will influence city size in the next 10 to 20 years.

Nevertheless, the urban population in the developing world is growing at astounding rates. Even though the developed regions of the world are more urbanized overall than the less developed regions, the sheer scale and rate of growth in absolute numbers reveal a reversal in this pattern. According to geographer David Drakakis-Smith, there are now twice as many urban dwellers in the developing world as there are in developed countries. For example, the population of urbanites in the countries of Europe, North America, Latin America, and the Caribbean (according to the United Nations, 1.2 billion) is smaller than the population of urbanites in Asia (1.5 billion). And with this incredible increase in sheer numbers of urban dwellers in the less developed regions of the world comes a large list of problems. Unemployment rates in cities of the developing world are often over 50 percent for newcomers to the city; housing and infrastructure often cannot be built fast enough to keep pace with growth rates; water and sewage systems can rarely handle the influx of new people. Consequently, one of the world's ongoing crises will be this radical restructuring of population and culture as people in developing countries move into the cities.

The target for much urban migration is the **primate city.** This is a settlement that dominates the economic, political, and cultural life of a country and, as a result of rapid growth, expands its primacy or dominance. Buenos Aires is an excellent example of a primate city because it far exceeds Rosario, the second-largest city in Argentina, in size and importance. Although many developing countries are dominated by a primate city, often a former center of colonial power, urban primacy is not unique to these countries: think of the way London and Paris dominate their respective countries.

REFLECTING ON GEOGRAPHY

What types of historical, political, and economic factors account for nations that are dominated by a primate city? Why didn't Boston or New York City become the primate city for the United States?

We are fast becoming a predominantly urban world, and our cultural geography is increasingly dominated by urban landscapes. Next we investigate the rise and evolution of the earliest settlements to understand the phenomenon of urbanization better.

 # Origin and Diffusion of the City

Where did urban life begin, and how did it spread throughout the world? As we seek explanations for the origin of cities, we ultimately find a relationship among areas of early agricultural development, permanent village settlements, the emergence of new social forms, and urban life. The first cities resulted from a complicated transition that took thousands of years.

As early people, originally hunters and gatherers, became more successful at gathering their resources and domesticating plants and animals, they began to settle, first semipermanently and then permanently. In the Middle East, where the first cities appeared, a network of permanent agricultural villages developed about 10,000 years ago. These farming villages were modest in size, rarely with more than 200 people, and were probably organized on a kinship basis. Jarmo, one of the earliest villages, located in present-day Iraq, had 25 permanent dwellings clustered together near grain storage facilities.

Although small farming villages like Jarmo predate cities, it is wrong to assume that a simple quantitative change took place whereby villages slowly grew, first into towns and then into cities. In fact, true cities differed qualitatively from agricultural villages. All the inhabitants of agricultural villages were involved in some way in food procurement—tending the agricultural fields or harvesting and preparing the crops. Cities, however, were more removed, both physically and psy-chologically, from everyday agricultural activities. Food was supplied to the city, but not all city dwellers were involved in obtaining it. Instead, city dwellers supplied other services, such as technical skills or religious interpretations considered important in a particular society. Cities, unlike agricultural villages, contained a class of people who were not directly involved in agricultural activities.

Two elements were necessary for this dramatic social change: the creation of an **agricultural surplus** and the development of a stratified social system. Surplus food, which is a food supply larger than the everyday needs of the agricultural labor force, is a prerequisite for supporting nonfarmers—people who work at administrative, military, or handicraft tasks. Social stratification, the existence of distinct socioeconomic classes, facilitates the collection, storage, and distribution of resources through well-defined channels of authority that can exercise control over goods and people. A society with these two elements—surplus food and a means of storing and distributing it—was set for urbanization.

Models for the Rise of Cities

Some scholars who seek to understand the transition from village to city life prefer to construct models for the development of urban life based on one single factor as the "trigger" behind the change. These scholars ask what activity could be so important to an agricultural society that its people would be willing to give some of their surplus to support a social class that would specialize in that activity. In the next sections, we discuss answers to that question, and we clarify a multiple-factor explanation for the rise of cities.

Technical Factors The **hydraulic civilization** model, developed by Karl Wittfogel, sees the development of large-scale irrigation systems as the prime mover behind urbanization and a class of technical specialists as the first urban dwellers. Higher crop yields resulted from irrigated agriculture, and this food surplus supported the development of a large nonfarming population. A strong, centralized government, backed by an urban-based military, expanded power into the surrounding areas. Those farmers who resisted the new authority were denied water. Continued reinforcement of the power elite came from the need for organizational co-ordination to ensure continued operation of the irrigation system.

Class distinctions were reinforced by power differences, and labor specialization developed. Some people farmed; others worked on the irrigation system. Still others became artisans, creating the implements needed to maintain the system, or administrative workers in the direct employ of the power elite's court.

Although the hydraulic model fits several areas where cities first arose—China, Egypt, and Mesopotamia (present-day Iraq)—it cannot be applied to all urban hearths. In parts of Mesoamerica, for example, an urban civilization blossomed without widespread irrigated agriculture, and therefore without a class of technical experts. The hydraulic model also begs the question of how or why a culture might develop an irrigation system in the first place.

Religious Factors Geographer Paul Wheatley suggests that religion led to urbanization. In early agricultural societies, knowledge of such matters as meteorology and climate was considered an element of religion. Such societies depended on their religious leaders to interpret the heavenly bodies before deciding when and how to plant their crops. The propagation of this type of knowledge led to more successful harvests, which in turn allowed for the support of both a larger priestly class and a class of people engaged in ancillary activities. The priestly class exercised the political and social control that held the city together.

In this scenario, early cities were religious spaces. The first urban clusters and fortifications are seen as defenses not against human invaders but against spiritual ones: demons or the souls of the dead. This religious explanation is applicable in some ways to all the early centers of urbanization, although it seems especially successful in explaining Chinese urbanization.

Political Factors Other scholars suggest that the centralizing force in urbanization was not religious order but political order. Urban historian Lewis Mumford described the agent of change in emerging urban centers as the institution of kingship, which involved the centralizing of religious, social, and economic aspects of a civilization around a powerful figure who became known as the king. This figure of authority, who in the preurban world was accorded respect for his or her human abilities, ascended to almost superhuman status in early urbanizing societies. By exercising power, the king was able to marshal the labor of others. The resultant social hierarchy enabled the society to diversify its endeavors, with different groups specializing in crafts, farming, trading, or religious activity. The institution of kingship provided essential leadership and organization to this increasingly complex society, which became the city.

Multiple Factors At the onset of urbanization, and even much later in some places, sharp distinctions among economic, religious, and political functions were not always made. The king may also have functioned as priest, healer, astronomer, and scribe, thereby fusing secular and spiritual power. Critics of the kingship theory, therefore, point out that this explanation of urbanization may not be different from the religion-based model. Rather than attempting to isolate one trigger, a wiser course may be to accept the role of multiple factors behind the changes leading to urban life. Technical, religious, and political forces were often interlinked, with a change in one leading to changes in another. Instead of oversimplifying by focusing on one possible development schema, we must appreciate the complexities of the transition period from agricultural village to true city.

Urban Hearth Areas

The first cities appeared in distinct regions, such as Mesopotamia, the Nile River valley, Pakistan's Indus River valley, the Yellow River (or Huang Ho) valley of China, Mesoamerica, and the Andean highlands and coastal areas of Peru. These are called the **urban hearth areas** (see Focus On: Cahokia: An Early Urban Center on the Mississippi on page 342, and Figure 10.3)

REFLECTING ON GEOGRAPHY

Scholars are continually altering the dates for the emergence of urban life, as well as the location of the hearth areas. Why? Can you outline some of the reasons that it is so difficult to pinpoint the places and dates for the emergence of urban life?

It is generally agreed that the first cities arose in Mesopotamia, the river valley of the Tigris and Euphrates in what is now Iraq. Mesopotamian cities, small by current standards, covered 0.5 to 2 square miles (1.3 to 5 square kilometers) with populations that rarely exceeded 30,000. Nevertheless, the densities within these cities could easily reach 10,000 people per square mile (4000 per square kilometer), which is comparable to the densities in many contemporary cities.

The spatial layouts of the cities of the urban hearth areas that we can call **cosmomagical cities** were similar in three important ways (Figure 10.4). First, great importance was accorded to the city's symbolic center, which was also thought to be the center of the known world. It was therefore the most sacred spot and was often identified by a vertical structure of monumental scale that represented the point on Earth closest to the heavens. This symbolic center, or **axis mundi,** took the form of the ziggurat in Mesopotamia, the palace or temple in China, and the pyramid in Mesoamerica. Often this elevated structure, which usually served a religious purpose, was close to the palace or seat of political power and to the granary. These three structures were often walled off from the rest of the city, forming a symbolic center that both reflected the particular significance

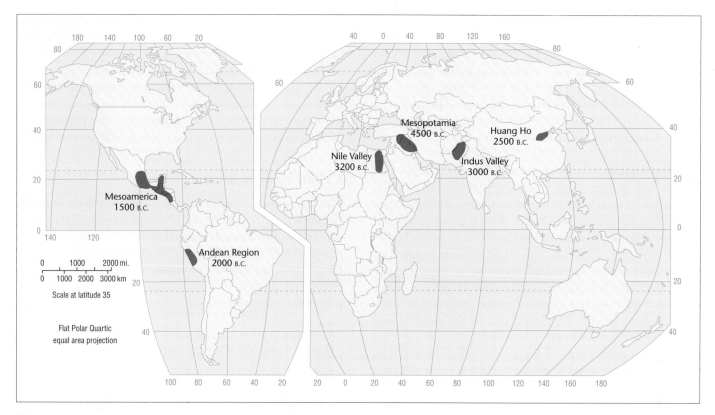

Figure 10.3 **The world's first cities arose in six urban hearth areas.** The dates shown are conservative figures for the rise of urban life in each area. For example, some scholars would suggest that urban life in Mesopotamia existed by 5000 B.C. Ongoing discoveries suggest that urban life appeared earlier in each of the hearth areas and that there are probably other hearth areas—in West Africa, for example.

of certain societal functions and dominated the city physically and spiritually (Figure 10.5). The Forbidden City in Beijing remains one of the best examples of this guarded, fortresslike "city within the city." The second spatial characteristic common to cosmomagical cities is that they were oriented toward the four cardinal directions. By aligning the city in the north-south and east-west directions, the geometric form of the city reflected the order of the universe. This alignment, it was thought, would ensure harmony and order over the known world, which was bounded by the city walls

In all these early cities, one sees evidence of a third spatial characteristic: an attempt to shape the form of the city according to the form of the universe. The ordering of the space of the city was thought to be essential to maintaining harmony between the human and spiritual worlds. In this way, the world of humans would symbolically replicate the world of the gods. This characteristic may have taken a literal form—a city laid out, for example, in a pattern of a major star constellation. Far more common, however, were cities that symbolically approximated mythical conceptions of the universe. Angkor Thom was an early city in Cambodia that presents one of the best examples of this parallelism. An

urban cluster that spread over 6 square miles (15.5 square kilometers), Angkor Thom was a representation in stone of a series of religious beliefs about the nature of the universe. Thus, the city was a microcosmos, a re-creation on Earth of an image of the larger universe.

Nevertheless, regional variations of this basic form certainly existed. For example, the early cities of the Nile were not walled, which suggests that a regional power structure kept individual cities from warring with one another. In the Indus Valley, the great city of Mohenjo-daro was laid out in a grid that consisted of 16 large blocks, and the citadel was located within the block that was central but situated toward the western edge.

The most important variations within the urban hearth areas occurred in the living conditions of Mesoamerican cities. Here, cities were less dense and covered large areas (Figure 10.6). Furthermore, these cities arose without benefit of the technological advances found in the other hearth areas, most notably the wheel, the plow, metallurgy, and draft animals. However, the domestication of maize compensated for these shortcomings. Maize is a grain that yields several crops a year without irrigation in the tropical

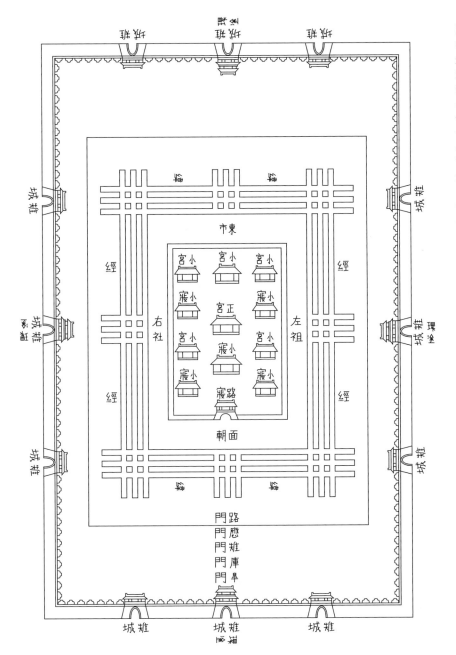

Figure 10.4 **Plan of the city of Wang-Ch'eng in China.** The city as built did not follow this exact design, but the plan itself is of interest because it suggests the symbolic importance of the three spatial characteristics of the Chinese cosmomagical city. The four walls are aligned to the cardinal directions, and the axis mundi is represented by the walled-off center city containing ceremonial buildings. The physical space of the city (microcosmos) replicates the larger world of the heavens (macrocosmos). For example, each of the four walls represents one of the four seasons. What do you think the gates to the city represent? *(Source: Wheatley, 1971.)*

climate; it can be cultivated without heavy plows or pack animals.

The Diffusion of the City from Hearth Areas

Although urban life originated at several specific places in the world, cities are now found everywhere: North America, Southeast Asia, Latin America, Australia. How did city life come to these regions? There are two possible explanations:

1. Cities evolved spontaneously as native peoples created new technologies and social institutions.

2. The preconditions for urban life are too specific for most cultures to have invented without contact with other urban areas; therefore, they must have learned these traits through contact with city dwellers. This scenario emphasizes the diffusion of ideas and techniques necessary for city life.

Diffusionists argue that the complicated array of ideas and techniques that gave rise to the first cities in Mesopotamia was shared with other people in both the Nile and the Indus river valleys who were on the verge of the urban transformation. Indeed, archaeological evidence suggests

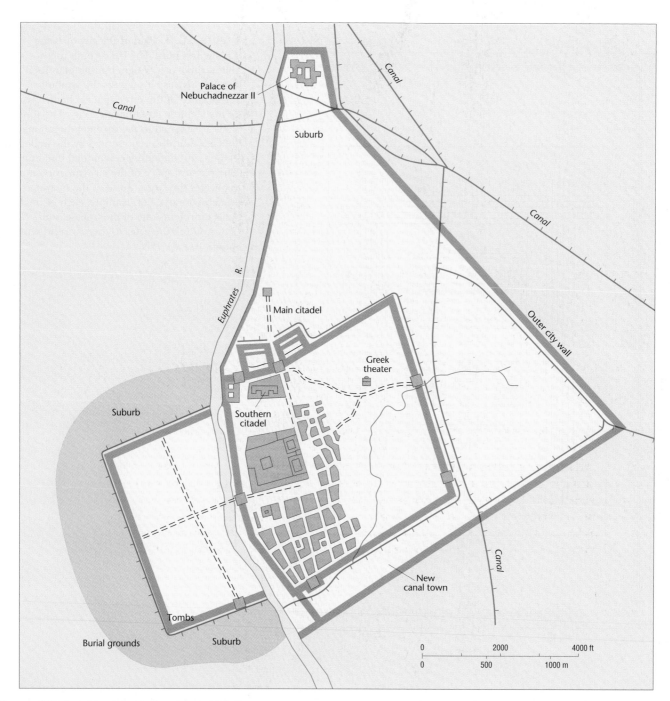

Figure 10.5 Map of Babylon, illustrating the urban morphology of early Mesopotamian cities. The citadel in the inner city is characterized by the ziggurat, main temple, palace, and granary. Beyond the citadel lay the residential areas; we can assume they extended out to the inner walls and occupied both sides of the river. Suburbs grew outside the major gates and were occupied by people not allowed to spend the night in the city, such as traders and noncitizens. *(After map in Encyclopaedia Brittanica, 1984: 555.)*

that these three civilizations had trade ties with one another. Soapstone objects manufactured in Tepe Yahya, 500 miles (800 kilometers) to the east of Mesopotamia, have been uncovered in the ruins of both Mesopotamian and Indus River valley cities, which are separated by thousands of miles. Writings of the Indus civilization have also been found in Mesopotamian urban sites. Although diffusionists use this artifactual evidence to argue that the idea of the city spread from hearth to hearth, an alternative view is that trading took place only after these cities

Figure 10.6 **Mayan city of Chichén Itzá.** Monumental and ceremonial architecture often dominated the morphology and landscape of urban hearth areas and reinforced ruling-class power. In what part of the city would you say this monument is located? Can you think of examples from your own daily life of monumental architecture that symbolizes some ruling authority? *(Malcolm Kirk/Peter Arnold, Inc.)*

were well established. There is also evidence of contact across the oceans between early urban dwellers of the New World and those of Asia and Africa, although it is unclear whether this means that urbanization was diffused to Mesoamerica or simply that some trade routes existed between these peoples.

Nonetheless, there is little doubt that diffusion has been responsible for the dispersal of the city in historical times (Figure 10.7), because the city has commonly been used as the vehicle for imperial expansion. Typically, urban life is carried outward in waves of conquest as the borders of an empire expand. Initially, the military controls newly won

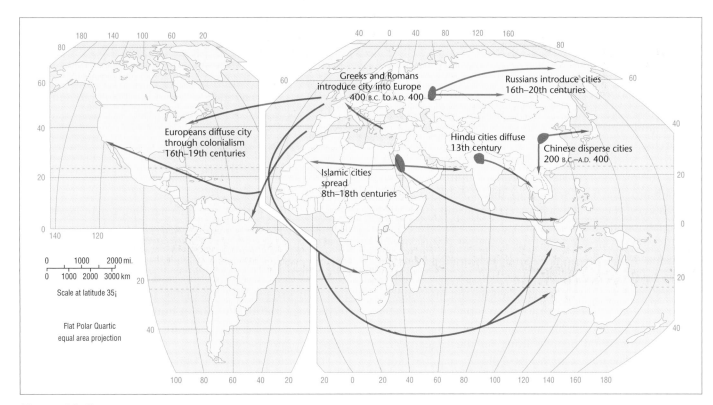

Figure 10.7 **The diffusion of urban life with the expansion of certain empires.** What does this map tell us about the importance of urban life to military conquest?

Cahokia: An Early Urban Center on the Mississippi

Cahokia, a pre-Columbian urban center on the Mississippi, shows that not all early cities were found in the six urban hearth areas mentioned in the text. Instead, Cahokia illustrates the process of independent city origin and can be taken as an example of events duplicated in hundreds of areas around the world.

The Cahokia settlement is an aggregation of mounds and living structures dating from about A.D. 100, located in the American Bottoms region of the Mississippi River valley, close to St. Louis. It is the largest of 10 large population centers and some 50 smaller farming villages that flourished between A.D. 900 and 1500.

How did this city arise? Archaeologists maintain that the city resulted from a complicated feedback process that involved population growth and an increase in agricultural productivity. In the late eighth century, the hoe replaced a less effective digging stick, and a new variety of maize—one that was better suited to the environmental conditions of the warm river valley—diffused into the American Bottoms region.

Peak population came centuries later, probably between 1150 and 1250, when Cahokia may have approached a population of 40,000. Archaeological evidence suggests that houses were mainly of pole-and-thatch construction and varied in size according to the status of the occupants. The settlement also contained many ceremonial structures, most notably large earthen mounds similar to the pyramids of Mesoamerican cities. Close to the largest mound was an enclosed area of large public structures that reminds one of the citadel areas of Mesopotamian cities.

Cahokia flourished because it was an ideally located central place, situated on fertile agricultural lands, with access to local and long-distance trade moving through the network of sloughs and rivers. Scholars who have investigated the site believe that Cahokia declined in importance around 1250. Perhaps this decline resulted from exhaustion of local resources, or perhaps Cahokia's trade hinterland was eclipsed by the growing strength of other Mississippi River cultures. Whatever the reason, further investigation is bound to shed light on the complicated processes that led to the rise and fall of cities.

Adapted from Fowler, 1975

---

lands and sets up collection points for local resources, which are then shipped back into the heart of the empire. As the surrounding countryside is increasingly pacified, the new collection points lose some of their military atmosphere and begin to show the social diversity of a city. Artisans, merchants, and bureaucrats increase in number; families appear; the native people are slowly assimilated into the settlement as workers and may eventually control the city. Finally, the process repeats itself as the empire pushes farther outward: first a military camp, then a collection point for resources, then a full-fledged city expressing true division of labor and social diversity.

This process, however, did not always proceed without opposition. The imposition of a foreign civilization on native peoples was often met with resistance, both physical and symbolic. Expanding urban centers relied on the surrounding countryside for support. Their food was supplied by farmers living fairly close to the city walls, and tribute was exacted from the agricultural peoples living on the edges of the urban world. The increasing needs of the city required more and more land from which to draw resources. However, the peasants farming that land may not have wanted to change their way of life to accommodate the city. The fierce resistance of many Native American groups to the spread of Western urbanization is testimony to the potential power of folk society to defy urbanization, although the destructive long-term effects of such resistance suggest that the organized military efforts of urban society were difficult to overcome.

The Evolution of Urban Landscapes

What do cities look like? Understanding urban landscapes requires an appreciation of large-scale urbanizing processes and local urban environments both past and present. The patterns we see today in the city, such as building forms, architecture, street plans, and land use, are a composite of past and present cultures. They reflect the needs, ideas, technology, and institutions of human occupancy. This section examines major stages in the evolution of urban landscapes around the world.

Two concepts underlie our examination of urban landscapes. The first is **urban morphology,** or the physical form of the city, which consists of street patterns, building sizes and shapes, architecture, and density. The second concept is **functional zonation,** which refers to the pattern of land uses within a city or, put another way, the existence of areas with differing functions, such as residential, commercial, and governmental. Functional zonation also includes social patterns—whether, for example, an area is occupied by the power elite or by people of low status, by Jews or by Christians, by the wealthy or by the poor. Both concepts are central to understanding the cultural landscape of cities, because both make statements about how cultures occupy and shape space (Figure 10.8).

What we try to do in the following sections, then, is to devise some categories for understanding the range of urban landscapes at present, and then we provide a historical framework to help explain that range of urban forms.

World/Global/Globalizing Cities

Three categories of cities—world, global, and globalizing—often overlap. World cities, as we've already discussed, are the largest cities in the world in terms of population (see Table 10.1). Although the list of world cities provided in Table 10.1 is not comprehensive, it reveals the range of locations of the world's largest cities. **Global cities** are defined as those world cities that have become the control centers of the global economy—in other words, the places where major decisions about the world's commercial networks and financial markets are made. These cities house a concentration of multinational and transnational corporate headquarters, international financial services, media offices, and related economic and cultural services. While many industries have become global in the sense that their sites of production and consumption are spread throughout the world, the sites of decision making are now centralized. According to sociologist Saskia Sassen, there are only three such cities now operating at this level: New York City, London, and Tokyo. These cities have become, in many ways, the headquarters for a global economy.

Globalizing cities are cities being shaped by the new global economy and culture (see Doing Geography at the end of the chapter). This includes just about every city, present and past, to one degree or another. As geographer Brenda Yeoh indicates, cities have almost always been important hubs of activity beyond the national scale, and therefore it is not surprising that they figure prominently in contemporary discussions of globalization. But the degree of globalization in the last 30 years has sharpened and enhanced the ways in which global economies and cultures shape cities. As geographer Kris Olds points out (see Practicing Geography), there are five interrelated dimensions of current globalizing processes that are shaping our cities: the development of an international financial system, the globalization of property markets, the prominence of transnational corporations, the stretching and intensifying of social and cultural networks, and the increased degree of international travel and networking. As he argues, it is impossible to understand developments in the urban landscapes of cities as diverse as Jakarta and London without referring to these global processes.

Yet not all cities are affected by these globalizing processes in the same way. Some cities like London, as we've just discussed, are the control centers of this economy, while others, like Jakarta, provide sites of production for the global economy. The differences between these two types of cities emerge out of cultural uniqueness and historical circumstance, particularly the colonial relationships that developed

Figure 10.8 San Francisco. This photo shows how the concepts of urban morphology and functional zonation can be used in examining cities. To the left, close to the shoreline, are older factories, some of which have been converted for the tourist trade associated with the Fisherman's Wharf area. The residential areas exhibit two morphological characteristics: high-rises on the hills to the right and blocks of low-rise apartments in the middle ground. The skyscrapers of the central business district show up in the background. *(Steve Proeh/The Image Bank.)*

Kris Olds

(Courtesy of Kris Olds.)

Singapore and Vancouver are thousands of miles apart, in two very different areas of the world, but as urban geographer Kris Olds reminds us, they are being shaped by similar processes: economic restructuring, transnational migrations, and new social policies. A professor of geography at the University of Wisconsin, Madison, Olds studies the interdependence of global cities around the world. His work intelligently undermines the distinctions we used to make between cities in the developed and developing worlds. "My research primarily focuses on the geographical organization of power in relation to contemporary urban transformations. Much of this work takes place in multiple locations that are tied together via the processes I am examining in my research."

This type of research allows Olds to indulge two of his passions at the same time: traveling and solving real-world problems. "I've always had the travel bug. When I almost got kicked out of the University of British Columbia for atrocious grades (I thought that I would be better off becoming an engineer or a geologist instead of a geographer), I took some time off, traveled the world, and then returned to UBC . . . and stumbled into some great courses, all of them taught by urban geographers. Now, I get to travel while 'working.' " His "work" takes him to Bristol, Berlin, Singapore, and Hong Kong, but also to Vancouver, Philadelphia, Chicago, and Madison. In all of these places, his interest is in understanding the global power relationships that are disrupting people's lives in fundamental ways, such as forced housing evictions that often accompany large-scale mega-events, such as the Olympic games, and access to education and other social services. "I am particularly interested in the processes underlying urban change and the role of elites and networks of elites in shaping the development process."

Olds finds qualitative methods the best for getting at these processes, since what makes these global networks "tick" are the interests and motivations of people. "I've got nothing against quantitative techniques (some of which I used to use), but they simply cannot help me shed light on the issues that I find to be important. I now prefer to work with in-depth semistructured interviews, observation, and participant observation." Currently, he's observing and interviewing some of the key players involved in Singapore's push to become a global education hub, as well as working with an international nongovernmental organization to formulate concrete mechanisms that will prevent future forced housing evictions caused by mega-events. One of the most exciting things about being a "practicing" geographer, Olds says, is that "I am able to work on issues of real importance in the world."

---

in the eighteenth and nineteenth centuries. In the following discussion, we analyze those circumstances by suggesting a historically based series of categories of urban form. We realize that the list is selective, not exhaustive. In other words, we provide only an overview of some of the important historical phases of urban landscapes in both the developed and developing worlds.

The Greek City

Western civilization and the Western city both trace their roots back to ancient Greece. City life diffused to Greece from Mesopotamia. By 600 B.C., there were more than 500 towns and cities on the Greek mainland and surrounding islands. As Greek civilization expanded, cities spread with it throughout the Mediterranean, reaching as far as the north shore of Africa, Spain, southern France, and Italy.

These cities were of modest size, rarely containing more than 5000 inhabitants. Athens, however, may have reached a population of 300,000 in the fifth century B.C.

Greek cities had two distinctive functional zones: the acropolis and the agora. In many ways, the acropolis was similar to the citadel of Mesopotamian cities. Here were the temples of worship, the storehouse of valuables, and the seat of power. The acropolis also served as a place of retreat in time of siege (Figure 10.9). If the acropolis was the domain of power, the agora was the province of the citizens. As originally conceived, the agora was a place for public meetings, education, social interaction, and judicial matters. In other words, it was the civic center, the hub of democratic life for Greek men (women were excluded from political life).

The early Greek cities probably were not planned but rather grew spontaneously, without benefit of formal guidelines. However, some scholars think that many ceremonial

Figure 10.9 **The Acropolis in Athens.** The Acropolis dominates the contemporary city and reminds us that many cities throughout the world have been centered on fortified places that eventually became more symbolic than functional. How does this landscape compare with other defensive acropolis sites? *(James Hanley/Photo Researchers.)*

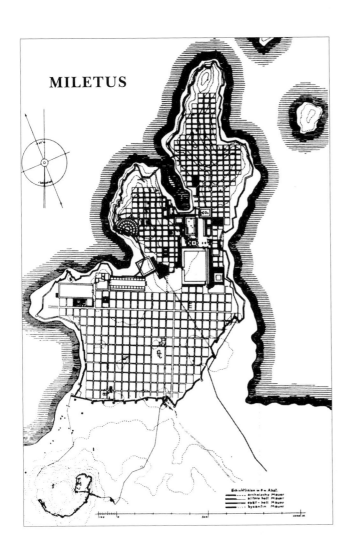

MILETUS

Figure 10.10 **The plan of the city of Miletus by Hippodamus, circa 450 B.C.** Notice how the strict grid is imposed on the irregular coastline. The central agora is also regularized, characteristic of this colonial phase of the Greek city. *(Source: Vance, 1990.)*

areas within these cities were designed to be seen according to prescribed lines of vision and that those lines of vision included not only the buildings but also the natural landscape that surrounded it. The human aesthetic sense was given a degree of authority that it did not have in the cosmo-magical city.

More formalized city design and plan are apparent in later Greek cities that were built in areas of colonial expansion. One of the best examples of such planned cities is Miletus, on the eastern shore of the Mediterranean, in Ionia (present-day Turkey). The city was laid out in a rigid grid pattern, imposing its geometry onto the physical conditions of the site (Figure 10.10). Although the source of such a plan is debatable, clearly this orderly and coherent layout indicates an abstract and highly rational notion of urban life and seems to fit well with the functional needs of a colonial city.

Roman Cities

By 200 B.C., Rome had replaced Greece as the chief urbanizing force in the West. The Romans adopted many urban traits from the Greeks as well as from the Etruscans, a civilization of central Italy that Rome had conquered. As the

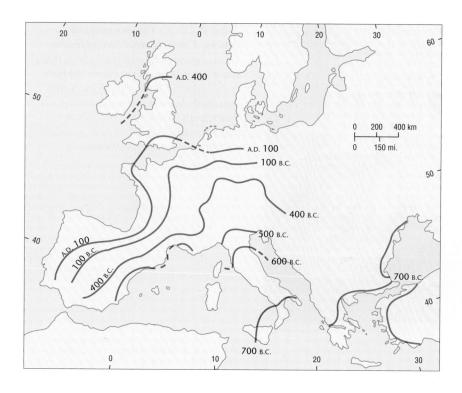

Figure 10.11 The diffusion of urbanization in Europe. The early spread of urban development moved in waves across Europe. The nucleus of city life was well established in the Greek lands by 700 B.C. In the following centuries, urbanization diffused westward and northward until it reached the British Isles. What do you think were some of the effects of this imposition of urban life on agricultural peoples? *(Reproduced by permission from Pounds, 1969.)*

Roman Empire expanded, city life diffused farther into France, while also reaching Germany, England, interior Spain, the Alpine countries, and parts of eastern Europe—areas that had not previously experienced urbanization. Most of these cities were military and trading outposts of the Roman Empire. The military camp, or *castrum*, was the basis for many of these new settlements. In England, the Roman trail of city building can be found by looking for the suffixes *-caster* and *-chester*—as in Lancaster or Winchester, cities orig-

inally founded as Roman camps. Figure 10.11 shows the diffusion of urban life into Europe as the Greek and Roman frontiers advanced.

The landscape of these Roman cities shared several traits with that of their Greek predecessors. The gridiron street pattern, used in later Greek cities, was fundamental to Roman cities. This pattern can still be seen in the heart of such Italian cities as Pavia (Figure 10.12). The straight streets and right-angle intersections make a striking contrast

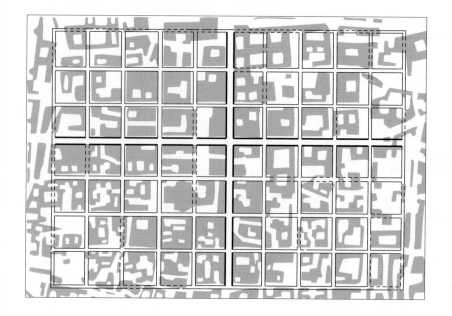

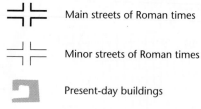

Main streets of Roman times

Minor streets of Roman times

Present-day buildings

Figure 10.12 The Roman grid street pattern in Pavia, Italy. Many of the straight streets from Roman times remain in use 20 centuries after they were first built. The dotted lines indicate the Roman streets that do not exist today. Beyond the Roman core, the streets developed in irregular patterns. Why do the present-day buildings not necessarily follow the Roman grid?

Figure 10.13 **The Colosseum in Rome.**
Crowds of 60,000 were entertained in the Colosseum by mock battles, circuses, gladiators, and sports events. Most large Roman cities had similar structures. Today, most cities have stadiums and coliseums that continue the tradition of public spectacles started by the Romans.

to the curved, wandering lanes of the later medieval quarters or the streets of Rome itself. At the intersection of a city's two major thoroughfares was the *forum*, a zone combining elements of the Greek acropolis and agora. Here were not only the temples of worship, administrative buildings, and warehouses, but also the libraries, schools, and marketplaces that served the common people.

Rome's most important legacy probably was not its architectural and engineering feats, although they remain landmarks in European cities to this day (Figure 10.13), but rather the Roman method for choosing the site of a city, which remains applicable today. The Romans consistently chose sites with transportation in mind. The Roman Empire was held together by a complicated system of roads and highways linking towns and cities. In choosing a site for a new settlement, the Romans made access to transportation a major consideration. The significance of Roman location was such that even though urban life declined dramatically with the collapse of the empire, many cities—such as Paris, London, and Vienna—were established centuries later on the same old Roman sites because they offered the advantage of access to the surrounding countryside.

With the decline of the Roman Empire by A.D. 400, urban life also declined. Historians attribute the fall of Rome to internal decay, the invasion of the Germanic peoples, and other factors. Cities were sapped of their vitality. The highway system that linked them fell into disrepair, so that cities could no longer exchange goods and ideas. When Roman cities were invaded, they could no longer count on

outside military support as the administrative structure of the empire collapsed. As symbols of a conquering empire, Roman outposts were either actively destroyed or, devoid of purpose, simply left to decay.

Yet there were exceptions. Some cities of the Mediterranean survived because they established trade with the Eastern Roman Empire centered in Constantinople. After the eighth century, some cities—particularly those in Spain—were infused with new vigor by the Almohad and Almoravis empires of Morocco, which spread across the Mediterranean from northern Africa. The cities of northern regions were unable to survive, however. Cities became small villages. Where thousands had formerly thrived, a few hundred eked out a subsistence living from agriculture.

Urban decline occurred only in the areas that had been under Roman rule. Other civilizations continued to thrive throughout this period. The achievements of Chinese civilization and the great cities of the Mayan Empire remind us that this collapse was limited to a particular area of Europe.

The Medieval City

The medieval period, lasting roughly from A.D. 1000 to 1500, was a time of renewed urban expansion in Europe that also deeply influenced the future of urban life. As the Germanic and Slavic peoples expanded their empires, urban life spread beyond the borders of the former Roman Empire, into the north and east of Europe. In only four centuries, 2500 new German cities were founded. Most cities of present-day Europe were established during this period; although many were on old Roman sites, others were new.

Scholars have debated why urban life began to regain vigor in the eleventh century. In essence, it was the result of the revival of both local and long-distance trade, which was itself the consequence of a combination of factors, including population increase, political stability and unification, and agricultural expansion through new land reclamations along with the development of new agricultural technologies. Sustained trading networks required protected markets and supply centers, functions that renewed life in cities. In addition, trading—particularly over long distances—led to the development of a new social class: the merchant class. Members of the merchant class breathed new life into early medieval cities, providing the impetus and the wealth for sustained city building.

The medieval city can be characterized by the presence of four features: the charter, the wall, the marketplace, and the cathedral. The *charter* was a governmental decree from a regional power, usually a feudal lord, granting political autonomy to the town. This act had important implications, as it freed the population from feudal restrictions, made the city responsible for its own defense and government, and often allowed it to coin money. The *wall* served a defensive purpose, but it was also a symbol of the sharp distinction between country and city (Figure 10.14). Within the wall, most inhabitants were, by charter, free; outside, most were serfs. A city of free citizens, not based on a vast pool of slave labor, was a first in the history of the Western world.

Another central feature was the *marketplace*. It symbolized the important role of economic activities in the medieval city. The city depended on the countryside for its food and produce, which were traded in the market. The market was also a center for long-distance trade. Textiles, salt, ore, and other raw materials were bought and sold in the marketplace. At one end of the marketplace stood the town hall, a fairly tall structure that provided meeting space for the city's political leaders. The town hall often served as a market hall as well, with many of its rooms used to store and display the finer goods that could not be exposed to the natural elements outside on the market square. Yet, in many of the larger commercial cities, civic and economic functions were located in separate buildings. Brugge, Belgium, an important trading center for northern Europe, had two distinct complexes of buildings at its center (Figure 10.15).

The crowning glory of a medieval town was usually the *cathedral*, a dominating architectural symbol of the importance of the church. Often the cathedral, the marketplace, and the town hall were close together, indicating close ties among religion, commerce, and politics. However, the church was frequently the prevailing political force in medieval towns.

The functional zonation of the medieval city differs markedly from that of our modern cities. The city was divided into small quarters, or districts, each containing its own center that served as its focal point. Within each of these districts lived people who were engaged in similar occupations. Coopers (people who made and repaired wooden barrels), for example, lived in one particular

Figure 10.14 The medieval hill town of Carcassonne in southern France. Notice the double set of fortified walls that surround this medieval town. *(Jonathan Blair/Corbis.)*

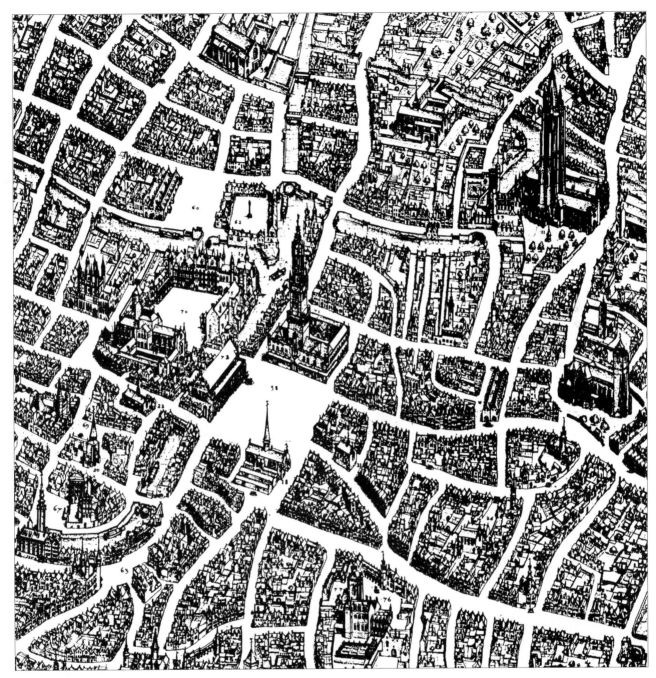

11. Cathedral of Notre Dame	58. Fish market	72. Waterhalle
12. Church of St. Sauveur	60. Grain market	75. Prison
18. Chapel of St. Christopher	62. Leather market	76. Prince's Hall
20. Chapel of St. John	63. Bourse	77. Mint
21. Chapel of St. Amanda	70. Castle, with the Town Hall and	88. So-called Castle of the Seven
22. Chapel of St. Peter	Chancellery	Turrets
26. Chapel of the Painters	71. Halle	

Figure 10.15 **Part of a 1562 panoramic map of the city of Brugge, Belgium, showing the central area.** Directly in the center of the image is the great Halle building, the economic heart of the city. Just in front of it and to the left is the waterhall, so named because it straddled the canal, allowing goods to be delivered directly into the building. To the left is the old castle surrounded by guildhalls and the town hall. To the extreme right is the cathedral building. How do the reasons for this organic urban plan compare and contrast with the reasons for the grid plan of Roman cities? (See Figure 10.12.) *(Source: Benevolo, 1980.)*

district, attended the same local church, and belonged to the same guild. Their church and guildhall were located in the small center area of their district. Along the narrow, winding streets surrounding this center area were the houses and workplaces of the coopers (Figure 10.16). Many worked in the first story of their houses and lived above the shop, with their apprentices living above them. The more prestigious groups lived in occupational districts close to the center of the city, whereas those who were involved in noxious activities, such as butchers and leather workers, lived closer to the city walls.

Some of these districts, however, were defined not by occupation but by ethnicity—these areas have been referred to as ghettos. The origin of the term *ghetto* is somewhat unclear, although one plausible explanation suggests that the word dates from the early sixteenth century, when Venetians decided to restrict Jewish settlement in the city to an area already known as Ghetto Nuovo, or the "new foundry." This area was physically separated from the rest of the city and had a single entrance that could be guarded. The practice of spatially segregating the Jewish population was not limited to Venice. In most medieval cities, Jews were forced to live in their own districts. In Frankfurt am Main, Jews lived on the *Judengasse,* a street that was formed from the dried-up moat that had run along the old wall to the city. The *Judengasse* was enclosed by walls with only one guarded gate for entrance and exit. Because the area was not allowed to expand beyond those walls, a growing population led to denser living conditions. In 1462, the population of the *Judengasse* was only 110 inhabitants; but by 1610, 3000 people lived in the Jewish ghetto, creating one of the densest districts in the city.

In summary, there are three fundamental points to be made about the role of the medieval period in the evolution of the Western city: (1) most European cities were founded during this period; (2) many of the traditions of Western urban life began then; and (3) the medieval landscape is still with us, providing a visible history of the city and a distinctive form into which twenty-first-century activities are placed.

The Renaissance and Baroque Periods

During the Renaissance (approximately 1500–1600) and Baroque (1600–1800) periods, the form and function of the European city changed significantly. Absolute monarchs arose to preside over unified countries. The burghers, or rising middle class, of the cities slowly gave up their freedoms to join with the king in pursuit of economic gain. City size increased rapidly because the bureaucracies of regional power structures came to dominate cities and because trade patterns expanded with the beginnings of European imperial conquest. One city, the national capital, rose to prominence in most countries.

A new concern with city planning went hand in hand with these developments. Rulers considered the city a stage on which to act out their destinies, and as a stage, the city could be rearranged at will. Most planning measures, then, were meant to benefit the privileged classes. Typical of the time was the infatuation with wide, grandiose boulevards.

Figure 10.16 **Heidelberg, Germany, showing the typical narrow, winding street pattern of the medieval period.** Besides the pedestrian-scale inner city, we see other typical medieval features, such as churches and residences located above street-level shops. Can you identify any other characteristic features of a medieval city? (*Source: Ulrike Welsch/Photo Researchers.*)

The rich could ride along them in carriages, and the army could march along them in an impressive display of power. Other features of the Baroque city were large, open squares; palaces; and public buildings.

Although the height of Baroque planning was between 1600 and 1800, the autocratic spirit in which it was pursued carried into the nineteenth century, as illustrated by Paris (Figure 10.17). There, Napoléon III had Baron Haussmann build a system of boulevards designed, among other reasons, to control the populace. Streets were straightened and widened, and cul-de-sacs were broken down to give the army—should the people rise up—space to maneuver, with ordered sight lines for its artillery. Whole neighborhoods were torn down to build these avenues, and thousands of residents were displaced. They had to seek new shelter without assistance, and many ended up in the congested working-class sections of east and north Paris. Even today, these areas are overcrowded, and much of the blame can be assigned to the Baroque planners.

The Capitalist City

Underlying many of the innovations in Renaissance and Baroque city planning was a sweeping socioeconomic transformation that reshaped western Europe. The transition from a feudal order to a capitalist one, which stretched from the mid-sixteenth century to the mid-eighteenth century, involved drastic changes in class structure, economic systems, political allegiances, cultural patterns, and human geographies. The countryside was reordered with the intro-duction of commercialized and specialized agriculture and with the enclosure of individual land units. The city was also reshaped, as the value of two-dimensional location and three-dimensional form in the city acquired economic significance.

Perhaps of greatest significance was how the capitalist mind-set introduced a notion of urban land as a source of income. Proximity to the center of the city, and therefore to the most pedestrian traffic, added economic value to land. Other specialized locations, such as areas close to the river or harbor, or along the major thoroughfares into and out of the city, also increased land value. This fundamental change in the value accorded to urban land led to the gradual disintegration of the medieval urban pattern.

In the emerging capitalist city, the ability to pay determined where one would live. The city's residential areas thus became segregated by economic class. The wealthy lived in the desirable neighborhoods; those without much money were forced to live in the more disagreeable parts of the city. In addition, places of work were separated from home, so that a merchant, for example, lived in one part of the city and traveled to another to conduct his business. This spatial separation of work from home, of public space from private space, both reflected and helped to shape the changing social worlds of men and women. In general, men generated economic income from work outside the home and therefore came to be associated with the public space of the city. Women, who were primarily engaged in domestic work, were considered the keepers of the private world of the home. This association of women with private domestic space and

Figure 10.17 A view of Paris, showing boulevards designed by Baron Haussmann. The boulevard was a favorite of Baroque planners. It was a ceremonial street that often led to public buildings and monuments, was lined with trees and upper-income housing, and offered public space for the wealthy. Boulevards were often created at the expense of thousands of poorer citizens, who were displaced as older housing was destroyed by the boulevard builders. Has this happened in your city or one near you as freeways have been built? *(Jeff Greenberg/Photo Researchers.)*

men with public work space deepened and became more complex throughout the next few hundred years.

REFLECTING ON GEOGRAPHY

How did (and does) the association of private domestic space with women and of public work space with men affect the daily lives of men and women? Can you think of counterexamples, that is, instances of the merging of private and public spaces?

The center of the capitalist city was not the cathedral or town hall, but instead the buildings devoted to business enterprises. A downtown defined by economic activity emerged that, with the coming of industrialization, eventually expanded and subdivided into specialized districts. The new upper classes of the city, whose status was based on their accumulation of wealth, not only made money from buying and selling urban land but also used urban land as a basis for expressing their wealth. With the downtown devoted to mercantile and emerging industrial uses, the upper classes sought newer land on the edge of the city for their residential enclaves. These new areas often acted as three-dimensional symbols of relatively recent wealth, conferring on their residents the legitimacy of upper-class membership.

One of the first and finest of these new enclaves for the wealthy was London's Covent Garden Piazza, a residential square designed by Inigo Jones in the early 1630s. The inhabitants of Covent Garden included some of London's nobility and wealthier bourgeoisie. The presence of nobility lent an aristocratic aura to the area and provided social legitimacy to the newly affluent who lived there. The economic success of this speculative real estate venture led to many imitations, and similar residential squares cropped up throughout the West End of London (Figure 10.18). These upper-class squares were transplanted to America throughout the seventeenth and eighteenth centuries, arising in such cities as Boston, New York, Philadelphia, and Savannah.

The Colonial City

A **colonial city** is an administrative, commercial, and often military outpost for an external power. During the eighteenth and nineteenth centuries, many European nations extended their power over other parts of the world to create empires, and much of this empire building was accomplished by and took shape through the development of new cities. These colonial cities were established not to serve the local population but to subdue local peoples economically or militarily, a purpose that was often expressed in the design of these cities.

The Symbolism of Colonial Space When colonial cities were built near already existing cities, the Europeans would either weld their city onto the existing settlement or, in a few extreme cases, build a totally new city nearby. The British built New Delhi adjacent to the original Delhi, and today the two still illustrate the contrast between colonial and indigenous cities. In old Delhi, density is 213 persons per acre

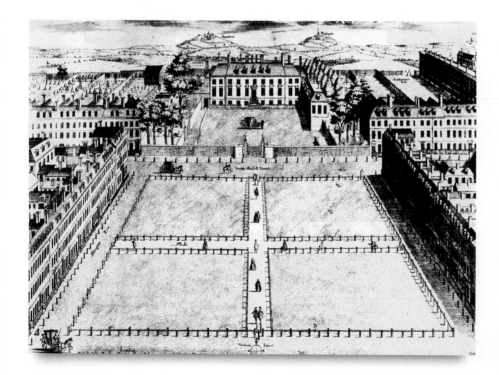

Figure 10.18 **A 1730 view of Bloomsbury Square, laid out in 1661 by the Earl of Southampton.** Southampton House occupies the far end of the square, lending an aristocratic air to this speculative, mercantile development. Notice the men and women parading in their finery, suggesting the wealthy and leisurely life of the inhabitants. What other signs of wealth are evident in this image? *(Source: Hayes, 1969.)*

(526 per hectare); in New Delhi, it is 13 persons per acre (32 per hectare). Old Delhi is medieval, with narrow, winding streets; little open space; and cramped residences (Figure 10.19). New Delhi, on the other hand, has wide streets, gardens surrounding the spacious houses of administrative staff, and parks and squares ringing government buildings. All this reminds one of the Baroque period in Western urban development—and well it should, for much European colonialism was coincidental with the Baroque era. As the Baroque style was used in Europe to express the power of the elite, so it was used in colonial cities. Grandiose boulevards were often cut through native residential quarters, large monumental buildings demonstrated the presence of the new power, and the Europeans lived in elaborate residences that constantly reminded locals of their new masters.

In his study of the city of Kandy, Sri Lanka, geographer James Duncan shows how British colonial rulers in the nineteenth century consciously manipulated the urban landscape to symbolize, reinforce, and legitimize their claims to authority. All the symbols of the former kingdom were either replaced by symbols of British rule or allowed to fall into disrepair (see Focus On: Colonial Rule Symbolized in the Urban Landscape of Kandy, Sri Lanka). For example, as Duncan notes, the king's audience hall, located on hallowed ground between the Temple of the Relic and the palace, became the civic court during the week and the Anglican church on Sundays. In the alcove where the king of Kandy's throne once sat stood the pulpit, and behind it hung a picture of the English king. The palace of the king's relatives became the European hospital, and the queen's bath became a European library.

When new colonial cities were founded, they were often based on a standardized plan. For example, all Spanish cities in the New World were constructed according to the Laws of the Indies, drafted in 1573. The document explicitly outlined how colonial cities were to be constructed. According to the laws, a gridiron street plan was to be centered on a church and central plaza, and all individual lots were to be

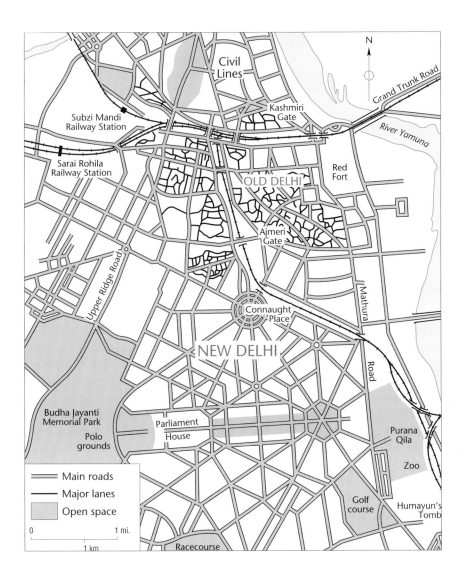

Figure 10.19 Map of Delhi and New Delhi, India. This map shows the contrast between the morphology and landscape of the indigenous city, Delhi, and the British colonial addition, New Delhi. Note the straight, symmetrical ceremonial boulevards and open space in the colonial city, expressions of Baroque planning in the colonial age. How does it compare with the morphology of old Delhi? (*After Drakakis-Smith, 1987: 20.*)

Colonial Rule Symbolized in the Urban Landscape of Kandy, Sri Lanka

With the advent of British rule in Sri Lanka, the meaning of the urban landscape of Kandy was changed. A new cultural and political system had been ushered in, and the old landscape model that spoke of what had been important under the old system was being transformed or allowed to fall into ruination. Kandy was no longer the city of the god king, for he had been unceremoniously sent into exile. It was becoming a British colonial town and it had to look the part. The British realized that if they were to achieve legitimacy it would have to be largely on their terms. And while they never achieved the degree of legitimacy that they sought, they achieved a degree of cultural hegemony among the Sinhalese elites. This cultural hegemony was achieved in part through a conscious attempt to change the Sinhalese elites, but very largely it was achieved through an attempt to transform Kandy into an outlier of British culture. The assimilation was left to the Sinhalese themselves who were often all too ready to emulate the British. This creation of a bit of British culture in Kandy involved a transformation of the landscape of the place and the natural environment of the Kandyan area lent itself admirably to this task. Because of the elevation and topography of Kandy it was possible to create a facsimile of the landscape of home. One could see in residents' diaries and official plans the conscious attempt to transform Kandy into a hybrid that was part English and part Sinhalese. Their success in doing so was attested to in the journals and paintings of travelers who visited Kandy throughout the 19th century. Kandy was designed to resemble a romanticized image of a pre-industrial England. The landscape model of the English lake district was superimposed upon the mountains and the Kandy lake to recreate a place where English ladies and

gentlemen could somehow escape the tropics and the native culture and symbolically return home.

And how exactly was this done? Promenades, such as Lady Horton's Walk, carriage drives such as Victoria Drive, and riding paths such as The Green Gallop, were created. The dense jungle around Kandy was pruned to reveal the best views of the town, the lake and the surrounding mountains. Travelers and residents alike often wrote about how one might "find enchanting views suddenly opening from the various points where the thick verdure of the trees has been judiciously cut away" (Dougherty 1890, p. 102) and that these openings, created an "exquisite framework through which . . . [to] see the distant landscape" (Cave 1912, p. 303). The term *sublime* was commonly used to describe the Kandyan landscape. English vegetables, fruits and trees were introduced and both formal and informal English gardens and parks were laid out. The Governor's Pavilion was laid out like an English country house situated in a parklike expanse of lawns and shrubbery overlooking the town, the lake and the mountains. Exclusive European residential quarters were located around the lake. English architect–designed bungalows, with their gardens full of roses and other English flowers climbed the hills from the lakeside. English style buildings predominated on the main thoroughfares such as Ward Street which contained the European stores like Cargills, Walker and Company, the Merchantile Bank, the Queen's Hotel, the Kandy Club, the Lawn Tennis Club, and the Planters Association of Ceylon.

From Agnew and Duncan, 1989: 192–193. Copyright © 1989 by John A. Agnew and James S. Duncan. Reprinted by permission of Routledge

---

walled. Smaller plazas were to dot the neighborhoods, occupied by parish churches or monasteries, so that religious teaching would be evenly spread around the new city. In many ways, the formal guidelines for Spanish colonial cities duplicate the planning rules used by the Romans.

In some instances, the Spanish would superimpose their colonial cities on indigenous cities. For example, Mexico City was constructed on top of Tenochtitlán, the religious and political center of the Aztec culture (Figure 10.20). As a type of cosmomagical city, Tenochtitlán had been laid out in a rectilinear pattern and was therefore easily adaptable to the Spanish grid pattern.

Gendered Space and the Colonial City The goal of extending political control over foreign nations, which was common to the policies of many western European nations in

the nineteenth and early portions of the twentieth centuries, is called **imperialism**. As we have seen, this entailed the construction of colonial cities and often the creation of landscape symbols to visually express the legitimacy of colonial rule. On close examination, we can see that ideas about gender played important roles in the processes of imperialism and in the creation of colonial spaces.

Although the actual process of conquering other nations and controlling them politically and economically was viewed through nineteenth-century European eyes as a masculine job, the process of bringing "civilization" to what these Europeans considered to be "savage" peoples was seen as a feminine job. In nineteenth-century Europe, women were considered the guardians of the home and as such were thought to be essentially more moral and spiritual than men. European powers found it imperative that women

Figure 10.20 **A view of the center of Mexico City.** The central plaza and surrounding buildings were constructed by the Spanish on the site of the ancient ceremonial center of Tenochtitlán. *(Danny Lehman/Corbis.)*

should move to the colonies so that they could continue the civilizing mission. For example, geographer Morag Bell has documented how English schoolgirls in the early portion of the twentieth century were convinced of their importance to the maintenance of the British Empire. If they moved to South Africa, for example, they could fulfill both their patriotic and their feminine duties at the same time. Their presence in the empire ensured that British values would be implanted; at the same time, it gave visual evidence that the British Empire was bringing "enlightenment" to those it thought required it. As Bell argues, "Overseas emigration would not only provide an alternative source of scarce work opportunities for women, an 'elevation of morals' would also 'inevitably' result from 'the mere presence in the colony of a number of high class women.'" According to Vron Ware, more than 20,000 women emigrated to British colonies between 1862 and 1914.

Even so, the presence of women in the British Empire was fraught with difficulties, particularly because it was thought that women needed protection from the physical danger presented by the diversity of urban life. If this was true in a city like London, it was even truer in Calcutta (now Kolkata), for example, because those dangers were "foreign" and more threatening. As such, specific spaces were set up for women to keep them from direct contact with foreign danger. In fact, part of the explanation for doing so was to protect the women from foreign eyes. Indeed, in India, the British built entirely new cities just for women and children. They designed what became known as hill stations, fairly small residential compounds in the hills, to provide cooler and purportedly better air and to keep separate their domestic world, including women and children, from the native cultures.

Yet none of these attempts to demarcate and separate women from native peoples worked at the level of everyday life. Even within the colonial portions of the city, Indian servants often lived in or close to the British sections, and Indian soldiers were stationed nearby. British women also performed missionary and benevolent work in the Indian city. Moreover, even in the most private of settings—the homes of proper Englishwomen in the hill stations—Indian servants, cooks, and gardeners were present (Figure 10.21). As Sara Mills and Judith Kenny have both pointed out, many of the houses built in these settings were designed in the bungalow style—an open floor plan with plenty of windows and doorways to capture the cool breezes. Thus, even the most private spaces of the home were open to view by native peoples. Women's domestic duties—how they treated their husbands, their gardens, their guests, their pianos—were part of the rituals of behavior that represented the civilized world of the British Empire. Gender and space, therefore, were important tools in representing and legitimizing imperial rule.

Class, "Race," and Gender in the Industrial City

Most of the Western cities that controlled these empires were being reshaped by the new power of industrialization (see Chapter 9), fueled by resources brought in from their colonies. Until the industrial period, the rate of urbanization in Western countries was relatively low. For example, in 1600, urban dwellers made up only 2 percent of the German, French, and English populations; in the Netherlands and Italy, 13 percent of the population were urban dwellers. However, as millions of people migrated to the cities over

Figure 10.21 **The MacNab family in front of their bungalow in the hill station of Ootacamund in the province of Madras, India, circa 1910.** This photo depicts a fairly typical example of a middle- to upper-class English family living in India under imperial rule. Notice the poised and elegant women, one with parasol in hand, and the Indian servant standing at the doorway. Can you think of other examples of how traditional notions of femininity were used to legitimize British imperial expansion? *(Source: India Office Library and Records Office, London.* MacNab Collection 752/4 No. 58. *Reprinted by permission of The British Library.)*

the next 200 years, the rate of urbanization skyrocketed. By 1800, England was 20 percent urbanized, and around 1870 it became the world's first urban society. By the 1890 census, 60 percent of its people lived in cities. The United States was 3 percent urbanized in 1800, 40 percent in 1900, and 51 percent in 1920 (when it became an urban country); today about 75 percent of its population live in towns and cities.

The industrial revolution and the triumph of capitalism turned the city from a public institution into private property—spoils to be divided with an eye to maximum profits. A new philosophy emerged: **laissez-faire utilitarianism.** Lewis Mumford, in *The City in History,* defined this philosophy as a belief that divine providence ruled over economic activity and ensured the maximum public good through the unregulated efforts of every private, self-seeking individual. One expression of this new philosophy was a changed attitude toward land and the buildings on that land. Once raw materials such as coal and iron ore could be brought to the city by rail, factories began to cluster together to share the benefits of **agglomeration**—that is, to share labor, transportation costs, and utility costs—and to take advantage of financial institutions found in the city. Industry concentrated in the city itself, around labor, the commercial marketplace, and capital. Land use intensified drastically. With the increased competition for land in the industrial period, land transactions and speculation became an everyday part of city life. Land parcels became the property of the owner, who had no obligations to society in deciding how to use them. The historical urban core was often destroyed, the older city replaced. The result was a mosaic of mixed land uses: factories directly next to housing, slum tenements next to public buildings, open spaces and parks violated by railroad tracks. A planned attempt to bring order to the city

came only in the twentieth century with the concept of zoning (see Focus On: The Origins of Zoning in America: Race and Wealth). Yet even this idea was rooted in some of the same forces—profit, bigotry, and individualism—that had already made the industrial city unresponsive to the needs of most of its inhabitants.

Class Laissez-faire industrialism did little for the working classes that labored in shops and plants. In their slum dwellings, direct sunlight was seldom available and open spaces were nonexistent. In Liverpool, England, for instance, one-sixth of the population reportedly lived in "underground cellars." A study from the middle of the nineteenth century showed that in Manchester, England, there was but one toilet for every 212 people. Running water was usually available only on the ground floors of apartment buildings. Disease was pervasive and mortality rates ran high. In 1893, the life expectancy of a male worker in Manchester was 28; his country cousin might live to 52. The death rate in New York City (Figure 10.22) in 1880 was 25 per 1000, whereas it was half that in the rural counties of the state. The infant mortality rate per thousand live births rose from 180 in 1850 to 240 in 1870. Legislation correcting such ills came only in the latter part of the nineteenth century.

"Race" With all its faults, industrialization created some of the most vibrant centers of urban activity in modern times. American industrial cities relied on a diverse labor force, and each social group fought for its place in the urban land market. Despite the harsh living conditions, various groups of laborers carved out identities in the urban landscape.

Industrialization in the United States drew its workforce not only from European immigrants but also from African-

FOCUS ON

The Origins of Zoning in America: Race and Wealth

The standard zoning ordinance of American cities was originally conceived from a union of two fears—fear of the Chinese and fear of skyscrapers. In California, a wave of racial prejudice had swept over the state after Chinese settlers were imported to build the railroads and work in the mines [in the mid-nineteenth century]. Ingenious lawyers in San Francisco found that the old common law of nuisance could be applied for indirect discrimination against the Chinese in situations where the constitution of the state forbade direct discrimination. Chinese laundries of the 1880s had become social centers for Chinese servants who lived outside the Chinatown ghetto. To whites they represented only clusters of "undesirables" in the residential areas where Chinese were living singly among them as house servants. By declaring the laundries nuisances and fire hazards, San Francisco hoped to exclude Chinese from most sections of the city. . . . Such nuisance-zone statutes spread down the Pacific coast. . . .

[Meanwhile,] in New York [City,] the Fifth Avenue Association, a group composed of men who owned or leased the city's most expensive retail land, demanded that the city protect their luxury blocks from encroachment by the new tall buildings

of the garment district. . . . The Fifth Avenue Association feared that the ensuing decades would see the [skyscraper] lofts invading their best properties, bringing with them [lower-class] lunch-hour crowds and a blockade of wagons, trucks, and carts. In short, they feared that skyscraper lofts, low-paid help, and traffic congestion would drive their middle-class and wealthy customers from the Avenue.

The combination of West Coast racism plus the fears of wealthy New York merchants resulted in the New York Zoning Law of 1916, a prototype zoning statute for the nation. These were the roots of the first American attempts to deal coherently with urban growth. Not surprisingly, the zoning law was no sooner passed than it was seized on in the South and elsewhere as a way to extend [the] laws and practices of racial segregation. . . . A land or structure limitation . . . became a financial, racial, and ethnic limitation by pricing certain groups out of particular suburbs. Italians were held at bay in Boston, Poles in Detroit, Blacks in Chicago and St. Louis, Jews in New York.

Abridged from Warner, 1972: 28–32, 117–118. Copyright © 1972 by Sam Bass Warner, Jr.

Americans. After the Civil War, many former slaves in the South either migrated to northern cities to work in a diverse array of skilled and semiskilled jobs or moved from the countryside to industrializing cities. In both northern and southern cities, the African-American population lived in segregated neighborhoods, forced by discrimination and often by law to keep its distance from Anglo-American residential districts.

Although the services provided to these neighborhoods were usually minimal, many people did find opportunities for cultural expression in the new urban mosaic. A study of African-Americans in Richmond, Virginia, after the Civil

Figure 10.22 New York City, looking southwest from the Bronx. The rows and rows of working-class housing in the foreground and the factories visible to the left indicate the horizontal spatial expansion of industrial urban form; the massive skyline indicates the degree of vertical expansion. *(Courtesy of Mona Domosh.)*

War found that residents effectively used public rituals in the streets and buildings of the city to carve out their own civic representations as well as to challenge the dominant Anglo-American order. For example, African-American militias were formed that marched through the streets of Richmond on holidays certified by the African-American community as their own political calendar: January 1, George Washington's birthday, April 3 (Emancipation Day), and July 4. As urban historians Elsa Barkley Brown and Gregg Kimball state: "White Richmonders watched in horror as former slaves claimed civic holidays white residents believed to be their own historic possession, and as black residents occupied spaces, like Capitol Square, that formerly had been reserved for white citizens." Other spaces, such as churches, schools, and beauty shops, served as both community centers and public statements of an African-American identity. In this way, the urban landscape acted as one arena for the struggle to control the meanings and uses of an environment often thought to be totally dominated by Anglo-American culture (Figure 10.23).

REFLECTING ON GEOGRAPHY

Consider how important the appropriation of space is to forming and maintaining cultural identity in the city. Why might such appropriation be more important for groups that are not dominant in a society? What do examples from your city tell you about struggles to control the meaning of its built environment?

Gender Industrialization, as we have seen, not only destroyed sections of cities to make way for railroads and factories but also made possible the creation of new urban identities and neighborhoods. Throughout the nineteenth century, the industrial city became increasingly segregated by function; large areas of the city were dedicated to the production of goods and services, surrounded by working-class neighborhoods. At the same time, the center of the city was remade into an area of consumption and leisure, with large department stores, theaters, clubs, restaurants, and nightclubs. In New York City during the last half of the nineteenth century, one of the foremost displays of such a culture of consumption was located along Broadway and Sixth Avenue between Union and Madison squares. This area was called Ladies' Mile because, as the new class of consumers, middle-class women were the major patrons of the large department stores that architecturally dominated the streets.

Although industrialization led to the creation of separate spheres—the female sphere centered on the home and domestic duties, the male sphere dominating the public spaces and duties—it also created the need for mass consumption to keep the factories running profitably. With men as the class of producers, the duties of consumption fell to the women. Moreover, the locational logic of the urban land market meant that retailers were located in the most central parts of the city. This established what some scholars have referred to as a feminized downtown, meaning not only that the downtown was characterized by the

Figure 10.23 Sketch of an African-American congregation in Washington, D.C. African-American churches often served as centers of community organizations and as public statements of identity in the industrializing cities of the north.

Figure 10.24 **Stewart's department store.** One of the most ornate department stores along Ladies' Mile in New York City was Stewart's, located on Broadway at 10th Street. Because the store catered to the needs of Victorian women, it can be considered an example of "feminine" space. Can you think of other examples of such "feminine" spaces in your city or in a city with which you are familiar?

presence of middle- and upper-class women but also that the retailers themselves created spaces considered appropriately "feminine." Interiors were orderly and well arranged, the facades of buildings were heavily ornamented, and streets were paved and well lit (Figure 10.24).

Although this type of ornate and "feminine" downtown retailing area is still evident in large cities such as New York and San Francisco, the decentralizing forces in the twentieth-century city led to the abandonment of many of these areas, which have been replaced by the suburban shopping mall (see Chapter 11). It would be interesting to speculate in what ways the shopping mall is also a "feminine" space.

Megalopolis

In the nineteenth century, cities grew at unprecedented rates because of the concentration of people and commerce. The inner city became increasingly dominated by commerce and the working class. In the twentieth century, particularly after World War II, new forms of transportation and communication led to the **decentralization** of many urban functions. As a result, one metropolitan area blends into another, until supercities are created that stretch for hundreds of miles. The geographer Jean Gottmann coined the term **megalopolis** to describe these supercities.

This term is now used worldwide in reference to giant metropolitan regions such as Tokyo-Yokohama in Japan and the Ruhr region of Germany that includes Dortmund, Essen, and Düsseldorf. These urban regions are characterized by high population densities extending over hundreds of square miles or kilometers; concentrations of numerous

older cities; transportation links formed by freeway, railroad, air routes, and rapid transit; and an extremely high proportion of the nation's wealth, commerce, and political power.

Edge Cities

The past 20 years have witnessed an explosion in metropolitan growth in areas that had once been peripheral to the central city. Many of the so-called bedroom communities of the post–World War II era have been transformed into urban centers, with their own retail, financial, and entertainment districts (Figure 10.25). Author Joel Garreau refers to these new centers of urban activity as **edge cities,** although many other terms have been used in the past, including "suburban downtowns," "galactic cities," and "urban villages" (see Focus On: Cities on the Edge, Cities of the Future?). Most Americans now live, work, play, worship, and study in this type of settlement. What differentiates an edge city from the suburbs is that it is a place of work, of productive economic activity, and therefore is the destination of many commuters. In fact, the conventional work commute from the suburbs to the inner city has been replaced by commuting patterns that completely encircle the inner city. People live in one part of an edge city and commute to their workplace in another part of that city.

Many scholars are wary of referring to these new nodes of activity as cities because they do not resemble our nineteenth- or early-twentieth-century vision of a city. Edge cities contain all the functions of old downtowns, but they are spread out and less dense, with clusters along major freeways and off-ramps. This new form is attributable to changes

Figure 10.25 **Edge city.** These new centers of economic activity are located on the "edges" of traditional downtowns. *(Source: Walter Jimenez/TexStock Photo Inc.)*

in Americans' lifestyles and to the development of new transportation and communication technologies. The interstate highway system made possible an effective trucking system to transport consumer goods, thereby enabling new industries to locate outside the downtown. Breakthroughs in computer and communication technologies have allowed corporate executives to move company headquarters out of the downtowns and into sleek new glass buildings with parking garages, jogging paths, and picnic tables under the trees. Real estate speculation in emerging edge cities has fueled their development, resulting in an environment that many people feel is ugly and chaotic. As Garreau points out, however, even a place as revered by designers as Venice, Italy, began as an ad hoc mercantilist adventure; the Piazza San Marco was the result not of great urban planning but of the coincidence of centuries of building and rebuilding by people concerned with making money.

Globalizing Cities in the Developing World

With the end of colonialism and the movement toward political and economic independence, developing countries entered a period of rapid, sometimes tumultuous change. Cities have often been the focal point of this change. Millions of people have migrated to cities in search of a better life. Economic activities clustered in and around cities have often changed their orientation from external to local markets. Political and social unrest have also been centered in these cities.

Some scholars think that cities in the developing world will duplicate the changes experienced by cities that underwent industrialization in the nineteenth century. Though there are similarities, the differences are much greater. One of the primary differences is that population growth is more rapid in today's globalizing cities than it was in Europe in the nineteenth century. This rapid growth results partly from high birthrates but mainly from extremely high rates of migration to the cities. And although people flock to the cities in search of jobs, there is less of a correlation between economic growth and urbanization than there was in Europe. Cities increase in size not necessarily because there are jobs to lure workers, but rather because conditions in the countryside are much worse. In India, for example, rural poverty has exacerbated the rapid population increase in such cities as Mumbai (formerly Bombay) and Kolkata. People leave in hope that urban life will offer a slight improvement, and often it does. Given the new global economy, however, many of the jobs that are available in these cities are low-skilled and low-paying manufacturing jobs with harsh working conditions. The result is that rural-to-urban migrants often find themselves either unemployed or with jobs that barely provide them a living.

Sociologist Alejandro Portes argues that the large internal migrations that bring impoverished agricultural people into the city are not a new phenomenon but one that can be traced back to colonial times. In colonial Latin America, for example, the city was essentially home to the Spanish elite. When preconquest agricultural patterns were disrupted, peasants came to the city looking to improve their economic situation. These people usually lived on the margins of the city. Moreover, they were completely disenfranchised because only landowners had the right to hold office. The reaction by the elite to this ongoing pattern of movement of large masses of people into the city was a mixture of tolerance and indifference, with no one taking responsibility to integrate the migrants into the city. This pattern continues today in many globalizing cities such as Arequipa in Peru (see Culture in a Globalizing World on page 368).

The combination of large numbers of migrants and widespread unemployment leads to overwhelming pressure

Cities on the Edge, Cities of the Future?

Edge City is any place that:

1. *Has five million square feet or more of leasable office space—the workplace of the Information Age.* Five million square feet is more than downtown Memphis. The Edge City called the Galleria area west of downtown Houston—crowned by the sixty-four-story Transco Tower, the tallest building in the world outside an old downtown—is bigger than downtown Minneapolis.

2. *Has 600,000 square feet or more of leasable retail space.* That is the equivalent of a fair-sized mall. That mall, remember, probably has at least three nationally famous department stores, and eighty to a hundred shops and boutiques full of merchandise that used to be available only on the finest boulevards of Europe. Even in their heyday, there were not many downtowns with that boast.

3. *Has more jobs than bedrooms.* When the workday starts, people head toward this place, not away from it. Like all urban places, the population increases at 9 A.M.

4. *Is perceived by the population as one place.* It is a regional end destination for mixed use—not a starting point—that "has it all," from jobs, to shopping, to entertainment.

5. *Was nothing like "city" as recently as 30 years ago.* Then, it was just bedrooms, if not cow pastures. This incarnation is brand new.

An example of the authentic, California-like experience of encountering such an Edge City is peeling off a high thruway, like the Pennsylvania Turnpike, onto an arterial, like Route 202 at King of Prussia, northwest of downtown Philadelphia. Descending into traffic that is bumper to bumper in both directions, one swirls through mosaics of lawn and parking, punctuated by office slabs whose designers have taken the curious vow of never placing windows in anything other than horizontal reflective strips. Detours mark the yellow dust of heavy construction that seems a permanent feature of the landscape.

Tasteful signs mark corporations apparently named after Klingon warriors. Who put Captain Kirk in charge of calling companies Imtrex, Avantor, and Synovus? Before that question

can settle, you encounter the spoor of the mother ship. On King of Prussia's Route 202, the mark of that mind-boggling enormity reads MALL NEXT FOUR LEFTS.

For the stranger who is a connoisseur of such places, this Dante-esque vision brings a physical shiver to the spine and a not entirely ironic murmur of recognition to the lips: "Ah! Home!" For that is precisely the significance of Edge Cities. They are the culmination of a generation of individual American value decisions about the best ways to live, work, and play—about how to create "home." That stuff "out there" is where America is being built. That "stuff" is the delicate balance between unlimited opportunity and rippling chaos that works for us so well. We build more of it every chance we get.

If Edge Cities are still a little ragged at the fringes, well, that just places them in the finest traditions of Walt Whitman's "barbaric yawp over the rooftops of the world"—what the social critic Tom Wolfe calls, affectionately, the "hog-stomping Baroque exuberance of American civilization." Edge Cities, after all, are still works in progress.

They have already proven astoundingly efficient, though, by any urban standard that can be quantified. As places to make one's fame and fortune, their corporate offices generate unprecedentedly low unemployment. In fact, their emblem is the hand-lettered sign taped to plate glass begging people to come to work. As real estate markets, they have made an entire generation of homeowners and speculators rich. As bazaars, they are anchored by some of the most luxurious shopping in the world. Edge City acculturates immigrants, provides child care, and offers safety. It is, on average, an improvement in per capita fuel efficiency over the old suburbia-downtown arrangement, since it moves everything closer to the homes of the middle class.

That is why Edge City is the crucible of America's urban future. Having become the place in which the majority of Americans now live, learn, work, shop, play, pray, and die, Edge City will be the forge of the fabled American way of life well into the twenty-first century.

From Garreau, 1991. Copyright © 1991 by Joel Garreau. Used by permission of Doubleday, a division of Bantam Doubleday Dell Publishing Group, Inc.

---

for low-rent housing. Governments have rarely been able to meet these needs through housing projects, so one of the most common folk solutions has been construction of illegal housing: **squatter settlements,** or **barriadas** (Figure 10.26). In greater Cairo, for example, scholars estimate that 5.5 million people live in squatter settlements. It is important to note, however, that such statistics often be misleading be-

cause what is considered unacceptable housing, or squatter settlements, varies by country and by household.

Squatter settlements usually begin as collections of crude shacks constructed from scrap materials; gradually, they become increasingly elaborate and permanent. Paths and walkways link houses, vegetable gardens spring up, and often water and electricity are bootlegged into the area so

Figure 10.26 **Squatter settlements in Mexico City (*left*) and Kuala Lumpur (*right*).** Migration to cities has been so rapid that often illegal squatter settlements have been the only solution to housing problems. *(Cameramann International, Ltd.)*

that a common tap or outlet serves a number of houses. At later stages, such economic pursuits as handicrafts and small-scale artisan activities take place in the squatter settlements. In many instances, these supposedly temporary settlements become permanent parts of the city and function as many neighborhoods do—that is, as social, economic, and cultural centers.

Squatter settlements are not just located in downtown areas; they also develop close to places where people work. In many cities, this means places that just five years were considered rural. Because of growing populations and pressures on space, many globalizing cities in the developing world are expanding outward. Some of these cities, such as Mexico City, Hanoi, and Manila, are expanding so rapidly out into the countryside that the city is encompassing or swallowing up smaller villages and rural areas. In this way, these new urban forms are blurring the distinction between the rural and the urban, creating what some scholars have called **extended metropolitan regions** (EMRs). Multinational corporations often rely on the labor of new urban migrants, and so the city grows rapidly at the margins as factories are built in export processing zones (EPZs) (see Chapter 9) and squatter settlements emerge around them. At the same time, the downtowns of these cities often experience not dispersal but concentration: high-rises accommodate the regional offices of corporations and the services associated with them (media, advertising, personnel management, and so forth), and upper-class housing developments accommodate this new class of white-collar workers.

In addition, landscape forms associated with the global consumer, entertainment, and tourist economy are emerging: American-style shopping districts (with American stores) and new airports, hotels, restaurants, and entertainment facilities. Many of these landscape developments are funded by international investments. Entrepreneurs and governments in many parts of the world look to these new globalizing cities of the developing world as good places to make financial and real estate investments. The extended metropolitan region of Hanoi, for example, is being built with funds from a range of countries (Figure 10.27): an export processing zone and a golf and entertainment facility are partly funded by Malaysia; South Korea is investing in a hotel, another golf course, and a business center; Taiwan is involved in a tourism project and an industrial park. Hanoi's downtown is being developed with more hotels and office construction funded by Japan and Singapore. Finland provided the infrastructure for the water supply to one of these new developments.

These new urban regions are complex in both their landscape form and function because they developed rapidly, without any planning, and have in many cases incorporated preexisting places. These EMRs, therefore, include multiple nodes of economic activity, with few of those nodes any older than a decade. Scholars who write about Mexico City, for example, find it impossible to speak of the city as one place; rather, they suggest that it can now only be represented as a pastiche of different places, each with its own center and outlying neighborhoods.

The new global economy, then, is reshaping many cities. Some, as we have seen, are becoming global cities: control centers for transnational corporations, services, and media. Others are heavily impacted by global investments in the manufacturing and consumer sector. The future of globalizing cities such as Hanoi (Figure 10.28) remains open, dependent partly on the success of differing sectors of foreign investment in jockeying for position within the global economy and partly on the success of national and urban governments in planning for and dispersing economic growth.

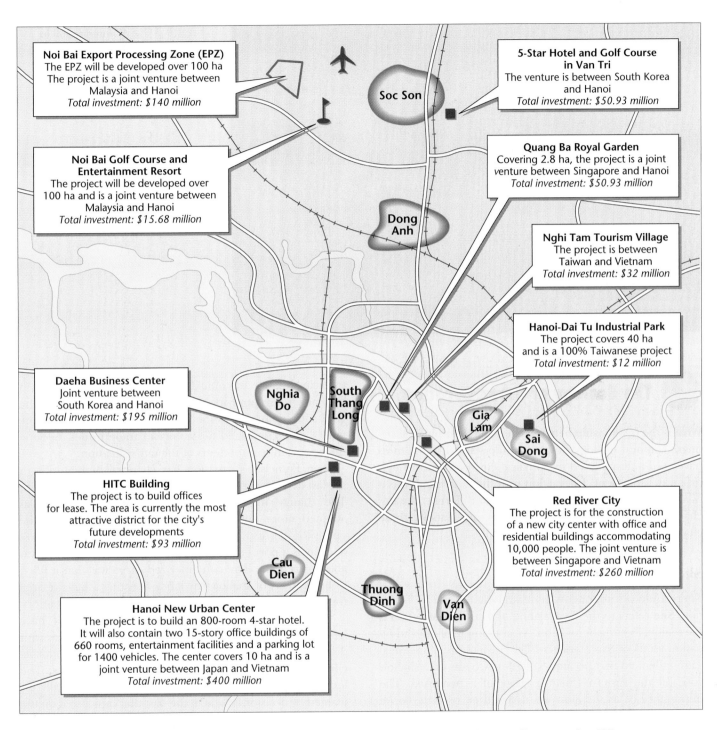

Noi Bai Export Processing Zone (EPZ)
The EPZ will be developed over 100 ha
The project is a joint venture between
Malaysia and Hanoi
Total investment: $140 million

**5-Star Hotel and Golf Course
in Van Tri**
The venture is between South Korea
and Hanoi
Total investment: $50.93 million

**Noi Bai Golf Course and
Entertainment Resort**
The project will be developed over
100 ha and is a joint venture between
Malaysia and Hanoi
Total investment: $15.68 million

Quang Ba Royal Garden
Covering 2.8 ha, the project is a joint
venture between Singapore and Hanoi
Total investment: $50.93 million

Nghi Tam Tourism Village
The project is between
Taiwan and Vietnam
Total investment: $32 million

Hanoi-Dai Tu Industrial Park
The project covers 40 ha
and is a 100% Taiwanese project
Total investment: $12 million

Daeha Business Center
Joint venture between
South Korea and Hanoi
Total investment: $195 million

HITC Building
The project is to build offices
for lease. The area is currently the most
attractive district for the city's
future developments
Total investment: $93 million

Red River City
The project is for the construction
of a new city center with office and
residential buildings accommodating
10,000 people. The joint venture is
between Singapore and Vietnam
Total investment: $260 million

Hanoi New Urban Center
The project is to build an 800-room 4-star hotel.
It will also contain two 15-story office buildings of
660 rooms, entertainment facilities and a parking lot
for 1400 vehicles. The center covers 10 ha and is a
joint venture between Japan and Vietnam
Total investment: $400 million

Soc Son, Dong Anh, Nghia Do, South Thang Long, Gia Lam, Sai Dong, Cau Dien, Thuong Dinh, Van Dien

Soc Son: Noi Bai International Airport is located in this area. Malaysia is investing in two projects there: a golf course and an EPZ.
Dong Anh: At the moment the area is one of the main vegetable-supplying sources for residents in Hanoi.
Nghia Do: Only five minutes from the West Lake, a property development area.
South Thang Long: Attracts a lot of foreign investment. The infrastructure is good, with the water supply system aided by the Finnish government.
Gia Lam Area: Called the "Daewoo area," it will soon become a satellite city of Hanoi.
Cau Dien: Recently approved project of traditional cultural tourism villages.
Thuong Dinh: Local industrial area.
Van Dien: An industrial park with infrastructure not yet developed. No foreign investment at present.

Figure 10.27 Diagram of Hanoi's extended metropolitan region. Foreign investment has been crucial to the spatial expansion of Hanoi, as you can see from the various projects under construction. In what ways is this urban expansion different from that in edge cities? *(Source: Drakakis-Smith, 2000: 24.)*

Figure 10.28 **Intersection in Old Quarter, Hanoi.** Economic development is visible even in the Old Quarter of Hanoi, as you can see by the presence of neon lights. *(Macduff Everton/Corbis.)*

 The Ecology of Urban Location

What is the relationship between cities and their physical settings? Cultural ecology helps us understand how cultures have used and modified the physical environment through urban development. Interaction with the environment is a two-way street: humans may respond to different physical characteristics; at the same time, they may modify those characteristics to suit their needs.

Site and Situation

There are two components of urban location: site and situation. **Site** refers to the local setting of a city; the **situation** is the regional setting or location. As an example of site and situation, think of San Francisco. The original site of the Mexican settlement that became San Francisco was on a shallow cove on the eastern (inland) shore of a peninsula. The importance of its situation was that it drew on waterborne traffic coming across the bay from other, smaller settlements. Hence the town could act as a transshipment point.

Both site and situation are dynamic, changing over time. For example, both the site and the situation of San Francisco have changed over the years. During the gold rush period of the 1850s, the small cove was filled both to create flatland for warehouses and to facilitate extending wharves into deeper bay waters. The filled-in cove is now occupied by the heart of the central business district (Figure 10.29). The geographical situation has also changed as patterns of trade and transportation technology have evolved. The original

transbay situation was quickly replaced during the gold rush by a new role: supplying the mines and settlements of the gold country. Access to the two major rivers leading to the mines, plus continued ties to ocean trade routes, became the important components of the city's situation.

San Francisco's situation has changed dramatically in the last decade, for it is no longer the major port of the bay. The change in technology to containerized cargo was adopted more quickly by Oakland, the rival city on the opposite side of the bay, which resulted in San Francisco's decline as a port city. One of the reasons that Oakland was able to accommodate containerized cargo was that it filled in huge tracts of shallow bay lands, creating a massive area for the loading, unloading, and storage of cargo containers.

Certain attributes of the physical environment have been important in the location of cities. Those cities with distinct functions, such as defense or trade, sought out specific physical characteristics in their original sitings. The locations of many contemporary cities can be partially explained by decisions made in the past that capitalized on the advantages of certain sites. The following classifications detail some of the different location possibilities.

Defensive Sites

There are many types of defensive sites for cities (some are diagrammed in Figure 10.30). A **defensive site** is a location that can be easily defended. The *river-meander site*, with the city located inside a loop where the stream turns back on itself, leaves only a narrow neck of land unprotected by water. Cities such as Bern, Switzerland, and New Orleans are

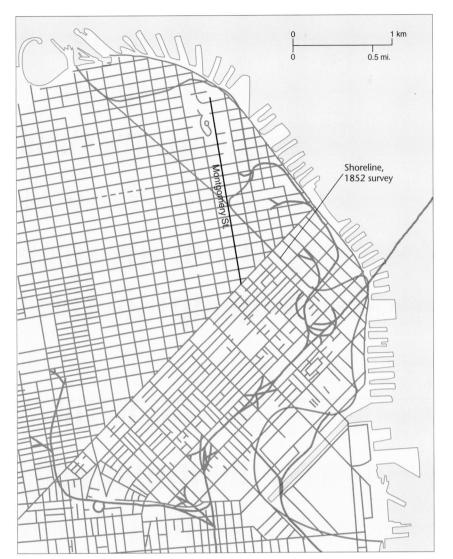

Figure 10.29 **This map shows how San Francisco's site has been changed by human activity.** During the late 1850s, shallow coves were filled, providing easier access to deeper bay waters as well as flatland near the waterfront for warehouses and industry.

situated inside river meanders. Indeed, the nickname for New Orleans, Crescent City, refers to the curve of the Mississippi River.

Even more advantageous was the *river-island site,* which, because the stream was split into two parts, often combined a natural moat with an easy river crossing. For example, Montreal is situated on a large island surrounded by the St. Lawrence River and other water channels. The *offshore-island site*—that is, islands lying off the seashore or in lakes—offered similar defensive advantages. Mexico City began as an Indian settlement on a lake island. Venice is the classic example of a city built on offshore islands in the sea, as is Hong Kong. *Peninsula sites* were almost as advantageous as island sites, because they offered natural water defenses on all but one side (Figure 10.31). Boston was founded on a peninsula for this reason, and a wooden palisade wall was built across the neck of the peninsula.

Danger of attack from the sea often prompted sheltered-harbor defensive sites, where a narrow entrance to the harbor could be defended easily. Examples of *sheltered-harbor sites* include cities such as Rio de Janeiro, Tokyo, and San Francisco.

High points were also sought out. These are often referred to as *acropolis sites;* the word *acropolis* means "high city." Originally the city developed around a fortification on the high ground and then spilled out over the surrounding lowland. Athens is the prototype of acropolis sites, but many other cities are similarly located.

Trade-Route Sites

In many other instances, defense was not a primary consideration. Instead, urban centers were often built on **trade-route sites**—that is, at important points along already

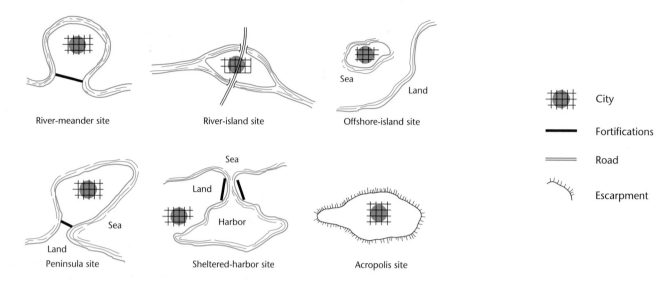

Figure 10.30 **Types of defensive city sites.** Natural protection is afforded by physical features. The Greek city of Miletus (see Figure 10.10) is an example of which type of defensive sites?

established trade routes. Here, too, the influence of the physical environment can be detected.

Especially common types of trade-route sites (Figure 10.32) are *bridge-point sites* and *river-ford sites,* places where major land routes could easily cross over rivers. Typically,

Figure 10.31 **The classic defensive site of Mont St. Michel, France.** A small town clustered around a medieval abbey, which was originally separated from the mainland during high tides, Mont St. Michel now has a causeway that connects the island to shore, allowing armies of tourists to penetrate the town's defenses easily. *(Photo Researchers.)*

these were sites where streams were narrow and shallow, with firm banks. Occasionally, such cities even bear in their names the evidence of their sites, as in Frankfurt ("ford of the Franks"), Germany, and Oxford, England. The site for London was chosen because it is the lowest point on the Thames River where a bridge—the famous London Bridge—could easily be built to serve a trade route running inland from Dover on the sea.

Confluence sites are also common. They allow cities to be situated at the point where two navigable streams flow together. Pittsburgh, at the confluence of the Allegheny and Monongahela rivers, is a fine example (Figure 10.33). *Head-of-navigation sites,* where navigable water routes begin, are even more common, because goods must be transshipped at such points. Iquitos, Peru, is located at the head-of-navigation site for the Amazon River, and Minneapolis-St. Paul, at the falls of the Mississippi River, also occupies a head-of-navigation site. *Portage sites* are very similar. Here, goods were portaged from one river to another. Chicago is near a short portage between the Great Lakes and the Mississippi River drainage basin.

In these ways and others, an urban site can be influenced by the physical environment. Of course, many nonenvironmental factors can also influence the choice of site. Here, it is useful to distinguish between the specific urban site and the general location, or **spatial distribution,** of cities. Spacing implies a broader overall view of the pattern of urban centers. Site is often influenced by the environment, but the spacing of cities is less likely to be. The theme of cultural interaction will help us understand why cities are spaced as they are.

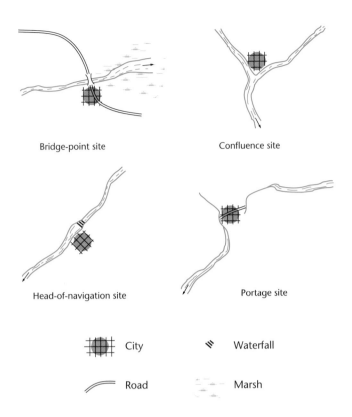

Bridge-point site

Confluence site

Head-of-navigation site

Portage site

⊞ City   ≋ Waterfall

⌒ Road   ≈ Marsh

Figure 10.32 **Trade-route city sites.** These sites are at strategic positions along transportation arteries. Is your city or one near you located on a trade-route site?

Figure 10.33 **Pittsburgh's Golden Triangle.** At the confluence of the Allegheny and Monongahela rivers, Pittsburgh is a classic example of how an early trade-route site has evolved into a commercial center. *(Henryk Kaiser/Leo de Wys, Inc.)*

 Cultural Interaction in Urban Geography

How can we understand the spatial arrangement of cities as an integrated system? In recent decades, urban geographers have studied the spatial distribution of towns and cities to determine some of the economic and political factors that influence the pattern of cities. In doing so, they have created a number of models that collectively make up **central-place theory.** These models represent examples of cultural interaction.

Most urban centers are engaged mainly in the service industries. The service activities of urban centers include transportation, communication, and utilities—services that facilitate the movement of goods and that provide the networks for the exchange of ideas about those goods (see Chapter 9 for a more detailed examination of these different industrial activities). Towns and cities that support such activities are called **central places.**

In the early 1930s, the German geographer Walter Christaller first formulated central-place theory as a series of models designed to explain the spatial distribution of urban centers. Crucial to his theory is the fact that different goods and services vary both in **threshold,** the size of the population required to make provision of the service economically feasible, and in **range,** the average maximum distance people will travel to purchase a good or service. For example, a larger number of people are required to support a hospital, university, or department store than to support a gasoline station, post office, or grocery store. Similarly, consumers are willing to travel a greater distance to consult a heart specialist, record a land title, or purchase an automobile than to buy a loaf of bread, mail a letter, or visit a movie theater. Because the range of central goods and services varies, urban centers are arranged in an orderly hierarchy. Some central places are small and offer a limited variety of services and goods; others are large and offer an abundance. At the top of this hierarchy are regional metropolises—cities such as New York, Beijing, or Mumbai—that offer all services associated with central places and that have very large tributary trade areas, or hinterlands. At the opposite extreme are small market villages and roadside hamlets, which may contain nothing more than a post office, service station, or café. Between these two extremes are central places of various degrees of importance. Each higher rank of central place provides all the goods and services available at a lower-rank center, plus one or more additional goods and services. Central places of lower rank greatly outnumber the few at the higher levels of the hierarchy. One regional metropolis may contain thousands of smaller central places in its tributary market

CULTURE IN A GLOBALIZING WORLD

One Family's Tale

One of the primary causes of rapid population growth in globalizing cities is massive rural-to-urban migration. In Arequipa, Peru, as in many cities, that rapid population growth has led to the development of squatter settlements on the outskirts of the town. Many migrants have few options for housing and must live in these settlements, which are often illegal. The following story explains how the negotiations over housing take place in the case of one family.

Sebastiano and Maria used to live in a small village about 30 miles from Arequipa with Maria's parents. Work was difficult to obtain as the prices for the sugar that was grown in the area had been falling for years and only those with strong personal ties to the overseers were recruited. Sebastiano initially moved to Arequipa on his own in order to try to get work in the new factories in the city.

Sebastiano first moved into an inner-city barrio with one of his distant cousins, but he only stayed there until he found out how the employment situation operated in Arequipa. Each day he would go to the western edge of the long-distance bus terminus where foremen from the building contractors would recruit their casual labor. Soon Sebastiano moved to his own rented room in a small house nearby. The accommodation was simple, even primitive, compared to his rural home. He had a bed, a cupboard and a recess for hanging his clothes. Washing was done at the tap in the yard.

All in all Sebastiano was reasonably happy with his rented room in the city center—he was near to his main source of work and to cheap services, and he had an understanding landlord. The advertisements for the new low-cost housing schemes on the edge of the city held no appeal for him. He could not afford the regular rental demands, or the transport costs to get into the city to find work.

However, Sebastiano did not want to live alone in the city. He missed his wife, Maria, and their young son, Pedro. After a couple of years in the inner city he began to make inquiries about a plot in a new squatter barrio that was planned on some unused public land. His landlord knew someone who knew the local councilor and advised Sebastiano to go and talk to him. The councilor was impressed with Sebastiano's carpentry and building skills and recommended him to the informal committee that was organizing the 'invasion.' Sebastiano was accepted and with about 90 other families occupied the small piece of floodplain down by the river on the Ascension Day holiday when they knew the police would be busy elsewhere. Each family managed to put up basic walls and a roof on their allotted plot and, with the support of their councilor, were permitted to stay and improve their shelter as and when they could. They named the settlement St. Christopher as they were all travelers to the city. The municipal authorities knew better than to enforce the letter of the law. After all, these were determined, hard-working people who were housing themselves at no cost to the city government.

Eventually, sheer numbers forced the municipal authority to recognize the de facto rights of the settlement and to extend electricity, water, and sanitation services to the barrio. Access to regular water was a particularly important improvement, as residents had hitherto been forced to purchase from private water trucks at ten times the cost of the piped supply, but all of the upgraded services had resulted in a substantial improvement in the community's health and well-being. Sebastiano and Maria were now established members of the urban community.

From Drakakis-Smith, 2000: 158–159

---

area (Figure 10.34). The size of the market area is determined by the distance range of the goods and services it offers.

With this hierarchy as a background, Christaller then tried to measure the influence of three forces in determining the spacing and distribution of urban centers by creating models. His first model measured the influence of market and range of goods on the spacing of cities. To simplify the model, he assumed that the terrain, soils, and other environmental factors were uniform; that transportation was universally available; and that all regions would be supplied with

goods and services from the minimum number of central places. In such a model, the shape of the market area was circular, encompassing the range of goods and services, with the city at the center of the circle. However, when central places of the same rank in the hierarchy were nearby, the circle became a hexagon (Figure 10.35a). If market and range of goods were the only causal forces, the distribution of towns and cities would produce a pattern of nested hexagons, each with a central place at its center.

Then Christaller created a second model. In this model, he tried to measure the influence of transportation

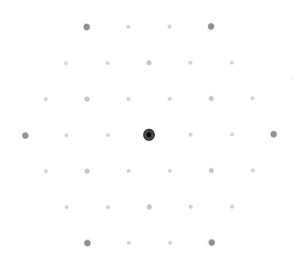

Figure 10.34 **Christaller's hierarchy of central places shows the orderly arrangement of towns of different sizes.** This is an idealized presentation of places performing central functions. For each large central place, many smaller central places are located within the larger place's hinterland.

- ⬤ First-order place (regional metropolis)
- ● Second-order place
- ◦ Third-order place
- · Fourth-order place

on the spacing of central places. He no longer assumed that transportation was universally and equally available in the **hinterland.** Instead, he assumed that as many demands for transport as possible would be met with the minimum expenditure for construction and maintenance of trans-

portation facilities. Thus, as many high-ranking central places as possible would be on straight-line routes between the primary central places (Figure 10.35b). The pattern of central places created by considering the transportation factor is rather different from that created by the market

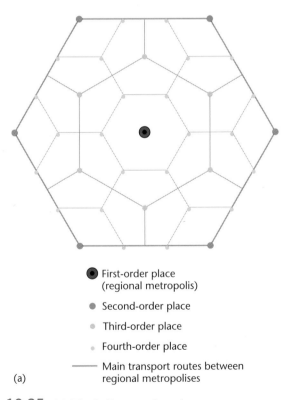

- ⬤ First-order place (regional metropolis)
- ● Second-order place
- ◦ Third-order place
- · Fourth-order place
- — Main transport routes between regional metropolises

(a)

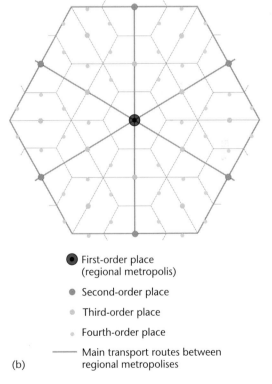

- ⬤ First-order place (regional metropolis)
- ● Second-order place
- ◦ Third-order place
- · Fourth-order place
- — Main transport routes between regional metropolises

(b)

Figure 10.35 **(a) The influence of market area on Christaller's arrangement of central places.** If marketing were the only factor controlling the distribution of central places, this diagram would represent the arrangement of towns and cities. Why, in this model, would hexagons be the shape to appear instead of a square, circle, or some other shape? **(b) The distribution of central places according to Christaller's model.**

If the availability of transportation is the determining factor in the location of central places, their distribution will be different from the distribution that would result if marketing were the determining factor. Note that the second-order central places are pulled away from the apexes of the hexagon and become located on the main transport routes between regional metropolises. (*After Christaller, 1966. By permission of the publisher.*)

factor. This pattern occurs because direct routes between adjacent regional metropolises do not pass through central places of the next-lowest rank. As a result, these second-rank central places are "pulled" from the points of the hexagonal market area to the midpoints to be on the straight-line routes between adjacent regional metropolises.

Christaller hypothesized that the market factor would be the greater force in rural countries, where goods were seldom shipped throughout a region. In densely settled industrialized countries, however, he believed that the transportation factor would be stronger because there were greater numbers of central places and more demand for long-distance transportation.

Christaller devised a third model to measure a type of political influence: the effect of political borders on the distribution of central places. He recognized that political boundaries, especially within independent countries, would tend to follow the hexagonal market-area limits of each central place that was a political center. He also recognized that such borders tend to separate people and retard the movement of goods and services. Such borders necessarily cut through the market areas of many central places below the rank of regional metropolis. Central places in such border regions lose rank and size because their market areas are politically cut in two. Border towns are thus "stunted," and important central places are pushed away from the border, which distorts the hexagonal pattern.

Many other forces influence the spatial distribution of central places. Market area, transportation, and political borders are but three. For example, in all three of these models, it is assumed that the physical environment is uniform and that people are evenly distributed. Of course, neither of these is true. Nevertheless, certain assumptions are necessary to construct a theoretical model that integrates different components of culture.

REFLECTING ON GEOGRAPHY

If Christaller's assumptions did not hold, in what ways would central-place theory need to be altered?

Conclusion

The first cities arose as new technologies, particularly the domestication of plants and animals, facilitated the concentration of people, wealth, and power in a few specific places. This transformation from village to city life was accompanied by new social organizations, a greater division of labor, and increased social stratification. These characteristics still distinguish rural from urban life. Although the first cities developed in specific hearths, urban life has now diffused

worldwide, and all indications are that our planet will become increasingly urban in the decades to come.

Many of the problems now plaguing our cities are consequences of uncorrected ills from the past. Traffic and housing problems in Europe, for example, may be understood in the context of the medieval urban landscape. Even though this landscape evolved well over 500 years ago, the narrow streets and cramped housing conditions of the period still pervade the typical European central city today.

Many problems of cities in the developing world are products of the twentieth century. Such cities are bursting at the seams as thousands of new migrants crowd into them each day, seeking jobs, housing, and schooling. Because jobs are scarce, unemployment rates are often very high. Housing is also a problem. In some cities, over a third of the population lives in hastily constructed squatter settlements. But even many of these problems have historical roots, as an examination of the political and social history of colonial cities demonstrates. For example, massive rural-to-urban migration is not a new phenomenon. The disruptions caused by nineteenth-century colonial settlements deprived many people of their land and forced rural inhabitants into the city. This pattern (with modified causes) continues today.

The future of the world's cities is uncertain. Strong governmental planning measures might alleviate many present-day ills, but the long-range hope lies with decreased population growth and increased economic opportunities. Whether this is possible under contemporary conditions remains to be seen.

DOING GEOGRAPHY

Connecting Urban Population Growth with Globalization

As we've suggested in this chapter, most cities today are global in the sense that they are being shaped by global economic, cultural, and political forces. But sometimes it is difficult to actually see in what ways this is happening or in what ways this matters. In this exercise, you will focus on one simple measure of urbanization—population growth—in order to analyze how it is being affected by globalization.

Choose one city from the list of world cities in Table 10.1. First, to provide context, track its population change over the past 50 years and determine its growth rate every decade (you will probably need to use online data, from the United Nations Statistics Division or other sources). Now, concentrating on the past 20 years, see if you can determine the sources of its population growth. In other words, are people migrating to the city from rural areas? From other countries? Or is it natural population growth? Third, link that population growth to global changes. Are people moving to this city to work for transnational companies? Because their rural homes are experiencing decline due to environmental degradation? Because they must leave their homes in one country due to global uneven development? Finally, try to understand in what ways these population shifts are shaping the cultures of this city.

The City on the Internet

You can learn more about the city in time and space on the Internet at the following web sites:

City Beautiful: The 1901 Plan for Washington, D.C.

http://xroads.virginia.edu/~CAP/CITYBEAUTIFUL/dchome.html

This provides an introduction to the City Beautiful movement, a late-nineteenth- and early-twentieth-century movement that attempted, through urban planning, to create more efficient and aesthetic cities.

Cyburbia: The Urban Planning Portal

http://www.cyburbia.org

This site provides a comprehensive directory of Internet resources about urbanism, planning, and architecture.

United Nations Statistics Division

http://www.un.org/Depts/unsd/

The source for world population statistics, this site contains a comprehensive section on urbanization as a social indicator.

U.S. Department of Housing and Urban Development

http://www.hud.gov

Here you can find information about housing issues and urban economic development and about how to get involved personally in your own local community.

Sources

Agnew, John A., and James S. Duncan (eds.). 1989. *The Power of Place: Bringing Together Geographical and Sociological Imaginations.* Boston: Unwin Hyman.

Bell, Morag. 1995. "A Woman's Place in 'a White Man's Country.' Rights, Duties and Citizenship for the 'New' South Africa, c. 1902." *Ecumene* 2: 129–148.

Benevolo, Leonardo. 1980. *The History of the City.* Cambridge, Mass.: MIT Press.

Brown, Elsa Barkley, and Gregg D. Kimball. 1995. "Mapping the Terrain of Black Richmond." *Journal of Urban History* 21: 296–346.

Christaller, Walter. 1966. *The Central Places of Southern Germany.* C. W. Baskin (trans.). Englewood Cliffs, N.J.: Prentice-Hall.

Cosgrove, Denis. 1984. *Social Formation and Symbolic Landscape.* London: Croom Helm.

de Planhol, Xavier. 1959. *The World of Islam.* Ithaca, N.Y.: Cornell University Press.

Domosh, Mona. 1995. "The Feminized Retail Landscape: Gender Ideology and Consumer Culture in Nineteenth-Century New York City," in Neil Wrigley and Michelle Lowe (eds.), *Retailing, Consumption and Capital.* Essex, U.K.: Longman, 257–270.

Doxiades, C. A. 1972. *Architectural Space in Ancient Greece.* Cambridge, Mass.: MIT Press.

Drakakis-Smith, David. 1987. *The Third World City.* London: Methuen.

Drakakis-Smith, David. 2000. *Third World Cities,* 2nd ed. London: Routledge.

Duncan, James S. 1989. "The Power of Place in Kandy, Sri Lanka: 1780–1980," in John A. Agnew and James S. Duncan (eds.), *The Power of Place.* Boston: Unwin Hyman, 185–201.

Encyclopaedia Britannica. 1984. "Babylon." *New Encyclopaedia Britannica,* vol. 2. Chicago: Encyclopaedia Britannica.

Fowler, Melvin. 1975. "A Pre-Columbian Urban Center on the Mississippi." *Scientific American* (August): 93–102.

Garreau, Joel. 1991. *Edge City: Life on the New Frontier.* New York: Doubleday.

Gottmann, Jean. 1961. *Megalopolis.* Cambridge, Mass.: MIT Press.

Hayes, John. 1969. *London: A Pictorial History.* New York: Arco Publishing Company.

Kenny, Judith T. 1995. "Climate, Race and Imperial Authority: The Symbolic Landscape of the British Hill Station in India." *Annals of the Association of American Geographers* 85: 694–714.

Mills, Sara. 1996. "Gender and Colonial Space." *Gender, Place and Culture* 3: 125–148.

Mumford, Lewis. 1961. *The City in History.* New York: Harcourt Brace Jovanovich.

Pirenne, Henri. 1996. *Medieval Cities.* Garden City, N.Y.: Doubleday (Anchor Books).

Portes, Alejandro. 1977. "Urban Latin America: The Political Condition from Above and Below," in Janet Abu-Lughod and Richard Hag, Jr. (eds.), *Third World Urbanization.* New York: Methuen, 59–70.

Pounds, Norman J. G. 1969. "The Urbanization of the Classical World." *Annals of the Association of American Geographers* 59: 135–157.

Samuels, Marwyn S., and Carmencita Samuels. 1989. "Beijing and the Power of Place in Modern China," in John A. Agnew and James S. Duncan (eds.), *The Power of Place.* Boston: Unwin Hyman, 202–227.

Sassen, Saskia. 1991. *The Global City: New York, London, Tokyo.* Princeton, N.J.: Princeton University Press.

Simon, D. 1984. "Third-World Colonial Cities in Context: Conceptual and Theoretical Approaches with Particular Interest to Africa." *Progress in Human Geography* 8: 493–514.

Sjoberg, Gideon. 1960. *The Preindustrial City.* New York: Free Press.

Spain, Daphne. 1992. *Gendered Spaces.* Chapel Hill: University of North Carolina Press.

Summerson, John. 1946. *Georgian London.* New York: Charles Scribner's Sons.

Vance, James E., Jr. 1990. *The Continuing City: Urban Morphology in Western Civilization.* Baltimore: Johns Hopkins University Press.

Vance, James E., Jr. 1971. "Land Assignment in the Pre-Capitalist, Capitalist and Post-Capitalist City." *Economic Geography* 47: 101–120.

Ware, Vron. 1992. *Beyond the Pale: White Women, Racism and History.* London: Verso.

Warner, Sam Bass, Jr. 1972. *Urban Wilderness.* New York: Harper & Row.

SEEING GEOGRAPHY

What are some of the major environmental and social impacts of an increasingly urbanized world?

View of Rio de Janeiro from Sugarloaf Mountain.

Rio de Janeiro

Few cities boast such a spectacular site as Rio de Janeiro, located between the mountains and Guanabara Bay along the Atlantic Ocean. This view looking southwest highlights the dramatic siting: the night lights of a bustling city, the colorful neon of the beaches, the outlines of rugged mountain peaks against the night sky. One can barely discern in this image the "other" side of Rio: the favelas, or squatter settlements, located on the mountainsides (although see Figure 10.2). Perched above the centers of economic activity and the middle- and upper-class residential areas located along the southern coastal areas of Rio, the favelas are an ever-present part of the urban landscape and are home to approximately one-fifth of the city's population.

The information in this chapter should help us to "read" this image of Rio de Janeiro. As a city of the developing world, Rio experienced rapid population growth in the twentieth century, and its metropolitan area now exceeds 11 million people. More striking is the dramatic increase in the urban population of Brazil. The percentage of the population living in metropolitan areas rose from approximately 31 percent in 1940 to about 84 percent in 2005. In Rio, that population growth is evident in the intensity of land use within the city, which is marked by the presence of skyscrapers; the metropolitan sprawl that extends well beyond the parameters of this image; and the presence of the favelas, home to many of the rural-to-urban migrants. Like other cities of the developing world, population growth has strained the city's infrastructure and its ability to provide services, which has led to traffic congestion, pollution, and crime. It has also exacerbated ecological problems. When vegetation covered the hillsides, the heavy summer rains Rio experiences were absorbed into the soil. Now the summer rains often flood the streets of the low-lying areas of the city and lead to landslides on the slopes that house the favelas. One such episode in 1996, for example, led to the death of 71 people, with approximately 2000 people left homeless. Yet Rio, like its larger neighbor 230 miles (370 kilometers) to the south, São Paulo, is now experiencing much slower population growth as a result of lower birthrates and less rural-to-urban migration.

Founded as a Portuguese colonial city in 1565, Rio grew quickly in the eighteenth century, when it became the primary port for exporting the gold and diamonds discovered in the interior of the country. Later, in the first decades of the twentieth century, Rio underwent industrialization. The southern and coastal portions of the city that we see in this image became home to the elite, while the factories and working classes moved north and west of the downtown (out of the view of this image).

Today, Rio is part edge city (transit networks and economic nodes extend well beyond the frame of this image), part colonial city, and part global city. It is home to the regional headquarters of 10 multinational firms, marking it as a second- or third-level world city. Its beaches, particularly Ipanema and Copacabana, are icons for global jet-setters. Yet its favelas, some of which have now been recognized by the government as legal communities, continue to grow, with little infrastructure and few public services. Like other globalizing cities, it experiences both the "bright lights" and the grimmer realities of the twenty-first-century economic order. ∎

Wheatley, Paul. 1971. *The Pivot of the Four Quarters*. Chicago: Aldine Publishing Company.

Wittfogel, Karl. 1957. *Oriental Despotism: A Comparative Study of Total Power*. New Haven: Yale University Press.

Yeoh, Brenda, S. A. 1999. "Global/Globalizing Cities." *Progress in Human Geography* 23: 607–616.

Ten Recommended Books
on Urban Geography

(For additional suggested readings, see *The Human Mosaic* web site: www.whfreeman.com/jordan)

Boyer, M. Christine. 1996. *The City of Collective Memory: The Historical Imagery and Architectural Entertainments*. Cambridge, Mass.: MIT Press. A wide-ranging analysis of the role of history and memory in the shaping and function of contemporary Western cities.

Harvey, David. 1985. *The Urban Experience*. Baltimore: Johns Hopkins University Press. A study of the relationship between capitalist economics and the cities it produces.

King, Anthony. 1990. *Urbanization, Colonialism and the World Economy*. Routledge: London. An examination of how colonialism shaped the geography of cities.

Knox, Paul, and Peter J. Taylor (eds.). 1995. *World Cities in a World System*. Cambridge: Cambridge University Press. An edited collection that examines the social and economic role of cities within the contemporary world system.

Legates, Richard T., and Frederic Stout (eds.). 1999. *The City Reader*, 2nd ed. New York: Routledge. An extensive edited collection of readings covering the evolution of cities and the contemporary forces that are restructuring them.

Marcuse, Peter, and Ronald Van Kempen (eds.). 2000. *Globalizing Cities: A New Spatial Order?* Oxford: Blackwell. A collection of studies of the impact of globalization on the spatial form of cities, from Singapore to Kolkata to New York.

Ogborn, Miles. 1998. *Spaces of Modernity: London's Geographies 1680–1780*. New York: Guilford Press. A historical study of the making of modernity within the spaces of eighteenth-century London.

Olds, Kris. 2001. *Globalization and Urban Change: Capital, Culture, and Pacific Rim Mega-Projects*. New York: Oxford University Press. An in-depth examination of how globalization actually operates in terms of large-scale urban developments in Vancouver and Shanghai.

Rose, Gillian, and Alison Blunt (eds.). 1994. *Writing Women and Space: Colonial and Postcolonial Geographies*. New York: Guilford Press. An edited collection that analyzes relationships between gender and colonial space, with several case studies focusing on urban space.

Sassen, Saskia (ed.). 2003. *Global Networks, Linked Cities*. New York: Routledge. A collection of essays that examine the emerging networks of global commerce and communication that are reshaping the world's cities.

Journals in Urban Geography

International Journal of Urban and Regional Research. Published by Edward Arnold, London. Volume 1 appeared in 1987.

Urban Geography. Published by Belwether Press, Lanham, Md. Volume 1 appeared in 1976.

How has globalization affected urban ethnic neighborhoods?

A street in Chinatown, New York City. *(Bojan Breceli/Corbis.)*

Turn to Seeing Geography on page 408 for an in-depth analysis of the above question.

INSIDE THE CITY
11
A Cultural Mosaic

FINDING AND UNDERSTANDING patterns in a city is a difficult matter. As you walk or drive through a city, its intricacy may dazzle you and its form can seem chaotic. It is often hard to imagine why city functions are where they are, why people cluster where they do. Why does one block have high-income housing and another, slum tenements? Why are ethnic neighborhoods next to the central business district? Why does the highway run through one neighborhood and around another? Just when you think you are beginning to understand some patterns in your city, you note that those patterns are swiftly changing. The house you grew up in is now part of the business district. The central city that you roamed as a child looks abandoned. A suburban shopping center thrives on what was once farmland.

Chapter 10 focused on cities as points in geographical space. In this chapter, we try to orient ourselves within cities to gain some perspective on their spatial patterns. In other words, the two chapters differ in scale. Chapter 10 presented cities from afar, as small dots diffusing across space and interacting with one another and with their environment. In this chapter, we use the five themes of cultural geography to study the city as if we were walking its streets.

Through culture region, we examine spatial differences within cities. Cultural diffusion shows how these internal and regional differences develop. Cultural ecology permits us to see the role of the physical environment within the structure of a city. Through cultural interaction, we come to appreciate what a finely woven fabric a city really is. Of course, the visual impact of these elements is revealed in the urban landscape, which is perceived in different ways by different people.

Urban Culture Regions

How are areas within a city spatially arranged? Much of the fascination with urban life comes from its diversity, from the excitement created by different groups of people and different types of activities packaged in a fairly small area. Yet within this diversity, it is possible to discern regional patterns, for cities are composed of a series of districts, each of which is defined by a particular set of land uses.

Downtowns

In the center of the typical city is the **central business district (CBD),** a dense cluster of offices and shops. The CBD is formed around the point within the city that is most accessible. As such, businesses and services located in the CBD experience the most "action" as measured by the volume of people, money, and ideas moving through this space. Competition for this space often leads to the construction of skyscrapers, creating a skyline that characterizes and symbolizes a city's CBD and the activities that are often located there: financial services, corporate headquarters, and related services such as advertising and public relations firms. The tallest buildings in the world are located in Asian cities such as Shanghai, Kuala Lumpur, and Taipei—cities that are vying to be major financial centers (Figure 11.1). Just beyond the skyscrapers are often four- and five-story buildings that comprise the city's main shopping district, traditionally centered around several department stores. Also within the CBD are concentrations of smaller retail estab-

lishments, transportation hubs such as railroad stations, and often civic centers such as a city hall and main library. Surrounding the CBD is a transitional zone, because it is situated between the core commercial area and the outlying residential areas. It is a district of mixed land uses, characterized by older residential buildings, warehouses, small factories, and apartment buildings.

Residential Areas

Beyond the transitional zone are various types of residential communities, or regions. Geographers have studied these culture regions in depth, trying to discern patterns of the distribution of diverse peoples. Some have focused on the idea of a **social culture region:** a residential area characterized by socioeconomic traits, such as income, education, age, and family structure (Figures 11.2 and 11.3). Other researchers, who use the notion of **ethnic culture region,** highlight traits of ethnicity, such as language and migration history. Obviously the two concepts overlap, because there can be social regions within ethnic regions and vice versa. Remember also that some researchers treat both social and ethnic culture regions as functions of the political and economic forces underlying and reinforcing residential segregation and discrimination. (More information on ethnic areas is found in Chapter 5.)

One way to define social culture regions is to isolate one social trait and plot its distribution within the city. The U.S. census is a common source of such information because the districts used to count population, called **census tracts,** are small enough to allow the subtle texture of social regions to

Figure 11.1 **Skyline of Shanghai, China.** The skyline is a clear marker of the global importance of Shanghai as a new financial center. Compare these very recent skyscrapers to those of an American or Canadian city. *(Photographer's Choice/Getty.)*

Figure 11.2 An inner-city neighborhood near the Capitol in Washington, D.C. One of the most pressing problems facing the United States is reversing the continued decay of inner cities. What factors have led to this decay of the inner city? (For help, look at the section on suburbanization and decentralization.) *(Cameramann International, Ltd.)*

show. Income is one of the more common social traits to be mapped. Such maps form the basis of many urban land-use models that are discussed later in the chapter (see the section on cultural interaction and models of the city).

In addition to income, another important characteristic that often distinguishes one urban residential area from another is ethnicity. This is certainly not surprising, given the history of immigration to North America in the nineteenth and twentieth centuries and the propensity of immigrants to move to cities. During the middle to late nineteenth century,

when waves of immigrants left eastern and southern Europe, North American port cities were a common destination and employment as laborers in factories was the norm. With limited affordable housing available, most immigrants settled close to one another, forming ethnic communities or pockets within the mosaic of the city. These ethnic urban regions—with names such as Little Italy in New York and Chinatown in San Francisco—often allowed the immigrants to maintain their native languages, holidays, foodways, and religions. Although the names of these urban enclaves still

Figure 11.3 Middle-income neighborhood in Reston, Virginia. Social areas within the city can be delimited by certain traits taken from the census, such as income, education, or family size. How would the social characteristics of this neighborhood differ from those in Figure 11.2? *(Cameramann International, Ltd.)*

exist today, most of them have been transformed by new and different waves of immigrants arriving in North America in the past 20 years. Little Italy, for example, is now home to people from East and Southeast Asia, with Italian restaurants vying for space with noodle houses.

It is important to recognize that urban ethnic enclaves are not limited to U.S. or Canadian cities. Many cities around the world are experiencing the effects of immigration as people from other countries seek employment in thriving metropolitan areas. As we've learned from previous chapters, globalization has created conditions that support the movement of peoples across national and ethnic boundaries (Figure 11.4). There are North African communities in Paris, Turkish neighborhoods in Berlin, and Kurdish neighborhoods in Istanbul, and each of these is impacting the culture, economy, and landscape of these cities in profound ways (see Culture in a Globalizing World).

REFLECTING ON GEOGRAPHY

As we look at these urban regions, various questions concern the cultural geographer: How do ethnic and social regions differ? Why do people of similar social traits cluster together? What subtle patterns might be found within these regions?

Social culture regions are not merely statistical definitions. They are also areas of shared values and attitudes, of interaction and communication. **Neighborhood** is a concept often used to describe small social culture regions where people with shared values and concerns interact daily. For example, if we consider only census figures, we might find that parents between 30 and 45 years of age, with two or three children, and earning between $50,000 and $75,000 a year cover a fairly wide area in any given city. Yet, from our own observations, we know intuitively that this broad social area is probably composed of numerous neighborhoods where people associate a sense of community with a specific locale.

A conventional sociological explanation for neighborhoods is that people of similar values cluster together to reduce social conflict. Where a social consensus exists about such mundane issues as home maintenance, child rearing, acceptable behavior, and public order, there is little daily worry about these matters. People who deviate from this consensus will face social coercion that could force them to seek residence elsewhere, thus preserving the values of the neighborhood.

However, many neighborhoods have more heterogeneity than this traditional definition would allow. Consequently, the current understanding of neighborhoods is more flexible. While it embraces traditional components of locality, such as political outlook and shared economic char-

Figure 11.4 **A Muslim family in the neighborhood of Belleville in Paris.** Many cities have ethnic enclaves where immigrants from other countries live, creating a different scale of community within the larger scale of the city. How are these ethnic enclaves related to globalization? *(Peter Turnley/Corbis.)*

acteristics, it also emphasizes the consensus that comes from both insiders and outsiders perceiving a certain area as a neighborhood. So although a neighborhood might be ethnically and socially diverse, its residents may think of themselves as a community that shares similar political concerns, holds neighborhood meetings to address these problems, and achieves recognition at city hall as a legitimate group with political standing. A recent article in the *New York Times* documenting the new ethnic composition of Woodside, Queens, was titled "From a Babel of Tongues, a Neighborhood" (Figure 11.5). For much of the late nineteenth century and into the late twentieth century, Woodside was predominantly an Irish-American community, but recent immigration has created a diverse neighborhood. In 1990, 55 percent of its residents were foreign-born: 29 percent from Europe, 37 percent from Asia, 23 percent from South and Central America, and 11 percent from other regions of

CULTURE IN A GLOBALIZING WORLD

Spaces of Inclusion and Exclusion: Urban Ethnic Enclaves

Globalization has created political and economic conditions that support the movement of peoples across national and ethnic boundaries. For example, many Kurdish-identified people from southeastern Turkey have migrated to Istanbul to escape the political and military turmoil surrounding the ongoing conflict between the state and the Kurdish separatist movement. In Istanbul, they seek ways to feel at home in a city that is divided into ethnically, religiously, and regionally segregated neighborhoods. Approximately 60 percent of Istanbul's 12 million inhabitants were born elsewhere, creating a city that resembles a patchwork of ethnic regions. Some Kurds are able to establish their "own" neighborhoods, while others find themselves living among people who consider them different and would prefer to exclude them. As geographer Anna Secor found, most would rather live in Kurdish-identified neighborhoods, since they provide a "safe haven" within an often hostile urban environment. For these migrants, the city provides a space of affiliation, one where they can identify as Kurdish and as Turkish. One of the women Secor interviewed said:

I feel most comfortable in the place where I live. It is a housing development of 75 homes, mostly Kurds and Alevis. . . . Our culture is the same, our language is the same. I feel very comfortable there.

For others, faced with discriminatory and exclusionary housing practices, the city becomes a space of alienation. Unable to find adequate housing in their "own" ethnic neighborhood, some Kurds are put in the position of "hiding" their identity. Here is how another woman migrant put it:

We came from Bitlis here, and being Kurds, everyone excluded us. At the moment it is still like this. In the neighborhood where we live, we are the only Kurds. If we had said we were Kurds they wouldn't even had given us the house. . . . I am Kurdish, okay. I am proud of my Kurdishness. But did something happen to make me say "Kurd, Kurd" constantly?

Ethnic neighborhoods, in other words, can be both spaces of identification and spaces of exclusion.

Based on Secor, 2004

Figure 11.5 Woodside, Queens, New York City. Once home to Irish immigrants, Woodside is now the destination of immigrants from a wide range of countries. In what ways are these new ethnic neighborhoods different from those of the Irish-Americans? In what ways do you think they are similar? (*James Estrin/NYT Pictures.*)

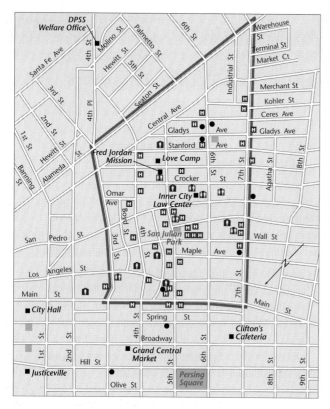

Overnight shelter facilities: men only

Overnight shelter facilities: women only or men and women

Hotels

Social service providers (no shelter facilities)

Park

Skid row boundary

0   0.25 km

0   0.25 mi.

Figure 11.6 **The distribution of services for the homeless in the skid row district of Los Angeles.** The population of the area is difficult to estimate, ranging from 6000 to 30,000. There are approximately 2000 shelter beds in the area, half of which are available to women. Single-room-occupancy hotels provide about 6700 units of longer-term housing. More than 50 social service programs are run through agencies, missions, and shelters. Love Camp and Justiceville are the sites of informal street encampments of homeless people. *(After Rowe and Wolch, 1990.)*

the world. In struggling for decent schools, housing, and jobs, many residents have united and forged a coalition of interests and a sense of communal identity—keystones of a neighborhood.

Neighborhoods are usually comprised of people that have access to a permanent or semipermanent place of residence. In the cities of the United States, however, homelessness, and with it the loss of neighborhood, is increasingly common. It is nearly impossible to determine the exact number of homeless people in the United States because definitions of **homelessness** vary. For example, does living in

a friend's house for more than a month constitute a homeless condition? How permanent does a shelter have to be before it is considered a "home"? To some people, home connotes a suburban middle-class house; to others, it simply refers to a room in a city-owned shelter.

REFLECTING ON GEOGRAPHY

Why is home such a difficult concept to define? How does it differ from the concept of a house?

In addition, homeless people are often not counted in the census or other population surveys. Estimates of the number of homeless, therefore, are only rough approximations. Recent studies suggest that there are up to 3 million homeless people in the United States, concentrated in the downtown areas of large cities, often in what we call the transitional zone (see the section on cultural interaction and models of the city).

The causes of homelessness are varied and complex. Many homeless people suffer from some type of disorder or handicap that contributes to their inability to maintain a job and obtain adequate housing. Most have been marginalized in some way by the economic problems that have plagued the United States since the early 1980s, and therefore they have been left out of the housing market. Deprived of the social networks that a permanent neighborhood provides, the homeless are left to fend for themselves. Most cities have tried to provide temporary shelter, but many homeless people prefer to rely on their own social ties for support to maintain some sense of personal pride and privacy. In a study of the Los Angeles skid row district, Stacy Rowe and Jennifer Wolch explored how homeless women formed new types of social networks and established a sense of community to cope with the day-to-day needs of physical security and food (Figure 11.6). This study points to the importance of social ties in maintaining personal identity and helps us understand the magnitude of a problem that deprives people of their home and neighborhood.

 Cultural Diffusion in the City

How can we understand the spatial movement of people and activities in the city? The patterns of activities we see in the city are the result of thousands of individual decisions about location: Where should we locate our store—in the central city or the suburbs? Where should we live—downtown or outside the city? And so on. The result of such decisions might be expansion at the city's edge or the relocation of activities from one part of the city to another. The cultural geographer looks at such decisions in terms of expansion and relocation diffusion (see Chapter 1).

To understand the role of diffusion, let us divide the city into two major areas—the inner city and the outer city. Those diffusion forces that result in residences, stores, and factories locating in the inner or central city are **centralizing forces.** Those that result in activities locating outside the central city are called **decentralizing forces,** or suburbanizing forces. The pattern of homes, neighborhoods, offices, shops, and factories in the city results from the constant interplay of these two forces.

Centralization

Centralization has two primary advantages: economic and social.

Economic Advantages An important economic advantage of central-city location has always been accessibility. For example, imagine that a department store seeks a new location. If its potential market area is viewed as a full circle, then naturally the best location is in the center. There, customers from all parts of the city can gain access with equal ease. Before the automobile, a central-city location was particularly necessary because public transportation—such as the streetcar—was usually focused there. A central location is also important to those who must deliver their goods to customers. Bakeries and dairies were usually located as close to the center of the city as possible to maximize the efficiency of their delivery routes.

Location near regional transportation facilities is another aspect of accessibility and is thus an economic advantage. Many a North American city developed with the railroad at its center. Hence, any activity that needed access to the railroad had to locate in the central city. In many urban areas, giant wholesale and retail manufacturing districts grew up around railroad districts, producing "freight-yard and terminal cities" that supplied the produce of the nation. Although many of these areas have been abandoned by their original occupants, a walk by the railroad tracks today will give the most casual pedestrian a view of the modern "ruins" of the railroad city.

Another major economic advantage of the inner city is **agglomeration,** or clustering, which results in mutual benefits for businesses. For example, retail stores locate near one another to take advantage of the pedestrian traffic each generates. Because a large department store generates a good deal of foot traffic, any nearby store will also benefit.

Historically, offices clustered together in the central city because of their need for communication. Remember, the telephone was invented only in 1875. Before that, messengers hand-carried the work of banks, insurance firms, law-

yers, and many other services. Clustering was essential for rapid communication. Even today, office buildings tend to cluster because face-to-face communication is still important for businesspeople. In addition, central offices take advantage of the complicated support system that grows up in a central city and aids everyday efficiency. Printers, bars, restaurants, travel agents, and office suppliers are within easy reach.

Social Advantages Three social factors have traditionally reinforced central-city location: historical momentum, prestige, and the need to locate near work. The strength of historical momentum should not be underestimated. Many activities remain in the central city simply because they began there long ago. For example, the financial district in San Francisco is located mainly on Montgomery Street. This street originally lay along the waterfront, and San Francisco's first financial institutions were established there in the mid-nineteenth century because it was the center of commercial action. In later years, however, landfill extended the shoreline (see Figure 10.29). Today, the financial district is several blocks from the bay; consequently, the district that began at the wharf head remained at its original location, even though other activity moved with the changing shoreline.

The prestige associated with the downtown area is also a strong centralizing force. Some activities still necessitate a central-city address. Think how important it is for some advertising firms to be on New York's Madison Avenue or for a stockbroker to be on Wall Street. This factor extends to many activities in cities of all sizes. The "downtown lawyer" and the "uptown banker" are examples. Residences have often been located in the central city because of the prestige associated with it. Most cities have remnants of high-income neighborhoods close to the downtown area. Although this trend has weakened in North America—downtown areas have become congested and noisy, and transportation has encouraged suburban residences—it is still important elsewhere. London and Paris have very prestigious neighborhoods in the downtown area.

Probably the strongest social force for centralization has been the desire to live near one's place of employment. Until the development of the electric trolley in the 1880s, most urban dwellers had little alternative but to walk to work, and as most employment was in the central city, people had no choice but to live nearby. Upper-income people had their carriages and cabs, but others had nothing. Even after the introduction of electric streetcar lines in the 1880s, which made possible the exodus of some middle-class residents, many people continued to walk to work, particularly those who could not afford the new housing being constructed in what Sam Bass Warner has called "streetcar suburbs."

Suburbanization and Decentralization

The past 40 years have witnessed massive changes in the form and function of most Western cities (Figure 11.7). In the United States in particular, the suburbanization of residences and the decentralization of workplaces have emptied many downtowns of economic vitality. How and why has this happened? Geographer Neil Smith argues that the processes of suburbanization and decline of the inner city are fundamentally linked: capital investment in the suburbs is often made possible by disinvestment, or the removal of money, from the central city. In post–World War II America, investors found greater returns on their money in the new suburbs than they did in the inner city, and therefore much of the economic boom of this time period took place in the suburbs at the expense of the city. Smith refers to these processes as **uneven development** (Figure 11.8). This type of explanation gives us a broad picture of the economic reasons that many cities are now decentralized. We will now look more closely, and examine the specific socioeconomic and public policy causes for the decentralization of our cities and for the problems that have resulted.

Socioeconomic Factors Changes in accessibility have been a major reason for decentralization. The department store that originally located in the central city may now find that its customers have moved to the suburbs and no longer shop downtown. As a result, the department store may move to a suburban shopping mall. The same process affects many other industries as well. The activities that were located downtown because of its proximity to the railroad may now find trucking more cost-effective. They relocate closer to a freeway system that skirts the downtown area. Finally, many offices now locate near airports so that their executives and salespeople can fly in and out more easily.

Although agglomeration once served as a centralizing force, its former benefits have now become liabilities in many downtown areas. These disadvantages include rising rents as a result of the high demand for space; congestion in the support system, which causes delays in getting supplies or means standing in endless lines for lunch; and traffic congestion, which makes delivery to market time-consuming and costly. Some downtown areas are so congested that traffic moves more slowly today than it did at the turn of the twentieth century. Often dissatisfied with the inconveniences of central-

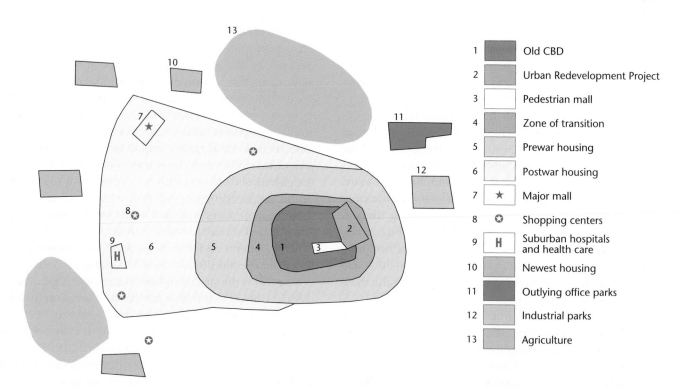

1	Old CBD
2	Urban Redevelopment Project
3	Pedestrian mall
4	Zone of transition
5	Prewar housing
6	Postwar housing
7 ★	Major mall
8 ✪	Shopping centers
9 H	Suburban hospitals and health care
10	Newest housing
11	Outlying office parks
12	Industrial parks
13	Agriculture

Figure 11.7 **A hypothetical decentralized city.** While the old central business district (CBD) struggles (vacant stores and upper floors), newer activities locate either in the Urban Redevelopment Project (offices, convention center, hotel) or in outlying office parks, malls, or shopping centers. However, some new specialty shops might be found around the new downtown pedestrian mall. New industry locates in suburban industrial parks that, along with outlying office areas, form major destinations for daily lateral commuting. In what ways does your city follow this hypothetical pattern? In what ways does it differ?

Figure 11.8 Abandoned row houses in North Philadelphia. Often the economic neglect of these areas is directly linked to economic investment in the suburbs. *(Associated Press.)*

city living, employees may demand higher wages as compensation. This adds to the cost of doing business in the central city, and many firms choose to leave instead. For example, many firms have left New York City for the suburbs. They claim that it costs less to locate there and that their employees are happier and more productive because they do not have to put up with the turmoil of city life.

Clustering in new suburban locations can also have benefits. In industrial parks, for example, all the occupants share the costs of utilities and transportation links. Similar benefits can come from residential agglomeration. Suburban real estate developments take advantage of clustering by sharing the costs of schools, parks, road improvements, and utilities. New residents much prefer moving into a new development when they know that a full range of services is available nearby. Then they will not have to drive miles to find, say, the nearest hardware store. It is to the developer's advantage to encourage construction of nearby shopping centers.

The need to be near one's workplace has historically been a great centralizing force, but it can also be a very strong decentralizing force. At first the suburbs were "bedroom communities" from which people commuted to their jobs in the downtown area. This is no longer the case. In

many metropolitan areas, most jobs are not in the central city but in outlying districts. Now people work in suburban industrial parks, manufacturing plants, office buildings, and shopping centers. Thus, a typical journey to work involves **lateral commuting:** travel from one suburb to another. As a result, most people who live away from the city center actually live closer to their workplaces (see the discussion of edge cities in Chapter 10).

The prestige of the downtown area might once have lured people and businesses into the central city. But once it begins to decay, once shops close and offices are empty, a certain stigma develops that may drive away residents and commercial activities. Investors will not sink money into a downtown area that they think has no chance of recovery, and shoppers will not venture downtown when streets are filled with vacant stores, transients, pawnshops, and second-hand stores. One of the persistent problems faced by cities is how to reverse this image of the downtown area so that people once again consider it the focus of the city.

REFLECTING ON GEOGRAPHY

Identify some of the efforts that your city has undertaken to create a better image of itself. Have these efforts been successful? Does this reimagining of the city actually help residents of the inner city?

Public Policy Many public policy decisions, particularly at the national level, have contributed greatly to the decentralization and abandonment of our cities. Both the Federal Road Act of 1916 and the Interstate Highway Act of 1956 directed government spending on transportation to the advantage of the automobile and the truck. Urban expressways, in combination with the emerging trucking industry, led to massive decentralization of industry and housing. In addition, the ability to deduct mortgage interest from income for tax purposes favors individual homeownership, which has tended to support a move to the suburbs.

The federal government in the United States has also intervened more directly in the housing market. In *Crabgrass Frontier,* Kenneth Jackson outlines the implications of two federal housing policies for the spatial patterning of our metropolitan areas. The first was the establishment of the Federal Housing Administration (FHA) in 1934 and its supplement, known as the GI Bill, enacted in 1944. These federal acts, which insured long-term mortgage loans for home construction, were meant to provide employment in the building trades and to help house the returning soldiers from World War II. Although the FHA legislation contained no explicit antiurban bias, most of the houses it insured were located in new residential developments in the suburbs, thereby neglecting the inner city.

Jackson identifies three reasons that this happened. First, by setting particular terms for its insurance, the FHA favored the development of single-family over multifamily projects. Second, FHA-insured loans for repairs were of short duration and were generally small. Most families, therefore, were better off buying a new house that was probably in the suburbs than updating an older home in the city.

Jackson regards the third factor as the most important. To receive an FHA-insured loan, the applicant and the neighborhood of the property had to be assessed by an "unbiased professional." This requirement was intended to guarantee that the property value of the house would be greater than the debt. This policy, however, encouraged bias against any neighborhood that was considered a potential risk in terms of property values. The FHA explicitly warned against neighborhoods with a racial mix, assuming that such a social climate would bring property values down, and encouraged the inclusion of **restrictive covenants** in property deeds, which prohibited certain "undesirable" groups from buying property. The agency also prepared extensive maps of metropolitan areas depicting the locations of African-American families and predicting the spread of that population. These maps often served as the basis for **redlining,** a practice whereby banks and mortgage companies demarcated areas (often by drawing a red line around them on these maps) considered to be at high risk for loans.

These policies had two primary effects. First, they encouraged construction of single-family homes in suburban areas while discouraging central-city locations. Second, they intensified the segregation of residential areas and actively promoted homogeneity in the new suburbs.

The second federal housing policy that had a major impact on the patterning of metropolitan areas, the United States Housing Act, was intended to provide public housing for those who could not afford private housing. Originally implemented in 1937, the legislation did encourage the construction of many low-income housing units. Yet most of those units were built in the inner city, thereby contributing to the view of the suburbs as the refuge of the white middle class. This growing pattern of racial and economic segregation arose in part because public housing decisions were left up to local municipalities. Many municipalities did not need federal dollars and therefore did not want public housing. In addition, the legislation required that for every unit of public housing erected, one inferior housing unit had to be eliminated. Thus, only areas with inadequate housing units could receive federal dollars, again ensuring that public housing projects would be constructed in the older, downtown areas, not the newer suburbs. As Jackson claims, "The result, if not the intent, of the public housing program of the United States was to segregate the races, to concentrate the disadvantaged in inner cities, and to reinforce the image

of suburbia as a place of refuge for the problems of race, crime, and poverty."

The Costs of Decentralization Decentralization has taken its toll on North American cities. Many of the urban problems they now face are the direct result of the rapid decentralization that has taken place in the last 50 years. Those people who cannot afford to live in the suburbs are forced to live in inadequate and run-down housing in the inner city, areas that currently do not provide good jobs. Vacant storefronts, empty offices, and deserted factories testify to the movement of commercial functions from central cities to suburbs. Retail stores in North American central cities have steadily lost sales to suburban shopping centers. Even offices are finding advantages to suburban location when they can capitalize on lower costs and easier access to new transportation networks.

Decentralization has also cost society millions of dollars in problems brought to the suburbs. Where rapid suburbanization has occurred, sprawl has usually followed. A common pattern is leapfrog or **checkerboard development,** where housing tracts jump over parcels of farmland, resulting in a mixture of open lands with built-up areas. This pattern occurs because developers buy cheaper land farther away from built-up areas, thereby cutting their costs. Furthermore, home buyers are often willing to pay premium prices for homes in subdivisions surrounded by farmland (Figure 11.9). The developer's gain is the area's loss, for it is more expensive to provide city services—such as police, fire protection, sewers, and electrical lines—to those areas that lie beyond open parcels that are not built up. Obviously, the most cost-efficient form of development is the addition of new housing directly adjacent to built-up areas so that the costs of providing new services are minimal.

Sprawl also extracts high costs because of the increased use of cars. Public transportation is extremely costly and inefficient when it must serve a low-density checkerboard development pattern—so costly that many cities and transit firms cannot extend lines into these areas. This means that the automobile is the only form of transportation. More energy is consumed for fuel, more air pollution is created by exhaust, and more time is devoted to commuting and everyday activities in a sprawling urban area than in a centralized city.

Moreover, we should not overlook the costs of losing valuable agricultural land to urban development. Farmers cultivating the remaining checkerboard parcels have a hard time earning a living. They are usually taxed at extremely high rates because their land has high potential for development, and few can make a profit when taxes eat up all their resources. Often the only recourse is to sell out to subdividers. So the cycle of leapfrog development goes on.

Figure 11.9 **Suburban sprawl.** Suburbanization gives us a familiar landscape of look-alike houses and yards; automobile-efficient street and transportation patterns; and, in the background, remnants of agriculture, awaiting the day that they are converted into housing tracts. *(Cameramann International, Ltd.)*

Many cities are now taking strong measures to curb this kind of sprawling growth. San Jose, California, for example, one of the fastest-growing cities of the 1960s, is now focusing new development on empty parcels of the checkerboard pattern. This is called **in-filling.** Other cities are tying the number of building permits granted each year to the availability of urban services. If schools are already crowded, water supplies inadequate, and sewage plants overburdened, the number of new dwelling units approved for an area will reflect this lower carrying capacity.

Gentrification

Beginning in the 1970s, urban scholars began to observe what seemed to be a trend opposite to suburbanization. This trend, called **gentrification,** is the movement of middle-class people into deteriorated areas of city centers. Gentrification often begins in an inner-city residential district, with gentrifiers moving into an area that had been run down and is therefore more affordable than suburban housing (Figure 11.10). The infusion of new capital into the housing market usually results in higher property values, and this, in turn, often displaces residents who cannot afford the higher prices. Displacement opens up more housing for gentrification, and the gentrified district continues its spatial expansion.

Commercial gentrification usually follows residential, as new patterns of consumption are introduced into the inner city by the middle-class gentrifiers. Urban shopping malls and pedestrian shopping corridors bring the conveniences of the suburbs into the city, and bars and restaurants catering to this new urban middle class provide entertainment and nightlife for the gentrifiers.

The speed with which gentrification has proceeded in many of our downtowns and the scale of landscape changes that accompany it are causing dramatic shifts in the urban mosaic. What factors have led to this reshaping of our cities?

Economic Factors Some urban scholars look to broad economic trends in the United States to explain gentrification. Throughout the post–World War II era, most investments in metropolitan land were made in the suburbs; as a result, land in the inner city was devalued. By the 1970s, many home buyers and commercial investors found land in the city much more affordable, and a better economic investment, than in the higher-priced suburbs. This situation brought capital into areas that had been undervalued and accelerated the gentrifying process.

In addition, most Western countries have been experiencing **deindustrialization,** a process whereby the economy is shifting from one based on secondary industry to one based on the service sector. This shift has led to the abandonment of older industrial districts in the inner city, including waterfront areas. Many of these areas are prime targets of gentrifiers, who convert the waterfront from a noisy, commercial port area into an aesthetic asset. In Buenos Aires, for example, one of the new gentrified neighborhoods is

Figure 11.10 **Gentrification in Vancouver, Canada.** Gentrification often occurs in older neighborhoods with historical buildings. These Victorian-styled houses have been carefully restored to reflect their new owners' interest in preserving the past, although this might have come at the cost of displacing the previous tenants. As you can see from this image, this neighborhood is also very close to downtown. Why? *(Canada Stock Photographs.)*

Puerto Madero, an area that was once home to docking facilities and a wholesale market. The shift to an economy based on the service sector also means that the new productive areas of the city will be dedicated to white-collar activities. These activities often take place in relatively clean and quiet office buildings, contributing to a view of the city as a more livable environment.

Social Factors Other scholars look to changes in social structure to explain gentrification. The maturing of the baby-boom generation has led to significant modifications of our traditional family structure and lifestyle. With a majority of women in the paid labor force and many young couples choosing not to have children or to delay that decision, a suburban residential location looks less appealing. A gentrified location in the inner city attracts this new class because it is close to their managerial or professional jobs downtown, is usually easier to maintain, and is considered more interesting than the bland suburban areas where they grew up. Living in a newly gentrified area is also a way to display social status. Many suburbs have become less exclusive, while older neighborhoods in the inner city frequently exploit their historical associations as a status symbol.

Political Factors Many metropolitan governments in the United States, faced with the abandonment of the central city by the middle class and therefore with the erosion of their tax base, have enacted policies to encourage commer-

cial and residential development in downtown areas. Some policies provide tax breaks for companies willing to locate downtown; others furnish local and state funding to redevelop central-city residential and commercial buildings.

At a more comprehensive level, some larger metropolitan areas have devised long-term planning agendas that target certain neighborhoods for revitalization. Often this is accomplished by first condemning the targeted area, thereby transferring control of the land to an urban-development authority or other planning agency. Such areas are often older residential neighborhoods that were originally built to house people who worked in nearby factories, which are usually torn down or transformed into lofts or office space. The redevelopment authority might locate a new civic or arts center in the neighborhood. Public-sector initiatives often lead to private investment, thereby increasing property values. These higher property values, in turn, lead to further investment and the eventual transformation of the neighborhood into a middle- to upper-class gentrified district.

Sexuality and Gentrification Gentrified residential districts are often correlated with the presence of a significant gay and lesbian population. It is fairly easy to understand this correlation. First, the typical suburban life tends not to appeal to people whose lifestyle is often regarded as different and whose community needs are often different from those of people living in the suburbs. Second, gentrified inner-city neighborhoods provide access to the diversity of city life and amenities that often include gay cultural institutions. In fact, the association of urban neighborhoods with gays and lesbians has a long history. For example, urban historian George Chauncey has documented gay culture in New York City between 1890 and the Second World War, showing that a gay world occupied and shaped distinctive spaces in the city, such as neighborhood enclaves, gay commercial areas, and public parks and streets.

Yet, unlike this earlier period, when gay cultures were often forced to remain hidden, the gentrification of the postwar period has provided gay and lesbian populations with the opportunity to reshape entire neighborhoods actively and openly. Urban scholar Manuel Castells argues that in cities such as San Francisco, the presence of gay men in institutions directly linked to gentrification, such as the real estate industry, significantly influenced that city's gentrification processes in the 1970s.

Geographers Mickey Lauria and Lawrence Knopp emphasize the community-building aspect of gay men's involvement in gentrification, recognizing that gays have seized an opportunity to combat oppression by creating neighborhoods over which they have maximum control and that meet long-neglected needs. Similarly, geographer Gill Valentine argues that the limited numbers and types of lesbian spaces in cities also serve as community-building centers for lesbian social networks.

According to geographer Tamar Rothenberg, the gentrified neighborhood of Park Slope in Brooklyn is home to the heaviest concentration of lesbians in the United States. Its extensive social networks are marking the neighborhood as both a center of lesbian identity and a visible lesbian social space.

The Costs of Gentrification Gentrification often results in the displacement of lower-income people, who are forced to leave their homes because of rising property values. This displacement can have serious consequences for the city's social fabric. Because many of the displaced people come from disadvantaged groups, gentrification frequently contributes to racial and ethnic tensions. Displaced people are often forced into neighborhoods more peripheral to the city, a trend that only adds to their disadvantages. In addition, gentrified neighborhoods usually stand in stark contrast to surrounding areas where investment has not taken place, thus creating a very visible reminder of the uneven distribution of wealth within our cities.

The success of a gentrification project is usually measured by its appeal to an upper-middle-class clientele. This suggests that gentrified neighborhoods are completely homogeneous in their use of land. Residential areas are consciously planned to be separate from commercial districts and are themselves sorted by cost and tenure type

(homeownership versus rental). Thus, gentrification often draws on the suburban notion of residential homogeneity and eliminates what many people consider to be a great asset of urban life—its diversity and heterogeneity (see Focus On: The Social Costs of Gentrification on page 390).

 Cultural Ecology of the City

How can we understand the relationships between the urban mosaic and the physical environment? The physical environment affects cities, just as urbanization profoundly alters natural environmental processes (Figure 11.11). The theme of cultural ecology helps us to organize information about these city-nature relationships. Although we discuss these topics in general terms in the next pages, one should not lose sight of how the differing cultural fabric within and between cities affects the relationship between city and nature. Urban ecology differs greatly from place to place because of different physical environments and varying cultural patterns.

Urban Weather and Climate

Cities alter virtually all aspects of local weather and climate. Temperatures are higher in cities, rainfall increases, the incidence of fog and cloudiness is greater, and levels of atmospheric pollution are much higher.

The causes of these changes are no mystery. Because cities cover large areas of land with streets, buildings, parking lots, and rooftops, about 50 percent of the urban area is a hard surface. Rainfall is quickly carried into gutters and sewers, so that little standing water is available for evaporation. Because evaporation removes heat from the air, when moisture is reduced, evaporation is lessened and air temperatures are higher.

Moreover, cities generate enormous amounts of heat. This heat comes not just from the heating systems of buildings but also from automobiles, industry, and even human bodies. One study showed that on a winter day in Manhattan, the amount of heat produced in the city is two and a half times the amount that reaches the ground from the sun. This results in a large mass of warmer air sitting over the city, called the urban **heat island** (Figure 11.12). The heat island causes yearly temperature averages in cities to be 3.5°F (2°C) higher than in the countryside; during the winter, when there is more city-produced heat, the average difference can easily reach 7°F to 10°F (4°C to 5.6°C).

Urbanization also affects precipitation (rainfall and snowfall). Because of higher temperatures in the urban area, snowfall will be about 5 percent less than in the surrounding countryside. However, rainfall can be 5 to 10 percent

Figure 11.11 **Suburban homes built on landfills, Treasure Island, Florida.** When land values are high and pressure for housing intense, terrain rarely stands in the way of the developer. In fact, particular physical site characteristics can actually increase land values. What site characteristics evident in this photo tell you that Treasure Island is a very expensive place to live? *(Cameramann International, Ltd.)*

higher. The increased rainfall results from two factors: the large number of dust particles in urban air and the higher city temperatures. Dust particles are a necessary precondition for condensation, offering a nucleus around which moisture can adhere. An abundance of dust particles, then, facilitates condensation. That is why fog and clouds (**dust domes**) are usually more frequent around cities (Figure 11.13).

Urban Hydrology

Not only is the city a great consumer of water, but it also alters runoff patterns in a way that increases the frequency and magnitude of flooding. Within the city, residential areas are usually the greatest consumers of water. Water consumption can vary, but generally each person in the United States uses about 60 gallons (264 liters) per day in a residence. Of course, residential demand varies. It is greater in drier climates as well as in middle- and high-income neighborhoods. Higher-income groups usually have a larger number of water-using appliances, such as washing machines, dishwashers, and swimming pools.

Urbanization can increase both the frequency and the magnitude of flooding because cities create large impervious areas where water cannot soak into the earth. Instead, precipitation is converted into immediate runoff. It is forced into gutters, sewers, and stream channels that have been straightened and stripped of vegetation, which results in more frequent high-water levels than are found in a comparable area of rural land. Furthermore, the time between rainfall and peak runoff is reduced in cities; there is more lag in the countryside, where water runs across soil and vegetation into stream channels and then into rivers. So, because of hard surfaces and artificial collection channels, runoff in cities is concentrated and immediate.

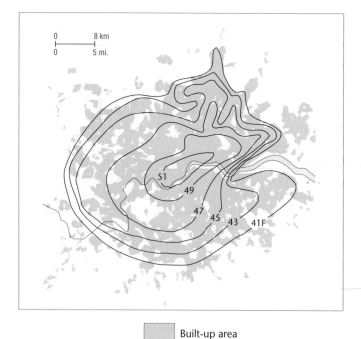

Built-up area

Figure 11.12 **The London heat island forms a dome over the city.** Notice the marked contrast in temperature between the built-up central part of the city and the surrounding "Green Belt" in the outer three rings. *(After Chandler, 1961.)*

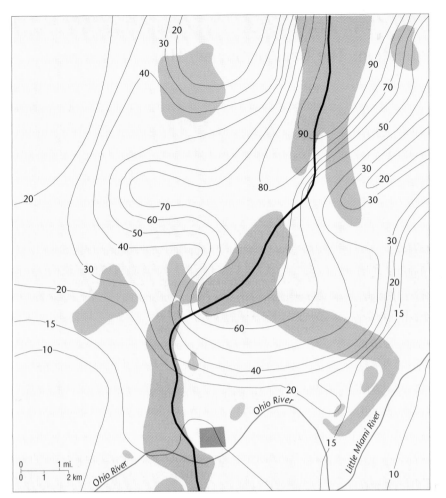

Figure 11.13 **The dust dome over Cincinnati, Ohio.** Numbers show the concentration of particulate matter in the air at an elevation of 3000 feet (914 meters). The higher the value, the greater the amount of particulate matter. Does land use (industrial, central business district, and so on) have an effect on the concentration of particulate matter in the air? (*After Bach and Hagedorn, 1971.*)

Urban Vegetation

Until a decade ago, it was commonly thought that cities were made up mostly of artificial materials: asphalt, concrete, glass, and steel. Studies, however, show that about two-thirds of a typical North American city is composed of trees and herbaceous plants (mostly weeds in vacant lots and cultivated grasses in lawns). This urban vegetation is usually a mix of natural and introduced species and is a critical component of the urban ecosystem because it affects the city's topography, hydrology, and meteorology.

More specifically, urban vegetation influences the quantity and quality of surface water and groundwater; reduces wind velocity and turbulence and temperature extremes; affects the pattern of snow accumulation and melting; absorbs thousands of tons of airborne particulates and atmospheric gases; and offers a habitat for mammals, birds, reptiles, and insects, all of which play some useful role in the urban ecosystem. Furthermore, urban vegetation influences the propagation of sound waves by muffling out much of the city's noise; affects the distribution of natural and artificial

light; and, finally, is an extremely important component in the development of soil profiles—which, in turn, control hillside stability.

Our urban settlements are still closely tied to the physical environment. Cities change these natural processes in profound ways, and we must understand these disturbances in order to make better decisions about adjustments and control.

Cultural Interaction and Models of the City

Are there generalizable spatial patterns or models that describe types of cities? Geographers are interested in understanding both the uniqueness of each city's urban pattern and the similarities that a particular city may have to others. For example, most cities have central business districts and neighborhoods with comparable socioeconomic traits. The positioning of the CBD in relationship to

The Social Costs of Gentrification: The Case of Society Hill, Philadelphia

Society Hill, an old residential area in Philadelphia that dates from the colonial era, represents one of the earliest gentrification projects and is considered one of the more successful. The following account, however, points out that this first phase (Unit One) of Philadelphia's redevelopment brought many social costs with it.

The physical appearance itself of the redeveloped Society Hill manifests the special difficulty of marketing this inner-city neighborhood in the midst of the suburban age. Advertisements highlighted stereotypically nonurban attributes of the neighborhood, such as marinas and green pathways. The conscious re-sorting of heterogeneous into homogeneous land-use patterns unlike any of the other older neighborhoods of the city, is, we claim, drawn from a prominent motif in suburban design. The anthropologist Constance Perin, in *Everything in Its Place* (1977), an exploration of cultural and social symbolism in metropolitan land-use patterns, argues that one of the keys to the successful marketing of American suburbia has been the appeal of clearly ordered and discrete land-use units. Prospective homebuyers, who were not only purchasing shelter, but also deeply committing themselves financially, were reassured by the evident presence of neighbors "just like themselves." Thus in the design of Society Hill, residential tracts were separated from most other uses and also were internally sorted by cost and tenure type. In addition, building design was such as to maximize both privacy and physical security. The inward-facing plans of several new housing clusters, for example, with parking and entrance on the interior of blocks, exemplify one of the earliest applications of "defended space" principles.

Having ensured that "everything was in its place," so too the Society Hill concept carefully saw to it that everybody was in their place; social homogeneity, equally a stereotypically suburban attribute, was relentlessly pursued. Part of the appeal of homogeneity was to snobbery: the advertisements invited one to come live with Philadelphia's top people: a 1957 advertisement (early in Society Hill's redevelopment) insinuates, "The mayor is,

why can't you?" (*Philadelphia Inquirer,* May 19, 1957). Just as important was the need to assuage fears about stereotypical in-city sub-cultures. ("See, you have to understand [that] the fundamental feeling in suburbia is fear [of the impingement of the city], let's face it," a realtor had informed Perin [1977:87].) So, in a suburban age, the advertisements felt they had to stress "nice people . . . coming to live in Society Hill."

It is a commonplace that the Society Hill renewal, so evidently "top-down" in conception and execution, imposed social costs upon preexisting residents of lower socioeconomic status. The prior residents of Unit One could remain only if the Redevelopment Authority was disposed to resell their property back to them with inevitably expensive contractual stipulations: a timetable for any of a number of specific repairs, mandatory upkeep requirements, plus remodeling to exacting and detailed "historically authentic" standards for facades. Unbending application of these criteria expelled all but a few of the original lower-income residents. Thus, at the public meeting held in conjunction with the unveiling of the Unit One plan (April 28, 1958), the complaint was heard from one resident that it was "a plan for an area of wealthy poodled people," and it was reported that "many [residents] . . . didn't like what they saw, or thought they saw, looming in the future." John P. Robin, president of the Old Philadelphia Development Corporation (the body that had contracted to implement the renewal) responded that "residents would have to compromise their desires with those of others and the city" (*Evening Bulletin,* April 29, 1958). This captures the general tone; in many cases the record documents a degree of insensitivity to or lack of concern with the special needs and claims of pre-existing Society Hill residents.

It was high-income people who were required in Unit One; any possibility of income mix was intendedly minimized.

Abridged from Cybriwsky, Ley, and Western, 1986. Copyright © 1986 Neil Smith, Peter Williams, and contributors. Reprinted by permission of Allen & Unwin.

---

high-income, middle-income, and low-income neighborhoods produces similar spatial patterns in cities as diverse as Chicago, Frankfurt, and Sydney. Yet this type of urban pattern, or model, differs significantly from the spatial arrangement of such cities as Mexico City and Buenos Aires, which have been shaped by quite different economic, cultural, and political circumstances. To provide insights into the diverse urban mosaic, geographers have tried to describe some spatial models of land use within cities, each of which helps us understand a particular type of city.

Concentric-Zone Model

The **concentric-zone model** was developed in 1925 by Ernest W. Burgess, a sociologist at the University of Chicago. Figure 11.14 shows the concentric-zone model with its five zones. At first glance, you can see the effects of residential decentralization. There is a distinct pattern of income levels from zone 1, the CBD, out to the commuter residential zone. This pattern shows that even at the beginning of the automobile age, American cities expressed a clear separation of social

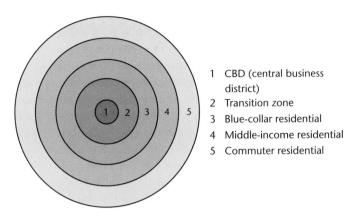

Figure 11.14 **The concentric-zone model.** Each zone represents a different type of land use in the city. Can you identify examples of each zone in your community?

1 CBD (central business district)
2 Transition zone
3 Blue-collar residential
4 Middle-income residential
5 Commuter residential

groups. The extension of trolley lines into the surrounding countryside had a lot to do with this pattern.

Zone 2, a transitional area between the CBD and residential zone 3, is characterized by a mixed pattern of industrial and residential land use. Rooming houses, small apartments, and tenements attract the lowest-income segment of the urban population. Often this zone includes slums and skid rows. Many ethnic ghettos took root here as well. Landowners, while waiting for the CBD to reach their land, erected shoddy tenements to house a massive influx of foreign workers. An aura of uncertainty was characteristic of life in zone 2, because commercial activities rapidly displaced residents

as the CBD expanded. Today, this area is often characterized by physical deterioration (Figure 11.15).

Zone 3, the "workingmen's quarters," is a solid blue-collar arc, located close to the factories of zones 1 and 2. Yet zone 3 is more stable than the zone of transition around the CBD. It is often characterized by ethnic neighborhoods: blocks of immigrants who broke free from the ghettos in zone 2 and moved outward into flats or single-family dwellings. Burgess suggested that this working-class area, like the CBD, was spreading outward because of pressure from the zone of transition and because blue-collar workers demanded better housing.

Zone 4 is a middle-class area of better housing. From here, established city dwellers—many of whom moved out of the central city with the construction of the first streetcar network—commute to work in the CBD.

Zone 5, the commuters' zone, consists of higher-income families clustered together in suburbs, either on the farthest extension of the trolley or on commuter railroad lines. This zone of spacious lots and large houses is the growing edge of the city. From here, the rich press outward to avoid the increasing congestion and social heterogeneity brought to their area by an expansion of zone 4.

Burgess's concentric-zone theory represented the American city in a new stage of development. Before the 1870s, an American metropolis, such as New York, was a city of mixed neighborhoods where merchants' stores and sweatshop factories were intermingled with mansions and hovels. Rich and poor, immigrant and native-born rubbed shoulders in the same neighborhoods. However, in Chicago,

Figure 11.15 **An abandoned building in the uptown area of Chicago.** The transitional zone in the city contains vacant and deteriorated buildings. Why has this area become a likely target for gentrifiers? (See the section on gentrification.)
(Cameramann International, Ltd.)

Burgess's hometown, something else occurred. In 1871, the Great Chicago Fire burned down the core of the city, leveling almost one-third of its buildings. As the city was rebuilt, it was influenced by late-nineteenth-century market forces: real estate speculation in the suburbs, inner-city industrial development, new streetcar systems, and the need for low-cost working-class housing. The result was more clearly demarcated social patterns than existed in other large cities. Chicago became a segregated city with a concentric pattern working its way out from the downtown in what one scholar called "rings of rising affluence." It was this rebuilt city that Burgess used as the basis for his concentric zone model.

However, as you can see from Figure 11.16, the actual residential map of Chicago does not exactly match the simplicity of Burgess's concentric zones. For instance, it is evident that the wealthy continue to monopolize certain high-value sites within the other rings, especially Chicago's "Gold

Coast" along Lake Michigan on the Near North Side. According to the concentric-zone theory, this area should have been part of the zone of transition. Burgess accounted for some of these exceptions by noting how the rich tended to monopolize hills, lakes, and shorelines, whether they were close to or far from the CBD. Critics of Burgess's model also were quick to point out that even though portions of each zone did exist in most cities, rarely were they linked in such a way as to totally surround the city. Burgess countered that there were distinct barriers, such as old industrial centers, that prevented the completion of the arc. Still other critics felt that Burgess, as a sociologist, overemphasized residential patterns and did not give proper credit to other land uses—such as industry, manufacturing, and warehouses—in describing urban patterns.

Sector Model

Homer Hoyt, an economist who studied housing data for 142 American cities, presented his **sector model** of urban land use in 1939. He maintained that high-rent residential districts (*rent* meaning capital outlay for the occupancy of space, including purchase, lease, or rent in the popular sense) were instrumental in shaping the land-use structure of the city. Because these areas were reinforced by transportation routes, the pattern of their development was one of sectors or wedges (Figure 11.17), not concentric zones.

Hoyt suggested that the high-rent sector would expand according to four factors. First, a high-rent sector moves from its point of origin near the CBD, along established routes of travel, toward another nucleus of high-rent buildings. That is, a high-rent area directly next to the CBD will naturally head in the direction of a high-rent suburb, eventually linking the two in a wedge-shaped sector. Second, this sector will progress toward high ground or along waterfronts when these areas are not used for industry. The rich have always preferred such environments for their residences. Third, a high-rent sector will move along the route of fastest transportation. Fourth, it will move toward open space. A high-income community rarely moves into an occupied lower-income neighborhood. Instead, the wealthy prefer to build new structures on vacant land where they can control the social environment.

As high-rent sectors develop, the areas between them are filled in. Middle-rent areas move directly next to them, drawing on their prestige. Low-rent areas fill in the remaining areas. Thus, moving away from major routes of travel, rents go from high to low.

There are distinct patterns in today's cities that echo Hoyt's model. He had the advantage over Burgess in that he wrote later in the automobile age and could see the tremendous impact that major thoroughfares were having on cities.

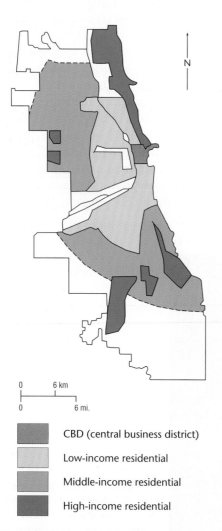

N

0 ── 6 km
0 ── 6 mi.

■ CBD (central business district)

▢ Low-income residential

▨ Middle-income residential

■ High-income residential

Figure 11.16 **Residential areas of Chicago in 1920** were used as the basis for many studies and models of the city. Compare this pattern with the concentric-zone and sector models.

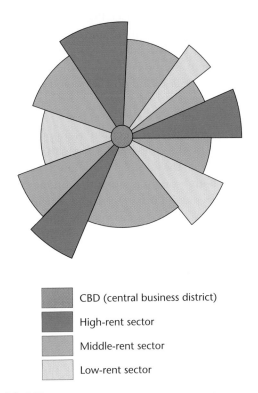

CBD (central business district)

High-rent sector

Middle-rent sector

Low-rent sector

Figure 11.17 The sector model. In this model, zones are pie-shaped wedges radiating along main transportation routes.

However, when we look at today's major transportation arteries, which are generally freeways, we see that the areas surrounding them are often low-rent districts. According to Hoyt's theory, they should be high-rent districts. Freeways are rather recent additions to the city, coming only after World War II, which were imposed on an existing urban pattern. To minimize the economic and political costs of construction, they were often built through low-rent areas, where the costs of land purchase for the rights-of-way were less and where political opposition was kept to a minimum because most people living in these low-rent areas had little political clout. This is why so many freeways rip through eth-

nic ghettos and low-income areas. Economically speaking, this is the least expensive route.

Multiple-Nuclei Model

Both Burgess and Hoyt assumed that a strong central city affected patterns throughout the urban area. However, as cities increasingly decentralized, districts developed that were not directly linked to the CBD. In 1945, two geographers, Chauncey Harris and Edward Ullman, suggested a new model: the **multiple-nuclei model.** They maintained that a city developed with equal intensity around various points, or multiple nuclei (Figure 11.18). In their eyes, the CBD was not the only focus of activity. Equal weight had to be given to an old community on the city outskirts around which new suburban developments clustered; to an industrial district that grew from an original waterfront location; or to a low-income area that developed because of some social stigma attached to the site.

Harris and Ullman rooted their model in four geographical principles. First, certain activities require highly specialized facilities, such as accessible transportation for a factory or large areas of open land for a housing tract. Second, certain activities cluster together because they profit from mutual association. Car dealers, for example, are commonly located near one another because automobiles are very expensive and so people will engage in comparative shopping—moving from one dealer to another until their decisions are made. Third, certain activities repel each other and will not be found in the same area. Examples would be high-rent residences and industrial areas, or slums and expensive retail stores. Fourth, certain activities could not make a profit if they paid the high rent of the most desirable locations and would therefore seek lower-rent areas. For example, furniture stores may like to locate where pedestrian traffic is greatest to lure the most people into their showrooms. However, they need large amounts of space for showrooms and storage. Thus, they cannot afford the high rents that the most accessible locations demand.

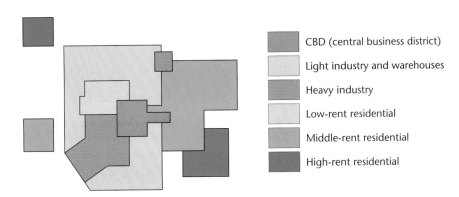

CBD (central business district)

Light industry and warehouses

Heavy industry

Low-rent residential

Middle-rent residential

High-rent residential

Figure 11.18 The multiple-nuclei model. This model was devised to show that the CBD is not the sole force in creating land-use patterns within the city. Rather, land-use districts may evolve for specific reasons at specific points elsewhere in the city—hence the name *multiple nuclei.* Compare this model to Figure 11.16. How and why are they different?

They compromise by finding an area of lower rent that is still relatively accessible.

The multiple-nuclei model, more than the other models, seems to take into account the varied factors of decentralization in the structure of the North American city. Many geographers criticize the concentric-zone and sector models as being rather simplistic, for they emphasize a single factor (residential differentiation in the concentric-zone model and rent in the sector model) to explain the pattern of the city. But the multiple-nuclei model encompasses a larger spectrum of economic and social factors. Harris and Ullman could probably accommodate the variety of forces working on the city because they did not confine themselves to seeking simply a social or economic explanation. As geographers, they tried to integrate the disparate elements of culture into a workable model. Most urban scholars agree that they succeeded.

Critiques of the Models

Most of the criticisms of the models just discussed focus on their simplification of reality or their inability to account for all the complexities of actual urban forms. More recently, feminist geographers have noticed some flaws in the models and in how they were constructed that call into question their descriptive power.

All three models assume that urban patterns are shaped by an economic trade-off between the desire to live in a suburban neighborhood appropriate to one's economic status and the need to live relatively close to the central city for employment opportunities. These models assume that only one person in the family is a wage worker—the male head of the family. They ignore dual-income families and households headed by single women, who contend with a larger array of factors in making locational decisions, including distances to child-care and school facilities and other services important for other members of a family. For many of these households, the traditional urban models that assume a spatial separation of workplace and home are no longer appropriate.

For example, a study of the activity patterns of working parents shows that women living in a city have access to a wider array of employment opportunities and are better able to combine domestic and wage labor than are women who live in the suburbs. Many of these middle-class women will choose to live in a gentrified inner-city location, hoping that this type of area will offer the amenities of the suburbs (good schools and safety), while also accommodating their work schedules. Other research has shown that some businesses will locate their offices in the suburbs because they rely on the labor of highly educated, middle-class women who are spatially constrained by their domestic work. As geographers Susan Hanson (see Practicing Geography) and Geraldine Pratt found in their study of employment practices and gender in Worcester, Massachusetts, most women seek employment locations closer to their homes than do men, and this applies to almost all women, not just those with small children.

The traditional models are also criticized for being created by men who all shared certain assumptions about how cities operate and thus presented a very partial view of urban life. Geographers David Sibley and Emily Gilbert, for instance, have both brought to our attention the development of other theories about urban form and structure during the same time. These theories incorporate the alternative perspectives of female scholars. Drawing on the urban reform work done by Jane Addams at Hull House in Chicago, scholars in the first decades of the twentieth century examined the causes of and possible solutions to urban problems. For example, Edith Abbott, Sophonisba Breckinridge, and Helen Rankin Jeter, faculty at the School of Social Service Administration at the University of Chicago, worked with their mostly female students to produce a number of studies about "race," ethnicity, class, and housing in Chicago. These studies differed in several ways from those of such theorists as Burgess and Hoyt. For instance, they emphasized the role of landlords in shaping the housing market and included an awareness of how racism is related to the allocation of housing and a sensitivity to the different urban experiences of ethnic groups.

Much of what these researchers at the School of Social Service uncovered in the 1930s is applicable to urban areas today. For example, a study by urban historian Raymond Mohl chronicles the making of black ghettos in Miami between 1940 and 1960. His research reveals the role of public policy decisions, landlordism, and discrimination in that process—forces identified by Abbott and others that continue to operate today.

REFLECTING ON GEOGRAPHY

Consider why the insights gained from the studies done by these women have been ignored until recently. How do you think our knowledge of urban life would have been different if these studies had become part of our accepted urban curriculum?

The Apartheid and Postapartheid City

As we have seen, racism and the residential segregation that often results from it can have profound effects on urban patterns. In South Africa, the state-sanctioned policy of segregating "races," known as **apartheid,** significantly altered the urban patterns that we outlined earlier. Although racial seg-

Susan Hanson

(Courtesy of Susan Hanson.)

Going out into the "field" doesn't necessarily mean donning stout boots and tromping along muddy paths or through dense stands of trees to reach mountain summits. For urban geographer Susan Hanson, it means talking to ordinary people about their differing experiences of the city. "All of my research involves fieldwork—yes, fieldwork in the city. Why? Because the questions I'm interested in all have to do, in one way or another, with how the everyday lives of people are shaped by, and in turn help to shape, the urban environment."

Even though Hanson is a world-famous geographer, a member of the National Academy of Sciences, and the former president of the Association of American Geographers, her passions about her work keep her close to the ground and in touch with her students. Given that she's a professor of geography at Clark University, located in the heart of Worcester, Massachusetts, she and her students only have to walk out the door to find an urban field project worthy of exploration. And those explorations with her undergraduates are the most exciting part of her job as a "practicing" geographer. "In my undergraduate courses students carry out original empirical research on a question that fascinates them; these students later tell me that they

never dreamed they could do this kind of work, nor did they realize how meaningful it could be." Perhaps her keen interest in sharing her work with students derives partly from her own experiences as a student, experiences that led her to become a geographer. "As a sophomore [at Middlebury College] I discovered geography when I took an intro course from a marvelous teacher, Rowland Illick, who emphasized links between human activity and the environment."

Hanson adopts a variety of methods for understanding the relationships between the everyday lives of people and the cities in which they live, including surveys, questionnaires, and in-depth interviews. For example, her current research focuses on understanding how cities assist and/or constrain male and female entrepreneurs differently when they launch and sustain their businesses. "I've used a range of secondary data sources on self-employment and entrepreneurship, and with the help of many student research assistants, I've also collected a lot of primary data, via both personal interviews and mailed survey questionnaires." By mixing her methods—using both quantitative and qualitative data—she and her students produce studies of cities and people that explore specific meanings and processes on the one hand but also seek generalizations on the other. "Combining these analytical approaches is, to me, an insightful and rewarding way to learn about the world."

regation was not the only force shaping the apartheid city, it certainly was a dominant one. The intended effects of this policy on urban form are delineated in Figure 11.19. To understand this illustration fully, we need to outline some of the important components of the apartheid state.

The policies of economic and political discrimination against non-European groups in South Africa were formalized and sharpened under National Party rule after 1948. To segregate the "races," the government passed two major pieces of legislation in 1950. The first was the Population Registration Act, which mandated the classification of the population into discrete racial groups. The three major groups were white, black, and colored, each of which was subdivided into smaller categories. The second piece of major legislation was called the Group Areas Act; its goal was, in the words of geographer A. J. Christopher, "to effect the total urban segregation of the various population groups defined under the Population Registration Act."

Cities were thus divided into sections that were to be inhabited only by members of one population group.

Although the effects of these acts on the form of South African cities did not appear overnight, they were massive nonetheless. Members of nonwhite groups were by far the ones most adversely affected. Almost without exception, the downtowns of cities were restricted to whites, whereas those areas set aside for nonwhites were peripheral and restricted, often lacking any urban services, such as transportation and shopping. Large numbers of nonwhite families were displaced with little or no compensation (estimates suggest that only 2 percent of the displaced families were white). Buffer zones were established between residential areas to curtail contact between groups, further hindering access to the central city for those groups pushed into the periphery. In effect, this created a city similar to that described by the sector model, only here it was organized along racial lines.

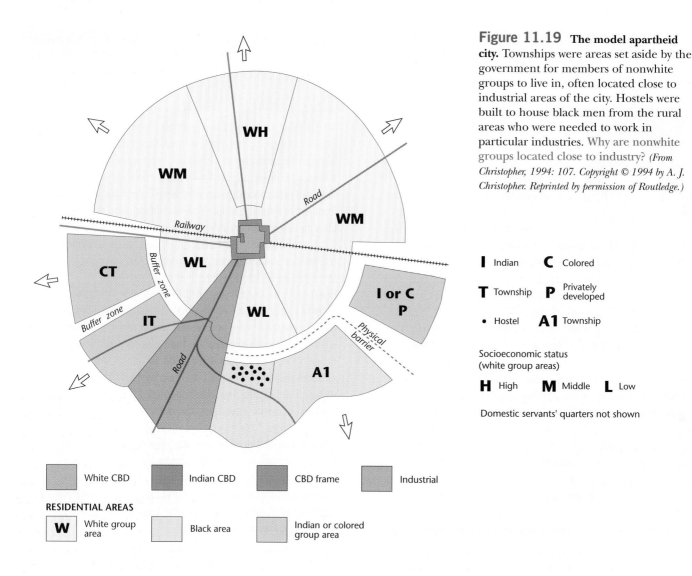

Figure 11.19 **The model apartheid city.** Townships were areas set aside by the government for members of nonwhite groups to live in, often located close to industrial areas of the city. Hostels were built to house black men from the rural areas who were needed to work in particular industries. Why are nonwhite groups located close to industry? *(From Christopher, 1994: 107. Copyright © 1994 by A. J. Christopher. Reprinted by permission of Routledge.)*

I Indian   **C** Colored

T Township   **P** Privately developed

• Hostel   **A1** Township

Socioeconomic status (white group areas)

H High   **M** Middle   **L** Low

Domestic servants' quarters not shown

White CBD   Indian CBD   CBD frame   Industrial

RESIDENTIAL AREAS

W White group area   Black area   Indian or colored group area

The Soviet and Post-Soviet City

The effects of centralized state policies on urban land-use patterns are also evident in the cities of the countries that formed the Soviet Union. With the Bolshevik Revolution of 1917 came attempts by the state to confront and solve the urban problems attendant upon industrialization (see Chapter 10). Socialist principles called for the nationalization of all resources, including land. Further, centralized planning replaced market forces as the means for allocating those resources. These ideas had profound effects on the form of Soviet cities. The principles that underlie the three models outlined earlier—that land is held privately and that the economic market dictates urban land use—were no longer the prime influences on urban form. Instead, Soviet policies attempted to create a more equitable arrangement of land uses in the city. The results of those policies included (1) a relative absence of residential segregation according to socioeconomic status, (2) equitable housing facilities for

most citizens, (3) relatively equal accessibility to sites for the distribution of consumer items, (4) cultural amenities (theater, opera, and so on) located and priced to be accessible to as many people as possible, and (5) adequate and accessible public transportation. Although these results created better living and working conditions for many people, the situation was far from ideal. By the 1970s and 1980s, many Soviet citizens realized that their standards of living were well below those in the West and that the centralized planning system was not successful.

National policies of economic restructuring introduced in the late 1980s, referred to as *perestroika,* led to mandates to privatize resources and the land market. In the post-Soviet city, market forces are once again dominant in shaping urban land uses, and the pace and scale of urban change are unprecedented (Figure 11.20). One of the most significant of those changes is the privatization of the housing market. In Moscow, for example, the percentage of the housing stock that is in private hands grew from 9.3 percent

Figure 11.20 **Downtown Moscow.** The post-Soviet city, rekindled by market forces, demonstrates unprecedented urban change. *(Sean Sprague/Impact Visuals.)*

in 1990 to 49.6 percent in 1994. However, this privatization does not necessarily mean better housing. In the new housing market, flats and homes are allocated according to market forces, and many people cannot afford the high prices. Apartments are particularly expensive in the center of Moscow, and most people have no choice but to continue to live in the communal apartments assigned to them under the Soviet system.

Post-Soviet cities are also taking on the look of Western cities. The downtowns are increasingly dominated by retailing outlets of familiar Western companies, such as Nike and McDonald's. Tall office buildings that house financial service businesses are replacing industrial buildings. Processes akin to gentrification (see pp. 385–387) are taking place in the center of cities such as Moscow, displacing residents to the peripheral portions of the city while housing others in Western-style elegance.

It is not yet clear whether Moscow will begin to follow the previously described three models of land-use forms or whether the combination of state policies and market forces will create new models of urban land use. Future research by geographers will undoubtedly yield insights into the effects of these massive socioeconomic and spatial transformations in post-Soviet cities on urban form.

Latin American Model

To illustrate cultural interaction in cities of the developing world, we draw upon a model specific to one region, Latin America—while keeping in mind that several other models can be applied to other parts of the developing world.

The model of the Latin American city is shown in Figure 1.15. Refer to the illustration as you read this section. This model is a generalized scheme that is sensitive to local cultures in Central and South America and also articulates the pervasive influence of international forces, both Western and non-Western, on urban structure. In contrast to contemporary cities in the United States, the CBDs of Latin American cities are vibrant, dynamic, and increasingly specialized. The dominance of the CBD is explained partly by widespread reliance on public transit and partly by the existence of a large and relatively affluent population close to the CBD. Outside the CBD, the dominant component is a commercial spine surrounded by an elite residential sector. Because these two zones are interrelated, they are referred to as the *spine/sector*. This combination is an extension of the CBD down a major boulevard, along which the city's important amenities, such as parks, theaters, restaurants, and even golf courses, are located. Strict zoning and land controls ensure continuation of these activities and protect the elite from incursions by low-income squatters.

Somewhat less prestigious is the inner-city *zone of maturity*, a collection of homes occupied by people unable to afford housing in the spine/sector. This is an area of upward mobility. The *zone of accretion* is a diverse collection of housing types, sizes, and quality, which can be thought of as a transition between the zone of maturity and the next zone. It is an area of ongoing construction and change, emblematic of the explosive population growth that characterizes the Latin American city. Although some neighborhoods within this zone have city-provided utilities, other blocks must rely on water and butane delivery trucks for essential services.

The most recent migrants to the Latin American city are found in the *zone of peripheral squatter settlements*. This fringe of poor people and inadequate housing contrasts dramatically with the affluent and comfortable suburbs that ring North American cities. Streets are unpaved, open trenches carry waste; residents haul water from distant locations, and electricity is often pirated by attaching illegal wires to the closest utility pole. Although this zone's quality of life seems marginal, many residents transform these squatter settlements over time into permanent neighborhoods with minimal amenities (see Chapter 10).

 ## Urban Landscapes

What do the urban patterns we have been discussing look like? How can we recognize different types of cities from their three-dimensional forms, and how are these forms changing? Cities, like all places humans inhabit, demonstrate an intriguing array of cultural landscapes, the reading of which gives varied insights into the complicated interactions between people and their surroundings. In this section, we offer some thoughts about how to view urban landscapes. We begin by discussing some themes—geographical reference points, one might say—for investigating **cityscapes**. A brief discussion of the new components in urban landscapes then follows. Much of what we say will strike a familiar chord, because our urban scene is the basis of so much of our life. You will find that you have a great deal of intuitive knowledge about cityscapes.

Themes in Cityscape Study

Cultural geographers look to cityscapes for many different kinds of information (see Doing Geography at the end of the chapter). Here we discuss four interconnected themes that are commonly used as organizational frameworks for landscape research (Figure 11.21).

Landscape Dynamics Think of some familiar features of the cityscape: downtown activities creeping into residential areas, deteriorated farmland on a city's outskirts, older buildings demolished for the new. These are all signs of specific processes that create urban change; the landscape faithfully reflects these dynamics.

When these visual clues are systematically mapped and analyzed, they offer evidence for the currents of change expressed in our cities. Of equal interest is where change is *not* occurring—those parts of the city that, for various reasons, remain relatively static. An unchanging landscape also conveys an important message. Perhaps that part of the city is stagnant because it is removed from the forces that pro-

Figure 11.21 **Boston's central city.** There are various ways of looking at cityscapes: as indicators of change, as palimpsests, as expressions of visual biases, and as manifestations of symbolic traditions. This photo offers evidence of all approaches. Which clues would you select to illustrate each cityscape theme? *(Steve Dunwell/The Image Bank.)*

duce change in other parts. Or perhaps there is a conscious attempt by local residents to inhibit change—to preserve open space by resisting suburban development, for example, or to preserve a historic landmark. Documenting landscape changes over time gives valuable insight into the paths of settlement development.

The City as Palimpsest Because cityscapes change, they offer a rich field for uncovering remnants of the past. A **palimpsest** is an old parchment used repeatedly for written messages. Before a new missive was written, the old was erased, yet rarely were all the previous characters and words completely obliterated—so remnants of earlier messages were still visible. This record of old and new is called a *palimpsest*, a word geographers use fondly to describe the visual mixture of past and present in cultural landscapes.

Cities are full of palimpsestic offerings, scattered across the contemporary landscape. How often have you noticed an old Victorian farmhouse surrounded by new tract homes, or a historic street pattern obscured or highlighted by a recent urban redevelopment project, or a brick factory shadowed by new high-rise office buildings? All of these give clues to past settlement patterns, and all are mute testimony to the processes of change in the city.

Our interest in this historical accumulation is more than romantic nostalgia. A systematic collection of these urban remnants provides us with glimpses of the past that might otherwise be hidden. All societies pick and choose, consciously or not, what they wish to preserve for future generations, and, in this process, a filtering takes place that often excludes and distorts information. But the landscape does not lie.

The urban palimpsest, then, offers a way to find the past in the contemporary landscape. We can evaluate these remnants to glean a better understanding of historical settlements.

Symbolic Cityscapes Landscapes contain much more than literal messages. They are also loaded with figurative or metaphorical meaning and can elicit emotions and memories. To some people, skyscrapers are more than high-rise office buildings: they are symbols of progress, economic vitality, downtown renewal, or corporate identities. Similarly, historical landscapes—those parts of the city where the past has been preserved—help people to define themselves in time; establish social continuity with the past; and codify a largely forgotten, yet sometimes idealized, past.

D. W. Meinig, a geographer who has given much thought to urban landscapes, maintains that there are three highly symbolic townscapes in the United States: the New England village, with its white church, commons, and tree-lined neighborhoods; Main Street of Middle America, a string street of a small midwestern town, with storefronts, bandstand, and park (Figure 11.22); and what Meinig calls California Suburbia, suburbs of quarter-acre lots, effusive garden landscaping, swimming pools, and ranch-style houses. As Meinig explains: "Each is based upon an actual landscape of a particular region. Each is an image derived from our national experience . . . simplified . . . and widely advertised so as to become a commonly understood symbol. Each has . . . influenced the shaping of the American scene over broader areas."

More politically and problematically, the cultural landscape is an important vehicle for constructing and maintaining, subtly and implicitly, certain social and ethnic distinctions. For example, geographers James and Nancy Duncan have found that because conspicuous consumption is a major way of conveying social identity in our culture, elite landscapes are created through large-lot zoning, imitation country estates, and the preservation of undeveloped land. They see the residential landscapes in upper-income areas as controlled and managed to reinforce class and status categories. Their study of elite suburbs near Vancouver and New York sensitizes us to how the cultural landscape can be thought of as a repository of symbols used by our society to differentiate itself and protect vested interests.

Perception of the City During the last 20 years, social scientists have been concerned with measuring people's perceptions of the urban landscape. They assume that if we really know what people see and react to in the city, we can ask architects and urban planners to design and create a more humane urban environment.

Figure 11.22 **Main Street, Ferndale, California.** The symbolism of Main Street, USA, is a powerful force in shaping communities today, particularly because an ersatz Main Street is the central element of Disney World. Think of the ways this symbol is used in art, literature, film, and television and of the messages and emotions conveyed by this landscape. (*ChromoSohm/Sohm/Photo Researchers, Inc.*)

Kevin Lynch, an urban designer, pioneered a method for recording people's images of the city. On the basis of interviews conducted in Boston, Jersey City (New Jersey), and Los Angeles, Lynch suggested five important elements in mental maps (images) of cities:

1. *Pathways* are the routes of frequent travel, such as streets, freeways, and transit corridors. We experience the city from the pathways, and they become the threads that hold our maps together.

2. *Edges* are boundaries between areas or the outer limits of our image. Mountains, rivers, shorelines, and even major streets and freeways are commonly used as edges. They tend to define the extremes of our urban vision. Then we fill in the details.

3. *Nodes* are strategic junction points, such as breaks in transportation, traffic circles, or any place where important pathways come together.

4. *Districts* are small areas with a common identity, such as ethnic areas and functional zones (for instance, the CBD or a row of car dealers).

5. *Landmarks* are reference points that stand out because of shape, height, color, or historical importance. The city hall in Los Angeles, the Washington Monument, and the golden arches of a McDonald's are all landmarks.

Using these concepts, Lynch saw that some parts of the cities were more **legible,** or easier to decipher, than others. Lynch discovered that, in general, legibility increases when the urban landscape offers clear pathways, nodes, districts, edges, and landmarks. Further, some cities are more legible than others. For example, Lynch found that Jersey City is not very legible. Wedged between New York City and Newark, Jersey City is fragmented by railroads and highways. Residents' mental maps of Jersey City have large blank areas in them. When questioned, they can think of few local landmarks. Instead, they tend to point to the New York City skyline just across the river.

The New Urban Landscape

Within the past 25 to 30 years, our cityscapes have undergone massive transformations. The impact of suburbanization and decentralization has led to an emerging new urban form that we have called the edge city (see Chapter 10). In the older downtown areas, we have seen that gentrification, redevelopment, and immigration have also created novel urban forms. What we see emerging in our cityscapes, then, is a new urban landscape, composed of distinctive elements that we have not yet discussed.

New Ethnic Neighborhoods As many middle- and upper-class families continue to move out of traditional neighborhoods near urban centers, they are being replaced by new immigrants. According to the Population Reference Bureau, 9.8 million people immigrated to the United States between 1990 and 2000: 51 percent came from Latin America, 30 percent from Asia, 13 percent from Europe, and 6 percent from other regions. The vast majority of these immigrants found job opportunities and cultural connections that drew them to major metropolitan regions in six states—California, New York, Texas, Florida, New Jersey, and Illinois (Figure 11.23). This spatial concentration of America's new immigrants has created diverse communities with distinctive landscapes, both within the downtown areas of these cities and in the suburban regions. Miami's Little Havana, for example, is easily recognized by the commercial signs in Spanish, Spanish street names, and the colors and styles of buildings. Parts of what were once run-down neighborhoods of the city have been remade into vibrant commercial and residential communities. Another example is Los Angeles: 80 years ago, a Saturday morning stroll through the CBD of Los Angeles would have led through streets lined with department stores, movie theaters, and offices. Now it is filled with the sounds of Latin music and vendors selling everything from electronics to mango ice cream.

But these new ethnic landscapes are not limited to the central city. Portions of America's suburbs have also become diverse. The decentralization of the downtown has created new economic centers in suburban regions, and immigrants are drawn to these centers. According to the 2000 census, immigrants make up 27 percent of the suburban populations of large cities in the United States (those with populations over 500,000). In Montgomery County, Maryland, a suburban community outside of Washington, D.C., almost a quarter of all households are headed by a person who is foreign-born. Instead of the dense residential and commercial districts that characterize downtown ethnic enclaves, the new suburban ethnicity is proclaimed within shopping centers, suburban cemeteries, and dispersed churches and temples. According to geographer Joseph Wood, their presence in the landscape is often not visible to observers precisely because it is suburban. For example, most of the 50,000 Vietnamese-Americans who migrated to the Washington, D.C., area from the 1970s through the 1990s settled in suburbs in northern Virginia. The focal point of the Vietnamese community here is the Eden Center, a typical L-shaped shopping center that has been transformed into a Vietnamese-American economic and social center (Figure 11.24). This pattern of shopping plazas serving as ethnic community markers for a dispersed immigrant population is not peculiar to northern Virginia; it is commonplace in the metropolitan areas of most major North American cities.

New York	92,361
Dominican Rep.	10.6%
China	7.4%
Jamaica	5.5%
Haiti	4.2%
Ecuador	4.0%

San Jose	28,715
Mexico	19.8%
India	12.3%
Vietnam	11.8%
China	10.9%
Philippines	6.6%

Chicago	44,888
Mexico	25.9%
India	10.3%
Poland	9.2%
Philippines	6.1%
China	4.8%

Washington, D.C./ Maryland/Virginia	39,815
El Salvador	12.7%
India	9.6%
China	5.7%
Pakistan	3.8%
Philippines	3.7%

Los Angeles	98,997
Mexico	33.8%
El Salvador	8.7%
Philippines	8.1%
China	5.4%
Guatemala	4.5%

Miami	48,797
Cuba	37.8%
Nicaragua	20.1%
Haiti	11.8%
Colombia	5.4%
Peru	2.3%

Figure 11.23 **Map indicating place of origin of legally admitted immigrants to six metropolitan areas in the United States.** Why is immigration focused on these six cities? *(Source: U.S. Immigration and Naturalization Service, 2001.)*

Shopping Malls Many people consider the image of the shopping mall, surrounded by mass-produced suburbs, to be one of the most distinctive landscape symbols of modern urbanity. Yet, oddly, most malls are not designed to be seen from the outside. As a matter of fact, without appropriate signs, a passerby could proceed past a mall without noticing any visual display. Unlike the retail districts of nineteenth- and early-twentieth-century cities, where grand architectural displays along major boulevards were the norm, shopping malls are enclosed, private worlds that are meant to be seen

Figure 11.24 **Eden Shopping Center in Fairfax, Virginia.** This shopping plaza serves as a social and cultural center for the Vietnamese community of northern Virginia. *(Courtesy of Joseph Wood.)*

from the inside. Often located near an off-ramp of a major freeway or beltway of a metropolitan area, and close to the middle- and upper-class residential neighborhoods, shopping malls can be distinguished more by their extensive parking lots than by their architectural design.

For all that, shopping malls do have a characteristic form. The early malls of the 1960s tended to have a simple, linear form, with 2 department stores at each end that functioned as "anchors" and 20 to 30 smaller shops connecting the two ends. In the 1970s and 1980s, much larger malls were built, and their form became more complex.

Malls today are often several stories high and may contain 5 or 6 anchor stores and up to 400 smaller shops. In addition, many malls now serve more than a retail function—they often contain food courts and restaurants, professional offices, movie complexes, hotels, chapels, and amusement arcades and centers (Figure 11.25). A shopping center in Kuala Lumpur, known simply as The Mall, contains Malaysia's largest indoor amusement park, a replica of the historic city of Malacca, a cineplex, and a food court, in addition to hundreds of stores. Many scholars consider these megamalls to be the new centers of urban life (see Focus On: The Shopping Mall as Social Center) because they seem to be the major sites for social interaction. For example, after workplace, home, and school, the shopping mall is where most Americans spend their time.

However, unlike the open-air marketplaces of an earlier era, shopping malls are private, not public, spaces. The use of the shopping mall as a place for social interaction, therefore, is always of secondary importance to its private, commercial function. If a certain group of people were considered a nuisance to shoppers, the mall owners could prevent them from what Jeffrey Hopkins calls "'mallingering'—the act of lingering about a mall for economic and noneconomic social purposes."

Office Parks With the connection of metropolitan areas by major interstate highways and with the development of new communication technologies, office buildings no longer need to be located in the central city. Cheaper rent in suburban locations, combined with the convenience of easy-access parking and the privacy of a separate location, has led to the construction of **office parks** throughout suburban America. Figure 11.26 shows the location of office parks in metropolitan Atlanta in relation to the freeway network. Many of these office parks are occupied by the regional or national headquarters of large corporations or by local sales and professional offices. To take advantage of economies of scale, many of these offices will locate together and rent or buy space from a land development company.

The use of the word *park* to identify this new landscape element points to the consciously antiurban imagery of these complexes. Many of these developments are surrounded by a well-landscaped outdoor space, often incorporating artificial lakes and waterfalls (Figure 11.27). Jogging paths, fitness trails, and picnic tables all cater to the new lifestyle of professional and managerial employees.

Many office parks are located along what have been called **high-tech corridors:** areas along limited-access highways that contain offices and other services associated with new high-tech industries. As our discussion of edge cities suggests (see Chapter 10), this new type of commercial landscape is gradually replacing our downtowns as the workplace for most Americans.

Figure 11.25 **Food court at the Fashion Mall in Plantation, Florida.** A large percentage of the third story of this mall is devoted to fast-food outlets. The fountain and natural lighting are meant to create a gardenlike setting for mall dining. Why do you think these fast-food outlets are all clustered together within the mall? *(Courtesy of Mona Domosh.)*

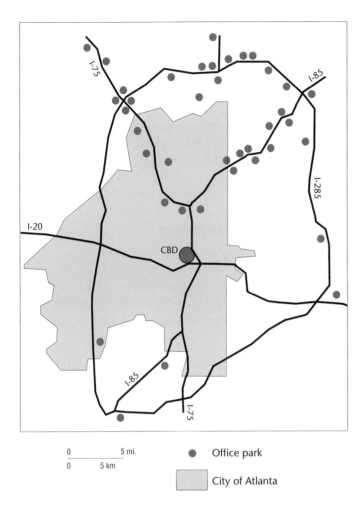

Figure 0 5 mi.
0 5 km

● Office park

City of Atlanta

Figure 11.26 Office park locations in Atlanta, Georgia. This map clearly shows their locational ties to major freeways. *(After Hartshorn and Muller, 1989.)*

Master-Planned Communities Many newer residential developments on the suburban fringe are planned and built as complete neighborhoods by private development companies. These **master-planned communities** include not only architecturally compatible housing units but also recreational facilities (such as tennis courts, fitness centers, bike paths, and swimming pools) and security measures (gated or guarded entrances). In Weston, a master-planned community that covers approximately 10,000 acres (4000 hectares) in southern Florida, land use is completely regulated not only within the gated residential complexes but also along the road system that connects Weston to the interstate (Figure 11.28). Shrubbery is planted strategically to shield residents from views of the roadway, and the road signs are uniform in style and encased in stylish, weathered-gray wood frames. This massive community—Weston is now home to 50,000 people—contains various complexes catering to particular lifestyles, ranging from smaller patio homes to equestrian estates. For example, in the mid-1990s, homes in one such complex—Tequesta Point—cost $250,000–$300,000 and came with gated entranceways, split-level floor plans, and Roman bathtubs. Those in Bermuda Springs, on the other hand, which cost $115,000–$120,000, were significantly smaller and did not offer the same interior features. Typical of master-planned communities, the name of the development itself was chosen to convey a hometown feeling. In this instance, developers carried out an extensive marketing survey before they settled on the name Weston.

Festival Settings In many cities, gentrification efforts focus on a multiuse redevelopment scheme that is built around a particular setting, often one with a historical association.

Figure 11.27 Compare this suburban office building in Yonkers, New York, with your image of downtown skyscrapers. Notice the green space around the building and its horizontal rather than vertical appearance. Why do you rarely find very tall office buildings in the suburbs? *(Michael Melford/The Image Bank.)*

Figure 11.28 The master-planned community of Weston, Florida. These automated gates keep "undesirables" out of many subdivisions in master-planned communities. The more expensive areas have guardhouses at their entrances, whereas less expensive ones may have privately installed security systems. *(Courtesy of Donna Faranda.)*

Waterfronts are commonly chosen as focal points for these large-scale projects, which Paul Knox has referred to as **festival settings.** These complexes integrate retailing, office, and entertainment facilities and incorporate trendy shops, restaurants, bars and nightclubs, and hotels. Knox suggests that these developments are "distinctive as new landscape elements merely because of their scale and their consequent ability to stage—or merely to be—the spectacular." Such festival settings as Faneuil Hall in Boston, Bayside in Miami, and Riverwalk in San Antonio serve as sites for concerts, ethnic festivals, and street performances; they also serve as focal points for the more informal human interactions that we usually associate with urban life (Figure 11.29). In this sense, festival settings do perform a vital function in the attempt to revitalize our downtowns. Yet, like many other gentrification efforts, these massive displays of wealth and consumption often stand in direct contrast to neighboring areas of the inner city that have received little, if any, monetary or other social benefit from these projects.

"Militarized" Space Considered together, these new elements in the urban landscape suggest some trends that many scholars find disturbing. Urbanist Mike Davis has called one such trend the "militarization" of urban space, meaning that increasingly space is used to set up defenses against people the city considers undesirable. This includes landscape developments that range from the lack of street furniture to guard against the homeless living on the streets, to gated and guarded residential communities, to the complete segregation of classes and "races" within the city. Par-

ticularly in downtown redevelopment schemes, the goal of city planners and others is usually to provide safe and homogeneous environments, segregated from the diversity of cultures and lifestyles that often characterizes the central area of most cities. As Davis says, "Cities of all sizes are rushing to apply and profit from a formula that links together clustered development, social homogeneity, and a perception of security." Although this "militarization" is not completely new, it has taken on epic proportions as whole sections of such cities as Los Angeles, Atlanta, Dallas, Houston, and Miami have become "militarized" spaces (Figure 11.30).

REFLECTING ON GEOGRAPHY

Some scholars might argue that the increasing "militarization" of our urban spaces will lead to situations little different from what happened to South African cities under apartheid (see Figure 11.19). Identify similarities and differences between these two urban situations.

Decline of Public Space Related to the increase in "militarized" space is the decline of public spaces in most of our cities. For example, the change in shopping patterns from the downtown retailing area to the suburbs indicates a change of emphasis from the public space of city streets to

Figure 11.29 Quincy Market, an early-nineteenth-century wholesale market near Faneuil Hall in Boston. The market is re-created as a festival setting, complete with upscale shops, restaurants, and bars. In what ways do you think this cultural landscape differs from the original Quincy Market in the early nineteenth century?

The Shopping Mall as Social Center:
"Mallingering" and Consuming at the West Edmonton Mall (WEM)

The role of WEM as a social center cannot be divorced from the popularity of shopping centers in our consumer society. The popularity of "mallingering"—the act of lingering about a mall for economic and noneconomic social purposes—can be partly attributed to the rapid proliferation of shopping centers during the economic and demographic booms of the post–World War II era and the ensuing rise in consumerism as a way of life. In an age in which consumerism is the dominant lifestyle and material consumption is a popular life objective, shopping malls—the dominant forum for commerce—become the principal forum for consumption and, thus, a popular place to spend money as well as time.

A more tempered explanation of mallingering considers the secondary social and recreational roles associated with retailing. The marketplace has traditionally played the role of communal meeting place. Given the latent social function of the marketplace in general and the congregative and community role of shopping malls in particular, WEM is not merely a mega-shopping mall, nor a mega-recreation center, but a mega-social center, which is claimed to bring together as many as 60,000 people per day from Edmonton and around the world. When placed in the context of the traditional role of the marketplace and the cultural context of consumerism and mallingering, WEM's popularity as a social center is not surprising. The formal introduction of social activities (e.g., leisure and entertainment facilities) into a shopping center is more a confirmation of the social role of the marketplace than it is a novel marketing ploy. The socially congregative pull—"the sociopetal" factors—exerted by WEM's size, scale, and leisure factors, however, renders the megamall functionally and socially unique relative to other shopping malls. The fact that social interaction is under the control of a single corporation, like most indoor urban space, makes understanding the freedoms and constraints—the socially divisive or "sociofugal" factors—imposed upon patrons by WEM's physical design and operation all the more pertinent.

Theatres of Consumption

To suggest that shopping malls are manipulating wizards able to induce unsuspecting patrons into money-spending frenzies or irrational purchases not only insults the public's intelligence but also pays unwarranted homage to mall designers and management. There is growing recognition, nonetheless, that physical design and atmosphere are important factors influencing customer behavior. Shopping malls in this latter sense are literally theatres of consumption staged within a carefully contrived set designed to promote retail drama. Enclosure, protection, and control are the basic design formula, and organized happenings assist in promoting an exciting friendly atmosphere. Herein lie factors that may promote and retard social interaction at WEM.

The mega-mall (indeed most shopping malls and indoor space) offers a pleasant alternative to some of the discomforts of the world outside. Enclosure provides freedom from climatic extremes, clear signage, ease of mobility, and access to hundreds of stores and services. Pay telephones, plants, statues, fountains, washroom facilities, and benches further contribute to the value of WEM as a social centre. The many and varied sights and objects in the corridors promote "triangulation," whereby external stimuli may provide links between people and prompt strangers to talk to one another. A combination of sophisticated electronic security systems and uniformed and plain-clothes personnel ensures, according to the management, "a safe and secure atmosphere for [the] entire family" (WEM security brochure). No city street can as yet match the 24-hour protection provided by "480 computer monitored security points,1600 fire detectors, 42 strategically placed 'help phones' and hidden cameras that keep an eye on 38 locations throughout WEM at the same time" (WEM security brochure). Control is, therefore, a key ingredient in the success of WEM; its environment can more easily conform to the tastes, needs, and preferences of patrons, as perceived by mall management, than, say a city street of independent shopowners.

From Hopkins, 1991. Reprinted by permission of the Canadian Association of Geographers

---

the privately controlled and operated shopping malls. Similarly, many city governments, often joined by private developers, have built enclosed walkways either above or below the city streets. These walkways serve partly to provide a climate-controlled means of passing from one building to another and partly to provide pedestrians with a "safe" environment that avoids possible confrontations on the street. Again, the public space of the street is being replaced by controlled spaces that do not provide the same access to all members of the urban community. It remains to be seen whether this trend will continue or whether new public spaces will be formed that accommodate all groups of people within the urban landscape.

Figure 11.30 **The Metro Dade Cultural Center in downtown Miami.** Inside this literal fortress is Dade County's public library and Center for the Fine Arts. The building was designed to be completely removed from the street, with the few entrances heavily monitored by cameras. Does this seem like a welcoming space? Should it be? *(Courtesy of Mona Domosh.)*

Conclusion

We have examined various components of the intricate urban mosaic. Culture regions are found at a smaller scale than others that we've previously explored; in the city, neighborhoods and census units can be thought of as social regions and culture regions.

We also see two major forces at work in the city that can be considered diffusion processes. One works to centralize activities within the city, the other to decentralize activities into the suburbs. The costs of decentralization run high, not just in the suburbs, where unplanned growth takes its toll, but also in the inner cities, which are left with decayed and stagnant cores.

The ecology of the city is a complicated issue because urbanization has modified natural ecosystems profoundly. The results of these changes—air pollution and even floods, for example—cause significant problems for urban dwellers everywhere. Solutions to these problems will require long-term commitments of energy and resources.

Models of the internal structure of cities describe how social and economic activities sort themselves out in space. The simplification of these models calls into question their usefulness for describing the contemporary American city, as well as cities of the former Soviet Union, South Africa, and the world generally

As dense collections of human artifacts, cities offer a fascinating array of cultural landscapes that tell us much about ourselves and our interaction with the environment. These cityscapes reveal contemporary change, the past, prevalent scenic values, and our storehouse of symbols. New elements in the urban landscape relay information about our current social, economic, and political reality, and they indicate trends for the future that many scholars find disturbing.

DOING GEOGRAPHY

Reading "Your" Urban Landscape

Even without extensive training in geography, most of us are avid "readers" of our landscapes. We drive through residential neighborhoods and make judgments about the types of people who live there; we walk downtown and, finding that the streets get narrower, surmise that they were built a long time ago, before automobile traffic was a factor; we marvel at how high buildings rise into the sky, knowing that those with offices at the top make "top" dollar. But, as Culture in a Globalizing World in Chapter 1 taught us, reading landscapes can be tricky business; what we see in front of us may not always be as it appears, nor built when and for whom we think. This exercise, then, is about interpreting your own urban landscape and about understanding the limitations of that interpretation.

Your goal in this exercise is to create an interpretative walking tour of part of your city that could be used by tourists (or anyone, really) and that is both informative and engaging. In other words, the idea is to get people to look, think, and make connections—but also to understand the limitations of "just looking." First, pick your place. Decide on a route that takes people through a particular part of your city—downtown, an ethnic landscape, a commercial area, a local neighborhood, suburban sprawl, and so on. Almost anywhere will work. From reading this chapter you should have a pretty good idea of the types of urban landscapes and the ones that are of interest to you. Second, walk the route yourself, marking places where you want people to stop, look, and think. Third, you must now investigate these places. You should be able to use the information in this chapter and elsewhere in the book to do a good bit of this work, but the specifics of your city will require more information: archival research, perhaps some informal interviews, or something else altogether. At each point, you should be asking yourself: what can I learn from looking at this landscape and what could I never have guessed? Fourth, based on what you've found out, write your interpretative tour, providing information and questions for each particular stop on the route. Finally, try it out—give your route map and written descriptions and questions to a friend, and see what happens.

The Urban Mosaic on the Internet

You can learn more about cities and suburbs on the Internet at the following web sites:

Burbs, Blockbusting, and Blacks

http://www.rut.com/mjalbert/burbs/index.html

This site provides a fascinating look at the relationships among racism, blockbusting, and the formation of American suburbs.

Levittown: Documents of an Ideal American Suburb

http://www.uic.edu/~pbhales/Levittown

Here you can find a history of Levittown, New York, the first mass-produced suburb, with interesting historical and contemporary photographs.

Literature on Race, Ethnicity, and Multiculturalism

http://ethics.acusd.edu/race.html

This site provides an annotated list of Internet resources on issues pertaining to race, ethnicity, and human rights.

The State of the Nation's Cities: A Comprehensive Database on American Cities and Suburbs

http://www.policy.rutgers.edu/cupr/sonc/sonc.htm

This site is a comprehensive database on 77 American cities and suburbs that you can download onto your computer and display in graphic form.

Sources

Abbott, Edith, and Mary Zahrobsky. 1936. "The Tenement Areas and the People of the Tenements," in E. Abbott (ed.), *The Tenements of Chicago*. Chicago: University of Chicago Press, 72–169.

Agnew, John, John Mercer, and David Sopher (eds.). 1984. *The City in Cultural Context*. Boston: Allen & Unwin.

Anderson, Kay. 1987. "The Idea of Chinatown: The Power of Place and Institutional Practice in the Making of a Racial Category." *Annals of the Association of American Geographers* 77: 580–598.

Bach, Wilfred, and Thomas Hagedorn. 1971. "Atmospheric Pollution: Its Spatial Distribution over an Urban Area." *Proceedings of the Association of American Geographers* 3: 22.

Bater, James H. 1980. *The Soviet City: Ideal and Reality*. Beverly Hills, Calif.: Sage Publications.

Bater, James H. 1996. *Russia and the Post-Soviet Scene*. New York: John Wiley.

Bell, David, and Gill Valentine (eds.). 1995. *Mapping Desire: Geographies of Sexualities*. London: Routledge.

Burgess, E. W. 1925. "The Growth of the City: An Introduction to a Research Project," in Robert E. Park, Ernest W. Burgess, and Roderick D. McKenzie (eds.), *The City*. Chicago: University of Chicago Press, 47–62.

Castells, Manuel. 1983. *The City and Grassroots: A Cross-Cultural Theory of Urban Social Movements*. Berkeley: University of California Press.

Chandler, T. J. 1961. "The Changing Form of London's Heat Island." *Geography* 46: 295–307.

Chauncey, George. 1994. *Gay New York: Gender, Urban Culture, and the Making of the Gay Male World, 1890–1940*. New York: Basic Books.

Christopher, A. J. 1994. *The Atlas of Apartheid*. London: Routledge.

Clay, Grady. 1973. *Close-Up: How to Read the American City*. New York: Praeger.

Cybriwsky, Roman A., David Ley, and John Western. 1986. "The Political and Social Construction of Revitalized Neighborhoods: Society Hill, Philadelphia, and False Creek, Vancouver," in Neil Smith and Peter Williams (eds.), *Gentrification of the City*. Boston: Allen & Unwin, 92–120.

Daniell, Jennifer, and Raymond Struyk. 1997. "The Evolving Housing Market in Moscow: Indicators of Housing Reform." *Urban Studies* 34: 235–254.

Davis, Mike. 1992. "Fortress Los Angeles: The Militarization of Urban Space," in Michael Sorkin (ed.), *Variations on a Theme Park: The New American City and the End of Public Space*. New York: Hill & Wang, 154–180.

Drakakis-Smith, David. 2000. *Third World Cities*, 2nd ed. London: Routledge.

Duncan, James, and Nancy Duncan. 1984. "A Cultural Analysis of Urban Residential Landscapes in North America: The Cause of the Anglophile Elite," in John Agnew, John Mercer, and David Sopher (eds.), *The City in Cultural Context*. Boston: Allen & Unwin, 255–276.

Gilbert, Emily. 1994. "Naturalist Metaphors in the Literatures of Chicago, 1893–1925." *Journal of Historical Geography* 20: 283–304.

Gordon, Margaret T., et al. 1981. "Crime, Women, and the Quality of Urban Life," in Catherine R. Stimpson, Elsa Dixler, Martha J. Nelson, and Kathryn B. Yatrakis (eds.), *Women and the American City*. Chicago: University of Chicago Press, 141–157.

Griffin, Ernst, and Larry Ford. 1983. "Cities of Latin America," in Stanley Brunn and Jack Williams (eds.), *Cities of the World: World Regional Urban Development*. New York: Harper & Row, 199–240.

Hanson, Susan. 1992. "Geography and Feminism: Worlds in Collision?" *Annals of the Association of American Geographers* 82: 569–586.

Hanson, Susan, and Geraldine Pratt. 1995. *Gender, Work, and Space*. New York: Routledge.

Harris, C. D., and E. L. Ullman. 1945. "The Nature of Cities." *Annals of the Association of American Academy of Political and Social Science* 242: 7–17.

Hartshorn, Truman A., and Peter O. Muller. 1989. "Suburban Downtowns and the Transformation of Metropolitan Atlanta's Business Landscape." *Urban Geography* 10: 375–395.

Hopkins, Jeffrey S. P. 1991. "West Edmonton Mall as a Centre for Social Interaction." *The Canadian Geographer* 35: 268–279.

Hoyt, Homer (ed.). 1939. *Structure and Growth of Residential Neighborhoods in American Cities*. Washington, D.C.: Federal Housing Administration.

Jackson, Kenneth T. 1985. *Crabgrass Frontier*. New York: Oxford University Press.

Knopp, Lawrence. 1995. "Sexuality and Urban Space: A Framework for Analysis," in David Bell and Gill Valentine (eds.), *Mapping Desire*. London: Routledge, 149–161.

Knox, Paul L. 1991. "The Restless Urban Landscape: Economic and Sociocultural Change and the Transformation of Metropolitan Washington, D.C." *Annals of the Association of American Geographers* 81: 181–209.

Lauria, Mickey, and Lawrence Knopp. 1985. "Toward an Analysis of the Role of Gay Communities in the Urban Renaissance." *Urban Geography* 6: 152–169.

Lynch, Kevin. 1960. *The Image of the City*. Cambridge, Mass.: MIT Press.

SEEING GEOGRAPHY

How has globalization affected urban ethnic neighborhoods?

A street in Chinatown, New York City.

Chinatown, New York City

"Reading" this urban landscape is relatively simple: the signs of the stores and restaurants leave no doubt that this place is marked as a "Chinatown." Interpreting this scene is easy for most Americans because Chinatown has become a symbolic landscape: a place that connotes America's history and geography of immigration, the idea of the melting pot, and now a commitment to cultural pluralism. But there are other ways to understand this landscape as well, ways that rely on a keen eye and an urban geographical analysis. That some of the writing is in English and some in Chinese tells us that this streetscape is located in a place where both languages are spoken; the style of architecture, the types of cars, the street signs, and the American flag indicate a location in the United States. This Chinatown happens to be in New York City, but one could have guessed San Francisco, Boston, or Philadelphia.

Based on our understanding of the models of urban land use, we could surmise that Chinatown is located in a transitional zone, just outside the CBD. This certainly was the case in the late nineteenth and early twentieth centuries, when most of the brick buildings in this photograph were built. In this part of New York City, land values were relatively low. The financial center of Wall Street was to the south, and the retail areas along Broadway and Fifth Avenue were farther north, as were the middle- and upper-class residences. With few choices available, Chinese immigrants (and many others, including Italians and eastern European Jews) settled into this area and found jobs in the small industries and businesses nearby. The result was a series of neighborhoods of mixed land uses, on the edge of both the financial CBD and the retail CBD, in the zone of transition. Each of these neighborhoods came to be defined by the dominant Anglo culture as an ethnic region—in this case, Chinatown.

Today, Chinatown is still home to new migrants, but many of them come from other East Asian countries: Vietnam, Korea, the Philippines. In the United States between 1980 and 1997, the Vietnamese population grew 327 percent, the Korean population 175 percent, and the Filipino population 155 percent. Although we know that an increasing proportion of new immigrants to the United States move to suburban areas, Chinatown in New York City still attracts many immigrants because of its accessibility to a fairly diverse job market and to the services available for immigrants who may not speak English and do not drive automobiles.

The Häagen-Dazs sign reminds us of the presence of globalizing forces and also indicates that Chinatown has become a tourist destination for visitors to the city. After a trip to the top of the Empire State Building or to the Metropolitan Museum of Art, tourists might go downtown for "authentic" Chinese food, stopping off for ice cream afterward. If they really wanted to sample the avant-garde club scene of the city, they might find themselves in a trendy bar on the edge of Chinatown. Much of the Lower East Side is already gentrified, and Chinatown is a likely next target. If that happens, the Mandarin Court sign might soon read Starbucks Coffee. ∎

Martin, Philip, and Elizabeth Midgley. 1999. "Immigration to the United States." *Population Bulletin* 54: 1–44.

McDowell, Linda. 1983. "Towards an Understanding of the Gender Division of Urban Space." *Environment and Planning D: Society and Space* 1: 59–72.

Meinig, D. W. (ed.). 1979. *The Interpretation of Ordinary Landscapes: Geographical Essays.* New York: Oxford University Press.

Mohl, Raymond A. 1995. "Making the Second Ghetto in Metropolitan Miami, 1940–1960." *Journal of Urban History* 21: 395–427.

Portes, Alejandro, and Ruben G. Rumbaut. 1996. *Immigrant America: A Portrait,* 2nd ed. Berkeley: University of California Press.

Pratt, Geraldine. 1990. "Feminist Analyses of the Restructuring of Urban Life." *Urban Geography* 11: 594–605.

Robinson, Jennifer. 1997. "The Geopolitics of South African Cities: States, Citizens, Territory." *Political Geography* 16: 365–386.

Rothenberg, Tamar. 1995. "'And She Told Two Friends': Lesbians Creating Urban Social Space," in David Bell and Gill Valentine (eds.), *Mapping Desire.* London: Routledge, 165–181.

Rowe, Stacy, and Jennifer Wolch. 1990. "Social Networks in Time and Space: Homeless Women in Skid Row, Los Angeles." *Annals of the Association of American Geographers* 80: 184–204.

Secor, Anna. 2004. "'There Is an Istanbul That Belongs to Me': Citizenship, Space and Identity in the City." *Annals of the Association of American Geographers* 94: 352–368.

Sibley, David. 1995. "Gender, Science, Politics and Geographies of the City." *Gender, Place and Culture: A Journal of Feminist Geography* 2: 37–49.

Smith, Neil. 1984. *Uneven Development.* New York: Blackwell.

Smith, Neil. 1996. *The New Urban Frontier: Gentrification and the Revanchist City.* New York: Routledge.

Sorkin, Michael (ed.). 1992. *Variations on a Theme Park: The New American City and the End of Public Space.* New York: Hill & Wang.

U.S. Immigration and Naturalization Service. 2001. *2001 Statistical Yearbook.* Washington, D.C.: U.S. Government Printing Office.

Valentine, Gill. 1993. "Desperately Seeking Susan: A Geography of Lesbian Friendships." *Area* 25: 109–116.

Ward, David. 1971. *Cities and Immigrants.* New York: Oxford University Press.

Warner, Sam Bass. 1962. *Streetcar Suburbs: The Process of Growth in Boston, 1870–1900.* Cambridge, Mass.: Harvard University Press.

Warr, Mark. 1985. "Fear of Rape Among Urban Women." *Social Problems* 32: 238–250.

Watson, Sophie, with Helen Austerberry. 1986. *Housing and Homelessness: A Feminist Perspective.* London: Routledge & Kegan Paul.

Women and Geography Study Group of the Institute of British Geographers. 1997. *Feminist Geographies: Explorations in Diversity and Difference.* London: Prentice Hall.

Wood, Joseph. 1997. "Vietnamese-American Place Making in Northern Virginia." *The Geographical Review* 87: 58–72.

Ten Recommended Books on the Urban Mosaic

(For additional suggested readings, see *The Human Mosaic* web site: www.whfreeman.com/jordan)

Allen, James P., and Eugene Turner. 1997. *The Ethnic Quilt: Population Diversity in Southern California.* Northridge, Calif.: Center for Geographical Studies. A fascinating visual exploration of Southern California's diverse population.

Davis, Mike. 1990. *City of Quartz: Excavating the Future in Los Angeles.* New York: Verso. A rough-and-tumble historical guide through the past, present, and possible future of the landscape of Los Angeles.

Dear, Michael. 2000. *The Postmodern Urban Condition.* New York: Blackwell. A fascinating look at the postmodern and global forces that are structuring our twenty-first-century megacities.

Fincher, Ruth, and Jane M. Jacobs. 1998. *Cities of Difference.* New York: Guilford Press. A series of case studies that examine the relationships between urban space and social identities and differences.

Ford, Larry. 2003. *America's New Downtowns: Revitalization or Reinvention?* Baltimore: Johns Hopkins Press. An interesting assessment of 16 contemporary American downtowns.

Harvey, David. 2003. *Paris, Capital of Modernity.* New York: Routledge, 2003. A revealing look at Paris during its mid-nineteenth-century political turmoil.

Hayden, Dolores. 2003. *Building Suburbia: Green Fields and Urban Growth, 1820–2000.* New York: Pantheon. A critical historical treatment of American suburban development.

Jacobs, Jane M. 1996. *Edge of Empire: Postcolonialism and the City.* London: Routledge. An examination of how imperialism has shaped and continues to shape cities in the developed world.

McDowell, Linda. 1997. *Capital Culture: Gender at Work in the City.* Oxford: Blackwell. An exploration of how masculinities and femininities are created within the contemporary urban workplace.

Soja, Edward W. 2000. *Postmetropolis: Critical Studies of Cities and Regions.* Oxford: Blackwell. A wide-ranging examination of the restructured form of Western megacities.

What do these images convey about empire and globalization and their connections and differences?

Two images of global reach, more than a century apart (Queen Victoria with world map; a JVC advertisement). *(Left: Enslow Publisher; Right: Eric Nash.)*

Turn to Seeing Geography on page 433 for an in-depth analysis of the above question.

ONE WORLD OR MANY?

12

The Cultural Geography of the Future

T HIS FINAL CHAPTER IS ABOUT the future. Unless one is precognizant, writing about the future is "a fool's game." The best we can do is collect evidence about past and present conditions, examine ongoing trends, and then let our imaginations go to work. Even when we do this well, it is difficult to predict the outcome of anything with certainty. Who, for example, would have thought that we would still be combating slavery and the slave trade in the twenty-first century? It is even more difficult to predict wholly new phenomena. Who would have predicted the dramatic social changes that the revolution in *information technology* is bringing about, especially the ascendance of the *World Wide Web* in daily life?

Despite the lack of certainty, looking ahead is a necessary activity if we want to be at all prepared for the world in which we will build our careers, raise our families, and work toward the fulfillment of ourselves and others. We are posing perhaps the most essential and difficult cultural geographical questions of all in this chapter. Will our future contain one world or many? Will we face a world where more people will have more opportunities and choices, or where deprivation and powerlessness will spread? Will we witness a global-scale process of cultural diversification or of homogenization? Are we headed toward a human mosaic or a human monochrome?

Some observers argue that geography is dead. They point out that every suburban strip mall, from Tucson to Terra Haute, looks identical and suggest that we are headed toward a condition of *placelessness*. They argue that globalization has led to the homogenization and standardization of landscapes around the world. For example, new middle-class housing developments in India are being modeled on North American–style suburbs, using identical architecture and street plans. In contrast, some geographers argue that the effects of globalization are highly uneven across the landscape and have not led to homogenization on a global scale. Others retain faith in the human capacity for creativity and endless innovation. New forms of cultural expression, such as Tejano, grunge, and hip-hop music, will continually spring from people's experiences in particular *places*. As these everyday examples suggest, both sides can call on plenty of evidence to back up their claims. Continued heated debate about the future is the thing we feel most confident in predicting.

Globalization: The End of Geography?

The debate over one-world-or-many hinges on *globalization*, a phenomenon that we have touched upon in almost every chapter. It is vital, therefore, that we begin our thoughts about the future with a fuller exploration of what people mean when they talk about globalization. Perhaps we can start by presenting the positions taken by geographers and then spend some time looking for common themes. Carolyn Cartier began her book on the economic growth and sociocultural transformation of South China, *Globalizing South China*, with a description of globalization. For Cartier, it includes many different cultural, economic, and political phenomena, both material and symbolic. Globalization is most closely associated with the transnational activities of large corporations, which operate sometimes in alliance with and sometimes against states.

In *Global Shift*, Peter Dicken views globalization as a complex of interrelated processes working on a global scale to produce effects that can vary greatly from place to place. He distinguishes "internationalization"—a decades- if not centuries-old practice of simply extending economic activities beyond state borders—from globalization. He explains that globalization is qualitatively different from internationalization because it involves the full integration of human activities on a global scale. Many examples of this may come to mind. Recall Chapter 9's Culture in a Globalizing World feature describing professionals in southern India conducting financial services for Wall Street firms in New York. Increasingly, globalization processes are linking far-flung places around the world in a complex, integrated system for the production, transport, and marketing of many everyday commodities

Our last view of globalization comes from R. J. Johnston, Peter Taylor, and Michael Watts's *Geographies of Global Change*. They think the most important element of globalization is the global scale of social activities. Similarly to Dicken, they differentiate between the international aspects of social interaction and globalization, arguing that the latter is constituted by "trans-state" processes. That is, under globalization, activities and outcomes "do not merely cross borders, these processes operate as if borders were not

there." They suggest that we carefully examine the processes of globalization from a "geohistorical perspective" to find out what, exactly, is different now and what the historical precedents are. This involves tracing the flow of things, people, and information through time and across spaces. It also involves identifying and explaining how specific places respond to and are transformed by globalization in different and unique ways.

You may be thinking that ideas about globalization are confusing and complicated. That's because they are! Globalization is an extremely complex and variable phenomenon involving many cultural, economic, and political processes. Globalization is a relatively recent occurrence that cultural geographers are just beginning to debate and examine. The best way for us to reach a better understanding is to look at concrete examples.

History, Geography, and the Globalization of Everything

From these ideas we can identify several defining features of globalization. First, it involves global-scale interactions among cultural, political, economic, and environmental phenomena. Second, globalization is characterized by relentless movement—a constant flow of money, people, information, ideas, goods, and services through all parts of the world. (For an example of how geographers study these movements, see Practicing Geography on page 425.) Third, the effects of globalization are felt unevenly in different places at different times. Fourth, transnational corporations are the primary institutions driving globalization. While states remain important, the relevance of international borders has diminished; several transnational corporations now have total sales greater than entire national economies (Figure 12.1). Fifth, local- and global-scale movements have formed to oppose globalization, hoping to limit or mitigate its effects. Sixth, globalization, although historically rooted in processes of internationalization, is qualitatively different.

Many scholars trace the origins of globalization to the age of European exploration and imperialism or to the *industrial revolution*. While its historical roots may run deep, globalization is a recent phenomenon. The processes of globalization first became prominent in the 1960s, when the capitalist world economy, increasingly dominated by huge multinational corporations and high technology, produced a new, efficient, and integrated system of production, marketing, transportation, communications, and information processing. Globalization functions as a single system—dynamic, yet highly organized. Globalization—unlike, say, the British Empire—has no single seat of power, and no single country can control it. In that sense, globalization repre-

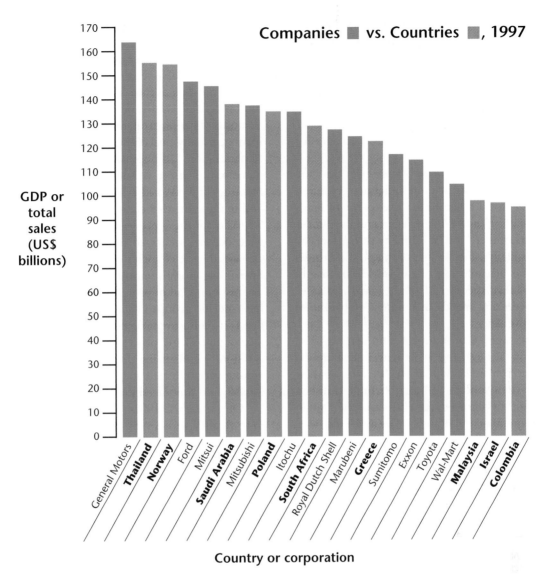

Figure 12.1 The economic power of global corporations.
The annual sales of the world's largest privately owned
corporations are greater than many countries' GDPs. How
might this affect these countries' abilities to regulate the
activities of foreign companies? *(Source: Elwood, Wayne. 2001. The
No-Nonsense Guide to Globalization. London: Verso.)*

sents something radically new and quite different from
older forms of empire.

Geographers are interested in globalization because it
bears so profoundly upon the central geographical issue of
human diversity. It produces a multitude of historically
unique, contradictory, and paradoxical cultural conditions.
The most evident paradox is that globalization—which
would seem to erase cultural difference—has been accompanied by a reassertion of distinct religious, national, and
ethnic identities. The start of the twenty-first century has
been marked by heightened ethnic divisions and conflicts,
the resurgence of nationalisms, and numerous highly visible
identity movements—gay, feminist, green, and born again.

Contradictions and paradoxes such as these lead geographers to ask whether we are headed for one world or many.

The Case for One World

Many geographers think that globalization possesses the
power to produce one world, to destroy human variety. As
long ago as 1951, before *globalization* had even entered our
vocabulary, geographer George Kimble suggested that in
the future there would be "no independent, discrete units
. . . no worlds within worlds." Half a century later, a special
issue of *National Geographic*, edited by Joel Swerdlow, was
devoted to "global culture," which would seem to confirm

Kimble's prediction of one world. It was filled with such phrases as "vanishing cultures," "a world together," and "we are all in each other's backyard." Considering the impact of globalization on place identity, James Kunstler speaks of the "geography of nowhere" and Edward Relph of "placelessness." Linda McDowell wonders whether we are "undoing place." William Greider warns of "one world, ready or not," and Pico Iyer notes that "everywhere is so made up of everywhere else."

Indeed, throughout *The Human Mosaic*, we have witnessed the transformation of folk and indigenous cultures, the spread of a few world religions at the expense of many local ones, the rise of a handful of languages and the demise of countless others, the erosion of ethnicity through acculturation and assimilation, the decline of the power of independent states, the urbanization of the world, the rise of corporate agribusiness, the spread of the *green revolution,* and other homogenizing trends that reflect globalization and undermine diversity.

Pick up a newspaper almost any day and you can read about globalization, though the word may not always be used. Ecuador and Panama adopt the U.S. dollar as their official currencies; new suburbs in India are built to resemble those in Southern California; the citizens of the United Kingdom lament membership in the European Union, worrying that the forces of globalization will erode their distinct English identity; commercial loggers deforest Rendova Island in the Solomon Islands and in the process destroy the culture and lifestyle of the native Haporai people; and so on—endlessly, it seems.

Globalization and Its Discontents

Many people view the consolidation of transnational corporate power, global environmental decline, and cultural homogenization as threatening to local livelihoods and cultural practices. We see on television and in newspapers the accounts of people from many countries and cultures participating, usually peacefully, in mass demonstrations against "globalization." In popular news accounts, we learn of antiglobalization protests, such as those trying to disrupt the meetings of the World Trade Organization in Seattle in 1999 and in Cancún, Mexico, in 2003.

Who are these protestors, what are they protesting, and what do they want? To find an answer, we need to move beyond the six o'clock news footage and front-page headlines of big, noisy demonstrations. Recognizing that there is not just one kind of protestor, we need to carefully examine how specific groups in specific locations organize to maintain local cultural practices, identities, and landscapes in the face of globalizing processes. Let us take a look at local opposition to globalizing processes in two different locations, among very different social groups: indigenous peoples in Mexico and unionized workers in New York City.

On January 1, 1994—the day that the North American Free Trade Agreement (NAFTA) between Canada, the United States, and Mexico took effect—hundreds of indigenous Mayan peasants forcibly occupied government offices in the southern Mexican state of Chiapas. Calling themselves *Zapatistas,* they declared that they had no choice but to take up arms (Figure 12.2). The impoverished Mayan

Figure 12.2 Local resistance to globalization. *Zapatista* commanders sit at the negotiating table in San Andres Larrainzar, Mexico, in 1996. The Mayan-based *Zapatista* leaders have been periodically involved in talks with the Mexican government over cultural and economic rights since NAFTA began in 1994. *(AP Photo/Scott Sady.)*

farmers saw globalization in the form of NAFTA as sounding the death knell for their culture and way of life. Globalization meant that cheap corn from the U.S. Midwest would flood Mexico, making it impossible for Mayas to continue farming for a living and to maintain their communities. Interestingly, the initial armed rebellion soon gave way to a skillful campaign that used key instruments of globalization—satellite TV and the Internet—to gain worldwide support for their campaign. The *Zapatistas* have won some concessions from the Mexican government, but their struggle to protect their culture and homeland continues. Their home page details the latest developments.

The response of the International Ladies' Garment Workers' Union (ILGWU) to globalization provides an example of protest and resistance very different from that of the *Zapatistas*. In this case, manufacturing jobs in the garment district in New York City began to disappear in the 1980s under the demands of the new global economy. At the same time, the new economy raised demand for office space and upscale urban housing, encouraging landlords to convert garment factories to more profitable spaces. Labor geographer Andrew Herod showed how the union fought job losses by lobbying for changes in the city zoning laws that would prevent the conversion of factories to high-rent offices and condos. A special garment center District was created that prohibited conversions, thereby giving the workers increased job security. The ILGWU managed to slow New York City manufacturing job losses resulting from globalization by defending the local historical urban landscape.

Many more examples of local efforts to resist globalization or at least mitigate its worst effects could be recounted. Some movements mobilize globally; others, locally. Some movements take up arms; others work through existing democratic institutions. In most cases, however, these movements are rooted in place and are expressed through local cultural values and beliefs. They all ultimately seek to gain a voice in controlling the speed and extent of globalization's transformative forces. As a consequence, the effects of globalization are not predetermined; cultural homogeneity is not the only possible outcome. Rather, the actions of local culture groups—be they made up of indigenous peoples, urban workers, or rural farmers—also shape its effects. The local-global link, it seems, operates in two directions.

Many Worlds

A careful and thoughtful student of geography might wonder whether the transnational corporations and the new systems of production, communication, marketing, and transportation really possess the power to produce one world. Does globalization truly have the ability to render cultural differences irrelevant? Can't groups of people selectively choose from what globalization has to offer and still retain their cultural identity and attachment to place (Figure 12.3)? Does globalization act to homogenize the world or, instead, to widen the differences between haves and have-nots? In fact, much of the resistance to globalization is based in the belief that it enriches and empowers the few at the expense of the many, heightening class differences.

Figure 12.3 **Australian aboriginal children at play with a laptop.** The blending of modern technology and traditional culture is increasingly common under globalization. Will such interactions enhance or reduce the world's cultural heterogeneity? (*Robert Essel NYC/Corbis.*)

Many—perhaps most—geographers believe that the future will continue to contain many worlds. They speak of profound and irreducible cultural contrasts and of the capacity of indigenous peoples to weave Western elements into their own cultures, creating new and distinct hybrids. Globalization, they argue, produces different results in different lands. The global need not and cannot abolish the regional or the local. In fact, throughout the chapter we will explore many examples of groups using the technologies and networks of globalization in campaigns that defend local cultural geographies and reassert the relevance of the local. Often local cultures are not merely defending ancient tradition but rather are interacting with outside influences to produce new and distinctive forms of cultural expression. So which view is correct or most likely? Will it be one world or many? We can gain some insight by going back to the five themes of cultural geography: region, diffusion, ecology, interaction, and landscape. What do these themes tell us about globalization?

 # Culture Regions

Are culture regions weakening and fading? Do the diverse hues of the human mosaic as revealed in maps shine less brightly than before? Can we detect any such trends, using the theme of culture region? Some geographers look at the maps and do indeed see fading colors. David Nemeth, for example, suggests that regions are "being crushed and recycled into a bland, ambiguous amalgam," producing "something akin to a vast parking lot of global scale." And without question, people in all parts of the world must seek a new form of self-identity, torn as they are between their traditional attachment to place and local culture on the one hand and their inevitable attraction to globalization-driven cosmopolitanism on the other. They feel the opposite tugs of hearth (region) and cosmos (world).

The Uneven Geography of Globalization

Most cultural geographers, by contrast, believe that culture regions will persist. In particular, the familiar *core-periphery* concept is just as relevant as ever. Globalization, it seems, is not a geographically even process. Some regions—forming the core—are moving ahead and prospering, while many others—the periphery—fall further and further behind. Global interdependence has not evened out the differences between the haves and have-nots; in many ways it increases them. There is now a transnational class of the super-rich, the 0.25 percent of the world's population that owns as much wealth as the other 99.75 percent. Most of them live in a First World core consisting of Anglo-America, the European

Union (EU), the coastal zone of East Asia, and Australia-New Zealand. As the greatest beneficiaries of globalizing processes, these regions are moving ahead of the remaining Third World peripheral lands.

Not all observers, however, agree that the global income gap is widening. In a recent study, *The New Geography of Global Inequality*, Glenn Firebaugh argues that careful analysis contradicts the widespread belief that world core-periphery differences are increasing. This belief, he points out, is based on the fact that the incomes of the richest nations are increasing at a greater rate than those of the poorest. Yet this overlooks another fact: the many countries that are falling behind contain only 10 percent of the world's population while those few that are closing the gap (mostly Asian countries) contain more than 40 percent. Taking national population numbers into account, global income gaps are in fact decreasing.

In the meantime, income gaps *within* nation-state boundaries are growing rapidly. Instead of core-periphery, another way to think about the unevenness of globalization is in terms of "fast" and "slow" worlds. The fast world is fully wired for the Internet; located in the world's megacities; adaptable to rapid shifts in global trends of investment, trade, production, and consumption; and home to the transnational super-rich. The slow world consists of the hollowed-out rural landscapes, declining or abandoned manufacturing zones, and slums and shantytowns. Little pieces of the periphery that lie adjacent to the core, such as Mexico's northern border, scramble to join the privileged part of the world, to be fast rather than slow. As Mexico's border cities' recent experience with job loss to China demonstrates, for such regions, membership in the fast world can be fleeting.

British geographer Rob Shields, in *Places on the Margin*, concentrates on an array of places and regions, of varying geographical extent, that have been "left behind in the modern race for progress." He finds peripheries even within the core. Often these places and regions become sites of illicit or stigmatized activities, such as the international trades in sex and illegal drugs. Says Shields, such "margins become signifiers of everything centers deny or repress."

Tragically, these places on the margin are key sites in the international trafficking of slave labor. Slavery, it turns out, is not a shameful practice consigned to the distant past, but an increasing phenomenon under globalization. Some believe that as many as 27 million people live in slavery worldwide, on every continent in the world save Antarctica. Traffickers prey on the most desperate and powerless of globalization's castoffs. In the United States, California, Texas, and Florida lead the way in the increase in slave labor cases. Some of Florida's famous orange juice, for example, was recently found to be harvested by illegal Mexican immigrants held against their wills in remote rural camps. The insatiable international demand for Brazil's timber and beef has been met through the labor of captive workers held deep in the Amazon. Labor recruiters in Brazilian cities lure jobless workers to cut remote forestlands through false promises of good wages and housing. Once there, workers' wages are withheld and they are prevented from leaving. Some are forced to work for years clearing forests to make way for cattle ranching. According to one Brazilian labor official, "slave labor in Brazil is directly linked to deforestation." The uneven distribution of the benefits of globalization is one, but not the only, way in which culture regions are maintained.

One Europe or Many?

Looking at just one small part of the world, geographer Ray Hudson echoes our question: "One Europe or many?" Local identities are asserting themselves within states, suggesting many culture regions, at the same time that supranationalism is touted as the path to "one Europe." He opts decidedly for "many," concluding that power and wealth will not be evenly distributed geographically within Europe and that one main role of the European Union should be to promote "complex geographies of identities."

A similar outlook leads geographer Michael Keating to speak of a "new regionalism" in Europe, and David Hooson goes so far as to suggest that globalization actually *strengthens* people's bond between place and identity. This strengthening is suggested by the rise of ethnic separatism in countries as diverse as Spain, the United Kingdom, and Serbia & Montenegro. The recent expansion of the EU is likely to bring a host of unintended and surprising outcomes for culture regions. In some former Soviet territories, for example, ethnic Russian immigrants have become a disadvantaged minority group. New post-Soviet states have used their membership in the EU to reassert national ethnic heritage and redefine themselves culturally as "Western."

Glocalization

The theme of culture region, then, seems to suggest that a new human mosaic is forming in the age of globalization. Rapid change is pervasive, but its direction differs from one location to the next. The future will not be like the past, but it will also not be monochromatic. As geographers Jessie Poon, Edmund Thompson, and Philip Kelly say, "opposed forces are operating simultaneously," producing new constellations of places and regions. These forces pit local against global, and the important thing is that the results differ from one region to another.

The interaction between global and local prompted geographer Erik Swyngedouw to promote the term **glocalization** to describe the consequences (see Focus On: Glocalization Comes to Nunavut). In brief, he argues that the outcome of this interaction involves change both in the regional way of life *and* in the globalizing force. For example, transnational corporations often have to adapt their product lines to local norms and preferences or adjust their production practices to local labor and environmental laws. Put differently, glocalization is a process that ensures the survival of culture regions and places in the future. These considerations, prompted by the culture region theme, lead us to conclude that a planetary culture is almost certainly illusory and that potent forces are at work to prevent homogenization.

The Geography of the Internet

Has the Internet rendered geography or culture regions obsolete? The Net is widely perceived "as being everywhere, yet nowhere in particular." That is how *The Economist* described it in its 2001 special report on the subject, "Geography and the Internet." The Internet can cross borders, both political and cultural; it breaks down barriers; it

---

FOCUS ON

Glocalization Comes to Nunavut

Zacharias Kunuk, 44, is an Inuit living at the village of Igloolik, well north of the Arctic Circle in Canada's Nunavut Territory (see Chapter 5). He knows and practices many of the traditional folkways. Kunuk prefers to live in the tundra, among his people. He believes in shamans and their powers.

But Kunuk also makes movies. His film *Atanarjuat* (*The Fast Runner*) uses Inuit actors speaking only Inuktitut and tells a traditional folktale. It is also about identity and cultural survival. The film won several prizes, including one at the Cannes Film

Festival in France, and in 2002 it was shown in Europe, Canada, Australia, and the United States.

Kunuk daily uses e-mail and the Internet and makes long-distance telephone calls. He has access to a bank ATM. But he is just as likely to go out on his snowmobile and hunt seals. Kunuk finds no difficulty in "picking and choosing from distinct cultures as if they were platters on a buffet." This interaction between global and local culture epitomizes glocalization.

Source: Kraus, 2002

Internet Connections

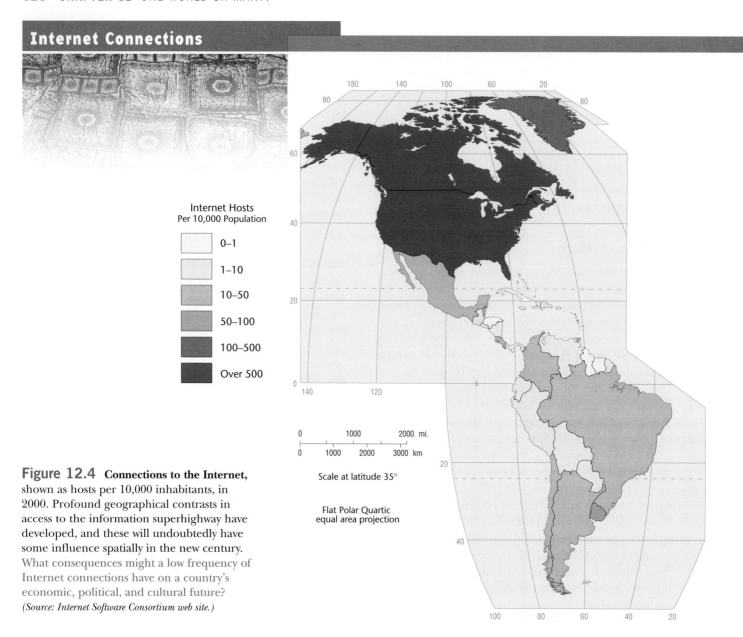

Internet Hosts
Per 10,000 Population

	0–1
	1–10
	10–50
	50–100
	100–500
	Over 500

0   1000   2000 mi.
0   1000   2000   3000 km

Scale at latitude 35°

Flat Polar Quartic
equal area projection

Figure 12.4 Connections to the Internet, shown as hosts per 10,000 inhabitants, in 2000. Profound geographical contrasts in access to the information superhighway have developed, and these will undoubtedly have some influence spatially in the new century. What consequences might a low frequency of Internet connections have on a country's economic, political, and cultural future? *(Source: Internet Software Consortium web site.)*

eliminates the effects of distance. *The Economist*'s "The Revenge of Geography," its updated 2003 report in *The Economist Technology Quarterly,* draws the opposite conclusion. Perhaps it was naive of people to think that the Internet would make geography irrelevant. Geography is "far from dead," *The Economist* concludes.

The reality of the Internet's influence is very complex and ultimately leaves culture regions intact. In truth, the Internet is much "constrained by the realities of geography." Rather than making national borders irrelevant, the Internet can now be screened, censored, regulated, and blocked by governments. Moreover, the fiber-optic cables of the Internet have a location, and in fact the whole enter-

prise remains largely city-bound. A high-speed digital subscriber line requires proximity to a telephone exchange. As the 2003 *Economist* report sums up, "so much for the borderless internet."

Internet companies are currently developing new strategies and technologies to address the importance of culture regions. For example, the focus of Internet businesses is now on *geolocation* technology, which in essence serves to link together the virtual and actual worlds. Companies now offer services that enable web sites to establish the geographic location of users. In addition, so-called hotspots—those locations where wireless Internet connections are available to passersby—are being mapped out

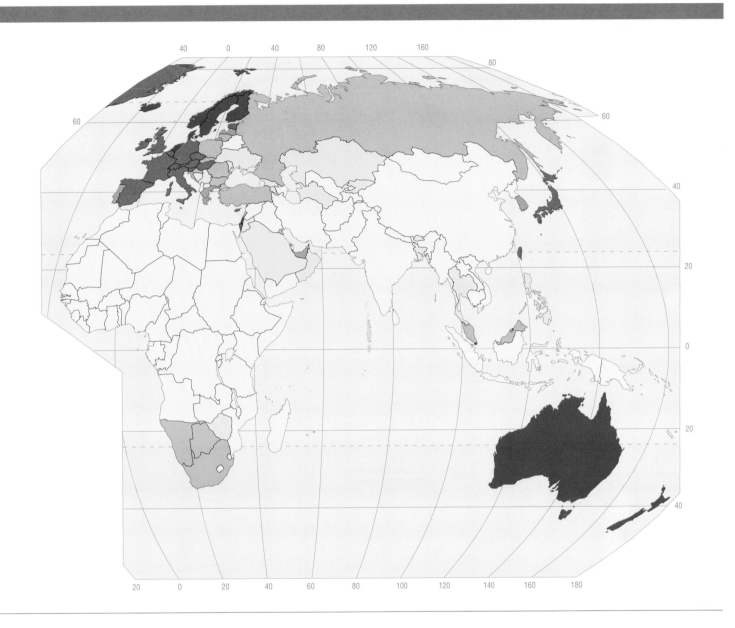

in color codes that indicate the relative strength of the connection. In some cases there have been local citizen initiatives to chalk-mark hotspot locations on walls and sidewalks, revealing the sites where the parallel worlds converge. We are finding that the Internet does not eliminate regional cultural differences but rather serves to connect multiple worlds, both actual and virtual.

Some observers suggest that the very computer systems that drive and power globalization have produced culture regions of their own, perhaps even entirely new kinds of places. Many of the words and phrases we use to describe the Internet imply that it possesses a geography: *cyberspace,* the *virtual community, cyberhood, cyberbia,* and even *virtual geography,* to mention a few. The Internet connects not just two points but *all* points, creating a new sort of "virtual" place in the process.

We might ask, as John Barlow does, "is there a *there* in cyberspace?" Does the Internet contain a geography at all? Certainly, *places*—at least as understood by cultural geographers—cannot be created on the Internet. For starters, these "virtual places" lack a cultural landscape and a cultural ecology. In the broader context, on a worldwide scale, human diversity is poorly portrayed in cyberspace. "Old people, poor people, the illiterate, and the continent of Africa" seem not to be "there," as Barlow notes (Figure 12.4). Users usually end up "meeting" others pretty much like themselves on the

Diffusion of the Internet

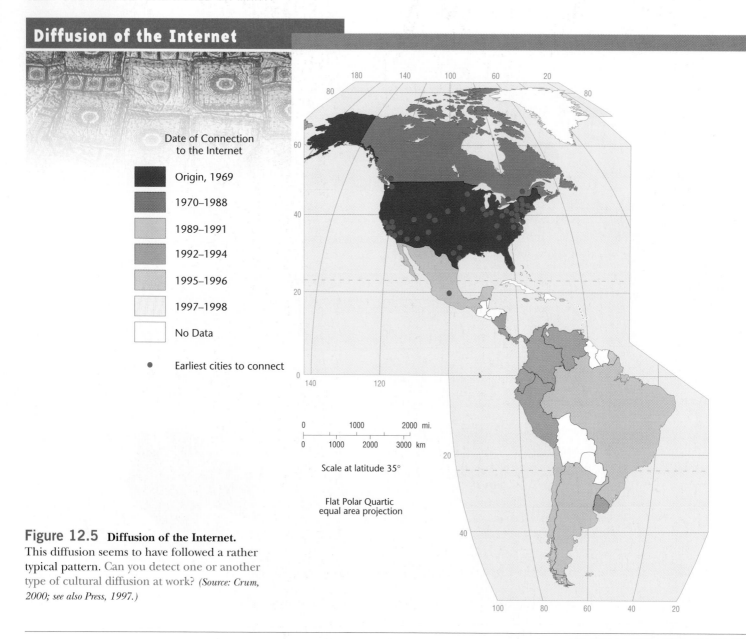

Date of Connection
to the Internet

■ Origin, 1969

■ 1970–1988

□ 1989–1991

■ 1992–1994

■ 1995–1996

□ 1997–1998

□ No Data

● Earliest cities to connect

0   1000   2000 mi.
0   1000   2000   3000 km

Scale at latitude 35°

Flat Polar Quartic
equal area projection

Figure 12.5 **Diffusion of the Internet.**
This diffusion seems to have followed a rather
typical pattern. Can you detect one or another
type of cultural diffusion at work? (*Source: Crum,
2000; see also Press, 1997.*)

Internet. More important, the breath and spirit of place cannot exist in cyberspace. Barlow, resorting to a Hindu term,
calls this missing essence *prana.* These are not real places,
nor can they ever be.

Other critics point out that virtual communities do not
have the defining qualities of geographic communities: communion among citizens, shared responsibilities, and civic
duty. Communication across the Internet does not a community make. Nevertheless, people can use virtual communities
to establish bonds that carry over into the real world. To keep
things in historical perspective, we should remember that
throughout the modern period families and individuals have
left their geographic communities and dispersed widely.
However, these people have constructed social networks to
maintain cultural and emotional ties with their geographic

communities of origin. From this perspective we might view
the Internet as just another vehicle for maintaining those ties
and preserving cultural identities.

 **Cultural Diffusion**

**Is the theme of cultural diffusion relevant to the debate over
"one world or many"?** Almost certainly it is. Economic and
industrial diffusion in many ways define globalization. The
computer, the Internet, satellite television, compact discs,
and other globally available technologies greatly facilitate
access to and the diffusion of ideas and information, while
also accelerating their spread. At the same time, the spread

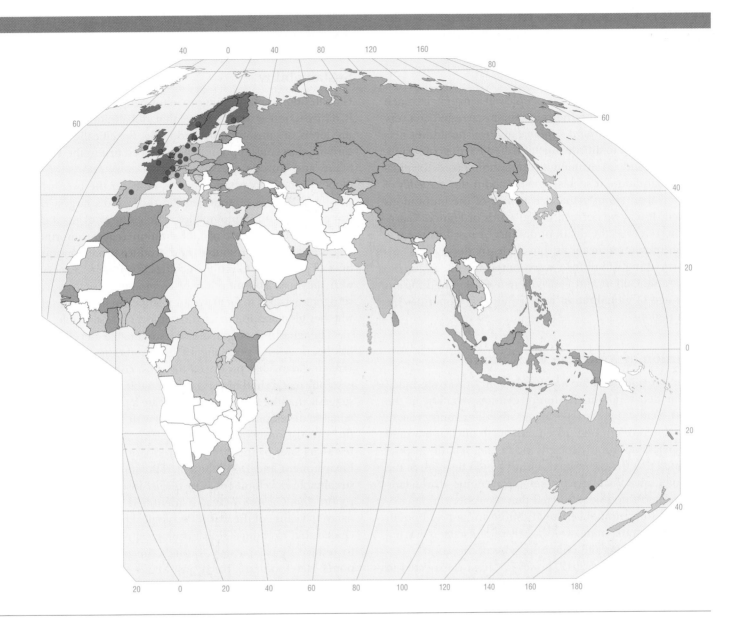

of new ideas and innovations often produces disruptions that change the world in unexpected and unintended ways. At the very least, the theme of cultural diffusion cautions us against counting on predetermined outcomes.

The Information Superhighway

Terms such as *information superhighway* and *infobahn* imply the enhanced ability to achieve cultural diffusion. Moreover, the use of more efficient transportation systems, such as containerized cargo units, has greatly increased "the spatial dispersion of the production and consumption of economic goods," in the words of geographer Christopher Airriess.

The spread of democracy has accompanied the more rapid diffusion of information, goods, and services in the age

of globalization. Dictatorships thrive by controlling and manipulating information—an increasingly difficult task in the age of the Internet. And the Internet is certainly not the only means by which information spreads rapidly. Cellular telephones, satellite-beamed cable television, and news channels such as CNN contribute to the diffusion of information, as does the increased volume of international travelers.

Diffusion of the Internet

The theme of cultural diffusion also applies to the spread of the Internet itself. If the future is to bring the universal diffusion of cultural elements, then surely this new homogenizing tendency ought to be revealed in the spread of this most essential element of globalization (Figure 12.5). The diffusion of the Internet has now spread across much of the world, obeying the models set down in Chapter 1.

But although the Internet now reaches into almost every land, its use varies profoundly (compare Figures 12.4 and 12.5). Just because an innovation is available does not mean that most or even many people will accept it. In much of the world, use of the Internet remains arrested at a very early phase of *hierarchical diffusion,* and we should not necessarily expect it to diffuse much further. Barriers of wealth, education, and governmental opposition prove formidable. Globalization, it seems, is more about the *possibility* of diffusion than about actual acceptance of the innovations diffused. It may be correct, in the words of Frances Cairncross, to refer to "the death of distance" caused by the revolution in communications, but it clearly does not follow that everything will diffuse everywhere. Indeed, as geographers Anne Gilbert and Paul Villeneuve ask, will diffusion in the age of globalization instead "amplify disparities between regions"?

Diffusion of American Car Culture

Back in the middle of the twentieth century, there was much popular debate about the future of transportation in the United States. People speculated that anything from a national network of high-speed railways to nuclear-powered flying machines would replace automobiles. Hardly anyone predicted that the twenty-first century would be more of the same old thing: the internal combustion engine–driven family car. Almost no one predicted that the American fascination with the automobile would diffuse to East and South Asia, which, at that time, were largely rural, facing recurring famine, and among the poorest regions of the world.

Between now and 2012, however, China is expected to account for 18 percent of the growth in worldwide auto sales. India, while expected to account for only 9 percent of the growth, will not be far behind the expected 11 percent of the United States. American auto manufacturers are scrambling to get a foothold in China, the world's hottest car market. Carmakers are betting that the symbolic importance of the luxury automobile will diffuse to these regions of East and South Asia. It appears as though a prime status symbol in American middle-class culture is poised to become the same for a new global middle class (see Culture in a Globalizing World).

 **Cultural Ecology**

How is the theme of cultural ecology related to the question of "one world or many"? The central issue is the impact of

globalization processes on ecosystems and local communities worldwide.

Sustainability

Globalization is many things to many people. Love it or hate it, desire it or fear it, most agree that globalization means rising levels of consumption worldwide. Specifically, the cultures of mass consumption that developed first in the United States and Europe are spreading to every corner of the globe. China is a case in point. As we enter the twenty-first century, China is or soon will be the world's largest consumer of coal and automobiles. The cultures of mass consumption at the heart of globalization require enormous amounts of natural resources and produce prodigious quantities of pollutants. Given the ecological problems associated with the mass consumption of commodities such as cars, refrigerators, and so forth, we are compelled to ask ourselves whether globalization in its current form is sustainable.

The question of global-scale sustainable development has been around since the 1970s. Cambridge geographer William Adams has produced the most comprehensive and carefully researched history of sustainable development. He suggests that the first attempt to create a plan for global sustainable development came in 1980 with the publication of the World Conservation Strategy. This idea was refined a few years later by the UN-sponsored World Commission on Environment and Development. The commission brought sustainable development into the mainstream through its report *Our Common Future.* It identified poverty as a fundamental cause of the world's ecological problems and concluded that to reduce global ecological problems, we need to reduce global poverty through the promotion of economic development. Today, just about everyone from the barefoot tree hugger to the well-heeled international bank executive advocates sustainable development.

But let us take a closer look at this "mainstream" approach to sustainable development. In essence it says that the geographic expansion of the Western model of economic growth is the cure for both global poverty and ecological problems. However, while globalization has brought new prosperity and higher levels of consumption to some parts of the world, ecological problems only seem to be increasing. China's rising coal consumption has led to increased emissions of carbon dioxide, a leading greenhouse gas. It is now second only to the United States in total greenhouse gas emissions. Furthermore, as we noted previously, the rewards of globalization are distributed unevenly, with the majority of poor people remaining poor and only a few people becoming richer.

Some observers conclude that the term *sustainable development* is an oxymoron. Given the ecological record of mod-

CULTURE IN A GLOBALIZING WORLD

China's New Car Culture

For most of his 70 years, You Xiaoyi pedaled his bike to work in one of China's state-run factories. Following the country's efforts to boost economic growth by shifting to private enterprise, he became a factory owner himself. Now he's driving himself to work in a brand-new Volkswagen Jetta, having passed on the Buicks and Audis that he test-drove.

Well-heeled new capitalists like You are turning China into the hottest car market in the world. China is now the third-largest market and is poised to become the second-largest, behind only the United States. General Motors is moving into China in a big way, having introduced its Cadillac line in June 2004 with the hope of capitalizing on the wealth of the new middle class. Along with five other of the largest carmakers, GM is committed to investing $17 billion to build new factories in China in anticipation of rising demand.

General Motors and the other carmakers are counting on the winners in China's phenomenal economic expansion to adopt the ultimate status symbol of the middle class. Just a decade ago, the notion that the expansion of global car sales would be driven by a Chinese version of American car culture was unthinkable. Then only state bureaucrats bought cars and had only six models from which to choose. Now there are 90 models on the market and businessmen like You, flush with profits from the economic boom, are paying cash. China's new millionaires have adopted the "Beemer," the Yuppie status symbol of the go-go 1980s in the United States, as their own. They have made China the world's number one market for BMW's 760Li model.

General Motors Corporation launches its Cadillac line at the 2004 Beijing Auto Show. What brand name better symbolizes America's car culture than Cadillac? China's nouveaux riches will now enjoy urban gridlock in grand American style. *(Ng Han Gua/AP Photo.)*

The stiff competition with BMW, Audi, and others for the hearts and minds of middle-class consumers pushed GM to pull out all the stops in launching its Cadillac luxury line. The company descended on the 2004 Beijing Auto Show with a dazzling ceremony, staged by filmmaker Ang Lee. If autos are any indication, it looks like cultural diffusion is as important as ever under globalization.

Source: Naughton, 2004

ern industrialization, the faith in economic growth as a cure for environmental ills seems misplaced (Figure 12.6). Cultural and political ecologists have been strong critics of mainstream sustainable development. They claim that the sustainable development idea does not take into account the larger-scale historical and structural causes of poverty, such as the lasting effects of European colonialism Unless these are addressed, it is unlikely that mainstream sustainable development will substantially decrease poverty levels. A further criticism is that the focus on the link between poverty and ecological degradation downplays the environmental impact from high levels of consumption in affluent countries. For instance, Americans alone consume one-fourth of the world's petroleum output and generate one-fourth of the carbon dioxide pollution.

One suggested alternative is to formulate sustainable development "from below" rather than through a top-down global program. The idea is to assist local initiatives and employ local knowledge to craft different economic paths for developing countries and communities that will not degrade land and resources along the way to higher living standards. Such alternatives, because they are informed by the communities they most immediately concern, would also be designed to maintain cultural identities, landscapes, and regions. Across the globe there are now hundreds of such efforts, which go by a variety of titles, such as "community

Figure 12.6 **Mountaintop mining in West Virginia.** Landscapes and ecosystems are permanently altered to meet the industrial demand for increasing amounts of fossil fuels. A popular technique in "sustainable" coal mining involves the removal of entire mountaintops to access the deposit. *(Vivian Stockman.)*

conservation," "joint forest management," and "indigenous peoples' reserves." Approaching sustainable development from below means that the future will be defined by cultural heterogeneity, not homogenization.

Think Globally, Act Locally

Perhaps sustainable development from below can mitigate widespread poverty while minimizing the ecological degradation that accompanies many top-down development initiatives. But what about the environmental effects of modern affluence—how can those be addressed? Throughout the 1990s a series of international conferences were held that sought to identify the world's most pressing environmental problems and propose global-scale initiatives to address them. The most prominent of these was the United Nations Conference on Environment and Development, held in Rio de Janeiro in 1992. Now known simply as the Rio Conference, it produced international conventions that sought to reduce global ecological problems such as species extinction and global warming. The most prominent of these was the Convention on Biological Diversity. The Biodiversity Convention committed signatory states to protecting wildlife habitats and pursuing economic development policies that minimize species loss.

The approach taken at the Rio Conference is best captured in the slogan "think globally, act locally." If we plan carefully, actions taken at the local scale in places around the world will collectively result in an improved global environment. For example, the establishment of local parks and reserves will provide a global network of protected habitats that will help to maintain the Earth's biodiversity.

The recent introduction of hybrid cars—vehicles that combine traditional fossil-fuel engines with electric motors to greatly reduce gas consumption and pollution—are another case in point. When the state of California passed a law requiring 10 percent of all car sales to be hybrids, it forced carmakers to produce more fuel-efficient cars. Since California is the largest car market in the United States, its action has had ripple effects nationwide and, ultimately, worldwide. China is now promoting hybrid cars for its burgeoning market, and several of the new auto factories will produce hybrids. These local- and national-level initiates should help considerably in reducing global levels of carbon dioxide and other pollutants.

 Cultural Interaction

Can we learn something about the one-world-or-many debate from the theme of cultural interaction? One of globalization's greatest impacts has been to accelerate and expand the level of interaction within and among culture regions.

The Internet allows ideas, music, artwork, and indeed any form of cultural expression that can be turned into digital data to be transmitted around the world in a matter of seconds. The circulation of people and things, although it takes considerably longer, can nonetheless reach virtually any part of the globe in only a matter of hours or days. With the development of the Internet and rapid global transportation systems, transnational corporations are able to advertise, market, and deliver virtually anywhere. Every *Fortune* 500 company now has its own web site, allowing them

PRACTICING GEOGRAPHY

Susan Mains

(Courtesy of Susan Mains.)

Cultural geographer Susan Mains gets around. Raised in Scotland, educated in Kentucky, and now a member of the faculty at the Department of Geography and Geology at the University of West Indies-Mona in Kingston, Jamaica, she personifies the curious, itinerant geographer. In fact, being able to "learn about and travel to new places" was one of the things that influenced her to study geography as an undergraduate.

Perhaps an even more powerful motivation for practicing cultural geography was her desire to understand the rapid changes in the landscape and social life of Uddingston (her hometown) that she witnessed growing up. In nearby Glasgow she was exposed to a very dynamic urban, political, and artistic landscape. "Glasgow has a long history of trade unionism, social activism, and community theater," she explains. "The arts have been a forum for expressing and affecting political change in the city for many years, and I became increasingly intrigued by the links between the social, architectural, and artistic changes that were taking place."

Her research and teaching constantly provide her with opportunities to experience new cultures and places or to experience familiar landscapes in unfamiliar ways. Even when just "having a lime" ("hanging out" in Jamaican) with her students after class, she discovers new ideas and ways of thinking about landscapes and cultural change. Her research and teaching provide her with opportunities to address topics of deep personal concern for her, such as social justice and social exclusion. "As a cultural geographer, I believe it is important to think reflexively about what we explore and to try to empathize with people and cultures whose experiences may be different from our own, for example, refugees, political prisoners, sites of civil unrest, children, and various recipients of discrimination."

Professor Mains found in cultural geography an academic discipline in which she could fully utilize her many talents and interests. She has strong interests in analyzing and producing documentary films, both of which she has incorporated into her research. Of her study of Jamaican migration, she explains that "I collected census data outlining the characteristics of migration, and I've been watching film and television footage (from the 1950s to the present) that addresses the topic of West Indians in the United Kingdom. I also . . . analyze key imagery, language, and themes addressed—and omitted—in media coverage." She combines film analysis with a wide range of other methods, such as open-ended interviews, the analysis of historical archives, and the analysis of demographic data.

Her current research explores the experiences of Jamaican migrants to New York, London, and Toronto, and of those who return to the island. "I'm examining what makes people decide to move," she explains, "what their experiences are like during that process and, once they are living overseas, how they keep in touch with Jamaica." As part of the study she is making a documentary film that will feature interviews with research participants and events organized by various Jamaican communities. On completing this project, she hopes to "give something back" to her Jamaican participants by providing access to her results through her web site and the distribution of the film. With committed and creative scholars like Professor Mains entering the field, the future of cultural geography is assured.

to market cultural products directly to consumers in every corner of the globe. What's more, nongovernmental organizations, art museums, indigenous peoples, individual artists and musicians, and just about all imaginable culture groups or producers of culture have their own web sites. Globalization clearly has the potential to profoundly alter the speed and character of cultural interaction, but to what effect is an open question.

The Place(s) of the Global Tourist

Arguably the most common face-to-face interactions between distantly located cultures will take place in the twenty-first century through people's participation in the global tourism industry. By some estimates, tourism is or soon will be the largest industry in the world, second only to oil as the most important source of revenue for the Third World. Cultural geographers are increasingly interested in understanding this phenomenon, as exemplified in the volume *Leisure/Tourism Geographies* edited by David Crouch. What sort of cultural interactions will take place under global tourism? Will the end result be the preservation, conversion, or elimination of distinct culture regions?

As with many globalized cultural interactions, there are distinct differences in power that are important to structuring the tourist encounter. The most glaring inequality is that between the visiting and visited cultures. The vast majority of global tourists originate in the First World. The cultures visited are often located in the marginalized sites of the global economy, such as on the famed African safaris or the spring-break excursions to Cancún, Mexico.

The global tourist industry presumes the existence of unique places that appear "exotic" to the Westerner—or at least serve to emphasize the difference between the experience of home and the experience of the travel destination. Tourism can thus be a double-edged sword. On the one hand, there is an imperative to preserve and nurture folk and indigenous cultures, and, on the other, an imperative to merely create the illusion of cultural difference (Figure 12.7). Some cultural geographers have concluded from these observations that tourism conforms to the tastes of the affluent global tourist and so results in an "inauthentic" experience of place.

It would be wrong, however, to simply view local cultures as "made up" or "invented" by the global tourism industry or to suggest that only inauthentic cultural interactions are possible. Geographers Peggy Teo and Lim Hiong Li's study of global and local interactions at a tourist site in Singapore—a former private mansion and fantasy garden—provides an excellent case in point. They favor the view that local groups can use the forces of global tourism to strengthen their cultural identities and traditions. Their study focused on a government-sponsored effort to create from the mansion and garden an "Oriental Disneyland," a Western-style theme park loosely based on Disney's technologically enhanced tourist attractions. Teo and Li found that

after the venture failed, local people successfully lobbied the government to redesign the site to more closely replicate its original condition. The motivation behind these efforts was to defend local cultural and historical meanings associated with the site. They conclude that "the global does not annihilate the local." Rather, tourism can result in "unique outcomes in different locations."

World Music

Whatever your tastes, if you buy music CDs, you will likely have run into a category titled "world music." The implicit suggestion of this title is that there is a pan-global sound, a musical genre that unites us all. On closer inspection of such CDs, it might be more accurate to call it "music of the (non-Western) world." In fact, this label better reflects the 1960s origins of the term among academics who wanted to raise the cultural status of non-Western musical traditions and diversify Western conservatories. World music, then, is an everything-but term: all musical forms but Western. A variety of other labels—such as "folk," "primitive," "tribal," "ethnic," and "traditional"—were subsumed by the category of "world music."

Some cultural geographers have celebrated the idea of a world music culture while others have been repelled by the thought of a homogenized global soundscape. As far back as 1973 geographer William Bunge predicted that the future would produce a "world culture of international youth" with "African music and dance forms" likely to provide the dominant ingredient in a globalized musical mix. A response from geographer Donald Fryer bemoaned the neglect of Western classical music traditions and the bland homogenization of music driven by a profit-motivated industry.

In the era of globalization, many consumers have come to associate world music with Western pop stars who collaborate with non-Western musicians and experiment with non-Western musical genres. Established performers such as Paul Simon, who recorded with South African musicians in 1986 for *Graceland*, and David Byrne, who recorded *Rei Momo* with Latin American musicians in 1989, were key in launching a global market for world music. Many other musicians have followed, enough so that in 1991 a world music category was created for the Grammy awards. In most cases musicians such as Simon and Byrne share royalties with Third World musicians, whose individual careers are often boosted by the exposure to new audiences and markets that collaboration can bring.

The emergence of world music as an identifiable commodity cannot be separated from the global expansion of the entertainment industry, which is increasingly controlled by a few large multinational corporations. This is not to say that economic forces have determined the content of world music. In *The Place of Music*, geographers Andrew Leyshon,

Figure 12.7 Global tourism and local culture. Tourists line up to photograph a colorfully dressed "native." What do such encounters suggest about the effects of global tourism on local cultures? *(AP World Wide Photos.)*

David Matless, and George Revill explain that transnational corporations are trading on local creativity and thus need to avoid homogenizing the global soundscape. "The majors are reliant on the global-local interplay of economic and cultural processes," they observe. It is also important to note that not all world music is distributed by large multinationals. Many small independent CD labels are involved. So far world music has not produced a single, homogenous sound but rather serves to circulate diverse sounds globally. Access to world music results in a cultural interaction that stimulates local creativity to produce new musical genres formed in place, which corporations in turn "discover" and circulate as new cultural innovations for commercial consumption.

There is a dark side to treating cultural and cross-cultural innovations as no more than a means to further economic gains. It follows from the kinds of unequal relations of power that inflect these interactions. Copyright laws and teams of lawyers back transnational corporate interests and protect their property rights. Many local cultures are often unaware of their rights and in many cases have no say in how their music is appropriated and profited from. Critics suggest that world music is more about the fame of the Western musicians and less about celebrating the creativity and protecting the cultural property rights of local people. Too much emphasis, they claim, is placed on the Western musician "discovering" the authentic tribal rhythm or melody and too little on the collaborative interactions between cultures (Figure 12.8).

In spite of such concerns, it is actually fairly difficult to find a truly "authentic" or "pure" locally bound musical genre. Distinctive regional sounds, such as Memphis soul or Tibetan throat singing, can definitely be identified. In many cases these musical genres are associated with culture regions. At the same time, musical genres rarely develop in geographic isolation. Cultural interaction has produced all manner of blending of ideas, styles, and genres—probably since the time humans began imitating the rhythms and sounds of nature. Modern technological innovations, from the invention of the gramophone to the release of online file-sharing software, have accelerated, intensified, and added to the complexity of cultural interaction.

Take the case of soukous, a musical genre centered in Africa's Congo River basin. Soukous originated in the folk music and dance traditions of various Congolese ethnic groups. Some of these performers began to adopt Western instruments and jazz arrangements during the Belgian colonial period of the early twentieth century. As the population urbanized in the 1950s, record companies found a burgeoning market and began importing Cuban "rumba" 78 rpm vinyl recordings. These "Latin" rhythms were incorporated and helped launch soukous as the first pan-African sound. It is interesting to note that this transfer was part of a historical process of multidirectional diffusion, since the rhythms

Figure 12.8 **World music and Western performers.** This cartoon originally appeared in *Spy Magazine*. The original caption, "On a search for new musical inspiration, David Byrne unexpectedly runs into Paul Simon," is a comment on the nature of Western musicians' relationship to local musicians. Are these relationships collaborative or exploitative? (*Reproduced by permission of Lawrence Rose for* Spy Magazine.)

imported from Cuba originated among African slave laborers who had carried them from West Africa a century earlier. Congolese musicians were given record contracts and brought to Paris studios, where they continue to blend new sounds and techniques and pump out the pulsing soukous beat for the world music scene. One can get dizzy just trying to keep track of the many multidirectional pathways of cultural interaction across time and space.

Cultural interaction in music has been ongoing for centuries but has been greatly speeded up and geographically expanded under globalization. From one perspective, globalization has sparked a creative cultural interaction by mixing musical traditions from around the world to produce new hybrid forms, many of which are highly localized. As a result, new and innovative regionally based soundscapes emerge continuously, reinforcing old or helping to construct new culture regions. From another perspective, globalization has enriched First World transnational entertainment corporations without providing due compensation for the creative labor of local cultures.

The debate over which perspective best reflects the actual effects of globalization on music is complex and will undoubtedly continue. Of course, music is only one arena of cultural interaction affected by globalization. Food, clothing, and language, to mention only a few, are all important subjects for geographers investigating cultural interaction in a globalizing world.

Cultural Landscape

Is the debate over whether the future will reflect one world or many visible? Can we get some clue about the outcome by observing the cultural landscape under globalization? Of course we can. Philip Kelly even speaks of "landscapes of globalization" (Figure 12.9).

Globalized Landscapes

Geographer David Keeling sought visible evidence of globalization in the landscape of Buenos Aires, Argentina—the capital of a country that desperately wants to become enmeshed in the world economy but struggles, perhaps in vain, against its peripheral location. He found abundant evidence of "a homogenized landscape" of glass-and-steel corporate office towers, of luxury hotels and conference centers for the economic power brokers, of megamalls and supermarkets. Global capitalism further announced its presence in neon signs projecting corporate brand names into the southern night.

Clearly, urban landscapes—cityscapes—can serve as an index to the level and type of engagement with the globalization process. We have now begun witnessing the diffusion of California-style suburban housing tracts to affluent regions of India. Still, Keeling notes, these homogenizing processes are neither omnipresent nor omnipotent. Certain other Latin American capitals—such as Quito, Ecuador; La Paz, Bolivia; and Havana, Cuba—reveal minimal global influences in their cityscapes. Given the improbability of a global culture, visible differences among cities seem likely to persist. Moreover, people all over the world value their cultural landscapes, whether as visual reminders of their heritage or as lucrative attractions in the global tourism industry, and will thus want to preserve them. Landscape and place still matter in a globalizing world.

Striving for the Unique

Urban landscapes in the age of globalization reveal another element: the enduring spirit of place. One city after another has preserved or erected some building or monument so unique as to be a symbol or icon of that particular city. When you see a photograph of this structure, you know at once where it is located (Figure 12.10). Television journalists often stand in front of such visible icons to convince viewers that they are actually reporting on site. Examples would include the opera house in Sydney, Australia; the arch linking east and west in St. Louis; the Space Needle in Seattle; and the Eiffel Tower in Paris. True, many or most of these icons predate the era of globalization, but that is not the issue. Rather, their retention and protection offer the relevant message. The Kremlin walls in Moscow may retain few if any of their original red bricks, as they fall victim to weathering and are replaced, but the structure is renewed and endures as a symbol of the city.

Neolocalism is the desire evident in many local communities to reembrace the uniqueness and authenticity of *place*. Governments and electorates at all levels—from local to national—have a far bigger say about globalization than you might imagine. A backlash against chain stores and con-

Figure 12.9 **Granville Square, Canada Place, and the Waterfront Centre Hotel,** a luxury complex designed for international business conferences, in Vancouver, British Columbia, Canada. Globalization has produced such complexes in many cities and countries. *(Gunter Marx Photography/Corbis.)*

Figure 12.10 **The opera house at Sydney, Australia,** has become a symbol for the city. Its unique design helps establish Sydney's identity as a city different from others. Uniqueness of design, a feature of much modern architecture, stands in opposition to cultural homogenization. *(Courtesy of Terry G. Bychkov-Jordan.)*

formity can find strength in local ordinances. A community can actually prevent McDonald's or Wal-Mart from establishing outlets. Neolocalism, then, pits the cultural power of place against the economic power of globalization.

Wal-Martians Invade Treasured Landscape!

Local communities and their governments attempt to preserve cultural landscapes in numerous ways. Zoning laws, architectural guidelines, minimum lot-size requirements, building codes, and conservation easements can all be used to maintain the distinct character of landscapes. At the global scale we have World Heritage Sites, places that the United Nations Educational, Scientific, and Cultural Organization (UNESCO) has deemed to be of such cultural significance that they should be given international protection. The temples at Angkor Wat in present-day Cambodia and the "Old Stone Town" on Zanzibar Island, Tanzania, are two examples of dozens of UNESCO World Heritage Sites worldwide (Figure 12.11).

Globalizing processes are putting new pressures on cultural landscapes. Often small community groups and town governments are pitted against powerful transnational corporations whose investment choices can profoundly transform a landscape. The phenomenal expansion of Wal-Mart Stores, Inc., is an often-cited example of how small-town landscapes are transformed by corporate investment. The biggest impact is the "hollowing out" of small-town main streets. Owner-run small businesses cannot compete with the giant retailer and soon have to lock their doors, turning the old downtowns into empty shells.

Some communities have welcomed Wal-Mart and others have tried hard to keep it out. Perhaps the most novel opposition campaign has been conducted in Vermont. In a confrontation that author Barbara Ehrenreich labeled "Earth

Figure 12.11 **Angkor Wat, UNESCO World Heritage Site.** Located 192 miles from Phnom Penh, Cambodia, and built between A.D. 1113 and 1150, this temple is regarded as the pinnacle of the Khmer Empire's architecture. UNESCO named it and surrounding structures a World Heritage Site in 1992. Such a designation helps efforts to safeguard and restore cultural landscapes of global significance. *(Courtesy of Ari Dorfsman.)*

People vs. Wal-Martians," the National Trust for Historic Preservation declared the entire state of Vermont to be an endangered landscape. Vermont is the only state ever to make the list of endangered historic places, which generally comprises individual buildings and historic urban districts. According to the National Trust, building more supersized Wal-Mart stores in Vermont would degrade the state's "sense of place." The National Trust had employed a similar strategy in 1993, which forced Wal-Mart to build stores more appropriate to Vermont's landscape

Protecting Europe's Rural Landscape

Another aspect of globalization, the drive to eliminate territorial barriers to the free trade of commodities, threatens rural landscapes in Europe. The fear is that cheap food imports will put small farmers out of business, which in turn will lead to the demise of treasured rural landscapes. European farmers and their national and EU representatives have argued that agriculture is not solely about food production—that it performs multiple functions, such as maintaining cultural landscapes and providing environmental services. Geographer Gail Hollander has observed that farmers and their advocates are using what they call agriculture's "multifunctionality" to gain exemptions from the World Trade Organization's (WTO) strict rules on free trade. The exemptions are warranted, they argue, in order to preserve the character of cultural landscapes that agriculture supports. Hollander concludes that multifunctionality could be used to preserve the landscapes of a few communities in Europe or, in stronger form, to challenge the very logic of the WTO's rules on the global trade of agricultural products. Given their symbolic value, the preservation of cultural landscapes may be a key tool used to slow or mitigate globalization's homogenizing effects.

Conclusion

As powerfully transformative as the processes of globalization are, they are unlikely to result in cultural homogenization any time soon. As we learned by examining globalization's interaction with each of cultural geography's five themes, we do not yet live in a placeless world. In fact, we have observed many trends suggesting that globalization will produce more geographic diversity and many unintended and unforeseen outcomes in our future.

In closing, it is our hope that we have excited your interest in the world's cultural diversity. To borrow and paraphrase the words of Aldous Huxley, we hope that our vicarious world travels have left you "poorer by exploded convictions" and "perished certainties," but richer by what

you have seen. Perhaps we, like Huxley, set out on this journey with preconceptions of how people should best "live, be governed, and believe." When one travels—even if just through the pages of a geography book as we have—such convictions often get mislaid. The main message of *The Human Mosaic* is that we will best be prepared to enter the new millennium if we maintain a willingness to question even our most closely held convictions and remain open to the boundless capacity of human cultural expression to surprise and amaze.

DOING GEOGRAPHY

Interpreting the Imagery of Globalization

The mandate of large corporations today, nearly regardless of the type of service or good they produce, is to go global or go bankrupt. In addition to staying competitive, going "global" gives a company a certain cachet and consumer appeal, the way that being "modern" did in previous decades. Transnational corporations also stress other popular notions related to globalization, such as respect for the world's cultural diversity and concern for the global environment.

This activity requires you to use your interpretive skills to look at the way the processes of globalization are represented in corporate-produced visual imagery and text. Try to find representations of globalization in more than one medium, including product packaging, magazine advertisements, and corporate web sites. You may concentrate on one type of industry, such as pharmaceuticals or automobiles, or several. Look for materials that include visual and textual representations of the globe, the Earth, or the world, and remember to make use of the five themes of cultural geography.

Set up a series of questions to systematically interpret each of the samples that you select. What popular notions about globalization are emphasized? How much validity do their representations carry? This is not the same as asking about the truth or falseness of an ad. Rather it is to ask, for example, what going to the Hard Rock Café and buying a T-shirt have to do with "saving the planet"? In the cases of visual imagery, look carefully at the way objects are arranged and scaled in relation to one another. How is power represented in the imagery? Does it lie with the individual consumer or the corporation? How are local-global linkages represented? Are the activities of global corporations given a moral authority, and if so, how? As you do this exercise, bear in mind the power of transnational corporations in an era of globalization. Think about the importance of understanding how the images and texts they produce give meaning to our world, our places, and our landscapes.

Globalization
on the Internet

You can learn more about globalization on the Internet at the following web sites:

An Atlas of Cyberspaces, Martin Dodge
http://www.cybergeography.org/atlas/atlas.html
Here cyberspaces are made visible: graphic representations of the geography of the electronic territories of the Internet, the World Wide Web, and other new cyberspaces help you to visualize and comprehend the digital "landscapes" beyond your computer screen in the age of popular culture.

Global Policy Forum
http://www.globalpolicy.org/
GPF is nonprofit organization that monitors policy making at the United Nations, promotes accountability of global decisions, educates and mobilizes for global citizen participation, and advocates on vital issues of international peace and justice. The site provides up-to-date coverage of the UN plus a variety of background briefs on globalization.

Internet Systems Consortium
http://www.isc.org/ds/new-survey.html
This site offers the Internet Domain Survey, an index to use of the Internet by country.

Yale Center for the Study of Globalization
http://www.yaleglobal.yale.edu/
The center publishes an informative online magazine, announces symposia and conferences, and serves as a clearinghouse for a wide variety of discussions on globalization. Magazine articles feature the latest in the globalization debate, such as the relationship between globalization and terrorism and national government responses to citizen discontent over the effects of globalization.

Sources

Adams, William. 2001: *Green Development: Environment and Sustainability in the Third World*, 2nd ed. London: Routledge.

Airriess, Christopher A. 2001. "Regional Production, Information-Communication Technology, and the Developmental State: The Rise of Singapore as a Global Container Hub." *Geoforum* 32: 235–254.

Barber, Benjamin. 1995. *Jihad vs. McWorld: How Globalism and Tribalism Are Reshaping the World*. New York: Ballantine.

Barlow, John P. 1995. "Cyberhood Versus Neighborhood." Special issue of *Utne Reader* 68(3): 52–64.

Beaverstock, Jonathan, Phillip Hubbard, and John Short. 2004. "Getting Away with It? Exposing the Geographies of the Super-Rich." *Geoforum* 35(4): 401–407.

Brewer's Digest Buyers' Guide and Directory. 1992. Chicago: Siebel Publishing Co.

Bruntland, H. 1987. *Our Common Future*. Oxford: Oxford University Press (for the World Commission on Environment and Development).

Bunge, William. 1973. "The Geography of Human Survival." *Annals of the Association of American Geographers*. 63: 275–295.

Cairncross, Frances. 1997. *The Death of Distance: How the Communications Revolution Will Change Our Lives*. Cambridge, Mass.: Harvard Business School Press.

Cartier, Carolyn. 2001. *Globalizing South China*. Oxford: Blackwell.

Cosgrove, Denis. 2001. *Apollo's Eye: A Cartographic Genealogy of the Earth in the Western Imagination*. Baltimore: John Hopkins Press.

Crouch, David (ed.). 1999. *Leisure/Tourism Geographies: Practices and Geographical Knowledge*. London: Routledge.

Crum, Shannon L. 2000. "The Spatial Diffusion of the Internet." Ph.D. dissertation, University of Texas at Austin.

Dicken, Peter. 2003. *Global Shift: Reshaping the Global Economic Map in the 21st Century*, 4th ed.. New York: Guilford.

Drummond, Ian, and Terry Marsden. 1999. *The Condition of Stability: Global Environment Change*. New York: Routledge.

Economist Technology Quarterly. 2003. "The Revenge of Geography" (March 15): 19–22.

Ehrenreich, Barbara. 2004: "Earth People vs. Wal-Martians." *New York Times* (July 25), p. 11.

Feld, Stephen. 2001. "A Sweet Lullaby for World Music," in Arjun Appadurai (ed.), *Globalization*. Durham, N.C.: Duke University Press, 189–216.

Ferguson, Andrew. 2004. "Wal-Mart Opponents Launch Two-Front Attack." *Pittsburgh Post-Gazette* (June 20), p. C2.

Ferry, Luc. 1995. *The New Ecological Order*. Carol Volk (trans.). Chicago: University of Chicago Press.

Flack, Wes. 1997. "American Microbreweries and Neolocalism." *Journal of Cultural Geography* 16(2): 37–53.

Fryer, Donald. 1974. "A Geographer's Inhumanity to Man." *Annals of the Association of American Geographers*. 64: 479–482.

"Geography and the Internet." 2001. Special report. *The Economist* (August 11): 18–20.

Gilbert, Anne, and Paul Villeneuve. 1999. "Social Space, Regional Development, and the Infobahn." *Canadian Geographer* 43: 114–117.

Greider, William. 1997. *One World, Ready or Not: The Manic Logic of Global Capitalism*. New York: Touchstone Books.

Hardt, Michael, and Antonio Negri. 2000. *Empire*. Cambridge, Mass.: Harvard University Press.

Herod, Andrew. 2001. *Labor Geographies: Workers and the Landscapes of Capitalism*. New York: Guilford.

Hollander, Gail. 2004. "Agricultural Trade Liberalization, Multifunctionality, and Sugar in the South Florida Landscape." *Geoforum* 35: 299–312.

Hooson, David (ed.). 1994. *Geography and National Identity*. Oxford: Blackwell.

Hudson, Ray. 2000. "One Europe or Many? Reflections on Becoming European." *Transactions of the Institute of British Geographers* 25: 409–426.

Huxley, Aldous. 1926. *Jesting Pilate: An Intellectual Holiday*. New York: George H. Doran.

Iyer, Pico. 2000. *The Global Soul: Jet Lag, Shopping Malls, and the Search for Home*. New York: Alfred A. Knopf.

James, Harold. 2001. *The End of Globalization*. Cambridge, Mass.: Harvard University Press.

Johnston, R. J., Peter Taylor, and Michael Watts (eds.). 2002. *Geographies of Global Change: Remapping the World*, 2nd ed. Oxford: Blackwell.

Keating, Michael. 1998. *The New Regionalism in Western Europe*. Northampton, Mass.: Edward Elgar.

Keeling, David J. 1999. "Neoliberal Reform and Landscape Change in Buenos Aires." *Yearbook, Conference of Latin Americanist Geographers* 25: 15–32.

Kelly, Philip F. 2000. *Landscapes of Globalization*. London: Routledge.

Kimble, George H. T. 1951. "The Inadequacy of the Regional Concept," in L. Dudley Stamp and Sidney W. Wooldridge (eds.), *London Essays in Geography: Rodwell Jones Memorial Volume*. Cambridge, Mass.: Harvard University Press, 151–174.

Kitchen, Rob, and Martin Dodge. 2002. "Emerging Geographies of Cyberspace," in R. J. Johnston, Peter Taylor, and Michael Watts (eds.), *Geographies of Global Change: Remapping the World*, 2nd ed. Oxford: Blackwell, 340–354.

Knox, Paul. 2002. "World Cities and the Organization of Global Space," in R. J. Johnston, Peter Taylor, and Michael Watts (eds.), *Geographies of Global Change: Remapping the World*, 2nd ed. Oxford: Blackwell, 328–339.

Kraus, Clifford. 2002. "Returning Tundra's Rhythm to the Inuit, in Film." *New York Times* (March 30), p. A4.

Kunstler, James H. 1993. *The Geography of Nowhere: The Rise and Decline of America's Man-Made Landscape*. New York: Simon & Schuster.

Leyshon, Andrew, David Matless, and George Revill (eds.). 1998. *The Place of Music*. New York: Guilford.

McDowell, Linda (ed.). 1997. *Undoing Place? A Geographical Reader*. London: Arnold.

Naughton, Keith. 2004. "China Hits the Road." *Newsweek* (June 28): E22.

Nemeth, David J. 2000. "The End of the Re(li)gion?" *North American Geographer* 2: 1–8.

O'Loughlin, John, et al. 1998. "The Diffusion of Democracy, 1946–1994." *Annals of the Association of American Geographers* 88: 545–574.

Poon, Jessie P. H., Edmund R. Thompson, and Philip F. Kelly. 2000. "Myth of the Triad? The Geography of Trade and Investment Blocs." *Transactions of the Institute of British Geographers* 25: 427–444.

Press, Larry. 1997. "Tracking the Global Diffusion of the Internet." *Communications of the Association of Computing Machinery* 40(11): 11–17.

Relph, Edward. 1976. *Place and Placelessness*. London: Pion.

Rohter, Larry. 2002. "Brazil's Prized Exports Rely on Slaves and Scorched Land." *New York Times* (March 25), pp. A1, A6.

Sessions, George (ed.). 1995. *Deep Ecology for the 21st Century*. Boulder, Colo.: Shambala Press.

Shields, Rob. 1991. *Places on the Margin: Alternative Geographies of Modernity*. London: Routledge.

Suvantola, Jaakko. 2002. *Tourist's Experience of Place*. Aldershot, U.K.: Ashgate.

Swerdlow, Joel L. (ed.). 1999. "Global Culture." Special issue of *National Geographic* 196(2): 2–132.

Swyngedouw, Erik. 1997. "Neither Global nor Local," in Kevin R. Cox (ed.), *Spaces of Globalization: Reasserting the Power of the Local*. New York: Guilford, 137–166.

Teo, Peggy, and Lim Hiong Li. 2003. "Global and Local Interactions in Tourism." *Annals of Tourism Research* 30(2): 287–306.

"Used and Abused: Five Recent Cases with Slavery Convictions." 2003. *Palm Beach Post* (December 7), p. 2.

Wood, William B. 2001. "Geographic Aspects of Genocide: A Comparison of Bosnia and Rwanda." *Transactions of the Institute of British Geographers* 26: 57–75.

Ten Recommended Books
on Globalization

(For additional suggested readings, see *The Human Mosaic* web site: www.whfreeman.com/jordan)

Crang, Mike, Phil Crang, and Jon May (eds.). *Virtual Geographies: Bodies, Space and Relations*. London: Routledge. Explores how new communications technologies produce new types of space and even new geographies.

Firebaugh, Glenn. 2003. *The New Geography of Global Inequality*. Cambridge, Mass.: Harvard University Press. Makes the argument that income inequalities among and within world regions are misunderstood. There is a lot of economic data to wade through, but they make the case stronger. The author raises important questions about the effects of globalization.

Gabel, Medard, and Henry Bruner. 2003. *Global Inc.: An Atlas of the Multinational Corporation*. New York: The New Press. A wonderful atlas mapping everything from the historic rise of multinational companies to the latest geographic expansions of Wal-Mart. It's full of facts on every important global industry, including food, cars, and pharmaceuticals. It also maps the impacts of multinational corporations, including cultural and environmental.

Goudie, Andrew S., et al. (eds.). 2001. *Encyclopedia of Global Change*. 2 vols. New York: Oxford University Press. A standard reference on the ecological changes accompanying globalization, written mainly by geographers.

Johnston, R. J., Peter Taylor, and Michael Watts (eds). 2002. *Geographies of Global Change: Remapping the World*, 2nd ed. Oxford: Blackwell. Considers such issues as post–cold war geopolitics, global environmental governance, and cultural changes related to mass consumption, the Internet, and ethnic identity.

Jussila, Heikki, Roser Majoral, and Fernanda Delgado-Cravidao. 2001. *Globalization and Marginality in Geographical Space*. Aldershot, U.K.: Ashgate. Case studies from Europe, the Americas, Africa, and Australia illustrate how geographical research aids our understanding of the way in which the policies and politics of globalization affect the more marginalized areas of the world.

Kotkin, Joel. 2000. *The New Geography: How the Digital Revolution Is Reshaping the American Landscape*. New York: Random House. Argues that computer and telecommunication technology has freed people and businesses to locate wherever they wish, thereby weakening venerable core-periphery patterns but strengthening place distinctiveness.

Norwine, Jim, and Jonathan M. Smith (eds). 2000. *Worldview Flux: Perplexed Values Among Postmodern Peoples*. Lanham, Md.: Lexington Books. An irreverent, occasionally funny look at how groups as diverse as Cajuns, South African whites, and

SEEING GEOGRAPHY

What do these images convey about empire and globalization and their connections and differences?

Global Reach

Before we explore an answer, let us pause to recall our Practicing Geography profile of Denis Cosgrove in Chapter 1. Remember that Professor Cosgrove's primary interest in cultural geography is in "interpreting" rather than "explaining." His book *Apollo's Eye* is a good example. In it, Cosgrove attempts to interpret the power represented in images of the globe and to show how the practices of globalization are historically rooted in a Western cultural history of imagining, seeing, and representing the globe. We will try a little of this interpretive method on these two images.

Two images of global reach, more than a century apart (Queen Victoria with world map; a JVC advertisement).

The image on the left shows Queen Victoria around 1850 in front of a world map oriented so that the majority of Britain's territorial empire is displayed. We know that during this period of European history the queen was sovereign, meaning that she personified, even embodied, Britain and its colonial empire. The image is scaled such that queen's arm span matches the span of the British Empire. She is positioned in front of the map, emphasizing her authority and power over it. With power and authority comes responsibility; the viewer is meant to read in the queen's pose and dress a moral role as protector and civilizing force. Foregrounded as she is, then, all lines of power, authority, and moral right and responsibility in the empire run through her.

The image on the right is an advertisement for JVC, a transnational consumer electronics company that began as the Victor Talking Machine Company of Japan, Ltd., in 1927. In the advertisement, photographed in 2004, the company's logo—JVC—is scaled to continental size. The message conveyed is one of global dominance and global reach. It is also conveys the message of one company bringing the world together, a goal that JVC's web site describes as "contributing to the global community through cultural activities" with corporate underwriting. Finally, the advertisement is meant to express through the image of the globe the fact that JVC now has a network of manufacturing sites throughout Asia, the Americas, and Europe and sales subsidiaries in many more regions.

So what do these images tell us about continuity and change from empire to globalization? We see a common theme in the claim of global reach. In the JVC ad, it is expressed as the company's ability to span the globe with its products and services. In the image with Queen Victoria, it is expressed in the cartographic representation of England's global empire. We can also identify significant differences between the emotional and affective meaning of British Empire and globalization conveyed by these images. Under empire, the queen personifies British imperial rule, and allegiance to the queen is required of all imperial subjects. Under globalization, on the other hand, allegiance is constructed between the consumer and transnational corporations. Corporations are faceless rather than personified, represented by abstract logos rather than by living, breathing sovereigns. In summary, we can see in these images both the roots of globalization in empire and the significant differences between the two kinds of global power. ■

Pacific coast Native Americans are coping with the new age of globalization and the need to restructure their self-identities and place attachments.

Schaeffer, Robert K. 1997. *Understanding Globalization: The Social Consequences of Political, Economic, and Environmental Change*. Lanham, Md.: Rowman & Littlefield. Studies the complicated interplay of factors as diverse as agribusiness, climate change, the illegal drug trade, and economic fluctuations.

Skelton, Tracey, and Tim Allen (eds.). 1999. *Culture and Global Change*. London: Routledge. No fewer than 27 authors consider the interaction of culture and globalization, in the process rejecting both cultural and economic determinism.

absorbing barrier   A barrier that completely halts diffusion of innovations and blocks the spread of cultural elements. [Chapter 1]

acculturation   The adoption by an ethnic group of enough of the ways of the host society to be able to function economically and socially. [Chapter 5]

acid rain   Rainfall with much higher acidity than normal, caused by sulfur and nitrogen oxides derived from the burning of fossil fuels being flushed from the atmosphere by precipitation, with lethal effects for many plants and animals. [Chapter 9]

adaptive strategy   The unique way in which each culture uses its particular physical environment; those aspects of culture that serve to provide the necessities of life—food, clothing, shelter, and defense. [Chapter 1 and throughout]

agglomeration   A snowballing geographical process by which secondary and service industrial activities become clustered in cities and compact industrial regions in order to share infrastructure and markets. [Chapters 9, 10, 11]

agribusiness   Highly mechanized, large-scale farming, usually under corporate ownership. [Chapter 8]

agricultural landscape   The cultural landscape of agricultural areas. [Chapter 8]

agricultural surplus   The amount of food grown by a society that exceeds the demands of its population. [Chapter 10]

agriculture   The cultivation of domesticated crops and the raising of domesticated animals. [Chapter 8]

agroforestry   A cultivation system that features the interplanting of trees with field crops. [Chapter 2]

agro-region   A culture region based on characteristics of agriculture, within which a given type of agriculture occurs. [Chapter 8]

animism   The belief that inanimate objects, such as trees, rocks, and rivers, possess souls. [Chapter 3]

apartheid   In South Africa, a policy of racial segregation and discrimination against non-European groups. [Chapter 11]

assimilation   The complete blending of an ethnic group into the host society, resulting in the loss of all distinctive ethnic traits. [Chapter 5]

axis mundi   The symbolic center of cosmomagical cities, often demarcated by a large, vertical structure. [Chapter 10]

barriadas   Illegal housing settlements, usually made up of temporary shelters, that surround large cities; often referred to as *squatter settlements.* [Chapter 10]

bilingualism   The ability to speak two languages fluently. [Chapter 4]

birthrate   The annual number of births per thousand population. [Chapter 7]

buffer state   An independent but small and weak country lying between two powerful countries. [Chapter 6]

cadastral pattern   The shapes formed by property borders; the pattern of land ownership. [Chapter 8]

carrying capacity   The maximum number of people that can be supported in a given area. [Chapter 7]

census tracts   Small districts used by the U.S. Census Bureau to survey the population. [Chapter 11]

central business district [CBD)   The central portion of a city, characterized by high-density land uses. [Chapter 11]

centralizing forces   Diffusion forces that encourage people or businesses to locate in the central city. [Chapter 11]

central place   A town or city engaged primarily in the service stages of production; a regional center. [Chapter 10]

central-place theory   A set of models designed to explain the spatial distribution of urban service centers. [Chapter 10]

centrifugal force   Any factor that disrupts the internal order of a country. [Chapter 6]

centripetal force   Any factor that supports the internal unity of a country. [Chapter 6]

chain migration   The tendency of people to migrate along channels, over a period of time, from specific source areas to specific destinations. [Chapter 5]

checkerboard development   A mixture of farmlands and housing tracts. [Chapter 11]

cityscape   An urban landscape. [Chapter 11]

cleavage model   A political-geographical model suggesting that persistent regional patterns in voting behavior, sometimes leading to separatism, can usually be explained in terms of tensions pitting urban against rural, core against periphery, capitalists against workers, and power group against minority culture. [Chapter 6]

colonial city   A city founded by colonialism or an indigenous city whose structure was deeply influenced by Western colonialism. [Chapter 10]

colonialism   The forceful appropriation of a territory by a distant state, often involving the displacement of indigenous populations to make way for colonial settlers. [Chapter 2]

concentric-zone model   A social model that depicts a city as five areas bounded by concentric rings. [Chapter 11]

consumer services   The range of economic activities that facilitate the consumption of goods. [Chapter 9]

contact conversion   The spread of religious beliefs by personal contact. [Chapter 3]

contagious diffusion   A type of expansion diffusion in which cultural innovation spreads by person-to-person contact, moving wavelike through an area and population without regard to social status. [Chapter 1]

convergence hypothesis   A hypothesis holding that cultural differences among places are being reduced by improved transportation and communications systems, leading to a homogenization of popular culture. [Chapter 2]

core area   The territorial nucleus from which a country grows in area and over time, often containing the national capital and the main center of commerce, culture, and industry. [Chapter 6]

core-periphery   A concept based on the tendency of both formal and functional culture regions to consist of a core or node, in which defining traits are purest or functions are headquartered, and a periphery that is tributary and displays fewer of the defining traits. [Chapters 1 and others]

cosmomagical city   A type of city that is laid out in accordance with religious principles, characteristic of very early cities, particularly in China. [Chapter 10]

cottage industry   A traditional type of manufacturing in the pre–industrial revolution era, practiced on a small scale in individual rural households as a part-time occupation and designed to produce handmade goods for local consumption. [Chapter 9]

creole   A language derived from a pidgin that has acquired a fuller vocabulary and become the native language of its speakers. [Chapter 4]

cultural determinism   The viewpoint that the immediate causes of all cultural phenomena are other cultural phenomena. [Chapter 1]

cultural diffusion   The spread of elements of culture from the point of origin over an area. [Chapter 1]

cultural ecology   Broadly defined, the study of the relationships between the physical environment and culture; narrowly (and more commonly) defined, the study of culture as an adaptive system that facilitates human adaptation to nature and environmental change. [Chapter 1]

cultural geography   The description and explanation of spatial patterns and ecological relationships in human culture. [Chapter 1]

cultural interaction   The relationship of various elements within a culture. [Chapter 1]

cultural landscape   The artificial landscape; the visible human imprint on the land. [Chapter 1]

cultural maladaptation   Poor or inadequate adaptation that occurs when a group pursues an adaptive strategy that, in the short run, fails to provide the necessities of life or, in the long run, destroys the environment that nourishes it. [Chapter 5]

cultural preadaptation   A complex of adaptive traits and skills possessed in advance of migration by a group, giving them survival ability and competitive advantage in occupying the new environment. [Chapters 5, 7]

cultural simplification   The process by which immigrant ethnic groups lose certain aspects of their traditional culture in the process of settling overseas, creating a new culture that is less complex than the old. [Chapter 5]

culture   A total way of life held in common by a group of people, including such learned features as speech, ideology, behavior, livelihood, technology, and government; or the local, customary way of doing things—a way of life; an ever-changing process in which a group is actively engaged; a dynamic mix of symbols, beliefs, speech, and practices. [Chapter 1]

culture hearth   A focused geographic area where important innovations are born and from which they spread. [Chapter 3]

culture region   An area occupied by people who have something in common culturally; or a spatial unit that functions politically, socially, or economically as a distinct entity. [Chapter 1]

death rate   The annual number of deaths per 1000 persons in the population. [Chapter 7]

decentralization   The tendency of people or businesses and industry to locate outside the central city. [Chapters 10, 11]

defensive site   A location where a city can be easily defended. [Chapter 10]

deindustrialization   The decline of primary and secondary industry, accompanied by a rise of the service sectors of the industrial economy. [Chapters 9, 11]

demographic transition   A change in population growth that occurs when a nation moves from a rural, agricultural society with high birth and death rates to an urban, industrial society in which death rates decline first and birthrates decline later. [Chapter 7]

demography   The statistical study of population size, composition, distribution, and change. [Chapter 7]

desertification   A process whereby human actions unintentionally turn productive lands into deserts through agricultural and pastoral misuse, destroying vegetation and soil to the point where they cannot regenerate. [Chapter 8]

dialect   A distinctive local or regional variant of a language that remains mutually intelligible to speakers of other dialects of that language; a subtype of a language. [Chapter 4]

dispersed   A type of settlement form where people live relatively distant from each other. [Chapter 1]

domesticated animal   An animal kept for some utilitarian purpose whose breeding is controlled by humans and whose survival is dependent on humans; domesticated animals differ genetically and behaviorally from wild animals. [Chapter 8]

domesticated plant   A plant deliberately planted and tended by humans that is genetically distinct from its wild ancestors as a result of selective breeding. [Chapter 8]

double-cropping   Harvesting twice a year from the same parcel of land. [Chapter 8]

dust dome   A pollution layer over a city that is thickest at the center of the city. [Chapter 11]

ecofeminism   A new doctrine proposing that women are inherently better environmental preservationists than men because the traditional roles of women involved creating and nurturing life, whereas the traditional roles of men too often necessitated death and destruction. [Chapter 1]

ecosystem   The functional ecological system in which biological and cultural *Homo sapiens* lives and interacts with the physical environment. [Chapter 1]

ecotheology   The study of the influence of religious belief on habitat modification. [Chapter 3]

ecotourism   Responsible travel that does not harm ecosystems or the well-being of local people. [Chapter 9]

edge city   A new urban cluster of economic activity that surrounds nineteenth-century downtowns. [Chapter 10]

electoral geography   The study of the interactions among space, place, and region and the conduct and results of elections. [Chapter 6]

enclave   A piece of territory surrounded by, but not part of, a country. [Chapter 6]

environmental determinism   The belief that cultures are directly or indirectly shaped by the physical environment. [Chapter 1]

environmental perception   The belief that culture depends more on what people perceive the environment to be than on the actual character of the environment; perception, in turn, is colored by the teachings of culture. [Chapter 1]

ethnic culture region   An area occupied by people of similar ethnic background who share traits of ethnicity, such as language and migration history. [Chapter 11]

ethnic geography   The study of the spatial and ecological aspects of ethnicity. [Chapter 5]

ethnic group   A group of people who share a common ancestry and cultural tradition, often living as a minority in a larger society. [Chapter 5]

ethnic homeland   A sizable area inhabited by an ethnic minority that exhibits a strong sense of attachment to the region and often exercises some measure of political and social control over it. [Chapter 5]

ethnic island   A small ethnic area in the rural countryside; sometimes called a "folk island." [Chapter 5]

ethnic neighborhood   A voluntary community where people of like origin reside by choice. [Chapter 5]

ethnic religion   A religion identified with a particular ethnic or tribal group; does not seek converts. [Chapter 3]

ethnic substrate   Regional cultural distinctiveness that remains following the assimilation of an ethnic homeland. [Chapter 5]

ethnographic boundary   A political boundary that follows some cultural border, such as a linguistic or religious border. [Chapter 6]

exclave   A piece of national territory separated from the main body of a country by the territory of another country. [Chapter 6]

expansion diffusion   The spread of innovations within an area in a snowballing process, so that the total number of knowers becomes greater and the area of occurrence grows. [Chapter 1]

export processing zones (EPZs) Designated areas of countries where governments create conditions conducive to export-oriented production. [Chapter 9]

extended metropolitan region (EMR) A new type of urban region, complex in both landscape form and function, created by the rapid spatial expansion of cities in the developing world. [Chapter 10]

farmstead The center of farm operations, containing the house, barn, sheds, and livestock pens. [Chapter 7]

farm village A clustered rural settlement of moderate size, inhabited by people who are engaged in farming. [Chapter 7]

federal state An independent country that gives considerable powers and even autonomy to its constituent parts. [Chapter 6]

feedlot A factorylike farm devoted to either livestock fattening or dairying; all feed is imported and no crops are grown on the farm. [Chapter 8]

festival setting A multiuse redevelopment project that is built around a particular setting, often one with a historical association. [Chapter 11]

folk Traditional, rural; the opposite of "popular." [Chapter 2]

folk architecture Structures built by members of a folk society or culture in a traditional manner and style, without the assistance of professional architects or blueprints, using locally available raw materials. [Chapter 2]

folk culture A small, cohesive, stable, isolated, nearly self-sufficient group that is homogeneous in custom and race; characterized by a strong family or clan structure, order maintained through sanctions based in the religion or family, little division of labor other than that between the sexes, frequent and strong interpersonal relationships, and a material culture consisting mainly of handmade goods. [Chapter 2]

folk fortress A stronghold area with natural defensive qualities, useful in the defense of a country against invaders. [Chapter 6]

folk geography The study of the spatial patterns and ecology of traditional groups; a branch of cultural geography. [Chapter 2]

foodways Customary behaviors associated with food preparation and consumption. [Chapter 5]

"footloose" Industries that are able to shift the location of their facilities in order to take advantage of cheap labor. [Chapter 9]

formal culture region A region inhabited by people who have one or more cultural traits in common. [Chapter 1]

functional culture region An area that functions as a unit politically, socially, or economically. [Chapter 1]

functional zonation The pattern of land uses within a city; the existence of areas with differing functions, such as residential, commercial, and governmental. [Chapter 10]

fundamentalism A movement to return to the founding principles of a religion, which can include literal interpretation of sacred texts, or the attempt to follow the ways of a religious founder as closely as possible. [Chapter 3]

Gaia hypothesis The theory that there is one interacting planetary ecosystem, Gaia, that includes all living things and the land, waters, and atmosphere in which they live; further, that Gaia functions almost as a living organism, acting to control deviations in climate and to correct chemical imbalances, so as to preserve Earth as a living planet. [Chapter 3]

generic toponym The descriptive part of many place-names, often repeated throughout a culture area. [Chapter 4]

genetically modified (GM) crops Plants whose genetic characteristics have been altered through recombinant DNA technology. [Chapter 8]

gentrification The displacement of lower-income residents by higher-income residents as buildings in deteriorated areas of city centers are restored. [Chapter 11]

geodemography Population geography; the study of the spatial and ecological aspects of population, including distribution, density per unit of land area, fertility, gender, health, age, mortality, and migration. [Chapter 7]

geography The study of spatial patterns and of differences and similarities from one place to another in environment and culture. [Chapter 1]

geolinguistics The cultural geographical study of languages and dialects. [Chapter 4]

geometric boundary A political border drawn in a regular, geometric manner, often a straight line, without regard for environmental or cultural patterns. [Chapter 6]

geopolitics The influence of the habitat on political entities. [Chapter 6]

gerrymandering The drawing of electoral district boundaries in an awkward pattern to enhance the voting impact of one constituency at the expense of another. [Chapter 6]

ghetto Traditionally, an area within a city where an ethnic group lives, either by choice or by force. Today in the United States, the term typically indicates an impoverished African-American urban neighborhood. [Chapter 5]

global city A city that is a control center of the global economy. [Chapter 10]

globalization The binding together of all the lands and peoples of the world into an integrated system driven by capitalistic free markets, in which cultural diffusion is rapid, independent states are weakened, and cultural homogenization is encouraged. [Chapters 1 and 12 especially, but throughout]

globalizing city A city experiencing significant economic and social changes related to the global economy. [Chapter 10]

global warming The pronounced climatic warming of the Earth that has occurred since about 1920 and particularly since the 1970s. [Chapter 9]

glocalization The process by which global forces of change interact with local cultures, altering both in the process. [Chapter 12]

greenhouse effect A process in which the increased release of carbon dioxide and other gases into the atmosphere, caused by industrial activity and deforestation, permits solar short-wave heat radiation to reach the Earth's surface but blocks long-wave outgoing radiation, causing a thermal imbalance and global heating. [Chapter 9]

green revolution The recent introduction of high-yield hybrid crops and chemical fertilizers and pesticides into traditional Asian agricultural systems, most notably paddy rice farming, with attendant increases in production and ecological damage. [Chapter 8]

Greens Activists and organizations, including political parties, whose central concern is addressing environmental deterioration. [Chapter 9]

guild industry A traditional type of manufacturing in the pre–industrial revolution era, involving handmade goods of high quality manufactured by highly skilled artisans who resided in towns and cities. [Chapter 9]

hamlet A small rural settlement, smaller than a village. [Chapter 8]

heartland The interior of a sizable landmass, removed from maritime connections; in particular, the interior of the Eurasian continent. [Chapter 6]

heartland theory A 1904 proposal by Mackinder that the key to world conquest lay in control of the interior of Eurasia. [Chapter 6]

heat island An area of warmer temperatures at the center of a city, caused by the urban concentration of heat-retaining concrete, brick, and asphalt. [Chapter 11]

hierarchical diffusion A type of expansion diffusion in which innovations spread from one important person to another or from one urban center to another, temporarily bypassing other persons or rural areas. [Chapter 1]

high-tech corridor An area along a limited-access highway that houses offices and other services associated with high-tech industries. [Chapters 9, 11]

hinterland The area surrounding a city and influenced by it. [Chapter 10]

homelessness A temporary or permanent condition of not having a legal home address. [Chapter 11]

hunting and gathering The killing of wild game and the harvesting of wild plants to provide food in traditional cultures. [Chapter 8]

hydraulic civilization A civilization based on large-scale irrigation. [Chapter 10]

imperialism The extension of political control by one country over foreign nations, often through military means. [Chapter 10]

independent invention A cultural innovation that is developed in two or more locations by individuals or groups working independently. [Chapter 1]

indigenous culture A culture group that constitutes the original inhabitants of a territory, distinct from the dominant national culture, which is often derived from colonial occupation. [Chapter 2]

indigenous technical knowledge Highly localized knowledge about environmental conditions and sustainable land-use practices. [Chapter 2]

industrial landscape Landscape forms that result from industrial activity. [Chapter 9]

industrial revolution A series of inventions and innovations, arising in England in the 1700s, that led to the use of machines and inanimate power in the manufacturing process. [Chapter 9]

infant mortality rate The number of infants per 1000 live births who die before reaching one year of age. [Chapter 7]

in-filling New building on empty parcels of land within a checkerboard pattern of development. [Chapter 11]

intensive agriculture   The expenditure of much labor and capital on a piece of land to increase its productivity. In contrast, *extensive agriculture* involves less labor and capital. [Chapter 8]

intercropping   The practice of growing two or more different types of crops in the same field at the same time. [Chapter 8]

isogloss   The border of usage of an individual word or pronunciation. [Chapter 4]

labor-intensive industry   An industry for which labor costs represent a large proportion of total production costs. [Chapter 9]

laissez-faire utilitarianism   The belief that economic competition without government interference produces the most public good. [Chapter 10]

language   A mutually agreed-upon system of symbolic communication that has a spoken and usually a written expression. [Chapter 4]

language family   A group of related languages derived from a common ancestor. [Chapter 4]

lateral commuting   Traveling from one suburb to another in going from home to work. [Chapter 11]

legible city   A city that is easy to decipher, with clear pathways, edges, nodes, districts, and landmarks. [Chapter 11]

lingua franca   An existing, well-established language of communication and commerce used widely where it is not a mother tongue. [Chapter 4]

linguistic refuge area   An area protected by isolation or inhospitable environmental conditions in which a language or dialect has survived. [Chapter 4]

livestock fattening   A commercial type of agriculture that produces fattened cattle and hogs for meat. [Chapter 8]

marchland   A strip of territory, traditionally one day's march for infantry, that served as a boundary zone for independent countries in premodern times. [Chapter 6]

market   The geographical area in which a product may be sold in a volume and at a price profitable to the manufacturer. [Chapter 9]

market gardening   Farming devoted to specialized fruit, vegetable, or vine crops for sale rather than consumption. [Chapter 8]

master-planned communities   Large-scale residential developments that include, in addition to architecturally compatible housing units, planned recreational facilities, schools, and security measures. [Chapter 11]

material culture   All physical, tangible objects made and used by members of a cultural group, such as clothing, buildings, tools and utensils, instruments, furniture, and artwork; the visible aspect of culture. [Chapter 2]

mechanistic view of nature   The view that humans are separate from nature and hold dominion over it and that the habitat is an integrated mechanism governed by external forces that the human mind can understand and manipulate. [Chapter 3]

megalopolis   A large urban region formed as several urban areas spread and merge, such as Boswash, the region including Boston, New York, and Washington, D.C. [Chapter 10]

model   An abstraction, an imaginary situation, proposed by geographers to simulate laboratory conditions so that they may isolate certain causal forces for detailed study. [Chapter 1]

monoculture   The raising of only one crop on a huge tract of land in agribusiness. [Chapter 8]

monoglot   A person who speaks only one language. [Chapter 4]

monotheistic religion   The worship of only one god. [Chapter 3]

multiple nuclei model   A model that depicts a city growing from several separate focal points. [Chapter 11]

nationalism   The sense of belonging to and self-identification with a national culture. [Chapter 6]

nation-state   An independent country dominated by a relatively homogeneous culture group. [Chapter 6]

natural boundary   A political border that follows some feature of the natural environment, such as a river or mountain ridge. [Chapter 6]

natural hazard   An inherent danger present in a given habitat, such as flooding, hurricanes, volcanic eruptions, or earthquakes; often perceived differently by different peoples. [Chapter 1]

neighborhood   A small social area within a city where residents share values and concerns and interact with one another on a daily basis. [Chapter 11]

neighborhood effect   The rapid acceptance of an innovation in a small area or cluster around an initial adopter. [Chapter 1]

neolocalism   The desire to reembrace the uniqueness and authenticity of place, in response to globalization. [Chapter 12]

node A central point in a functional culture region where functions are coordinated and directed. [Chapter 1]

nomadic livestock herder A member of a group that continually moves with its livestock in search of forage for its animals. [Chapter 8]

nonmaterial culture The wide range of tales, songs, lore, beliefs, superstitions, and customs that passes from generation to generation as part of an oral or written tradition. [Chapter 2]

nonrenewable resource A resource that must be depleted to be used, such as petroleum. [Chapter 9]

nucleation A relatively dense settlement form. [Chapter 1]

office park A cluster of office buildings usually located along an interstate, often forming the nucleus of an edge city. [Chapter 11]

organic view of nature The view that humans are part of, not separate from, nature and that the habitat possesses a soul and is filled with nature spirits. [Chapter 3]

orthodox religion A strand within most major religions that emphasizes purity of faith and is not open to blending with other religions. [Chapter 3]

outsource The physical separation of some economic activities from the main production facility, usually for the purpose of employing cheaper labor. [Chapter 9]

paddy rice farming The cultivation of rice on a paddy, or small flooded field enclosed by mud dikes, practiced in the humid areas of the Far East. [Chapter 8]

palimpsest A term used to describe cultural landscapes with various layers and historical "messages." Geographers use this term to reinforce the notion of the landscape as a text that can be read; a landscape palimpsest has elements of both modern and past periods. [Chapter 11]

peasant A farmer belonging to a folk culture and practicing a traditional system of agriculture. [Chapter 8]

permeable barrier A barrier that permits some aspects of an innovation to diffuse through but weakens and retards continued spread; an innovation can be modified in passing through a permeable barrier. [Chapter 1]

personal space The amount of space that individuals feel "belongs" to them as they move about their everyday business. [Chapter 7]

physical environment All aspects of the natural physical surroundings, such as climate, terrain, soils, vegetation, and wildlife. [Chapter 1]

pidgin A composite language consisting of a small vocabulary borrowed from the linguistic groups involved in international commerce. [Chapter 4]

pilgrimage A journey to a place of religious importance. [Chapter 3]

place A term used to connote the subjective, idiographic, humanistic, culturally oriented type of geography that seeks to understand the unique character of individual regions and places, rejecting the principles of science as flawed and unknowingly biased. [Chapter 1]

placelessness A spatial standardization that diminishes regional variety; may result from the spread of popular culture, which can diminish or destroy the uniqueness of place through cultural standardization on a national or even worldwide scale. [Chapters 2, 12]

plantation A large landholding devoted to specialized production of a tropical cash crop. [Chapter 8]

plantation agriculture A system of monoculture for producing export crops requiring relatively large amounts of land and capital; originally dependent on slave labor. [Chapter 8]

political geography The study of the spatial and ecological aspects of political behavior, from nationalism and the independent country to voting patterns, sectionalism, and regional separatism. Sometimes called *geopolitics*. [Chapter 6]

polyglot A mixture of different languages. [Chapter 4]

polytheistic religion The worship of many gods. [Chapter 3]

popular culture A dynamic culture based in large, heterogeneous societies permitting considerable individualism, innovation, and change; having a money-based economy, division of labor into professions, secular institutions of control, and weak interpersonal ties; producing and consuming machine-made goods. [Chapter 2]

population density The number of people in an area of land, usually expressed as people per square mile or per square kilometer. [Chapter 7]

population explosion The rapid, accelerating increase in world population since about 1650 and especially since 1900. [Chapter 7]

population geography Geodemography; the study of the spatial and ecological aspects of population, including distribution, density per unit of land area, fertility, gender, health, age, mortality, and migration. [Chapter 7]

population pyramid A graph used to show the age and sex composition of a population. [Chapter 7]

possibilism A school of thought based on the belief that humans, rather than the physical environment, are the primary active force; that any environment offers a number of different possible ways for a culture to develop; and that the choices among these possibilities are guided by cultural heritage. [Chapter 1]

postindustrial phase A society characterized by the dominance of the service sectors of economic activity. [Chapter 9]

primary industry An industry engaged in the extraction of natural resources, such as agriculture, lumbering, and mining. [Chapter 9]

primate city A city of large size and dominant power within a country. [Chapter 10]

producer services The range of economic activities required by producers of goods. [Chapter 9]

proselytic religion A religion that actively seeks converts and has the goal of converting all humankind. [Chapter 3]

push-and-pull factors Unfavorable, repelling conditions and favorable, attractive conditions that interact to affect migration and other elements of diffusion. [Chapter 7]

race A classification system that is sometimes understood as arising from genetically significant differences among human populations, or visible differences in human physiognomy, or as a social construction that varies across time and space. [Chapter 5]

ranching The commercial raising of herd livestock on a large landholding. [Chapter 8]

range In central-place theory, the average maximum distance people will travel to purchase a good or service. [Chapter 10]

redlining A practice by banks and mortgage companies of demarcating areas considered to be a high risk for housing loans. [Chapter 11]

refuge area A region in which the physical habitat has provided natural protection for a minority cultural group. [Chapter 4]

region A grouping of like places or the functional union of places to form a spatial unit; see also *culture region*. [Chapter 1]

regional trading blocs Agreements made among geographically proximate countries that reduce trade barriers in order to better compete with other regional markets. [Chapter 6]

relic boundary A former political border that no longer functions as a boundary. [Chapter 6]

religion A social system involving a set of beliefs and practices through which people seek harmony with the universe and attempt to influence the forces of nature, life, and death. [Chapter 3]

relocation diffusion The spread of an innovation or other element of culture that occurs with the bodily relocation (migration) of an individual or group that has the idea. [Chapter 1]

renewable resource A resource that is not depleted if wisely used, such as forests, water, fishing grounds, and agricultural land. [Chapter 9]

restrictive covenant A statement written into a property deed that restricts the use of the land in some way; often used to prohibit certain groups of people from buying property. [Chapter 11]

return migration A type of ethnic diffusion that involves the voluntary movement of a group of migrants back to its ancestral or native country or homeland. [Chapter 5]

rimland The maritime fringe of a country or continent; in particular, the western, southern, and eastern edges of the Eurasian continent. [Chapter 6]

sacred space An area recognized by a religious group as worthy of devotion, loyalty, esteem, or fear to the extent that it becomes sought out, avoided, inaccessible to the nonbeliever, and/or removed from economic use. [Chapter 3]

satellite state A small, weak country dominated by one powerful neighbor to the extent that some or much of its independence is lost. [Chapter 6]

secondary industry An industry engaged in processing raw materials into finished products; manufacturing. [Chapter 9]

sector model An economic model that depicts a city as a series of pie-shaped wedges. [Chapter 11]

sedentary cultivation Farming in fixed and permanent fields. [Chapter 8]

services The range of economic activities that provide services to industry. [Chapter 9]

sex ratio The numerical ratio of males to females in a population. [Chapter 7]

shatter belt A zone of great cultural complexity containing many small cultural groups. [Chapter 4]

site The local setting of a city. [Chapter 10]

situation The regional setting of a city. [Chapter 10]

slang Words and phrases that are not part of a standard, recognized vocabulary for a given language but that are nonetheless used and understood by some of its speakers. [Chapter 4]

social culture region An area in a city where many of the residents share social traits such as income, education, and stage of life. [Chapter 11]

social science The branch of learning that seeks to apply the scientific method to the study of humankind, seeking universal principles, theories, and laws of behavior, often through the use of mathematics. [Chapter 1]

sovereignty The right of individual states to control political and economic affairs within their territorial boundaries without external interference. [Chapter 6]

space A term used to connote the objective, quantitative, theoretical, model-based, economics-oriented type of geography that seeks to understand spatial systems and networks through application of the principles of social science. [Chapter 1]

spatial distribution The arrangement of a particular landscape feature or features throughout a unit of space. [Chapter 10]

squatter settlement An illegal housing settlement, usually made up of temporary shelters, that surrounds a large city. [Chapter 10]

state A centralized authority that enforces a single political, economic, and legal system within its territorial boundaries. Often used synonymously with "country." [Chapter 6]

stimulus diffusion A type of expansion diffusion in which a specific trait fails to spread but the underlying idea or concept is accepted. [Chapter 1]

subsistence A livelihood system that provides only basic food, clothing, and shelter requirements. [Chapter 2]

subsistence agriculture Farming to supply the minimum food and materials necessary to survive. [Chapter 8]

suitcase farm In American commercial grain agriculture, a farm on which no one lives; planting and harvesting is done by hired migratory crews. [Chapter 8]

supranationalism Occurs when states willingly relinquish some degree of sovereignty in order to gain the benefits of belonging to a larger political-economic entity. [Chapter 6]

supranational organization A group of independent countries joined together for purposes of mutual interest. [Chapter 6]

survey pattern A pattern of original land survey in an area. [Chapter 8]

sustainability The survival of a land-use system for centuries or millennia without destruction of the environmental base, allowing generation after generation to continue to live there. [Chapters 8, 9, and others]

swidden cultivation A type of agriculture characterized by land rotation, in which temporary clearings are used for several years and then abandoned to be replaced by new clearings; also known as "slash-and-burn agriculture." [Chapter 8]

symbolic landscapes Landscapes that express the values, beliefs, and meanings of a particular culture. [Chapter 1]

syncretic religion Religions, or strands within religions, that combine elements of two or more belief systems. [Chapter 3]

technopole A center of high-tech manufacturing and information-based industry. [Chapter 9]

teleology A philosophy proposing that the Earth was created specifically as the abode for humans, that the Earth belongs to humans by divine intention. [Chapter 3]

territoriality A learned cultural response, rooted in European history, that produced the external bounding and internal territorial organization characteristic of modern states. [Chapter 6]

theocracy A government guided by a religion. [Chapter 3]

threshold In central-place theory, the size of the population required to make provision of services economically feasible. [Chapter 10]

time-distance decay The decrease in acceptance of a cultural innovation with increasing time and distance from its origin. [Chapter 1]

toponym A place-name, usually consisting of two parts, the generic and the specific. [Chapter 4]

total fertility rate (TFR) The number of children the average woman will bear during her reproductive lifetime (15–44 years old). A TFR of less than 2.1, if maintained, will cause a natural decline of population. [Chapter 7]

trade-route site A place for a city that is at a significant point on transportation routes. [Chapter 10]

transnational corporations Companies that have international production, marketing, and management facilities. [Chapter 9]

transportation/communication services   The range of economic activities that provide transport and communication to businesses. [Chapter 9]

uneven development   The tendency for industry to develop in a core-periphery pattern, enriching the industrialized countries of the core and impoverishing the less industrialized periphery. This term is also used to describe urban patterns in which suburban areas are enriched while the inner city is impoverished. [Chapters 9, 11, 12]

unitary state   An independent state that concentrates power in the central government and grants little authority to the provinces. [Chapter 6]

urban agriculture   The raising of food, including fruit, vegetables, meat, and milk, inside cities, especially common in the Third World. [Chapter 8]

urban hearth area   A region in which the world's first cities evolved. [Chapter 10]

urbanized population   The proportion of a country's population living in cities. [Chapter 10]

urban morphology   The form and structure of cities, including street patterns and the size and shape of buildings. [Chapter 10]

vernacular culture region   A region perceived to exist by its inhabitants; based in the collective spatial perception of the population at large; bearing a generally accepted name or nickname (such as "Dixie"). [Chapters 1, 2]

world city   One of the largest cities in the world, generally with a population of over 10 million. [Chapter 10]

zero population growth   A stabilized population created when an average of only two children per couple survive to adulthood, so that, eventually, the number of deaths equals the number of births. [Chapter 7]